**Teaching Science
to the Ordinary Pupil**

Teaching Science to the Ordinary Pupil

K. Laybourn O.B.E., M.Sc., Ph.D.
formerly Deputy Education Officer, Manchester
formerly Chief Inspector of Schools, Bristol and Manchester

C. H. Bailey M.Sc.
formerly Head of Science Department
Didsbury Training College, Manchester

BARNES & NOBLE BOOKS · NEW YORK
(a division of Harper & Row Publishers, Inc.)

Published in the U.S.A. 1972 by
HARPER & ROW PUBLISHERS, INC.
BARNES & NOBLE IMPORT DIVISION

ISBN 06 4941086

First printed 1957
Reprinted 1958 (twice), 1962, 1964, 1966
Second Edition 1971

Copyright © 1971 K. Laybourn and C. H. Bailey
All rights reserved. No part of this publication may be reproduced or transmitted in any form or by any means, electronic or mechanical, including photocopy, recording, or any information storage and retrieval system, without permission in writing from the publisher.

Printed and bound in Great Britain

Preface

The education of the ordinary pupil—neither the ablest nor the least able—remains the central problem of teaching. This is no less true now that more and more boys and girls are staying on longer at school, and indeed it may become more evident with the development of comprehensive schools, where the spread of ability presents a special challenge. We believe that the teacher's basic task is to foster interest ("given interest, at any level of ability, learning follows"—to quote our original Preface), and that the pupils with whom we are chiefly concerned are interested in their everyday surroundings, benefit by using their hands in support of their minds, and learn best through practical experience and personal involvement. Our aim in writing this book has been to show how science in all its aspects may be presented in secondary schools in close association with practical work, making maximum use of situations and materials familiar in daily life.

Since the publication of our first edition, in 1957, a good deal of attention has been focused on the education of pupils of average and near-average ability. The work of the Schools Council, the introduction of the Certificate of Secondary Education examinations (with their three "Modes"), and the establishment of curriculum development centres, have transformed the approach of many teachers to their subjects. In science, a particular debt is owed to the Association for Science Education and to the Nuffield Science Teaching Projects. The Policy Committee of the A.S.E. has repeatedly stressed the importance of ensuring that science education is made available to every boy and girl, and the Association's publications in recent years have contained much that is helpful to teachers at all levels. Meanwhile, the Nuffield Combined Science Project, for the 11–13 age-group, and the Nuffield Secondary Science Project, for the 13–16 range, have produced text-books and materials which will undoubtedly prove to be of great value to those planning integrated science courses for pupils in the middle-ability streams.

It is far from our intention to overlook these very important contributions to science teaching; rather would we urge every teacher to acquaint himself with the Nuffield material and to profit from membership of the A.S.E. But science teachers face ever more difficult problems associated with the phenomenal growth of scientific knowledge and the need to select, from the mass of material available to them, what is most appropriate to their particular purposes. Every day they are offered new textbooks, new materials and new techniques. They are invited to attend in-service training courses and teachers' study centres, and even to spend periods in industry. Not a small proportion of teachers must still attempt science subjects for which their initial training gave them little or no specific training. It is in these circumstances that we hope that this new edition of our book will prove timely, dealing as it does with the whole field of practical science teaching method in a simple and straightforward way.

The main body of each chapter centres around some likely topic from any integrated science course, which is treated by a detailed description of practical work arranged in a logical teaching sequence. However, neither the sequence of topics nor the chapter contents should be regarded as any kind of directive. As we have said before, practical work will generally prove futile without the skill of the teacher to interpret its meaning and its relation to the pupil's everyday experience. The teacher alone can see his scheme of work as a whole; without his integrating influence, best seen in the art of question and answer, practical science can become a jumble of unrelated activities and an expensive waste of time. The teacher must know his syllabus and his treatment of it through and through, and such mastery seldom comes unless the scheme is his own.

A few of the original experiments have been omitted in favour of more effective alternatives, and the total number of experiments has been considerably increased. A new chapter has been added which should enable interested teachers to exploit some of the many uses of transistors in school science teaching. The main changes, however, are in two directions: (a) the book has been revised throughout to bring information of all kinds up to date and has been rewritten in SI units; (b) chapter introductions have been greatly enlarged to provide a much more complete source of information and advice on such matters as aims and methods, techniques, and the everyday problems of science teaching and laboratory management. We reiterate our claim that what we have written is grounded in our own practical experience.

We again offer our sincere thanks to all those science teachers, past and present, whose work is the source of so many of our own ideas. Especially would we renew our thanks to the Committee of Head-teachers and Science teachers in Manchester from which we drew our original inspiration.

Note. The occasional mention of particular films or filmstrips is intended only as a reminder that much excellent material of this kind is available. Unless otherwise stated, references are to the catalogue, *Visual Aids*, of the Educational Foundation for Visual Aids (1964 Edition), in Parts V and VI of which will be found listed strips and films on a great variety of science topics. The catalogue may be obtained from 33 Queen Anne Street, London W.1. A booklet, *Educational Films*, 1946–66, is available from the same address and lists material produced in co-operation with the National Committee for Audio-Visual Aids in Education. The monthly journal *Visual Education* carries up-to-the-minute information in this field.

Contents

1. The Air — 9
2. Burning and Respiration — 27
3. The Practical Study of Living Things — 44
4. The Structure of Living Things — 61
5. A First Study of Plants — 74
6. Foodstuffs from Plants — 85
7. History of a Simple Meal — 98
8. The Circulation of the Blood — 118
9. Fuel, Diet and Growth — 138
10. The Preservation of Food and the Prevention of Disease — 154
11. Water in Nature — 168
12. The Water Supply to our Homes — 185
13. Heating our Homes — 199
14. Electricity in the Home — 219
15. The Generation and Distribution of Electricity — 237
16. Music and Noise — 266
17. Optical Instruments — 282
18. Sight and Colour — 304
19. Stars and Space — 323
20. Force and Movement — 345
21. Balance and Stability — 362
22. Common Materials — 376
23. Machines and Engines — 391
24. Soil — 419
25. How Life is Handed On — 432
26. Transistors and Radio — 448

Index — 465

"Wonders and treasures come floating in on every tide"
Richard Church

"Early in life he hit upon the profound truth that enjoyment and education are very nearly one and the same"
Neville Cardus

"Yet all experience is an arch, wherethro'
Gleams that untravell'd world, whose margin fades
For ever and for ever when I move.
How dull it is to pause . . ."
Alfred Lord Tennyson

"We had a 'lab' of a sort, but the teacher did all the experiments"
Dorothy Checketts

"It is the man that counts. All obstacles he pushes aside"
F. W. Westaway

Chapter One

The Air

Air and the Nature of Matter

Experience of the nature of air comes early, and even in nursery days it presents its mysteries. The young child chases paper caught up by the wind, puffs out the candles on his birthday cake, or runs along with his toy "windmill". As soon as he begins to notice and to ask questions his education in science has begun. At the Infant stage he finds that he can collect his breath in a jam jar; he sees that it is the wind that drives his boat along; and he knows the delight of a bouncing ball or rubber balloon.

The Junior school has not always followed up such splendid beginnings. Yet the teacher who understands the natural interest of boys and girls of this age in parlour tricks and simple mechanisms has a wide range of exciting happenings connected with air pressure at his disposal, whether he turns to a consideration of paper darts, penny whistles or pop-guns. He will seize the opportunity to encourage the making of kites and gliders; to talk about and wonder at the destruction caused by high winds; to give simple instructions on how to put out a fire; to discuss the function of the weed in the classroom aquarium; and to emphasize the importance of fresh air and deep breathing. Under such a teacher a child will be well prepared for his Secondary school course.

Even average pupils today are often considerably better informed than the most learned of early seventeenth-century philosophers. Three hundred years ago the very name "air" did not mean what it does to us. Included by the Greeks as one of the four "elements", it was yet regarded as something not quite material in the sense that earth and water are material (the young child has the same idea, and we seek to provide experiences to correct it). We owe the term "gas" to van Helmont (c. 1620):

"... I call this Spirit ... by the new name of Gas, which can be neither restrained by vessels nor reduced to a visible body."

Galileo (1564–1643) was probably the first man to weigh air, doing it by weighing a bottle into which extra air had been compressed, and reweighing the bottle after it had been opened again to the atmosphere. It was his pupil Torricelli who made the first mercury barometer and gave thereby the earliest clear proof that a vacuum can exist—confounding Aristotelian doctrine. The famous Frenchman Pascal arranged to have Torricelli's experiment repeated on the 3,000-ft. Puy-de-Dome and recorded that the mercury stood 3 (French) in. lower at the summit than at the bottom of the mountain. Also about this time, Otto von Guericke, in Magdeburg, made the first air pump and astonished everyone with "the force of the vacuum". So we come to Robert Boyle, founder-member of the Royal Society, whose researches on "The Spring of the Air" (1660) established the Law that bears his name. Newcomen's steam engine, in which atmospheric pressure was the moving force, followed Boyle's work directly and was the immediate precursor of the developments which we associate with the name of James Watt (1736–1819).

The nature of air is bound up with the nature of matter in general. The Greek philosopher Democritus (5th century B.C.) had argued an atomic theory, pictured later by the Roman poet Lucretius when he wrote of "primal atoms"—

". . . driven on
In ceaseless varied motion some rebound,
Leaving large gaps, while some are knit together
With hardly any interspace at all;
And these more closely bound with little space
Locked close by their own intertangled forms,
These form the rocks, the unyielding iron mass,
And things like these: But those which spring apart
Rebounding with great intervals between,
These give us the thin air . . ."

During the Middle Ages atomism suffered eclipse but it was inevitably readopted with the development of experimental science. One of the strongest general arguments in its favour is based upon the compressibility of matter, especially of gases. It is very difficult to see how a gas can be reduced to a small fraction of its original volume on any other hypothesis. The well-known school experiments on gaseous diffusion, on diffusion between liquids and into jellies, and the Brownian motion, are illustrations of the further development (during the nineteenth century) of the idea of matter consisting of particles in motion. Dalton's atomic theory had begun to put the particulate description of substances upon a quantitative basis and gradually, through the work of men like Gay-Lussac and Avogadro, the notion of molecules emerged. Now however the kinetic theory of gases was developed, which could offer a rational interpretation of the observed facts about the relation of the volume of a gas to temperature and pressure, gaseous energy and the many phenomena (such as diffusion) to which reference has already been made.

Today the teacher thinks of molecules as being in constant motion whether in gases, liquids or solids. In solids they are in regular array, though in rapid vibration; in liquids they have sufficient energy to intermingle; but in gases the individual molecules fly about in all directions at high speeds. The behaviour of air—its ubiquity, its compressibility, the pressure it exerts and its expansion when heated—can be well understood in these terms.

The Reality of Air and its Existence Everywhere

1 *Air from the Lungs*
Fill a Winchester quart bottle with water and invert it in water in a basin or sink. After a deep inspiration, expel the air from the lungs into the bottle via a 50-cm length of rubber tube (each pupil is supplied with his own glass mouth-piece). Read off the volume of air from a scale marked out on white adhesive tape down the side of the bottle, the scale having been calibrated beforehand by pouring known volumes of water into the bottle from a measuring-jar.

2 *Air in Sand or Soil*
Paste a graph-paper scale along the side of a test-tube and about one-third fill the tube with dry sand (or soil). Pour water into a second, similar, tube to the same height. Mark the top level of the sand on the scale and then pour the water on to the sand and shake sand and water together. Finally, mark the top level of the liquid.

From the two scale readings the fraction of the sand or soil which was air is readily calculated.

3 *Air Resistance*
Make a 1-cm deep saw-cut diametrically across one end of a cotton reel and mount the reel on a horizontally clamped large nail so that it will run as a drum on an axle. Drive a small tack into the curved surface of the reel and attach to it one end of a piece of fine string about a metre long. Fasten a small weight to the other end of the string and wind up the string on to the reel. Now allow the weight to fall from bench level to the floor, so that it turns the reel as the string unwinds: notice the very short length of time required—a fraction of a second. Next, rewind the string on to the reel and fit a piece of card, about 10 cm × 20 cm, into the saw-cut so that it acts as a vane; it will be necessary to cut out a small piece of card so that the vane clears the axle. Again note the time required for the weight to fall. The effect of air resistance on the turning vane is very marked.

4 *Air Pressure*
Float a small coloured ball (wood or cork) on water in a jam jar. Cork one end of a wide glass tube (e.g. 20 cm × 2 cm) and push the other end down-

wards over the ball and into the water. Notice that the ball sinks with the level of the water inside the tube, so that it floats below the level outside. Now remove the cork—the ball jumps upwards with the water in the tube.

5 *Air has Weight*
Construct the balance shown in the diagram. The beam (cane or dowel-rod, and about a metre long) pivots at its mid-point on a length of knitting needle which is supported horizontally. A second knitting needle pierces the beam vertically, just to one side of the pivot, and by sliding this needle upwards or downwards the sensitivity of the balance may be varied.

Suspend a scale-pan (syrup-tin lid) from one end of the beam and from the other end hang a rubber play-ball (*c.* 20 cm diameter) encased in a stout felt or canvas cover. Load the pan until the beam is balanced; then adjust the vertical needle until the pan falls about 20 cm when 1 gramme is added. 1 gramme is the weight of about ¾ litre of air, and this is the volume of air which must be pumped into the ball so that there shall be an adequate change in weight when it is released.

Pump the ball up hard, using a football inflator. Balance the beam by adding weights to the pan. Unscrew the clip on the ball until air is escaping slowly and notice how the ball steadily rises.

The Pressure of the Air

6 *Rubber Sucker*
Moisten the rim of a sink-pipe cleaner (rubber hemisphere on wooden handle) and press it firmly on to the top of a light table or on to the flat seat of a laboratory stool. Lift the table or stool by means of the cleaner.

7 *Fountain-pen Filler*
Soften the middle of a 20-cm length of glass tubing in a batswing flame. When the glass begins to fall, withdraw it from the flame and at once pull the two ends apart as far as desired (up to arm's length for very fine tubes; in the present experiment it is sufficient to extend the tube a few centimetres). Cut the capillary portion at the middle to make two tubes, each with a jet. Attach a small rubber teat to the wide end of each tube, so making a pair of fountain-pen fillers or simple syringes. Examine how the syringe works.

Rubber teats may be bought; but a teat may be contrived by using a 3-cm length of soft rubber tubing closed at one end by a 2-cm length of glass rod or dowel rod.

8 *Chicken Fountain*
Fill a medicine bottle with water and invert it in a saucer of water, fixing it

THE AIR 13

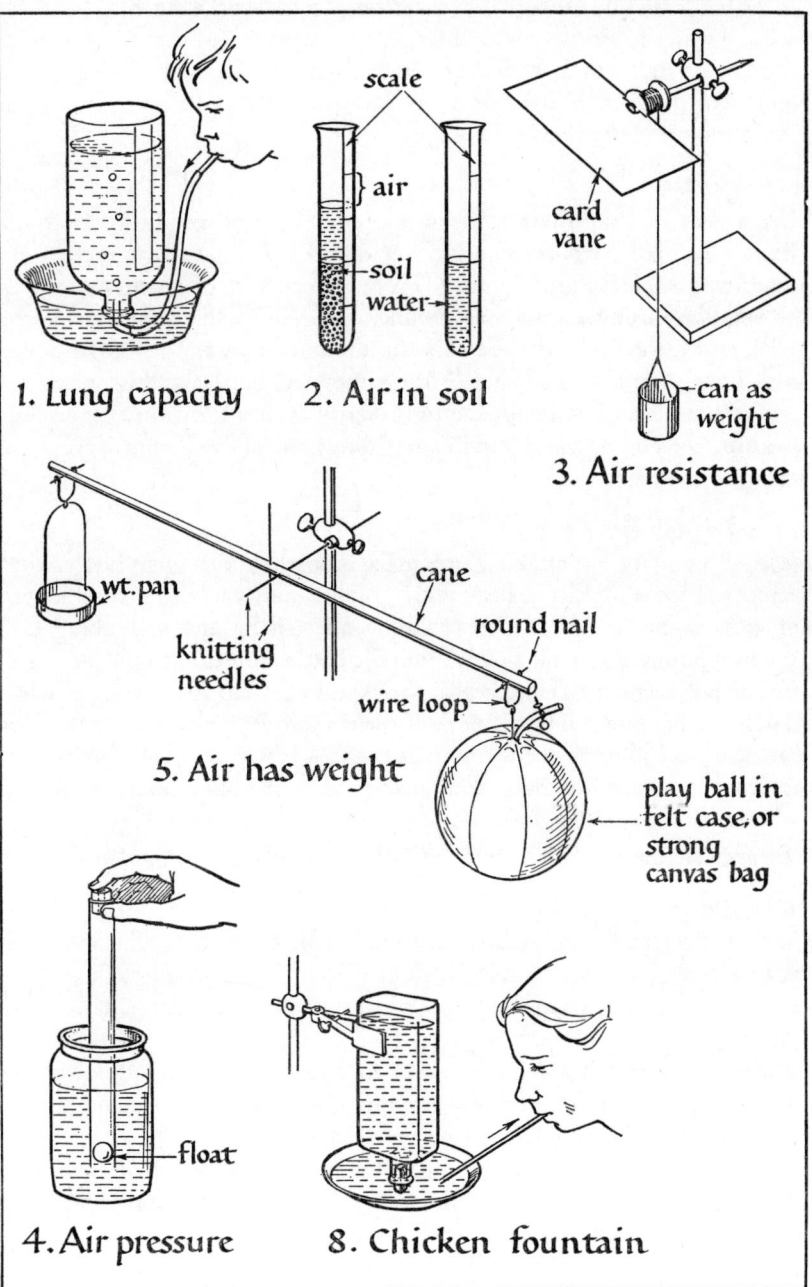

with its mouth just below the surface of the water in the saucer. The neck of the bottle may be supported by insertion of a half-cork (Fig. 8).

Suck water from the saucer through a milk straw (or use the syringe of Expt. 7). Notice that whenever the level in the saucer falls below the mouth of the bottle, air bubbles up into the bottle and water runs down into the saucer until the mouth is again sealed.

9 *Popgun*

Use a glass or aluminium tube, or a 30-cm length of metal tube from the frame of an old cycle. Select a piece of dowel rod about half a metre long that just fits loosely into the tube. From a thick slice of potato cut a plug of potato by using the tube as a punch; the plug will remain inside the tube, and it should be pushed along to the middle by means of the dowel rod. Punch out a second plug in the same way, but leave this one at the end of the tube. Now thrust the rod smartly against the centre plug while pointing the gun upwards and in a safe direction. The end plug is projected at high speed.

10 *Collapsing Vessels*

(a) Use a polythene bottle (e.g. a SquEzy household detergent bottle, after removing the cap). Fit the neck with a rubber bung carrying a short length of glass or metal tube which can be connected by pressure tubing to a vacuum pump. Pump air slowly from the bottle. Substitute a tin can (litre) for the polythene bottle and repeat the experiment. (b) Alternatively, select a solid rubber bung to fit the neck of the tin can. Run about 2 cm of water into the can and bring the water to the boil. When steam issues freely from the outlet, remove the flame and at once force the bung home. Run cold water over the can in a sink.

Topics: Action of a milk-straw, self-filling fountain-pen, garden syringe.

11 *Vacuum Pump*

Saw off the bottom of the barrel of an old cycle pump and fit the open tube with a rubber stopper carrying a short length of glass tubing; the tubing should project only from the outer (wider) end of the stopper. Cut a rubber patch to fit over the inner face of the stopper and stick half of one face to the stopper (rubber solution or Evostik) to form a flap-valve. Remove the leather washer from the end of the pump piston, grease it well, and replace it in the reversed position.

Attach a length of rubber tubing to the pump and show that air can be withdrawn from an inverted jam-jar standing in a trough of water. The pump is used in Expts. 12 and 23.

12 *Aneroid Barometer*

Refer to the diagram. Screw a doubly-bent strip of tin and an ink-bottle cap

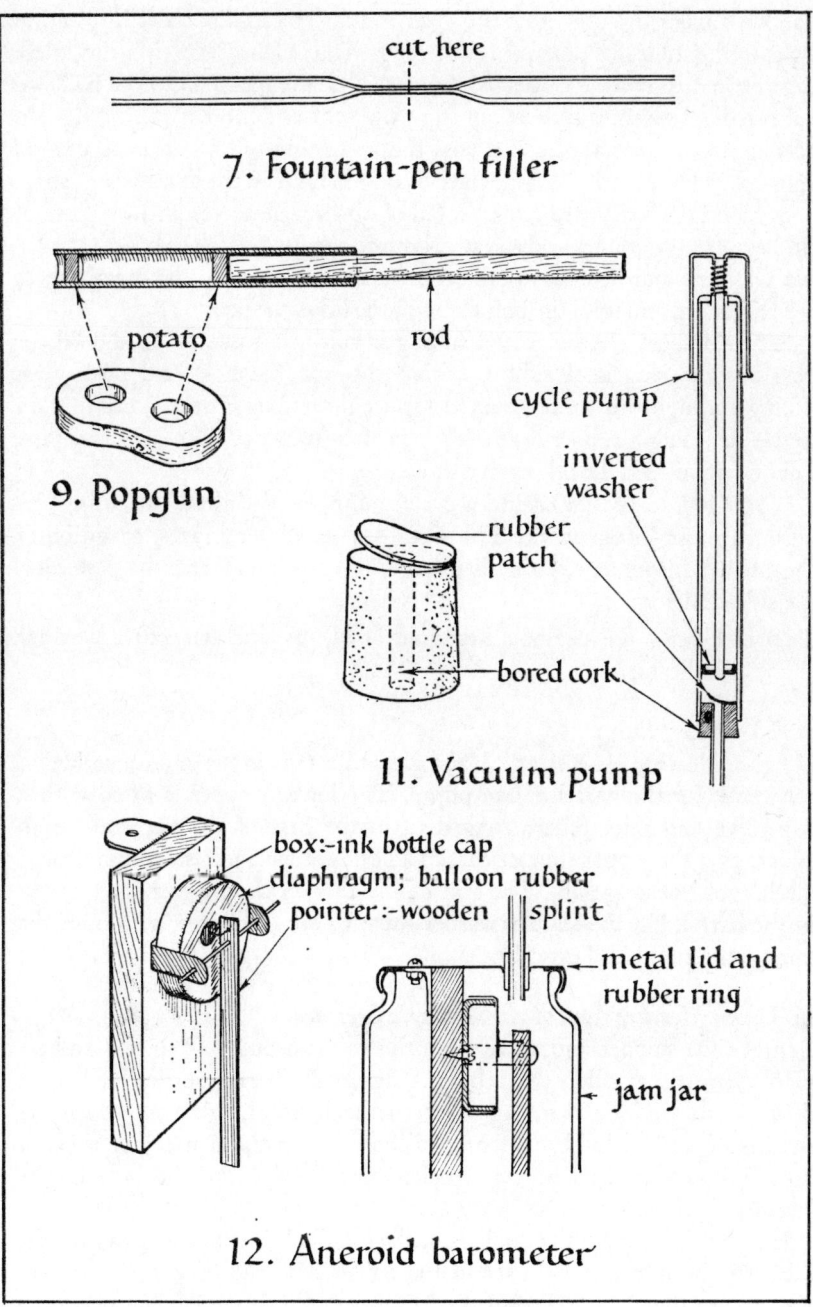

together on to a wooden baseboard (10 cm × 5 cm) as shown. Stretch balloon rubber tightly across the open top of the cap and fix it in position by running adhesive tape round the edge. Run a pin through a tiny piece of cycle patch (from the sticky side) and stick the patch on to the balloon-rubber diaphragm, a little away from the centre. Bend the projecting end of the pin at right angles and pass the point through one end of a wood splint which is pivoted on a needle running in holes in the doubly-bent strip.

Suspend the baseboard from the lid of a 2-litre preserves jar by a piece of tin bent at right angles and screwed both to the lid and to the board. A rubber washer should be used both with the screw fastening the metal cap to the baseboard and with the bolt through the lid of the jar.

Solder a short piece of metal tubing into a hole punched in the lid; or pass a short length of rubber tubing through the hole and push glass tubing through this to make an airtight connection. Fit the lid tightly on to the jar, using a rubber ring such as is often provided with preserves jars. Let one pupil hold the lid down firmly.

Blow air into the jar, using a cycle pump; or withdraw air, using the vacuum pump of Expt. 11. The wood-splint pointer moves, magnifying the smaller movement of the diaphragm. A paper scale may be pasted on the side of the jar.

Topics: Discuss the use of an aneroid as (a) an altimeter, (b) a weather indicator.

13 *Model Lift Pump*

No glass-blowing is necessary. Use a glass tube (15 cm × 2½ cm), corked at each end, for the barrel of the pump. The lower stopper is fitted with a flap-valve and inlet tube arranged as in the case of the vacuum pump (Expt. 11). The upper stopper carries an outlet tube and also a plunger rod (cycle spoke or long nail). The aluminium disc on the plunger is a loose fit in the barrel, but the leather washer must be cut to fit closely. Mount the pump on a stand in Terry clips.

14 *Direct Measurement of Atmospheric Pressure*

Remove the stopper and valve from the vacuum pump (Exp. 11) and replace them by a solid-rubber bung. Clamp the barrel vertically, handle downwards, and fix a strong hook to the handle: this may consist of strands of wire twisted together and looped over the handle; or a metal hook may be screwed into a wooden plug driven into the hole in the handle.

Hang weights from the hook until the handle is just pulled downwards. Measure the internal diameter of the barrel with callipers, and calculate the cross-sectional area. Thence find the atmospheric pressure in grammes per square centimetre.

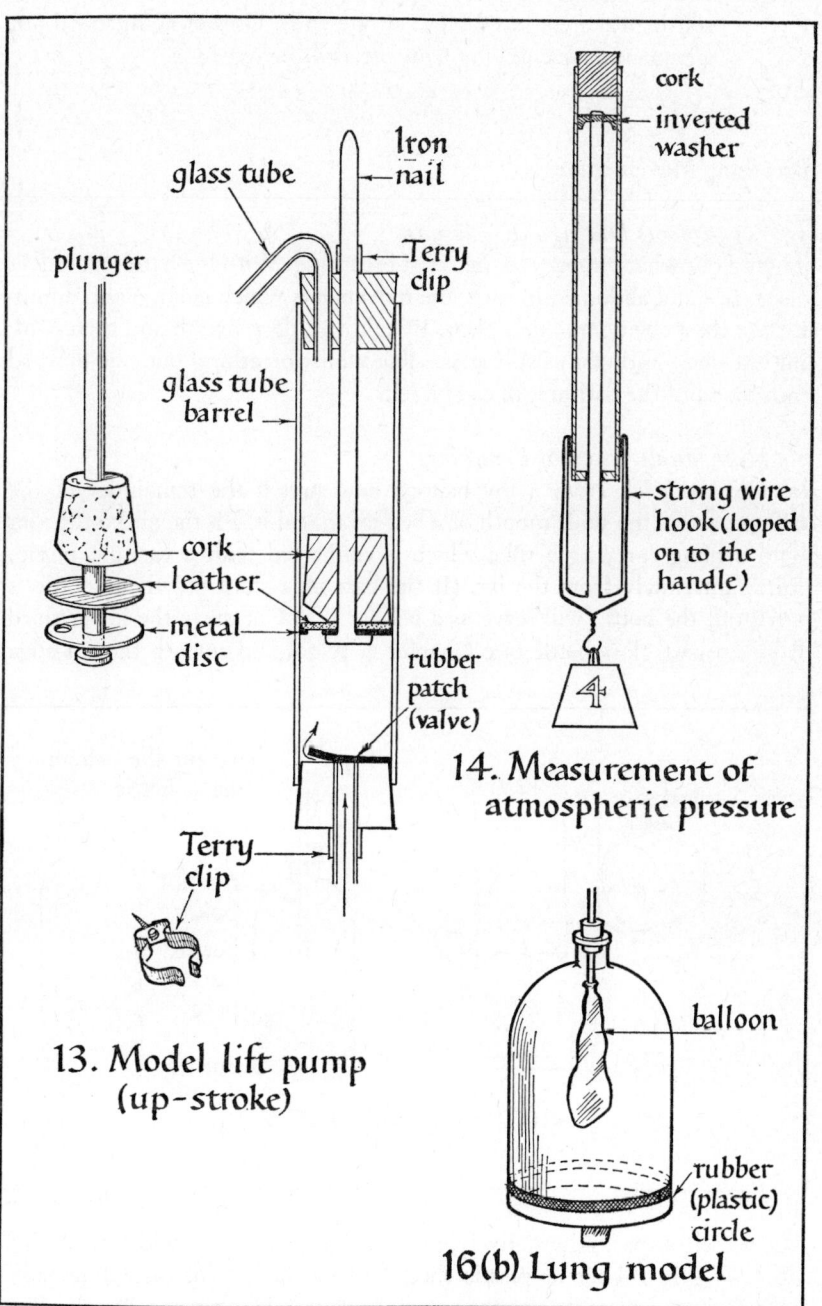

13. Model lift pump (up-stroke)

14. Measurement of atmospheric pressure

16(b) Lung model

Topics: Bourdon gauge (make a long narrow paper tube from newspaper, roll it into a coil, and blow at one end). Uses of compressed air, e.g. pneumatic chipping hammer, drilling machine.

Breathing Movements

15 *Experiments During P.E. Lessons*
To find out what happens in the act of breathing. With the hands placed on chest, ribs and abdomen in turn, the movements which enlarge and diminish the chest cavity are fairly clear. By taking a deep breath and then holding the chest and ribs as still as possible whilst breathing out, the upward movement of the diaphragm can be felt.

16 *Mechanical Action of Breathing*
(a) Cut the neck from a toy balloon and stretch the remainder of the balloon across the wide mouth of a bell-jar to seal it. Fit the neck of the jar with a bung carrying a tube which is connected with a vacuum pump. Pump air slowly from the jar. (If the base of a stout polythene bottle is sawn off, the bottle will serve as a bell-jar.) (b) Cut away the lower third from a quart glass bottle (see Chapter 2, p. 30) and smooth the cut edge

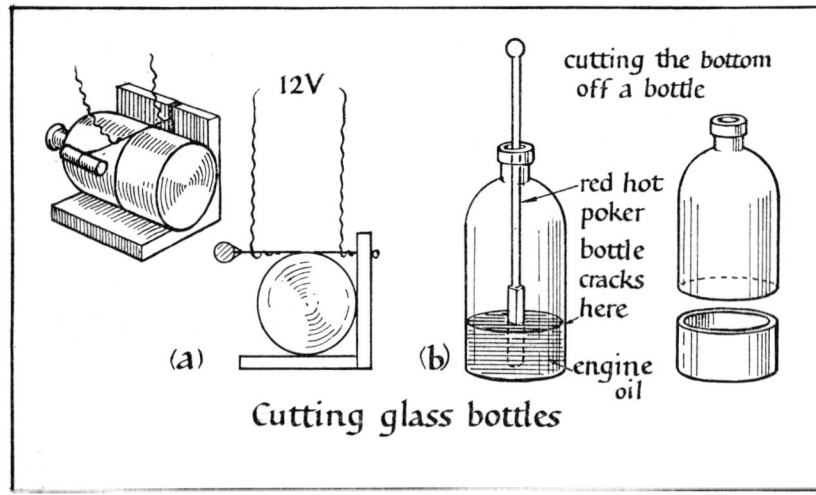

with emery paper. Alternatively, use a bell-jar. Cover the wide end with a circle of thin rubber or plastic sheet and secure it with insulating tape. Stick a short rubber strip to the middle of the circle to act as a handle (Fig. 16).

Fit the neck of the bottle with a cork carrying a length of glass tubing to the lower end of which a toy balloon is fixed, so that the balloon is inside the bottle.

Pull the diaphragm downwards: the "lung cavity" is thus enlarged and the "lung" (the balloon) expands. Release the diaphragm: the lung collapses. Show the passage of air in and out of the "windpipe" (the glass tube) by holding a smoking twist of brown paper at the outlet.

17 Iron Lung Model

Fig. 17 shows the assembly. The pump is a soft plastic bottle (e.g. household detergent bottle) from which the cap has been removed and replaced by a cork carrying a short length of glass tubing. The "head" may be made in Plasticine. The "thorax" is represented by a toy balloon.

Compress the plastic bottle before connecting it with the "lung". When the bottle is allowed to spring back to its normal shape the balloon will be seen to expand; on squeezing the bottle again the balloon collapses. Test the movement of air in and out of the "mouth" by means of a small flame (match).

Prior to assembling the model, fully inflate the balloon in order to render the rubber easily flexible. It may be fixed to the glass tube by means of a rubber band.

18 *Tidal Capacity of the Lungs*

Although we can breathe out, in a single breath, 2 litres or more of air (and even this represents only about half the total lung capacity), we normally breathe only a fraction of this. Deep breathing is obviously helpful in changing the air in the lungs more quickly.

Breathe a normal "breath" into a flat football bladder and apply a clip so that the air is trapped. Connect the bladder by rubber tubing to the interior of an inverted Winchester bottle filled with water and standing in a trough of water. Open the clip and squeeze the air from the bladder into the bottle. Cork the bottle, stand it upright and find how much water (measuring jar) must be poured in to fill it; this is the volume of air which was breathed into the bladder.

Compare the result with that of Expt. 1.

Repeat Expt. 18 after running up and down stairs or after other physical exertion.

Topics: Lessons in artificial respiration. The iron lung. Breathing mechanisms in other animals. (Note—the efficiency of the breathing mechanism varies according to the needs of different animals. Frogs swallow air; in reptiles rib movements occur; but in mammals rib action is assisted by contraction of abdominal muscles acting on the diaphragm. Spasmodic movements of the diaphragm in man result in hiccups.)

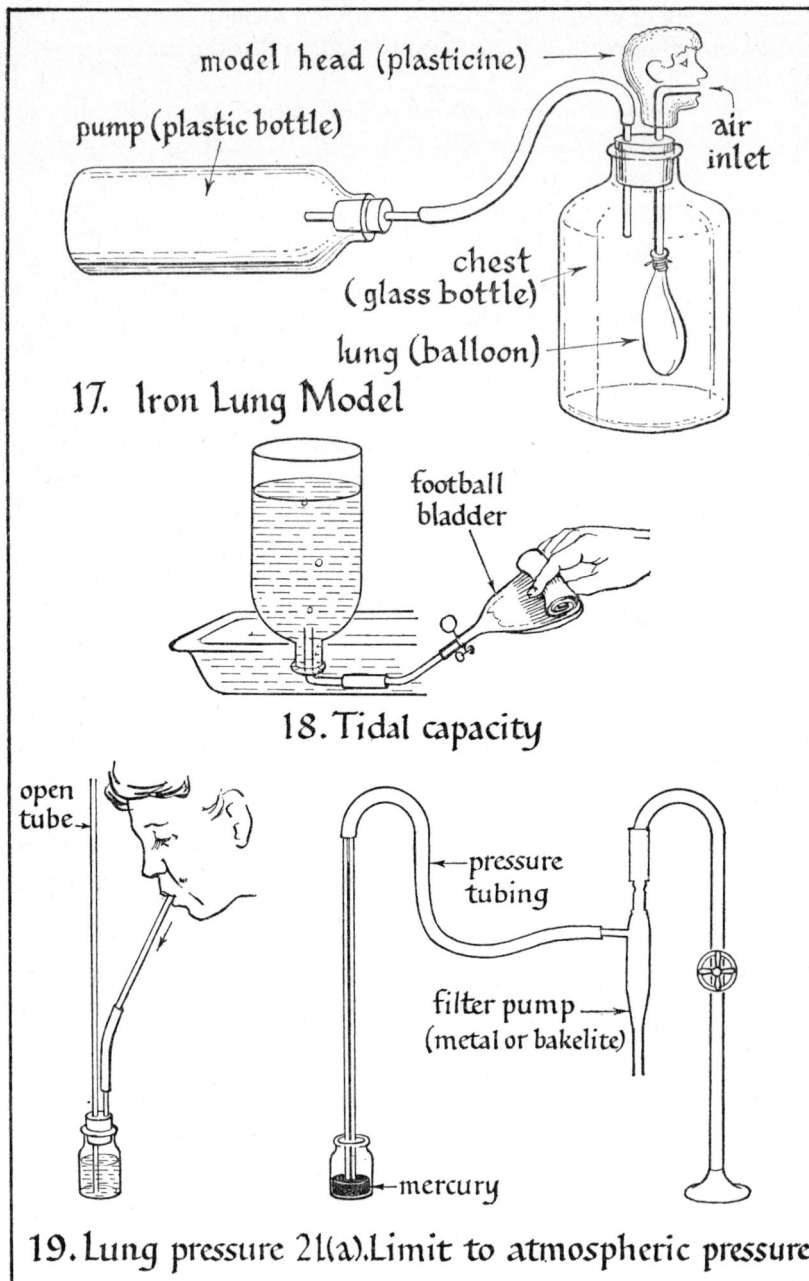

The Barometer

19 *Lung Pressure*

Measure the pressure in terms of a column of water or mercury by using the apparatus shown in the diagram; the pressure is given by the difference in the liquid levels.

20 *Gas Pressure*

(a) Connect a 25-cm length of glass tubing, standing in a tall jar of water, by rubber tubing to the gas supply. Turn on the gas slowly. The water level inside the tube is depressed, and the difference between the final levels in the tube and in the jar is a measure of the gas pressure. (b) Bend fairly narrow-bore polythene tubing into the form shown in Fig. 20(b), clipping the U to a wooden backboard by Terry clips. Half fill the U with water coloured with methyl orange and join the apparatus to a gas tap. Turn the gas on slowly.

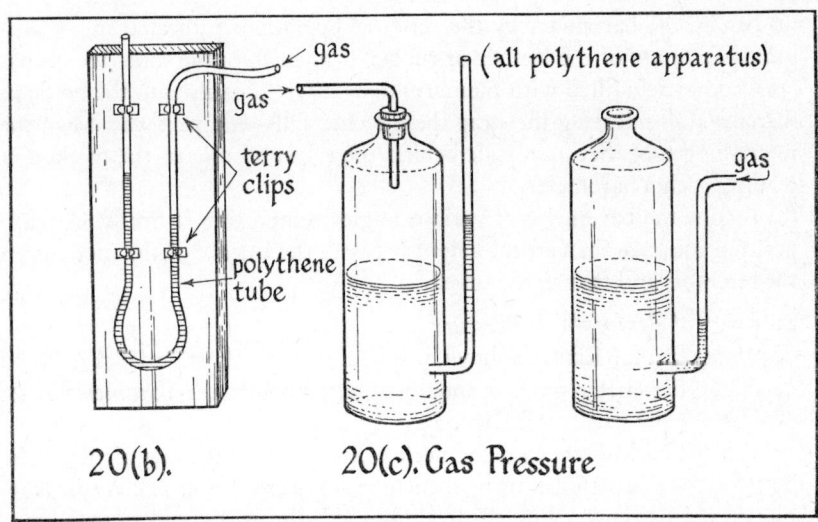

20(b).   20(c). Gas Pressure

This form of gas pressure gauge is called a manometer. Compare the difference in the liquid levels with the result you obtain in Expt. 20(a).

Express the results in the form:

Pressure of gas supply = ———— cm of water.

(c) Fit up the two arrangements indicated in Fig. 20(c). Use polythene bottles and tubes: a neat 6 mm hole is easily drilled in the side of each bottle; polythene tubes may be chosen to fit these holes and the necks of the bottles tightly. Discuss the significance of what you find when the gas supply is turned on.

21 *Limit to Atmospheric Pressure*

(a) Use a piece of barometer tubing about a metre long, open at both ends, standing in a bottle of mercury. Draw mercury up the tube by attaching a vacuum pump (e.g. filter pump) to the upper end. Notice that the mercury cannot be drawn more than a certain height up the tube. (b) Use a 20-metre length of flexible transparent plastic tubing. Immerse one end in water in a bucket and suck at the other until water syphons through; then immerse the free end in water in a second bucket.

Have the two ends held firmly under water (with the tube completely filled) and haul the middle section of the tube to an upper window, so that the tube forms an inverted U against the outer wall of the building.

Report on the height of the water in each limb. What are the bubbles in the water? What effect will these have on the height of the water columns? What is the limiting height to which water might be raised by an efficient lift pump?

22 *Mercury Barometer*

(a) Set up the barometer by the series of operations indicated in the diagrams. The use of the leather or rubber strap enables the tube (which has been completely filled with mercury) to be inserted easily into the bottle of mercury. On releasing the strap the mercury falls only part-way down the metre-long tube. Set up a scale behind the tube and discuss the method of reading such a barometer.

(b) Incline the barometer at various angles, supporting it firmly. At each position measure the vertical height between the surface of the mercury in the reservoir and that in the tube.

23 *Effect of Atmospheric Pressure*

(The diagram for Expt. 22 shows a cork, carrying a short outlet tube, fitted on to the barometer tube. It should be fitted before the barometer is set up, but it is not used until Expt. 23.)

Push the cork down into the neck of the bottle and draw air from the bottle via the outlet tube, using a suction pump (see Expt. 11). As air is removed the barometer "falls". If air is suddenly readmitted to the bottle, mercury shoots up the barometer tube.

Topics: How to read a gas-meter. How a gasholder (gas-works) operates. Use of barometer as weather indicator. Weather reports and reference to simple charts showing cyclonic and anti-cyclonic conditions.

Expansion by Heat

24 *Heated Air Rises*

(a) Investigate the way in which the heated air moves about a flame by

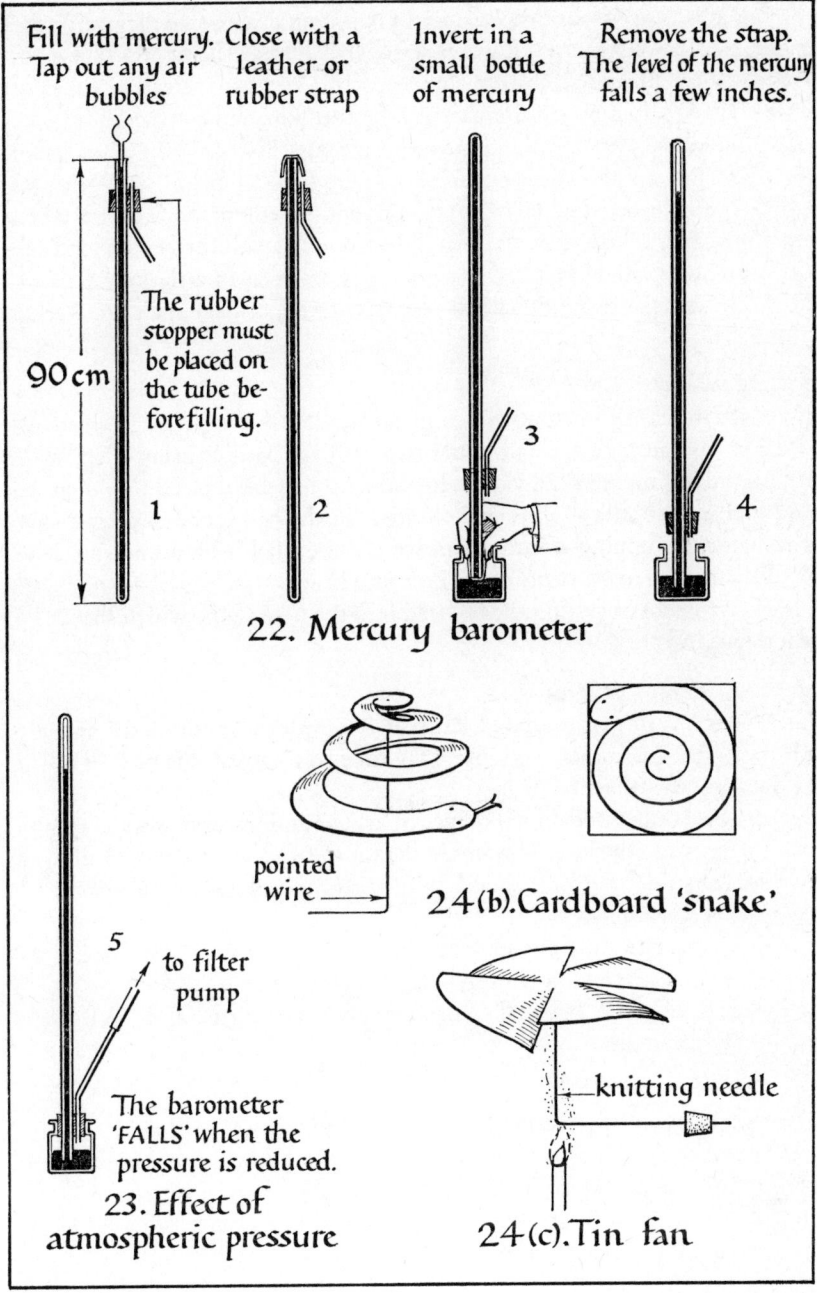

holding the hand in successive positions above and around a Bunsen flame. (b) Cut a "snake" from thin card and pivot it on a wire (see diagram); the snake revolves continuously when set over a Bunsen flame. (c) Cut a tin fan with four blades from tinplate (cocoa tin) and use instead of the card snake. (d) Set up a model fireplace, using a tin box and cardboard tube. A small piece of lighted candle represents the fire. Use smoking corrugated paper to indicate the draught. Smoke enters the "fireplace" and emerges from the top of the "chimney"—but it no longer enters the fireplace when the chimney is taken away. (e) Use light from a 12-volt car head-lamp bulb to throw the shadow of a red-hot poker on a screen in a darkened room. Move the poker up and down; the rising currents of heated air are plainly indicated.

25 *Expansion of Air*
Fit a 50-cm length of stout-walled glass capillary tubing (say 2 mm bore) through the neck of a small bottle (e.g. aspirin bottle), using a collar of rubber tubing to effect a good fit. Introduce a tiny bead of oil into the tube and warm the bottle slightly by holding it in the hand, or standing it over a radiator, or dipping it into warm water, etc. Cool it by immersing it in ice. Observe the movements of the indicator bead.

(The problem of getting the oil bead into the tube is one which should be put to pupils.)

26 *Expansion of Liquids*
Use apparatus similar to that of Expt. 25 but omit the oil drop. Completely fill the bottle with water and insert the tube so that water is pushed about halfway up the tube.

Dip the bottle suddenly into warm water and observe very carefully what happens to the level of water in the tube. Pupils should not be allowed to miss the initial fall in the level, which is followed by a steady rise. Discuss the observations.

It is worth repeating the experiment with a Pyrex test-tube in place of the bottle. There is no initial drop in level: why?

Other liquids may be tried: purple methylated spirits, and "Westron" coloured with iodine.

27 *Thermometer*
Use the classroom thermometer (Fahrenheit) to take series of readings (e.g. outdoor shade temperature at 9.00 a.m. for a month; classroom temperature at half-hourly intervals during a day; temperature of water as it is being heated in a pan). In each case take parallel readings with a Celsius instrument. Graph each series of readings.

28 *Expansion of Metals*
(a) Drill a small dent in an iron nail and use it to hold a knitting needle

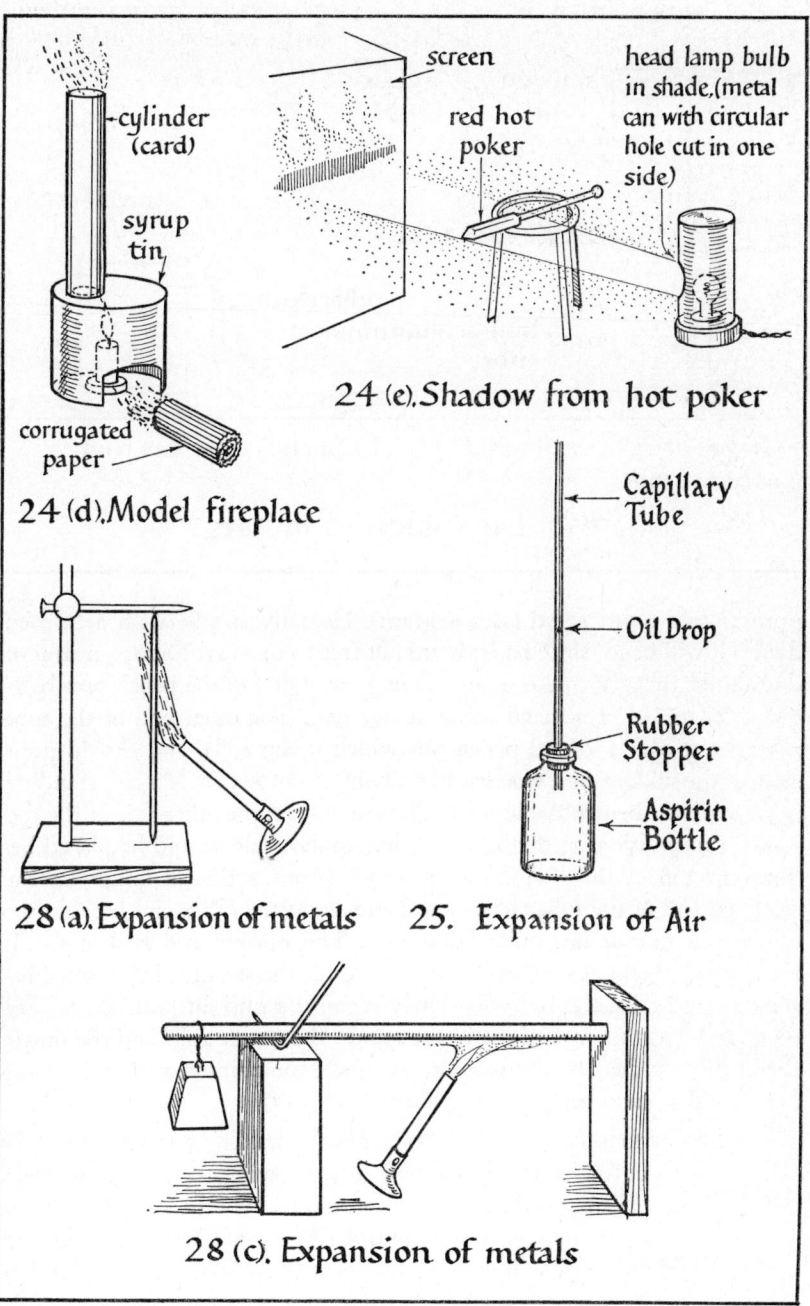

24 (d). Model fireplace

24 (e). Shadow from hot poker

28 (a). Expansion of metals

25. Expansion of Air

28 (c). Expansion of metals

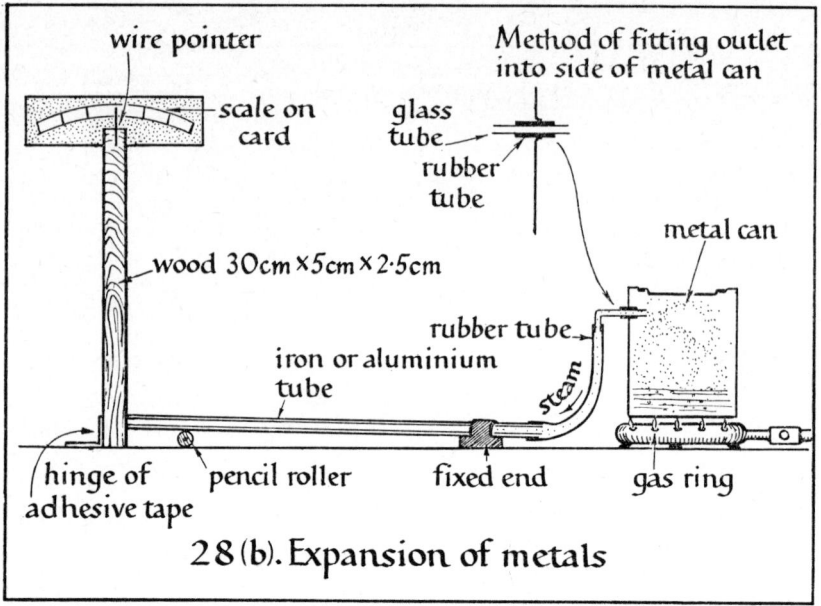

28 (b). Expansion of metals

upright in a retort stand (see diagram). Heat the needle with a Bunsen flame; it will bend, since its ends are not free to move. (b) Strap an iron or duralumin tube ($\frac{1}{2}$ metre long, about 1 cm wide) to the bench or a baseboard by means of a metal collar at one end. The other end of the tube should rest over a round pencil (on which it can roll), and should press against the bottom of a wooden bar, about 30 cm × 5 cm × 2 cm, standing upright on the bench. A hinge of adhesive tape on the other side of the rod holds it in position on the bench. A horizontal scale should be placed behind the top of the rod. Blow in steam (from a tin-can boiler) at the strapped end of the tube; it can escape easily at the other end because the duralumin tube is not quite horizontal. The upright rod is seen to tilt slowly and, finally, to fall over with a bang. If the steam is interrupted before the rod falls, the rod will slowly regain its upright position. (c) See diagram: Heat the rod of the retort stand—the needle rolls and the movement is made clear by the pointer. To make the pointer, simply heat the needle red-hot and bend it, using pliers.

Topics: How to loosen a tight nut or screw (by holding a red-hot poker in contact for half a minute and then allowing the nut or screw to cool). How tyres are fitted to locomotive wheels. Aquarium thermostat or Regulo oven control. Allowance for expansion in bridges, railway lines, etc. Use of heat-resistant glass in the kitchen and laboratory.

Chapter Two

Burning and Respiration

Apparatus and Equipment for Science Lessons: Self-help
As the importance of science education becomes better appreciated local education authorities make more money available for science courses. For example, initial equipment in the many new schools has often been quite generous. In some areas schools have been enabled, through a substantial allocation, to take part in pilot schemes of the Nuffield Science Teaching Project and to establish the Nuffield approach. Lists and specifications have been published, and information about sources of supply, which are of great value to the schools concerned in helping them to build up stock of equipment. Laboratory furnishers have been made aware that schools' apparatus design is a specialized field. The development group of the Consortium of Local Education Authorities for the Provision of Science Equipment (CLEAPSE) was commissioned to assist in defining and solving the problems which arise.

As a result, many teachers will be offered a prospect of more, and more appropriate, commercially manufactured items of equipment. All this is excellent: it is time that we got away from a pattern of practical work in schools' science laid down half a century and more ago.

There remain very sound reasons for saying that the science teacher must continue to help himself. One of these, though not the most significant for the teacher of the ordinary pupil, is that he is never likely to be in a position to buy more than a fraction of his real requirements. Reports on the early Nuffield trials showed that the capital cost of apparatus for a single year of the O-level Physics programme might be £750 or more; and although schools will already own some proportion of what is required, and large-scale production may do something to hold down rising costs, the prospect is bound to be daunting to many.

Even more cogent are the educational arguments. In the Nuffield Junior Science Source Book *Apparatus* (Collins) the case is presented for improvisation and the use of homely apparatus and materials in primary schools. It is a fact that there are very many boys and girls in secondary schools who profit from a similar approach; who are not yet ready for the maturity and sophistication of thought that specialized, ready-made equipment often represents. Such equipment, indeed, may often prove a positive barrier between the pupil and the principle it was designed to demonstrate.

Much traditional laboratory apparatus fails with many pupils simply because it is unfamiliar; the main object is missed in the effort to master the mechanics.

The teacher's task is not of course confined merely to the selection of material and apparatus. He must often make and improvise. This is time-consuming but, within limits, eminently worthwhile. A man who devises something himself is likely to use it well and to commend its use to his pupils because of his personal enthusiasm. His demonstrations are more effective when pupils see that he does not call upon "special" gadgets, but is content to use tools and apparatus familiar to them. Given opportunity, some pupils will wish to follow his lead, trying out things for themselves either in school or at home. Their teacher's skill and ingenuity set a standard by which they may measure their own efforts.

Many have attempted the task of listing what equipment is necessary in a school science laboratory, and it is entirely right that teachers should press for a comprehensive range of basic material. Even in a well-stocked department they will inevitably be faced with a formidable programme if they conscientiously undertake class practical work, and obstacles should not be put in their way. But schools must often trim their spending to an inelastic requisition allowance, and there may be other reasons why, in some schools, Science stock has not been properly built up. From the descriptions of experiments provided in this book teachers will select those basic items without which even a modest course cannot be begun, but it should be clearly understood that there must be steady building upon this foundation if value is to be gained from Science lessons. Science equipment is expensive, and costs continue to rise; yet good teaching cannot be done on the cheap and schools will only reap in proportion to what is provided. This book sets out the thesis that improvised methods and homely apparatus are the very things likely to be understood by the majority of our pupils, but it would be disastrous if this were to be used as an excuse for "saving" on the requisition account. The enthusiasm that will "make do and mend" will sooner or later evaporate unless the essential tools are provided. Every Science room needs corks and tubing, burners, stands, weighing and measuring apparatus, thermometers, a selection of tools, reagents ... to mention but a few of the essentials; and it needs *sets* of many things, so that group-work and individual-work may both be encouraged. Some necessary items are inevitably expensive; for example, a drying oven, a micro-projector (or microscopes), various meters, a low-voltage source and a properly-equipped workbench. Attempts to teach without adequate equipment will be costly failures when success is measured in the real terms of substantial progress by a majority of pupils. At the same time it should be recognized that much apparatus advertised by laboratory furnishers is quite unsuitable for our work, and was never intended for such work. Even in regard to basic equipment, simpler and more suitable apparatus might well be chosen as, for example, plastic containers in place of fragile glass vessels; specimen tubes in place of gas jars; and (for some purposes) tin-cans instead of beakers.

A fully-equipped bench (better still, a workshop) for working in wood and metal is very desirable. It is one of the aims of Science teaching to bring pupils to the point where they regard it as normal to carry out simple handyman jobs for themselves. Practical training is often slow work, and not infrequently expensive in materials; yet neither consideration should deflect the teacher from his goal.

Simple Techniques

Science teachers need to master certain techniques which are not difficult given care and practice. Improvisation should not imply untidiness or inefficiency. Today the job of construction is often greatly simplified because of the availability of new materials—metals, plastics, adhesives and solvents, for example—and of tools and gadgets for special purposes; while the effectiveness of apparatus for demonstration is commonly improved if the material is carefully mounted or arranged. Quick-drying paints may be used to bring out important features.

(a) Cork Boring:

(i) A power drill provides the quickest and best method, but the cork or rubber bung MUST be held in a suitable clamp: it is highly DANGEROUS to attempt to bore a stopper held in the hand.

(ii) Alternative method, using cork borer: press the cork against a mat of soft card so that the borer is not blunted as it emerges; always sharpen the borer before use (a proper sharpener must be purchased); bore from the narrow end and be careful to keep the borer parallel to the axis of the cork throughout boring; keep the cutting edge flooded with water (water may be poured inside the borer tube); when the borer is almost through keep the cork firmly against the mat and finish the cutting slowly and carefully so that the edges of the hole are not torn.

With rubber stoppers, the secret is to use a really sharp borer. Vaseline should be used instead of water as a lubricant.

Rubber bungs are superior to corks for most purposes and especially where apparatus must be reasonably gas-tight. If corks are the only thing available they should be dipped in hot molten paraffin wax for a few seconds and then allowed to cool thoroughly before use.

(b) Bending a Glass Tube:

Practise with a 15-cm length of narrow tubing and always use a batswing (fishtail) burner. Hold each end of the tube lightly between thumb and forefinger and heat the middle of the tube in the upper part of the flame—so that it is quickly covered with a layer of soot (an uncovered space means that it is being held too low). Turn the tube continually, slowly and steadily, but avoid left or right movement. When the glass shows a tendency to bend, stop turning it, remove it from the flame and allow one end to fall under its own weight (do not push it) until the desired angle is obtained. Hold the tube in this position until the glass hardens; then set it down against a support so that the hot part is not touching anything.

All bending should be done out of the flame and in one operation.

(c) *Cutting Glass Tubing*:

Hold the tube in the left hand so that the point at which it is to be cut lies just beyond where it is gripped between thumb and forefinger. Make a file scratch across the tube, as near to the thumb as possible; any difficulty will probably be due to a blunt file. Grip the tube with a thumb on either side of the mark and the forefingers beneath, and *pull* the tube apart (in reality there is a slight bending action); the tube will break cleanly at right angles to its length. Rotate each cut end in the Bunsen flame until a yellow flame is seen, and continue heating for only a few seconds more. By this means the sharp edges are removed but the tube is not deformed.

(d) *Cutting a Glass Bottle or Wide Glass Tube*: See Figure, p. 18:

(i) Use part of a 1000-watt 230-volt electric fire spiral as the heating element. Cut off one-twentieth of the spiral plus about 4 turns (perhaps 24 turns in all) and use this part; it will provide a heater suitable for a 12-volt supply.

Straighten out the wire. Attach one end to a nail on a baseboard and the other to a wooden handle. Loop the wire round the bottle, pulling it tight by means of the handle, and being careful to avoid a short circuit. Connect the nail and the wire on the handle to a 12-volt supply; the bottle should crack in about 1 minute. If the wire does not get hot enough, reduce its length.

(ii) An alternative method is to pour engine oil into the bottle up to the level at which the cut is required. Make the end of a poker red hot and push it down into the oil in the bottle. Usually the bottle cracks very cleanly at the oil level, but a cold wet rag folded round the bottle just above the oil level is sometimes helpful.

(e) *Sealing a Glass Tube*: See Expt. 34, p. 34.

(f) *Blowing a Hole in a Glass Tube*: See Expt. 151, p. 132.

(g) *Making a Glass Jet or a Capillary Tube*: See Expt. 7, p. 12.

(h) *Making a Hole in a Metal Can to Carry a Delivery Tube*:

(i) Arrange the can on a suitably shaped wooden anvil (block of wood) held in a vice and use a hand-drill to bore through the metal on to the anvil.

Plastic bottles, if firmly held, may be drilled directly with a power-drill, giving clean holes.

(ii) Alternatively, file the point of a large nail to a smooth conical shape and use it to punch a hole in the metal can at the desired place. Syrup—or fruit—cans are suitable; thinner tins may yield a ragged hole and should be avoided. Enlarge the hole with a reamer, such as the tang of a metal file or the spike of a scout knife. If done carefully, a clean flanged hole results into which rubber tubing may be fitted to make an air-tight joint. Holes may be made in plastic containers in the same way; they may also be cut with nail scissors or fine-toothed saws.

(i) Making a Larger Hole in a Metal Can:

Mark out the position of the hole (2 cm diameter or larger) with a pencil, make a cross cut or a small hole at the centre, and then with curved tin-snips cut spirally, finishing round the marked circumference.

(j) Tin-plate:

Cut out the top and bottom plates from a tin can with a rotary tin-opener; if the can has a press-in lid, remove the top ledge similarly. Then cut down each side of the seam, using straight tin-snips, and finish by cutting off the upper and lower rims.

(k) Tin Cans as Beakers:

Cut out the top ledge from a can with a press-in lid (e.g. syrup tin), using a rotary-type tin-opener. Remove any sharp projections by tapping with a small hammer.

(l) Soldering: See Expt. 29, 31.

(m) Annealing, Hardening and Tempering Steel: See Expt. 302, p. 247.

(n) Cutting Metal Tubing (gas-piping, copper, duralumin, etc.):

Grip in a vice and use a hack-saw.

(o) Plaster of Paris Casts: See Expt. 80, p. 78.

(p) Preparation and Mounting of Microscopic Sections:

See Chapter 4.

(q) Use of Gummed Paper:

Gummed paper strip is very useful: stock it in various widths. Use it for model making, hinging paper or card, fixing paper tubes, holding coils of wire, strapping apparatus in position, labelling, etc. White adhesive tape is handy for scales on tubes and bottles, and Sellotape for mounting colour filters and for a host of other jobs.

Safety First in the Laboratory

Whenever a demonstration experiment offers any risk of breakage or explosion, safety screens should be erected. Perspex screens, say $\frac{1}{2}$ metre wide and 1 metre high are suitable; they may be supported in slotted bases.

29 Bimetal-strip Fire Alarm

First make a bimetal strip as follows: Cut strips of thin brass and tin-plate, about 10 cm × 1 cm. Emery a strip of each metal until it is perfectly clean on the face to be joined, then smear a trace of Fluxite (or of "killed spirits of salt") all over this face. Heat a soldering-iron, dip the tip into flux, and then touch it on a stick of solder until it becomes "tinned" (covered with a film of solder); if the solder will not melt, the iron is not hot enough, but it must not be made red-hot. If the iron is very dirty it may have to be cleaned with an old file before heating. Now hold the tinned iron and the solder together on the prepared face of one of the strips until a little solder melts; spread this all over the face by rubbing it with the soldering iron. Repeat with the second strip. Next smear a trace of flux over the two "tinned" surfaces, lay them face to face, and heat the bimetal "sandwich" by pressing the freshly heated iron on top of it (the strips may be held in position with a short wooden stick). The heat will travel through the sandwich and melt the solder, and when the iron is removed the solder will set, binding the two strips together.

In the fire alarm (Fig. 29), the copper contact wire is held in position by winding it over a layer of paper round a clamped nail. An electric lamp is used as the source of heat. As the bimetal strip is heated it bends upwards and touches the contact wire, so completing the electric circuit and starting the bell ringing. If the heating lamp is switched off the ringing soon stops.

30 *Fire Precautions*

Arrange a bonfire on a piece of waste land well away from any building. Use a little paraffin *before* lighting, to ensure a strong blaze. Show how such a fire may be rapidly put out by covering with earth or sand.

Burn rubbish in a dust-bin (away from buildings) and show that the flames are extinguished when the lid is put on the bin.

31 *Laboratory First-aid Box*

Examine the contents of the laboratory box: check from the list of contents whether the box is complete: make good any deficiencies. Practise the treatment of minor injuries: (a) Bleeding from a slight wound: Wash well under running water to remove dirt. Cover with a "sterilized dressing" to maintain the aseptic conditions. (b) An acid burn: Flood the burn with cold water in quantity. Dust with sodium bicarbonate to neutralize any traces of acid. Cover with a sterilized burn dressing. (c) A dry burn or scald: Cover with a sterilized burn dressing soaked in a solution of picric acid. Avoid the use of grease or oil.

Discuss the correct use of other items in the box and practise simple bandaging. Refer to Expts. 187 and 188.

Topics: Use of water in fire-fighting and of a blanket on a person whose clothes have caught fire. Safety measures at home. Fire-breaks in

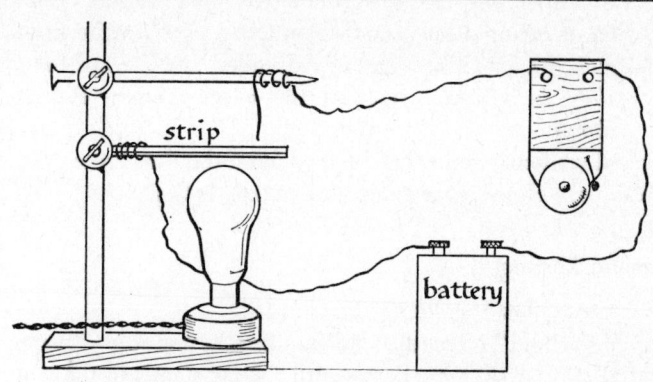

29. Bimetal-strip fire alarm

32. Air is altered when something burns

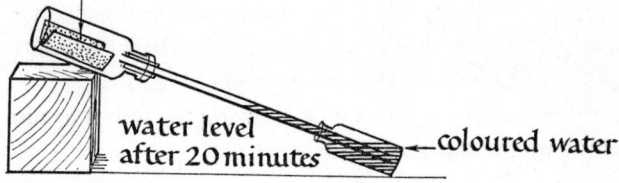

33(b). Air used up during rusting

forests. Safety in the laboratory: the handling of bottles, reagents and flames; the need for order and a good routine. Note the position of extinguishers, sand, blankets, exits. Practise fire-drill. See also Expt. 250. The Dept. of Education and Science Pamphlet 53, *Safety in Schools*, replaces the earlier *Safety Precautions in Schools*.

Films and wall-charts may be obtained from the Fire Protection Association, Aldermary House, Queen Street, London, E.C.4.

Burning and Rusting

32 *Air Altered when Something Burns in It*

Light a "night-light" or candle-end standing in a saucer of water. Lower an inverted jam jar over the flame until the jar stands in the water. Note the appearance of mist in the jar. When the flame begins to die, lift the jar away gently (note how the flame enlarges again) and thrust a strongly burning taper into it: the taper is extinguished. Analysis of the residual air shows that the candle is extinguished when about 3–4 per cent of carbon dioxide is present, leaving about four-fifths of the oxygen unused.

33(a) *Air Necessary for Rusting*

Almost fill a small conical flask with water and boil the water vigorously for five minutes to expel all air both from the water and from the space above it in the flask. Polish a short length of iron strip (or steel knitting needle) with emery and drop the metal into the boiling water. Remove the flame and at once close the flask with a rubber bung. Set up a control by repeating the operations except that the second flask is left unstoppered. Allow both flasks to stand and observe the contents during several days.

Discuss the importance of the control experiment.

33 (b) *Air Used Up During Rusting*

Sprinkle iron filings on a moistened strip of card and push the strip into a small wide-mouthed bottle. Fit the bottle with a cork carrying a 30-cm length of narrow glass tubing. Invert the bottle and support it so that the lower end of the tube dips into coloured water in a small jar. The rise of water in the tube will be obvious after a short time.

The action may be accelerated by allowing the filings to rust slightly before setting up the experiment.

34 *Proportion of Oxygen in Air*

(i) First seal one end of a 1-cm wide glass tube (about half a metre long), as follows: Rotate the tube evenly with one end in the hottest part of a blowpipe flame (a foot-bellows blowpipe is very desirable in the laboratory); the best position is just beyond the tip of the inner blue cone. Heat also one end of a length of glass rod. When rod and tube are softening, join rod and tube end to end and at once remove from the flame. When cold this gives a tube with a "handle" sticking out from one end. Holding the tube in one hand and the "handle" in the other, and rotating both steadily, heat the tube about 5 cm from the handle. When softening occurs, remove the tube from the flame whilst gently continuing the rotation, but in addition pull the two ends apart slowly (increasing the pull somewhat as the glass cools) so that a fairly narrow constriction is obtained. When cold, cut the tube at its narrowest point. Now heat the shoulder of the jet on the main part of the tube in a hot pointed flame, rotating the tube all the time. When the glass is well softened, pull the jet off sharply (e.g. with tongs), turn the tube to a more acute angle to the flame (still rotating), and heat the sealed end until the glass shows signs of collapse. Blow gently into the open end to prevent collapse and by alternately heating and blowing, always continuing the rotation, shape the sealed end to a smooth curve with walls equally thick all round. Allow the tube to cool slowly.

(ii) Moisten the inside of the tube and sprinkle iron filings into it so that the inner walls are covered. Support the tube with its open end dipping downwards into a jar of water. Read the water level either by using a ruler or from an adhesive tape scale attached to the tube. Note how much of the air in the tube has been used up after an hour, a day, and a week. For accuracy the tube should be positioned so as to make the water levels the same in tube and jar before each reading is made.

The residual gas extinguishes a flame; it is principally nitrogen. The active gas which was used up is called oxygen.

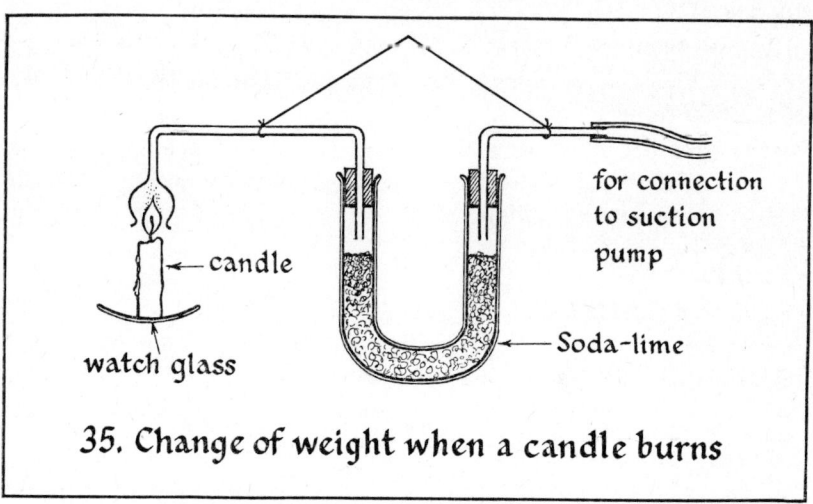

35. Change of weight when a candle burns

35 *Changes in Weight when a Candle Burns*

When a candle burns it gets gradually smaller and obviously diminishes in weight. Is this the full story? What about the weight of the products of combustion—the invisible gases which escape from the flame?

Suitable apparatus for an investigation of this point is shown in the diagram. The U-tube is packed with granules of soda-lime, a substance which readily absorbs both moisture and carbon dioxide.

First weigh the entire apparatus, including the candle and watch-glass. Then support the thistle funnel/U-tube section by a clamp and join it to a suction pump. Arrange the candle under the funnel, light it and then turn on the pump. Let the candle burn for 3 to 4 minutes, then extinguish the flame and simultaneously disconnect the pump but leave the pump running. When the apparatus has cooled, reweigh it, together with the candle and watch-glass.

As a control, run the operation through again but this time without lighting the candle. Maintain the same airflow by reconnecting the pump for exactly the same length of time.

Discuss the reason for the increase in weight when the candle was burning.

36 *Prevention of Rusting*

Use 5-cm × 1-cm strips of iron, or use nails. Polish thoroughly with emery paper. Treat different strips with Vaseline, machine oil, water paint, distemper, whitewash, etc., covering one half of the strip only in each case. Half of one strip may be "tinned" (Expt. 29); half of another may be copper-plated (Expt. 292). The strips can be held apart by sticking them into a lump of Plasticine, the nails by hammering them part-way into a small block of wood.

Rest the Plasticine or wood over the top of a jam jar in which there is a little water, so that the strips or nails hang down into the jar. Observe the effect of the damp atmosphere over a few days.

Topics: Priestley's discovery of oxygen. The use of painting, tinning, galvanizing, electro-plating, greasing, plastic spraying, etc. in the prevention of rusting.

Oxygen

37 *Priestley's Method*

Use a 5-cm ignition tube (made by drawing out and sealing ordinary glass tubing). Gently heat a tiny quantity of "red calx of mercury" (red mercuric oxide) in the tube. Beads of metal appear on the walls and a glowing wood splint held at the mouth of the tube bursts into flame.

38 *Making Oxygen without Heat*

Use an ink bottle fitted with a cork and delivery tube; the gas is collected

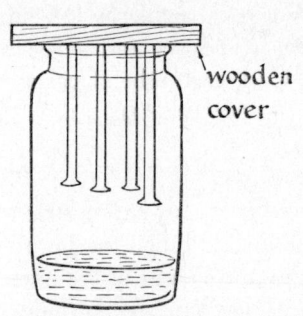

36. Prevention of rusting

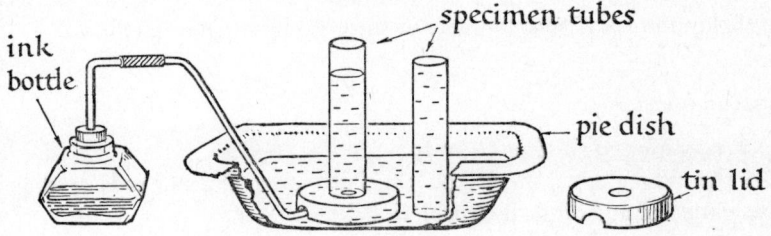

38. Preparation of oxygen from hydrogen peroxide

42. Fire extinguisher

in specimen tubes (10 cm × 2 cm) over water in a pie-dish. A beehive shelf may be fashioned from a tin lid.

Put 20-volume hydrogen peroxide in the bottle, add a pinch of manganese dioxide powder (catalyst), and at once insert the cork. Gas is evolved immediately. Cork each tube of gas as it is collected and use the samples for the following experiments.

39 *Properties of Oxygen*
(a) Bend up the end of a 15-cm × 1-cm tin strip to serve as a spoon, and set fire to a little sulphur in it. Plunge the burning sulphur into a tube of oxygen. Note the colour and vigour of the flame and the smell of the gas produced. (b) Repeat using charcoal; the flame is feeble and there is no smell. Test the residual gas by adding a few drops of clear lime-water and shaking; the liquid turns milky (chalky) because of the presence of carbon dioxide in the gas. (c) Heat a few iron filings to redness in the spoon and plunge them into oxygen; or use a wad of steel wool, in which case some of the strands are welded together by the great heat that is developed.

Carbon Dioxide

40 *Preparation of Carbon Dioxide*
Use the oxygen apparatus (Expt. 38). Put marble chips or soda crystals in the bottle and add dilute hydrochloric acid.

41 *Properties of the Gas*
(a) Add lime-water to a tube of the gas and shake. (b) Ignite a small splint of wood. Pour a tube of carbon dioxide over the flame; the flame is extinguished and the gas itself does not catch fire. (c) Pour the gas from one tube to another; use lime-water to prove that the transfer has occurred. (d) Invert a tube of carbon dioxide in a small dish of caustic-soda solution. Joggle the tube about and notice that the liquid rapidly rises up the tube. What is any gas left in the tube likely to be?

42 *Fire Extinguisher*
Place a rag soaked in paraffin in the bottom of a metal basin. Take two jam jars, put a few soda crystals in each, add a little dilute acid and cover each jar with a piece of card. After a few minutes ignite the rag and pour the gas from the two jars simultaneously over the flames. Try to relight the rag while it is still in the dish.

43 *Soda-water Syphon*
Use a half-litre bottle (e.g. a lemonade or milk bottle) three-quarters filled with water. Put a teaspoonful of powdered tartaric acid into the water and shake until dissolved. Wrap up a similar amount of sodium bicarbonate

in tissue paper, drop the packet into the bottle, and quickly stopper the bottle with a cork through which passes a delivery tube, closed by a clip, descending to the bottom of the bottle. Hold the cork in and observe what takes place inside the bottle. Open the clip and again watch the liquid in the bottle. The experiment must be carried out over a sink and with the exit tube pointing downwards into the sink. Taste the effervescing liquid.

44 Foam Extinguisher
Repeat Expt. 43, but add a little of some foaming agent (saponin, or one of the modern detergents) to the water and tartaric acid. Invert the bottle before opening the clip and use the jet of foam as a fire-extinguisher.

Hydrogen

45 Preparation of Hydrogen
Use the oxygen preparation apparatus (Expt. 38), with granulated zinc and dilute sulphuric or hydrochloric acid. EXTINGUISH ALL FLAMES in the laboratory before adding the acid. Collect some tubes full of gas and some about one-third filled.

46 Explosive Nature of Hydrogen–Air Mixtures
Empty all hydrogen generators before using any flame. (a) Use a small tube one-third filled with hydrogen, holding it corked and with the mouth

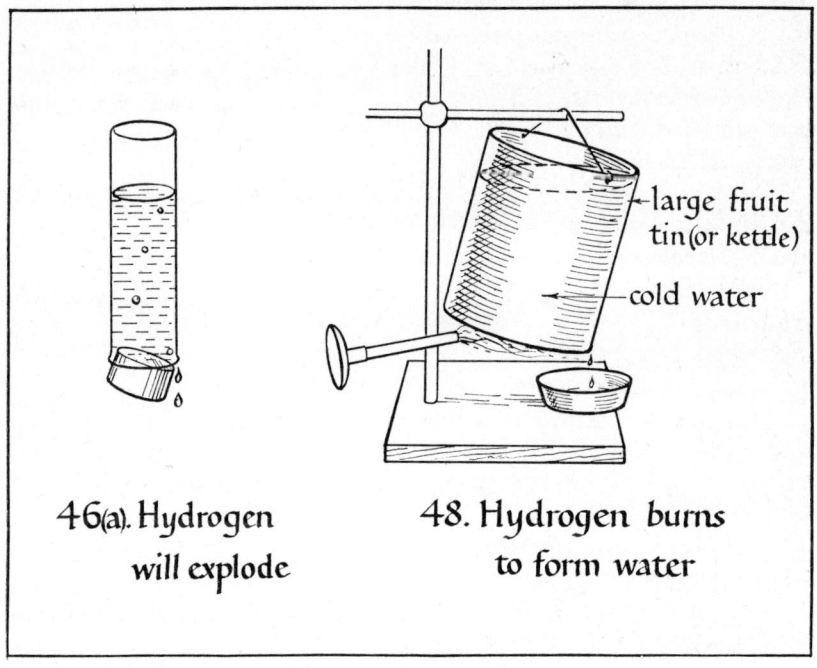

46(a). Hydrogen will explode

48. Hydrogen burns to form water

downward. Loosen the cork so that the water drips away slowly; in this way a roughly 2:1 mixture of air and hydrogen is formed in the tube. What is this in terms of oxygen and hydrogen? Turn the tube upright, extract the cork and apply a flame; the mixture explodes. (b) Ignite a small tube filled with hydrogen; there is only a slight pop (what causes it?) and the gas burns quietly, with a blue flame. (c) Set a tube of hydrogen cork upwards and remove the cork. Wait 2 seconds and then apply a flame. Comment upon the result.

47 *Hydrogen Bubbles*

Coal-gas or North Sea gas may be used in place of hydrogen for this experiment. Make a "soap" solution by shaking a modern detergent with cold water in a jam jar, and then blow bubbles on the end of a rubber tube connected to the gas supply. The bubbles are best released by turning the end of the tube upwards and drawing it sharply downwards; they float rapidly to the ceiling and may be ignited as they rise.

Topics: Oxy-hydrogen and oxy-acetylene flames. Balloons and airships.

Respiration

48 *Hydrogen Burns to Form Water*

In this experiment, as in the previous one, coal-gas is used instead of pure hydrogen. In both cases hydrogen itself could be used as a demonstration, but the class experiment is preferred.

Adjust a Bunsen to give a small blue flame and allow the flame to play on one side of the base of a large canned-fruit tin suspended from a support and filled with cold water. Liquid forms on the base of the can and may be collected as it drips off.

Transfer some of the liquid to a test-tube and bring it gently to the boil with the bulb of a thermometer immersed in it. Test another portion with blue cobalt chloride paper (which turns pink in the presence of water).

Refer to what is observed when a saucepan of cold water is heated on the gas-stove.

49 *Products of Burning Common Fuels*

The fuel may be methylated spirits, paraffin, olive-oil, etc. burning at a small wick. Push the wick through a hole in the lid of a small metal box containing the fuel. Invert a jam jar over the flame for a few seconds, then gently remove the jar and cover it with a lid or card. A film of moisture is seen on the walls (try rubbing the inside of the jar with a finger); and if lime-water is put into the jar it turns milky.

A similar result is obtained if the jar is inverted over a small gas flame or if a burning wood splint is thrust into the jar. It is not easy to burn solid

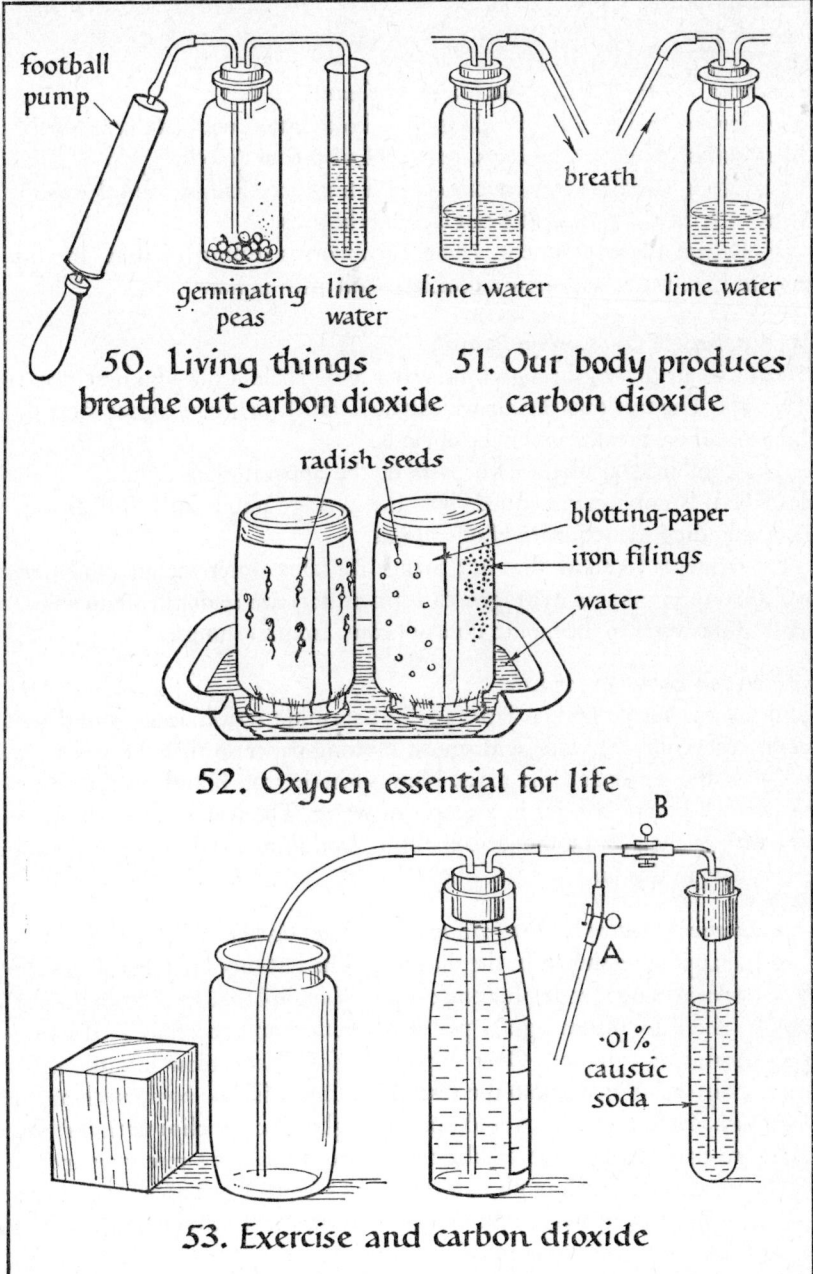

food in this experiment but satisfactory results have been obtained by using a few strands of a shredded breakfast cereal, ignited and thrust (by hand) into the jar.

50 *Living Things Breathe Out Carbon Dioxide*
(a) Allow soaked peas to germinate in a bottle fitted with stopper and delivery tubes. After several days, gently blow the air (football pump) from the bottle into lime-water contained in a test-tube. Run a control experiment with the same apparatus but lacking the peas.

(b) Repeat the experiment, using earthworms instead of peas. In this case the lime-water will show a positive result after an hour or so.

51 *We Breathe Out Carbon Dioxide*
Breathe in air drawn through lime-water and exhale it through lime-water (Fig. 51). The fact that the air we exhale is much richer in carbon dioxide than the air we breathe in will be obvious.

The combination of the two parts of the apparatus into one (as often described) is not recommended since the average pupil finds difficulty in understanding the sequence of operations.

Experiments to show that our breath contains water-vapour (and that we, therefore, oxidize hydrogen to form water) are seldom convincing—most of the water in the mouth does not come from the lungs.

52 *Oxygen Essential for Life*
Moisten the inside of two jam jars and sprinkle radish seeds round the walls; then line the walls with moist blotting-paper so that the seeds are between the paper and the glass. Now sprinkle iron filings on the paper in one jar. Invert each jar in a saucer of water. The water eventually rises one-fifth of the way up the jar containing iron filings and the seeds do not germinate in this jar.

53 *Exercise Increases the Proportion of Carbon Dioxide in the Breath*
Use the apparatus shown in the diagram. The test-tube contains 40 cm^3 of 0·01 per cent caustic soda plus one drop of phenolphthalein solution (make up the alkali by preparing a 1 per cent solution and successively diluting in a measuring cylinder). Open clip A (B closed) and blow into the milk bottle, displacing water into the reservoir; almost fill the bottle with air in this way. Then close clip A and open B slightly (screw clip) until bubbles begin to pass through the alkali; progressively raise the reservoir and so continue to force air through until the pink colour of the alkali is just discharged (use a comparison tube). Observe from the scale on the milk bottle how much breath was required.

Repeat the whole experiment after vigorous exercise. The volume of air required to decolorize the alkali will now be much reduced.

An alternative form of apparatus is described in the authors' *Practical Science for Secondary Schools* (U.L.P.), Book Three, p. 13.

Topics: Use of oxygen in hospitals, in high-altitude climbing and flying, in diving and in mine-rescue work. Value of physical exercise. See also the film "Animals Breathe in Many Ways" (*Educational Films Catalogue*, 1946–66: Reference 614 D27).

Chapter Three

The Practical Study of Living Things

The Importance of Nature Study

First-hand observation of living things—nature study—is essential to any real understanding of the science which we call biology. Unfortunately, many children (and not a few teachers) could neither identify a dozen common wild flowers nor tell a cock from a hen house-sparrow. The mistake is often made early and what is missed at the primary school stage is not easily made good later. Every teacher of young children would do well to read Margaret Hutchinson's *Children as Naturalists* (Allen and Unwin) and then reflect upon what is meant when we talk of a rich school experience. It is the teacher's job to open the eyes of boys and girls to a world in which, as Richard Church says, "wonders and treasures come floating in on every tide".

Today field work and environmental studies are discussed and developed as a means of interesting average and lower-than-average pupils in secondary schools. Nature rambles appear to have suffered a decline, perhaps not surprisingly in an age of urban sprawl. But whatever the form or title of the work, its basic significance remains. An interest in living things is almost universal when the right opportunities are presented; and upon interest knowledge and confidence grow.

For some, the more able, children nature study will give meaning to more than one science subject at school. But its value for the majority lies rather in the possibilities it offers for the development of life-long interests or hobbies which will take men and women out into the open air and combat the pressures of city life. In the hands of an inspired teacher we may look for even more—an appreciation of the wonder of nature and an aesthetic pleasure potentially more significant for the ordinary citizen than any formal scientific training. H. B. Miles has pointed out that the whole organism in its natural setting is the proper concern of biology and that the attitude of cold objectivity characteristic of the exact sciences is not always the most rewarding when dealing with living creatures. There are values which, amongst the sciences, only biology has to offer and which, in biology, can be brought out best in field studies. Knowledge alone is not enough in human life; it must be accompanied by feeling.

Nature Rambles

These and the general day in the country remain the most popular and often the most appropriate form of excursion for younger and for average pupils.

The first essential is careful planning of every aspect of the journey, even if it be only a visit to a local park. Certainly in the case of a park visit the need for preparation is no less, since the chances of boredom arising from absence of clearly seen purpose are usually greater. Having in his own mind decided his objectives, the teacher must go over the ground beforehand (preferably *shortly* beforehand: why?) so that he may plot the time required. For a country walk it will be necessary to refer to both an ordnance and a geological map, trying to account for particular features of the flora and fauna observed. The class should be given an outline of the route proposed, so that they may know in general terms what to expect.

The teacher's greatest single problem will be to ensure that every child's interest is sustained during the walk. It is a very great help if pupils take some part in preparing individual outline maps beforehand and if a sheet of "things to look for" (with hints about *where* to look) is supplied. Questions too may be posed. On the day of the outing pupils will need a satchel and a tin for specimens, and a pencil and notebook. The teacher, at least, should carry an illustrated handbook of the particular subjects of investigation—animals, flowers, trees, or whatever else may be appropriate.

A great part of the success of a nature ramble is dependent upon the teacher's ability to keep several different interests running at once: the search for specimens, advice on identification, encouragement to note and sketch what is seen, the pauses for discussion and (not least) for rest and refreshment. It will almost certainly be fatal to expect all the children to do much the same thing. It is far more profitable if various groups direct their attention to different aspects of the material available.

The importance of conservation and care should be one of the great lessons of nature study. A sense of personal responsibility is called for. To the Country Code (closing of gates, care for animals, no litter, etc.) the teacher will add warnings against taking any rare plant (or more of *anything* than is actually required) and of the need to handle and house even the most humble animals so as to cause least distress both in transit and back at school.

The pupil's record of his adventures is of prime importance. It may be illustrated by drawings or mounted specimens and it should call forth maximum effort, resulting in something which recalls a day well spent.

Field Work

Here, we refer to field work in the narrower sense of specific projects. It is, of course, for the teacher to decide the level at which such studies are undertaken, in relation to his own pupils, but there is a wealth of possibilities open. A most excellent first guide for beginners (teachers and pupils) is V. E. Ford's *How to begin your fieldwork* (John Murray; published for the Association of Science Education). Chapter 2 (*Studies in Natural History*) of the Ministry of Education Pamphlet No. 35, contains much useful advice. Examples of successful field work are often recorded in the pages of the Journal of the School Natural Science Society (*Natural Science in Schools*). Of many other interesting reference books, Philip Street's *Between the Tides* and T. H. Savory's *World of Small Animals* (both University of London Press and now unfortunately out of print) are especially interesting.

Observation of Living Things in the Classroom

The teacher should seize every opportunity to take his class into the fields and woods, or to the local pond or stream; and to the zoo if there be one in the vicinity. He should encourage the amateur bird-watcher and be prepared with help and advice for those of his pupils who keep pets at home. He should make the very fullest use of any plot of ground available, knowing that a school garden can become a laboratory in which experiments make sense to the ordinary child. Yet unless some form of vivarium is set up in the classroom or laboratory, many pupils will find few opportunities to watch animals and plants, and terms such as movement, growth, breathing, feeding, living together and reproduction are likely to remain academic abstractions. Throughout the school course the biological laboratory should provide a series of living exhibits for day-to-day study and care.

Classroom vivaria not only provide first-rate material around which to build lessons; they also make demands upon the patience, sense of responsibility and reliability of boys and girls. The regular attention which is required in connection with feeding, cleaning and restocking is invaluable social training, demanding intelligent reactions to changing situations and making constant calls upon resource. One golden rule must be observed if the vivarium is to live up to its name—scrupulous attention to the routines of cleaning and care is required.

Sources of Material

Ponds, ditches, hedges and the soil are rich sources of small creatures. Look for tiny animals in places such as the following:

Under bushes: Spread newspaper on the ground and gently beat the bushes with a stick.

Among ground litter: Make a sieve from a half metre square of fine wire netting. Fold the square in half and weave the side edges together so that the netting will open out into a boat-shape (and be flat after use): Scoop up fallen leaves and other litter and shake it in the sieve over newspaper.

Under stones or bark: Gently lift flat stones, and the bark of tree stumps or fallen branches.

In soil: Mark out a half metre square of land. Use a trowel to dig up all the plant material, but shake all the soil from the roots back on to the cleared area. Then collect the loose soil, spread it on paper and search among it, with a lens, for small animals.

Use a camel-hair brush to coax or push creatures into a collecting box or bottle. Back in school, compare them carefully with reference-book illustrations. Savory's book, referred to above, is useful both in respect of methods of collection and ways of identifying specimens. The Nuffield Foundation has produced a booklet *Keys to small organisms in soil, litter and water troughs.*

In the paragraphs which follow, guidance about the collection and treatment of pond creatures is a main feature. The simple techniques which are described should give satisfactory results in the hands of even the most inexperienced teacher. It is not, of course, expected that any school will undertake all this work; but there should be something here for everyone, however limited the environment.

Such work involves no departure from the basic curriculum needs; for when properly directed it calls for the keeping of accurate records, the oral and written description of personal experiences, the frequent use of reference books, and the ability to follow instructions faithfully.

Aquatic Plants and Animals

54 *Collecting*

Pond life is a particularly fascinating study for the classroom. Here we can make daily observations in a way which we could not do even if we could regularly visit the pond itself. For collecting, all that is needed is a pond net (which may be made from a broom-stave or stout cane, stout brass wire and a muslin flour bag), an enamel meat-dish (say 25 cm × 20 cm), and a jam jar or two. Insects and larvae may be skimmed from the surface, collected from the water, or scraped from the bottom mud, using the net, and then transferred to the dish for sorting. From the dish the living creatures and plants are removed to the jars, using a spoon for the animals. Harlequin-fly larvae will be found as red "blood worms" in the mud. Transport the animals in plenty of wet weed; only fish need water continually. But pond water will be required for setting up the miniature aquaria.

55 Miniature Aquaria

Use large jam jars or accumulator jars. Put a 2-cm layer of aquarium gravel (see Expt. 56) in each jar, root some water plant in the gravel, fill up with pond water and add one species of pond animal. Label. Cover with a loose lid to check evaporation.

Such aquaria must be reasonably well lit if the plants are to flourish: stand the jars on a window ledge, but not in bright sunlight. The water must *not* be changed.

Small aquaria of this kind are far better than larger ones for the observation of particular plants and small insects and larvae.

56 Larger Aquarium

A tank perhaps 60 cm long, 30 cm wide and 30 cm deep is suitable. The cover (needed to reduce evaporation) may be of frosted glass, since clear glass shows every trace of dust. Tap-water is usually satisfactory (provided that it is not strongly chlorinated) and about 2 litres is needed for every centimetre of fish. For small fish and other small water creatures growing weed will supply sufficient oxygen. The plants may be weighted down in the gravel by stones or by pieces of lead or zinc (not copper); they soon root themselves and produce new stems. Pebbles and gravel must be thoroughly washed before use; sand should be avoided—it holds decaying matter and is not readily cleaned. One or two larger stones may be placed on top of the gravel.

An aquarium always looks best when lit from the top, but in any case adequate daylight is necessary if the plants are to flourish. Mount two 25-watt lamps in lamp-holders, one at each end of a metal cover which rests about the glass cover. Make the metal cover from aluminium sheet cut and bent as indicated. The two lamps will run for 20 hours on 1 unit of electricity and they may be switched on for about 8 hours a day in the ordinary classroom. Even better visibility is achieved by backing the trough with black or grey paper.

Remove green algae from the walls of the tank by using a piece of fresh steel wool on the end of a stick. Water-snails help to keep this growth down. Unsightly refuse on the gravel can be taken up in a glass tube; close the top with the finger, push the tube down over the refuse, release the finger—so that the refuse is pushed up into the tube with the water—and then replace the finger and lift the tube from the tank.

57 Water-plants

A collection may be made in an aquarium; or single plants may be introduced into the miniature aquaria of Expt. 55, animal and plant being named on a label. Notes on a few of the commoner water-plants are given below:

(i) Duckweed: The leaf-like blades (round-leaved or ivy-leaved) float on

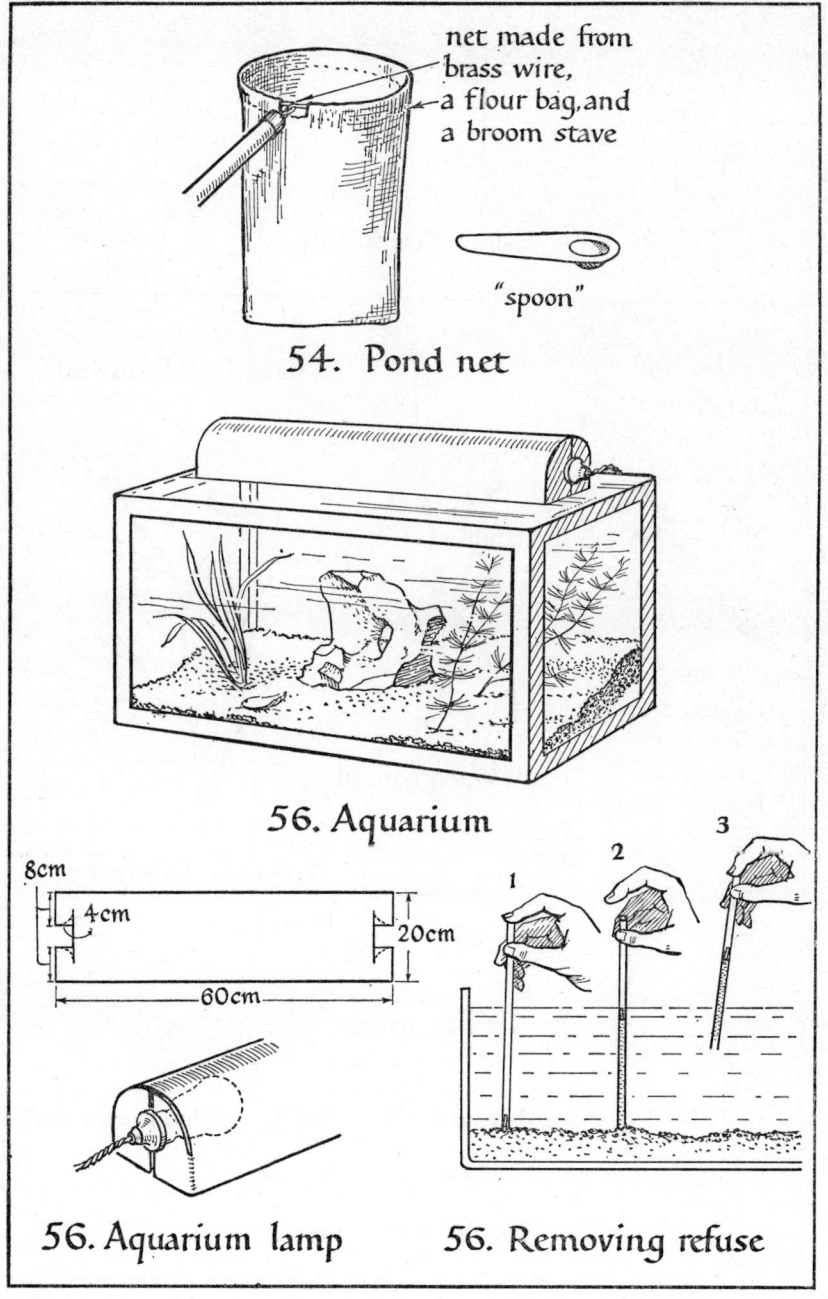

54. Pond net

56. Aquarium

56. Aquarium lamp

56. Removing refuse

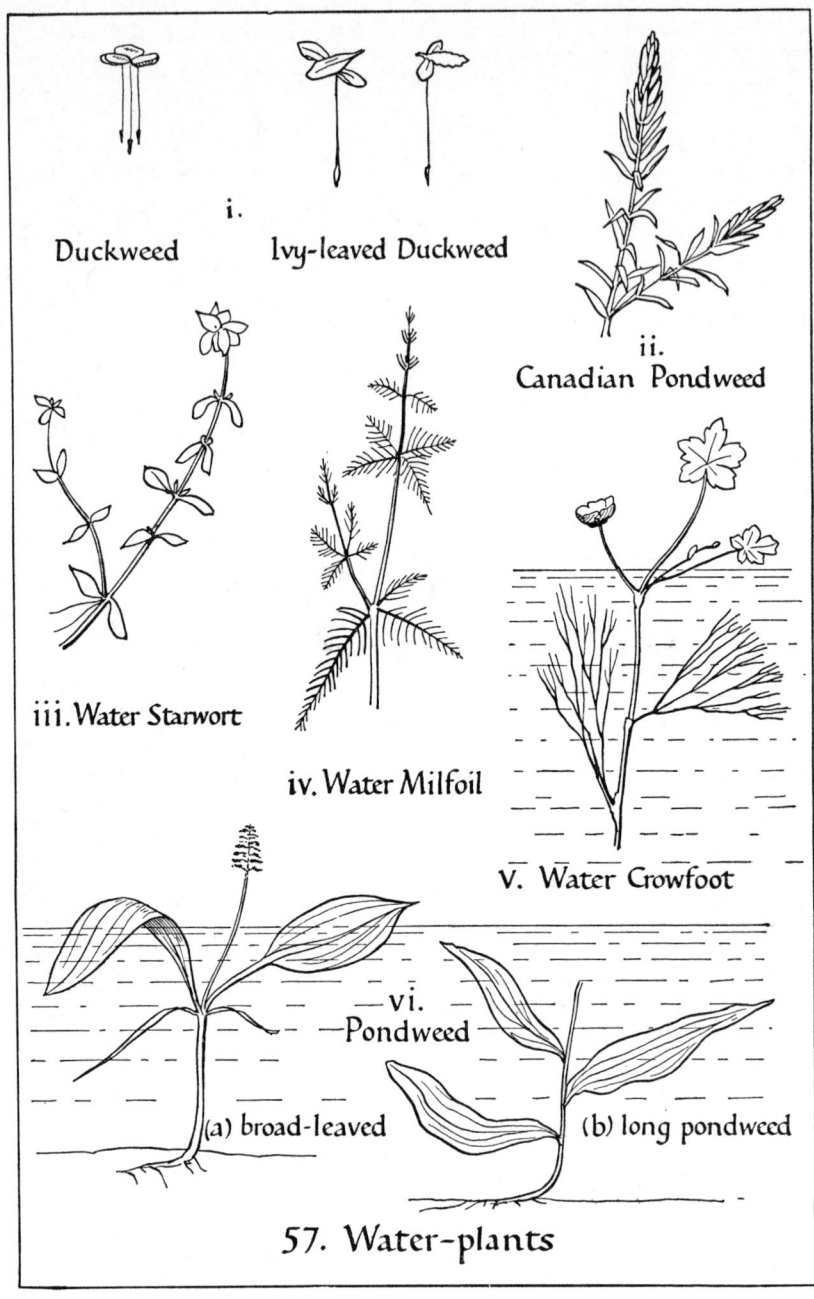

57. Water-plants

the surface and are useful as shade and shelter for small creatures in the aquarium. New plants grow out from the old, their rootlike fibres hanging downwards into the water.

(ii) Canadian Pondweed: The plant is totally submerged and its leaves grow in whorls of three; the stems are long and branched and readily anchor themselves by thread-like roots. Buds form in autumn which fall to the bottom of the pond and grow into new plants the following spring.

(iii) Starwort: The top leaves form a star on the surface of the water; below, the leaves grow in pairs and hair-like roots grow out from the stems.

(iv) Milfoil: The finely divided leaves grow in whorls of four; the plant multiplies rapidly.

(v) Water Crowfoot: This may be recognized in summer by the buttercup-like flowers (white petals) which float on the surface. The underwater leaves are very finely divided, but the leaves at the surface have broad green lobes.

(vi) Pondweed: The term covers a number of plants, all having long broad leaves. Flowers are borne on a stalk above water.

(vii) Creeping Jenny: A well-known garden plant; grows vigorously in water.

58 *Small Aquatic Animals*
See also Chapter 4. For the guidance of beginners a rough division into groups may be made:
(a) Crustaceans, having many legs.

(i) Water-fleas: Likely to be Daphnia; they may be seen swarming near the bottom of the jar. Each is about the size of a pin-head but they should be examined with a lens or under a microscope to see the single large black eye, the large feelers and the constantly moving legs. See Fig. 68.

(ii) Cyclops: Similar in size to Daphnia, but of different shape and having four pairs of legs instead of five. The female may show two large eggsacs; if placed in a dish of pond-water young Cyclops appear when the sacs burst. See Fig. 68.

(iii) Water Slater (or Water Louse): About 1 cm long when full grown, with segmented body and many legs. These animals do not swim, but crawl about. Like Cyclops and the Freshwater Shrimp, the Water Slater is a scavenger and is, therefore, useful in the aquarium.

(iv) Freshwater Shrimp: Found in running water and best kept in shallow, well-aerated aquaria. About 1 cm long, curved and with feelers and many legs; its movements are particularly interesting.

(b) Insects (three pairs of legs).

(i) Great Water-beetle (Dytiscus): Large dark-brown body with a yellow line just above its horny wings. Swims by paddling its hairy back legs and

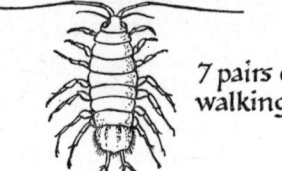

2 pairs of feelers

7 pairs of walking legs

58(a) iii. Water Slater

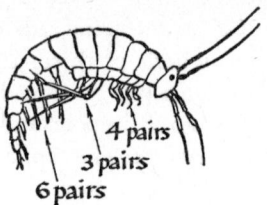

4 pairs
3 pairs
6 pairs

13 pairs of legs

58(a) iv. Freshwater Shrimp

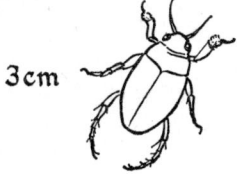

3 cm

1 cm

58(b) ii. Whirligig

2½ cm

tail tube

58(b) i. Great Water-beetle

58(b) iii. Water Scorpion

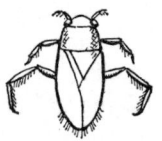

Notonecta
(back swimmer)
1½ cm

Corixa

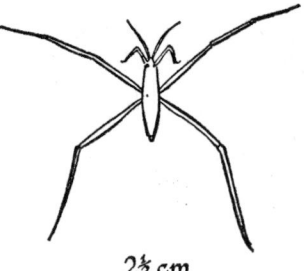

2½ cm

58(b) iv. Water Boatman

58(b) v. Pond Skater

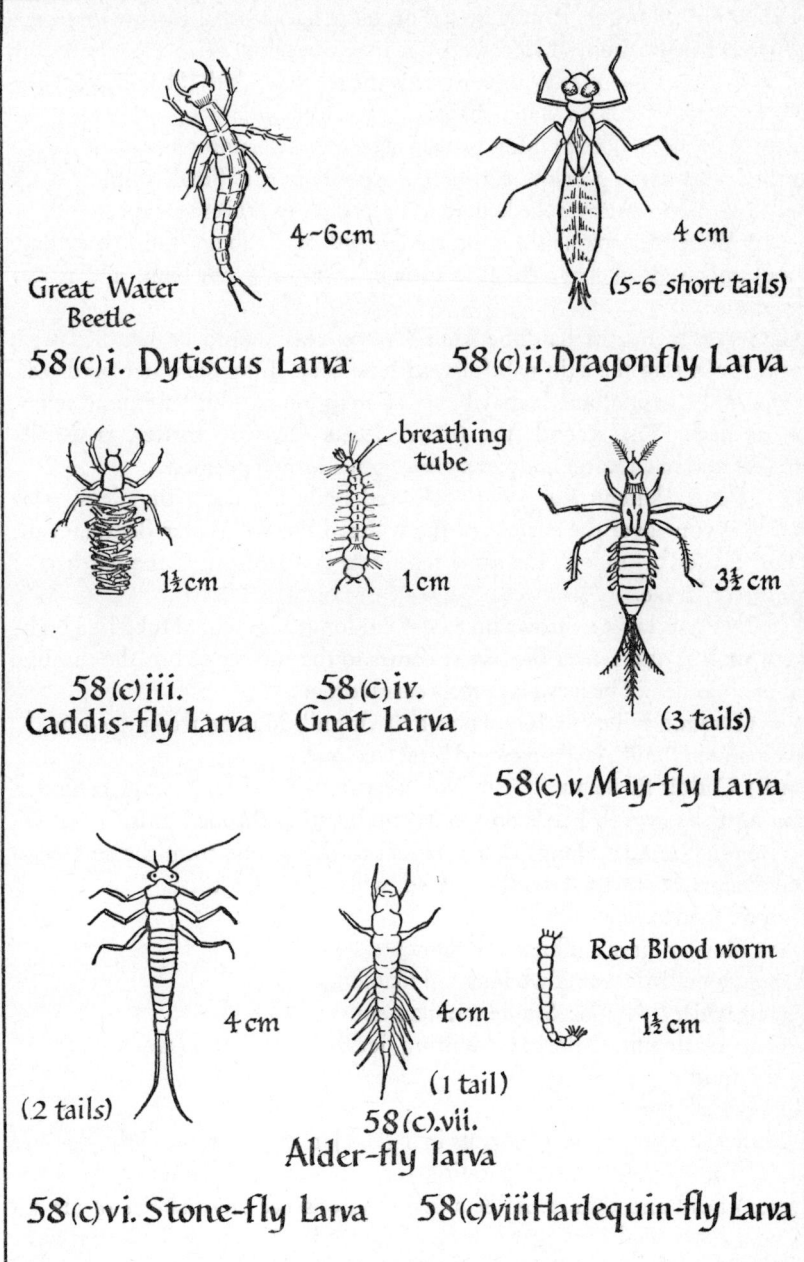

comes to surface to breathe, poking up the end of its abdomen to take air into the two breathing tubes there. This beetle must be kept apart from the other pond creatures. It may be fed on tadpoles or small earthworms; if a worm is held in front of it (forceps), it may be seen to seize the worm with its front legs. An equally large beetle is the shining black ("silver") Hydrophilus, which feeds on water-snails.

(ii) Whirligig Beetle: May be seen dancing and running over the water surface and darting below carrying a globule of air. Small shining black body; carnivorous; must be kept in a covered jar to prevent escape.

(iii) Water Scorpion: May be recognized by its long "tail" (breathing tube) and beak-like mouth. It is brown, about $2\frac{1}{2}$ cm long, and is carnivorous.

(iv) Water Boatman: One kind (Notonecta) should be handled with care; it can stab the skin painfully with its beak. Like the other predators, it should be kept alone. It may be up to 2 cm long and it habitually swims on its back. The second type (Corixa) eats decaying matter, is usually smaller and has a softer body; it swims in the normal position.

(v) Pond Skater: Long dark-coloured body and long thin legs, with which it runs over the surface of the water. Like the Water Boatman, the Pond Skater belongs to the same family as the greenfly of the garden.

(c) Insect larvae.

(i) Dytiscus larva: Grows up to 4–6 cm long; segmented tube-like body, with six legs and pincer-like jaws; comes to the surface to breathe through tip of abdomen. The larva is fiercely carnivorous.

(ii) Dragonfly larva: Known as a "nymph". May be recognized by the five-pointed "tail", large eyes and brown colour.

(iii) Caddis-fly larva: Grub-like creature, dragging its case behind it amongst the gravel. Feeds on weeds and breathes through gills.

(iv) Gnat larva: Hangs down by its breathing tube from the surface of the water; segmented body covered with hair-like tufts. The pupa is comma-shaped.

(v) May-fly larva: Three tail filaments.

(vi) Stone-fly larva: Two long tail filaments.

(vii) Alder-fly larva: Single tail filament.

(viii) Harlequin-fly larva: Twisting, jerking, red "blood-worms", found in the mud.

(d) Water Spiders

Place these among water plants in a glass jar. Look for the eight legs and notice the narrow waist separating the unsegmented abdomen from the (fused) head and thorax. After a few days observe any bubbles of air apparently stranded among the water plants; they may indicate the web, which forms a tiny "diving-bell" from which the animal sallies forth in search of prey.

59 Larger Pond Animals

(a) Horse-leech (a true worm): Note the flattened dark reddish-brown segmented body, which may be up to 10 cm long. There is a small sucker at the pointed head end and a larger sucker (by which the worm anchors itself) at the hind end. The animal sucks blood; it should be kept in a jar by itself and fed on earthworms. Remove each worm when the leech has left it.

(b) Pond Snails: There are many kinds, but most have spiral shells, often brownish-green. Put one into a dish with a little water and wait until the snail emerges. Observe the head, the eyes and mouth, the pair of triangular-shaped horns, and the foot on which the snail glides along.

(c) Fish: Sticklebacks (three spines protruding upwards from the back), minnows, gold-fish, dace and carp are all suitable aquarium fish. Observe especially how they swim and how the mouth and gills open in the breathing movements. Notice the streamlined body and the scales. Sticklebacks must be kept apart from other species.

Topics: Formal studies of the structure and classification of these plants and animals are out of place at this level. The creatures' habits and mode of life should be observed and discussed, including their ways of moving, breathing, feeding and reproducing, but in a manner which does not detract from the absorbing interest of keeping and watching living things.

Other Creatures

60 *A Wormery:* See also Chapter 24.

(a) Fill a large jam jar with alternate layers of soil and sand, or with layers of differently coloured soils; a thin layer of sawdust may be included. Keep the soil moist but not wet, and introduce two or three small worms. Tie black paper round the jar, and slip it off only for observation. Leave the jar undisturbed for a week or two: worm-casts on the surface, burrows meeting the glass sides of the jar, and the mixing effect of the earthworms' activities should then be visible. The experiment of putting small fragments of various kinds of food on the surface of the soil can be tried, and small leaves may be dropped into the jar to see whether the worms will try to drag them down.

(b) A larger wormery may be made from a rectangular, 5-litre oil-can by washing it thoroughly with soapy water, cutting away most of the front and lining the aperture with glass (which will be kept in place by the soil).

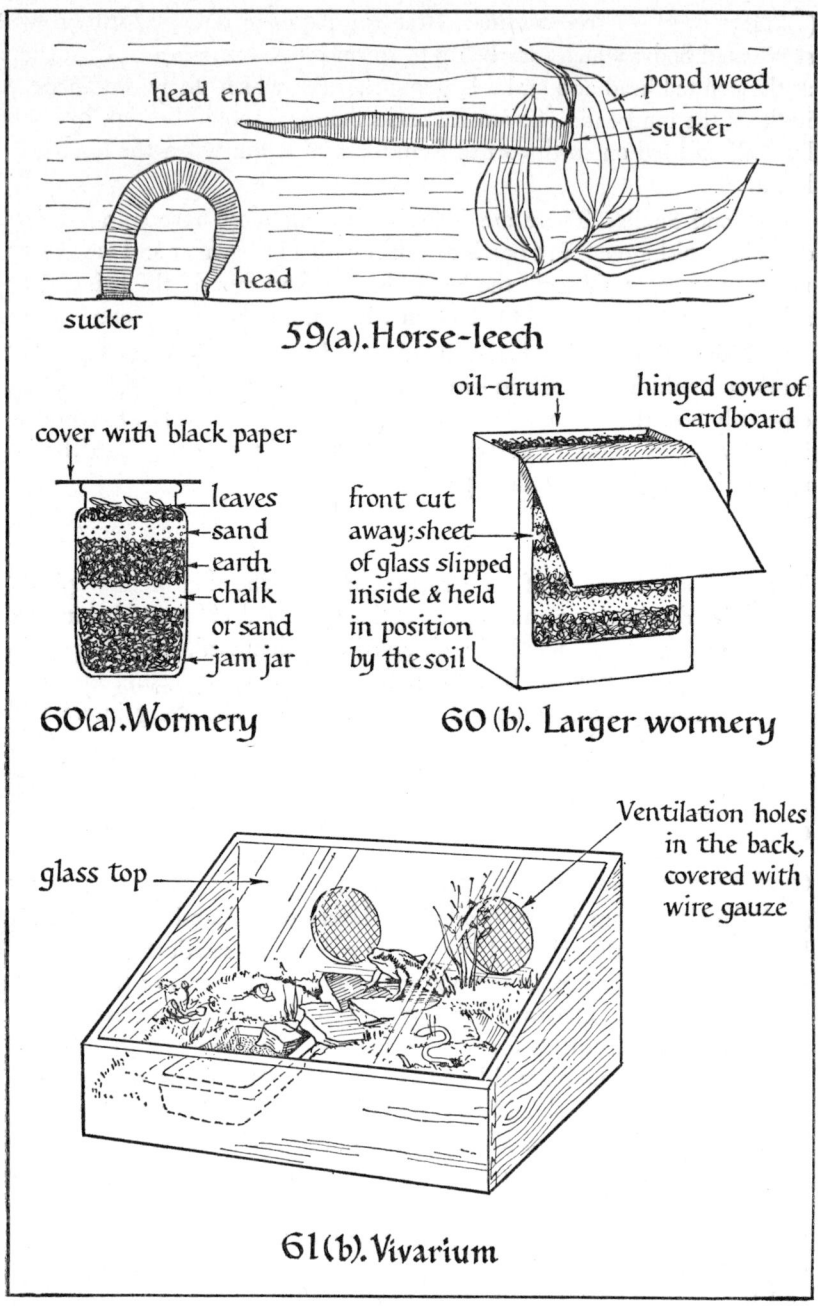

59(a). Horse-leech

60(a). Wormery

60(b). Larger wormery

61(b). Vivarium

61 Various Forms of Vivaria

(a) Aquarium for newts: See the authors' *Practical Science for Secondary Schools*, Book Three, pp. 28-9.

(b) Vivaria for reptiles, amphibians, etc.: Fig. 61. shows a useful type, shaped like a garden frame. A metal tray at the bottom is filled with living turf. Sink a saucer or small dish of water flush with the turf and arrange a few flat stones on the turf and in the water to serve as shelters and hiding places.

Here may be kept (preferably for short periods) snails, slugs, worms, lizards, toads, frogs, and perhaps a tortoise. Toads and frogs may be fed on caterpillars, slugs and living insects. Very young frogs often do well on greenfly.

Snails and slugs may lay eggs in damp soil, 20-50 at a time. Watch for them and see how long it is before the young hatch. Feed snails and slugs on fresh lettuce leaves every day.

(c) Tadpoles may be reared from frogspawn or toadspawn either in jam jars or in pie-dishes sunk in the turf of vivaria such as that described for reptiles. They need warmth, light and a few water plants to which the young tadpoles can attach themselves. As water evaporates it should be replaced by fresh pond-water, but if the water goes cloudy it should be syphoned away and replaced.

(d) Another form of vivarium, made from an old stoneware sink and suitable for lizards or a grass-snake or slow-worm, is described in *Practical Science for Secondary Schools*, Book Three, p. 30.

62 Insect Cages

(a) A good design consists of a wooden box, perhaps 30 cm high by 10 cm square, with a shelf across it 10 cm from the bottom. There is a small hole in the shelf and through this the stem of the food plant passes into a small jar of water beneath. If the insect falls off the twig, it is protected from falling into the water and from having to try to climb back up the jar. The front of the box is glass or acetate sheet. A few small holes are punched for ventilation. A small box of soil may stand on the shelf.

(b) A cylinder of acetate sheet closed at the ends with the lid and base of a floor-polish tin makes an attractive cage.

Insects, caterpillars and eggs may be found in the garden. Eggs of the Tropical Moonmoth can be purchased—the larvae will live on hawthorn, and the life-cycle is spectacular. Silk-worms may be fed with lettuce. Generally, rear insects on the plants on which you find them. The food plant will need frequent renewal. After some time the caterpillar will stop feeding and will prepare some kind of cocoon, in which as pupa or chrysalis it will undergo metamorphosis. When the winged insect emerges it should be given its liberty.

If you have a copy of *Foundations of Science* (Glasspool and Laybourn, U.L.P., now out of print), Book Two, pp. 66–70, you will find there full details of the method of rearing silk-worms and the Indian Moon-moth.

63 *Life-cycle of Fly*

Flies may be trapped in milk bottles by fitting a paper funnel in the top and supplying a suitable bait at the bottom—e.g. raw meat for the blow-fly, or ripe banana for fruit flies. Allow two or three flies to enter and then plug the top of each bottle with cotton-wool. When eggs are laid release the flies and observe the hatching and growth of larvae. The larvae should be well covered with sawdust for pupation. The whole life-cycle will be completed in two or three weeks. The adults may be fed on sugar, water and moist dog-biscuit.

64 *Keeping Ants*

A simple formicarium consists of a prepared honeycomb, made by cutting a winding path in a square of felt, clamped between a sheet of Perspex and a wooden baseboard. One end of the felt hangs out of the sandwich and dips into water, to keep the felt moist; the other end adjoins a closed space which serves as a food chamber. The formicarium is kept dark by means of a simple cloth or paper cover, except that the food chamber is not covered. Food consists of drops of honey, supplemented by occasional flies, cake crumbs, fruit fragments, etc.

Find an ants' nest (e.g. under flat stones) and dig into it with a trowel. Transfer soil, ants, eggs, larvae and pupae all together into a soup-plate standing in water. Place a matchbox, slightly open, on the plate. The ants will move into the dark box and may thence be emptied into the food chamber of the formicarium. In a few days (during which the ants have been left in the dark, undisturbed) changes will be noticeable. Tunnels will have been dug, the larvae and pupae will have been collected into special places by the workers, and it may be possible to observe a queen.

65 *Spiders*

These may be kept in jam jars darkened with black paper. Fed occasionally on houseflies, they rapidly fill the jars with their webs and show little desire to emigrate.

66 *Hamsters*

Golden hamsters thrive in captivity and are well-suited for life in the classroom; they take up little space, have no strong smell, and are very attractive in appearance. They are easy to feed, doing well on table scraps, grain of any kind, nuts, crushed dog-biscuit, hard bread, root vegetables, cabbage, dandelion, etc. Hard food is essential, since hamsters are rodents, but greenstuff should also be given daily. One feed a day is sufficient (about 30 g of dry food per animal), except in the case of breeding does. Water

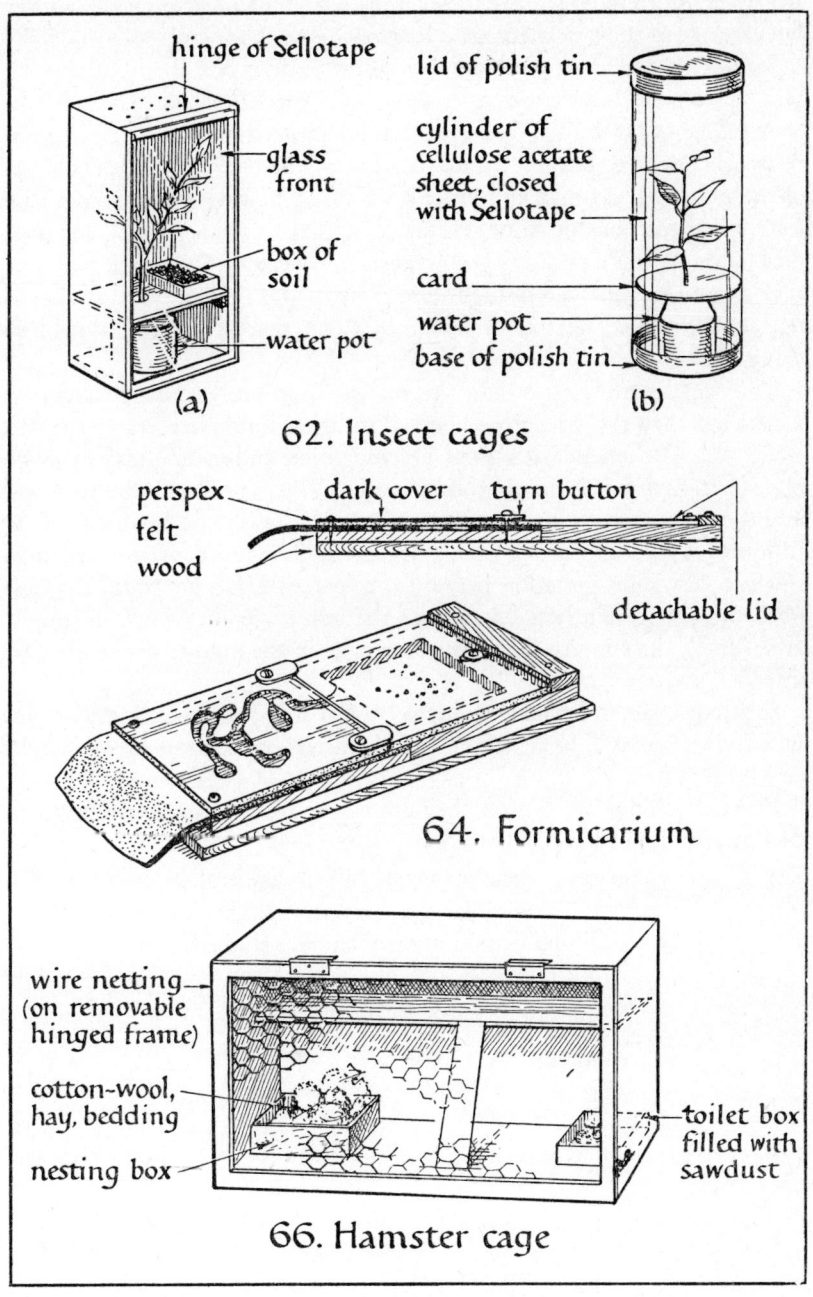

62. Insect cages

64. Formicarium

66. Hamster cage

should be available, and milk may be given on occasion. Hamsters instinctively store food, so that they can be left unattended over week-ends; but the cage must be cleaned out at least once a week.

Metal-wire cages are most suitable, but a wooden box about 50 cm long will serve provided that wire-netting is fastened over the inside of the frame door to protect the frame from the hamster's teeth. The mesh must be small enough to prevent the escape of young hamsters. Cover the bottom of the cage with sawdust and provide a shallow nesting-box, at least 15 cm long, filled with hay or straw. Hamsters will use a small "toilet" box (or a jar laid on its side), and this is a great help in keeping the cage clean. The cage should be kept in a draught-free position and the temperature should not be allowed to fall below about 15°C. A shaded position should be chosen.

The females are larger than the males. They are mature at about 10 weeks but they should not be allowed to breed until they are at least 12 weeks old. The female has a 4-day breeding cycle and mating may easily be observed. To prevent fighting after mating, the male should be removed and the doe left with ample nesting material; she should be disturbed as little as possible. Up to ten young are born, about 16 days after mating; this is a very short gestation period for a mammal. Do not touch the nest until the young hamsters come out in search of food (about a fortnight after birth), since interference usually results in the mother destroying the litter.

Separate male and female "kittens" when they are about 6 weeks old. Otherwise there will be fighting. Only hamsters of the same brood should be kept together.

Females seldom breed after they are a year old and hamsters begin to decline after two years.

Topics: Ants and bees (social insects). Insects harmful to man (see also Chapter 10). Insects in the garden—aphides, hover-flies, ladybirds, etc. Simple classification of animals studied.

Chapter Four

The Structure of Living Things

The Use of Magnifiers

Boys and girls (to say nothing of grown-ups) are often lamentably ignorant even of the general arrangement of the major organs in their own bodies, while their ideas on the structure of cells and tissues may be vague in the extreme.

Children in the primary school should be taught the proper use of a hand-lens, which will remain a most valuable aid throughout any science course. With the lens held close to the eye, the object to be examined is brought slowly up towards it (or the eye moved towards the object). A good light is essential and it will generally be found that the best way of avoiding casting a shadow on the object is to hold it and the head well up.

A single magnifier with a $\times 5$ lens is suitable. Not infrequently it is an advantage to have both hands free and simple dissecting microscopes may be purchased, or made in the school workshop.

In general the conventional compound microscope is not recommended for individual use by average pupils in the lower or middle school. What is seen through such a microscope requires a considerable interpretation and the teacher has no guarantee of the pupil's reaction. Moreover a battery of such microscopes is costly and lenses are easily damaged. However, the teacher himself should have a good microscope available, preferably with built-in illumination and a device to prevent the possibility of racking the lens into the slide. With this he may set the instrument and allow pupils to look at particular specimens. Magnification up to 200 diameters should be possible and suitable instruments may still be bought for as little as £20.

A more recent development is the inexpensive low-power stereoscopic microscope, giving magnification of $\times 10$ or $\times 20$ with a much more "lifelike" image. Instruments of this type can be obtained with built-in lighting and an adjustable arm by which the optical head may be moved over the field which is being examined.

There are, however, great advantages in communal viewing and for this the microprojector should be considered. A good instrument is not costly in comparison with a battery of microscopes and the teacher remains in touch with what the pupil sees, able to point out significant features. Pupils' own mounted specimens may be exhibited in rapid succession, so that the whole class is involved. Indeed, a microprojector should be used chiefly for the display of pupils' material. Permanent mounts of specimens difficult to prepare or to obtain locally will be kept on hand of course, but whenever possible boys and girls should mount their own objects. The average pupil may learn little from the contemplation of slides prepared by others. The simple mounting techniques described later in this chapter give good results and can be extended to a wide variety of material. Cheap instruments, of low resolving power, should be avoided. It is desirable to have eyepieces for ×5 and ×10, and a choice of objectives, bringing the cost to £120 or more.

Larger specimens of plant and animal dissections, suitable for naked-eye examination, have often been stored in formalin. Today excellent products are available embedded in transparent plastic. They are injected with attractive colours to bring out details. Such specimens may be passed from hand to hand and are virtually indestructible.

Finally, films and filmstrips are often useful in showing the structure and movements of small organisms. They are discussed in Chapter 17.

Mounting Microscopic Objects

67 *Preparation of a Section of Marrow Stem*

Use a new one-edged safety-razor blade for cutting. Hold the stem between the index finger and thumb of the left hand, with the finger nearly on a level with the surface to be cut but the thumb somewhat lower. Remove a slab of material to expose a flat face and then, with material and razor flooded with water, draw the razor across the surface so as to cut extremely thin slices of stem. Do not attempt to get whole cross-sections; small sector flakes will serve and the object is to get them not more than one cell thick.

When a number of sections have accumulated on the razor, slide them off into a shallow saucer of water. Select the very thinnest; to do this, stir the water and look for a section whose shadow on the bottom of the saucer is more obvious than the section itself. Transfer one or two such sections to the middle of a microscope slide, and allow one drop of glycerine jelly (liquefied by standing the bottle in hot water) to fall on to the material on the slide.

Rest one edge of a square cover-slip on the slide and bring it along until it just touches the drop of jelly. Then, steadying the slip with a needle, allow it to fall gently over the drop. The jelly should spread out evenly as the slip is lowered, excluding any air bubbles.

Such a slide will last for several weeks. To render it more permanent, remove any extruded jelly from round the edges of the coverslip and paint round the edges with stove black, using a fine brush. This will seal the jelly from the air. Glycerine jelly slides should not be used in the microprojector without a heat filter; otherwise the jelly will melt.

Sections of stems, roots, potato, etc. may be mounted by this method. Temporary water-mounts may be made as directed in Expt. 70, and for pollen tubes, yeast, etc. the method of Expt. 522 is useful. A simple staining technique, to bring out particular features, is described in Expt. 70.

For thin stems or leaves resort must be had to embedding when sections are to be cut. The material is gripped between two halves of a piece of carrot or elder pith, and the carrot or pith is cut at the same time as the material it supports.

Early Attempts at Formation of a Body

68 Hydra

During early summer, transfer a spoonful of pondweed to a litre jar (jam jar) filled with pond water over a 2-cm layer of aquarium gravel. Set up several such jars, preferably from a number of different sources. The water-fleas Daphnia and Cyclops usually develop within a week or two, and they are followed by Hydra, which feeds upon them. The Hydra (green or brown) will attach themselves to the walls of the jars and the tentacles can be seen waving about in search of food. For observing them a hand-lens is desirable.

If some Hydra are transferred to a jar of clean water and fed on Daphnia, they will multiply rapidly. The capture of Daphnia by Hydra is a good subject for the microprojector. One Hydra, preferably starved for several days, is transferred to a cavity cell which is then mounted (horizontally) in the projector. After focusing, a few Daphnia are pipetted into the cell; they are quickly captured and their ingestion may be observed.

The reproductive swellings on the body of Hydra are easily visible. The film "Life of a Freshwater Polyp" (646/A4) is recommended as an aid in studying the form, movements and methods of reproduction of Hydra and to introduce the idea of division of labour (specialization) among cells. Film 656/A42 (Daphnia) deals with several types of water-fleas.

Amoeba is not easily cultured in the laboratory but the film "Life of a One-celled Animal" (644/A2) well illustrates how this unicellular creature lives and carries out, without specialized organs, the vital functions of feeding, excreting and reproducing.

69 Paramoecium

A small supply should be bought from one of the biological supply agencies and then cultured for class work, as follows:

Boil about 10 g of chopped straw or hay in a litre of distilled water or rain water for a quarter of an hour. Allow to cool to room temperature and then drop in three or four crushed wheat grains. Let the preparation stand for a day. Filter the liquid and adjust the pH to between 6 and 7 (i.e. near neutral) by adding very dilute caustic soda solution drop by drop with stirring. A suitable indicator paper (Lypham) may be obtained from Camlab (Glass) Ltd., Milton Road, Cambridge. This operation is important. The stock medium may be preserved in a refrigerator.

In order to culture, pour about 250 cm^3 of the medium into a 400 cm^3 conical flask, shake it vigorously (to aerate it) and inoculate it with a few cm^3 of purchased Paramoecium liquor, using a clean teat pipette. Maintain the preparation at between 18°C and 25°C., keeping it away from strong light to diminish the risk of growth of algae. Sub-culturing may be undertaken after three or four weeks.

Paramoecium is just visible to the naked eye. Its movement through the water, backing to avoid obstacles, can be observed under a hand-lens. Its slipper shape and spiral motion are well seen under the low power of the microscope or on the microprojector.

70 *A Simple Plant (Spirogyra)*

Spirogyra is found floating as tangled masses of fine, slimy, bright-green threads near the surface of ponds. Mount one or two threads in a single drop of water on a slide, cover with a slip, and examine under the low power. Each thread is seen to consist of stout-walled cells joined end-to-end and crossed obliquely by narrow, parallel, green bands.

Stain the nucleus by putting a drop of iodine solution or methylene blue at one edge of the cover-slip and soaking up water from the opposite edge using blotting-paper. As the water is absorbed, iodine is drawn on to the filaments.

The Cellular Nature of Living Matter

All the following objects can be seen under the low power of the microscope, except Pleurococcus, which requires higher power.

71 *Plant Cells*

Suitable material can be obtained by tearing a leaf of laurel or lily obliquely across; the extreme edge of the tear will be translucent and may be only one cell thick. Snip off a tiny portion of this epidermal tissue with scissors, mount it in a drop of water on a slide under a cover-slip, and examine with the microscope or microprojector. Good results are also obtained by tearing off the thinnest possible strip of tissue from the inside of an onion; or by using a single leaf of common moss. Material such as privet leaves may first be boiled with very dilute caustic soda solution to assist removal of epidermis.

THE STRUCTURE OF LIVING THINGS 65

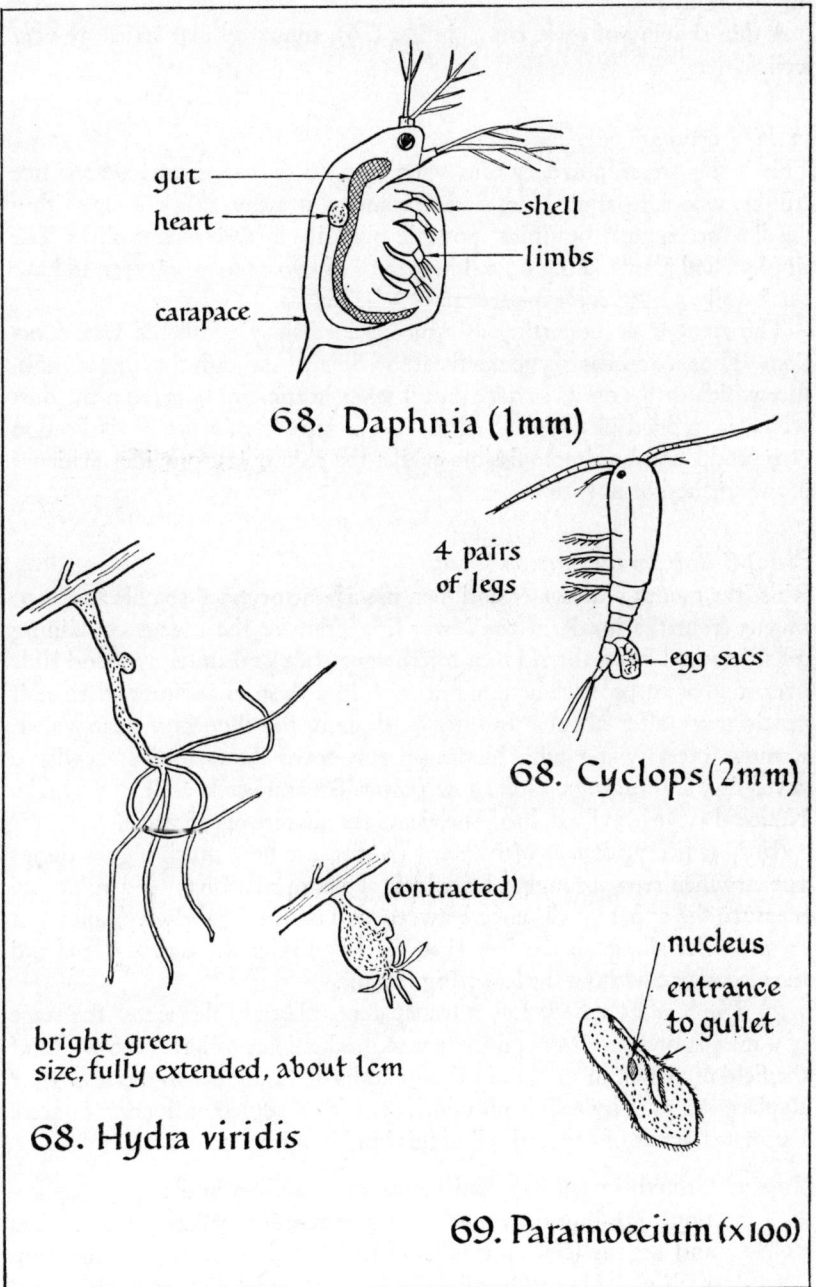

68. Daphnia (1mm)

68. Cyclops (2mm)

bright green
size, fully extended, about 1cm

68. Hydra viridis

69. Paramoecium (×100)

In all cases iodine may be used as a simple stain to bring out the cell nuclei (Expt. 70).

A thin shaving of cork, cut as in Expt. 67, shows cellular structure very well.

72 *Pleurococcus*

This is the green, powdery film often seen on the windward side of tree trunks, wooden palings, etc. Scrape some of it away, break it up with a needle and mount the tiniest possible quantity in water on a slide. The single-celled plants, often united in groups of two or four, are seen to have thick walls, a large chloroplast and a small nucleus.

The plant is as interesting as Amoeba in displaying all the vital functions. Thus it absorbs oxygen and carbon dioxide through the film of moisture which forms on its surface and it takes in mineral salts from the dust which is trapped in the same film. The groups of cells are an indication of reproduction by simple fission, whilst the chloroplast provides evidence of the method of nutrition.

73 (a) *Cells from the Human Mouth*

Rinse the mouth with water and then use a bone or metal spatula to scrape mucus from the inside of the lower lip. Transfer the mucus containing cells detached from the lip to a microscope slide and draw a second slide over it so as to produce a thin smear. Add a drop of iodine and rinse it gently away after about a minute by dipping the slide into clean water. Remove excess water with blotting-paper, cover the stained area with a cover-slip, and examine under low power. Separate cells are easily visible. Notice also the heavily stained nuclei and the absence of cell walls.

(b) *Magnifying Power of a Lens:* To measure how much bigger things appear when seen through a lens, look at 1 mm markings on a ruler and measure the apparent distance between two adjacent marks by holding a second ruler alongside the lens (you view one ruler through the lens and the second one without the lens: Fig. 73 (b)).

(c) *The Size of a Cell:* Lay a transparent (plastic) ruler across the stage of a microscope and focus on the 1 mm graduations. What is the width of the field of view i. in mm, ii. in thousandths of a mm (micro-metres, μm) ? Replace the ruler by a slide on which cells from your mouth are mounted. Estimate the size of a typical cell of this kind in micro-metres.

Topics: Growth in animals and plants (cell division and cell multiplication). Healing of wounds and regeneration of lost parts. Tissues and organs (cell specialization). Selected frames from filmstrips such as "About Ourselves" (670/G1) and "The Human Body" (670/G2).

THE STRUCTURE OF LIVING THINGS 67

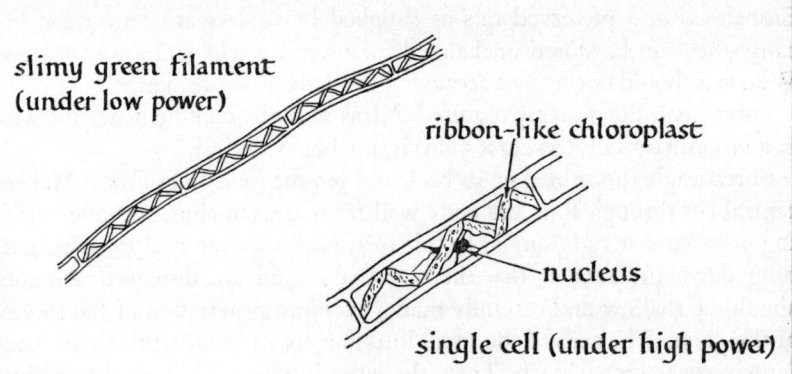

70. Spirogyra

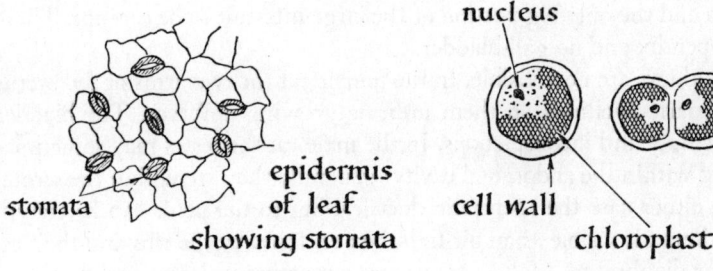

71. Plant cells

72. Pleurococcus (under high power)

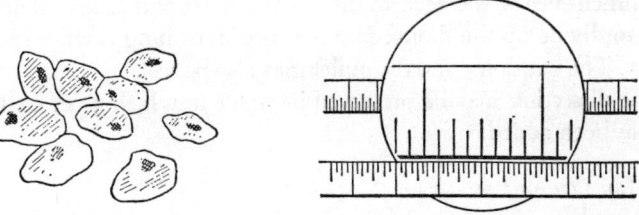

73(a). Cells from human mouth stained with iodine

73(b) Magnification

Principal Organs of the Mammal

74 *Dissection of Rat*

Embalmed and preserved rats as supplied by dealers are convenient because they can be stored unchanged for several weeks and are odourless. Wild rats should not be used because of the danger of infection.

Large dissection pins are required. A tray made by melting dissecting wax in a meat tin (25 cm × 20 cm × 5 cm) is suitable for the rat.

Spreadeagle the animal on its back and pin the four limbs down. Make a central cut through skin and body wall from anus to chin, and after making cross cuts at right angles to this turn back the skin and muscles, pinning down the flaps so that the digestive organs are displayed. All cuts should be shallow and carefully made, avoiding penetration of the thorax at this stage. The coils of the small intestine are prominent; the liver lobes largely cover the stomach. Trace the large intestine up from the rectum, across, and down to the caecum.

Cut the alimentary canal at the anus and just above the stomach; Remove it bodily after cutting other attachments as necessary. Note the stomach and the only big portion of the large intestine—the caecum. There is no appendix and no gall-bladder.

The kidneys are now visible. In the female rat the two arms of the uterus appear; dark swellings on them indicate growing embryos. The bladder will be empty and inconspicuous. In the male rat the testes may sometimes be found within the abdominal cavity; generally they are within the scrotal sacs. In either case the spermatic duct leading to the penis can be traced.

The thorax is visible as an air-tight box enclosed by the ribs and the thin muscular diaphragm. Make a transverse cut across its lower end to release the diaphragm from the ribs, and continue the cut up each side of the thorax to the neck. The latter operation involves cutting through the ribs, but is not difficult with sharp scissors. Finally, cut away the remaining attachment below the neck to display the heart and lungs. Membranes are seen to divide up the thorax into the pleural or lung cavities and the heart cavity. The windpipe and the gullet may also be seen.

The dissection may be preserved in water to which 5 per cent of formalin has been added.

75 *Man (cut-out model)*

This model is intended to show the relative sizes and positions of the main organs of the human body.

A duplicated sheet of drawings is pasted on thin card, coloured, and the separate organs cut out and fastened to the body background at the numbered positions.

To ensure that the parts fit correctly, proceed as follows: First draw the complete torso, with organs and other parts (some parts will overlap).

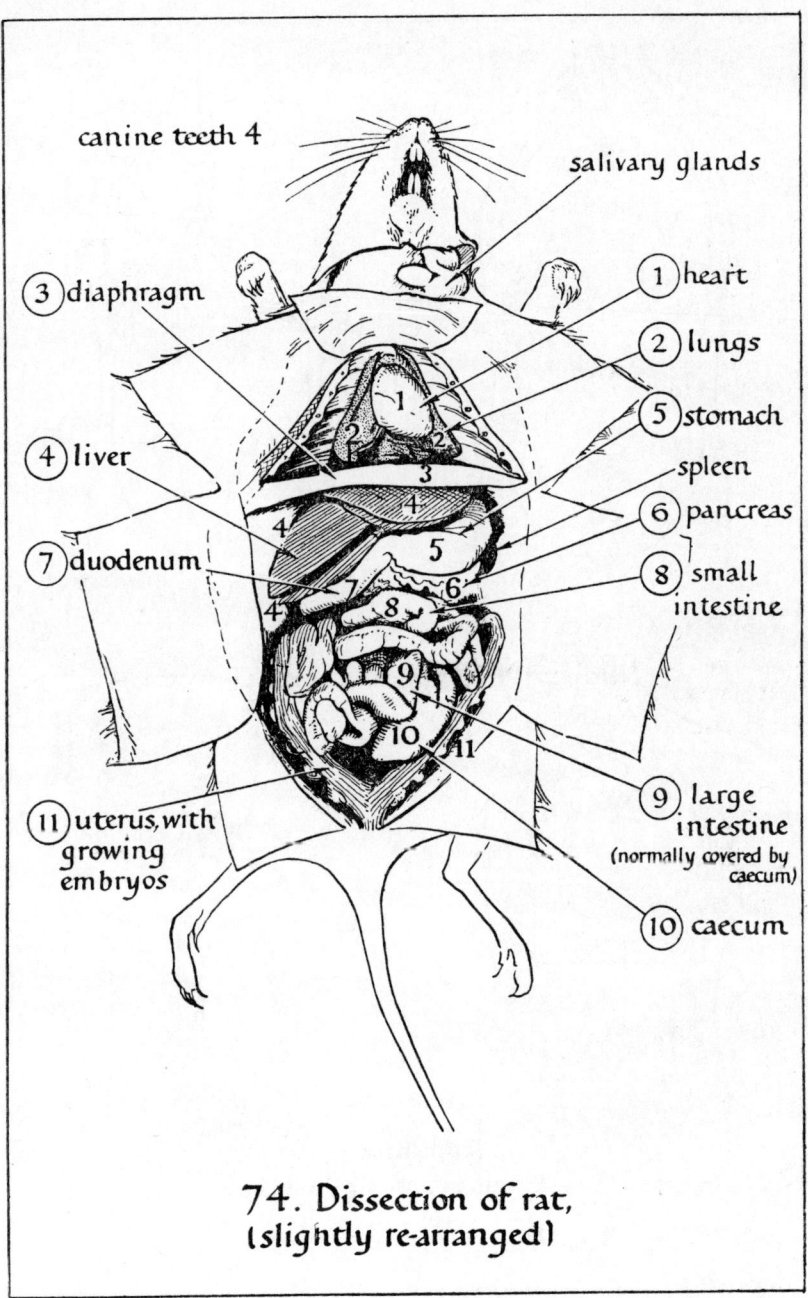

74. Dissection of rat, (slightly re-arranged)

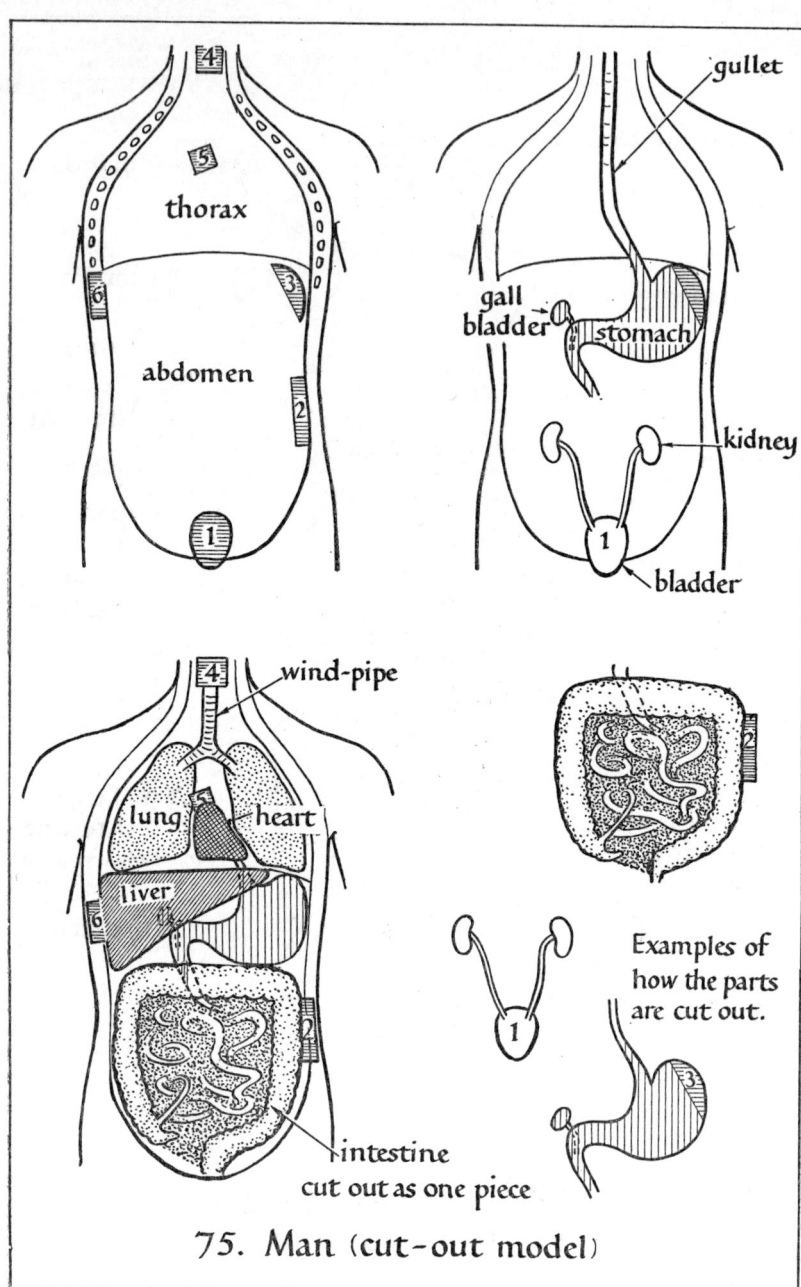

75. Man (cut-out model)

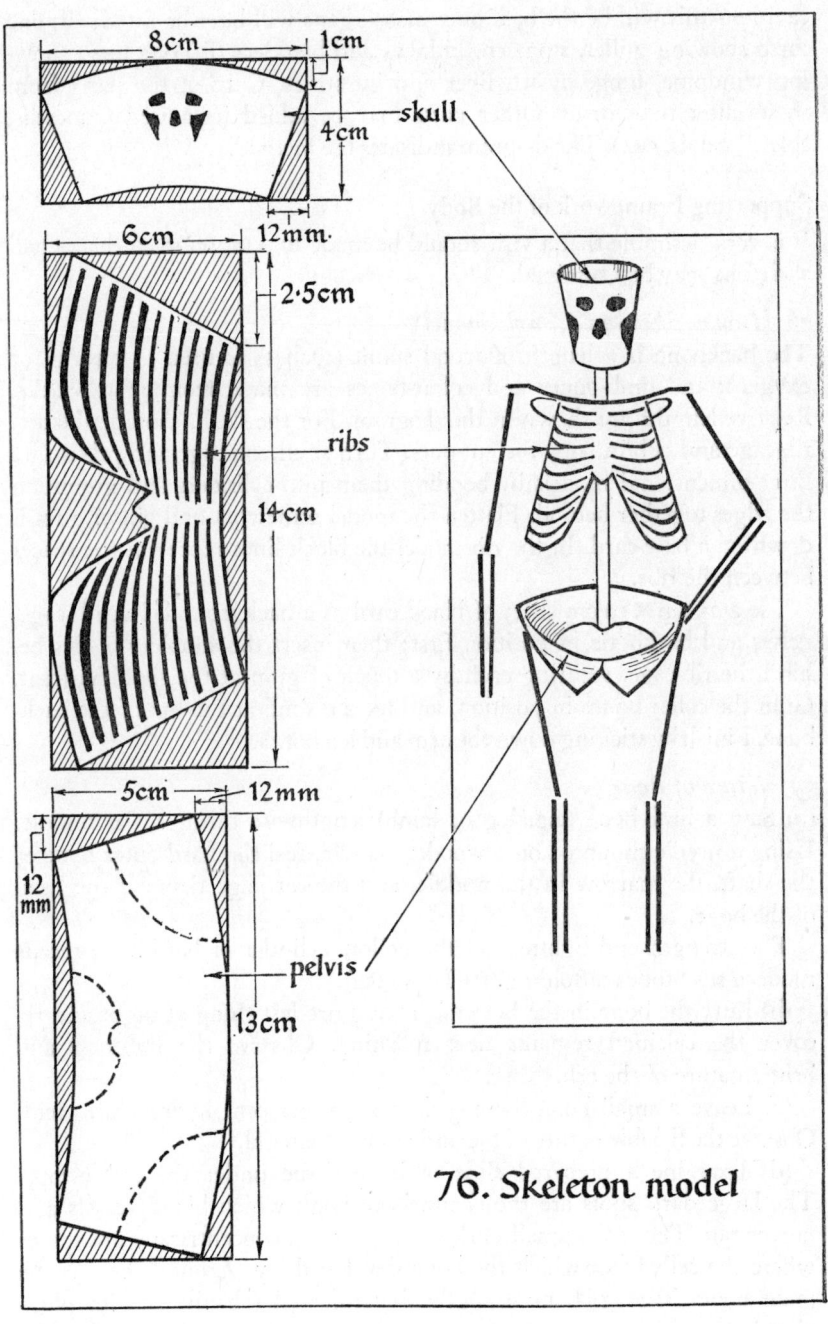

76. Skeleton model

From this trace (i) one torso showing only the thoracic and abdominal cavities—this will be the base on which organs will later be fitted; (ii) one torso showing gullet, stomach, kidneys and bladder; (iii) one torso showing windpipe, lungs, heart, liver and intestines. Cut out the parts from these latter two torsos. Other parts may be added if desired (pancreas, spleen, pelvis, etc.). The diagram indicates the method.

Supporting Framework of the Body
It is very desirable that a visit should be made to a museum so that actual skeletons may be examined.

76 *Human Skeleton (simple model)*
The backbone is a length of wood splint (such as is used in testing for oxygen); the limb-bones and collar-bones are made from match-sticks. Relative lengths are shown in the diagram. For the skull, shoulder-blades, rib-cage and pelvis, copy the cut-outs. Turn skull, rib-cage and pelvis into three-dimensional models by bending them into cylinders and gumming the edges together behind. Flatten the model somewhat and pin or gum it down on a base-card. In the rib model the black lines represent the spaces between the ribs.

Use a 25-cm × 10-cm sheet of black card as a background. Fix rib-cage, pelvis and backbone in position first; then insert the shoulder-blades behind the rib-cage, securing each by a touch of gum at the shoulder-joint. Gum the collar-bones in position, and fix the skull at the top of the backbone. Finish by sticking down the arm and leg bones.

77 *Nature of Bone*
(a) Saw a limb-bone (e.g. leg of lamb) lengthwise through the middle. Using a needle mounted on a wooden handle, feel the hard outer bone of the shaft, the marrow in the middle, and the cartilage tissue at the head of the bone.

The strength and lightness of the hollow cylinder of hard bone recalls modern steel-tube scaffolding (see Expt. 452).

(b) Bury the bone in the hot embers of a fire last thing at night and recover the calcined remains next morning. Observe the lightness and brittle nature of the ash.

(c) Leave a small bone for 2–3 days in 10 per cent hydrochloric acid. Observe the flexible nature of the undissolved material.

(d) Examine a prepared slide of bone tissue under the microscope. The large dark spots are the channels through which blood vessels and nerves ran. The many small dark spots arranged concentrically are spaces where the cells from which the bone developed lay. Around them is the main bone tissue, rich in strengthening material (chiefly calcium phosphate).

Topics: How the main organs of the body are protected (danger of "hitting below the belt"). Supporting function of skeleton. Lining and supporting membranes of the body; pleurisy and peritonitis. Mechanical action of skeleton (introductory reference to muscles). Fractured limbs and their repair: greenstick fractures; use of X-rays. Need for calcium and phosphorus in diet.

The film "Body Framework" may be hired from the British Medical Association, Tavistock Square, W.C.1.

Chapter Five

A First Study of Plants

The School Garden and Greenhouse

Nature Study as a subject is under an obvious handicap in city schools, yet access to the country-side is unlikely to become easier as the urban sprawl enlarges. Fortunately a secondary school built today is likely to have land for a garden and may well be provided with a greenhouse. Either amenity needs only the services of a keen and competent member of staff to transform it into one of the school's most valuable assets.

The words "cultivate" and "culture" both derive from the same Latin root and their literal meaning was originally the same. Culture is no longer used in the sense of tilling the soil, but the close relationship between the two words is well appreciated by school gardening enthusiasts. For cultivation in its literal sense can and should lead to culture in the figurative sense—"improvement and development by education and training". A well-planned and well-kept school garden is at once a training ground in methods of cultivation, a laboratory for experimental investigations and an aesthetic setting for at least a part of the school building. Its influence may be extended throughout the school when it provides decorative plants to brighten corridors and classrooms as well as botanical material for Science lessons. The garden is, too, a rich source of insect life and a potential basis for valuable work on the relationships between the highest classes of the invertebrate and vertebrate kingdoms.

A useful introduction for those considering starting school gardening work is provided in Chapter 5 of *Schools and the Countryside* (Ministry of Education Pamphlet 55; H.M.S.O.).

A greenhouse can add enormously to the decorative resources of a school, and this is a very proper use. But it can also be a prolific source of illustrative material for the laboratory and teachers are referred to an article by Irene Finch in *School Nature Study* (No. 226, January, 1962) where the author lists well over one hundred greenhouse plants with an indication of the use to which they may be put as lesson material.

Growing Plants in the Classroom

If neither a garden nor a greenhouse is available, it will be necessary to consider ways of growing plants in the classroom. Joyce M. Knight has a very valuable essay on this subject in *School Nature Study* (No. 221,

October, 1960). She considers such factors as the control of humidity, light, soil conditions, growing plants from seeds, methods of vegetative propagation and the choice of plants, especially for decoration. In poorly-lit rooms a Wardian case is helpful; this is a miniature greenhouse, somewhat resembling a fume cupboard in form, which is fitted in place of an existing window and which juts out a foot or more on the sunny side of the building.

Bulbs, corms, etc. are always popular both for the interest of growing them and for the material which they provide for lessons on food storage and plant reproduction. See Chapter 25.

More than half a century ago an article was contributed to *School Nature Study* which reappeared in 1933, revised and enlarged, and which was issued also as a separate leaflet: *The Greengrocer's Shop and What it Yields for Nature Study*. It stands as a reminder to every teacher that no school need be without resources. Of peanuts the writer remarks:

"They are of very useful size for examination, they germinate readily and it must come as a surprise ... to see delicate seedlings begin to emerge from the curiously wrinkled seed-case. Further, the fact of the parent plant setting its own seed by the bending down of the flower stalk cannot fail to arouse interest."

It would be a splendid thing if every child at school could at some time grow something "from seed to seed", tracing the course of germination, enlargement, flowering and fruiting, and finally collecting and packeting the seed for the following season. Peas and beans are good for the purpose; so are nasturtiums and many other common flowers; while the vegetable marrow has its own special lessons to convey. Pupils should make an illustrated diary of the stages of growth, including mounted specimens of plant material. The record would be judged not on scientific accuracy alone but also on artistic presentation and literary form.

Nature Table and Nature Records

A well-kept Nature Table (as distinct from the desultory collection which sometimes represents it) is an ornament to any Science room. Its arrangement and the labelling of its specimens are matters for selected pupils, but a high standard should be maintained. For living flowers, a 10-cm wide wooden shelf running 25 cm or so above bench height along one side of the room and bored at 20-cm intervals with suitable holes can be used as a support for large test-tubes which act as vases. An appropriate label is pinned to the front of the shelf whenever a new specimen is introduced; and flowers are removed as soon as they shown any signs of wilting.

Side by side with such work a classroom reference library is essential (Chapter 19). It should include not only books but also collections of pictures of trees, birds, flowers, etc., neatly mounted and indexed. The production of such collections is an important part of the work, since it satisfies the collecting and classifying instincts which are so marked in many of our pupils.

Whatever the position of a school, teachers may profit from occasional excursions and observations that children make themselves. Nature diaries need not consist only of written notes, and a pupil's own sketches and paintings are infinitely preferable to pasted-in cut-outs. In encouraging our pupils to report their findings orally, and with pen and brush, we are helping them to observe carefully, to draw simple conclusions and to attempt an expression of their thoughts—no mean introduction to the study of science. If, in addition, we can bring them to some appreciation of the beauty of Nature, and inspire them with a resolve to do what they can to defend the countryside from carelessness and vandalism, we begin to link science with citizenship.

Our work with plants might begin with the recognition of common trees or well-known wild flowers. It is suggested that a minimum list might be attempted for each year of the school course, so that a definite body of information is built up. How much richer is the boy or girl who can find and name a dozen common species than one who, having "studied" seed dispersal and photosynthesis, yet has not learned to *look* at a single living plant.

Recognition of Trees in Summer and in Winter

78 *Tree Census*

First prepare a map of the area to be studied—this in itself is an important exercise. Show the position of every tree by means of a small circle containing a letter identifying the kind of tree. Recourse to reference books may often be necessary; pupils may sketch individual trees and bring in leaves, twigs, etc. for identification purposes. Sketches or photographs of the same tree done both in summer and in winter are particularly valuable.

79 *Leaf Forms*

(a) Pin the leaf on drawing paper and either spray it with powder paint from a scent spray or dab it with a small piece of sponge which has been dipped in powder paint. As the paint overlaps on to the paper, a clear outline of the leaf shape is produced. (b) Smear the back of a leaf with a very thin layer of Vaseline and cover with carbon paper. Put leaf and carbon between newspaper sheets and rub over the leaf firmly with the fingers. Carefully peel off the leaf from the carbon paper and lay it (greasy side down) on drawing paper. Cover the leaf with newspaper again and rub it firmly. A clear print of the leaf shape and veining is obtained. (c)

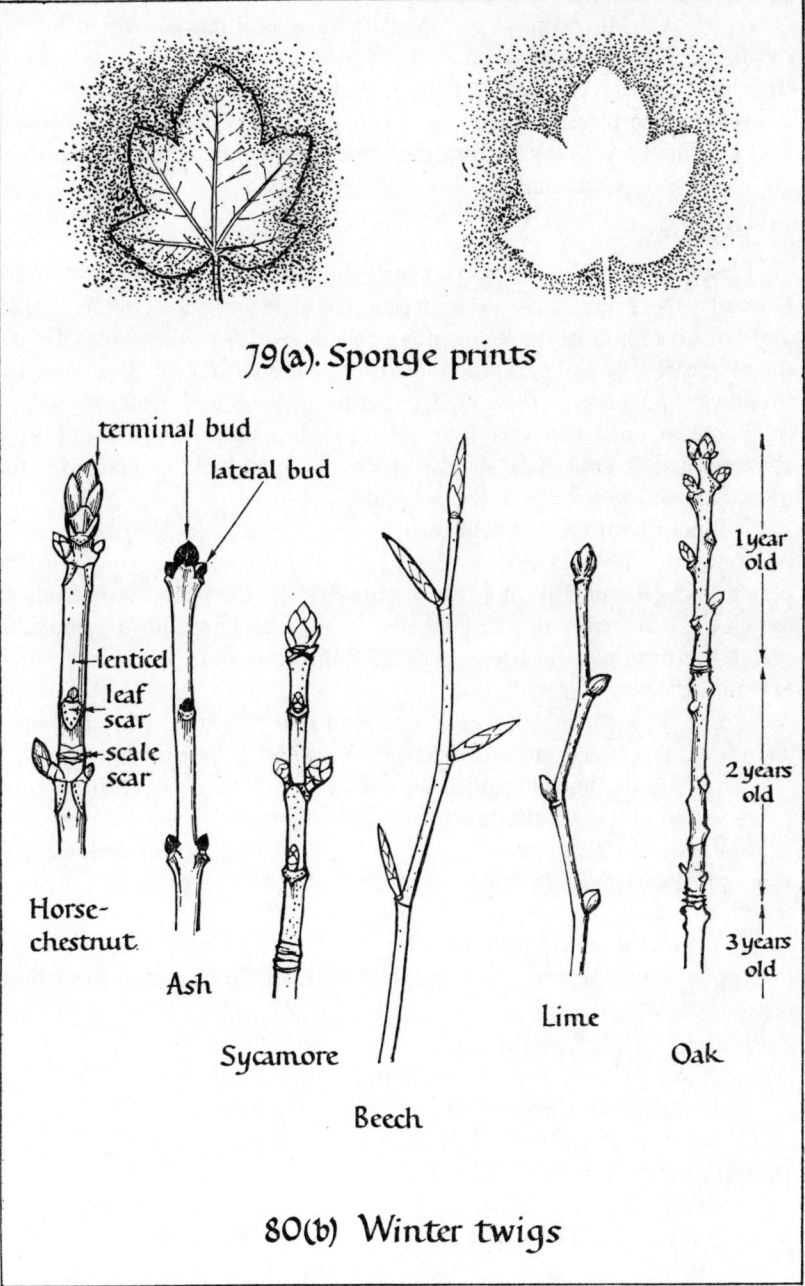

79(a). Sponge prints

80(b) Winter twigs

Instead of commercial carbon paper we may use paper prepared as follows. Coat a small sheet of newspaper with fat or lard and wipe away any excess grease. Move the paper about (greasy side down) over a lighted candle near the wick of which a small piece of mothball has been placed (this produces a very smoky flame), and so cover the paper with soot. Leaves may be placed directly on this paper and rubbed as in (b) above. Many prints may be taken from the same sheet of sooted paper, and they are reasonably permanent.

80 *Winter Twigs*

(a) Plaster Casts: Collect twigs which show the bud arrangements well. Choose a short and fairly straight twig. Dust it with talc (French-chalk) and press it to half its thickness into a rolled-out slab of Plasticine. Extract the twig carefully and paint the Plasticine mould with olive-oil or Vaseline (to prevent adhesion of plaster). Mix plaster of Paris with water to make a thick cream, and run this into the mould, which should stand in a shallow card or paper box so that excess plaster may be poured over the mould to form a backing for the twig cast.

Within an hour the cast will be hard and the box and Plasticine should be removed. The twig is now seen as a raised cast standing up from the plaster background. Give it a coat of glue size and then paint it carefully to match the real twig. Stick tiny labels on to the background to name such features as terminal and lateral buds, leaf and scale scars, lenticels, and the extent of the year's growth.

(b) Use of a Botanical Key: Ask pupils to examine twigs of horse-chestnut, birch, beech, etc. and to answer questions such as the following:

i. How are the buds arranged on the stem? (spirally—oak; in opposite pairs—sycamore, horse-chestnut; alternately—lime, elm).

ii. What is the shape of the buds? (Long and thin, large, small, etc.). A more precise description might be given, such as the approximate ratio of length to breath.

iii. What is the colour of the scale leaves which protect the bud?

Suggest how a very simple key might be made from such information, e.g. —

A. Buds occur singly on the stem.
    Short, pointed, dark-brown buds.   Birch.
    Long, pointed brown buds.   Beech.
    Short, oval, brown buds.   Oak.

B. Buds occur in pairs on the stem.
    Small, dull-black buds.   Ash.
    Large, sticky, brown buds.   Horse-chestnut.

Try other systems, e.g. one beginning: "A. Buds more than 4 times as long as broad."

Introduce other kinds of twigs and show how a key must be progressively adjusted to fit them.

81 Breathing Pores (Lenticels)
Attach a football-pump and valve via pressure tubing to the freshly cut end of a twig. The twig should be cut under water and the tubing attached whilst the cut surface is still under water. With the twig still submerged, work the pump. Bubbles appear all over the surface of the twig, enlarge, break away, and rise to the surface.

The surface pores should also be studied with a hand-lens.

Expt. 81 will recall the method of locating a puncture in a bicycle inner tube.

Topics: Follow the development of horse-chestnut or other twigs for two or three weeks: the twigs stand in water on the Nature Table, and may be sketched every two days. Drawings made of a particular bud will show the unfolding and growth of leaves and the extension of the spaces (internodes) between them.

The Roots and Stems of Plants

It is a good thing to look at roots in situ. This may be done by opening up a small trench in a patch of weedy grass so as to reveal a longitudinal section through the plant roots. By making suitable spade thrusts, tap-root systems (e.g. dandelion) and fibrous roots (e.g. grasses) may be clearly exposed.

82 Young Roots
(a) Germinate seeds of mustard, radish, etc. in a "germination sandwich" consisting of a backboard (plywood), about 15 cm × 10 cm, on which are laid, successively, a layer of cotton-wool, a sheet of blotting paper, a sprinkling of seeds and a sheet of Perspex, the whole sandwich being held together by screws or by rubber bands and suspended on the wall like a picture. The backboard should be painted before use since the cotton-wool must be kept permanently moist by daily watering.

Roots develop quickly, and in a few days root-hairs and root-caps are easily visible (hand-lens). By turning the sandwich through 90° when the roots are about half an inch long, the growth of roots towards the ground can be shown.

(b) For individual work, germinate seeds in tumblers. They are held against the inside of the glass by a roll of blotting-paper, and a little water in the bottom of the tumbler keeps them moist.

83 Growth of Roots and Stems
(a) Roots: Use a germination sandwich loosely filled with moist peat or vermiculite (instead of cotton-wool and blotting paper). Put a few soaked

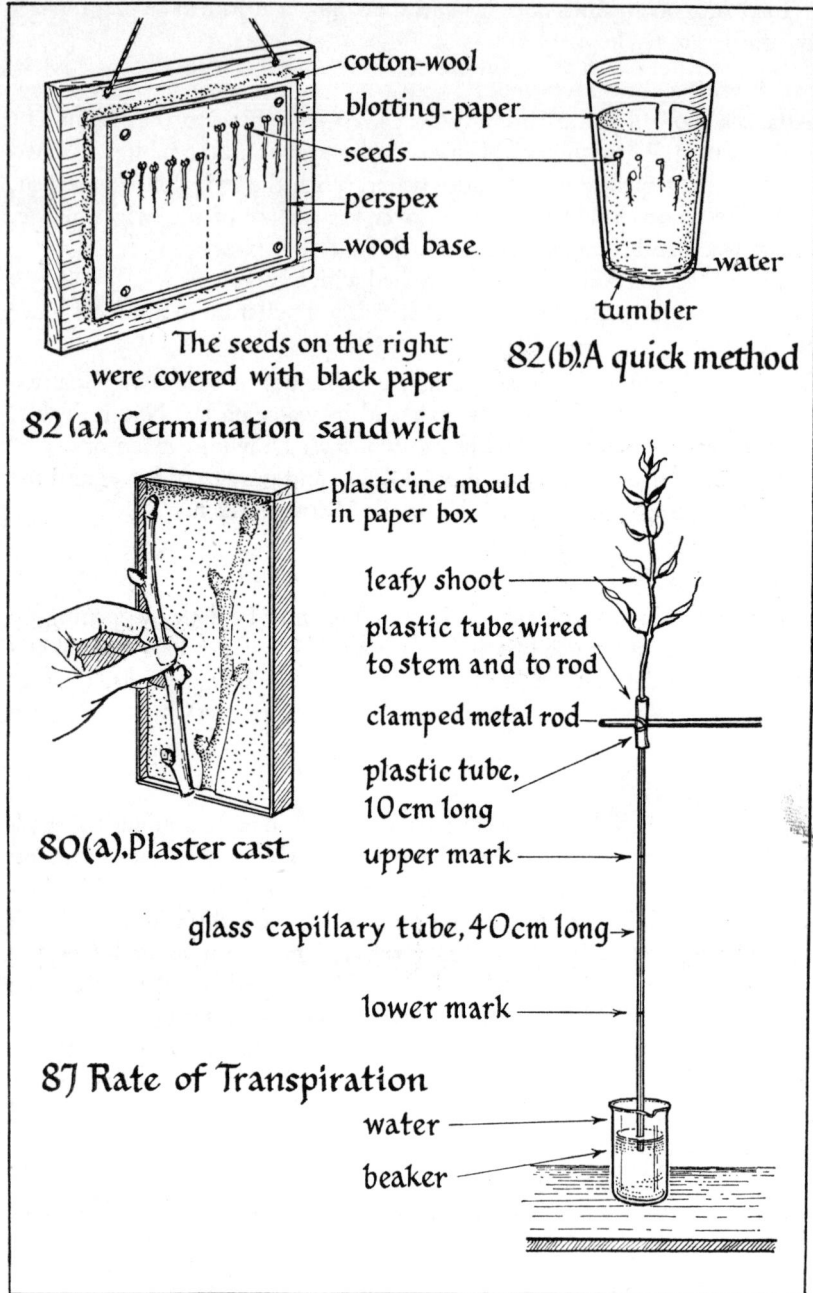

broad beans an inch deep in the peat, radicles downward, and leave for a few days until the young roots are an inch or so long.

Select a bean with a straight radicle, clean off particles of peat with a scrap of blotting paper and mark off the radicle with lines of waterproof Indian ink, say 1 mm apart. Use a pencil to dibble a hole in the peat sandwich and carefully insert the bean with the marked radicle in the hole. Observe the marks during the next few days.

(b) Age of Twigs: Examine winter twigs and look for the girdle scars which mark what was the position of each year's terminal bud before it burst and started to grow. Estimate the age of each twig you examine.

By studying the distance apart of the girdle scars, compare the rate of growth of twigs in different years.

(c) Annual Rings: In older stems the conducting woody bundles join up to form continuous rings (really cylinders) and new rings appear each year.

Select a twig which shows several years' growth according to the bud scars. Cut it across obliquely at points representing different years and count the rings in each section.

Count the rings on a tree-stump; and in a cross-section of a small branch of a tree.

(d) Examine a planed wood board; discuss the origin of the "grain" and the "knots". Make saw-cuts through a small log of wood (e.g. a short piece of branch) to show how a side branch is connected internally with the branch from which it springs.

84 *Internal Structure of Roots and Stems*

(a) Uproot a complete dandelion plant and wash the soil from the roots. Then stand the roots in a jar containing water coloured with red ink. After a few hours note that the leaf veins are coloured red. Cut slices across root and stem, using a razor-blade, and supply a slice of each kind to each pupil. Examine with a lens, and notice that whereas the root sections are stained red at the centre, the stem sections have a ring of red near to the outer edge (Fig. 84 (a)).

(b) Repeat the experiment, but in this case make vertical cuts through stem and tap-root. Suitable cuts will reveal how the soil solutions are carried from the rootlets to the centre of the root; how the root tubes merge into those of the stem; and how branches lead off from the stem into the leaves.

(c) Repeat the experiments, using *stems* of marrow or Brussels sprouts cut off under water. With these stout stems it is possible to see that the red colour is confined to a ring of small spots inside a green outer ring in the horizontal section.

(d) Cut sections across the leaf-stalk of the stained marrow. Under the hand lens (× 10), the woody bundles with the inner part stained red may be distinguished. Thin sections may be cut and mounted as described in Expt. 67 and examined microscopically.

Topics: Roots as anchors. Stems modified for special purposes (e.g. climbing). Preliminary reference to food storage in stems and roots (see also Chapter 25).

Water and the Plant

85 *Roots Take Up Water*

Support a groundsel plant in the neck of a sauce bottle with its roots dipping into water in the bottle and its shoot protruding above the bottle. Plug the neck of the bottle round the stem of the plant with Plasticine and mark the height of the water in the bottle. Set up a similar bottle containing water to the same marked level; there is no plant in this "control" bottle, but the neck is plugged with Plasticine.

Compare the levels of the water in the two bottles after several days.

86 *Leaves Give Out Water*

Support a groundsel or other plant in water in a jam jar, with the stem passing through a hole in a cardboard cover. Gummed paper is used to seal the slit which must be cut in the card in order to insert the stem, and the card is well Vaselined on both sides and round the stem to render joints air-tight.

Carefully dry and polish a second jam jar and invert it over the cardboard cover so that it encloses the leaves of the plant. The inside of this jar soon becomes misty, and after a few hours drops of water may be distinguished on the glass walls.

87 *Rate of Transpiration*

A simple form of potometer (Latin potio = to drink) is illustrated in Fig. 87. It is a device to measure the rate at which a leafy shoot loses water under various conditions, e.g. of temperature, light or wind. The 10-cm length of translucent plastic tube fits tightly round the stem of the shoot and the 2-mm bore glass capillary tube (it may be fixed over the stem with thin copper wire).

Michaelmas Daisy and common Willowherb have long smooth round stems suitable for this experiment. Choose a stem on the living plant, cut it off and at once plunge it under water in a bucket. With a sharp knife make a slanting cut across the stem, still under water, to remove the lower 15 cm or so and connect on the water-filled plastic tube and capillary tube. Avoid damaging the surface of the stem. By carrying out all these operations under water, air is prevented from entering the stem.

Seal the lower end of the glass tube with your finger and transfer the tube to a beaker of water which has been cooled after boiling (thus driving

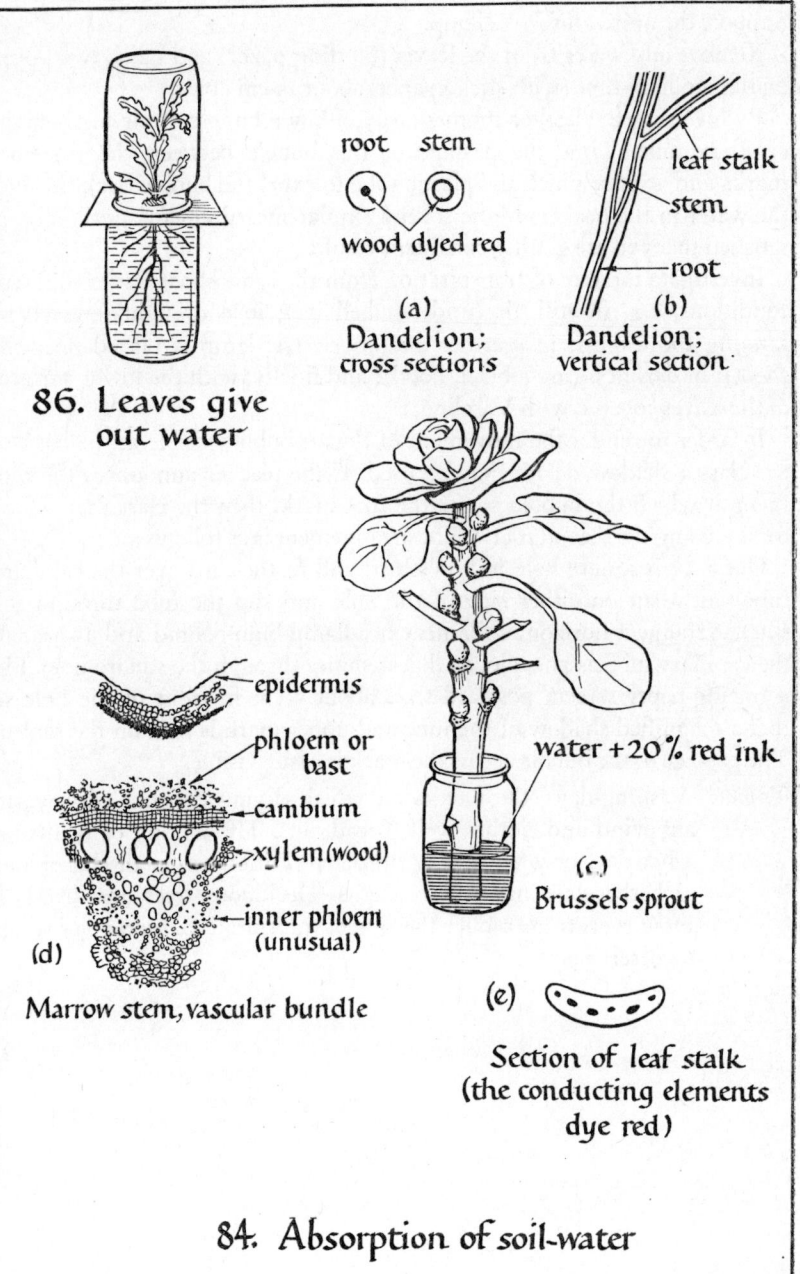

86. Leaves give out water

(a) Dandelion; cross sections

(b) Dandelion; vertical section

(c) Brussels sprout

(d) Marrow stem, vascular bundle

(e) Section of leaf stalk (the conducting elements dye red)

84. Absorption of soil-water

out dissolved air and avoiding later trouble with air bubbles in the stem). Support the apparatus in a clamp.

Remove any water from the leaves (blotting paper) and mark two points on the capillary tube (with sticky paper) about 15-cm apart.

By lowering the beaker momentarily, allow a bubble of air to enter the capillary tube. Time the passage of this bubble between the reference marks and at once pinch the plastic tube to expel the bubble back through the water in the beaker. Make several similar measurements until you are satisfied that you are getting consistent results.

Investigate the rate of transpiration from the same shoot under different conditions, e.g. in still air (under a bell jar); in a draught (created by fanning the leaves); in warmer air (an electric lamp is placed near the shoot); in darkness (use a black hood); and finally, with the lower surfaces of the leaves covered with Vaseline.

In order to render the movement of the air bubble visible at the back of the class a shadow device may be used. If the teacher announces the moment at which the bubble passes the first mark, then the class may watch for it passing the second mark. The arrangement is as follows:

Cut a 2-cm square hole in a postcard and fit the card over the capillary tube (cut a slit on either side of the hole and slip the tube through the slits). Arrange a horizontal-filament headlamp bulb behind and as near to the capillary tube as possible, so that it shines through the square hole. Fix a tracing-paper screen, postcard size, about 5 cm in front of the hole so that a magnified shadow of the tube and upper mark is seen on the screen. The passage of the bubble across the mark is easily visible.

Topics: Washing-day: the factors on which drying depends (dry warm air, wind and clothes well spread out). The wilting of plants on a hot day, or when cut or uprooted. Difference in the behaviour of herbaceous and woody stems. Deciduous trees and leaf-fall. How evergreens reduce the rate of transpiration. Storage of water by desert plants.

Chapter Six
Foodstuffs from Plants

The Nuffield Science Teaching Project
In 1962 the Nuffield Foundation made available £250,000 for a Project aimed at the reform of science teaching in Britain. Curriculum development would be supported by the provision of books, apparatus and other aids. Full-time organizers were appointed, backed by consultative committees bringing together expert opinion from the schools, universities, industry, professional scientific associations and local education authorities. Detailed work on the preparation of Teachers' Guides, Pupils' Tests and ancillary material was undertaken by teams of practising teachers, often seconded, while field trials were made in schools throughout the country. The final cost will exceed £1,000,000, apart from the very large investment in publication.

The first product related to courses in the separate sciences for 11–16 year-olds, aimed roughly at G.C.E. O-level (and aimed also at substantial modification in the examinations themselves). Later schemes dealt with science in primary schools and in sixth forms. Meanwhile, the Schools Council had produced, in 1965, Working Paper No. 1: *Science for the Young School Leaver*, intended as a starting point for a further Nuffield curriculum development project and a contribution in preparation for the raising of the school leaving age. The Working Paper analysed the existing position in regard to pupils "of average and below average ability between the ages of 13 and 16, i.e. the Newsom pupils". We remind our readers that these are also some of the Ordinary Pupils with which the present book is concerned, so that the ideas of the Schools Council paper are of particular interest. Of present teaching it was remarked that:

". . . work of an adventurous kind is relatively uncommon. The best is usually associated with teaching through topics in the later stages of the course, and some of the liveliest is to be seen where class teaching has largely given place to a more independent way of working, usually in pairs or in small groups, on associated aspects of a topic and using work sheets which set out the general lines of each part of the enquiry and probably pose questions to be answered or problems to be investigated. Although . . . it requires a keen and interested teacher, who would be likely to do good work in any case . . . it seems that much of the success achieved (for example a marked development of self-reliance) is inherent in the method itself."

In relation to course content the Paper says:

"There is often little to help pupils to appreciate the general drift and purpose of what they are doing. By the end of their school life much of what they have studied must seem trivial or artificial to them."

It is in this connection that the Paper reaches a main conclusion:

". . . the most dramatic of the changes which the Newsom Report envisages could well arise from concentration upon significance in all aspects of the work: by using it, indeed, as a touchstone at many points."

For what *significance* means in this context the reader is urged to turn again to the Newsom Report itself, Chapter 18, pp. 142–8.

The basis of the suggestions of the Working paper is that there are certain major themes in science with which Newsom pupils might be expected to have some measure of acquaintance. An outline is given of how some of these themes might be developed. Now the Nuffield Project is following up these ideas, for the benefit of the teacher of the ordinary pupil, treating Science as a whole and purposely blurring the subject boundaries.

Topics and Projects

Teaching through Topics or Centres of Interest is, of course, not new. Certain topics (notably those of Air and Water) appear in almost all elementary Science schemes because they provide obvious points of contact with everyday experience for most boys and girls. Others commonly met with include Engines, Clothing, Food, Health, Senses, etc. The teacher's choice will be determined by his own interests and background as well as by the needs of his pupils. It is a fact that well-chosen topics can focus interest without undue sacrifice of syllabus content, provided that the teacher undertakes careful analysis of the material available. Newsom reminded us that a great deal of real science can be extracted from relatively few enquiries. Unhurried discussion, reading and writing around the topic are essential components of the work, and the outcome is not measurable in terms of information alone.

When topics broaden into Projects, where the work of many subjects is concentrated in one study, the problem of ensuring that important fields of knowledge are not omitted altogether is sometimes acute. There is, of course, no suggestion that a Science scheme should be all-embracing in content; indeed, with the most generous time-allowance it is not possible to do more than touch upon much of what one would like to do. But there are certain matters which ought by common consent to appear in any scheme, and when a project eats up most of a school term more than usual vigilance must be exercised to see that the essentials are retained. Provided that the project does not drag on too long, and that the work is so planned that pupils of widely differing ability are all catered for (so that they all do actually participate to the extent to which they are capable), the interest aroused by the treatment may well compensate for some restriction of content.

The topic "Food" is a specially valuable one. It allows easy correlation between all three of the main branches of science (Chemistry, through the composition of foodstuffs and their identification; Physics, through calorific values; and Biology, through the relationships between nutrition and health); it lends itself very well to group and individual practical work; and it has an immediate appeal to children. For the practical work only the simplest apparatus is required and the materials used are inexpensive.

It seems important to discuss, at the outset, the sources of foods and the means by which plant foodstuffs become available to man. It is apparent that there is scope here for the teachers of Geography and of Science to work closely together. Class visits to a flour-mill, a margarine factory or a sugar-processing plant would serve the purposes of either subject equally well. The visits should be extended to include factories where plant materials are turned into textiles, floor-covering, paper, rope and string, oil-cake, varnishes, soap, cosmetics, and the like. Only after pupils have become familiar in this way with the substances concerned will many of them be ready to undertake chemical identifications (even of the simplest) with any real understanding, or to tackle the study of the role of the various foodstuffs within the body.

For a works visit to be a success, very careful preparation is essential. The ground must be so prepared that pupils both know what to look for and have sufficient knowledge to ask intelligent questions. The average works plant is not self-explanatory. It is important that the trip be so planned that pupils are taken round in quite small groups, and by men briefed for the work. The sight of twenty or so pupils tagging along behind a works foreman whose remarks can be heard by only two or three should convince any teacher that the majority of his charges are unlikely to learn much that way.

Carbohydrates
88 Sugar Testing
The sugar in sugar-cane and in sugar-beet is "cane-sugar". Other sugars, less sweet, are grape-sugar (glucose), fruit-sugar (fructose), and milk-sugar

(lactose). The following simplified version of the well-known Fehling's test has been found satisfactory for the detection of small amounts of sugar in common foods. Cane-sugar is the only common sugar that does not give the test, but its sweetness is usually sufficient indication of its presence. The chemical test for cane-sugar by hydrolysis with dilute acid followed by the Fehling's test is not recommended; it is likely to confuse the ordinary pupil.

(a) Prepare two solutions:

(i) Dissolve about 2½ g of copper sulphate crystals in half a litre of water.

(ii) Dissolve about 10 g of washing soda in half a litre of water.

Both solutions will store indefinitely. When required for testing, mix equal volumes of the two liquids and observe the precipitation of (basic) copper carbonate. Shake the mixture immediately before use.

Cut a toffee sweet into very small pieces, so that each member of the class may take a fragment. Dissolve the material in a little water in a test-tube, add about 2 cm^3 of the test reagent, and warm gently. The blue carbonate is reduced to orange-red cuprous oxide, which appears slowly.

Tubes tend to retain a coating of the red oxide. After each test, tubes should be washed out with a little dilute hydrochline acid, and then with water.

(b) Sugar may be detected in apple, carrot, honey, date, raisin, etc. in the same way. Crush the material with a few drops of water, decant, and test the liquid by warming with the test reagent.

(c) Detect sugar in grass (e.g. Cocksfoot, a grass recognizable by its pale flat juicy stem bases) by chopping up and mashing the swollen stem bases, boiling for a few minutes with a little water, decanting, cooling and testing with the reagent.

89 *Extraction of Starch*

Hold a large clean half of a potato upright in a small pie-dish and scrape it to pulp with a knife. Tilt the dish and push the pulp to the higher end; then press it with a spoon until it is as dry as possible. Liquid drains down the dish; allow this to settle and then carefully decant off the water from the white starch powder. Transfer the powder to a saucer or watch glass and allow it to dry.

90 *Starch for Washing-day*

Put a little household starch into a basin and add just enough cold water to form a smooth, thick paste when well worked in with the back of a wooden spoon. Pour on *boiling* water, steadily and with constant stirring, until the liquid turns clear.

FOODSTUFFS FROM PLANTS

91 How to Make Custard
~~Use the~~ following recipe:
1 heaped teaspoonful of starch (e.g. from potato, Expt. 89)
½ teaspoonful of sugar.
½ litre of milk.
I.C.I. "Edicol supra yellow" dye.

To the milk add an equal volume of water. Put the starch, sugar and dye into a basin, add a little of the milk and water, and mix to a smooth paste (only a trace of dye is required). Boil up the rest of the milk and water in a pan and pour the boiling liquid into the paste, stirring steadily.

92 Testing for Starch
Prepare a solution of iodine as described in Expt. 187. Using a 20-cm length of glass tubing as a pipette, transfer one drop of this solution to a test-tube. In the same way, using another piece of tubing, transfer one drop of starch solution (Expt. 90) to a second test-tube. Fill each tube to about one-third its height with water, shake, and pour one solution into the other. Notice the fine blue colour produced.

Now add a few drops of undiluted iodine solution to undiluted starch paste. The mixture is black.

93 Starch in Foodstuffs
Use carrot, turnip, potato, chestnut, acorn, peas, beans; or prepared foods such as flour, bread, breakfast cereals or rolled oats. Iodine solution may be spotted on directly, but it is much better to pour boiling water over the scrapings of the material and then to test the decanted liquid with diluted iodine solution after cooling.

Topics: Everyday uses of starch (laundering, bill-sticking, gravy-making). Staple foods of the world—rice, wheat, maize. Starchy foods that we eat in Britain.

94 Artificial Silk
The principal food of sheep and cattle is grass or hay, rich in cellulose. Cellulose exists in the main supporting fibres in many stems—we know it as straw, linen, jute and hemp. Cotton, coconut fibre, kapok (the fibre of a plant grown in Java), wood and cork are other forms of the same materials. Vast quantities of cellulose are used as wood and paper and in floor coverings, whilst "artificial silk" is also cellulose. The following experiment is suitable for teacher-demonstration or as part of a project in the Science Club:

Add strong ammonia solution (0·880) to copper hydroxide until the powder is just dissolved to give a deep blue solution of cuprammonium hydroxide. Add torn filter papers to this solution, with stirring, until a fairly viscous liquid is obtained; the papers dissolve only slowly. Put the solution of cellulose into a stoppered bottle fitted with an inlet tube passing just into the bottle and an outlet tube which dips below the surface of the liquid. Connect the outlet tube to a fine glass jet (Expt. 7) which dips below the surface of dilute sulphuric acid in a pie-dish.

Blow air into the bottle (football pump), and so force the blue jelly-like liquid into the acid. As the ammonia is neutralized the cellulose is reprecipitated as a fine white thread.

Fats

Emphasize the typical greasy nature of a fat by reference to lard, butter, margarine, tallow, coco-butter, lanoline, etc., as well as to substances made from fats (e.g. ointments). One or two pupils might undertake to arrange a display of fats and oils—e.g. in small, neatly labelled bottles. Liquids which might be shown include linseed, olive, palm, cotton-seed, castor, soyabean, groundnut and cod-liver oils.

95 *Tests for Fats*

(a) Examine the effects of vigorously rubbing small pieces of various fats (candle, suet, grease-paint, ointment) over small pieces of absorbent paper (duplicating paper). Spot single drops of various oils on to the paper and observe the results.

(b) If a fatty food is treated with alcohol the fat readily dissolves. If the solution of fat is poured into cold water the fat is thrown out of solution to form a milky emulsion.

Into a test-tube put about 2 cm^3 of industrial methylated spirit and just a little of the food to be tested (e.g. two or three crumbs of cake, a small pinch of cocoa, or a thin shaving from a nut, taken with a razor blade). Shake well, allow solid to settle and then pour off the liquid into a second tube. Add an equal volume of cold water.

Wash out the tubes with warm water and detergent.

Try the test also on milk from which the cream has been removed.

96 *Fat Extraction*

Hammer the lid of a syrup tin into a concave shape, almost fill the tin with hot water and fit the lid on the tin. EXTINGUISH ALL FLAMES in the laboratory.

Put a teaspoonful of desiccated coconut (or grated monkey-nut, grated sunflower seed, etc.) into a wide-necked 100 cm^3 round flask. Add 10 cm^3 (1 teaspoonful) of petrol and cork the flask. Stand the flask on the concave lid and shake it gently from time to time. After 10 minutes remove the flask from the hot tin, uncork it, and carefully decant the liquid into the hollow lid. The petrol rapidly evaporates and the process is complete when the smell of petrol has gone. Then the lid is lifted, and cooled by standing it on top of a second tin filled with cold water. The residue on the

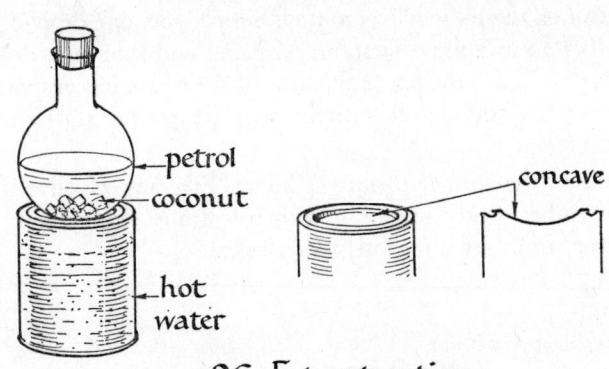

96. Fat extraction

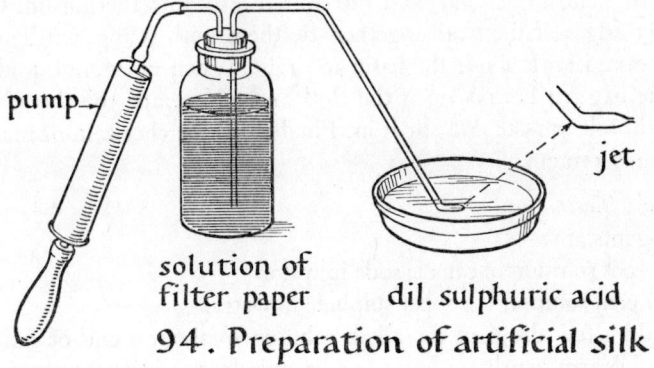

94. Preparation of artificial silk

99. Extraction of gluten from flour

lid solidifies to a white fat, which may be scraped out and tested (Expt. 95).

If it is only required to show that a food contains fat, the evaporation of the petrol on the lid may be omitted. Simply spot one drop of the petrol extract (after 10 minutes' digestion) on paper and spot on a drop of pure petrol near by. Wave the paper about until the petrol has evaporated: one spot (pure petrol) disappears entirely, whilst the other (fat) remains as a translucent stain.

Topics: The "rendering" of fats at home. Freezing of olive oil in cold weather. "Dry"-cleaning with petrol and similar solvents (need for care). List of the fatty foods we eat.

Proteins

97 *Cheese from Milk*

In the summer any milk which turns sour should not be wasted. Set it aside for a few days until it is "solid". Lay a piece of butter-muslin across the top of a clean dish and pour the clotted milk into the muslin. Gather the outer edges of the cloth together, tie them with string, and hang the bag of soured milk above the basin to drain. When no more liquid drips from the bag (24 hours), open the cloth out and scrape the cheese into a dish. Add salt to taste and stir it in. Finally, fill the cheese into small jars. It is mainly protein.

98 *Protein Test*

The reagents are:

2 per cent solution of caustic soda in water.

½ per cent solution of copper sulphate in water.

(a) Add a few drops of the alkali solution to about 2 cm^3 of milk in a test-tube. Warm gently and add one or two drops of the copper sulphate solution. A mauve coloration appears and indicates the presence of protein in the milk.

(b) Try the test on tinned peas or beans: boil one pea or bean with a little caustic soda for 2 minutes, cool and add 2 drops of copper sulphate. The colour here is reddish-purple. The cheese from Expt. 97 and the gluten from Expt. 99 may be tested.

(c) Boil up a single crystal of glue-size with water. The solution gives a fine purple colour in the protein test. The same protein (gelatin) can be identified in table-jelly or in the jelly found in tinned meats.

(d) Take a fragment of fresh lean meat. Boil it with water for 1 minute and then add a few drops of caustic soda reagent and boil up again. Decant the fluid into a test-tube and add 1 drop of copper sulphate solution. Note the delicate purple coloration. The protein here is largely myosin.

99 *Gluten from Flour*

Put a teaspoonful of flour into a square of clean cotton rag, gather the edges of the cloth between the fingers and keep dipping the bag into water in a small dish while gently kneading it and pressing it against the bottom of the dish. The water in the dish turns milky as starch powder washes through the cloth. After 15 minutes of kneading (more if possible), open the bag; the residue inside is a sticky mass consisting largely of gluten, which dries to a stringy solid. The starch in the dish may be allowed to settle, and may then be collected (Expt. 89).

Topics: The main food proteins (lean meat, fish, eggs, milk, cheese, seeds such as wheat, peas, nuts). Protein fibres (wool, silk, hair: see Chapter 22). Manufactured protein products—cattle-cake, bone-meal, glue, gelatine.

Wheat Project

100 *The Milling of Wheat*
Use a glazed brick of the kind with a hollow in one face. Put a teaspoonful of wheat grains into the hollow and grind the grains, using a selected hand-size pebble as a pestle. A rubbing action and considerable pressure are required. Alternatively, of course, a standard pestle and mortar may be used.

Pour the milled product into a gauze tea-strainer held over a sheet of paper. As the strainer is shaken white flour falls through, leaving the bran (seed-coat) behind.

101 *Soda-bread Rolls*
Contrive an oven from a large cubical biscuit tin supported open side downwards about 12 cm above the bench on two bricks. Protect the bench with a sheet of asbestos and stand a Bunsen burner under one corner of the tin so that the base of the flame will be about 3 cm within the tin. Light the burner some 15 minutes before the bread is put into the oven and adjust the flame to about 3 cm high.

Mix together, in a basin:
1 heaped dessertspoonful of flour.
1 level saltspoonful of baking powder.
Pinch of salt.

Make a well in the middle of the mixture and pour in a dessertspoonful of water. Mix the flour into the water with a fork until a light dough is obtained; it should hold together without sticking to the basin. Turn it out on to a floured board and knead it lightly into a flat smooth cake. Three or four such rolls may be placed on an inverted syrup tin and pushed under the heated oven. Raise the tin into the oven by sliding the two bricks underneath it, so that the rolls are at about the centre of the oven. Bake for about half an hour.

Break one of the baked rolls. Note that the interior is spongy, being full of tiny holes produced by the carbon dioxide given off by the heated baking powder.

Mineral Salts

102 *Mineral Residues*

(a) Burn a roll of plant leaves on a tin lid over a Bunsen flame. Notice the grey ash which remains when all the black carbon has been burnt away.

(b) Spear a 1-cm cube of potato on an iron wire and heat it directly in the flame. The material is reduced to a fused bead of mineral matter and the flame turns lilac, indicating the presence of potassium salts.

Topics: Refer to the ash left from a wood fire; and to the result of heating bone (Expt. 77 (b)). The importance of salt to man (its history as a key commodity). Iron and phosphate "tonic" medicines. Farmers' use of sulphate of ammonia, nitrate of potash, lime, etc. (See Expts. 172, 502–4, 510–11). Absorption of salts by roots of plants. Fruits and vegetables as sources of mineral salts in our diet.

How Plants Manufacture Starch and Other Foodstuffs

103 (a) *Extraction of Colouring Matter (Chlorophyll) from a Green Leaf*

With a sharp cork borer cut a number of discs from a thin green leaf (young beech or lime). Immerse the discs in boiling water for a minute or so, to rupture the cells. Transfer the discs, after removing adhering water with blotting paper, to a dry boiling tube. Just cover them with industrial spirit and stand the tube in warm water until the leaf is practically colourless: avoiding boiling the spirit. The green colouring matter will pass into solution.

(b) *Leaves Contain Starch*

Remove the decolorized discs (Expt. 103 (a)) from the spirit and wash them in water, making them less brittle. Then immerse them for a few minutes in dilute iodine/potassium iodide solution. Rinse the discs in a little benzene (CARE: no flame) to remove excess iodine and note the dark coloration which indicates starch.

Mount a disc in a drop of 50 per cent glycerine on a microscope slide and examine under low power.

104 (a) *Chlorophyll Necessary for Starch Formation*

Decolorize a variegated leaf (privet or geranium) by the method of Expt. 103 (a). Test for starch as in Expt. 103 (b). Only those parts of the leaf that were green turn black.

(b) *Light Necessary for Starch Formation*

Cut a hole the shape of a cross in a piece of metal foil. Cover both sides of

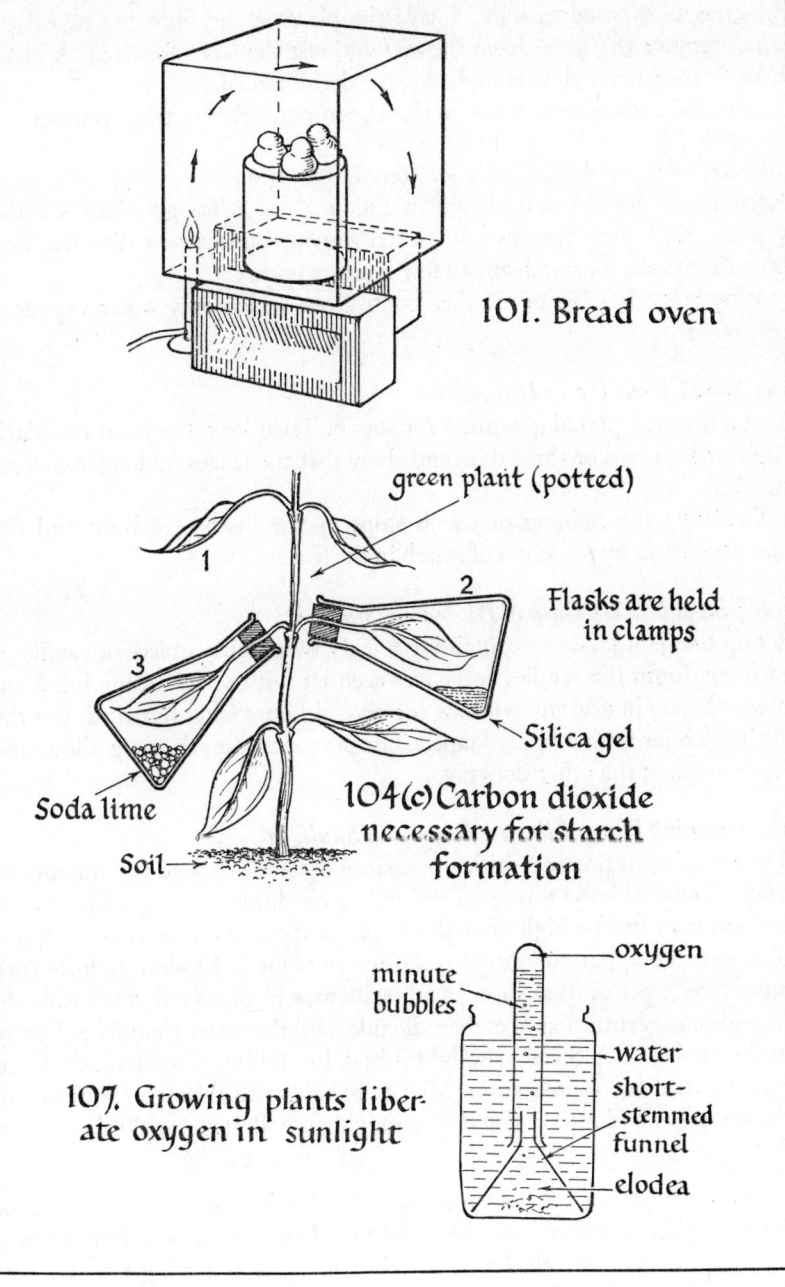

101. Bread oven

104(c) Carbon dioxide necessary for starch formation

107. Growing plants liberate oxygen in sunlight

one of the leaves of a potted plant with the foil (using a hair-grip or paper-fastener to keep the foil in position) so that only the part of the leaf under the cross is exposed to light. Leave the plant in the light for two days. Then remove the cover from the leaf and test the leaf for starch. A black cross forms when iodine is applied to the decolorized leaf.

Lilac leaves also are suitable for this experiment. Keep a twig in water.

(c) *Carbon Dioxide Necessary for Starch Formation*
Appropriate apparatus is shown in Fig. 104 (c). Silica gel absorbs water vapour; soda lime absorbs both water vapour and carbon dioxide. Test leaves 1, 2 and 3 for starch after a few hours exposure.

Why is it advisable to use the "control" in which only water vapour is removed?

105 *Starch Used Up in Darkness*
Test a leaf of a potted geranium for starch. Then keep the plant in a dark cupboard for two or three days and show that the leaves no longer contain starch.

Evidently the making of starch stops in the absence of light and the plant then uses up the stores of starch in the leaves.

106 *Leaves Use Up Carbon Dioxide in Sunlight*
Set up two jam jars, one containing a leafy twig, with a piece of candle in each jar. Light the candles and cover each jar with a well-fitting lid. Now place the jars in a sunny window for several hours and afterwards test the air in each jar with a lighted taper. The jar containing the twig allows the taper to burn; the other does not.

107 *Growing Plants Liberate Oxygen in Sunlight*
The experiment presents difficulties, since the gas liberated is a mixture of oxygen with (chiefly) nitrogen, and unless conditions are right the oxygen content may not be high enough (30 per cent) to give the glowing splint test. Use the apparatus shown: the water plant is Elodea. A little (not more than 1 per cent) sodium bicarbonate may be dissolved in the water to provide a concentration of carbon dioxide, and the water should be slightly warm (20–25° C.). Strong sunlight is best, but failing this a 100-watt lamp may be used for illumination. Minute bubbles rise through the water in the test-tube, and after a few days enough gas collects to apply the oxygen test.

Topics: Discussion on how food is formed and stored in the leaves of plants, and of how it is transported and stored in other tissues—as sugar, starch, fat or protein (the latter requiring mineral salts for its formation). The use of water-weed in the aquarium.

108 Growth Uses Up the Plant's Food Store

Grow an onion resting on the lip of a jam jar containing water; or an acorn in the neck of a medicine bottle; or a bean in moist sawdust. Examine the old tuber when potatoes are lifted; or a bulb grown in fibre when flowering is over. In every case the fact that the food store in the parent tissue has been depleted is very evident.

109 Leaf Surfaces

(See also Expt. 71.) Paint a single coat of coloured nail varnish on to about a square cm of each surface of a fresh privet leaf. When the varnish is dry, peel it away from the upper and lower surface in turn: it will bring away the "skin", or epidermis of the leaf with it.

Mount each of the two pieces for microscopic examination in a drop of water, under a cover-slip. Look especially for the stomata in the undersurface of the leaf.

110 Absorption of Light by Chlorophyll

Use the chlorophyll solution prepared in Expt. 103 (a); alternatively, grind up nettle leaves with industrial spirit.

Use a slide projector to throw the image of a thin slit on the screen. Focus sharply and then insert a 60° glass prism in the light beam and adjust the position of the projector until you get a good spectrum (see Expt. 375). For best results use a hollow prism filled with carbon bisulphide or ethyl cinnamate. Now pour some diluted chlorophyll solution into a flat container (glass or plastic) and insert it in the light beam.

Which colours does the chlorophyll absorb (i.e. which are now missing from the spectrum)?

Topics: The green plant as the only known device for using solar energy on a large scale, and therefore as our ultimate source of energy. Examples of food chains and of man's dependence upon the green plant. How man "steals" the food stores of plants.

Chapter Seven

History of a Simple Meal

Secondary School Examinations other than G.C.E.
The Beloe Committee, appointed to report on this subject, recommended (H.M.S.O., 1960) the establishment of regional examinations for pupils completing a five-year secondary school course, aimed at a band of candidates extending from those who just overlapped the group taking the Ordinary level of G.C.E. to those who were somewhat below average in ability.

As a result a number of Regional Examining Boards, effectively under the control of teachers, have been set up throughout the country to conduct examinations for the new Certificate of Secondary Education. Each Board is required to offer facilities for examinations of three types:

    i. An external examination on syllabuses provided by the regional subject panels (Mode I).

    ii. An external examination on syllabuses provided by a school or group of schools and approved by the regional subject panels (Mode II).

    iii. Examinations set and marked internally in a school or group of schools but moderated by the region (Mode III).

The Secondary School Examination Council supported these developments by producing a number of Examination Bulletins. No. 1 (1963) looked at general principles and problems of examining and went on to consider individual subjects. The attention of Science teachers is drawn to pp. 79–87 particularly. Bulletins No. 3 and 4 were concerned with techniques of examining and objective-type tests respectively; they should be of interest to many teachers.

Since 1964, when the S.S.E.C. was wound up, the work has been continued under the guidance of the Schools' Council and the series of Bulletins has been continued. No. 5 (*School-based Examinations*, 1965) related to the most revolutionary of the three permitted C.S.E. modes, Mode III, and quoted Bulletin No. 1 when it said:

> "The main advantages of this technique of examining are that there is more scope for flexibility of syllabus and teaching methods, and more opportunities for matching the examinations with local and individual needs . . . There is, however, a price to be paid . . . The inherent problem is that of establishing reasonably comparable standards between examinations that are conducted on different syllabuses . . ."

The Council proposed to rely on two methods of monitoring the various Boards' judgments on standards: the statistical procedure known as "goodness of fit", and samplings of the scholastic abilities of candidates from the different Boards. Many thousands of candidates have already been examined for C.S.E. and although the percentage of those tested by Mode III was small in the early years, it is certain that an increasing number of teachers are alive to the advantages, for the pupils, of internally-set examinations allied with continuous assessment of course work. With the raising of the school leaving age it may be expected that Mode III will commend itself for a growing proportion of pupils.

Pupils Not Considered Suitable for Regional Examinations

The Beloe Committee felt that it would not be right to deprive abler children of the opportunity to take examinations because there were other children for whom examination could not be recommended. These latter form a large proportion of the boys and girls considered in the Newsom Report (H.M.S.O., 1963), the "average and below average".

Science teachers no less than teachers of other subjects should from time to time remind themselves of the contents of the Newsom Report. The following quotations are taken from Chapter 10 ("Examinations and Assessments"):

"All pupils who remain at school till the age of sixteen should receive some form of internal school leaving certificate."

"We are convinced that many of the pupils with whom this report is concerned ought not to be entered for public examinations; and that for all the pupils a substantial part of the curriculum should be unexamined."

"For those pupils who do enter, we hope that oral work, course work and the teacher's assessment will play a significant part in the new examinations."

Events have already shown that the new examinations make heavy demands upon the energies of the many teachers who are involved in committee and panel work; and even in school the demands of examinations often tend to divert attention fron non-examination work. The Report observed that "If the schools are not to have a seriously depressed class of pupils on their hands, they will need to give a more positive, distinctive character to the programmes of these non-examinees".

". . . it will be more than ever urgent to experiment with interesting and demanding forms of work, if they are to be convinced that what they are doing is of any consequence."

"The attitude of the Head and of the Staff will be decisive . . . by ensuring, for example, that the heads of department take some non-examination work..."

We add two quotations from Chapter 13 of the Report:
"Speech is their main means of communication and always will be"
"The appropriate form of external incentive varies with the ability of the pupils; but getting ready to go to work is always a valuable spur which can be used in the last year of school to call forth a strong finish..."

A Topic of Interest to Everyone: Eating

Whereas it has been the custom in the past to include in the Science scheme formal lessons on such subjects as "Acids and Alkalis", "Solutions" and "Temperature Scales", it now seems clear that for a majority of children in Secondary schools this is not the best approach. The development of a logical argument does not attract them. On the other hand, they are at once interested in matters which appear to them "useful" or which link up with their personal experience.

It follows that experiments should be chosen to illustrate a human problem wherever possible, and they may call for much discussion and lead to many digressions. The present chapter deals with a topic of immediate importance to everyone, illustrates how the subject can be used to introduce a wide variety of useful scientific concepts, and retains the all-important basis of practical investigation.

Yet the teacher must always be careful to distinguish what is worth talking about from what is of only superficial interest: he must be convinced of the real significance of what he teaches. His digressions should not blind him to the main theme and he should remember that the test of a good lesson is still that it drives home one or two worth-while ideas.

Digestion in the Mouth

111 (a) *What You Should See when you Examine Your Teeth in a Mirror*
Small handbag mirrors are suitable. Let each pupil make a diagram of the teeth in his own mouth, using a semicircle as a base for each jaw and the following symbols:

Molars ⊞   Premolars ◇   Canines △   Incisors □

The full dental formula for an adult is:

$$\frac{(upper)\ \text{i.2; c.1; pm. 2; m. 3}}{(lower)\ \text{i.2; c.1; pm. 2; m. 3}}$$ on each side; total 32.

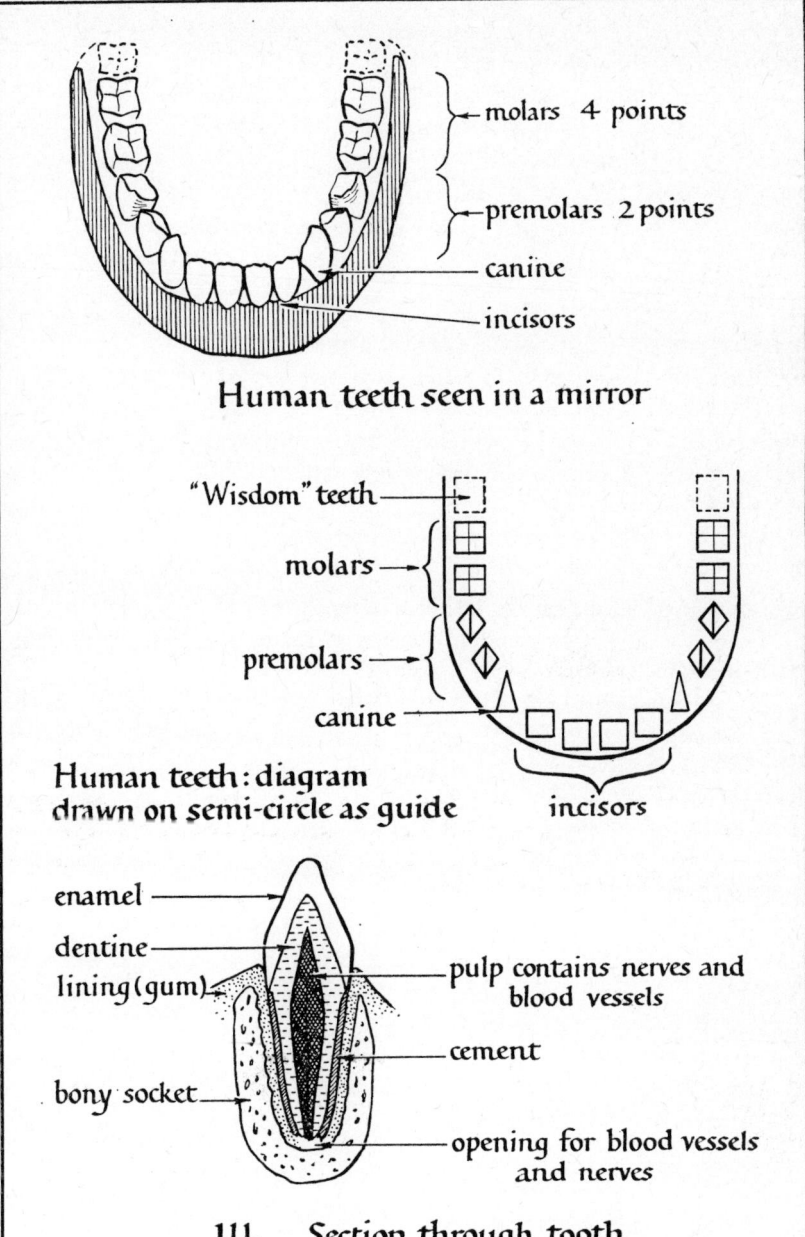

111. Section through tooth

Variations from this, due to immaturity (e.g. absence of "wisdom" teeth), extraction or accident should be discussed. A simplified diagram to show the structure of a tooth and how it is held in the jaw is useful.

(b) *Decay Due to Acid*

Use animal teeth (e.g. sheep) or an extracted human tooth. Dip the tooth in melted paraffin wax and let the wax harden. Then scrape the wax away from part of the enamel and leave the tooth in dilute hydrochloric acid for a few days.

Topics: How to care for one's teeth. Fluoride and tooth decay.

112 *Skulls and Teeth*

Allow the head of an animal (rabbit, sheep, cat, mouse) to simmer in water for some hours, so that the flesh is easy to remove. Take care to clean out the brain. Then stew the skull in 1 per cent hydrogen peroxide solution until the bones are white and free from grease. Rearticulation of the lower jaw can be effected using a fine drill and thin wire. Teeth may be set in the jaw with Evostik.

Note the general structure and function of the skull. Pay a visit to a museum to examine the skull and jaws of other animals.

  i. Rabbits (herbivorous): Canines absent (no prey to grasp); molars finely ridged (for grinding); hinge of lower jaw permits grinding movement; incisors grow continually (rodent).
  ii. Cat or dog (carnivorous): Molars have sharp-pointed cusps for crushing and tearing; large canines; no lateral movement of jaw, but certain teeth have a scissor-like action.
  iii. Cow or calf (ruminant): Flat molars for grinding; the jaw hinges are merely flat surfaces capable of wide lateral movement; no canines; crowded lower incisors (for biting herbage); hard pad replaces upper incisors.
  iv. Monkey (omnivorous): Teeth similar to Man, but large interlocking canines (for fighting); teeth of a carnivore, and hinge (ball and socket, with some lateral movement) of a herbivore.

113 *Beaks and Feet of Birds*

Encourage pupils to feed birds at home, to construct nesting boxes and to record the comings and goings of the birds.

Excellent coloured postcards of British birds can be obtained from (i) The Norfolk Naturalists' Trust, Assembly House, Norwich; (ii) The British Museum (Natural History), Cromwell Road, London, S.W.7; or through H.M.S.O. The complete list of cards obtainable from the British Museum is given in the pamphlet N.H.M., Form 170.

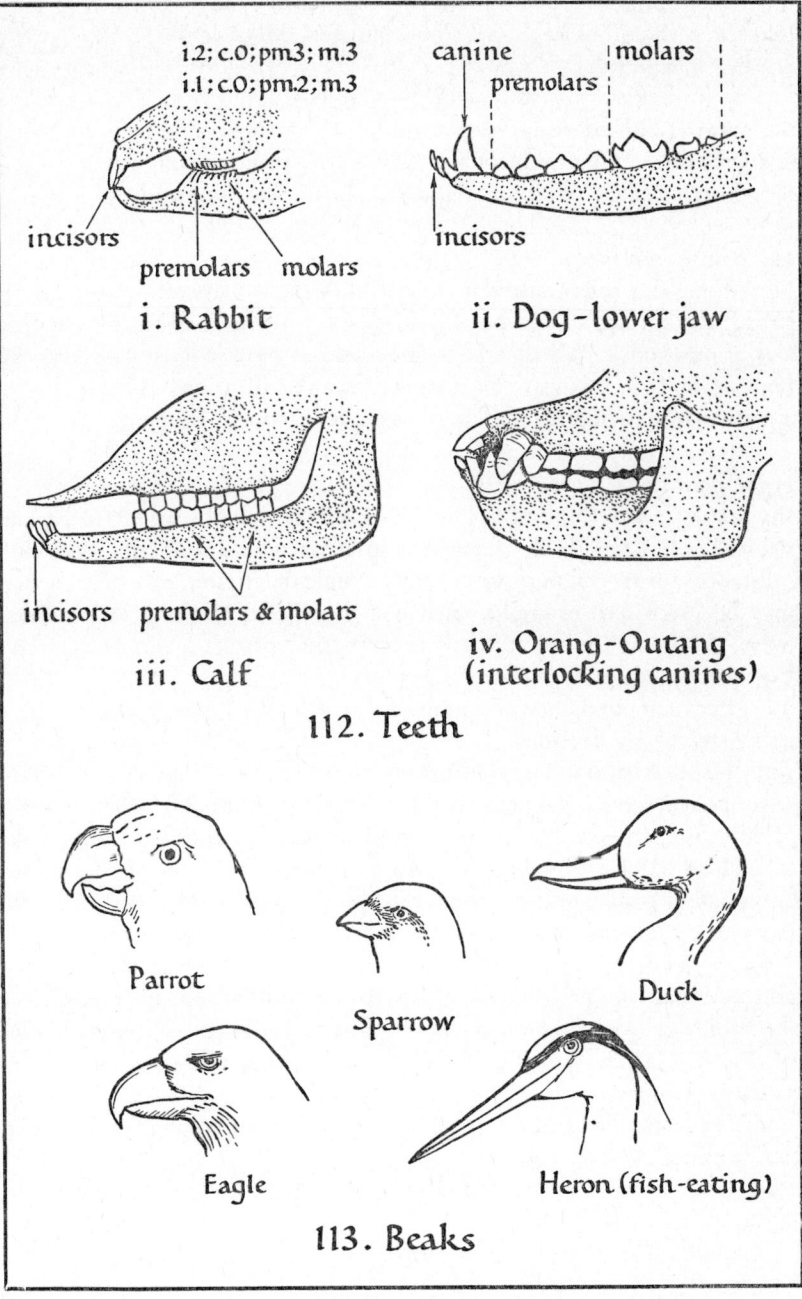

112. Teeth

113. Beaks

Let pupils make careful drawings of the beaks and feet of various birds. The seed-eating sparrow, the nut-cracking parrot, the mud-straining duck and the carnivorous eagle may be compared. Here again a museum trip can be most useful.

The study need not stop at birds or at beaks and feet. The lancets of the mosquito, the darting tongue of the frog or snake, and the long toothless jaws of the Giant Anteater of South America, with the sticky tongue on which it catches "white ants", suggest further fields of study.

114 *Bird Footprints*

Sieve some clay soil, moisten it and roll it out into a smooth layer on a flat board; the surface should be almost glossy. Put the board outside with a bait of meat on it. Watch it from indoors, but recover it as soon as a bird hops on to it; in this way the footprints may be identified as belonging to a particular kind of bird. Sketches and plaster-casts may be made.

115 *Digestion by Saliva*

Invite the class to think of the taste of a lemon; mouths water freely, and reference can be made to "glands" as specialized groups of cells producing substances for special purposes. A very simple description of a reflex action may be given and examples tried out (knee-jerk; blinking at a sudden noise; "jumping" when startled; sneezing). Construct a simple diagram. (See also Expt. 439.)

(a) Let each pupil chew a crumb of dry bread for a few minutes; notice that a sweet taste develops.

(b) Have at hand iodine solution for the starch test (Expt. 92), a suspension of basic copper carbonate for the sugar test (Expt. 88), and a solution of saliva prepared by diluting saliva with an equal quantity of water. Take a pinch of starch in a test-tube, "cream" it with two drops of cold water, and pour in boiling water to one-third fill the tube. Cool this starch solution and test a sample with iodine to confirm that it gives a blue colour.

Put about 1-cm depth of the starch solution into a clean test-tube and add an equal volume of the diluted saliva. Stand the tube in warm water for 2 minutes, cool, and test a portion of the liquid for starch; none should be found. Test the remainder of the liquid for sugar; a good positive reaction is obtained.

(c) Use a crumb of bread instead of the starch, pour boiling water over it, and continue as under (b).

(d) Use a tiny piece of potato (raw or boiled), treat it with boiling water, and continue as under (b).

In cases (c) and (d) tests for sugar on the original solutions obtained by pouring boiling water over the bread or potato may show faint positive reactions—but markedly different from the results after saliva treatment.

HISTORY OF A SIMPLE MEAL 105

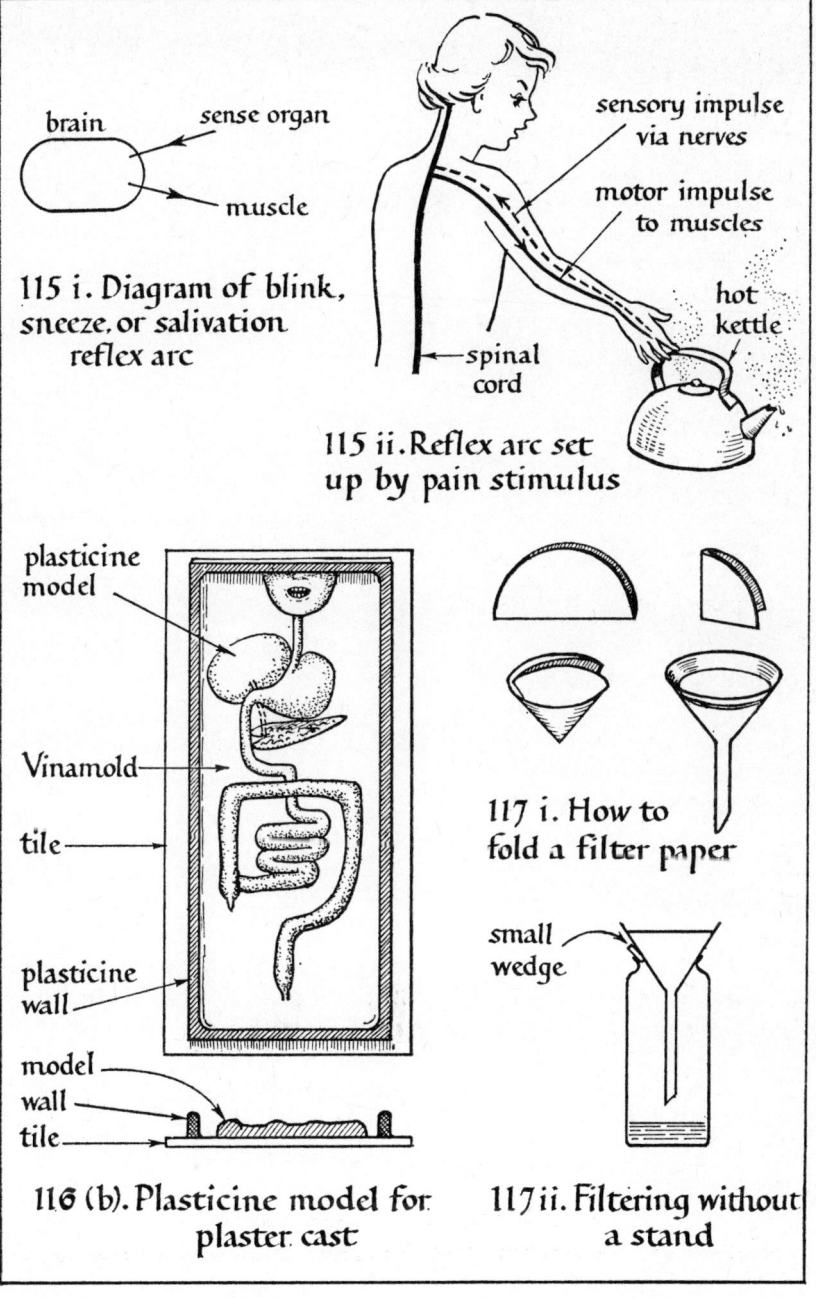

The Alimentary Canal

Refer to Expt. 74 (dissection of rat) and to Expt. 75 (main organs of man) in order to recall the main features of the food canal. See also Expt. 505 (b) (dissection of earthworm).

116 *Models of Alimentary Canal*

(a) Plasticine Model: Pupils may work from any good textbook diagram but they will need advice about proportions and about the third dimension. Some departure from strict accuracy will be necessary in the case of the small intestine. Gullet, stomach, duodenum, liver, pancreas and large intestine are readily modelled. An overall height of 15–20 cm is suitable, and the model may be laid out on a piece of heavy card. Tiny labels should be printed and pinned on to the parts.

(b) Plaster Models: First prepare a model in ordinary grey Plasticine; it may be as small as only 10 cm long. If the Plasticine is new, let the model stand on blotting-paper for about a week in order to draw out some of the oil; old Plasticine may be moulded at once. The moulding material is "Vinamold", particulars of which (descriptive leaflet and price list) may be obtained from Vinatex Ltd., Devonshire Road, Carshalton, Surrey. For the small model illustrated in Fig. 116 (b) about 250 g of Vinamold, type H.M.C. 1028 (red), is needed. The material is recoverable; old moulds may be melted down and made into new ones with little loss.

Support an aluminium bowl (say 12–15 cm in diameter and about 10 cm deep) in a hot-air bath consisting of a biscuit tin heated on a gas-ring. Dice the Vinamold and put a handful into the bowl; cover with a lid. Stir in more Vinamold as required. The temperature should not rise above 140°C. and a smooth fluid should be obtained.

Place the Plasticine model on a porcelain tile and build up a wall of Plasticine around it. Then pour the molten Vinamold into the space between the wall and the model until it covers the model completely. Rock the tile gently to encourage trapped air to escape. The mould should be ready for the next stage after a couple of hours. The Vinamold will then be solid and rubber-like, regaining its shape perfectly after deformation. It will come away easily from the model; if a cut is required it should be made with a razor-blade. After extracting the model dust any cut edges with talc to ensure perfect registration when the edges come together again.

The plaster of Paris used is called "dental white". Stir it into water to produce a fairly heavy cream and pour the cream at once into the Vinamold mould; setting is complete in a few minutes. The Vinamold strips away easily, leaving a perfect reproduction of the original model.

Any number of casts can be taken from one mould and every member of the class may be supplied with a model. Let pupils colour the various organs and label them suitably.

The Meaning of Digestion

Digestion is the process of preparing food, normally in the alimentary canal, for absorption into the body proper. It usually involves the conversion of insoluble materials into soluble form, although in the case of fats it may be that considerable absorption of the emulsified fat as such takes place. The only common soluble solid foodstuffs are sugar and salt, and even cane sugar must be broken down into simpler sugars by digestion.

117 Soluble and Insoluble Foodstuffs

Shake up a little starch powder with water in a test-tube. The liquid turns milky but the starch, which is insoluble in water, soon settles out. Shake up a little salt and water. The salt disappears, being soluble, and the solution tastes salty.

Separate salt from starch as follows: Shake up a little of the mixture with water for a minute or two. Filter the milky suspension and collect the clear liquid running through the filter paper. The starch remains on the paper; it should be treated two or three times with tiny amounts of cold water, to wash away all traces of salt solution, and then dried by putting the paper on a radiator or in a warm oven.

The filtered liquid tastes salty. The salt may be recovered by gently evaporating the solution in a dish—either over a small flame or supported on the open mouth of a can of boiling water.

Topics: The need to chew our food. Taste, smell and appearance of food important. Chewing and swallowing as exemplifying voluntary and involuntary movements. Reference to sickness, the use of emetics, ruminants and the muscular movements of earthworms to draw attention to the way in which food is moved along the alimentary canal.

The Digestion of Fats

It has already been suggested (p. 90) that a classroom display of fats and oils might be undertaken. Mineral oils will almost certainly find their way into such a collection, which might include:

Ceresine wax	castor oil	cream	cod-liver oil
paraffin wax	coconut oil	butter	halibut-liver oil
petroleum jelly	cottonseed oil	margarine	
medicinal paraffin	groundnut oil	lard	
burning oil	linseed oil	tallow	
petrol	olive oil	sperm oil	
	palm oil	spermaceti	
	soyabean oil	beeswax	

Here is valuable material for the study of foodstuffs (including animal feeding stuffs), vitamins, soap and glycerine, varnishes, paints and linoleum. Discussion of everyday experiences, such as the melting and setting of fats in the frying-pan, the solidification of olive oil in cold weather, the softening of butter in warm weather, and the ready melting of coco-butter when used to remove stage make-up, can lead to a clearer understanding of the use of the terms "fat" and "oil". The immediate melting of a flake of coconut "oil" when placed on the hand is always striking. Pupils may have seen fat vapour catch fire above an overheated frying pan, and the volatility of burning oils, e.g. in the internal-combustion engine, will be known to some.

118 *Emulsification of Fats by Alkalis*

Put about 2 cm of water into a test-tube and add three or four drops of olive oil (or cod-liver oil, etc.). Holding the tube upright, shake it to try to mix the oil and water; the oil quickly floats to the top when shaking is stopped. Now add a few drops of dilute caustic soda solution and shake again; a white emulsion is formed at once.

Repeat, using liquid paraffin instead of olive oil; there is no emulsification.

In this way alkalis are introduced as substances able to emulsify fats. A distinction between mineral oils and animal or vegetable oils is also established.

119 *Preparation of Hair Cream*

Cosmetic creams are emulsions and their preparation illustrates very well both the nature of an emulsion and the processes to which a fat is subjected in the food canal as essential preliminaries to digestion. The preparation of hair cream is an attractive experiment, easily performed by the pupils themselves, but it is important in such work that the product should be "the real thing", matching up to the commercial article in appearance and performance.

Some of the materials used in making cosmetic emulsions are not fats but are wax-like solids prepared by saponification of sperm oil. The proprietary products "Collone HV" and "Collone SE", made by Glovers (Chemicals) Limited, Wortley, Leeds, consist essentially of cetyl alcohol to which an emulsifying agent has been added.

A recipe for hair cream is:

Liquid paraffin ....88 g   Water .... 160 g
Collone HV .... 12 g   Caustic soda .... 0·4 g

Small tins, from which the upper rims have been removed with a modern type can-opener, are used instead of beakers. They are not only cheap and unbreakable, but they can be heated very quickly and conveniently by standing them in a pan of hot water. They are readily cleaned from oils by swabbing with cellulose wadding, obtainable from any chemist. Ordinary teaspoons are used for stirring.

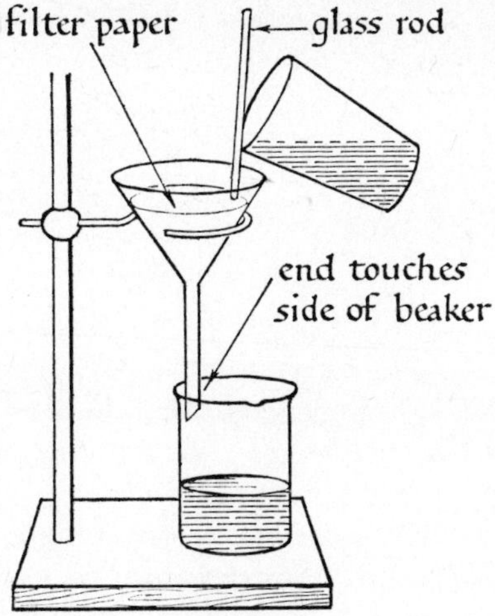

HISTORY OF A SIMPLE MEAL

117 iii. Filtration
- filter paper
- glass rod
- end touches side of beaker

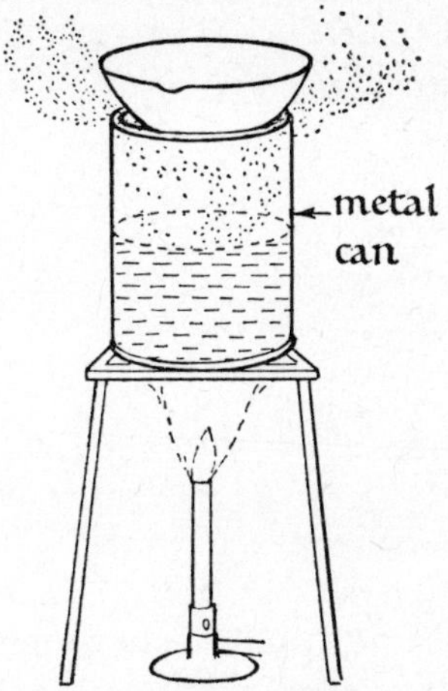

117 iv. Evaporation on steam bath
- metal can

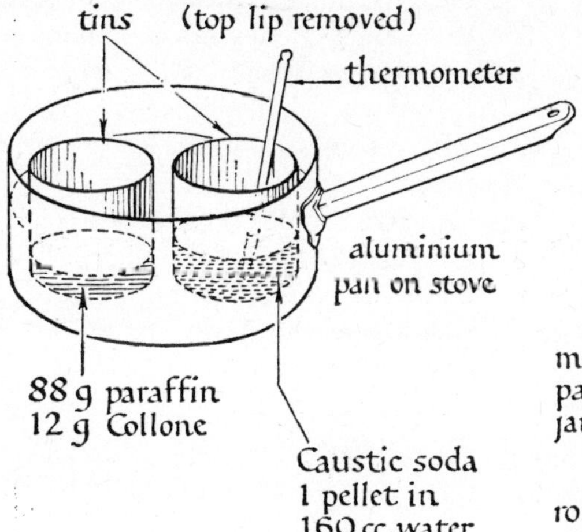

119. Preparation of hair cream
- tins (top lip removed)
- thermometer
- aluminium pan on stove
- 88 g paraffin
- 12 g Collone
- Caustic soda 1 pellet in 160 cc. water

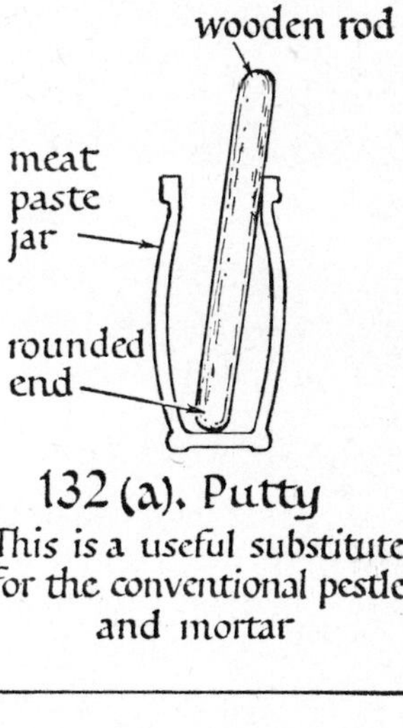

132 (a). Putty
- wooden rod
- meat paste jar
- rounded end

This is a useful substitute for the conventional pestle and mortar

Whenever a number of substances are to be weighed out into a can a standard procedure is adopted which greatly minimizes error by the pupils. The can is put on to a compression or lever balance and its weight noted; the necessary arithmetic is then done in advance by the pupils, thus:

Weight of can	52 g
Add 88 g paraffin	88 ,,
	140 ,,
Add 12 g Collone	12 ,,
	152 ,,

Liquid paraffin is run straight into the can, on the balance, until the reading of 140 g is just reached. Shredded Collone is then added until the balance reads 152 g. The method is speedy and effective, since the weights of material are not critical.

Using a similar procedure, weigh out the water into a second can and add a single pellet (about 1/3 g) of caustic soda. Stand the two cans in a pan of hot water and bring the contents of both to blood termperature or thereabouts (say 40°C.). Then pour the alkali solution steadily and with constant stirring into the clear mixture of oils. Emulsification is immediate and complete. Continue stirring while the mixture is cooled by standing the can in cold water; the white cream stiffens, and when it is cold a few drops of concentrated perfume are worked in. Finally the cream is filled into suitable jars, the top being levelled off with a knife-blade.

Suitable perfumes may be bought from Messrs. A. Boake Roberts & Co., Abrac Works, Walthamstow, London.

The Collone is best shredded with a pocket-knife. The process parallels the act of chewing a fat. The melting and stirring of the oils recalls the warming and churning action of the stomach. The process of emulsification in the presence of alkali is similar to the emulsification of fats by bile juice. The fact that the experiment takes place at blood temperature completes the analogy with digestion; it may also serve to introduce a lesson on the clinical thermometer or on temperature scales.

120 *Soap-making*
Unilever Ltd. recommend the following method for school laboratory work.

Use a mixture consisting of 25% cooking oil and 75% dripping. Heat 50 g of this with 1/4 g of household bar soap to 90–95°C. in an evaporating basin over a low Argand burner flame and then gradually add 20 cm^3 of 32% caustic soda solution, two or three drops at a time, stirring continuously. Continue stirring vigorously until the whole is emulsified and the mass stiffens to such an extent that it comes away from the basin and attaches itself to the glass stirring rod (roughly half an hour).

After cooling, scrape the saponified mass into a 400 cm³ tall beaker and add about 60 cm³ of hot water. Heat over a low flame with continuous stirring, for about another half-hour, when the material should be a thick, even paste. Now add hot saturated salt solution, with continuous stirring, until the soap just breaks quickly and evenly from a spatula dipped into it. If it breaks in a sticky manner, add a little more hot brine, always keeping the mixture nearly up to boiling point.

Remove the stirring rod and let the mixture stand overnight in the beaker. The soap will separate as a solid upper layer covered with some frothy material. Run a spatula blade round the inside wall of the beaker and so free and remove the cake of soap (the liquid "lye" beneath is discarded). Cut out the "neat soap"—i.e. the centre layer of the cake—and further improve it by placing it in a beaker with 50 cm³ of hot distilled water, heating over a low flame, and salting out as before.

121 *Further Properties of Alkalis*

Use a *very* dilute solution of caustic soda (one or two drops of bench solution in half a test-tube of water). Prepare also solutions of washing soda, bicarbonate of soda, slaked lime (lime-water) and household ammonia (much diluted); suspend a little "milk of magnesia" in water.

Notice the slimy feeling of caustic soda solution and of washing soda solution; discuss the term "caustic" and comment on the harsh action of washing soda on the hands. Test the "flat" taste of alkaline solutions, but remember that caustic soda *must* be very much diluted for this test; its intensely corrosive nature *must* be stressed.

Put different alkali solutions in each of 6 test-tubes standing in a rack. Drop a short strip of litmus paper (red) into each. Introduce the term "indicator".

122 *Common Acids*

Grate unripe apple or rhubarb and pulp the product by crushing it with a wooden rod in a meat-paste jar. Pour off the juice and dilute it with a little water. Dilute lemon juice, vinegar and sour milk similarly.

Confirm the sour taste of all these liquids. Then arrange them in test-tubes and test with blue litmus paper.

Make up weak solutions of citric acid and of acetic acid. Taste them and identify them as constituents of lemon juice and vinegar respectively. Demonstrate that solid citric acid, or tartaric acid (as used in baking), does not affect dry litmus paper.

Refer to the mineral acids. At this stage it is sufficient to demonstrate their corrosive action (e.g. on zinc or iron); to spot a little of each on to cloth and note what happens after a time; to show the effect of adding concentrated sulphuric acid VERY CAUTIOUSLY to water; and generally to emphasize that such acids must be handled with great care.

123 *Neutralization*

Have ready approximately normal solutions of caustic soda and hydrochloric acid.

The alkali is prepared by dissolving 40 g of the solid (which should be handled with care) in water and making up to 1 litre. The acid is roughly one-tenth the strength of concentrated acid; more accurately, dilute 90 cm^3 of concentrated hydrochloric acid to a total volume of 1 litre.

The reagents may be supplied to pupils in (labelled) test-tubes. Let pupils put a few cm of alkali into a small evaporating dish and add acid, cautiously, until a strip of litmus paper just turns red. Let them see that the original blue colour can be brought to the point where one drop of acid or alkali will affect it. A 15 cm length of glass tubing should be used, as a pipette, for the last stages of neutralization.

Remove the litmus paper and evaporate the liquid carefully to dryness on a sand-bath. Taste the residue when it is cold.

124 *Baking-powder and Health Salt*

(a) Weigh out 25 g sodium bicarbonate and 24 g tartaric acid powder into a dry tin box. Put on the lid and mix thoroughly by shaking.

The baking-powder may be used in making soda bread (Expt. 101). Add a little of the powder to water and test the gas that escapes (Expt. 41).

(b) Prepare baking-powder as in (a) and then add 10 g of finely powdered Epsom salt and 30 g of icing sugar. Mix as before.

Stir a teaspoonful into a tumbler of cold water and drink.

125 *Other Indicators*

(a) Shred purple pansy petals and crush them with very little alcohol (industrial spirit) in a mortar until you have a deep purple solution.

With a glass rod, spot a few drops of the coloured extract on to the middle of a filter paper laid over a watch glass. Let the coloured patch dry out.

Prepare dilute solutions (in water) of lemon juice, vinegar, bicarbonate of soda, washing soda, etc. Spot a drop of each in turn near the coloured patch on your filter paper and record any colour change when the liquid spreads to the patch.

Instead of pansy you may use such flowers as rose (red), iris and aquilegia. The juice of raspberries, blackberries and rhubarb may be tested similarly.

(b) Grate a little red cabbage and crush to a paste (Expt. 122). Put a tablespoonful into a beaker and pour on a little boiling water. Stir well and filter the liquid. Add a drop or two of oil of cloves as a preservative.

Add dilute sodium carbonate solution until the liquid just turns yellow/

green. Paint on to white-wove writing paper (*not* highly glazed), allow to dry, and then cut the paper into strips for use as test paper.

Just restore the red colour of the remaining solution by adding dilute vinegar drop by drop, and prepare red test papers from this liquid.

Use the papers to test alkalis and acids as in Expts. 121 and 122. See also Expt. 503.

(c) Using sodium carbonate solution and dilute acid, show that the pink colour of phenolphthalein in alkaline solution disappears when the alkali is neutralized.

126 *The Digestion of Cream*

Steapsin, the fat-splitting enzyme, may be purchased. Shake a little with cold water in a test-tube to make a solution of about 1–2 per cent strength.

Skim about 5 cm^3 of cream from a bottle of milk and divide it between two test-tubes. Add 3 drops of 1 per cent phenolphthalein solution to each tube, followed by very dilute sodium carbonate solution until the indicator just turns pink. Now run a few drops of steapsin solution into one of the tubes only, and let both tubes stand in a can of water kept at blood temperature. Within 5–10 minutes the liquid in the tube containing the steapsin, but not that in the other tube, loses its pink colour—the alkali in this tube, under the influence of the enzyme, having been used up by reaction with the fat.

Whilst the experiment is going forward a clinical thermometer may be used to take the temperature of the water bath and also of a member of the class.

The Digestion of Protein Foods

Prepare a list of the chief protein foods. Coloured cubes (children's building bricks) may be used in introducing the idea that proteins are built of smaller units (amino-acids) and that they must be broken down into these units by digestion before they can be absorbed. White blocks might represent those units which the body can use to build up its own proteins (muscle, etc.); red ones could represent units which cannot be so used. "First-class" protein (e.g. meat) contains a high proportion of the "white" units; "second-class" protein (e.g. plant protein) is richer in the "red" units, but is very useful as a complement to other protein. The idea of a satisfactory protein intake is considered further later (see Expt. 168).

Draw attention to the fact that most proteins are insoluble in water. Milk protein is exceptional; consider the action of rennin in the stomach.

127 *Preparation of Junket*

Warm a pint of milk in a pan to blood temperature and add one dessertspoonful of rennet (prepared from the calf's stomach and containing the enzyme rennin) and sufficient sugar. Stir to dissolve the sugar and pour the liquid into a clean dish to cool.

128 *Digestion of Milk Protein*
Suspend a teaspoonful of junket in water in a boiling tube. Shake well and allow the curdy material to settle; then decant off the liquid. Repeat the washing with water several times.

(i) Heat a little of the protein with water; shake well; note that the curds do not dissolve.

(ii) Add two drops concentrated hydrochloric acid to a test-tube one-third filled with water containing suspended curd. Warm slightly and shake—the protein rapidly dissolves. (Rennet contains pepsin as well as rennin.)

129 *Digestion of Cod Protein*
Prepare some of the muscle protein "fibrin" by boiling a little cod in water for two hours, flaking it, and washing the flaked material very thoroughly with water (this is best achieved by using very little of the protein and shaking it in a test-tube with water, decanting, rewashing, etc.). After this treatment the fibrin will appear as shining threads suspended in the water; it is colourless, quite insoluble, and is in a form which presents a large surface to enzyme action.

Pepsin solution is prepared by shaking about $\frac{1}{2}$ g of pepsin powder with 50 cm^3 cold water and filtering. To 5 cm^3 of this solution add 5 cm^3 of 0·4 per cent hydrochloric acid (prepared by adding 4 cm^3 concentrated HCl to 300 cm^3 water), so producing 0·2 per cent acid—which is the acid concentration in the stomach. Suspend a tiny amount of the washed fibrin in this liquid. In a second tube suspend a similar quantity of fibrin in 0·2% acid but add no pepsin. Keep both tubes at blood temperature for a few hours. The fibrin in the tube containing pepsin is completely dissolved, so that only a minute residue of fine powder remains at the bottom of the tube.

130. *Model to Illustrate the Passage of Digested Food through the Intestine Wall*
(a) Required: i. Visking tubing ($\frac{1}{2}$–1 cm diameter), made from regenerated cellulose and obtainable from laboratory suppliers. It acts as a membrane permeable to glucose molecules but not to the much larger starch molecules. Store moist once the tubing has been wetted. ii. Starch/glucose solution: cream about 5 g starch with a little cold water and pour on 100 cm^3 boiling water. Add about 10 g glucose and cool the solution to blood temperature.

The arrangement of apparatus required is shown in Fig. 130(a). The water in the two beakers is kept at about 37° C.

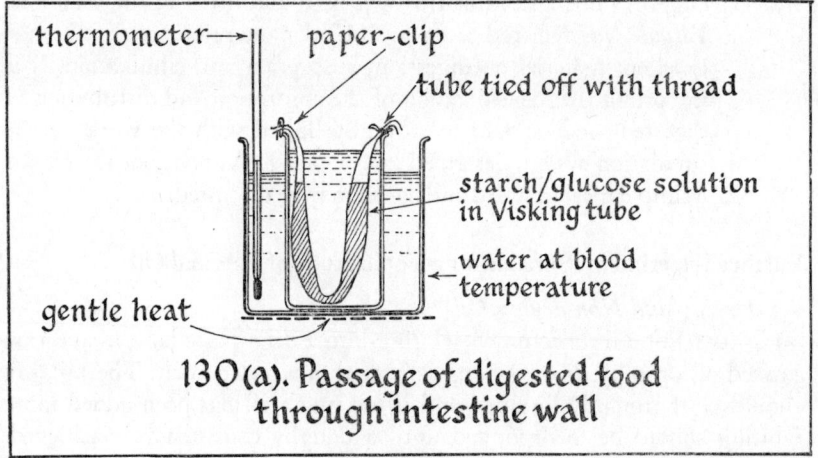

130 (a). Passage of digested food through intestine wall

Tie off one end of a 15-cm length of Visking tubing with thread and carefully run into the tube starch/glucose solution. Close the tube with a paper clip and rinse the outside free from any traces of starch or glucose. Arrange the tubing in a U form in the inner beaker.

After 15, 30, 45 . . . mins. test the water round the Visking tubing for starch (Expt. 92) and sugar (Expt. 88).

(b) Use the same apparatus as in the previous experiment but three-quarters fill the tube with a solution of starch only and top up the tube with fresh saliva. Test the surrounding water for sugar after 15, 30, 45 . . . minutes.

131 *Absorption (teacher demonstration only)*
Ask the chemist to make up a few gelatine capsules containing potassium iodide. Each should contain 0.2 g KI and they must be stored in a cool, dry place—e.g. in a tube containing silica gel.

Quickly swallow one capsule and wash it down with a glass of water. Rinse the mouth and at once test the saliva for the presence of potassium iodide, using acid starch reagent (see below). Then test saliva taken from the mouth at two minute intervals and record the time elapsed from swallowing the capsule to the first appearance of iodide in the saliva.

The potassium iodide is set free when the gelatine coating dissolves in the stomach. It is absorbed into the blood stream from the small intestine and is later excreted by the salivary and other glands.

(Acid starch reagent: Add 1 cm^3 dilute sodium nitrite solution and 1 cm^3 dilute sulphuric acid to 10 cm^3 starch solution prepared by pouring half a litre of boiling water on to 1 g starch made into a paste with a little cold water. The reagent will not keep.)

Topics: Helpful films and filmstrips will be found listed in the catalogue *Visual Aids* referred to on p. 6. Under the reference 673 there is excellent material on digestion, absorption and elimination. It is important that consideration of the absorption and distribution of digested foods should be carefully linked with the work on the circulation system described in Chapter 8. As revision, the fate of a simple meal of bread and bacon may be discussed.

Further Experiments Suitable for a Topic Study of Fats and Oils

132 *Drying and Non-drying Oils*

(a) Putty: Put a little common whiting into a meat paste jar and add raw linseed oil drop by drop, stirring it in with a wooden stick. The mixture should be thoroughly kneaded and if too much oil has been added more whiting should be incorporated until a doughy consistency is achieved. The experiment should be repeated using boiled linseed oil instead of the raw oil, and the behaviour of the two lots of putty on standing for several days compared.

(b) Using a variety of oils make spots on white paper, the name of the oil being written underneath the corresponding spot. Examine the spots after 24 hours and so classify the oils as "drying", "semi-drying" or "non-drying".

Suitable oils are: linseed, hemp, poppyseed, castor, olive, paraffin.

(Note: Drying oils are compounds of glycerol with unsaturated acids; they undergo oxidation on standing in the air and solidify. Compounds of lead, etc. accelerate the oxidation and are sold as "driers". Boiled linseed oil dries more quickly than the raw oil.)

133 *Paint*

Mix together in a small tin a little finely powdered zinc oxide, boiled linseed oil, turpentine, and "drier" (which is sold commercially as such). Stir well to produce a smooth mixture and then paint a strip of wood with the product. Repeat the experiment using red lead, lead chromate or lampblack instead of zinc oxide.

134 *Vanishing Cream*

The procedure is similar to that followed in the preparation of hair cream (Expt. 120). A solution of 1 g of caustic potash in 117 g water, at about 85° C. is poured into a mixture of 17 g stearic acid, 1 g cetyl alcohol and 1 g liquid paraffin at the same temperature—with stirring. A suitable perfume is incorporated when the cream is cold, and the cream is packed into attractive jars.

Vanishing creams are essentially emulsions of stearic acid. They do not in fact "vanish", but they spread easily over the skin to form a "foundation" for powder. The emulsifier is a soap, potassium stearate, formed by partial neutralization of the stearic acid.

Further examples of the preparation of cosmetic creams as part of the school science course may be found in the following articles appearing in the *School Science Review*:

November, 1953: "Cosmetics", by K. Laybourn.
June, 1962: "Cosmeticology", by J. Gostelow.
December, 1969: "Cosmetics for C.S.E.", by Mary Martinson.

The manufacture of linoleum is an important industry based on the use of drying oils. As a project for the science club the experiment may be tried of painting successive layers of boiled linseed oil on a small square of canvas stretched across a wooden frame (e.g. a small picture frame). Each layer of oil is allowed to dry before the next is put on. Meanwhile a quantity of cork dust is prepared by rubbing down old corks on coarse sandpaper. The dust is spread over the oiled canvas and is rolled in. Rolling is best done by turning the frame over, so that the oiled and corked surface is downwards on a board, and rolling from the back. Loose dust is brushed off and another layer of linseed oil is added. The process of rolling in cork dust and covering again with oil is repeated until a sufficient thickness has been obtained, and the linoleum is then allowed to dry thoroughly. It may be removed from the frame, the unfinished edges trimmed off, and the surface painted.

Chapter Eight

The Circulation of the Blood

History as an Aid to Science Teaching

Stories of great achievement thrill young people today no less than formerly. Our pupils respond to the genius of a Newton or a Faraday; to the courage of a Curie or a Gagarin. And whilst it is seldom that the practical investigations of the pioneers can be repeated in school, accounts of original discoveries and of the work which led up to them can sometimes be introduced into our teaching with most telling effect. Make some of the world's great scientists your familiar friends, says Westaway: "dwell on their lives not only as men of science but as personalities".

Some teachers advocate an historical treatment of certain topics, so that their pupils may arrive at a knowledge of a scientific idea or principle more or less by the stages through which it was first developed. Opportunities for this kind of approach are rare. Possibly the average pupil will come nearest to seeing it in action if he is studying some project, such as the history of the steam engine or the conquest of disease. Most frequently, it will be for the teacher to refer his pupils to the lives and discoveries of individual men of science.

Whatever method is used, we should recognize that besides stirring up interest we have opportunities to drive home the lesson that the search for truth is often hard and long, and that not all who embark upon it succeed. It has been said that perhaps the most difficult of all mental acts is that of re-arranging a familiar set of data in our minds; taking a new look at the facts. Galileo, Harvey and Rutherford managed it, so that concepts such as the planetary nature of the solar system, the circulation of the blood and the spontaneous disintegration of atoms are now accepted even by boys and girls at school. But these concepts originally demanded nothing less than genius in the face of prevailing ideas. For the ordinary pupil the lesson is an important one: that things are not always what they seem: that "authority" is not always right; and that our minds are our own, to use.

Several practical teaching aids suggest themselves in relation to teaching with a historical reference:

(a) A chart running along the classroom wall, recording the names and dates of great scientists over the centuries, not only displays the succession but draws attention to the extraordinary surge of scientific advance during the last few hundred years, most especially of course, in the present century. The chart may be embellished with sketches or photographs of many of those to whom it refers, and here the postcard series of the National Portrait Gallery can prove helpful.

Alternatively, the chart may show the dates of great discoveries or achievements: the invention of printing, the publication of the *Principia*, the introduction of vaccination, anaesthesia and antiseptic surgery, the voyage of the *Beagle* and of Luna-9; among many others.

(b) A science reference library should include plenty of popular books relating to the history of science, including the most recent discoveries. Many publishing houses issue series on great lives and great achievements, providing excellent material for simple research and individual study in preparation for writing up a topic, or delivering a classroom lecturette, or simply finding the answer to a question—e.g. *Newton* and *Galileo* (E.U.P.).

(c) Readings from the classics of science literature (usefully collected in such books as Mason's *Readings from the Scientists* and McKenzie's *Major Achievements of Science*) can be used in more ways than one. Here is an extract from the *School Science Review* of February, 1922:

"It occurred to me that since they were interested in Pasteur I might get them to produce some scenes from the play Pasteur by Sacha Guitry. I got some help, and by the time they had read the play about four times they caught the spirit of it . . . and the boys learned something about science from the play, of which a considerable portion consists of Pasteur's own words.

One of the boys, whose scene-painting for Pasteur was the best thing in the art exhibition of that term, wrote a paper on Leonardo da Vinci the artist and another on Leonardo the scientist. It then occurred to the boys that Leonardo might be a suitable subject for a play . . ."

The dramatization of famous episodes can provide excellent scope: The incident at the Leaning Tower, The Force of the Vacuum (Guericke's experiments) or The Discovery of Penicillin suggest themselves as possible titles.

(d) Good prints of great paintings add interest to the walls of the Science corridor: Breughel's *The Alchemist at Work*, Chardin's *Soap Bubbles* and Torun's *Portrait of Copernicus* are examples of pictures which might well hang side by side with good photographs of modern scientific developments.

(e) There is now a useful selection of films dealing with aspects of the history of science, such as Kepler and his Work (576 A6), Mirror in the Sky (501 A15), The Discovery of Radioactivity (555 D2) and Conquest of the Atom (557 D17).

One further point may be mentioned: the history of science provides us with an opportunity to bring out the international nature of scientific advance and the co-operative effort upon which progress depends. From the past we link the names of Tycho Brahe, Kepler, Galileo and Newton; of Darwin and Wallace; Lister and Pasteur. Today vast organizations and many research teams are working on problems as diverse as synthetic fibres, atomic power and the conquest of cancer.

Books and the Teacher of Science

It has long been a popular misconception that science cuts a man off from art. Yet great writing relies upon two qualities most typical of scientific thought—observation and imagination. It has been truly observed that the man without imagination may collect facts but has little prospect of making a discovery; and Karl Pearson has pointed out that the scientific classics are often the most intelligible of books because they speak of real things interpreted by artists. Certainly the teacher of science must make himself familiar with the writings of the masters. Here is Leonardo describing the action of climbing stairs:

> "The first thing that the man does when he ascends by steps is to free the leg which he wishes to raise from the weight of the trunk ... and at the same time he loads the other leg with his entire weight, including that of the raised leg. Then he raises the (freed) leg and places the foot on the step where he wishes to mount; having done this he conveys to the higher foot all the weight of the trunk and of the leg and leaning his hand upon his thigh, thrusts the head forward and moves towards the point of the higher foot, while raising swiftly the heel of the lower foot; and with the impetus so acquired he raises himself up; and at the same time, by extending the arm which was resting on the knee, he pushes the trunk and head upwards and thus straightens the curve of the back."

John Ruskin was not a scientist but he has much to offer a teacher. The latest edition of the Meteorological Office publication, *A Course in Elementary Meteorology*, warns its readers against regarding a cloud as "an entity drifting across the sky"; but Ruskin had made the point a century earlier:

> "Clouds, it is to be remembered, are not so much local vapour, as vapour rendered locally visible by a fall in temperature. Thus a cloud, whose parts are in constant motion, will hover on a snowy mountain, pursuing constantly the same track upon its flanks, and yet remaining the same size, the same form, and in the same place, for half a day together. No matter how violent ... the wind may be the instant (the vapour) approaches the spot where the chilly influence of the snow extends, the moisture it carries becomes visible, and then and there the cloud forms

on the instant ... the variations which take place in its outlines are not so much alternations of positions and arrangement of parts, as they are the alternate formation and disappearance of parts."

In the following extract Michael Faraday contemplates the steady flame of a candle shielded from draughts:

"You see then that in the first instance a beautiful cup is formed. As the air comes to the candle it moves upward by the force of the current which the heat of the candle produces, and it so cools all the sides of the wax as to keep the edge much cooler than the part within; the part within melts by the flame that runs down the wick as far as it can go before it is extinguished, but the part on the outside does not melt. If I made a current in one direction, my cup would be lop-sided, and the fuel would consequently run over. ... You see therefore, that the cup is formed by this beautifully regular ascending current of air playing upon all sides, which keeps the exterior of the candle cool."

Charles Darwin, in his *Journal of a Voyage Round the World*, describes Professor Owen's discovery on the coast of Argentina of the remains of nine great quadrupeds within a space of 200 yards square. The habits of these creatures had been a mystery: they fed on leaves of trees, but why the colossal breadth and weight of their hinder quarters? Darwin explains:

"With their great tails and their huge heels firmly fixed like a tripod on the ground, they could freely exert the full force of their most powerful arms and great claws. Strongly rooted indeed must that tree have been which could have resisted. The mylodon, moreover, was furnished with a long extensile tongue like that of a giraffe, which, by one of those beautiful provisions of Nature, enabled it, with the aid of its long neck, to reach its leafy food".

Let no young teacher feel that only modern science matters; that *New Scientist* and the *Scientific American* can fully meet his needs. Of course he must try to keep abreast, and he will carry more conviction with his pupils if he can at least recognize such terms as laser or lysozyme. But he cannot afford to neglect the heritage of the past; to cut himself off from works which not infrequently are classics not only of science but of teaching method too. We are reminded especially of men like Hooke, Tyndall, Herschel, T. H. Huxley and Sir James Jeans—all of whom wrote in a language which ordinary people could understand.

A paragraph from Professor Perry's *Spinning Tops* well illustrates the methods of the great teachers. The author records that he once showed some of his experiments with tops to a "coffee-drinking, tobacco-smoking" audience in the Victoria Music Hall in London. He used them to demonstrate the stability of the axis of a spinning body and illustrated the matter further by remarking that guns are rifled in the barrel so that the bullet leaves with a spin which stabilizes its direction, while the best way of throwing a quoit with certainty is to give it spin. He goes on:

> "But after my address was finished, and after a young lady in a spangled dress had sung a comic song, two jugglers came upon the stage. They sent hats and hoops, and plates, and umbrellas spinning from one to the other. One of them threw a stream of knives into the air, catching them and throwing them up again with the greatest precision and now my educated audience shouted with delight and showed in other unmistakeable ways that they had observed the spin which the juggler gave to every knife as it left his hand, so that he might have perfect knowledge of how it would come back to him again."

Breathing

The movements of breathing and the nature of the gas exchange have already been considered (Expts. 15–19 and 50–53); the film "Breathing" (672/A6) may be used for revision. "Lights" obtained from the butcher show the richness of the blood supply to the lungs and the branching nature of the air tubes and the blood vessels. The evils of breathing through the mouth and the value of breathing exercises can best be brought out in the P.E. lesson.

135 *Breathing Movements*

Closely observe the breathing movements of a fish in the classroom aquarium and of a frog in the terrarium. Next, time the breathing movements. In the case of the fish, do the gill covers move simultaneously with the mouth opening; do different types of fish breathe at the same rate; does artificial improvement of the aeration of the aquarium affect the rate of breathing?

A very simple but effective aquarium aerator has been described by Haswell. Place an old Bunsen burner in the sink and connect the gas inlet tube to the water tap. Join the barrel of the burner by rubber tubing to a glass tube which dips into the water of the aquarium. The jet of water inside the burner tube draws in air which passes up to the aquarium, the water falling back through the air-inlet hole.

136 *Seconds Ticker*

This is useful for timing breathing rate, pulse rate, etc.

Using a red-hot needle, bore a hole centrally through a 1-cm thick slice from a 2-cm diameter cork and hang a pendulum (thread and small metal nut) from a bent pin stuck into the edge of the slice. Remove one end from the tray of a match-box and pin the tray, open end downwards, to the edge

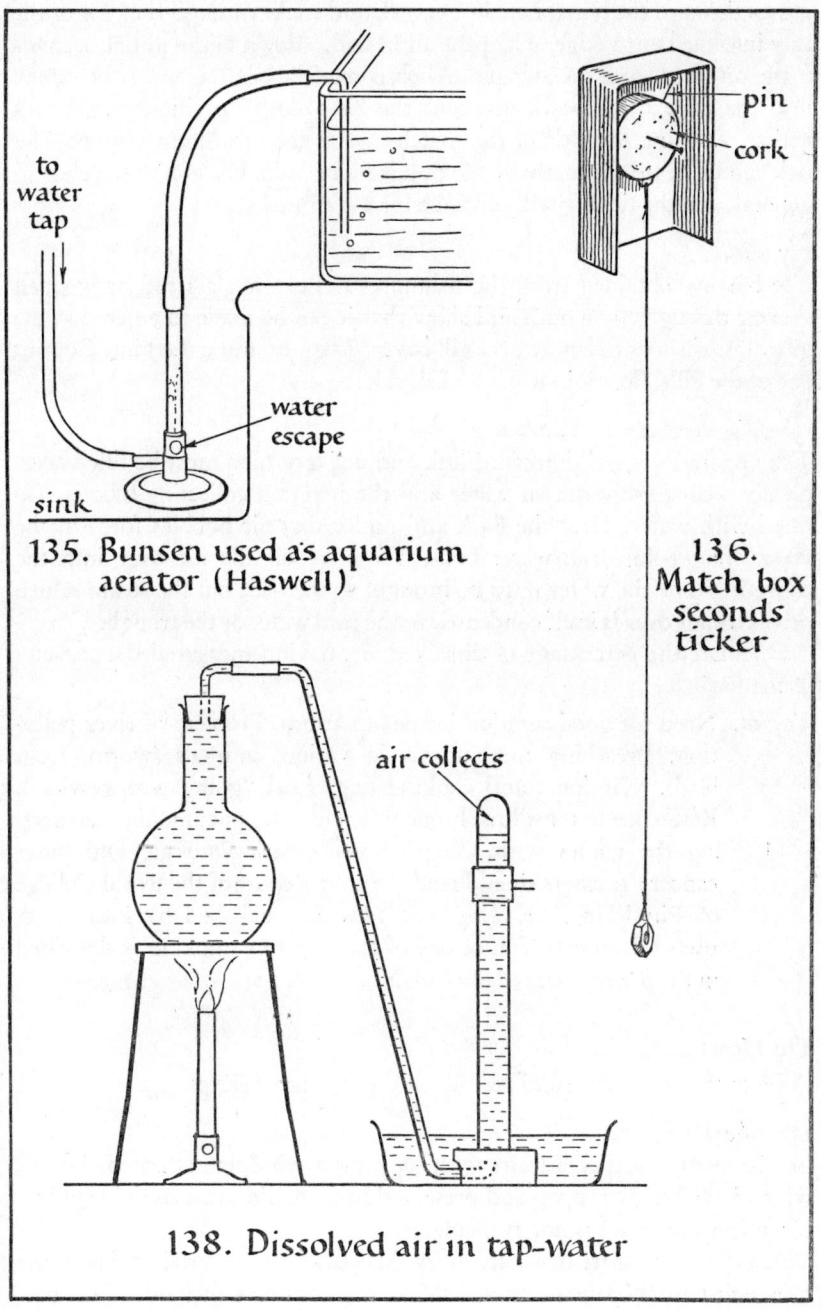

135. Bunsen used as aquarium aerator (Haswell)

136. Match box seconds ticker

138. Dissolved air in tap-water

of the laboratory bench. Pivot the cork slice inside the tray on a pin which passes through the bored hole in the cork and sticks through the base of the tray into the bench edge. The pendulum hangs down and will tick seconds if the distance from the axle-pin to bob is made about 100 cm. A pin stuck into the edge of the cork at about the "1 o'clock" position serves as a striker, catching the side of the match-tray as the pendulum swings. The tick can be heard distinctly by the pupils in a group, but not by the class in general, and the ticking will continue for 2–3 minutes.

137 *Gills*
Use herring obtained from the fishmonger. Push a glass rod or wooden skewer through the mouth and show that it can be made to emerge at the gills. Use scissors to cut away a gill-cover. Then examine the gills. Cut out one of the gills, float it in water and sketch it.

138 *Dissolved Air in Tap-water*
The apparatus is well-known. Flask and delivery tube must be filled completely with freshly drawn water and the inverted collecting-tube is also filled with water. Heat the flask and notice that air bubbles form in the water long before the water boils. To drive all the air over into the collecting-tube the water must be brought to the boil, but the steam which drives the air over is itself condensed in the cold water of the trough.

Calculate the percentage of dissolved air, having measured the capacity of the flask.

Topics: Need for good aeration in the aquarium. Problem of river pollution. Breathing mechanisms in various animals (worm, frog, bird). Windpipe and choking (e.g. food "going wrong way"). Reference to tonsillitis, bronchitis, pleurisy, pneumonia—connecting the names with the parts concerned. Smoking and lung-cancer: teachers should read the 1962 Report of the Royal College of Physicians, *Smoking and Health*, published by Pitman. A useful demonstration of one of the perils of smoking is described in the *School Science Review*, No. 155, p. 239.

The Heart
Refer to the appearance and position of the rat's heart (Expt. 74).

139 *Sheep's Heart*
Get from the butcher a heart with lungs and windpipe attached. Hearts which have been cut open and preserved in formalin are a useful stand-by when fresh material is not available.

From a fresh heart first pare away (scalpel) fatty material and note the muscular nature of the heart wall. Make incisions on either side of the narrow, lower end of the heart, and when the ventricles are entered cut away

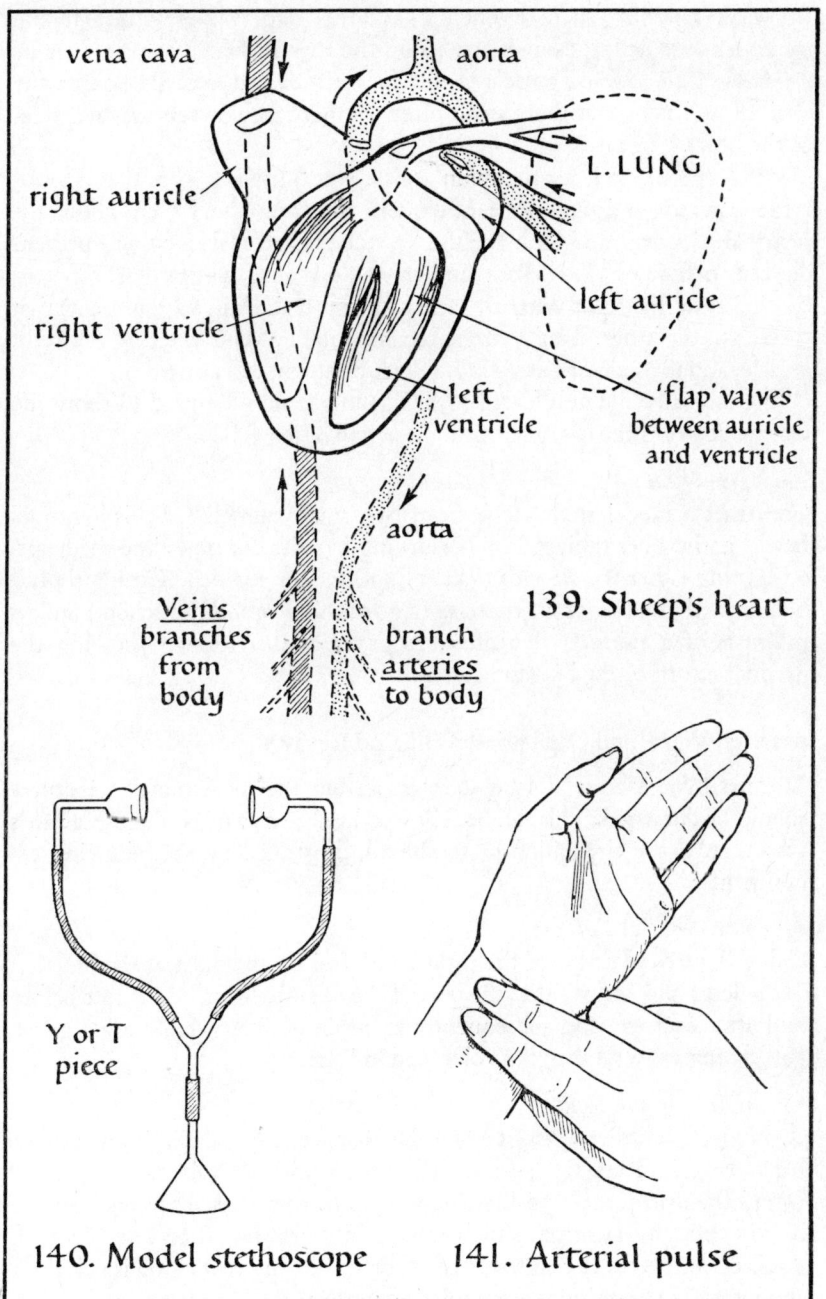

139. Sheep's heart

140. Model stethoscope

141. Arterial pulse

more materials to expose the cavities more clearly. Notice the thickness of the walls (especially the left ventricle) and the "flap" valves with their thin white tendons acting as anchors. From the way in which these valves lie the flow of blood from auricle to ventricle can be deduced. Probe into the auricles and note that there is no direct connection between the two sides of the heart.

With a probe, seek for the main artery (aorta) leading from the left ventricle upwards and out of the heart. Cut the aorta about 5 cm above the heart, slit its wall and look for the "watch-pocket" valves which prevent the return flow of blood. In a similar way examine the pulmonary artery leading from the right ventricle, and confirm (if the lungs are present) that it leads to the lungs. Lastly, probe the large flabby veins entering the right auricle, and the smaller ones joining the lungs to the left auricle.

The loop film "The Heart" (672/K4) might now be used to show the various stages of the heart-beat and the action of the valves.

140 *Heart-beat*

Construct a model stethoscope from two small funnels (or thistle-funnel heads) and rubber tubing. Pupils working in pairs can now time the heart-beat, using either the seconds ticker (Expt. 136) or a watch. Timing should be repeated after vigorous exercise (e.g. running round the school) and at intervals of 2 minutes thereafter. A graph is then drawn showing the gradual return of the beat to normal.

Arteries, Veins, and Capillaries: William Harvey

The need for a circulatory system in all but the most minute creatures should be discussed. This can be followed by the story of William Harvey's discovery of the circulation of the blood, illustrated by the following experiments:

141 *The Arterial Pulse*

Using the second finger of the right hand, feel for the pulse at the junction of the left hand and wrist at the base of the thumb. Measure the rate before and after exercise, and subsequently at 2-minute intervals. Draw a graph and compare it with the graph obtained in Expt. 140.

142 *Valves in the Veins*

(a) Notice the little swellings along the course of a large vein in the arm or leg: these indicate the position of "watch-pocket" valves. Tie a band round the arm just above the elbow so as to compress the veins (but not tightly enough to compress the deeper-seated arteries). The veins below it swell up and become knotted at the valves, showing that blood is still flowing into the arteries but is accumulating in the veins.

(b) With the band still in position, place a finger-tip on one of the large veins in the wrist or forearm and with another finger stroke the vein towards the elbow. Notice how easy it is to empty the vein of blood in this way. Lift the finger nearest the heart—the vein remains empty. Lift the finger nearest the hand—the vein at once fills.

143 Arteries and First-aid
(a) Tie a narrow bandage tightly round the base of a finger; notice that the finger becomes white and numb, showing that blood is no longer flowing into it.

(b) After commenting on the danger of a deep cut, practise the first-aid necessary in the case of a cut artery. Discuss the need for care in using a tourniquet.

Topic: Study and discuss the following quotation from Robert Boyle's report of his interview with William Harvey: "And when I remember that when I asked our famous Harvey, in the only Discourse I had with him (which was but a while before he died), what induc'd him to think of a Circulation of the Blood? He answer'd me, that when he took notice that the Valves in the Veins of so many several Parts of the Body were so plac'd that they gave free passage to the Blood towards the Heart, but oppos'd the passage of the Venal Blood the Contrary way: He was invited to imagine, that so provident a Cause as Nature had not Plac'd so many Valves without design: and no Design seem'd more probable than that, since the Blood could not well, because of the interposing Valves, be sent by the Veins to the Limbs; it should be sent through the Arteries and Return through the Veins, whose Valves did not oppose its course that way."

For reference see Singer, *The Discovery of the Circulation of the Blood* (Bell).

144 Capillaries and Corpuscles
Anaesthetise a tadpole by sprinkling a very small amount of ether on the surface of water in a beaker containing the creature. Then put the animal in a hollow slide and view the middle part of the tail (microscope or microprojector). Two main blood vessels and a number of capillaries may be seen, and the movement of blood corpuscles can be observed.

For anaesthesia the Nuffield text recommends M5.222, obtainable (with an information leaflet) from Sandoz Products Ltd., Pharmaceutical Department, 23, Great Castle Street, London, W.1. Supplies are recommended for all-round-the-year use.

Blood movement (and the beating heart) may also be observed in recently-hatched trout: see the authors' *Practical Science for Secondary Schools*, Book Four, pp. 37–8.

The Nature of Blood

145 *Blood Smear*

(a) Tie a piece of string fairly tightly round the index finger just below the last joint. Sterilize a needle by passing it through a flame and then, with the end of the finger bent, prick the skin behind the nail sharply. At once smear the drop of blood across a clean warm slide, cover it, and examine it under high power.

(b) Repeat, but do not cover the slide. Instead, wave it in the air for a few minutes until the film is dry. Then add 2 or 3 drops of Leishmann's stain and rinse off excess after 5 minutes under the tap. Dry the preparation gently near an electric lamp and examine with the microscope.

Most of the cells seen in the smears are red blood corpuscles. But the stained smear should show some rather larger and irregular cells—the leucocytes.

(c) Leave a drop of blood on a slide (do not smear), exposed to the air. What happens?

146 *Blood and Oxygen*

Shake a few drops of fresh blood with water in a test-tube. Add a few tiny grains of sodium hydrosulphite ("a chemical that readily absorbs oxygen"), and notice the colour change. Then shake the liquid vigorously for a time so as to dissolve fresh oxygen from the air; the colour change is reversed.

147 *Styptic Pencil*

Prepare a "former" from a 10-cm length of dowel rod (or a pencil stump) by shaping one end to a blunt point. Alternatively the end of a household "steel" (used for sharpening knives) is very suitable. Wrap metal foil (from a cigarette carton) tightly round the former, pressing it closely over the pointed end. Next, fill an egg-cup or fish-paste jar with flour, pressed down, and thrust the foil-covered former (pointed end first) into the flour to a depth of about 5 cm. On withdrawing the former the foil sheath will be left in the flour as a mould. Three or four such moulds may be prepared in one egg-cup.

Make a long-handled metal spoon by inserting the little handle of a metal measure such as is found in some baby-food tins into a slit cut in one end of a 10-cm length of cane. If the measure is without a pouring lip, then one should be contrived; otherwise pouring will prove difficult.

Powder some alum and fill it into the spoon. Heat it over an open flame. It melts in its own water of crystallization with some harmless spurting. Heat the lip of the spoon and pour the molten material quickly into the moulds—overflow does not matter. When the sticks are cool, extract them and remove the rough upper ends with a small saw. Strip away the foil

THE CIRCULATION OF THE BLOOD 129

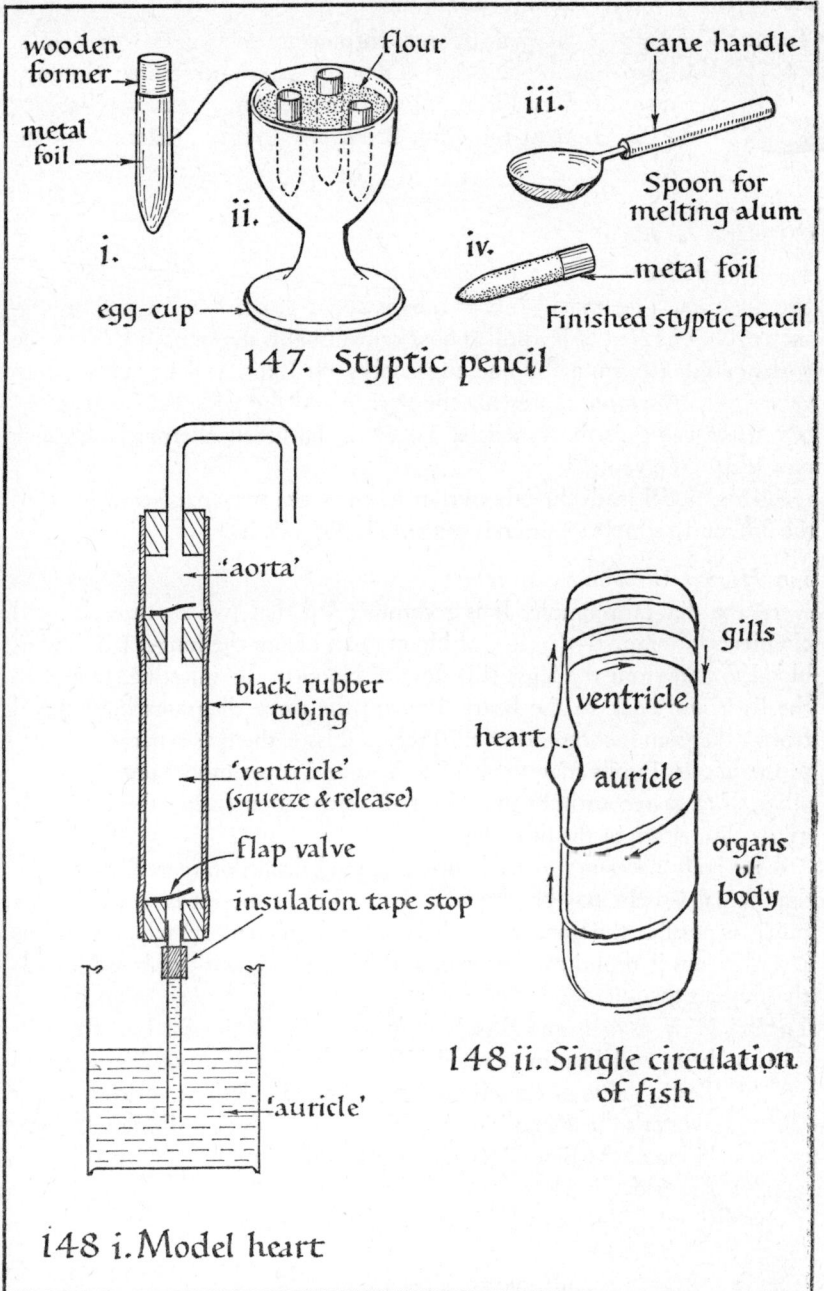

147. Styptic pencil

148 i. Model heart

148 ii. Single circulation of fish

and polish the pencils of alum with a damp cloth or with a scrap of fine emery paper. Wrap the blunt ends in metal foil.

Topics: Carriage of oxygen by red corpuscles; anaemia; iron tonics. White corpuscles; abscesses and pus. Plasma and serum: clotting; blood transfusion. Film, "Blood Transfusion" (Central Film Library, Government Building, Bromyard Avenue, Acton, London, W.3).

Circulation of Blood

148 *Model Heart*

See diagram. The (black) rubber tube is about 12 cm long $\times$ 1½ cm diameter. Put one coat of Evostik rubber cement on to the smooth faces of the corks before attaching (by one edge only: cf. Expt. 11) the rubber flap-valves. The reservoir represents the auricle and the wide rubber tube between the valves is the ventricle. To work the heart, alternately squeeze and release the ventricle.

Such a model leads directly to a mention of the two-chambered heart of the fish, and a simple diagram is suggested (Fig. 148, ii).

149. *Human Circulatory System*

Keep the diagram simple. It is recommended that two or three limited circuits be attempted—(i) flow of blood to and from the lungs; (ii) flow of blood to and from the legs; (iii) flow of blood to the intestine, thence to the liver and back to the heart. Prepare the three diagrams beforehand from a diagram incorporating all three, and issue them as separate systems to the pupils. Pupils may then trace them and superimpose one upon another so as to reconstitute the "figure-8" circulation (using the lung diagram with either of the other two).

It is vitally necessary to study a real animal dissection (e.g. Expt. 74) so that actual vessels may be observed. If the gut of the rat is spread out as much as possible the transparent sheet of tissue (mesentery) which supports it and wraps it round can be seen, and in it the network of blood vessels that invests the gut.

Topics: How oxygen and dissolved foods reach all tissues. Lymph. Diabetes and insulin (treated historically—the story of Banting and Best). Value of exercise in promoting circulation; varicose veins; aviator's "blackout"; first-aid in cases of fainting. Films: "Circulation of the Blood" (672/D1); "Blood" (672/A2); "Circulation of the Blood" (loop 672/K5). Excretion of the waste products via lungs, kidneys, and skin (see also Expt. 191).

Chemical Reactions and Energy: True Respiration

Refer to the work on cells (Chapter 4), to Expt. 144, and to the experiments

THE CIRCULATION OF THE BLOOD 131

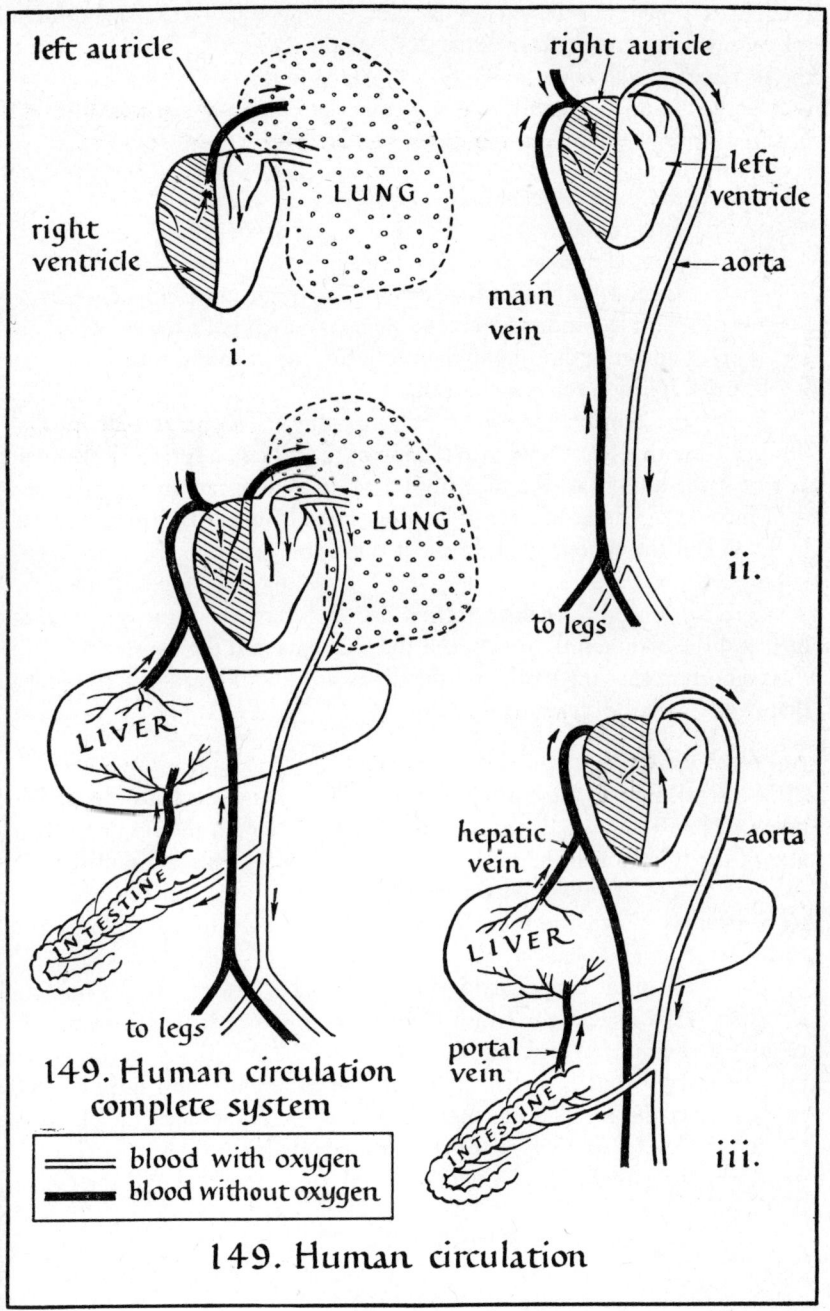

149. Human circulation

on respiration. Develop the idea of food as a fuel. Observe that when fuel burns in petrol or diesel engines, part of the product is useful mechanical energy, and only the remainder appears chiefly as heat. Hence promote the expectation that when food and oxygen combine in the body cells heat will be one product, keeping us warm, but that energy will also be released in other forms—to drive our movements and our body processes.

150 *Chemical Union between Iron and Sulphur*
Wash iron filings repeatedly with methylated spirit (before the lesson) until the washing liquid is almost clear; this treatment removes grease.

Two-thirds fill a test-tube with powdered sulphur (an element) and top the tube up with iron filings (another element); then pour the material out on to paper and mix thoroughly before returning it to the tube. For class work, small ignition tubes serve well.

Observe the appearance of the mixture—the constituents may be distinguished with a lens. Now grip the top of the tube in a spring clothes-peg and heat the bottom of the tube until a red glow appears in the mixture; then remove the flame at once. The glow spreads upwards throughout the mass. When the tube is cold, break it open and examine the new "compound".

There is no need to make a formal list of differences between the mixture and the compound, or between the elements and the compound. But it is important that the work and the discussion should lead to a clear idea that fundamental differences do exist.

151 *Decomposition*
Blow a small hole in the bottom of a soft-glass test-tube; pupils can undertake this job. Use a small roaring Bunsen flame, soften the tip of the bottom of the tube, touch the softened part with a glass rod, and pull sharply to form a "pip" of glass on the tube. Reheat this area quickly and then blow strongly down the tube; the glass blows out into a bubble, bursts and leaves a small hole.

Put a little black copper oxide inside the tube, near the hole, holding the tube horizontal in the hand. Connect one end of a length of rubber tubing to the gas tap and slip the other into the mouth of the tube (the tube should be chosen to fit). Turn on the gas gently and light it as it escapes from the small hole; then turn down the gas until the flame is about 2 cm long. Now warm the copper oxide with the tip of a small Bunsen flame and observe the formation of red copper powder and the escape of steam from the hole.

Allow the tube to cool while gas is still flowing (why?)

152 *Oxidation*
Connect the (cold) tube containing copper powder (Expt. 151) to the oxygen

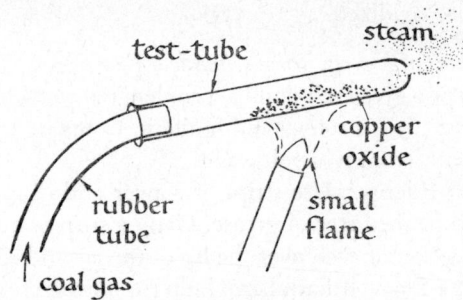

151. Decomposition of copper oxide

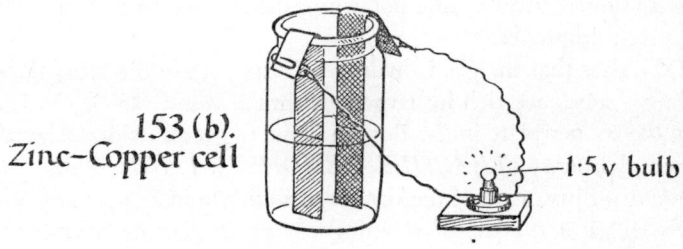

153 (b). Zinc-Copper cell

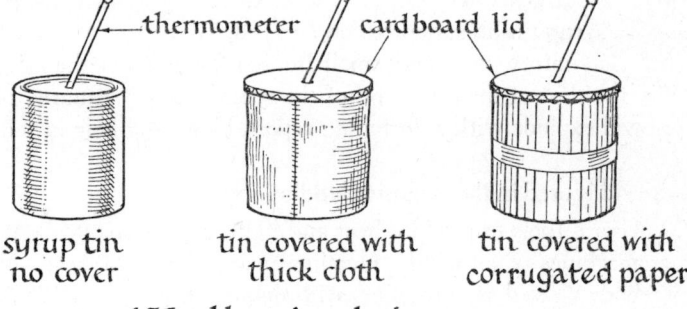

155 Heat insulation

apparatus (Expt. 38) instead of to the gas tap. Pass a brisk current of oxygen and heat the copper gently. The glow of chemical reaction is seen as the copper is "oxidized".

153 *Other Forms of Energy from Chemical Reaction*
(a) Light Energy: give each pupil a 3-cm length of magnesium ribbon. Let him hold it in a clip (or tongs) and ignite it. Compare the new compound with the elements from which it came.

(b) Electrical Energy: Use strips of copper and of zinc, each about 15 cm × 2 cm and washed free of grease. Hang a strip of each metal in a jam jar, bending the top of each over the lip of the jar and connecting the projecting lugs to a $1\frac{1}{2}$-volt flash-lamp bulb (in a holder); the connections to the lugs may be made with wire paper-clips.

Lift one strip out of the jar and then three-parts fill the jar with dilute ($\frac{1}{2}$ per cent) sulphuric acid. Replace the strip: the bulb glows for a short time, bubbles of gas appear on the copper plate, and the light fades. Stir the acid to brush the bubbles from the plate—the lamp glows whilst stirring is continued. Add a little potassium dichromate to the liquid in the jar: the light improves.

Tell the class that the gas is hydrogen (Expt. 45), and discuss the effect of adding a substance rich in oxygen. A similar result can be obtained by heating the copper plate in the Bunsen flame to get an oxidized layer.

(c) Sound Energy (*TEACHER DEMONSTRATION ONLY*): The experiment is illustrative of the danger of indiscriminate play with chemicals as well as of the use of chemical energy in blasting operations and in explosives generally.

Mix together, by shaking in a dry ignition tube (5 cm × 1 cm) dry picric acid powder and red lead, using not more than a centimetre depth of each. DO NOT RUB OR GRIND. Tip the mixture into a small heap in the middle of a syrup-tin lid supported on a tripod. With the class at the other end of the laboratory put a very small Bunsen flame under the lid, and at once join the class at the other end of the room. After a minute or so the mixture will explode with a deafening report, blowing a hole in the metal lid.

Picric acid is used in the explosive lyddite.

Topics: Use of fuels to produce heat and light, and mechanical energy in machines of all kinds. Heating-up of a compost heap. Human body viewed as a machine, with discussion of the various ways in which we use up energy. Fat storage; adipose tissue.

Warm- and Cold-blooded Animals
Man checks undue loss of heat by wearing clothing; other warm-blooded creatures have wool, fur or feathers. Make lists to show: (i) the kinds of

THE CIRCULATION OF THE BLOOD

material used by man for clothing; (ii) the nature of the covering on various mammals and birds.

154 Clinical Thermometer

Let one of each pair of pupils take his partner's temperature, using a clinical thermometer (i) under the tongue, (ii) under the arm-pit. Observe the proper precautions in resetting and sterilizing the instrument after use; why must hot water *not* be used?

Consider the collected results carefully and work out the class average (readings should be taken to one-fifth of a degree). Suggest also that a pupil should take his own temperature at hourly intervals throughout a day at home, reporting his findings back to the class.

In school, let pupils try using an ordinary thermometer in place of the clinical instrument—and so find out the advantage of the latter.

Discuss the temperature of the body in health and in sickness.

155 Heat Insulation

Use three approximately 2-litre cans—one bare, one wrapped in thick cloth, and the third wrapped in corrugated paper (Fig. 155). Cover each can with a cardboard lid having a hole through which a thermometer may be passed. Three pairs of pupils may work on the apparatus at once, each pair taking one of the three cans.

Pour boiling water into the cans until they are practically filled (each may stand on a cardboard mat), insert a thermometer into each, and start timing at once. Take temperature readings every 5 minutes, writing down the figures as they are obtained. Later, the results from the three pairs of pupils are brought together on one sheet of graph paper.

Minutes:	Start	5	10	15	20	25	30	35	Temp fall
Temperature:									
Bare									
Cloth									
Paper									

Topics: The use of blankets, gloves, the tea-cosy, oven-cloth, wood or plastic handles to tea-pots, etc. Keeping the car engine warm in cold weather; lagging the hot-water tank. The vacuum flask.

156 To Show that Chemical Reactions are Checked by Cold

(a) Pour vinegar (or other dilute acid) on to large soda crystals or marble chips; gas bubbles escape. Repeat using hot vinegar; the bubbling is very vigorous.

(b) About one-quarter fill each of two test-tubes with 20-volume hydrogen peroxide. Drop a strip of litmus paper into each tube and add enough

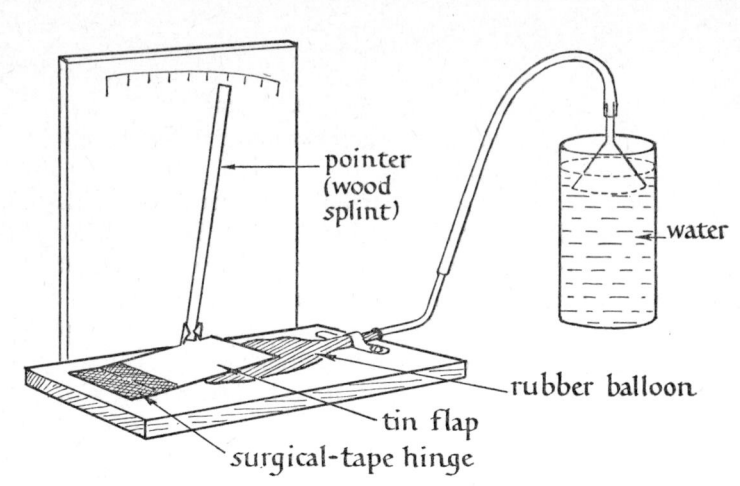

158 (a) i. Pressure in liquid increases with depth

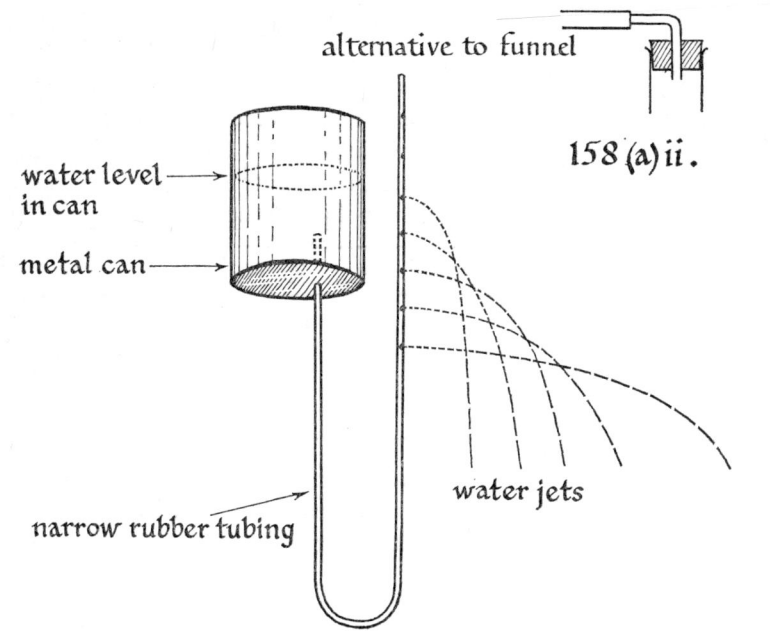

158 (b). Pressure and depth of water

caustic soda solution to turn the litmus blue. Stand one tube in fairly hot water; note the vigorous escape of gas (oxygen) and the bleaching of the litmus. Compare with the other tube.

Topics: Cold-blooded creatures and the need for hibernation (examples from the classroom vivaria—see Expt. 61).

Effects of Pressure upon the Body

157 *Diving-bell Principle*

Attach a length of rubber tubing to the stem of a small glass funnel or thistle funnel. Lower the funnel, mouth downwards and horizontal, into a jar of water; notice that the water level is the same inside and outside the funnel. Now squeeze the rubber tube to close it and repeat the experiment of lowering the funnel into the water; again observe the water levels. Finally, blow down the rubber tube while the funnel is being held under water; notice the greater pressure required to keep the funnel filled with air the lower it is in the water.

158 *Increasing Pressure Below the Surface of Water*

(a) Connect one end of a rubber tube to a small funnel (Expt. 157) and the other to a balloon held under a sheet-metal "flap" (see diagram), the movements of which are shown by a wood-splint pointer (held by a corner of the metal cut and bent round the splint); the neck of the balloon is anchored under a strip of metal pinned down to the baseboard.

Lower the funnel under water and observe the movements of the pointer. An alternative arrangement (shown in Figure 158 (a) ii) may be used instead of the funnel and gives rather steadier results.

(b) Push one end of a 50-cm length of fairly narrow rubber tubing up through a small hole drilled in the bottom of a tall tin can (see Chapter 2 on boring holes). The tube must fit the hole tightly. Using a red-hot knitting needle, bore holes 2 cm apart along 15 cm of the other end of the tubing. Hold the can and tube over a sink, almost fill the can with water, and bend the tube into a U-form (Fig. 158 (b)). Raise and lower the free end of the tube and discuss what is seen.

Topics: Diver, and diver's "Bends"; similar difficulty experienced by airmen. Refer to Expt. 43 (effect of pressure on solubility of a gas).

Chapter Nine
Fuel, Diet and Growth

The Pupil's Record of His Work in Science

A criticism often levelled against General Science (as opposed to the separate sciences) is that it largely excludes quantitative work—the implication being that science is sacrificed to generalities. A more penetrating analysis might suggest that by whatever method or at whatever stage Science is taught, it should lead to definite conclusions based upon carefully formulated evidence. Content may vary, but the fundamental aims of Science teaching remain. The pupil may do a great deal of practical work, qualitative and quantitative, but unless he is brought to the stage where he must think over and think out for himself what he has done and what it means, it is doubtful whether he will gain anything of lasting value.

Whether or not this thinking is done is often determined by the method of summing-up and recording the lesson. For the average pupil the copying of notes from the blackboard or the writing out of an account from the textbook is unlikely to produce the desired result. Recourse to books for information is a necessary and useful exercise, but most boys and girls require personal experience as the basis for constructive thought; and that experience having been gained, good oral work is one of the finest ways of ensuring that its significance is thoroughly understood. Generally it is the teacher who will do the questioning, anticipating difficulties, correcting misunderstandings and guiding the line of thought. But he must insist that the pupils do their part, so that they are called upon to formulate conclusions in words before any attempt is made to record them on paper. Occasionally it may be understood that two or three members of the class will be expected to deliver a brief oral account of their work from the front of the classroom. At other times the class may be divided into teams, the members putting questions to one another, with the teacher as arbitrator. Training is needed for such work, but once the class has come to realize both its attractiveness and its inevitability it can be very rewarding.

The value of good oral work extends far beyond the confines of the Science lesson, but Science has a special contribution to make. "Real communication", says the Newsom Report, "begins when the words are about experience, ideas and interests which are worth putting into language." Our pride is justified if we find our pupils talking about their work in Science and we should give them both the vocabulary and the opportunity.

Any definition of literacy for the ordinary boy or girl must include some ability to understand the basis of reasonable argument and some facility in expressing in words a point of view. There is no gift like the gift of speech; and the level at which people use it often determines the level at which their lives are lived.

Because of the difficulty which some pupils find with the mechanics of writing (even in Secondary schools), teachers have sought ways of minimizing written work in Science lessons. The class may be asked to complete tabulated summaries (e.g. Vitamin–Source–Function), or to fill gaps in prepared sentences (e.g. Green leaves take in ...... from the air and convert it into ......, which is stored as a food reserve in the leaves). Outline drawings may be provided, in which detail or labelling is to be added; or the pupil may be asked to make his own labelled sketch in lieu of a written account. Experience suggests that the "cartoon" type of drawing, advocated in some quarters, may easily lead to untidy and inaccurate work. For the very weakest children pictures cut from newspapers and magazines may serve as reminders of important facts and principles.

It should nevertheless be remembered that the Science lesson provides some of the finest material for the practice of written expression. Here is first-hand experience—the soundest basis for English composition. It is extremely difficult to match the power of a good written statement as a record and reminder of the results of practical work. The record may be quite brief: following good discussion, one or two carefully thought-out sentences are often sufficient, especially if supported by pictorial work.

Attention has been drawn, in one of the Nuffield Biology Guides, to a paper by Jean Bremner (*School Science Review*, June, 1962) in which the value of drawing as an aid to learning in biology lessons is seriously questioned. Thirty years ago Phillips & Cox wrote: "No form of record-making is better than drawing." Bremner's work is based on investigations with able children (I.Q.s 108 and above) and few teachers would quarrel with the suggestions which we have made for including sketches, diagrams, and clean line drawings as legitimate and useful devices with average and less-able pupils. For some pupils throughout the ability spectrum drawing is deeply satisfying.

Oversight and regular correction of note-books is most important. If written work goes unmarked we may expect its standard to deteriorate. It is accordingly essential that the record should be in a form that can be marked with reasonable ease. Undoubtedly the finest way to achieve this position is (a) to see that the work is thoroughly understood before it is reported, and (b) to encourage and applaud good writing and a neat layout. All drawings should be done in pencil; all writing (except labelling) in ink.

The ability to read a graph is more important to the average citizen than the ability to construct one, but both techniques are valuable in science and this particular method of expression is illustrated in the work of the present chapter.

The Composition of Common Foods

Reference should be made to the *Manual of Nutrition* (H.M.S.O.)—an invaluable source of information about foodstuffs and diet. Various reports of the National Milk Publicity Council (e.g. *The Teaching of Science and Household Subjects*) contain useful teaching material on nutrition and allied topics.

Tests to establish the presence of carbohydrates, fats, proteins and mineral salts in common food materials have already been described (Chapter 6).

159 *Percentage of Water in Food Materials*

Bread, potato, apple, cabbage, grass, wheat grain, etc. are suitable. Potato and apple are best sliced thinly; cabbage and grass should be chopped finely. Use a tin lid as a crucible. Weigh (see Expt. 160) enough prepared food material to fill the lid and transfer it to the lid (which is not weighed) by means of a brush. Heat the lid on a sand-bath (shallow layer of sand in larger lid) or in an oven (cf. Expt. 101); in either case only a very small flame should be used so that the food is not charred. After an hour allow the lid to cool, brush off the residue into the balance-pan and reweigh.

The loss in weight is due to evaporated water. Hence calculate the percentage of water in the original material.

160 *Simple Lever Balance (see also Expt. 214)*

The constructional details are shown in the diagram.

161 (a) *Test for Iron*

Dissolve about ½-cm length of thin iron wire, or an iron filing, in warm hydrochloric acid. Dilute with water and add a few drops of potassium ferrocyanide solution; a deep blue colour develops.

(The potassium ferrocyanide reagent may be prepared by dissolving about ½ g of the solid in 100 cm³ of water.)

161 (b) *Iron Compounds in Cereal Foods*

Burn a few shreds or flakes of a breakfast cereal on an inverted porcelain crucible lid, and continue heating strongly for a few minutes until part at least of the material has fallen to ash. Cool, tap the residue on to a sheet of paper, and powder it (e.g. by pressing with a knife blade). Put the powder into a small test-tube, warm with a drop or two of fairly strong hydrochloric acid, and dilute with a little water. Either filter or allow the charcoal particles to settle and then decant. To the clear solution add a few drops of ½ per cent potassium ferrocyanide solution.

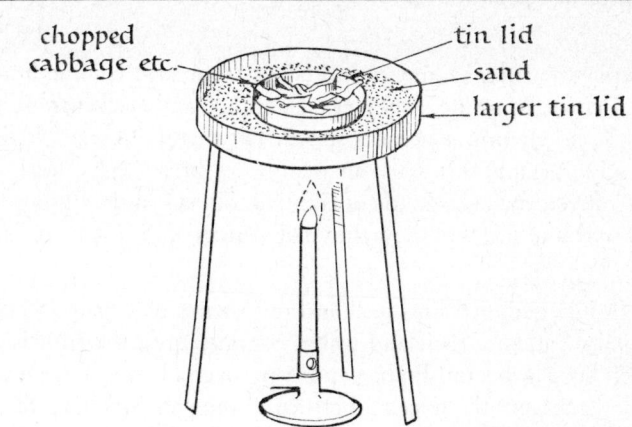

159. Percentage of water on sand-bath

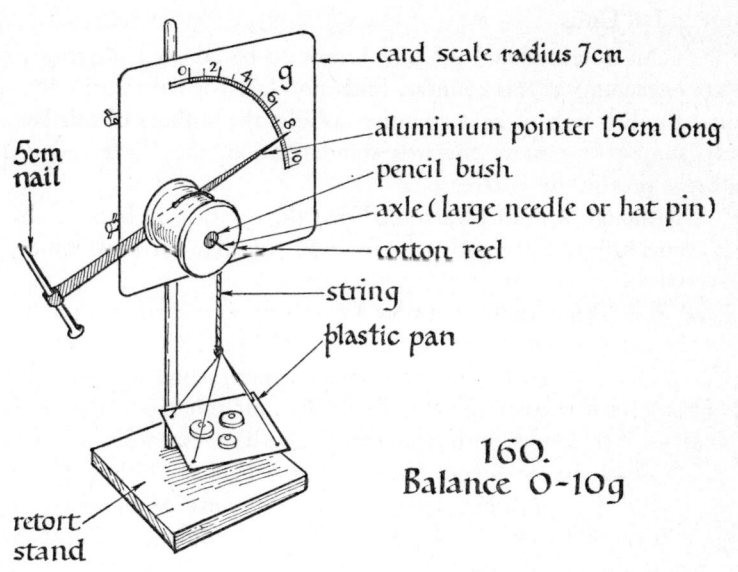

160. Balance 0-10g

The formation of a blue colour or precipitate in this test is an indication of the presence of an iron salt.

162 *Vitamins*
Ask pupils to collect wrappers and labels from such commodities as margarine, Bemax, Marmite, fish-liver oils, orange and blackcurrant juices, etc. on which the vitamin content is stated. Let them see a sample of pure ascorbic acid (Vitamin C). Cut out pictures of bread, eggs, fish, a bottle of milk, fruit, vegetables, a bottle of cod-liver oil, etc. and let groups of pupils paste them on to sheets to show the chief sources of the main vitamins.

163 *Rose-hip Syrup*
Wash freshly gathered hips well and put them into a pan with water, using equal weights of fruit and water. Simmer until the fruit is quite soft and then pour into a muslin bag and hang over a basin to strain overnight. Next day, measure the juice and return to the pan with 1 kg of sugar and the strained juice of 2 lemons to each litre of hip juice. Boil until the liquid will set when cooled.

Topics: Story of scurvy and of beri-beri. Reference to the history of the discovery and synthesis of the vitamins. "Protective" foods.

Heat and SI Units
SI (Système International d'Unités), now to be adopted progressively in Science teaching in this country, finds no place for the calorie, the traditional English unit of heat quantity. Whilst the authors of this book entirely support the move towards standarization, they have retained the calorie at present, for two reasons:

i. Although it must be assumed that the calorie will become obsolete, it seems safe to assume that its use will continue for some time yet in everyday life.

ii. The authors claim that they have themselves carried out and tested all the experiments described in their book. But they have not yet been able to devise to their satisfaction an experimental approach to heat quantity on the basis of the joule as the unit suitable to the needs and abilities of the pupils with whom they have been especially concerned. A recent article in the *School Science Review* ("Heat Without Calories"), by D. Shires; September, 1969) offers suggestions for an approach with O-level candidates which would certainly pose difficult problems for the teachers of the Ordinary Pupil.

See, however, Expts. 290 and 291.

Fuels and Foods
Open the topic by reference to the common fuels—coal, coke, gas, oil and petrol. All are plentiful, reasonably cheap, and give out heat in useful

amounts when burned. The heat may be converted into other forms of energy (as in the gas-engine, steam turbine, or motor-car), but their value as fuels is most readily assessed by measuring the amount of heat that a known weight of each produces when completely burnt.

164 *Heat Quantity*
Use two similar cans or beakers, and a quick-weighing balance. (a) Measure 500 g of water into one can and 1000 g into the other. Take the temperature of the water (Celsius) and give the cans equal quantities of heat, either by means of similar small Bunsen flames placed under them for equal times (e.g. 3 minutes) or by using a hand immersion heater. Note the final temperatures. (b) Repeat, but use 500 g of water in one can and 500 g of liquid paraffin in the other.

It becomes evident that in measuring heat we must take into account not only the rise in temperature but also the nature and weight of the substance which is being heated.

165 *Heat Units*
On the metric system only the Large Calorie need be used, since this is the unit which is always employed in connection with food value. Its relation to British units may be shown as follows (the definitions of the British Thermal Unit and the Therm should be given since both units continue in use at present).

Weigh out 1000 g of cold water into a large can. Into an exactly similar can weigh out 1 lb. of cold water. Put a Celsius thermometer into the first can and a Fahrenheit instrument into the second, and note the temperatures which they record.

Stand the cans on similar tripods and put similar Bunsen flames under them at the same instant. Stir each gently with the thermometer, and at the moment when the Celsius instrument shows a 10° rise remove the flames and note the rise on the Fahrenheit thermometer. Suppose this rise is T°F.

$$\text{Heat given to water in first can} = 10 \text{ Calories.}$$
$$\text{Heat given to water in second can} = T \text{ B.Th.U.}$$

But the amounts of heat were the same, since we used similar flames for the same length of time. Hence 1 Calorie $= T/10$ B.Th.U.

166 *Calorific Values*
Heat water in a tin box (lid on) over a small spirit stove. A syrup tin will serve, but greater efficiency is possible with a larger vessel such as a toffee tin about 20 cm diameter × 10 cm high. The stove is simply a metal lid or cap (perhaps 3 cm diameter × 1 cm deep) packed with cotton-wool. 5 cm³ of methylated spirit is run on to the wool from a pipette or burette immediately before the stove is lit.

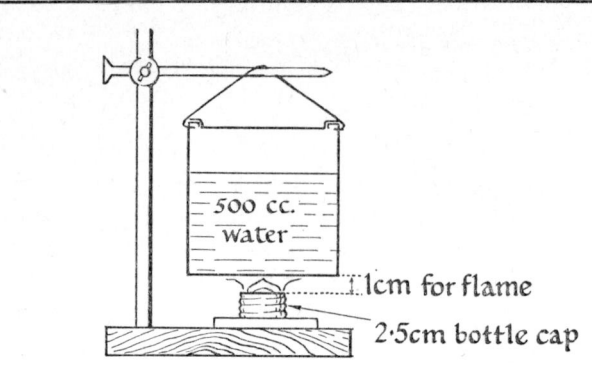

Syrup tin calorimeter 166.

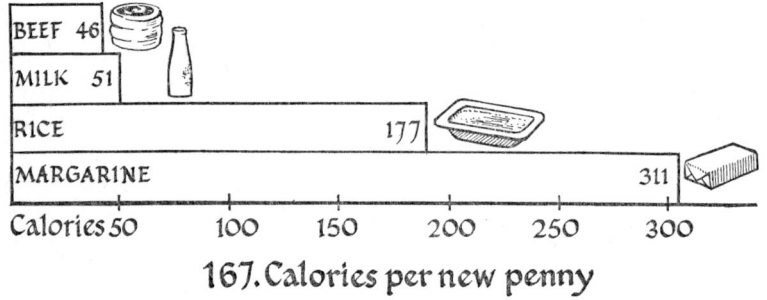

167. Calories per new penny

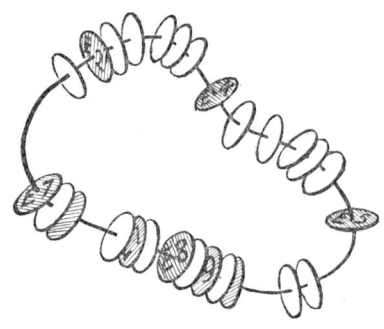

168. Protein structure

Take the temperature of the water, put the lid on the tin, and ignite the spirit. Take the water temperature again when the flame dies out. The following is a set of typical results from an experiment using a syrup tin:

Volume of spirit (alcohol)	$= 5 \text{ cm}^3 \ (= 4 \text{ g})$
Weight of water	$= 500 \text{ g}$
Starting temperature of water	$= 18°$ C.
Final temperature of water	$= 54°$ C.
Rise in temperature of water	$= 36°$ C.
Whence, heat taken in by water	$\dfrac{500 \times 36}{1000}$ Calories
	$= 18$ Calories
Thus 1 g of alcohol would have produced $\dfrac{18}{4}$ Calories	$= 4\frac{1}{2}$ Calories

In simple apparatus such as that used here a considerable proportion of the heat given out by the burning spirit is lost to the surroundings. When burnt in more elaborate apparatus, so that no such heat losses occur, it is found that 1 g of alcohol produces 8 Calories. Such an apparatus is called a fuel calorimeter, and we speak of the Calorific Value of alcohol as 8 Calories per g.

The efficiency of our experiment may be stated thus:

$$\text{Efficiency} = \frac{\text{Heat given to water}}{\text{Total heat supplied}} \times 100 = \frac{4\frac{1}{2}}{8} \times 100 = 56 \text{ per cent}$$

With a 20-cm diameter tin and a draught shield, an efficiency of perhaps 70 per cent may be obtained.

Instead of using cotton-wool and spirit, 4 g of meta-fuel can be substi-

Topics: Calorific value of foodstuffs. Although we often speak of food as "the fuel of the body" it is important to emphasize that food is not "burned" in the sense that a fire burns; it is oxidized, as coal or oil is oxidized, but there are complex intermediate stages, and only a small part of the energy liberated appears as heat. Indeed, any heat produced in excess of what is required to maintain the body temperature is wasted. The energy derived from the oxidation of food (respiration) is that required for standing, walking, chopping wood, eating digesting, breathing, and for all other activities of the living body. However, it is convenient to express all this energy, whether in the form of heat or not, in heat units. thus:

1 g of carbohydrate produces 4 Calories
1 ,, of fat ,, 9 ,,
1 ,, of protein ,, 4 ,,

167 Energy Value of Common Foods

Using the *Manual of Nutrition* or other reference books, let pupils prepare a simple table showing the number of grammes of carbohydrate, fat and protein respectively in 100 g of various common foods, e.g.:

	Carbohydrate	Fat	Protein
100 g rice	79·3 g	1·1 g	6·4 g
100 g milk	4·6 g	3·6 g	3·2 g

Nearly all the weight unaccounted for in the table is water, but pupils should be reminded that the small amounts of mineral salts and vitamins found in most foods are very important.

Next, pupils should calculate the energy value, in Calories, of the foods they have included in their table, e.g.

$$\begin{aligned}
\text{Rice: Energy-value of Carbohydrate} &= 79\cdot3 \times 4 \text{ Cal.} = 317\cdot2 \text{ Cal.} \\
\text{fat} &= 1\cdot1 \times 9 \text{ Cal.} = 9\cdot9 \text{ Cal.} \\
\text{protein} &= 6\cdot4 \times 4 \text{ Cal.} = 25\cdot6 \text{ Cal.} \\
\text{Total energy value of 100 g of rice} & \phantom{= 1\cdot1 \times 9 \text{ Cal.}} = 352\cdot7 \text{ Cal.}
\end{aligned}$$

Finally, list the current prices of the foods included in the table and thence work out the "Calories per (new) pennyworth" for each food. Set out the results (i) in a table and (ii) in the form of a simple bar graph (see diagram).

Food	Cost per kg (in new pence)	Cals. per kg	Cals. per new penny
Rice	20p.	3527 Cal.	3527/20 = 177
Margarine	25p.	7782 Cal.	7782/25 = 311
Beef	70p.	3193 Cal.	3193/70 = 46
Milk	12p.	607 Cal.	607/12 = 51

Topics: The energy requirements of various people. Figures may be obtained from the *Manual of Nutrition*.

Approximate average daily needs are:

Adults: Man, 3000 Cal. Woman, 2500 Cal.

Young children require considerably less than this, but boys and girls over fourteen years of age often need more. An active worker such as a blacksmith may use up twice as much energy as a clerk.

The following points should be mentioned:

(i) If a diet is lacking in fat it will tend to become very bulky; fat is also necessary to render food palatable (e.g. in frying, buttering bread, making cakes). At least a quarter of the daily energy needs should be supplied as fats.

(ii) Part of each day's food must be in the form of protein, since although protein can be used to supply energy its primary use is for body building and repair—for which purpose nothing can replace it.

FUEL, DIET AND GROWTH

168 First- and Second-class Proteins

Attention must be paid to the kind of protein eaten. Proteins are built up from simpler units called amino-acids, of which there are many kinds. Proteins differ in the kinds and arrangement of the amino-acid units within them, and among the hundreds of amino-acid units in a single protein there may be twenty or more different kinds. The human organism can usually convert amino-acid units which it does not need for its own structure into others which it does need, but there are ten amino-acids which it cannot make in this way and which must therefore be supplied in the proteins of the diet. Animal protein foods usually contain all these essential amino-acids in proportions more or less appropriate to human needs; but many vegetable proteins are lacking in one or several of the essential units. For this reason it is wise to include a proportion of meat protein in every diet, although a diet of mixed vegetables may serve the same end.

To illustrate protein structure use "bracelets" (Fig. 168) made from small cardboard discs threaded on to thin string. Each bracelet has many discs, each disc representing an amino-acid unit, but amongst them are certain coloured ones, marked E_1, E_2, ... E_{10}, representing "essential" amino-acid units. Each bracelet stands for a food protein; thus different bracelets are labelled "beef protein", "egg protein", "cabbage protein", etc. Ensure that each animal protein bracelet includes at least one of each of the ten essential units, and that the vegetable protein bracelets are deficient in one or more of these essential units. Let pupils select a protein food and then examine the corresponding bracelet to see whether this food alone would meet the protein requirements of the body.

169 Adequacy of a Daily Diet (graphical method)

Discuss the essentials of a daily diet and prepare a simple basic list of foods for one person for one day. Such a list might be:

Bread,	420 g	Beef,	110 g	Butter, etc.	35 g
Bacon,	15 g	Cheese,	10 g	Sugar, etc.	50 g
Milk,	560 g	Potato,	170 g		

Here "beef" represents all meat (except bacon); peas, beans, etc. are included with "bread" and "potato"; water and waste are not shown. Green vegetables have little calorific value and are omitted. Their importance in the diet, for their mineral salt and vitamin content, must be emphasized.

Divide the class into groups of eight pupils, and proceed with each group as follows. Let each member take one of the eight items in the above diet, so that the whole list is covered by the group. Using a table showing the composition of common foods, let each pupil work out the

	Protein g	Fat g	Carbo-hydrate g	Calcium mg	Iron mg	Vitamins A	B	C	D	Calories	% waste
Milk	3	4	5	120	–	✓	✓	✓	✓	64	–
Beef	15	28	–	10	4	✓	✓	–	–	220	17
Cheese	25	35	–	820	1	✓	✓	–	✓	420	5
Bacon	11	46	–	10	1	–	✓	–	–	460	12
Butter	0·4	84	–	14	–	✓✓	–	–	✓	750	–
Sugar	–	–	100	–	–	–	–	–	–	385	–
Potato	2	–	17	7	1	–	✓	✓	–	75	15
Bread (wholemeal)	9	2	50	18	2	–	✓	–	–	250	–
Cabbage	1·5	–	5	64	1	✓	✓	✓	–	25	30
Herring	16	12	–	100	1·5	✓	✓	–	✓✓	170	30

169(i). Composition of common foods
Values per 100g of edible parts

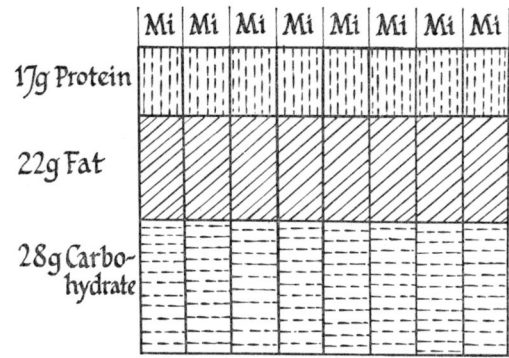

A block graph like this, made by one pupil, is then cut into 8 strips and distributed among other members of the group

169(ii). Constituents of part of daily diet
(560g Milk)

FUEL, DIET AND GROWTH

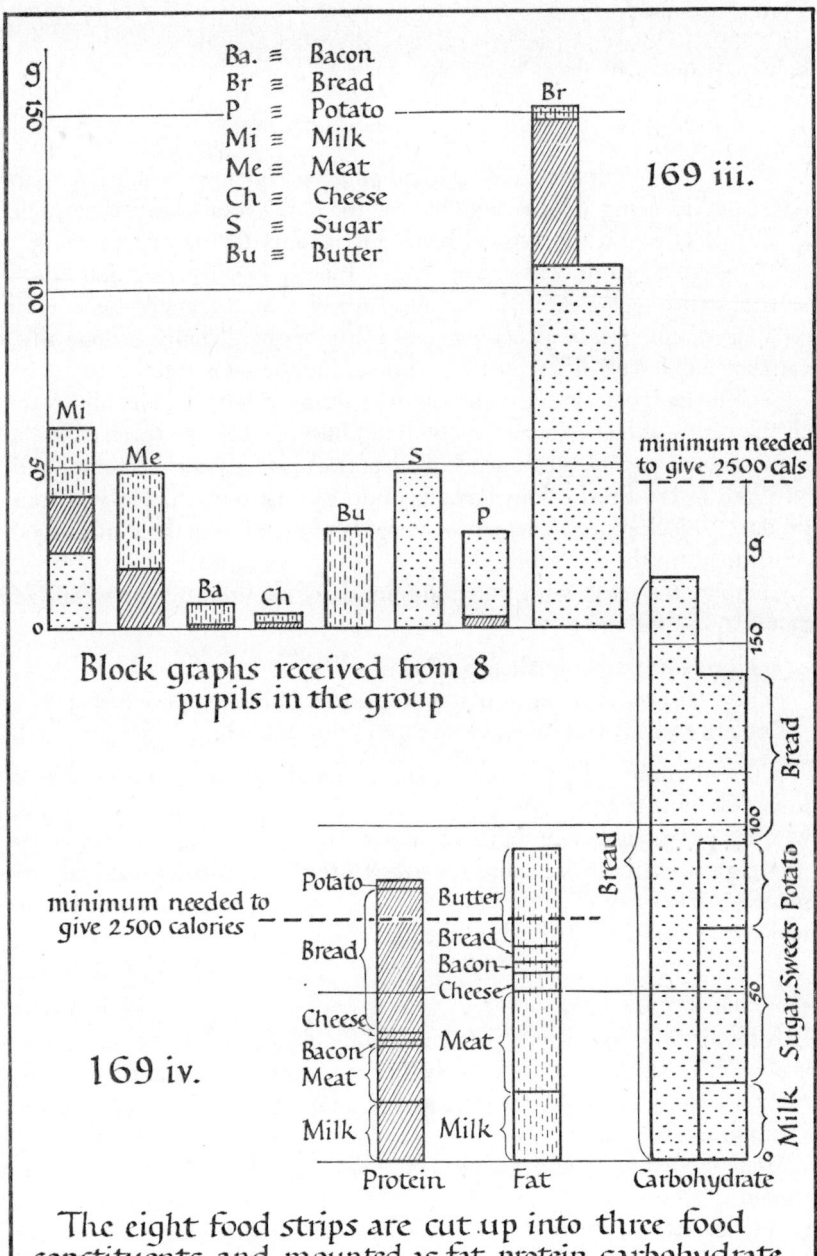

weight of carbohydrate, fat and protein (separately) in his food item. Thus, for bread:

>420 g bread contains 230 g carbohydrate
>3 g fat
>34 g protein

The pupil now draws a block graph on squared paper, making it 8 cm wide and marking off the amounts of the three food constituents, one above the other on the vertical scale. He colours the areas representing the different foods in contrasting shades. Finally he cuts his graph into 8 vertical strips, each 1 cm wide and all identical, and distributes one to each member of his group. When each member of the group has done this, each boy will have 8 different strips representing the 8 items in the diet.

Now let each boy cut his strips up into its three colours and let him paste all the pieces of one colour (carbohydrate) into one column (preferably on 1-cm squared paper), all those of another (fat) into a second column, and all those of the third colour (protein) into a third column. He will thus produce a block graph showing the weights of each of the three main food constituents in the day's diet.

Compare the result with the minimum daily requirement for a child of Secondary school age:

70 g protein (30 g animal, 40 g other);
70 g fat (equivalent to one-quarter of the daily Calorie requirement);
Enough carbohydrate to make up 2500 or more Calories.

These minimum figures can be shown on the block graph by dotted lines. The diet suggested will be found to contain excess fat and protein, whilst the carbohydrate is deficient. However, excess fat replaces $2\frac{1}{4}$ times its weight of carbohydrate and the excess protein will make good any remaining deficiency. The graph clearly indicates the importance of bread, which may truly be described as "the staff of life".

170 Balanced Meals

Let pupils write down typical menus for the meals they get at home and at school. Examine them to see whether they contain, in addition to fats, proteins, and carbohydrates, sufficient amounts of calcium, iron and the vitamins.

Make models of fruit, eggs, slices of bread, rashers of bacon, pork chops, shredded wheat, etc. from a dough of flour (2 parts), salt (1 part) and water, afterwards baked in the oven and coloured. Using such models (which will keep indefinitely), arrange specimen dishes and consider the adequacy of each as a meal. Attach a neat "flag" to each item, showing the calorific value, the content of mineral salts and the vitamins present.

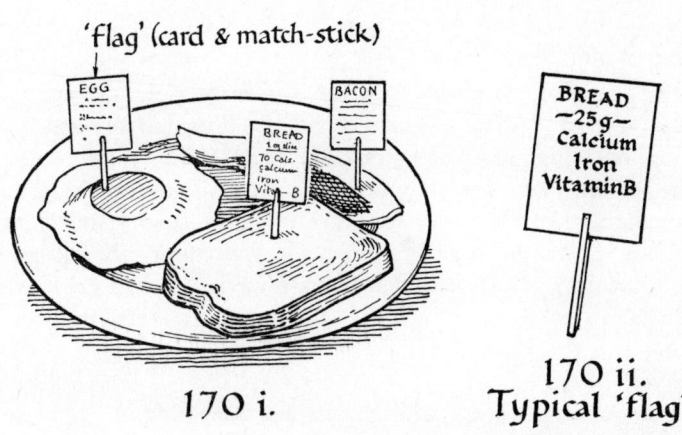

170 i.

170 ii. Typical 'flag'

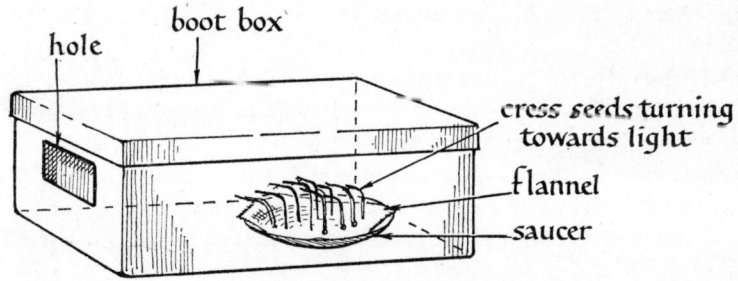

172 (a). Shoots grow towards light

Topics: Value of mineral salts in the diet (calcium and rickets; iron and anaemia); refer to Expts. 77 and 161. Effects of cooking: (i) improved digestibility, (ii) greater attractiveness, (iii) effect on vitamins. Importance of dainty serving. Milk, "the perfect food"; need to supplement baby's diet with orange-juice, cod-liver oil and green vegetables.

Growth in Animals and Plants

Charts may be obtained which show the increase in weight of the average baby from birth to perhaps eighteen months, and its development in other ways (e.g. crawling, first teeth, walking, etc.). A class might "adopt" a baby in the family of one of the pupils, keeping a class-room record of its development and comparing it with the average record. If mice, guinea-pigs, hamsters, etc. are born in school, the opportunity should be taken to weigh one or more daily (after about 2 weeks) and to graph weight against age.

171 Growth in size

Stick insects often grow at a remarkable rate, increasing in length at each moult. Measurement of various parts of the body and of the appendages may be made during the period when the nymph is developing into the full-grown insect.

For details of how to rear stick insects see the authors' *Practical Science for Secondary Schools*, Book Three, pp. 21–2.

172 Factors Affecting Plant Growth

(a) Refer to Expt. 82 for the effect of gravity on the growth of roots. The fact that garden flowers often turn to the light is well known; thus if a sunflower is observed through a sunny day it can be seen that the flower-head turns so that it always faces the sun. Sow cress seeds in a saucer on damp flannel, allow them to germinate in the dark, and then stand the saucer in one end of a covered shoe-box from which the other end has been cut away. The shoots grow toward the light. Turn the saucer round and observe again after a few days. (b) Set up two "germination sandwiches" (Expt. 82) containing mustard seeds. Keep one in the dark and one in the light and observe the appearance of the leaves as they develop. Alternatively, allow potatoes to sprout during spring, some in the light and some in the dark; contrast the appearance of the shoots. Refer to the "earthing-up" of celery. (c) It has already been shown that growing plants extract carbon dioxide from the air (Expt. 106) and absorb water from the soil (Expt. 85). Chemical analysis of the ash of plants indicates that various elements besides carbon, oxygen and hydrogen are present, and experiment shows that a number of elements are essential for healthy plant growth. Some are present in the plant as mineral salts and others are constituents of proteins. All are absorbed as mineral salts from the soil.

Make up a simple culture solution, using pure chemicals, as follows:
1 g potassium nitrate.
1 g calcium phosphate.
1 litre water.
1 iron nail (optional).

Sow grass or wheat seed on top of cotton-wool in cardboard ice-cream "tubs". Keep the seed in three cartons moist with pure water, but use the culture solution in three other cartons. The difference in the growth of the leaves is very striking.

The experiment may be repeated using a culture solution made up of about a teaspoonful of Growmore in 1 quart of water.

The composition of a commercial mixed fertilizer may be discussed and the influence of the various elements upon the development of root, leaf and flower indicated.

Topics: Storage of reserve food in adipose tissue (man) and in leaves, stems, roots and seeds. Refer to Chapter 25 for a study of this subject. Grow bulbs in the classroom.

The significance of youth, maturity and old age.

Chapter Ten

The Preservation of Food and the Prevention of Disease

Health Education

The education of the average citizen, so far at least as Science is concerned, is not to be measured by reproducible learning, nor yet by mastery of scientific skills—important as both of these may be. It is the degree to which he can be said to have made contact with his environment which determines a man's capacity for adjustment within the complexities of modern life. The effective working of society depends increasingly upon the intelligent and willing co-operation of men and women in many matters essentially scientific, and sporadic propagandist efforts by this Ministry or that are never likely to produce the results which could flow from an informed public opinion.

The ordinary citizen does not often require detailed knowledge of science. What he does need is a background of sound teaching about principles and opportunities for informed discussion such as will guide his thinking and his actions and save him from the bias of ignorance and inertia. This is particularly true in relation to health. Men and women should obviously have some understanding of the structure and functions of the bodily organs, but it is at least as important that they should appreciate the significance of living and working conditions. One can think also of many ways in which social services are dependent upon the co-operation of individuals. Clinics and welfare services need to be used; a clean water supply is of little advantage if crockery is contaminated; facilities for immunization rely heavily upon the attitude of parents; hygienic conditions for the preparation and preservation of food are of no avail if the food is subsequently displayed for sale on exposed shelves or kept unguarded against dirt and flies at home. When we consider the immense amount of working time lost through coughs and colds, it seems that even an elementary introduction to the principles and practice of hygiene might make a very considerable difference to the national economy.

Who is to teach these things? The Newsom Report says of health education:

"Its biological foundations belong to science, its practice and its proof lies to a great extent in the hands of the physical education department; its moral implications to the humanities; its reference to home surroundings—a difficult point where smoking is concerned—belong to the head in his dealings with parents; and its setting in a school that is clean and whose equipment makes cleanliness easy belongs to the head in his relations with the governors and his administrative staff..."

The Report refers also to the role of the school doctor and school nurse. "What is everybody's business can easily be nobody's business"; this is as true of health education as it is of English teaching. The Science master can scarcely be satisfied (and he is unlikely to be convincing) unless he is prepared to consider with his pupils the practical implications of their studies. He cannot preach cleanliness and neglect it in school; he cannot duck questions on smoking or sex; his lessons on food and on fertilizers must sometimes lead him to open up the topics of population, failures of distribution and the have-not peoples of the world. He has an essential contribution to make in trying to ensure that the taxpayer of tomorrow sees in biological research, for example, a direct contribution to practical problems.

An insight into the part which biology might play in health education is provided by Chapter 3 of Ministry of Education Pamphlet No. 31 (*Health Education*).

The study of bacteria, moulds and fungi presents difficulty for the ordinary pupil, unacquainted with the techniques of high-power microscopy, but it has sometimes been forgotten that what the ordinary pupil needs is not a proof but an experience. The effects of bacterial action are more significant to him than the bacteria themselves; methods of fighting bacteria or of profiting from their activities mean more than an agar plate. Realizing this, some schools have arranged that small groups of pupils should spend half a day in the local hospital, in the premises of a dispensing chemist, or in the offices of the borough engineer. Alternatively, the medical officer of health and other officials have been invited to come to school for talks followed by questions and discussion. Visits have been made to health departments, canning factories and sewage works. Valuable and indeed necessary as such experience is, it is nevertheless fatal to imagine that "social biology" conducted through the medium of visits and topic studies alone is an effective alternative to practical work in the laboratory. The compelling interest for the ordinary pupil of doing something for himself is never more in evidence than when the experiments can be seen to have a direct application to life—and this is particularly the case with work on health and disease.

It is desirable therefore that laboratory work and contacts with the social services should be regarded as complementary, the one interpreting the other. Some flexibility of time-tabling is required. Particularly is it important that the most careful preparation should precede any visit. Pupils must be briefed on what to expect, what to look for, and what questions to ask. They may be given cyclostyled sheets on which to take notes or summarize their findings, but in any case the main points arising from the visit must be brought out in subsequent discussion and in the pupil's own reports. Both preparation and follow-up demand that boys and girls be instructed how to use reference books, charts and graphs, and how to seek information by means of personal letters.

The range of material for study in this field is very great and some selection will probably have to be made from the following list:

The history of our knowledge of micro-organisms and their effects, built around such names of Jenner, Pasteur, Robert Koch, Lister, Ross, Fleming, Florey and Chain (the three last-named were Nobel Prize-winners). The germ theory of disease.

How disease spreads: the role of the protozoa (including bacteria), fungi and viruses as related to plants and animals. Insect carriers (housefly, malarial mosquito). Importance of clean air, clean water, clean food.

How disease is controlled: disinfectants, antiseptics, asepsis (hospital practice): the body's defences and how man assists them by means of various methods of inoculation and the use of antibiotics such as penicillin.

Methods of preserving food: salting, smoking, drying, pickling, canning, refrigerating; treatment of milk.

Use of compost in the garden. Processes of decay: nitrogen cycle; sewage disposal.

Manufacture of wines, beer, vinegar, cheese, etc.

The Conditions under which Moulds and Bacteria Flourish

173 *The Growth of Moulds on Food*

The general conditions are that the food should be left exposed in a warm damp atmosphere. In order to encourage growth it is convenient to place the food on an inverted meat-paste jar standing in a saucer of water under an inverted jam jar. The experiment is conducted in a warm place (e.g. near a radiator), and will take a week or so.

(a) Use bread, moistened with water: Mucor will appear (along with other moulds) and can be recognized (lens) by its white threads bearing black knobs (spore cases) at their tips.

Mount a tiny scraping of Mucor in a drop of water on a microscope slide, cover with a cover-glass, and examine with the microscope or microprojector. Note the tubular threads of the mycelium and the spores around the burst spore cases.

PRESERVATION OF FOOD, PREVENTION OF DISEASE 157

(b) Allow moulds to grow on cheese, jam, an orange, etc. The blue-green growths probably belong to the family Penicillium.

(c) Boil a potato in its skin for 15 minutes, cut it in two, and expose the half-cooked material to the air until it is cold. Now set it up on a meat-paste jar under a jam jar as described above, keeping it in a warm place. Mucor is likely to develop.

174 The "Damping-off" of Seedlings

Sow cress seeds thickly on moist cotton-wool in a cardboard ice-cream tub and cover with a jam jar, so that the seeds germinate in a damp atmosphere. Observe the fungus (Pythium) which grows on the seedlings, causing the shoots to rot at ground level and fall over.

175 The Compost Heap

Wherever there is a garden there will be, each autumn, large quantities of waste cuttings and fallen leaves. If such material is burned the ash forms a useful source of mineral salts, but the organic matter which is so essential for the formation of humus is lost. It is much better to convert the waste into organic manure by composting.

Mix coarser material (bean haulms, leaves) with finer (grass cuttings) so that fast-decaying elements will hasten the decomposition of the tougher matter. Add a little horse-dung or a sprinkling of sulphate of ammonia. Small quantities of lime are also of value. Cover with a thin layer of soil and water thoroughly. Further layers of plant material, nitrogenous "accelerator" and soil may be added until the heap is ½–1 metre high.

The heap soon begins to heat up, showing that the bacteria of decay are actively feeding on the nitrogenous matter and converting the plant material to humus. A less advantageous decomposition (accompanied by an unpleasant smell) may occur if air is lacking; the heap should therefore be turned about once a month.

In spring the dark-brown compost will be ready for digging into the soil of the garden.

Topics: How to protect food from moulds. Cream cheese (Expt. 97).

The Growth of Bacteria and Fungi

176 Preparation of Nutrient Jellies

The usual test for bacteria is to allow them to multiply on a food jelly until they have formed colonies large enough to be seen with the naked eye. Vessels containing the jelly must be carefully sterilized and kept sterile.

Sterilize small glass jars or test-tubes by putting them into a pan of cold

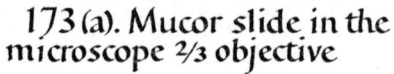
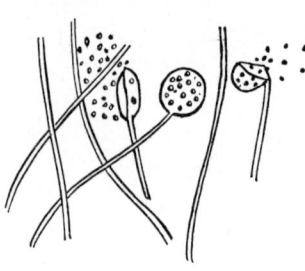

173 (a). Mucor slide in the microscope ⅔ objective

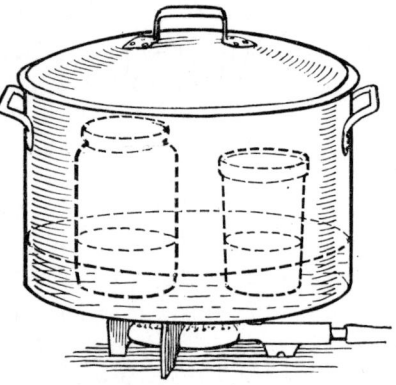

176. Sterilising vessels in boiling water

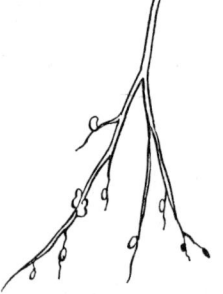

179. Root nodules on lupin

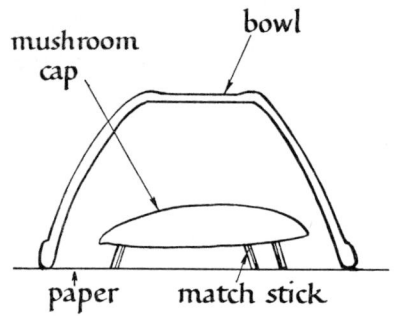

180. Fungal spores

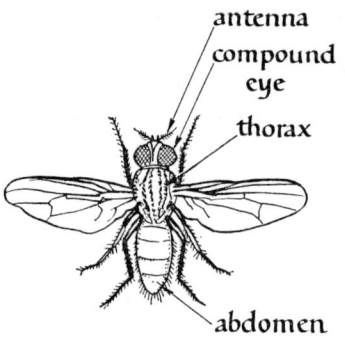

182. House-fly

water, heating, and allowing the water to boil for half an hour. Leave the jars or tubes in the water until they are required.

Different groups of pupils may prepare nutrient jellies by different methods:

(a) *Potato Jelly*: Put slices of scrubbed potato into a pan, just cover with water, and simmer for three hours (adding more water as necessary). Pour off the fluid through butter muslin into the sterilized vessels, where it will set to a jelly on cooling. A depth of a centimetre of jelly is sufficient in the jars; test-tubes can be one-quarter filled, and they should be set to cool in a slanting position. Immediately after pouring in the hot liquid cover the jars (watch-glass) or plug the test-tubes (cotton-wool).

(b) *Agar Jelly*: Nutrient agar can be bought from chemical suppliers. The agar is a seaweed extract, and it will have been incorporated with meat extract, peptone, etc. Weigh out about 2 g of agar, cover with water, and allow to soak until soft (overnight). Put the soaked material into a beaker with 100 cm^3 of warm water and bring gently to the boil, with constant stirring to prevent charring. Boil for half an hour and then transfer to sterile vessels as in (a) above.

(c) *Nutrient Gelatine*: Heat together, with constant stirring, the following materials:

500 cm^3 water

½ Oxo cube (or ½ teaspoon Bovril)

50 g powdered gelatine

1 teaspoon glucose (or a little grape juice)

Boil until all the gelatine has dissolved. Now add 1 per cent caustic soda solution drop by drop until a strip of litmus paper dipped into the liquid just turns blue (alternatively, powdered washing soda may be stirred in, a pinch at a time). Filter through muslin into sterile vessels and cover at once.

(d) *Flour Paste*: Mix 50 g (2 rounded tablespoons) of flour to a smooth paste with a little warm water, add a drop of phenolphthalein solution and then 1 per cent caustic soda solution drop by drop, with stirring, until the paste just remains pink. Now pour in half a litre of boiling water, with vigorous stirring, and transfer the liquid at once to sterile vessels. When infected (see below), the pink colour of this jelly disappears, the material becomes fluid, and growths develop on the surface.

177 *Growth of Moulds (Fungi)*

Suspend a little Mucor or Penicillium (Expt. 173) in water and paint a little of the suspension across the surface of nutrient jelly in a jar or flat dish (use a paint-brush which has been sterilized in boiling water); the spores should be well separated. Cover the jelly and examine daily with lens or microscope. The spores will swell as water is absorbed and they will put out filaments (hyphae) which spread in all directions under the surface of the jelly. Spore-bearing branches may be seen growing vertically.

178 *Growth of Bacteria*

In order to transfer microbe-containing material to nutrient jelly a sterile darning-needle should be used, prepared by passing the needle through a Bunsen flame and allowing it to cool without touching anything.

Using the needle, scrape a little film from the teeth and streak it across the jelly, uncovering the jelly for as short a time as possible. Dip a sterile needle into water which has been boiled and then cooled under cover, and streak a second jar of jelly. Label the first jar "Film from teeth" and the second "Control: boiled water". Keep the covered jars in a warm place and compare from day to day.

In all such work it is essential to avoid breathing into the jars, touching the inside of the jars with the fingers, or otherwise risking contamination and the teacher should carefully WARN PUPILS of the possible dangers.

179 *Bacteria on the Roots of Legumes*

Examine washed roots of peas, beans, clover, vetch, lupin, sweet peas, etc. and contrast them with the roots of non-leguminous plants. A lens is helpful in studying the nodules; they are found on the roots of legumes only.

Take a lupin rootlet bearing nodules and wash it repeatedly with water containing a little disinfectant. Cut off a nodule, wash it again, and crush it on a watch-glass with a few drops of water. Wash a microscope slide to remove grease (either alcohol or soapy water is effective), and transfer one drop of the bacterial suspension to the slide, using a glass rod. Spread the drop by drawing another washed slide over it. Now fix the preparation by passing the slide quickly two or three times through a flame.

Examine the slide under the high power of the microscope. Find a satisfactory area and mark this at the edge of the slide with Indian ink. Remove the slide from the microscope stage and spot with one drop of Indian ink (diluted with an equal volume of water) at the marked position. Tilt the slide so that the ink drains down to the opposite edge, staining the preparation; take up any excess with blotting-paper. When the film is dry, re-examine under the microscope. The bacteria now show up as a great number of identically shaped objects against a dark background.

How Germs Spread from Place to Place

180. *Fungal Spores*

Remove the stem from a freshly gathered and fully-opened mushroom. Support the cap above a sheet of clean white paper, using three matchsticks as "stilts". Cover the cap with a glass bowl and leave it undisturbed overnight. A dark print of the gills appear on the paper; it consists of masses of spores arranged in radiating lines.

If a ripe puff-ball is squeezed against a white background, a dark cloud is seen which rises in the air and disappears like smoke. The experience gives a good idea of how it is that the air always contains large numbers of fungal and bacterial spores.

181 *Infection of Nutrient Jellies*
Any of the jellies prepared in Expt. 176 may be used. They must be sterile, and if there is any doubt about this the material can be reheated in the jars or tubes standing in water. For all the following experiments one unexposed lot of jelly must be kept as a control.

(a) Expose one lot of jelly to the air for about an hour. Re-cover and set the jar and its control in a warm place. Both jars must be labelled.

After a day or two look for radiating masses of fungus and also for compact slimy colonies of bacteria.

(b) Expose jelly to the air of the room for 5 minutes and then cover. Now sweep the room vigorously and immediately expose a second lot of jelly for 5 minutes; cover. Set the jars in a warm place and count the number of colonies of bacteria in each after a given period.

Discuss the value of a vacuum cleaner in the home.

(c) Sneeze or cough into a jar of jelly; cover and label. Compare with the control after 24 hours' incubation.

(d) Rub a finger once across nutrient jelly; cover and label. Wash and rinse the hands and repeat the experiment on a second lot of jelly. Incubate in a warm place for 24 hours, and compare both results against a control.

(e) Capture a house-fly and introduce it quickly into a jar of jelly; cover and see that the fly touches the jelly; release the fly and cover again. Incubate, and compare with a control.

182 *Model of Housefly*
Model the body (head, thorax, abdomen) in Plasticine; the overall length might be 7–10 cm. Then proceed to lay all over it strips (say, 3 cm × 1 cm) of newspaper soaked in thin starch paste, or of muslin soaked in thin plaster of Paris cream. Press the material closely to the shape of the body and proceed until every part is covered with criss-cross strips to a thickness of about 1 mm. Allow to dry out completely and then saw the model into two halves. Dig out the Plasticine and attach legs and a wing to each half before joining the halves together again. The wings may be made from thin wire and covered with cellophane. The legs, made of wire, are thickened by rolling thin paper round each section. A proboscis is added to the head and the whole model is painted, eyes being shown. Finally, body and legs may be given a coat of paste and a dusting with fine black wool fragments to represent the hairy nature of the insect.

Models of the eggs, grubs and pupae of the fly may also be made. Refer to Expt. 63.

183 *Development of Gnat*

The gnat, or British mosquito (Culex), is related to the malaria-spreading mosquito (Anopheles).

Look for dark flakes on the surface of stagnant water (e.g in a water-butt which has not been disturbed for some time); examine with a lens to see whether the flakes are masses of gnat eggs ("egg-rafts"). Alternatively, larvae may be found hanging head downwards from the surface of the water. The larvae are only about 1 mm long when first hatched, but grow to more than 1 cm in a few weeks. They dart away and swim to the bottom when disturbed, but must shortly return to the surface for more oxygen.

Transfer some of the water with eggs or larvae to jam jars; keep these indoors, loosely covered. Tap-water should not be used, since it does not contain the minute organisms upon which the larvae feed. Observe the form and movements of the larvae, and watch for pupation and, a few days later, the emergence of the winged insect. Make sketches of all the stages and keep a diary of the successive changes.

184 *Surface Tension*

Fill a beaker with water. Clean a sewing needle from grease by washing it in soapy water, and then dry it. Float a scrap of filter paper or tissue paper on the surface of the water and rest the needle upon it. The paper becomes soaked and eventually sinks, leaving the needle floating on the water; notice the depression in which the needle rests.

By means of a glass rod introduce one drop of thin oil on to the surface of the water; it spreads, and as it reaches the needle the latter sinks.

Topics: "Coughs and sneezes spread diseases." The need for personal cleanliness. Protection of food in the home. The story of malaria and how it is kept in check. See also Expt. 344 (dust in the air), and Expt. 508 (soil bacteria).

Filmstrip: The House Fly (685 G1).

The Prevention of Disease and Decay

185 *Pasteurizing Milk*

In hot weather heat some milk rapidly to about 80°C. (avoid boiling, for this affects the flavour). Cool rapidly by standing the pan, covered, in a sink of cold water. Transfer the cooled milk to a bottle which has been well washed with soapy water and then rinsed; plug the mouth with cotton-wool.

Compare the keeping properties of this milk with those of a similar sample of unpasteurized milk.

Using sterile needles, streak nutrient jelly (Expt. 176) with (i) fresh milk, (ii) pasteurized milk, (iii) milk which has been exposed for a day.

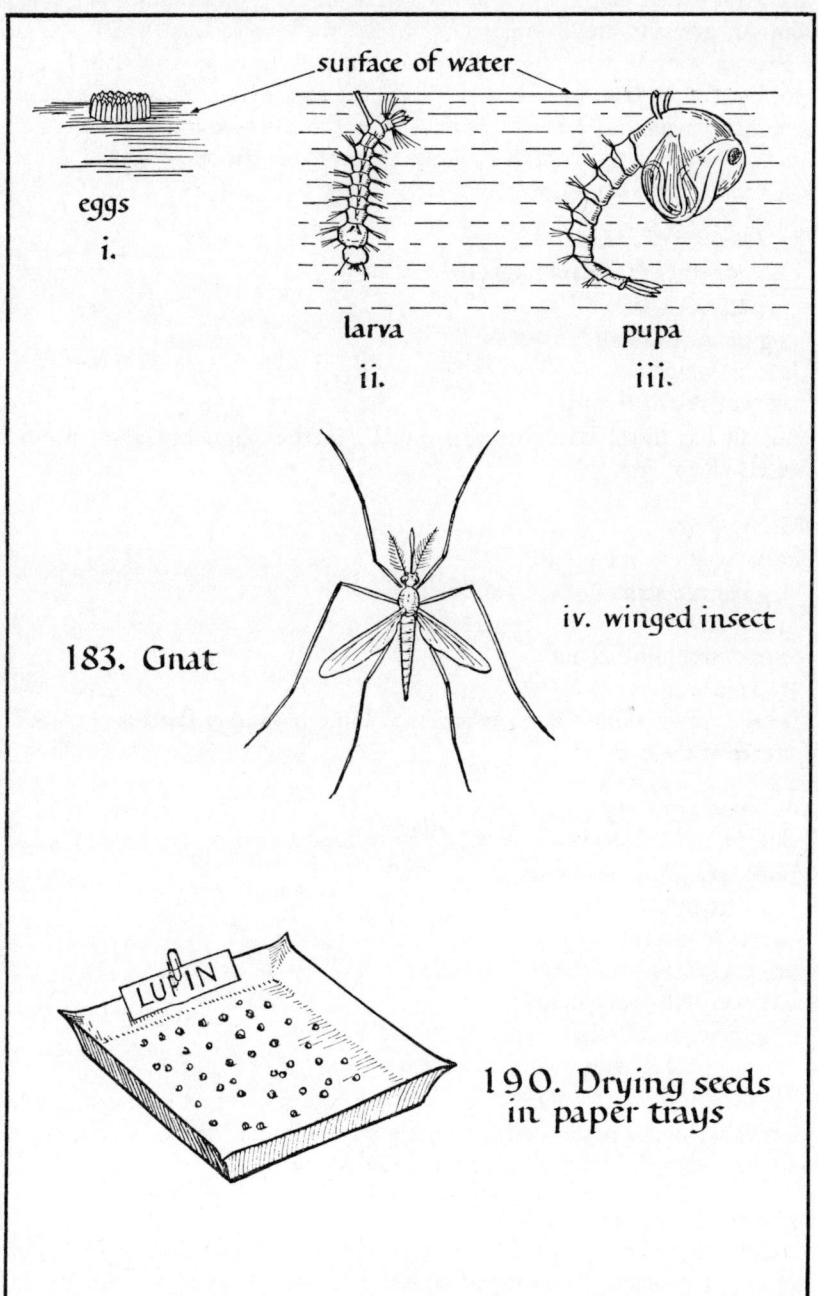

183. Gnat

190. Drying seeds in paper trays

186 *Disinfectants and Antiseptics*

Use boracic-acid solution, carbolic acid, tincture of iodine, strong salt solution, vinegar, and any commercial antiseptics. (See also Expt. 229.)

Prepare a number of "plates" of nutrient jelly (in jam jars) as in Expt. 176, but incorporate in some a little disinfectant or antiseptic. In all the experiments use a "control" which lacks the disinfectant or antiseptic. Infect by any of the methods of Expt. 177, 178, or 181, and compare, after incubation, with the controls.

187 *Tincture of Iodine*

Shake together in a glass-stoppered bottle:

 5 g iodine crystals.
 5 g potassium iodide crystals.
 10 cm^3 water.
 250 cm^3 rectified spirit.

until all has dissolved. Store the solution in the laboratory first-aid box (see also Expt. 31).

188 *Eye-lotion*

Shake together in a bottle:

 8 g boracic acid.
 4 g borax.
 2 cm^3 absolute alcohol.
 250 cm^3 water.

Use the lotion diluted with twice its volume of water. Discuss the need for care of the eyes.

189 *Salad Dressing*

(vinegar and salt as preservatives): The recipe is:

 4 teaspoonfuls cornflour.
 ¼ litre milk.
 4 teaspoonfuls olive oil.
 2 teaspoonfuls mustard.
 4 teaspoonfuls sugar.
 ½ teaspoonful salt.
 8 teaspoonfuls vinegar.

Mix the cornflour, mustard, sugar and salt in a jug with a little cold milk, to give a smooth paste. Boil the remaining milk and pour on to the paste while stirring. Add the oil and vinegar and stir well.

190 *Preservation by Drying*

Collect seeds of peas, broad beans, lupins, laburnum, nasturtium, etc. and set to dry on paper trays in the sunshine or in a warm dry shed. When thoroughly dried, packet and label the seeds; the packets may be suitably decorated with paintings of the plants. Use the seed for planting next spring.

191 *Outer Defences of the Body*
(a) Examine the skin under a hand lens, noting the hairs. (b) Press the fingers on cold glass or a polished bench and note the moisture prints. (c) Spread shoe polish on blotting-paper, press the fingers on it and then on a sheet of white paper; examine the "finger prints". (d) Press something against the back of the hand and notice how quickly blood is driven away and how quickly it returns when pressure is removed. (e) Spill a few drops of ether or methylated spirit on the back of the hand; notice the feeling of coldness, increased if the hand is waved to and fro. See also Expt. 437.

Discuss the results of these experiments—the toughness as well as the sensitiveness of the skin. Preliminary mention may be made of the cooling effect of the evaporation of sweat. A section of skin may be shown on the micro-projector.

Topics: The inner defences—white corpuscles and antibodies. The film "Immunization" (688/A1) discusses this subject as well as the preparation, use and effect of vaccines and toxoids; whilst "The Fight Against Disease (688/A5) gives a general survey of the methods used to combat disease.

192 *Burgundy Mixture*
This and the more popular Bordeaux Mixture are very widely used garden fungicides.

Dissolve 30 g of washing soda in half a litre of warm water; and dissolve 20 g of copper sulphate crystals separately in a little hot water, subsequently diluting to 2 litres. Then pour the soda solution into the copper sulphate solution, with stirring. The copper is precipitated as basic copper carbonate, and to make sure that precipitation is complete dip a bright steel blade into the liquid; there should be no red deposit of copper.

Shake the mixture before use.

Bacteria and Fungi in Useful Roles
The most important function of bacteria and fungi is in the process of decay—an essential part of the nitrogen cycle. In a narrower sense they are useful in several important industries—brewing, cheese-making, etc.

193 (a) *Fermentation of Sugar*
Either cane-sugar or glucose may be used; the former takes a little longer.

Fit a large flat-bottomed flask (2-litre), or a Winchester bottle, with a delivery tube bent twice at right angles so that it leads vertically downwards and dips just below the surface of some lime-water contained in a beaker or test-tube. Put 50 g of glucose and 500 cm^3 of warm water into

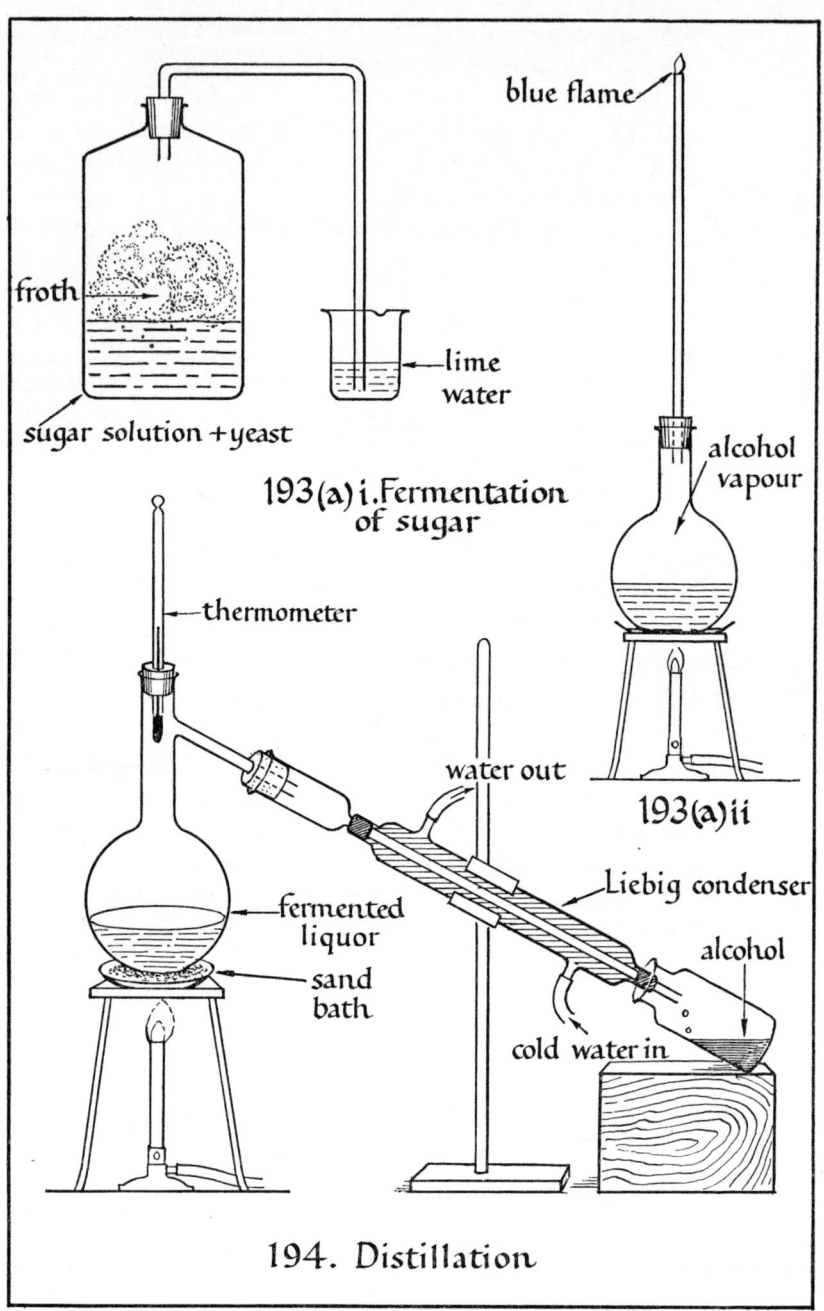

193(a)i. Fermentation of sugar

193(a)ii

194. Distillation

the flask, and swirl the liquid until the sugar is dissolved. Now add about 20 g of fresh brewer's yeast, shake well, and allow the flask to stand in a warm place (about 25°C.) for two or three days.

The mixture froths considerably and carbon dioxide is evolved—each bubble produces a cloud of chalk in the lime-water. When the liberation of gas appears to have stopped, remove the stopper from the flask and smell the mixture. Transfer a small portion of the liquid to a round flask fitted with a long (50 cm) upright tube; on gently heating, the vapour of alcohol escapes from the upper end of the tube and may be ignited.

193 (b) *Yeast Cells*
Transfer one drop of fermented sugar solution (e.g. from Expt. 193 (a) before heating to drive off alcohol) to a glass slide, apply a cover slip and examine under the high power ($\times$ 400) of the microscope. The yeast cells may be stained with methylene blue to bring out more detail. Look especially for budding cells.

194 *To Distil Alcohol from the Fermented Liquor*
A distillation flask and Liebig condenser may be used; alternatively to the Liebig condenser a long inclined glass tube cooled by sponging it with cold water will serve.

The fermented liquor from Expt. 193 is gently boiled in the flask and the readings of the thermometer in the neck of the flask are noted. Distillation is stopped when the temperature reaches about 97°C., by which time about one-tenth of the liquid will have distilled, the residue being largely water. The distillate is fairly strong alcohol.

195 *Rhubarb Wine*
Skin and cut up 1 kg of rhubarb and boil it for half an hour with 5 litres of water. Strain through muslin, and when the liquid has cooled somewhat add ¾ kg of sugar and stir to dissolve. Now add 15 g of citric acid and 15 g of yeast spread on toasted bread; leave the liquid several days to ferment.

Strain off the liquid into bottles (lightly corked) and leave to mature.

Topics: Micro-organisms—Friends or foes? The beneficial and harmful activities of micro-organisms are the subjects of two sound films, 632 D2 and 632 D3 respectively.

Chapter Eleven

Water in Nature

General Science or Science Singles?

The topic "Water" typifies the General Science treatment; certainly few syllabuses can omit it from their content. The outlook of Science teachers has been profoundly influenced by the movement towards a more generalized treatment of their subject, and the questions raised have by no means all been answered. Some acquaintance with the story behind the present position is helpful to any teacher who is considering what is his best line of attack with the particular pupils that he has to teach.

Early in the present century the Association of Public Schools Science Masters published its report *Science for All*, the forerunner of the General Science idea. At that time school Science faithfully reflected the interests of a generation dazzled by mechanical and physical progress; only girls studied botany. The spirit of this famous document was revived in the Thomson Report of 1918 (*Natural Science in Education*), which urged that "no boy should leave school with the idea that science consists of Physics and Chemistry alone".

The Educational Science Section of the British Association had from its inception in 1901 exerted its influence in the cause of a broadening of science teaching and in 1922 its President, Sir Richard Gregory, observing that less than 3 per cent. of pupils from state-aided schools proceeded to universities, protested that "the needs of the many are sacrificed to the interests of the few", criticized "the prevailing obsession in regard to quantitative work" and considered that "no teacher of school science should be unwilling or unqualified to impart instruction (over the whole field of Nature) to his pupils".

In 1924 the Science Masters' Association began to press for the inclusion of general science papers in the School Certificate examinations; such a paper was in fact offered by the Oxford and Cambridge Joint Board, but few pupils took it. The Board of Education *Report of an Enquiry into the Conditions affecting the Teaching of Science in Secondary Schools* (1925) noted that in an increasing number of schools Science was being begun at 11 +, but the first year work was often confined to Nature Study but might include Elementary Science—commonly "a very dull and uninteresting course in measurements . . . and manipulative exercises".

In 1932 the Secondary Schools Examination Council advocated a compulsory paper in elementary science to include questions on physics, chemistry and biology, but it was becoming increasingly clear that unless general science meant more than teaching the elements of the separate sciences it lost much of its force. The Science Masters' Association affirmed its support for the wider approach, publishing Parts I and II of *The Teaching of General Science* in 1936 and 1938 respectively, and the number of candidates taking General Science papers in the various School Certificate examinations mounted rapidly.

The Spens Report of 1938 contains an oft-quoted sentence: "We believe there is a general body of knowledge, not confined to either the physical or the biological field of science, which ought to be known by the average citizen and also by those who may ultimately specialise in a particular part of one of these fields and that we should aim, in general, at giving each boy and girl this minimum knowledge . . ." In reply to a question from the Norwood Committee, the S.M.A replied: "Assuming that general science means a broad course comprising at least physics, chemistry and biology and perhaps also astronomy and geology, then it should be adopted as the science of the main school. However, it does not necessarily mean that all these branches are to be taught by one teacher in any one set year. It would be true to say that a school is teaching general science even if its pupils study physics, chemistry and biology separately."

This latter was not everyone's view. There were many who saw integration of the separate subjects as essential, wishing to bring out the oneness of science and especially to teach it by an appeal to an environment —the everyday environment—which knows no distinction between chemistry, physics and biology. In 1947 and again in 1950 S.M.A. reports advocated General Science "where suitable staff and conditions are available" throughout the five-year course for pupils who will not continue beyond the age of 16, but regarded a shorter course, followed by the separate sciences, as "satisfactory where at least two full science subjects are studied in the last one or two years".

The opposite view was trenchantly put by Connell and James in an article in the *School Science Review* in March, 1958. The general science movement, they claimed, was a protest against something which no longer exists—against the narrow specialization of former years. They could discover no unity in published syllabuses, which were "always set out with the traditional divisions clear". Time-tables, they claimed, showed that "spells of physics, chemistry and biology follow each other". Examiners found great difficulty in framing questions which demanded an understanding of the interdependence of the different sciences. Recognizing some value in the topic method, these writers deprecated its "slavish adoption". The good teacher, they said, will always stress the links between different aspects.

Much of the opposition to General Science was crystallized in a resolution agreed upon at the annual business meeting of the A.S.E. in 1959: "That this meeting disapproves of the continued teaching of General Science on an inadequate time allowance". The periods allowed for the subject in the weekly time-table too often equated it with a single science, with especially disastrous effects upon practical work. Many teachers also were unhappy about the combined course as a preparation for Sixth Form studies: as early as 1936 Bradley (*School Science Review*, No. 70) had argued that co-ordination was being attempted at the expense of continuity in the specialist fields.

The claim for a proper time allowance is undeniable and we take up this point again in Chapter 13. The argument relating to advanced work is largely irrelevant to our present purpose, since our concern is with pupils of average and below-average ability. Today a majority of schools teach separate sciences in the upper forms, whatever the ability range, while many have accepted the challenge to broaden the syllabus in the first one or two years of the secondary course. The Nuffield projects approve a general science treatment throughout the secondary course for pupils who will not specialize in science; and even in the case of the specialists it is suggested that the first two years of the five-year run to "O" level might appropriately be treated on similar lines. It is interesting to notice that some C.S.E. Boards insist upon a Basic Science paper for all candidates taking other science subjects.

However, evolving patterns of teaching are rapidly eroding the impact of the general science *v.* separate science debate. Nuffield developments re-emphasize scientific enquiry rather than particular course content and the question is no longer so much whether a man knows enough of several aspects of science as whether he can adapt his teaching methods and laboratory practice to match the philosophy of the Nuffield approach. The entirely desirable change in attitude which will often be called for is unlikely to be any less demanding.

In this respect teachers of boys and girls of modest ability may sometimes find themselves at an advantage. The problem-solving type of work, through practical investigation, is not unfamiliar to those who have learned how much real science may be extracted from relatively modest enquiries in well-chosen fields. Discussion of "everyday" phenomena often ranges widely, whether thought of as "general" science or not.

This experience goes back a long way. Science in non-grammar schools was developed in the Higher Grade Schools with Science Departments in the eighteen-nineties, the forerunners of the Central Schools and Junior Technical Schools, but its availability to all pupils came only slowly. The Haddow Report (1926) observed that "the special equipment required for the teaching of science hardly exists in many (elementary) schools at the present time", and the Board's memorandum *Science in Senior Schools* showed that as late as 1932 biological teaching was largely excluded from boys' schools and physical science from girls' schools. Treatment was still academic and in the absence of equipment for practical work the object lesson predominated.

Here and there keen teachers, backed by sympathetic Heads, experimented with model-making and with group work, but the difficulties were many and progress was slow. It required a world war and an Education Act to bring about substantial change. The 1944 Act focused attention afresh upon aims and "education for citizenship" in the Modern schools provoked new thinking on the content of science courses. Training Colleges concentrated on the social aspects for another reason also: many of their students, fresh from the Forces or from industry, responded more readily to a treatment based on topics such as health and disease, food and the soil, or transport and power, as opposed to one typified by the traditional "Heat, Light and Sound". The theme studies of the Nuffield Secondary Science papers (*Harnessing Energy, Using Materials,* etc.) are not new ideas, any more than those of the introductory Combined Science course.

Underlying the new thinking of the 'forties was a fundamental consideration and one which is as relevant in the new comprehensive schools as it was in the Modern schools. Many pupils "do not love learning for learning's sake". They need to be convinced of the value of education. Their teachers' task is to kindle interest, the driving force behind effective learning. For many of them this means doing something with their hands; they "think with their fingers". Their minds need the focusing lens of practical experience and the mental floundering time that such experience can provide. It is necessary too that their laboratory work should not appear unrelated to real life, so that they can gain confidence in its significance for them.

It is not of course that General Science *must* be taught, but that the teacher should be free to teach whatever science citizenship calls for and by methods likely to be effective with average pupils. It is well to remember that a man usually succeeds best along the line of his own interests and skills. A good teacher uses his special knowledge as a spring-board. The chemist may dwell longer upon the phenomenon of hardness in water, the physicist upon water supply and the biologist upon the significance of water to living organisms. Given a sound basic syllabus, the emphasis may safely be left in the hands of the teacher.

As increasing numbers of boys and girls stay on at school, and with the raising of the leaving age the need to cash in on career interest becomes ever more obvious. Traditional science options may often prove inadequate and courses overlapping the boundaries of school, further education and industry need to be considered. In this connection the 1967 Schools Council bulletin *A School Approach to Technology*, though primarily directed towards young men and women who will go on to higher education, contains much of value for every teacher of science. Its suggestions on the organization of specific projects and on staff team-work, for example, are under-pinned by sound arguments related to creativity, design and craftsmanship. It reminds us also of a conclusion of the Crowther Report which is at the root of all our work—that there are many pupils who do not live up to their promise because the courses we offer fail to hold their interest, rather than because they have "exhausted their capacity to learn".

Moisture in the Atmosphere

196 *Drying Conditions*

Cut half a dozen similar squares of cotton cloth (or use similar handkerchiefs). Soak them in water and squeeze them out as thoroughly as possible. Roll one up into a tight ball. Hang the others to dry—one in the laboratory, one in the open air, one in a warm cupboard, one in a warm draught, etc. Compare and discuss the results.

197 *Formation of Dew*

Discuss familiar phenomena such as (a) what happens when we breathe on a mirror; (b) how we polish our spectacles; (c) the clouding-over of a tumbler of water when it is brought into a warm room; (d) the "steaming" of windows; (e) dew formation on grass (but note that transpiration also plays a part here).

Use a highly polished metal tube such as one of those in which shaving soap is sometimes packed. Pour into it 3 cm of petrol ether (which has no anaesthetic properties), taking care that all flames are extinguished beforehand. Blow air through the liquid (via a right-angled delivery tube) and note the temperature of the ether when a misty film first forms on the outside of the tube. Observe that the film clears away if the tube is allowed to warm up again.

198 *Wet and Dry Bulb Hygrometer*

Design and make a simple wooden stand (Woodwork room) consisting of an upright board on which two thermometers may be fastened, and a horizontal baseboard. Fix the thermometers upright and side-by-side; small-size Terry clips are useful. A hole cut in the upright board takes a small "non-spill" inkwell containing water; this stands below the bulb of the "wet" thermometer.

Fix a small strip of muslin round the bulb of the "wet" instrument (by means of a rubber band) and let the muslin dip down into the water in the inkwell.

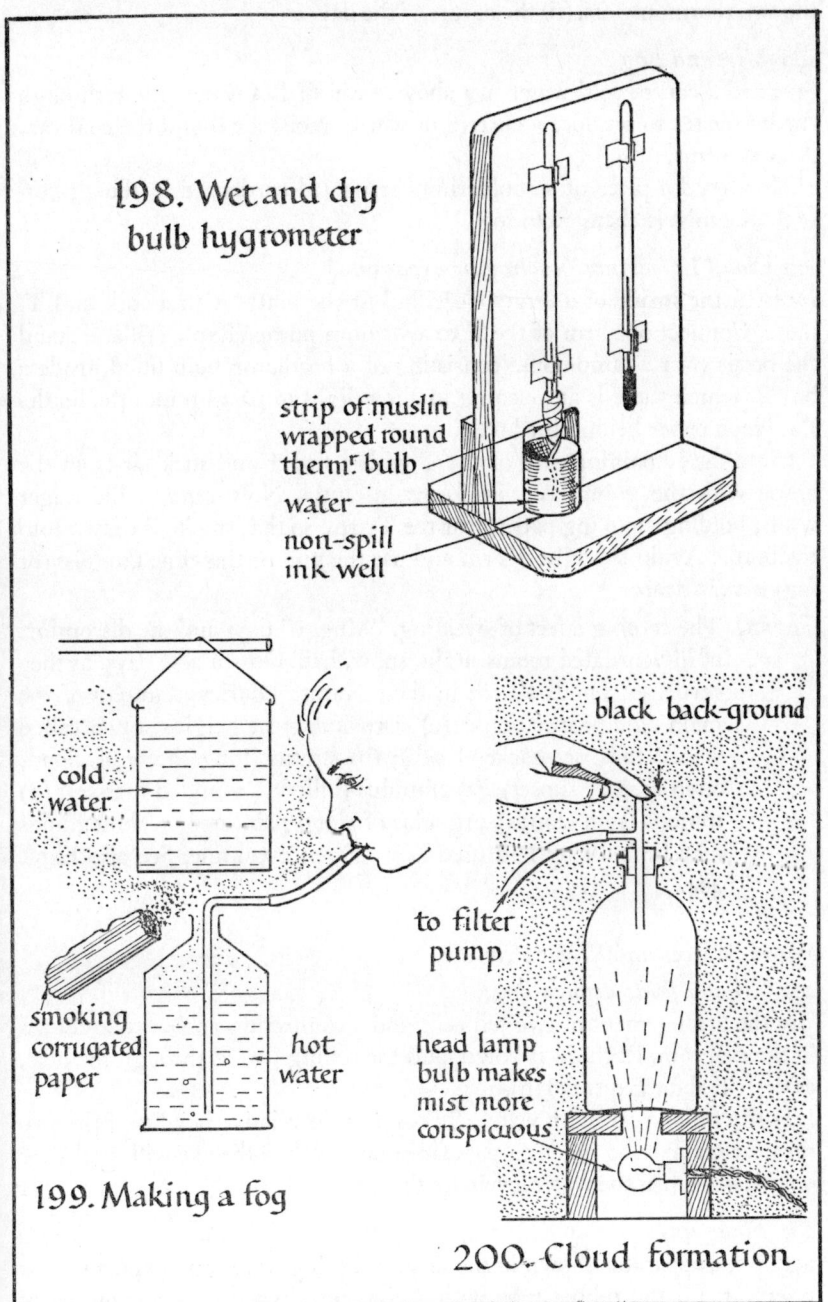

Set the hygrometer in an open place and record daily (i) the readings of the two thermometers, (ii) the nature of the day.

199 Mist and Fog

Suspend a can of cold water just above a can of hot water. Blow through the hot water to produce a current of warm, moist air round the cold can. A mist forms.

Now hold a piece of smouldering corrugated cardboard in the air current; the mist is changed to fog.

200 Cloud Formation (cooling by expansion)

Moisten the inside of a large bottle and fit the bottle with a cork and T-piece. Connect one arm of the T to a vacuum pump (Expt. 11), and stand the bottle over a lamp-house consisting of a headlamp bulb fitted inside a box in which there is an opening to allow light to pass up into the bottle. Put black paper behind the bottle.

Close the remaining arm of the T with a finger and suck air from the bottle with the pump. A mist forms instantly. Now remove the finger whilst holding smoking paper near the T-arm, so that smoke is drawn into the bottle. Again close the T-arm and use the pump; this time the mist (or fog) is very dense.

Topics: The cooling effect of sweating. "Muggy" days and the discomfort of ill-ventilated rooms. Rain, snow, hail. On suitable days, as they occur, let pupils sketch in their Nature Diaries examples of the main cloud formations: (a) cirrus (at great heights; often called mares' tails or mackerel sky); (b) stratus (long sheets of cloud, often seen at sunset); (c) cumulus (billowy, rounded masses); (d) nimbus (rain clouds). An atlas of cloud paintings or photographs may be built up and used as a reference volume. See also Expt. 404.

Water Sources and Water Pressure

201 "Water finds its own level"

Use the arrangement of two tall cans and a connecting rubber tube shown in the diagram. Each tin is bored, and the tubing passed through the hole, as described for Expt. 158 (b).

Partly fill one can with water. By varying the relative heights of the two cans, water may be made to pass from one to the other at will, and flow only ceases when the water levels are the same.

202 Fountains

Set up the apparatus shown in the diagram, using a tall can (Expt. 201) as a reservoir. Fit the rubber tube with a glass nozzle so that a narrow jet of water is produced; clamp the nozzle so that it points upwards above a sink.

Raise and lower the can (containing water) and observe the variations in the height of the jet. Support a ping-pong ball in the jet and notice that it can never rise quite as high as the level of water in the reservoir.

203 Overflow Can
The usual form of spouted can is often unsatisfactory in action, and is seldom large enough for effective work. The modification described below is used in subsequent experiments.

Set up a reservoir, made from a tall can (Expt. 201), on a tripod, with a rubber tube passing from its base and bent round and upwards to form a U. Join an inverted glass V-tube to the open end of the rubber tubing to form a nozzle. Clamp this at such a height that water flows from it when the can is about half-full of water. Allow the water to flow; notice that it gradually stops and that the V-tube remains filled with water when flow ceases.

Topics: Springs, wells, and reservoirs; storage cistern at home; water tower, water-table in soil. Artesian wells; oil wells. Rainfall (see Chap. 19).

Density and Floating Bodies
204 Density
Use large masses of iron, brass, glass, stone, etc. (e.g. iron weight, brass weight, glass block, large pebble). Weigh one specimen (spring balance) and lower it on a thread into the overflow can. Measure the volume of water displaced by collecting the overflow in a measuring jar.

Different groups of pupils may tackle different solids. Results will be expressed in grammes per cubic centimetre (g/cm^3).

205 Density of Water
Confirm the fact that a cubic centimetre of water weighs 1 g by weighing a tin can on a spring balance and repeating the weighing after pouring in 50, 100, 150, 200 ... cm^3 of water from a measuring cylinder.

The idea of relative density (specific gravity) may now be introduced by calculating the relative densities of the solids used in Expt. 204.

206 Density of Gas
It is important to draw attention at some point to the fact that the densities of gases are very low indeed as compared with those of solids or liquids. Gow (*School Science Review*, Vol. VII, p. 43) describes an interesting method which we have modified only slightly.

A Sparklet soda-water syphon is emptied of water and a Sparklet bulb containing liquid carbon dioxide is weighed, fitted to the syphon and pierced. The carbon dioxide vapourizes into the syphon, whence it may be delivered at regulated speed by pressing the lever. The volume of gas is

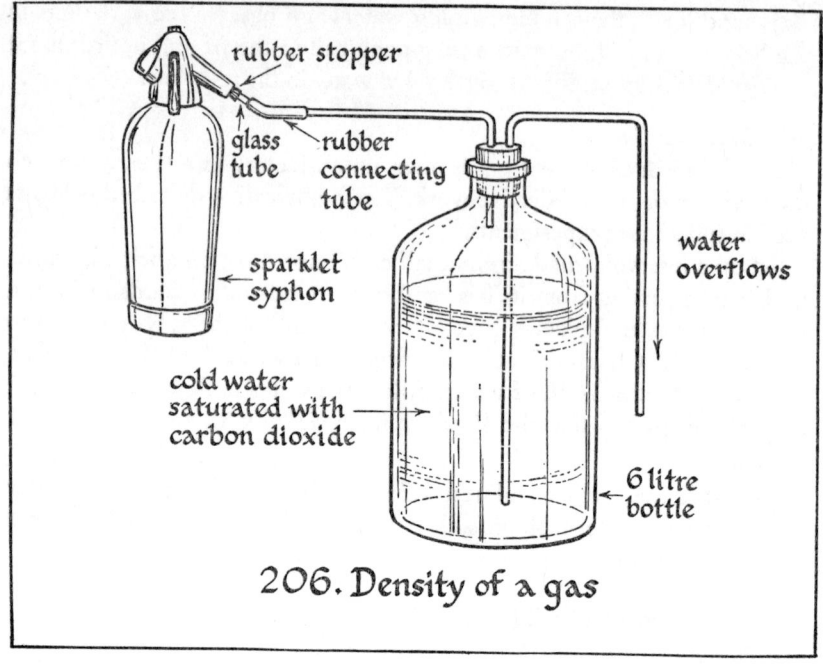

206. Density of a gas

measured by the volume of water displaced from a large bottle (6-litre) connected to the nozzle of syphon and for greater accuracy the water should be saturated with carbon dioxide beforehand.

The empty bulb is weighed, the loss representing the weight of carbon dioxide. The barometric pressure and the temperature of the gas should be noted and their significance discussed in qualitative terms.

(Ericson, *S.S.R.* Vol. 49, pp. 552–3, describes simple apparatus for measuring the density of air and for verifying Boyle's Law.)

207 *Density of a Substance that Floats*
(a) Cut a piece of wood roughly $25 \text{ cm} \times 10 \text{ cm} \times 4 \text{ cm}$ and then plane it accurately to this size so that its volume is exactly 1000 cm^3. Weigh it to the nearest gramme. Hence calculate the density.

Various woods may be studied by different groups of pupils. (b) Suggest that pupils devise their own method of finding the density of rubber (or other material that floats) by the displacement method (Expt. 204). The solution is to attach a "sinker", such as a piece of metal, to the rubber.

208 *The Supporting Action of Water*
Each group of pupils should be supplied with an extension spring balance, a large tin can or other container for water, and a large solid object.

Hang the object on the balance and note its weight. Then lower the object slowly into water and observe the readings on the balance.

WATER IN NATURE 177

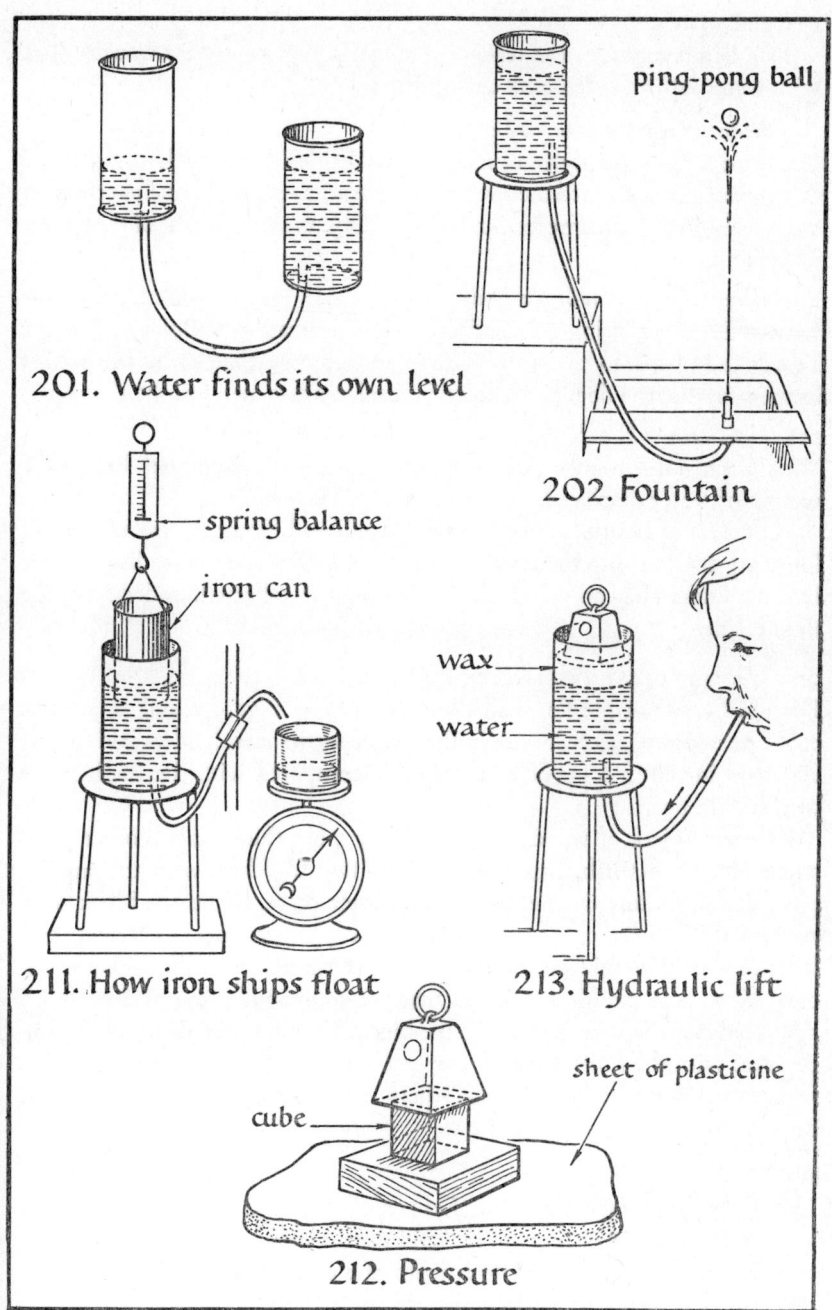

Particular attention should be paid to what happens in the case of a block of wood.

As a demonstration, the teacher may get a boy to lower a bucket filled with water into a garden tank containing water.

209 *What Happens when a Body Floats*
Use the overflow apparatus of Expt. 203. Weigh a large block of wood and then lower it gently into the overflow apparatus, collecting the overflow in a can standing on a compression balance. Observe the weight of water displaced.

210 *What Happens when a Body Sinks*
Repeat Expt. 209 using a large iron weight instead of the block of wood. Lower the iron into the water slowly and observe that, even when fully immersed, the iron does not succeed in displacing its own weight of water.

211 *How Iron Ships Float*
Weigh a metal can and lower it into the overflow apparatus; observe the weight of water displaced.

Puncture the bottom of the can with a nail and repeat the experiment of lowering the can into the overflow apparatus. Observe the readings of the balance under the can in which the overflow is collected, and discuss the final result.

212 *Meaning of the Term "Pressure"*
Discuss the use of needles, nails, knives and forks, garden stakes, arrows, etc. The opposite effect is seen in the use of snowshoes, ladders laid on ice, etc., and in the imprint of a shoe sole as compared with the mark made by a stiletto heel.

Prepare a piece of wood 5 cm square by 3 cm thick, and another 3 cm square by 3 cm thick. Screw or nail the two together, with the smaller piece at the middle of one face of the larger piece. Stand the block on a smooth thick sheet of Plasticine, with the 3 cm square face down, and balance a 5 kg weight on top of it. Observe the mark made in the Plasticine. Now turn the block over, so that the 5 cm square face is down, and again balance the 5 kg weight on the block. Compare the depth of the impression with the former mark.

State the force acting on each square centimetre of Plasticine in each case.

213 *Hydraulic Lift*
Use the tall-can reservoir again (Expt. 201). Remove the rubber tube and insert a rubber stopper instead. Half fill the tin with water and pour melted paraffin wax on to the water to a depth of 2 cm. Allow the wax to harden thoroughly (overnight) without disturbance.

Invert the tin (the wax will hold the water in position), extract the stopper, and reinsert the rubber tube. Set the reservoir upright on a tripod, bringing the rubber tube round to form an upright U. Press downwards gently on the wax plug until it just moves. Now put a 250 g weight upon it, and blow gently down the rubber tube; the wax plug carries the weight upwards. Find out what weight can be lifted in this way.

A certain amount of water may leak round the plug, but if an undamaged can is used this will not be sufficient to interfere with the general effect.

Topics: Swimming and floating. Ships and submarines. Plimsoll lines. Floating docks.

The Hardness of Water

214 *Home-made Spring Balance*

The balance is useful if the pupils are required to weigh small quantities of the order 0–10 g, great accuracy not being essential.

The construction is shown in the diagram. The lever arm is a 30-cm length of springy metal strip (such as is used for binding packing-cases), and the pan-holder is made of aluminium. The loose pan is simply a cone of paper. The 50-cm scale is fastened with paper clips to a polished aluminium bracket, the latter serving as a mirror to eliminate parallax errors when reading the pointer position.

Adjust the balance by bending the strip and moving the scale as required until the pointer stands at zero. Put a 10 g weight in the pan and slide the pan-holder to the left or right until the pointer stands exactly at the 50 mm mark: each millimetre now represents 0·2 g and the scale may be marked off in grammes.

215 (a) *Preparation of Talcum Powder*

The features of a good talcum powder should be discussed. Thus it should have (i) absorbing power, to remove perspiration and to hold the perfume; (ii) smoothness or "slip"; (iii) covering power or opacity; (iv) adhesive power or "cling". Precipitated chalk is absorbent and has fair covering power: talc is unique for providing "slip"; and the stearates of magnesium, lithium or zinc are unrivalled in adhesive properties.

Weigh out into a screw-topped glass jar:

talc	21 g
precipitated chalk	2½ g
magnesium stearate	1 g

Add a few drops of concentrated perfume (Expt. 119), screw on the cap, and shake the bottle well. Store the product in a decorative jar.

In speaking of talc, reference may be made to another solid lubricant, graphite; and in discussing covering power the use of lead oxide, zinc oxide, etc. in paints may be mentioned.

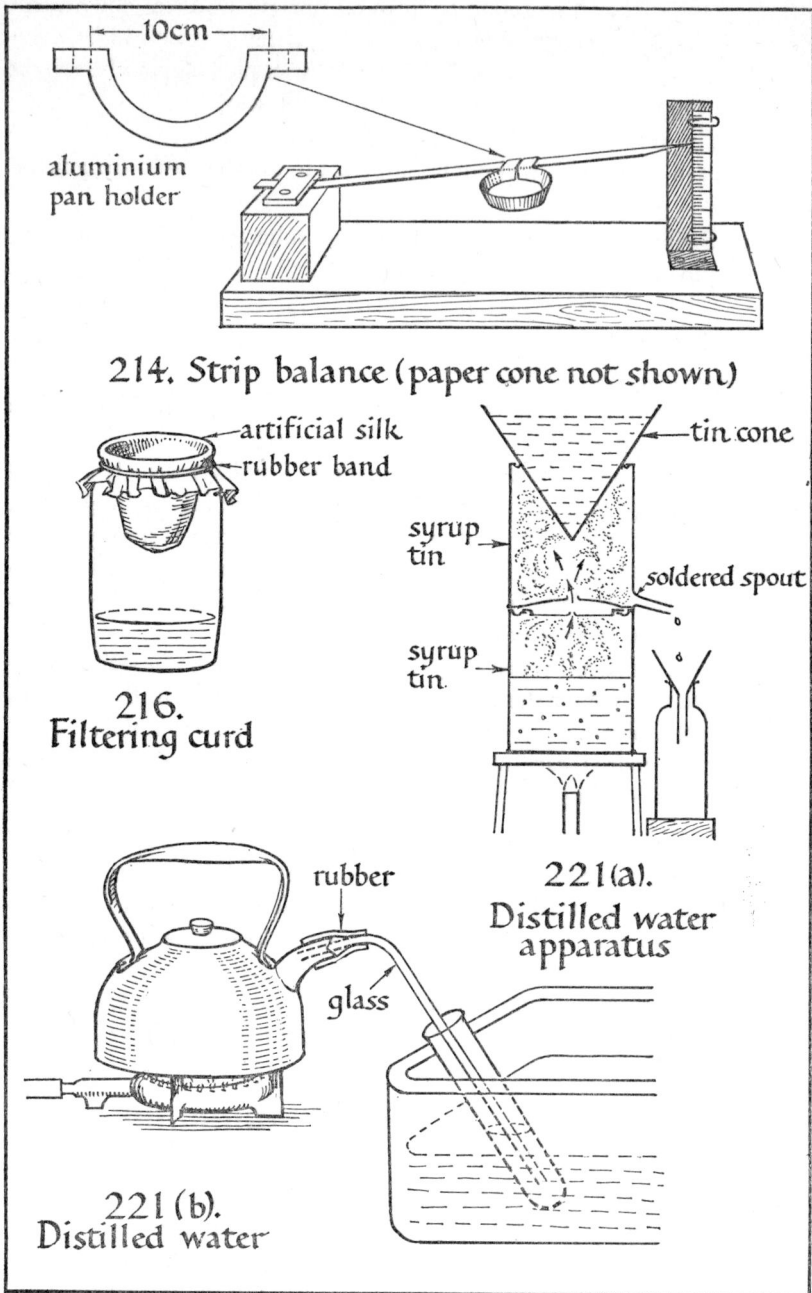

214. Strip balance (paper cone not shown)

216. Filtering curd

221(a). Distilled water apparatus

221(b). Distilled water

215 (b) *Preparation of Bath Salts*

The dye solution is made first. It is a 1 per cent solution in water and discussion on what this means is valuable—e.g. what weight of dye is required to make 50 cm³, 200 cm³, etc. of solution? Groups can use the home-made spring balance (Expt. 214) to weigh out the small quantities of dye required; 50 cm³ of solution will serve the whole class probably, but it is better to let each group make its own. Suitable dyes, such as azogeranine and naphthol yellow, have been obtained through Messrs. Boots or from I.C.I. Dyestuffs Division.

Weigh out approximately 100 g of sodium sesquicarbonate (very similar to washing soda but non-efflorescent and so retaining the pleasing feathery appearance of its crystals). A lever or compression balance is best. Transfer the crystals to a pudding basin or similar vessel and add about 20 drops of dye solution, using the fountain-pen filler of Expt. 7. The operator must now don a rubber glove and he should be introduced to the value of French chalk (talc) in doing so (compare Expt. 215 (a)). With the gloved hand mix the dye and crystals thoroughly, sifting the solid between the fingers. A delicate pleasing colour should result. Finally, perfume is added and the crystals are sealed up in a stoppered bottle. Later the bath salts may be packed into suitable cellophane packets.

Examine the power of the bath salts to soften hard water (Expt. 217).

216 *Curd Formation in Hard Water*

If pupils have used lime in the garden, reference might be made to the difficulty of washing the hands afterwards. A pupil might also be invited to try to wash his hands in a basin of water in which Epsom salt has been dissolved. Each group should then carry out the following experiment.

Prepare a sample of very hard water by dissolving about ½ g of Epsom salt in 100 cm³ of water. Make soap solution by dissolving about 1¼ g of Castile soap (or Pears' Transparent) in 100 cm³ of distilled water; the soap is best shredded, and warm water should be used.

When the soap solution is cold, pour it into the hard water. A very dense white curd forms; there is no lather.

Now divide the suspension (note the term) into two parts. Filter the first through a square of artificial silk stretched across the top of a jam jar or beaker and held by a rubber band. In this way the solid nature of the curd is amply demonstrated. Gently heat the second part in a beaker, stirring with a glass rod or spoon. Before long the curd flocculates, collecting on the stirring spoon and in a ring round the sides of the beaker; the remaining liquid is quite clear. The "ring" of curd around the bath at home, often not easy to remove, is now explained by the adhesive nature of the curd. This curd consists of stearates, oleates, etc. of calcium or magnesium.

217 (a) *Hardness of Water*

Soap solution should be prepared in advance. A ½ per cent solution of ordinary soft soap in distilled water has been found very suitable. Winchesters of distilled water, rain water, sea water, and of tap waters from various sources should be kept in the store-room. Specimens of water from named districts (e.g. Birmingham water) are much more interesting to pupils than samples prepared artificially or of unstated origin.

Various methods may be tried which avoid the use of a burette—e.g. the use of a dropping-bottle (the drops being counted), or the method of using thimblefuls of soap solution. Nevertheless this work provides an excellent opportunity to introduce the idea of exact analysis and the need for special instruments, without, of course, demanding too much technical skill in their use. Burettes should be of the simplest—the kind with a spring clip in place of a glass tap.

Issue about 150 cm^3 of soap solution to each group of pupils, and let them fill their own burettes via small funnels. Iron retort stands and clamps are quite satisfactory as burette stands if a wad of paper is used between the jaws of the clamp and the glass. The usual laboratory burette stands are often clumsy or expensive.

If it is desired to avoid the use of pipettes, try medicine bottles filled to a certain mark (or run 50 cm^3 of water in from a measuring cylinder). Let each group of pupils experiment with (a) distilled water and (b) one other named type of water.

Add soap solution from the burette, ½ cm^3 at a time, shaking the medicine bottle after each addition. Stop when a lather is formed which lasts for at least one minute (laboratory clock); note the volume of soap solution which has been used. Hence compare the "hardness" of various waters.

217 (b) *How Hard Water may be Softened*

There seems little point in distinguishing between "temporary" and "permanent" hardness at this stage. It is sufficient to show that water can be softened by various methods, some less expensive than others.

Shake up a teaspoonful of washing soda in a large bottleful of hard water and allow the curd to settle. Label the bottle. Boil another sample of the same water and allow this to cool in a second (labelled) bottle.

Test the relative hardness of the original water, the water treated with soda, and the boiled water, using the method of Expt. 217 (a).

218 *Removal of Grease and Dirt by Detergents*

The modern synthetic detergent is a complex mixture of substances, each incorporated for a specific purpose, but its main job is to loosen and disperse the grease that holds dirt to a fabric or other surface.

Use a large polythene washing-up bowl, rubber gloves, a hand-mop, teaspoon, egg-whisk, thermometer and a stack of cheap white dinner plates. Pour 5 litres of water into the bowl and mark the water level by a black line on the outside of the bowl; then pour away the water.

Prepare a "soil" by melting 100 g lard and stirring in 100 g flour and 5 g oleic acid. Colour with a little red ink. Keep the soil liquid by warming it and flick a teaspoonful on to each plate in turn. Wearing rubber gloves, smear the soil over each plate. After about an hour you may stack the plates, the soil having hardened.

Fill the bowl to the mark with water at about 47°C. and add 5 g of detergent. Agitate the water, using the whisk, for a timed 20 seconds. Then wash the plates, one after another and using the mop. Give each plate similar treatment and re-stack them as you go.

Look for the point at which a grease mark (pink) remains on a plate after washing and a cold water rinse.

Record:
    i Name of detergent under test;
    ii Number of plates washed free of grease;
    iii Price of detergent (weight per new penny)
    iv Efficiency (number of plates washed per new penny)

Figures should be the average of several tests. Let different groups of pupils work with different detergents brought from home.

219 *Wetting Action of a Detergent*

A detergent must come into intimate contact with the surface to be cleaned —i.e. it must wet the surface.

Prepare swatches of dish-cloth cotton or similar yarn; for each, wind 20 turns of yarn on a 10 cm former to make a skein, afterwards detaching from the former.

Attach a 3 g weight to a skein and use a glass rod to press the skein just beneath the surface of water contained in a 500 cm^3 measuring cylinder. Simultaneously run tests using detergent solutions ($\frac{1}{4}$ g per litre) instead of pure water: household detergents and also products such as sodium lauryl sulphate and dodecyl benzene sulphonate (British Drug Houses) may be tried.

Notice the air-bubble displacement as wetting proceeds and measure the time taken for the swatch to sink. The end-point is striking, the swatch moving sedately to the bottom of the liquid.

220 *Dissolved Solids in Water*

Let different class groups use different kinds of water (Expt. 217).

Transfer one teaspoonful (about 5 cm^3) of water to a watch-glass and evaporate over a syrup tin of boiling water. When dry, examine the residue against a black background. Compare the residues from different waters.

221 *Distillation of Water*

(a) A home-made still is shown in the diagram. A small hole is punched in the lid of the lower syrup tin (the boiler) and the base of the upper tin is hammered into a convex shape so that condensed water collects round the edges and runs easily from the soldered-in metal spout (short length of tin). The tin cone is soldered down the seam, but is not fixed to the upper syrup tin. It may easily be lifted and refilled with cold water. (b) Insert a glass delivery tube some distance into the spout of a kettle, joining it to the spout by a rubber tube. Boil water in the kettle and lead the steam into a flask or large test-tube standing in cold water in a sink.

The water may be tested as follows:

(i) Evaporate a little to dryness (Expt. 220); practically no residue is left.
(ii) Test the hardness with soap solution (Expt. 217).
(iii) Taste the water; it is "flat".

Examine the "fur" inside a kettle that has been in use for some time.

Topics: The water cycle in Nature; action of water on rocks; formation of caves; why the sea is salty. Household and industrial methods of softening (no detail). Value of dissolved salts to living things.

Chapter Twelve

The Water Supply to our Homes

Who will Teach Science?
"Tens of thousands of schoolboys have no idea in their heads but that they too will split the atom or ride on a rocket round the Moon. Ask the average science student what he wants to do and he will say 'Research', in the same tone one fancies as in the twelfth century he might have said 'Crusade'. As he sees it, science is an interesting and honourable profession, to be contrasted with the drabness of school teaching and municipal engineering..."

In this quotation from a Third Programme talk by John Ziman the conjunction of school teaching and municipal engineering is a reflection of the widely-held view that the work of a schoolmaster is at best a mechanical business, concerned with discipline rather than with design (though the slight on the city engineer is equally undeserved). It cannot be denied that science teaching fails to attract more than a small proportion of the ablest graduates and the fact must be faced that industry and research are likely to remain more attractive, intellectually and financially, to the most highly qualified people. This is not the real problem in most schools, where men and women of more modest academic attainment often do first-class work.

Ministry of Education statistics for 1961 showed that three out of four secondary modern schools, on average, were without a science graduate. Two years earlier an S.M.A. survey had concluded that in such schools one member in six of the science staff "had no pretensions at all to science qualifications". Certainly there has been no improvement since that time commensurate with the ever-growing need for science education. It is still true that there are secondary school pupils who miss science lessons simply because teachers of the subject are not available.

Women today probably represent the nation's only considerable reservoir of untapped science teaching potential. Unfortunately the view is still held, even by teachers, that science is not quite right as a career prospect for girls. Less than two-fifths of the science candidates of the 1964 G.C.E. O-level examinations were girls; and in the A-level entries the figure was two-ninths. When we remember that the majority of papers taken by girls are in biological subjects, the position of chemistry and physics is obvious. The almost non-existent future for girls in top engineering posts is a proper matter for criticism of industry; but there are things nearer home which need to be rectified.

But in boys' schools too there is small reason for satisfaction. The proportion of sixth-formers taking science courses is declining because, it is said, the interest in science which is so strong in many eleven-year-olds is killed in succeeding years. Both universities and colleges of education complain. The former speak of the poor quality of many applicants for places, and especially of the narrowness of their outlook; the colleges of education recruit too many students who see science teaching only in terms of their own academic experience. How many pupils are frightened off altogether because they see science teaching as a task of "drilling apparently useless facts into unenthusiastic minds"?

To the problem of the supply of teachers of science there is only one possible solution; it is that a far larger proportion of boys and girls in secondary schools should come to regard science as an attractive option. One of the most valuable outcomes of the Nuffield ferment would be an increased flow of students in training attracted to teaching science becuase the subject had recommended itself to them in their own school courses. Perhaps we ought to measure the success of a teacher not by the number of examination successes gained by his pupils, but by the number of those pupils who choose teaching as a career.

The colleges of education have, of course, a crucial role to play. There is every prospect that they will play it well, given a fair start. Yet here too it will be necessary to keep clearly in mind the objectives of science teaching so far as the majority of pupils are concerned.

The Importance of Science to the Ordinary Pupil

This book is not primarily concerned with the education of boys and girls who will become scientists or technologists; but changing patterns of school organization, and developments in the field of public examinations, emphasize certain common factors in science education. Every child today belongs to an age dominated by the devices of applied science and overshadowed by the political and social effects of a scientific revolution. We have to prepare all our pupils for life in a late twentieth century setting.

In selective schools the interests of science specialists have tended to operate against the science education of other able youngsters. Praiseworthy attempts to bridge the gap between "the two cultures" have seldom recorded any considerable success. In other kinds of secondary school it was the hope that pupils might be insulated from narrow academic pressures, but as secondary modern schools found it expedient to bring in

G.C.E. examinations the prospect faded, at least for some. The advent of the new Certificate of Secondary Education revived hope of avoiding the worst evils of examinations, but the curriculum research and development centres that have been established will find no lack of questions to discuss. With the coming of comprehensive schools the problems are sharply focused: the deployment (as well as the recruitment) of science staff; the organization of science classes; the G.C.E./C.S.E. boundary; the treatment of the unexaminable . . . Never was it more urgent for the science teacher to see clearly what his objectives are.

There are, it has been said, two ways of teaching science. In the one, statements are made and the pupil is exhorted to understand and learn them. Practical work, such as it is, is conducted as an illustration of the statements; but the real authority is the text-book. It is this method that has ruled the schools until now, in spite of efforts by many teachers to bring about reform. Only the very best schools, selective or non-selective, have escaped it. To it we may trace much of university criticism of sixth-form pupils, for it is fundamentally illiberal. In it we may see the death of science so far as the majority of boys and girls are concerned, for it does not interest them.

The second way is grounded in the conviction that science is not merely information, or laws, or the application of laws; but that it is a method of looking at things and thinking about things, founded upon personal observation. The areas of knowledge to be explored must vary with the interests and abilities of the pupils, but for all the attempt must be made to open their eyes to what lies around them and to promote discussion based on closer examination. To what extent this work can be extended to the testing of hypotheses and the formulation of general conclusions will again depend on the boys and girls concerned. The main thing is to convince pupils of the interest and relevance of the work for them.

Most of our effort will be addressed to pupils who will never again see or handle a Bunsen burner, a flat-bottomed flask or even a metre rule. They *will* see, and have to guard against, fires, dry-rot and pneumonia; they may have experience of agriculture, if only in the garden; they will pay for gas, water and electricity; and they will have the stars above their heads. It may be that we have too often advocated the teaching of science on grounds subsidiary to the main issue so far as the ordinary pupil is concerned. The fact is that these youngsters live in a world of questions to which they want to know the answers. Without our help they are likely to remain blind and dumb in the face of the world's news, the conversation of their fellows, their surroundings at home and at work, and the wonders and beauties of Nature. It is a question not only of knowledge but also of attitude. We want our future citizens to be interested in life and to ask questions; and science *is* modern life in one of its important aspects.

To deny it to any of our young people is to make nonsense of our educational ideals.

If science teaching is to commend itself, the first essentials are a syllabus built on commonsense lines related to pupils' experience, the use of simple apparatus, and methods which do not blind the pupil to the real issues. Many teachers would feel more confident if they realized that the criterion of a good experiment for average pupils is that it can be carried out in the kitchen at home. Yet while for most pupils science teaching should depart radically from the traditional Grammar School approach, it should reject with equal firmness the "householder hints and gadgets" type of treatment. It is important to a householder that he should be able to fit a washer on a tap, but we have no right to spend time in school on such a matter unless we are using the situation to teach our pupils more important lessons—to arouse their interest and to teach them something of scientific method, to show them the principles upon which water supply depends and to tell them something of the need for its conservation and purification. The appeal through the social significance of science can be very strong at the Secondary stage. Those who have tried it know that, far from the burden upon the child being increased, understanding of the impact of science upon everyday life is an essential preliminary to any substantial progress with the subject in the case of most boys and girls.

The Water Supply to Our Homes

The topic provides an excellent opportunity for collaboration in the fields of Science and Geography.

Wherever possible, maps and solid models of a watershed should be made. A holiday visit to the area would of course be ideal. The local waterworks should be visited and pupils should go prepared to seek answers to question such as the following:

(a) What is the source of the water—aqueduct (from a distant reservoir), river, or well?

(b) How is the water purified—filtration, chlorination or both?

(c) What is the elevation of the service reservoirs relative to the area they supply? What are stand-pipes and water-towers?

(d) What kinds of pump are used, and how is the water measured?

(e) By what kind and size of pipes is the water carried to houses and to factories?

Consult the catalogue *Educational Films, 1946–66* for details of the Ministry of Education (1951) Visual unit called "Water Supply"; see p. 6.

THE WATER SUPPLY TO OUR HOMES   189

222 *House Water Supply*
Pupils should be instructed to locate in their own homes:
    (a) The stop-cock on the branch service main outside the house.
    (b) The cold-water storage tank, its main inlet pipe (leading in via a ball-valve), its overflow pipe, and its other exit pipes.
    (c) The pipe leading from the bottom of the cold-water storage tank to the hot-water cistern.
    (d) The pipes supplying cold water to the upstairs taps and to the downstairs taps, noting whether the supply is from the storage tank or direct from the mains.
    (e) The supply to the lavatory cistern.

Note that the hot-water system will be studied later (p. 210). Make as realistic a picture as possible of the house water supply and then reduce this to a "flow diagram" on another sheet of paper.

223 *To Renew a Tap-Washer*
Means should be found of letting every pupil dismantle an actual tap, since this is an operation that the householder ought to be able to undertake.

Turn off the water at the main first. Then open the tap to its full extent and unscrew the cover C_p (diagram). Using a spanner, unscrew the tap collar C in which the spindle S runs. Care is needed, since the thread may be either left- or right-handed. Lift out the collar and spindle. The rubber (for hot water) or leather washer may be found either on the lower end of the spindle or on a loose "jumper", J, which can be lifted out separately. Unscrew the small nut which holds the washer in place, remove the old washer and fit a new one. The new one will go on quite easily if it is put on with a screwing motion, like a nut.

Notice that the householder ought to keep handy: (i) spare washers, (ii) spanners which will fit the two sizes of nut.

A means of rendering visible the action inside a water tap (by fitting a perspex window) is described in the *School Science Review*, No. 125, p. 116.

224 *Waste of Water*
Allow a tap to drip slowly. Collect the water in a jar over a period of an hour or more. From the volume collected in a known time calculate the amount of water wasted by such dripping in 24 hours. What is the waste with a thousand such taps?

225 *Syphon Action*
(a) Use the tall-can reservoir (Expt. 201) with a $\frac{1}{2}$-metre length of rubber tubing fixed into the outlet hole. Put a spring clip on the free end of the tube. Fill the can with water, allow water to flow out so as to fill the tube, and reclip it. Stand the reservoir on a tripod at the edge of a sink.

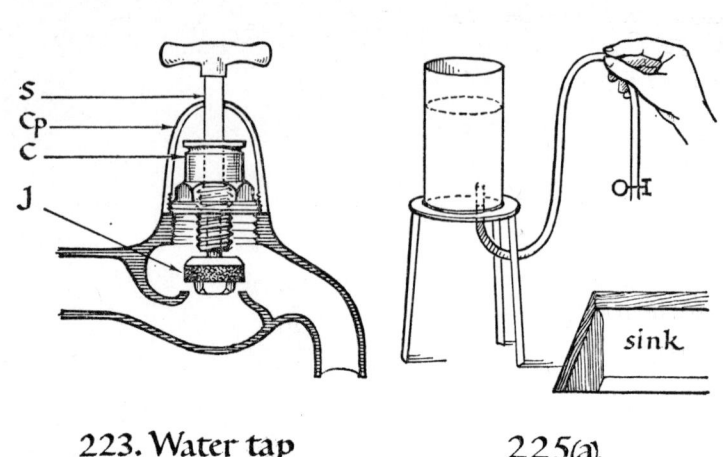

223. Water tap

225(a).

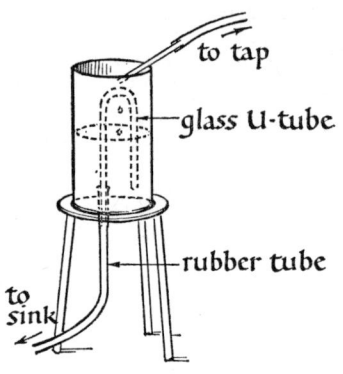

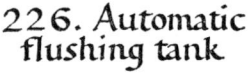

226. Automatic flushing tank

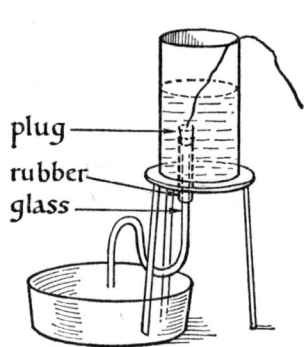

227. Sink waste pipe

Bend the tube upwards to form a double loop with the top bend above the level of the water in the reservoir and the free end of the tube hanging down into the sink. Open the clip and notice what happens: (i) when the loop is raised further, (ii) when the loop is lowered, comparing at each stage the position of the free end of the tube with the water level in the reservoir.

(b) Syphon water from one vessel to another, using the normal arrangement. There is no need to "suck" water into the tube: fill the tube by sinking it in the water, nip one end, and lift this end (only) out of the water and over the side of the can (compare Expt. 21 (b)).

226. *Automatic Flushing Tank*
Set up the arrangement shown in the diagram. A 25-cm length of glass tubing is bent to form a narrow U, one arm of which is pushed down into the rubber tube projecting into the reservoir can so that the U stands in an inverted position inside the can. The free end of the rubber tube hangs downwards into the sink.

Run water slowly into the open top of the can. Notice that as soon as the water level in the can reaches the top of the inverted U-bend the can is automatically emptied, "flushing" the sink.

227 *Sink Waste Pipe*
Use the reservoir can. Connect a piece of glass tubing, bent to represent the waste pipe of a sink, into the exit hole by means of a short collar of rubber tubing. Make a wooden plug (dowel rod) to fit the projecting end of the rubber tube inside the can, and fix a length of string to the top of the plug by means of a tack. Fit the plug lightly into the rubber tube. Stand the can on a tripod in a sink or basin.

Fill the can with water. Pull out the plug and notice that when water ceases to flow some still stands in the U-bend, forming a seal.

Now examine the U-bend under an actual sink. Put a bucket underneath it, unscrew the access cap and flush the waste pipe. Replace the cap. Test the action of the sink-pipe cleaner (see Expt. 6).

Topic: Examination of ball-valve in storage tank or lavatory cistern; the valve should be removed as for the replacement of the washer. The teacher is advised to carry out the job at least once before attempting a demonstration, so that he may grease the working parts and ensure that the split-pin will come out easily.

Purification of the Water Supply
Refer to the examples of filtration in Expts. 97, 117, and 216.

228 *A Sand Filter*
Use well-washed pebbles, gravel and sand; supplies of each should be kept

in separate containers in the laboratory. Thoroughly clean a plant-pot and fit a one-holed cork, carrying a length of glass tubing, into the hole at the bottom. Into the pot put 3-cm layers of pebbles, gravel, sand, and silver sand, in that order. Lay a piece of glass or slate on top, so that when water is poured in the sand is not disturbed. Run in muddy water, and collect the filtered water in a jar underneath the plant-pot.

229 *Chlorine Disinfectant*
"Milton" and similar chlorine disinfectants are solutions made by the electrolysis of brine; the chlorine formed during electrolysis dissolves to form a disinfectant and bleaching solution.

Set up two carbon rods (from an old cycle battery) about a centimetre apart by fixing them through a cork in a small bottle. Solder connecting wires to the brass caps on the carbons so that a current may be passed from a flash-lamp battery or (better) from a 6-volt supply. Put a fairly strong solution of common salt into the bottle so that the carbon rods dip into it.

Connect up the battery and note the smell of the chlorine (bubbles of chlorine may be seen at the positive electrode: hydrogen bubbles are given off at the other electrode). After current has been passing for a few minutes, disconnect the battery and test the solution as follows:

(i) Dip litmus paper into the liquid.
(ii) Use the liquid with a nutrient jelly (Expt. 186).
(iii) Pipette water containing Daphnia (Expt. 58) into a cavity cell and observe under the microprojector. Introduce one drop of the chlorine solution into the cell and observe again.

230 *Chlorine from Bleaching Powder*
Use a glass jam jar with a cardboard cover. Put a small teaspoonful of bleaching powder into the bottom of the jar and pour in a little dilute hydrochloric acid (or use vinegar); cover the jar and observe it as it stands undisturbed on the bench. Green chlorine gas can be seen collecting at the bottom of the jar.

Lower moistened litmus paper into the jar by means of a thread.

231 *Bleaching*
(a) Use stained white cotton cloth. Shake bleaching powder with water in a large bottle and allow the thin cream to settle overnight. Pour off the liquid into dishes. Soak the cloth in this "bleach" for ten minutes and then in very dilute hydrochloric acid for a similar time. Wash the cloth thoroughly in running water, dry and iron; compare with unbleached cloth.

(b) If you buy a second-hand book and the former owner's name is written on the fly-leaf you may remove it as follows: Paint the ink with a chlorine solution, such as Domestos, then with vinegar. When bleaching is complete, remove the liquid with blotting paper, paint with clean water

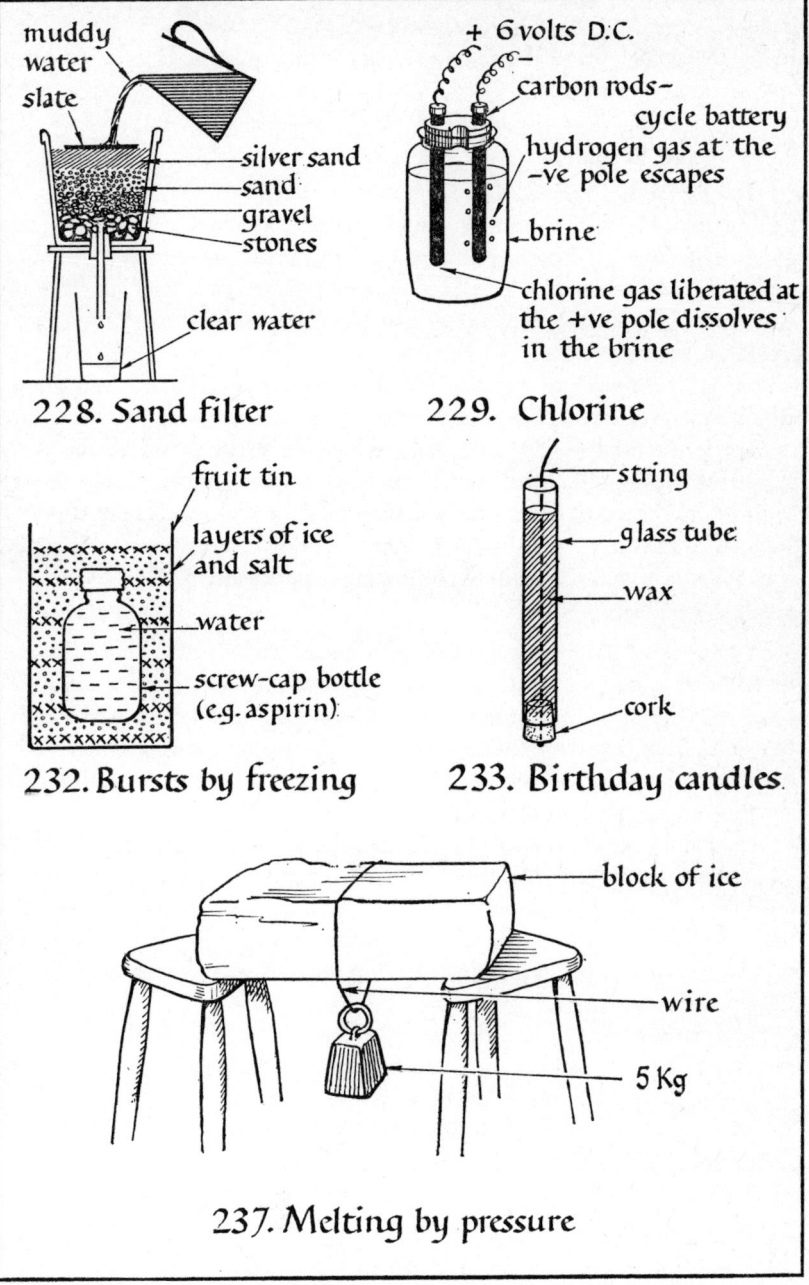

two or three times and dry off each time. A pad of paper should be placed under the fly-leaf during these operations, to protect the page beneath.

Topics: Chlorine as a disinfectant (waterworks; swimming-baths) and bleach. Other bleaching agents—sunlight, hydrogen peroxide (hair; toothpaste).

Freezing and Melting

232 *Bursts Caused by Freezing*

Fill an aspirin bottle completely with water and screw on the lid (best done under water). Immerse the bottle in a metal can and pack it round with alternate layers of crushed ice and salt. Examine after half an hour. Alternatively the bottle may be wrapped in cloth and left overnight in the freezing compartment of a refrigerator.

For a substance to expand on freezing is somewhat exceptional, although alloys have been developed for special purposes, where sharp casting is essential (e.g. type metal), which do expand and so fill every corner of the mould. Most metals contract as they solidify, and castings must be machined to exact size and shape. Coins and medals are stamped (pressed) into shape for a similar reason. The marked contraction of liquid wax as it sets is well shown in the following experiment.

233 *Birthday Candles*

Melt together 4 parts by weight of stearic acid and 1 part of paraffin wax (paraffin wax may be used alone, but the product will not be so hard). A small metal can may be used, on which a spout has been fashioned by squeezing two points on the top edge closely together. Add a pinch of lipstick pigment (Expt. 383)—e.g. Brilliant Rose—warm and stir until a clear rose-coloured liquid is obtained.

Meanwhile, cut a 7-cm length of glass tubing about 1 cm inside diameter and choose a cork to fit the tube. Thread thin string centrally through the cork (darning needle), and knot it on the wider side of the cork. Fit the cork into the tube so that the string falls through the tube. Clamp the tube vertically, cork downwards, and pour in molten wax whilst holding the string taut and central.

As the wax begins to set, considerable contraction takes place, so that the tube has to be "topped up" two or three times. Contraction away from the walls of the tube (plainly seen) enables the candle to be taken out easily. When the wax is quite cold—draw out the cork—the candle will follow. Cut off the cork, trim the other end of the candle to shape, and cut the wick to about ½ cm long.

234 *Melting-point*

Melt stearic acid, naphthalene (moth-balls), paraffin wax, cooking fat, dripping, or margarine by warming very gently in a small tin can (different class groups use different substances). Note the temperature when melting begins and when it is complete. Now allow the liquid to cool, stirring all the time, and take the temperature every minute until the substance is quite solid. Graph the results.

Single substances, like stearic acid or naphthalene, melt (and freeze) sharply; mixtures do not have such well-defined melting or freezing points. Which of the substances used are mixtures?

235 Solder
Melt together in a small spouted can (Expt. 233) approximately equal weights of scrap lead and tin. Stir with a wooden stick and run the clear liquid away from the scum into grooves in a block of wood, or into a thoroughly dry plaster of Paris mould, so as to form thin sticks of solder.

236 Freezing Mixtures
Put crushed ice into one can, and a mixture of ice and salt into another. Keep each stirred with a wooden stick and observe the temperature of each for 15 minutes. Different class groups should use different proportions of ice and salt.

As a demonstration, the teacher may use a mixture of finely crushed ice (100 parts) and crystalline calcium chloride (143 parts) to reach a much lower temperature.

237 Ice Melts Under Pressure
Support a large block of ice across two stools, pass a length of thin copper wire over the ice between the stools, and hang kilogramme weights from the end of the wire. Notice that the wire slowly sinks through the block as the ice beneath it melts, but that the block remains in one piece since the water formed escapes round the wire and at once freezes again.

238 Evaporation of Solid Substances
Moth-balls slowly get smaller in use; naphthalene dust, sprinkled on the soil as a pest control, gradually evaporates away.

(a) Clamp a test-tube upright and put a little solid ammonium chloride in the bottom. Heat gently. The solid disappears entirely from the bottom of the tube, most of it crystallizing again on the cooler upper parts.

(b) Fit a dry folded filter paper into a funnel and invert paper and funnel over a tin lid on which a little solid iodine or naphthalene (moth-ball) has been placed. Warm the lid very cautiously and examine the paper after a minute or two; it is covered with glistening crystals.

(c) Show how a mixture of common salt and ammonium chloride may be separated by sublimation. Put a gramme or so of the mixture at the bottom of a boiling tube and support a test-tube containing cold water inside the boiling tube with its base just above the mixture. Heat the mixture gently; the ammonium chloride collects on the inner tube.

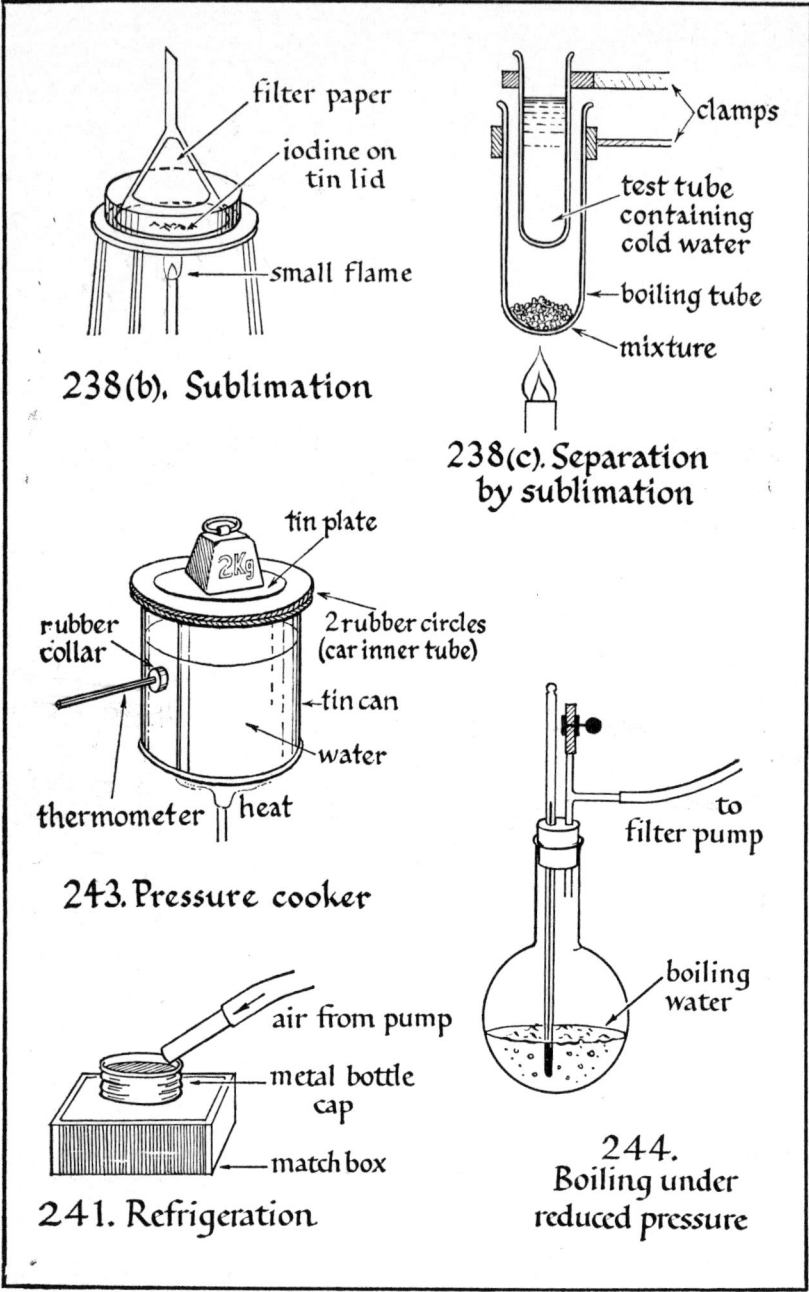

THE WATER SUPPLY TO OUR HOMES 197

Topics: Weathering action of frost on rocks and soil. Casting of metals. Solid carbon dioxide.

Evaporation and Boiling
When steam issues freely from a kettle there is a space between the end of the spout and the cloud of condensed steam. Hold a metal spoon in this space. Try heating the cloud with a Bunsen flame.

Contrast the great volume of steam from a kettle with the amount of water from which it comes.

239 *The Temperature of Boiling Water*
Boil water in a metal can and observe: (a) the steady rise in temperature to the boiling point and the constant temperature thereafter; (b) the fact that the temperature does not alter no matter how big a flame is applied to the boiling water.

Put a shield (metal can with top and bottom removed, and with gap cut for Bunsen tubing) round the flame and, starting again with about 2 cm of cold water in the metal can, note the time taken to bring the water to the boil and the time required to convert it entirely to steam.

240 *Scalds and Iced Drinks*
(a) Demonstration—Put a large can on a compression balance and pour in (say) 1000 g of water. Take the temperature of the water and then pass in steam until the weight has increased by 50 g. Again note the temperature.

Using the same weight of water to begin with, repeat the experiment, but pour in 50 g of boiling water instead of using steam. Note the final temperature. Comment on the severity of a scald by steam. Refer to Expt. 31 (c).

(b) Class experiment—Pour 100 cm^3 of water into each of two similar cans or beakers; note the temperature. To one can add a weighed lump of ice and to the other an equal weight of water in which ice has been standing. Stir until the ice has melted and note the temperature in each can.

Note: With the ablest pupils a rough calculation of the latent heat of steam may be made directly from Expt. 239 (second part) or from Expt. 240 (a).

Thus, in Expt. 239, if it takes 2 minutes to bring the water to the boil (from 20°C. to 100°C.) and 15 minutes thereafter to boil it all away, we can say:

For each gramme of water the flame supplies (100−20) = 80 calories in 2 minutes; it therefore supplies $7\frac{1}{2}$ times this amount of heat in 15 minutes, i.e. 600 calories per gramme of water changed to steam. This is the value we seek. The sources of error should be discussed, and the use of the small calorie will need explaining.

241 *Refrigeration*
Fill a small metal bottle cap with petrol ether and stand it in a drop of water on a match-box. Use a football pump and delivery tube to blow air over the ether so as to evaporate it rapidly. The cap freezes to the box.

242 *Cooling by Evaporation*
(a) Put some water into a glazed pot, and cover the pot with a cardboard lid through which a thermometer passes. Put a similar amount of water into a porous pot (as used for electric cells) or into a flower-pot (hole in base corked), and cover as before. Put each jar in the open or in a sunny spot and note the temperatures from time to time.

(b) Make a simple twisted junction of copper and Eureka resistance wire. Join the free ends of the two wires to a sensitive galvanometer. Dip the junction in ether and then expose it to the air.

Explain that metal junctions can be used as thermometers (cf. Expt. 483 (c)).

243 *A Pressure Cooker*
Drill a small hole in one side of a tin can (see Chapter 2) and insert through it a rubber tube or bung carrying a thermometer, so that the bulb is more or less centrally placed inside the can. Half fill the can with water, and cover it with a metal disc separated from the rim by two rubber discs cut from an old car inner tube. Heat over a Bunsen burner and read the temperature when steam is just lifting the lid. Repeat with weights of $\frac{1}{2}$ kg, 1 kg, 1$\frac{1}{2}$ kg ... 5 kg placed on the lid.

244 *Boiling under Reduced Pressure*
Fit a 500 cm^3 hard-glass round flask (containing a little water) with a rubber stopper carrying a thermometer (dipping into the water) and one limb of a glass T-piece. A second limb of the T-piece is fitted with a short length of rubber tubing and screw-clip; the remaining limb is connected to a filter-pump or vacuum pump (Expt. 11). Open the clip and boil the water in the flask; then remove the burner and close the clip. Use the pump to reduce the pressure on the flask. Observe that the water boils again, and that it can be kept boiling at temperatures far below 100°C.

Topics: Fixed points on a thermometer. Practical applications of the idea of latent heat. Refrigerators. Pressure cookers. Sterlization by steam (canning). Cold storage.

Chapter Thirteen
Heating Our Homes

Laboratory Assistance

"The Science Masters' Association has for its main object the improvement of the quality of science teaching in this country... no matter is more relevant to this object than the provision of proper laboratory assistance in the schools"

(From a report a quarter of a century ago)

"Work reaches its highest standards where adequate assistance is provided, and no single step which is immediately practicable could improve the standard of the teaching to a greater extent than the making of this provision more general"

(*Science in Secondary Schools*, Ministry of Education, 1960)

"... more than half the (grammar) school laboratories in the country are without laboratory assistance, skilled or unskilled"

(From a report dated 1929)

"Full-time assistance, though of widely varying degrees of skill, was provided in rather more than half of the grammar schools visited... In modern schools laboratory assistance of any kind at present appears rarely to be provided"

(*Science in Secondary Schools*, Ministry of Education, 1960)

A Gulbenkian Foundation inquiry (Kerr, *Practical Work in School Science*, 1963) again revealed the urgent need for action even in grammar schools; while the survey of secondary modern schools carried out by the Science Masters' Association in 1959 showed that laboratory assistance was provided in only 3 per cent of the 1500 schools that replied to the questionnaire. Since then it would appear that a number of local authorities have moved in this matter but the position in many schools is still poor.

Science teachers are right in their claim that not even good laboratories and a proper supply of teachers could fully compensate this problem. If it is agreed that laboratories built and equipped at great cost should be used to the fullest advantage, and that scarce teachers should employ their time most profitably, then neglect of the one condition which might best help is indefensible.

In some areas reorganization of schools and the blurring of distinctions between selective and non-selective streams may offer the opportunity for a fresh approach to the Education Committee. Teachers should know where to find authoritative support for their case. The reports of the Science Masters' Association and the Association of Women Science Teachers provide in handy form not only the arguments for laboratory assistance but also descriptions of the kinds and gradings of technicians required under various circumstances, their qualifications and training, details of their duties and working conditions and suggestions relating to salary scales and prospects. The main reports appeared in 1938, 1947 and 1955 (see *School Science Review*, Vol. 130, p. 392) and more recent information is contained in an interim report which appeared in Bulletin No. 28 (June 1968) of the Association for Science Education.

Another valuable source is the report of a Joint Working Party of Education Authorities (Oct., 1961) on the supply of laboratory technicians. It includes useful extracts from the schemes of a number of Authorities (which, however, serve to show the disparity between the treatment meted out to schools of different types). A note by one of us (K.L.) in *S.S.R.*, Vol. 151, p. 771, summarizes the case as actually presented to a local education authority and the scheme which emerged from it.

The Working Party report to which reference has been made included a powerful claim on behalf of the ordinary pupil :

"Every laboratory properly equipped for the teaching of science requires the services of a competent person other than the teacher, if the teaching potential of the room is to be fully realized. The needs of the science laboratory in the non-selective school must be recognized here ... With the growth of extended courses some of the science in these schools will be increasingly related to academic examination requirements; but whether this is the case or not it is important to appreciate that an imaginative teacher of science in a secondary modern school constantly needs special equipment or teaching machinery devised and provided for particular purposes."

The modest suggestion of the Thomson Report (1918)—"Wherever it could be afforded it would be an advantage to have a mechanic . . ."—is totally inadequate today. Fifty years after Thomson the Crowther Report called for "A realistic study of possible ancillary services of all kinds to save the teacher's scarcer skill" and listed laboratory technicians among such services.

It is, of course, absolutely necessary that salaries and prospects for laboratory technicians should be such as to attract the right kind of people (not excluding married women). The City and Guilds of London Institute has laid down syllabuses relating to their examinations for the Ordinary and Advanced Laboratory Technicians Certificate, and day release courses leading to these qualifications are available in many technical colleges. A booklet (*Laboratory Technicians and Assistants*) in the Choice of Careers series of the Central Youth Employment Executive sets out the wider prospects.

The attention of laboratory technicians should be drawn to the National Association of Educational Technicians (8, Bailey Road, Bilston, Staffs.), formed in 1967. The Handbook of the Association contains, in addition to much valuable technical data, advice on the functions, salary gradings and working conditions of laboratory technicians.

Time Allowance for Science Teaching

The claims of each and every subject in the curriculum are constantly pressed upon the Headmaster. Conscious as he must be of the urgent need to put English at the centre of the timetable, to give adequate time to Mathematics, to include a range of cultural and practical subjects, and not to forget physical education, he may well ask, "What is the minimum time that I can allocate to Science?"

The argument for the teaching of Science to all pupils today is a very strong one; yet still there are schools, and especially girls' schools, where only two periods a week (or even less) are given to the subject, a time allotment which mocks any attempt to treat it effectively. Even in 1931 the Board of Education memorandum *Science in Senior Schools* observed that:

"The time available for Science is very short . . . three lesson periods a week in such a course is little enough to ask . . . it is strongly urged that this should be regarded as the minimum weekly allowance for Science."

Since that time the conviction has grown that only if boys and girls are given opportunities to handle experimental work themselves will most of them gain any real understanding of the subject; the need for an allowance of time which will permit such an approach is, therefore, greater than ever. Let us consider what is likely to happen on a two-period-a-week timetable. Single periods for practical work are entirely uneconomic: the proportion of the lesson spent in preparing apparatus and in clearing it away is far too high. Hence our two periods are, at best, two consecutive periods, say of 35 minutes each. Of the 70 minutes, at least 10 must be spent in starting and in finishing; seldom will there be a full hour for the actual business of experimenting and recording results. During this time, if any considerable progress through a scheme of work is to be made, it might be hoped that class groups could work their way through three or four short exercises, or through two longer ones. There will scarcely be time for discussion, summary, or for consideration of next week's work. What will happen in practice is that next week's lesson will be spent in this necessary follow-up and preparation, and in consolidation—perhaps with incidental demonstration by the teacher. All this presupposes a very keen and able teacher, some time allocated to him for trying out and setting up apparatus, and none of the hundred-and-one interruptions which so often occur. At the very best, therefore, practical work and progress will fit into fortnightly stages—of which there are barely twenty in the school year! Small hope, indeed, of our future citizens receiving anything but a mere smattering of a few limited fields of science.

Three periods per week is thus the absolute minimum for any class, but four is undoubtedly desirable. For with four periods it is possible to arrange practical work for the class every week, with discussion, demonstration, revision and preparation properly dovetailed in. Beyond the first two years of a five-year course these minima will be inappropriate for boys and girls proceeding to C.S.E. examinations in Science.

It is, of course, an essential qualification that the science specialist should be given some free periods in which to prepare for practical work. He will in any case have to give much time to his job in out-of-school hours. The situation in which a master must enter a laboratory without adequate practical preparation is unpardonable; an experiment which goes wrong, or one which cannot be undertaken but which might have been, means that valuable time is lost, the teacher feels frustrated and the resources of the laboratory are wasted.

Fire in the Home

245 *How to Lay a Fire*
Where coal fires are still in use, pupils should be asked to lay and light a fire at home, and to report their experience.

Sweep the back and sides of the fireplace (note the heavy collection of soot after one day) and rake through the cinders in the grate so that ash and soot fall through; remove them from beneath the grate with a shovel. Pile the cinders to the back of the grate and put a torn and crumpled half-sheet of newspaper in front of them. Arrange over it a "wigwam" of several dry sticks and pile around the wigwam several lumps of coal or smokeless fuel, building smaller pieces above until only the top of the wigwam is showing. Sweep and wash the hearth.

246 *Temperatures at which Substances take Fire*
Discussions of the need to use paper, wood and coal in making a fire leads to the following experiments:

(a) Heat a wooden rod in a candle flame; it is unlikely to take fire. Cut a thin splint from the rod; this can easily be ignited. Note that paper is a very thin sheet of similar material.

(b) (Demonstration) Arrange *small* pieces of phosphorus, sulphur, wood and charcoal in a circle on a tin lid. Heat the lid centrally, using a small flame. The class should be warned of the extreme danger of handling phosphorus.

(c) (Demonstration) Stuff a tuft of asbestos wool loosely into the mouth of a test-tube and pour on 1 or 2 cm^3 of ether (care!). Heat one end of a

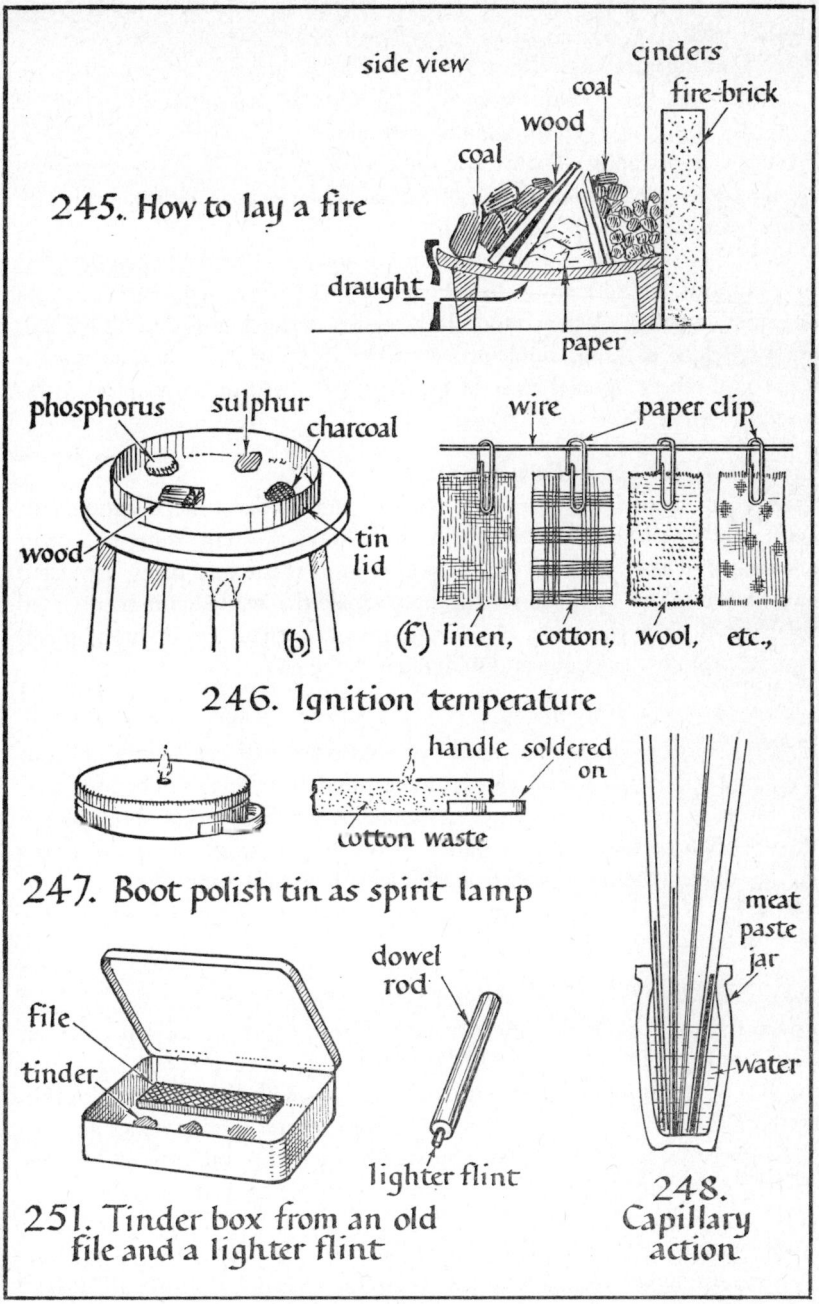

245. How to lay a fire

246. Ignition temperature

247. Boot polish tin as spirit lamp

251. Tinder box from an old file and a lighter flint

248. Capillary action

glass rod to softening point and hold it very close to, but not touching, the wool. The ether vapour takes fire. Repeat using petrol, lighter fuel, alcohol, etc.

(d) Use the same apparatus again, but add paraffin and carbon tetrachloride to the list of liquids used. This time use a lighted taper instead of the hot rod, and touch the wool if necessary.

(e) (Demonstration) Thrust a lighted splint of wood quickly into a few cubic centimetres of machine oil in a small dish. Repeat with paraffin and with petrol. Only the petrol takes fire.

(f) Stretch a length of wire horizontally 50 cm above the bench between two supports. Hang from it, using paper clips as pegs, 5-cm × 2-cm strips of paper, woollen cloth, cotton cloth, calico, flannel, muslin, silk, linen, rayon, nylon, sacking, linoleum, etc. Try lighting each in turn with a taper and report upon (i) ease of ignition, (ii) speed of burning when ignited.

247 *Methylated Spirits Burner*

Emery part of the side of a shoe polish tin and solder a metal handle (cut from another tin) on to the bright surface. Make a ½-cm diameter hole in the centre of the lid, stuff the tin with cotton waste and bring a twisted end of the waste up through the hole. Soak the waste with methylated spirits and light the wick. As a refinement, a small (1-cm high) metal chimney may be fashioned and soldered into the hole.

248 *Wick Action (Capillarity)*

Pupils may draw fine glass capillary tubes from delivery tubing or from test-tubes by the method of Expt. 7. Exceedingly fine tubes can be produced in this way, and the long lengths should be cut into pieces about 20 cm long. Support several tubes of different bores in a jar of coloured water— e.g. by fixing them on a card with sticky tape and supporting the card vertically. Notice that the liquid rises to a very considerable height in the finest tubes. (See also Exp. 501.)

249 *(DEMONSTRATION ONLY) Matches*

Powder BY ITSELF in a clean mortar about 2 g of potassium chlorate. Shake with it (DO NOT GRIND) in a small test-tube about 1 g of red antimony trisulphide. Tip the mixture into a small dish, add a little thin gum, and stir to a paste. Cut the heads from several used matches and dip the sticks to a depth of half an inch into melted paraffin-wax. Dip the paraffined heads into the prepared paste and then hang the matches, head downwards, in a warm place for a day.

Mix together equal weights of red phosphorus and silver sand and make into a paste with gum. Spread this on the plain side of an old match-box and set to dry (e.g. over the radiator).

HEATING OUR HOMES 205

See that the matches and striking surface are absolutely dry before testing them. Use the demonstration to emphasize the danger of playing with matches.

250 *(DEMONSTRATION ONLY) Petrol Fire*
Put about 25 cm^3 of petrol into a small metal pie-dish which stands on a large metal tray. Remove the bottle of petrol. Light the petrol in the dish and pour water gently on to it from a kettle. The petrol floats and burns, if anything more fiercely.

Repeat, using fresh petrol, but use pyrene (carbon tetrachloride) instead of water.

For Fire Precautions refer to Chapter 2 (Expts. 30, 42 and 44). A visit to the local fire station and contact with the chief officer there is very helpful. Actual extinguishers should be examined.

251 *Early Ways of Making Fire*
Refer to the heat generated by rubbing the hands together on a cold day. Try rubbing a brass button vigorously on the coat sleeve. Discuss ways in which early man made fire, emphasizing the enormous problem presented to him. Examine the parts of a modern petrol lighter.

Make a tinder box in the following way: Put a short piece of old, fairly smooth, metal file into a small tobacco tin (hinged lid) and add a few scraps of well-scorched linen. Drill the end of a short length of thin dowel rod and fit a lighter-flint tightly into the hole. Using the rod as a handle, strike the flint across the file against the tinder and blow gently when the tinder begins to smoulder. Thin splints of wood tipped with sulphur may be lit from the tinder.

Topics: The construction and form of modern fireplaces: air inlets, fireclay and brick, shape, need for poking. Safety precautions at home against fire, especially with small children (matches, fireguard); what to do if fire breaks out. Insurance against fire.

Coal Gas

An ordinary gas-ring and the burners of a gas-stove should be examined, with special attention to control of the air supply and the effect of varying the amount of air admitted.

252 *Coal-gas Flame*
Take a Bunsen burner to pieces, noting the upright chimney, the gas-inlet tube ending in a narrow jet, and the adjustable air-inlet hole.

Light the gas, close the air-hole, and notice the two main parts of the flame. Put a wood splint or match-stick horizontally across the flame (so as to cut both parts) for a second or so; it is evident that there is unburnt gas in the centre part. Confirm this by pushing the end of a 3-mm bore glass tube into the centre of the flame and lighting the gas which emerges at the other end of the tube. Hold a fragment of white porcelain in the yellow outer part of the flame and notice that soot is deposited. Would such a flame be acceptable in the kitchen?

Open the air-hole wide and repeat the tests.

253 *Model Bunsen Burner*

Use as a chimney a glass tube about 50 cm long and 2 cm diameter. If the glass at the top end is covered inside and out with asbestos paper (soaked in water-glass, moulded on to the glass and dried) the tube is much less likely to crack, and it is worthwhile to keep a number of prepared tubes in store. Clamp the chimney upright and lead gas in at the bottom via a narrow glass tube around which air can enter. Turn on the gas and after a second or two light it at the top of the chimney. Slowly turn down the gas (do not turn it out) until the flame "strikes back" to the jet at the bottom of the chimney. Close the air inlet around the jet with a rag and notice that the flame reappears at the top of the chimney.

Find a piece of rod or tube which will just fit loosely into the chimney. Mould over one end of it a cap of fine-mesh copper gauze. Remove the cap and push it into the top of the chimney. The burner will no longer strike back. Push the gauze cap half-way down the chimney; when the burner is lit and the gas lowered, the flame strikes back only as far as the gauze, being extinguished there. A continuous series of explosion waves can be arranged by fitting a pilot flame at the top of the chimney.

Most gas-fires have a similar device to ensure that, if the flame strikes back, it does not continue to burn at the inlet jet. The very poisonous nature of coal gas and of incompletely burned gas should be enlarged upon.

254 *Danger of Gas Explosion*

(a) One-quarter fill a medicine bottle with coal gas by displacement of water; cork the bottle loosely and let water trickle out past the cork so that air takes its place. Wrap the bottle in a thick duster, remove the cork, and apply a flame. A greater proportion of gas gives a feebler explosion.
(b) Use a syrup tin: with a nail make a small hole in the press-in lid and a larger (1-cm diameter) hole in the base. Stand the tin on two wood blocks, or on a tripod, pass in gas via a tube fitting very loosely into the bottom hole, wait for 10 seconds or so, and then light the gas issuing from the small hole in the lid. Now turn off the gas. Air enters round the gas inlet tube and in a minute or so the flame strikes back with a loud explosion, blowing the lid sky-high.

255 *How Gas is Made from Coal*

A visit to the gas-works should be arranged; very careful preparation and

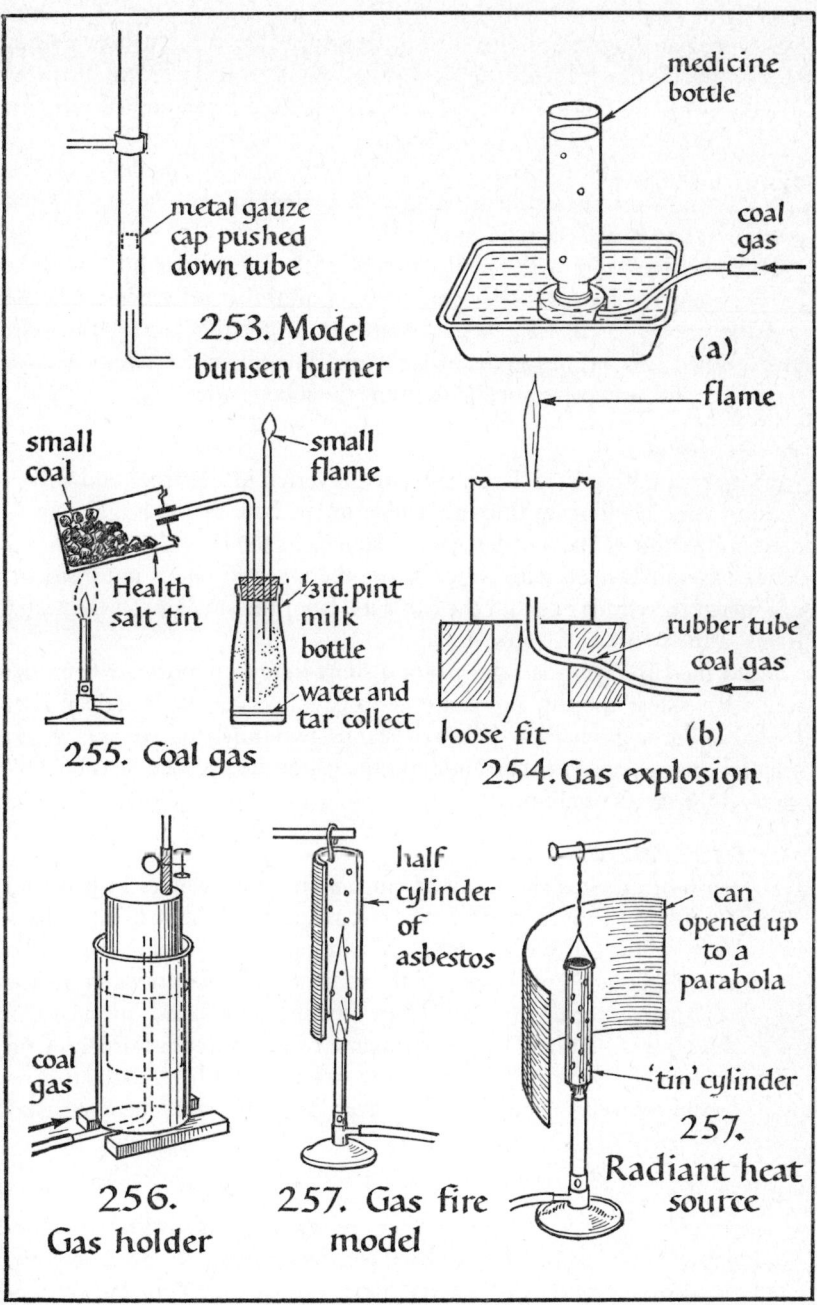

253. Model bunsen burner
254. Gas explosion
255. Coal gas
256. Gas holder
257. Gas fire model
257. Radiant heat source

briefing is essential. The literature obtainable from large gas undertakings is useful.

Use a small metal can with a press-in lid (health salts tin) as a retort. Make a hole in the lid with a large nail and widen it to say, 1 cm diameter with a file-tang. Fix into the hole, by means of a wrapping of asbestos paper, a glass delivery tube leading to a stoppered glass bottle from which leads an upright exit tube and jet. A better seal between the delivery tube and retort can be effected if the asbestos is soaked in water-glass solution, pressed tightly round the tube and dried.

Half fill the retort with small chips of coal, put on the lid, and heat fairly strongly. Observe the tar and watery liquid that collect in the bottle and the smoky gas that escapes from the jet. Light this gas after a short time. When heating has gone on for some time allow the retort to cool, remove the lid, and prize out and examine the solid residue.

256 *Gas Holder*
Arrange two tall cans (cf. Expt. 201), one inverted in the other and with a delivery tube leading up through a hole in the base of the larger can almost to the top of the smaller one, as shown in the diagram. The larger can is two-thirds filled with water before the inverted one is put inside it, and when the clip is open on the exit tube from the smaller can the water levels in the two are of course equal.

With the clip open, pass gas in for a short time to remove air from the inner can. Close the clip and continue to pass in gas. The inner can rises steadily, like a gas-holder. When it stands two-thirds out of the water, turn off the gas, open the clip and light the gas at the jet. The "gas-holder" sinks as the gas is used up.

257 *Gas Fire Model*
Cut a strip of asbestos sheet, say 15 cm x 4 cm, punch holes in it with a ½-cm cork-borer so as to give a lattice effect, and bend the strip into a half-cylinder by wetting it with water-glass solution and moulding it round a wooden rod about 3 cm diameter; the strip may be separated from the wood by paper, held in position by string, and dried in a warm place. Hang this "radiant" above the flame from a Bunsen burner. A tin cylinder punched with nail holes also works well, with or without a reflector. Alternatively again, a "tree" from a gas-fire may be used, suspended by iron wire.

258 *The Gas Bill*
Cards showing the dials of a gas-meter are sometimes delivered to householders; similar cards may be prepared for class practice in meter reading. Large model dials, with moveable pointers, may be made for class demonstration. In all cases pupils should be asked to copy on to a "dial blank"

the positions of the pointers of their own meter at home and to write alongside the meter reading in figures—not forgetting the "hundreds".

Refer back to Expts. 165 and 166, and discuss why we no longer pay for gas by the cubic foot. Study actual gas bills and make out duplicates; fill in the home readings for two successive weeks and complete the bill so as to show the cost of the week's gas. It will be necessary to consider items such as the meter rent and the nature of the tariff (see back of gas bill).

Topics: Precautions with gas appliances at home; deadly nature of gas; carbon monoxide formation in coke stoves. Industrial uses of gasworks products—a display chart may be prepared (with samples) to show the commoner derivatives, and it should make clear whether these are actually present in the tar, etc. or are prepared later by chemical processes. Benzene, carbolic acid, naphthalene, etc. are examples of substances actually present; aspirin, dyes, photographic chemicals, sulphate of ammonia, etc. are chemical derivatives. A similar chart to show the products of petroleum distillation will include petrol, paraffin oil, lubricating and heavy soils, Vaseline, paraffin wax, etc. Tar distillation in progress may be seen at the gas-works laboratory. Reference should be made to the origin of coal and petroleum.

North Sea gas: origin and nature; how obtained and distributed.

Convection, Conduction, Insulation

259 (a) *Convection Currents in a Liquid*
Fill a flat-bottomed flask as far as the base of the neck with water coloured with phenolphthalein; the solution should be just acid. Introduce a small pellet of caustic soda to the bottom of the flask via a glass tube; then remove the tube (and the liquid in it) carefully, having closed the top with a finger. The caustic soda dissolves with evolution of heat and a thin red column of liquid ascends in the flask, cools and falls as red streamers.

To repeat the experiment, simply re-acidify with a few drops of dilute acid. The currents are seen better if the liquid is illuminated from a small light source.

259 (b) *Convection Currents in Benzene*
(DEMONSTRATION ONLY) Almost fill a boiling tube with benzene and stir in a trace of fine aluminium powder (or a few drops of aluminium paint). Suspend the tube in a clamp and allow the particles to come to rest. Then touch the tube with a warm finger, or bring any warm body near (NOT a flame): convection currents are plainly visible.

259 (c) *Model Hot-water System*
Drill two 3-mm diameter holes in the base of a tin can and two similar

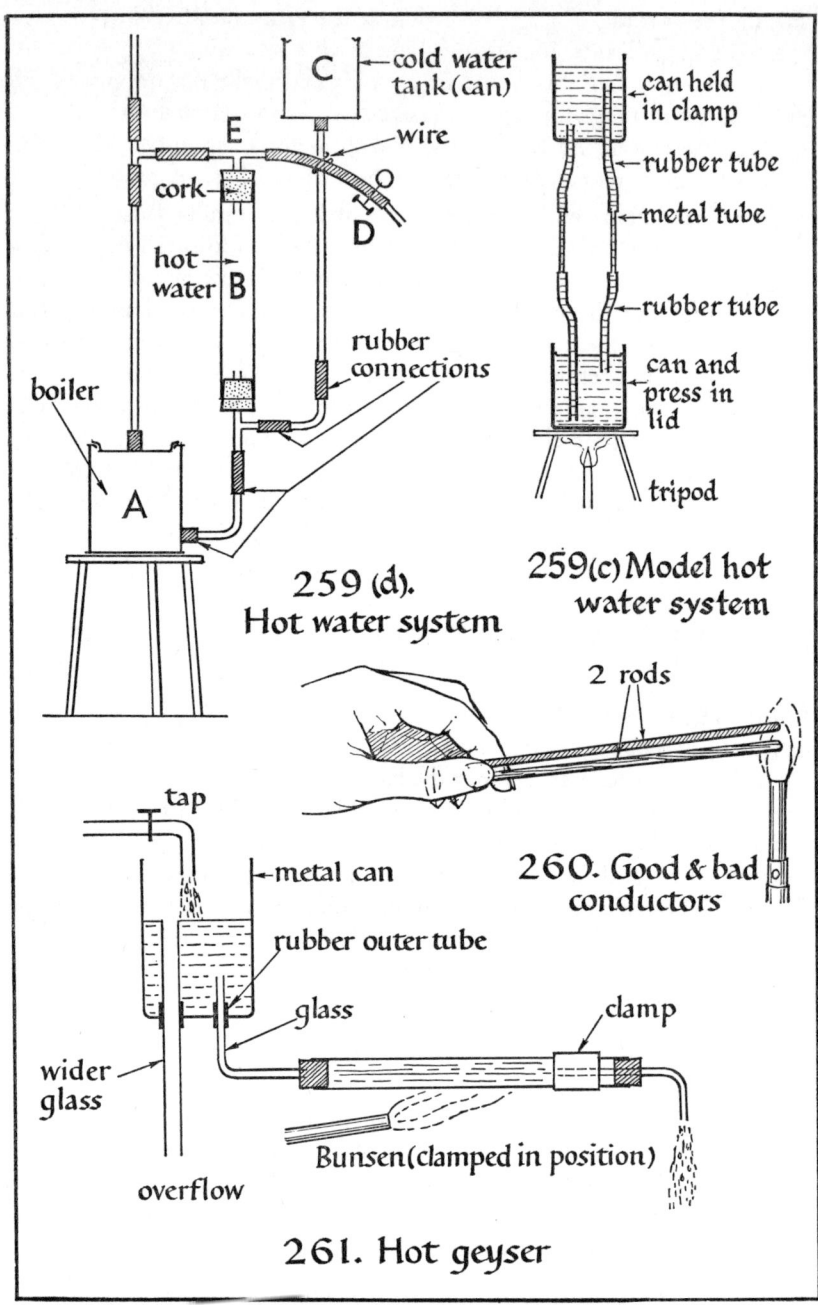

holes in the press-in lid of a second can. Join the cans by lengths of 3-mm black rubber tubing and short pieces of copper tubing arranged as shown in the diagram: note especially the position of the ends of the rubber tubes in the cans. For the method of fitting the tubes see Expt. 158 (b).

Remove the lid from the lower can, completely immerse the apparatus in water in a large sink, and refit the lid when the cans and tubes are full of water. Set the model up as indicated after pouring away just a little water from the upper can.

Gradually heat the water in the "boiler". Feel the metal connecting tubes with your fingers from time to time, and use a thermometer to take the temperature of the water at the top and bottom of the "storage tank".

259 (d) *Another Model Hot-water System*

The hot tank is a glass tube, say 20 cm × 3 cm. The cold tank is a small metal can with a rubber tube leading through a hole punched in the base. Extension of the system shown in the diagram to include upstairs and downstairs taps may be made as desired. Heating, by means of a Bunsen burner or spirit lamp, should be very gentle.

Put a few small permanganate of potash crystals into the boiler (metal can), replace the lid, and open clip D. Now steadily fill the system with cold water by running water into tank C. The water in the boiler A will become coloured, but that in the hot tank B will remain colourless. Any air bubbles which may become trapped (e.g. at E) should be cleared by tilting the apparatus before closing tap D. The T-tubes simplify construction.

Heat gently. Observe the circulation as shown by the coloured water. Draw off hot water from D.

260 *Good and Bad Conductors of Heat*

Refer to Expt. 155 (reason for lagging hot tank). Recall the use of wooden handles on metal tools; of straw and sacking on exposed water-pipes; of blankets, kettle-holders and tea cosies; of fur, feathers and clothes; of metals for boilers, pans, etc.

Use rods of aluminium, iron, copper, glass, wood, etc., each (say) 3 mm diameter. They should be given out in pairs to class groups or individuals so that every possible combination is covered (e.g. wood/iron; iron/copper; copper/wood). Hold the two rods in one hand and with one end of each in the same flame, so that both receive equal heating. After a moment or two cautiously run a finger along each rod towards the flame. Repeat once or twice, and so decide which material is the better conductor of heat. The class results may be collated, and a list showing the order of conductivity deduced. Which materials would be called heat insulators?

In this experiment softening of the glass rods and burning of the wooden rods need not interfere with the results.

261 *Hot-water Geyser*
The hard-glass heating tube through which the water runs is about 20 cm long × 2 cm diameter. Metal tubes may be tried also. The Bunsen burner is clamped beneath the tube in a sloping position and the temperature of the issuing water is measured after it has become steady. The device shown in the diagram may be used to get a constant rate of flow. A faster flow is secured by raising the height of the overflow tube.

262 *Insulating Powers of Building Materials*
Prepare heat-sensitive paper by soaking duplicating paper in a solution made up from the following formula:

Cobalt chloride, 25 g; calcium chloride, 25 g; water, ½ litre.

The paper is pale pink when dry and cold; on warming, it turns blue.

Cut 15-cm squares of wall-boarding, three-ply wood, sheet metal, asbestos, etc. and paste heat-sensitive paper on one side of each. When the paste is quite dry, lean the sheets against an electric lamp as shown in the diagram. Switch on the lamp and observe any changes in the paper.

263 *Cracking of Cooking Vessels by Heat*
(DEMONSTRATION ONLY) See also Expt. 16 (b).

Use a glass jam jar and a resistance glass beaker for each part of the demonstration.

(a) Pour boiling water into each vessel in turn (work with the vessels in a stone trough or metal bowl).

(b) Stand both vessels in a pan of cold water and bring the water to the boil. The vessels should stand on cloth to prevent bumping. Now pour boiling water into each vessel.

(c) Stand both vessels in ice in a trough or bowl. When they have been there for some time, pour in boiling water.

264 *Davy Lamp*
An actual lamp should be available for inspection. The well-known introductory experiments may also be made:

(a) (i) Coil one end of thick copper wire to form a helix. Bring this down over the flame of a candle—the flame is extinguished. (ii) Hold a square of copper gauze (e.g. by a spring clothes-peg) over a Bunsen burner, turn on the gas and apply a flame below or above the gauze—the flame does not immediately pass through the gauze.

(b) Make a cylinder of fine mesh copper gauze—say 15 cm long × 3 cm diameter—by wrapping the gauze round a wooden cylinder of these dimensions. Weave ends of wire into the gauze to join edges together; similarly, weave on a gauze cap at one end. Saw a 2-cm thick slice from the wooden former, stick a lighted candle-end on to it, and push the slice into the open end of the cylinder so that the candle is inside the cylinder.

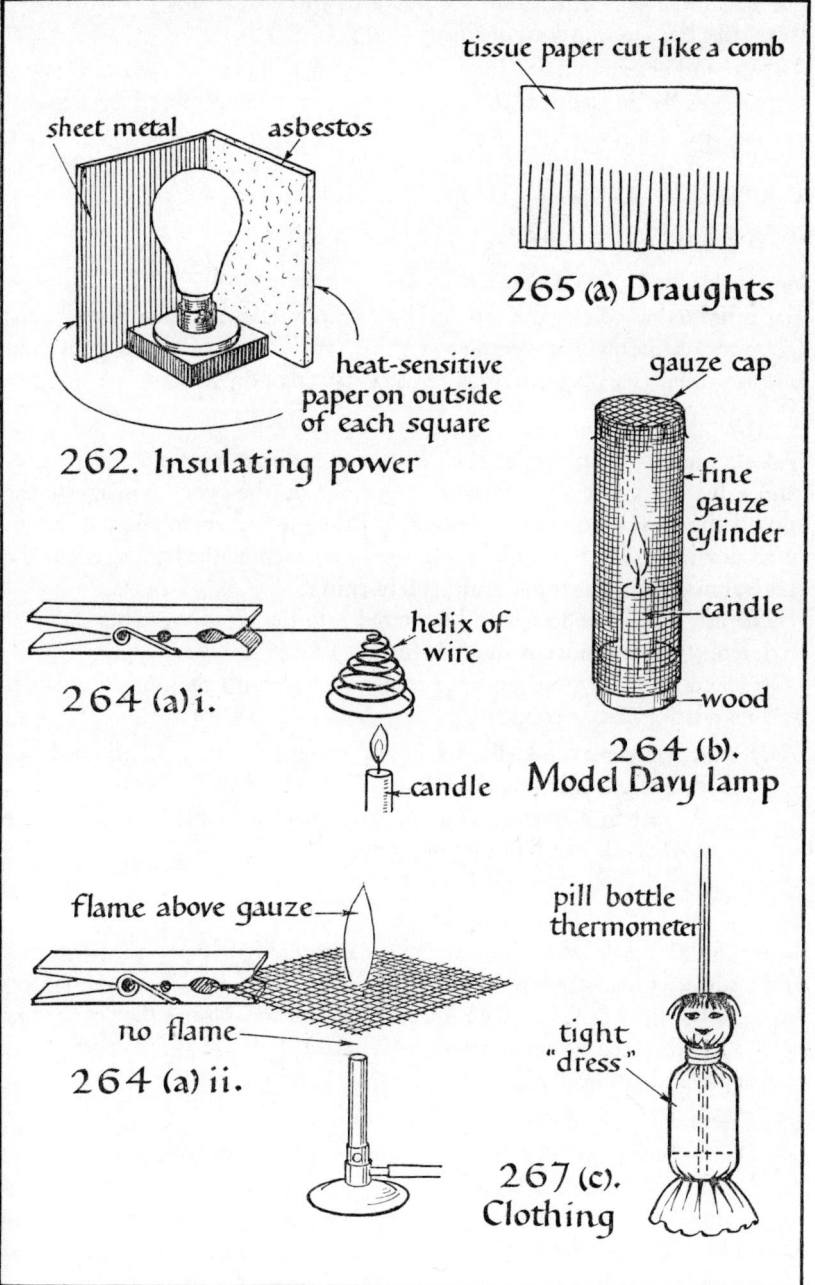

Play coal-gas from a Bunsen burner on to the outside of the gauze; the gas which passes through burns inside the cylinder, but the gas jet outside the gauze does not ignite.

Topics: Other examples of the use of good or bad conductors—e.g. cavity walls, incubators, loss of efficiency in boilers caused by deposits of "fur".

Ventilation of our Homes

Refer to Expt. 24 (heated air rises; action of a chimney).

265 (a) *Draughts in a Room*
Use a lighted candle at the top and bottom of a slightly open door, at the laboratory windows, at ventilation grids, etc. Pieces of tissue paper cut into streamers (see diagram) may be used instead of the flame.

265 (b) *Convection in Air*
Take a piece of tissue paper such as that in which oranges are wrapped. Roll a piece into a cylinder, stand it upright on the bench and ignite the top all the way round. In a reasonably draught-free room the paper will burn down steadily to within a fraction of an inch of the bench, when the last fragment will rise into the air, still burning.

The ash may be collected and scattered into the air above a hot radiator to demonstrate the movement of air there.

Refer to Expt. 197, 198 and 242 in connection with the humidity of air and its relation to our comfort.

Topics: Advantages and disadvantages of a coal fire. Land and sea breezes. Major wind systems of the the world. Ocean currents. A visit to a modern cinema or factory may enable pupils to see how an air-conditioning plant operates.

Radiant Heat

Refer to the way in which the sun's heat is immediately cut off as we pass from sunlight into shadow; there is a similar experience if we are sitting before a hot fire and interpose a sheet of newspaper. Notice that in neither case is the intervening air heated nearly as much as the (solid) body upon which the radiant heat falls.

266 *Characteristics of Radiant Heat*
(a) Use a bowl-type electric fire as a source of radiant heat (or use the radiant of Expt. 257). Hold a thermometer at a distance of about 15 cm in front of the hot element; note the rise in temperature. Now screen the thermometer by interposing a sheet of card; the temperature registered falls at once, showing that the air has not been greatly heated.

Show that radiant heat travels in straight lines by holding one thermometer just within the shadow of the card and one just outside it. The pill-bottle thermometer of Expt. 25 is suitable.

(b) Hold a hand 2–3 cm from a cold electric bulb; then switch on the current. Heat is felt immediately. At once clasp the bulb: it still feels cold. The evidence excludes transfer of heat by either conduction or convection.

267 *Absorbing Power of Various Surfaces*

(a) Use similar metal cans: those used for storing film-strips are admirable. Polish the outside of one very brightly and treat the others with whitewash, white enamel paint, soot (lampblack dissolved in bleached shellac), black enamel, etc. Make a small hole in the lid of each tin and insert a thermometer. Pour the same volume of cold water into each tin (so that each is almost full). Stand the tins in a circle with a heating element at the centre; the element may be from a bowl electric fire, or it may be a Bunsen flame playing on a gas-fire radiant. Observe the thermometers every 5 minutes. List the surfaces in order of absorbing power.

(b) Use an electric bowl fire as a radiant. In front of it mount a 30-cm square sheet of 6-mm thick asbestos board, at 3 cm distance and covered with thin aluminium sheet on the side facing the heater. A 2-cm diameter hole drilled through the centre of the asbestos shield allows radiation to escape in a controlled beam.

Let each pupil in turn present the back of his hand near to the hole for not more than, say, 5 seconds. Next lay a sheet of aluminium leaf on the moistened skin (i.e. licked), the hand being clenched and only slightly relaxed once the foil is in position. Again the hand is presented at the hole. Finally, paint the centre of the foil (still in position on the hand) with a thick mixture of soot and methylated spirit (using a soft brush), let the paint dry and test yet again before the radiator. How long now is it before the heat becomes uncomfortable?

(Paint and foil are best swept from the hand afterwards by water from a fast flowing tap.)

(c) Make several similar air thermometers (Expt. 25) and dress each in a different fabric (vary the material and the colour). Expose to a 100-watt lamp and compare the results. The experiment can suggest discussion on the effects of clothing.

268 *Radiating Power of Various Surfaces*

Use the cans of Expt. 267 (a). Into each pour the same quantity of boiling water, stand them well apart and observe temperatures every 5 minutes.

269 *Action of a Greenhouse*

Bury the top end of a thermometer downwards in the garden soil and cover the projecting bulb with a jam jar (sunny day). Arrange a second thermometer similarly just outside the jar. Put up a notice: "Experiment in progress." Read the thermometers with the aid of a lens after an hour or two in the sun.

270 *Uses of Phototransistors*
See *Practical Science for Secondary Schools*, Book Three, Chap. XVIII, and Book Four, pp. 106-9. Transistors are very sensitive to infra-red radiation. Transistors made earlier than 1962 (Mullard OC70, OC71, OC72) are cheap and make good detectors if the black paint is removed so as to expose the glass bulb. Transistors of more recent date may be filled with opaque material and special phototransistors (e.g. Mullard OCP71) must be used. There are a number of other more modern phototransistors which may be used, e.g. BPX25, but the makers' instructions as to polarity and mounting position must be carefully observed. Thus the BPX25 is a silicon phototransistor, with the collector connected to the *positive* battery terminal, and it is mounted in a horizontal position. This transistor is also sensitive to the visible spectrum but if used with a deep blue filter the response is mainly in the infra-red region.

Mount the transistor 8 cm high on a lens stand, bending it forward (i.e. towards the source of radiation) at about 30° to the vertical and so that the tip lies on the optical axis, 8 cm above bench level. A single dry cell is held to the stand between two metal (tin-plate) strips, as indicated in the diagram, the negative strip being shorter so that it will not make a connection if the cell is inserted wrongly: reversal of the cell connections will damage the transistor. Connect a 0-15 milliammeter in circuit with the cell and transistor.

(a) Use the transistor to investigate the region round a source such as an electric lamp or fire.

(b) Place a headlamp bulb two or three metres in front of the transistor (if the lamp is too close, the transistor will overheat) and focus the rays on to the transistor tip by means of a convex lens held in a stand a few centimetres away. Stand a medicine bottle in the path of the rays and note the meter reading when the bottle is (i) empty, (ii) filled with water, (iii) filled with acidified ferrous sulphate solution.

(c) Replace the medicine bottle of the previous experiment by two light filters—one red and one blue—so that the visible beam is absorbed. What does the meter reading tell you?

(d) Set up a spectrum apparatus (Fig. 375) but replace the screen by the phototransistor unit. Use a more sensitive meter (0-1 mA). Move the transistor through the spectrum from the blue to the red end and then beyond the visible red. Where is the meter reading highest?

(e) If a portion of the heat filter of a miniature projector is available, insert it in the path of the rays. The meter reading will be much reduced since the special glass employed absorbs most of the infra-red.

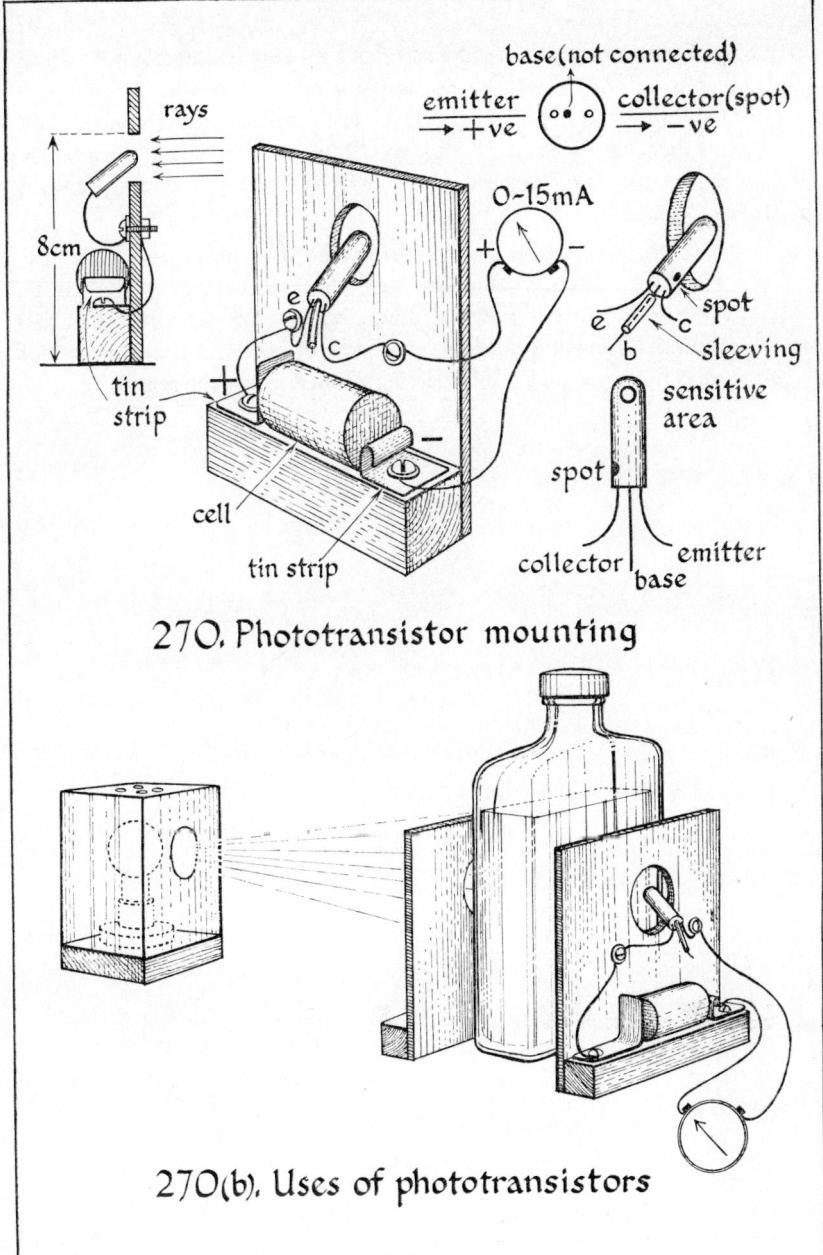

270. Phototransistor mounting

270(b). Uses of phototransistors

(Ordinary glass transmits infra-red radiation lying just outside the visible red, though it absorbs all the very wide band of infra-red of still longer wave-length).

(f) *Inverse Square law*: Use the standard 24-watt headlamp bulb as an infra-red source. The OCP71 phototransistor with a $1\frac{1}{2}$-volt cell will give suitable readings on a 0–15 milliammeter for distances up to about 30 cm. No lens is needed. Work out the values of the product: current × (distance)^2; or plot $1/s^2$ against meter readings. Results should confirm the inverse square law.

Topics: Use of reflector on electric fires. The Thermos flask. How the Earth is heated; reason for low temperatures at high altitudes. Summary study of how the school boiler heats the air in the classrooms. Discussion of the relative advantages and disadvantages of solid fuel, gas, oil and electric central heating in the home.

Chapter Fourteen
Electricity in the Home

Electricity in the Science Syllabus

The fact that so many electrical appliances are used at home is a good reason for including electricity in our Science schemes at school. But whilst all of us switch on lights, fires, radio and television without a thought until something goes wrong, it is usually the housewife who is the immediate sufferer when faults occur: her cooking, cleaning or ironing is interrupted, the water fails to heat, or the sewing-machine comes to a standstill. Here is a curious paradox: girls, more especially of course in single-sex schools, generally get far less opportunity than boys to study the elements of electricity and women teachers often appear very uncertain of their ability to handle even the simplest electrical apparatus. Men teachers, on the other hand, sometimes go to the other extreme and their enthusiasm for electrical gadgets of all kinds may lead them to bias the curriculum too much in that direction. We may recognize that few girls have boys' curiosity about mechanical contrivances, and that a teacher, man or woman, will probably teach best along the line of his or her interests, and yet still remember that we have a duty towards tomorrow's citizens which cannot be discharged with too narrow a conception of the syllabus.

Electricity, with magnetism, offers so many possibilities for school work that careful selection will be necessary. One is almost embarrassed by the multifarious applications even within one's own home. The sequence set out in the present chapter is only one of many that might be chosen, and indeed an alternative scheme is indicated in the authors' *Practical Science for Secondary Schools*. But however we tackle things it will probably be fairly generally agreed that a beginning might be made through the investigation of simple circuits by the pupils themselves, so that boys and girls become familiar with things such as cells and batteries, conductors and insulators, switches, meters, lamps and similar commonplace components, and with the various ways in which they are arranged for particular purposes. In the pages which follow materials are used of a kind which many youngsters will be able to find in their own homes and it is to be hoped that they will be encouraged to experiment for themselves out of school, using safe low-voltage sources. The simple circuit board of Expt. 272 is typical, but teachers may find a more permanent board useful and we refer them to the A.S.E. book *Teaching Science at the Secondary Stage* (Murray) for a description of a circuit board mounted on peg-board. Components such as lamps, switches, resistances and meters are mounted separately, with 4 mm plugs beneath spaced to match the spacing of sockets on the baseboard. A note in A.S.E. Bulletin No. 12, p. 19, gives information about sources of components for such work.

A ready source of low voltage is absolutely essential. The mains supply should be used ONLY by the teacher, and it is an important part of his work to demonstrate its dangers and the precautions which must always be taken with mains current. There is no doubt that a large-capacity accumulator bank is best if steady currents are required even though several groups of pupils may be tapping off from the system at one time; and details of such a system are to be found in the *Planning and Equipment of School Science Blocks*, by Sir Graham Savage (Murray, 1964). However, where space is limited, where laboratory assistance is not forthcoming and where teachers may lack something in practical experience themselves, it may well be that a central transformer-rectifier unit, wired to bench points, may be preferred. With such an arrangement, however, voltage fluctuations will occur as the demands of the benches vary and individual transformer-rectifier units, portable and safe to use, are more satisfactory in this respect. A few small accumulators should in any case be available in the laboratory and pupils should be taught how to maintain them in good condition. Torch batteries, useful in emergency, may prove rather expensive for general use, although in fact torch bulbs consume less than half an ampere.

A chapter on radio and transistors appears in the present edition of this book. It is suggested that the making of apparatus such as transformers, telephones and complicated radio sets is best undertaken out of school, perhaps in a Science Club; otherwise other important parts of a balanced science syllabus are likely to get pushed aside. Nevertheless, it is in making models which really work that the greatest satisfaction accrues and no part of the syllabus can be more productive in this respect than the electricity sections. Today, transistor devices, suitably arranged and mounted, might well be used as part of the course (see Chap. 26).

The generation, distribution and cost of electrical power is a matter of prime interest, and will lead us to a consideration of dynamos, transformers and motors as well as to an examination of the household electricity bill. Resistance and Ohm's Law are easily overstressed; some qualitative ideas are needed in connection with cables and heaters, and the practical use of resistances and shunts with voltmeters and ammeters can get some of our brighter pupils thinking, but beyond this we need not go. A working knowledge of the power equation (watts = volts × amperes) is more valuable, whether in connection with a safe load for household circuits or for the school stage-lighting set. With selected pupils we may introduce Joule's equivalent—a fundamental idea—provided that we link it with a well understood application (such as the immersion heater) and keep computation simple.

Group work in Science

It is often convenient to group experiments. Four different experiments dealing with the same theme are usually sufficient, and will serve for a group of eight pupils working in pairs. Assuming a class of thirty-two pupils, there will be four sets of apparatus for each experiment. It is useful to appoint one pupil for each experiment to act as monitor or liaison officer—it being his job to check that all the necessary apparatus for his experiment (and there may be four sets of it) is present at the start and is properly put away at the end. In this way even a class of thirty-six pupils may be employed. But it is extremely difficult to give really adequate attention to so many pupils and it is scarcely possible to maintain such a programme lesson after lesson unless there is laboratory assistance and a generous allowance of "free" periods. The principle of group work is an excellent one: each group of pupils deals with at least one of the four experiments in detail and has some time to examine the apparatus for the other experiments. The teacher brings all the work together in the course of his summing-up. Where experiments are short it is possible for groups to move from one experiment to another and so to carry out two, three, or even four experiments in one double lesson. Regular work of this kind (and it is the kind that really produces results) calls for small numbers and the splitting of large classes for Science will pay handsome dividends. Failing this, even the keenest teacher may be excused if he feels that he must confine his class practical work to a single experiment per topic.

The first four experiments described below form a typical group on the simple circuit. Instructions may be given on duplicated sheets pasted into paper or card folders, each pair of pupils being issued with a full copy covering all four experiments. Considerable work is demanded of the teacher in the first instance, but the method has great advantages. It frees the teacher to give his time to personal supervision during the lesson and it forces the pupil to attempt to read with comprehension—even if he is occasionally obliged to seek the help of his partner (two backward readers should not be paired). In simple cases instructions may be written on the blackboard. Oral instructions waste much time as a rule; they can be given only in small doses, and they must frequently be repeated.

The Electric Circuit

271 How to Make a Torch Bulb-holder from Card

Parts required: Thin card, 1 cm wide × 10 cm long, and 2½ cm wide × 12 cm long; this may be cut from a post card. Two 15-cm lengths of insulated copper wire; remove the cotton covering from one end of each wire. Gummed paper (the kind used for parcels). 2·5-volt torch bulb.

Roll up the 1-cm strip of card into a tight plug, making it the same diameter as the screw-in base of the torch bulb; secure it by means of gummed paper. Push one of the wires up through the centre of the roll of card and bend the bared end into a little knob at one end of the plug. Now roll the wider strip of card round this plug as shown in the diagram, so that a collar is formed to take the torch bulb, with the wire knob inside the collar. Secure this outer roll of card with gummed paper. Prick a hole through the collar, pass the second length of wire through and bend over the bared end inside the collar; this wire must not touch the wire knob.

Push the bulb into the collar and connect up the two wires to the bench terminals or to a torch battery. Make a careful diagram of the electrical circuit.

272 Conductors and Insulators

Parts required: Torch bulb holder (Expt. 271) and bulb. Cycle battery (or other low-voltage source). Connecting wire (say 24-gauge covered copper). Sheet of card, about 2 cm × 15 cm (e.g. one side of a breakfast-cereal box). Wire paper-fasteners and gummed paper strip. Handy objects—rubber, wood, paper, plastic, glass and metal.

Lay the card on the bench and assemble the parts as shown in the diagram. Join the connecting wires to the bulb holder and fasten them down to the card with gummed paper strip. Thread the free ends of the wire through two holes pricked in the card and join them to the battery terminals (by wire paper-fasteners if it is a cycle battery). Notice that the lamp lights up. Now cut the connecting wire so as to produce two ends, C and D; the lamp goes out. C and D together may be used as a switch, one end being touched on to the other to close the circuit.

Close the switch: the lamp lights up. Release the switch and join up CD by means of a pin, a two pence piece, a strip of wood, etc., trying in turn as many different materials as possible. Make a list of those substances (conductors) which allow current to pass; and another of those (insulators) that resist the passage of current.

Note: Use of wire paper-fasteners as connectors: twist (or solder) the bare end of the connecting wire to the fastener, then slip the fastener on to the flat-strip terminal of the torch battery (Fig. 273). The circuit card of Expt. 272 may be used in Expts. 275, 285 and 303.

ELECTRICITY IN THE HOME 223

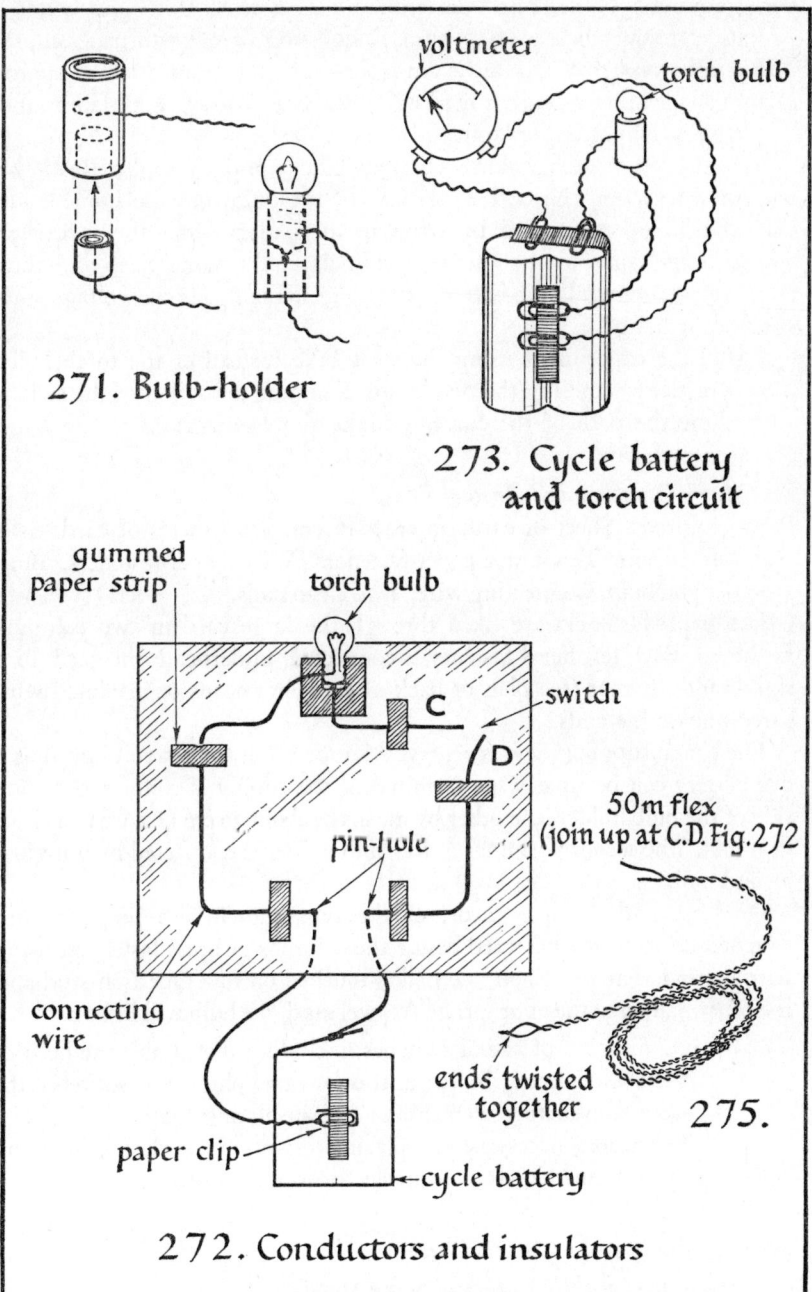

271. Bulb-holder

273. Cycle battery and torch circuit

272. Conductors and insulators

273 Cycle Lamp and Electric Torch

Parts required: Cycle-lamp bulb and battery. Electric torch and battery. Voltmeter. Bulb holder (Exp. 271). Connecting wires (with paper clips).

It is important that an electric lamp should be fed from a cell of appropriate voltage; this voltage is marked on the brass cap of small lamps and on the glass bulb of larger lamps.

Dismantle the torch, taking out the battery and the bulb. Read the voltage marked on the bulb cap. Now fit the bulb into the home-made bulb-holder and connect it by wires to the battery. Join the voltmeter terminals by wires to the battery terminals at the same time and thus read the voltage while the battery is feeding the lamp. Is the voltage suitable for the lamp?

Repeat the experiment using the cycle bulb instead of the torch bulb. Then practise assembling the two lamps. Examine the action of the switch and follow the path of the current. Make simple diagrams to show the circuit in each case.

274 Magic Question and Answer Board

Parts required: Sheet of card, 20 cm × 16 cm. Two sheets of card, each 15 cm × 5 cm. Ten brass paper-fasteners. Wire paper-fasteners. Bulb holder and bulb. Connecting wire. Two clean nails.

The paper-fasteners are fixed through the large card in two columns as shown. Each left-hand fastener is connected, underneath the card, to a right-hand fastener (see plan of back of card) by means of insulated wire bared only at the ends.

The bench supply (3 volt for 3·5 volt lamp; 2 volt for 2·5 volt lamp) or a dry battery can be used. One terminal of the supply is connected to one side of the bulb holder, the other by means of about 30 cm of wire to a clean iron nail. The second terminal of the bulb holder is connected by wire to a second nail.

Question and Answer cards, of the type shown, are prepared and fastened down to the basecard beside the columns of brass fasteners, using wire paper-fasteners. When one nail is touched on to a Question stud and the other nail on to the appropriate Answer stud, the bulb will light up.

Topics: Examination of actual switches, including the tumbler switch; of household electric bulbs; and of various plugs and sockets: the use of conducting elements and of insulating materials is noted. Precautions necessary in replacing a lamp in a socket or in fitting a plug connection (e.g. to an electric iron or lamp).

Heating Effect of the Electric Current

275 High Electrical Resistance of Some Metals

The circuit board of Expt. 272 is used (the switch wire D is bent back out

ELECTRICITY IN THE HOME 225

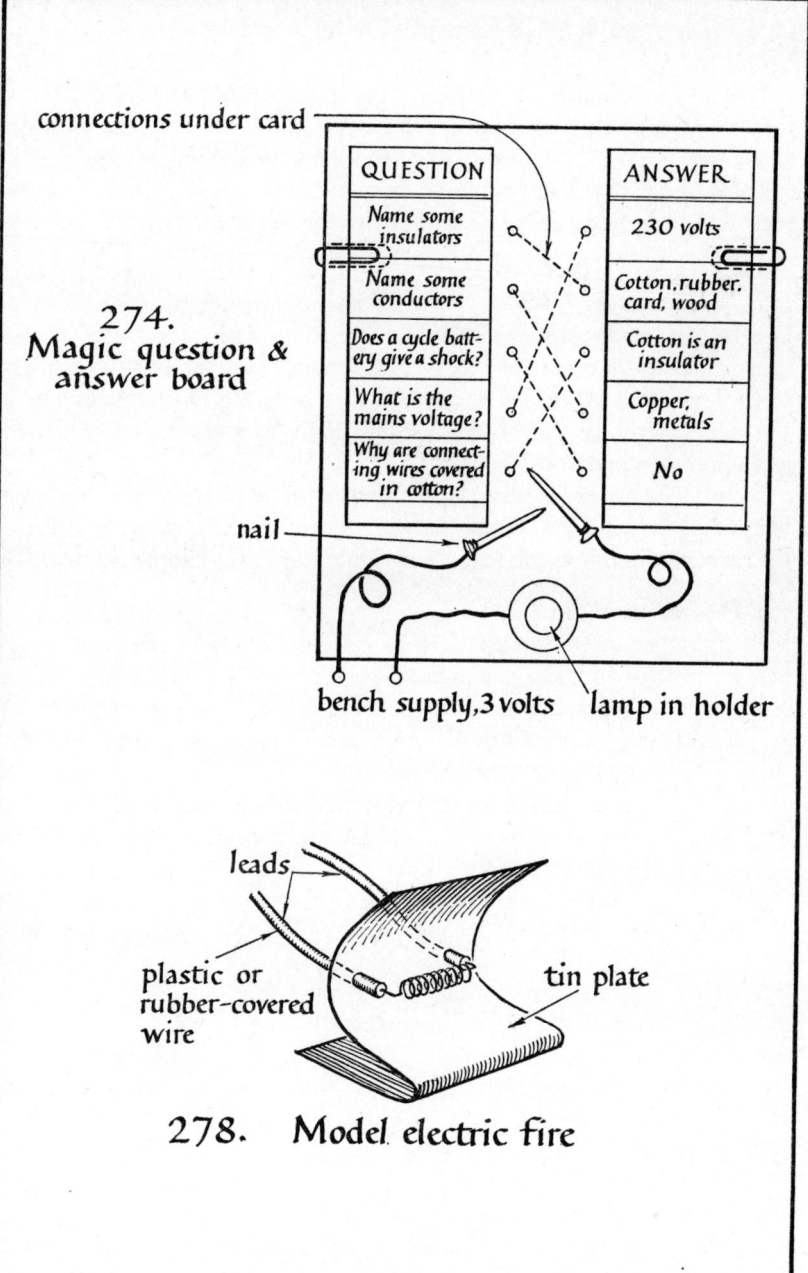

of the way). About a metre of bare copper wire, 24 S.W.G., is connected between C and D; to prevent short circuits, it may be taken round retort stands or wrapped into a loose spiral. The lamp will light at practically full brilliance.

Now replace the copper wire by a metre of (i) nichrome wire, (ii) thin iron wire, (iii) 5-amp. fuse wire. Notice that all these wires offer considerable resistance to the current, since the lamp glows much less brightly. Finally, show that even copper is not a perfect conductor; connect 50 metres of twin-flex across CD and twist together the (bared) distant ends of the flex.

276 Thin Wires Do Not Conduct as Well as Thicker Wires

Use the same apparatus as in Expt. 275 along with a metre of No. 24 copper wire and a metre of No. 36 copper wire. Join one end of each wire to C. Touch the other end of the No. 24 wire on to D—the lamp lights. Disconnect, and then touch the free end of the No. 36 wire on to D—the lamp lights again, but is less bright.

Now touch the same wire on to D but so as to put successively shorter lengths of the wire into circuit between C and D. The effect of reducing the resistance in this way is seen by a brightening in the lamp.

277 Production of Heat

The resistance offered to the flow of current results in electrical energy being expended and turned into heat.

Screw two terminals into a piece of wood about 10 cm long × 5 cm wide, so that the terminals are some 7 cm apart. Connect the terminals with a 4-volt supply and switch. Stretch a short length of No. 36 copper wire tightly between the terminals and close the switch. Notice anything that happens to the wire between the terminals. Repeat the experiment replacing the copper wire by (i) nichrome wire, (ii) thin iron wire. In each case open the switch as soon as the wire begins to get hot. Note the expansion of the wire.

278 Model Electric Fire

Obtain a replacement electric fire element (cheap stores). If it is designed for 230 volts, about one-twentieth of it will make a heater suitable for a 12-volt supply. Cut the spiral into such pieces and distribute them to the class groups.

Twist the bared end of a plastic-covered connecting wire to each end of the heating spiral. Cut from a tin can a sheet of metal about 12 cm × 6 cm. Pierce two holes (drill or nail) in the tin sheet about 4 cm apart and bend the sheet to represent an electric fire. Pass the connecting wires through the holes so that the plastic covering acts as an insulator between the wires and the fire "reflector". Connect the wires to a 12-volt supply and switch.

The model takes a considerable current (up to 4 amperes), so the number of class groups testing it any one time should be limited. With only a 6-volt supply available the model is still effective if a spiral only half as long is used. A 6-volt model may be made in any case and will provide a useful introduction to the meaning of "voltage".

279 *An Adjustable Resistance*

This model may be used for general circuit purposes, as a speed control for electric motors, or as a dimmer for a model stage. The maximum resistance can be varied by varying the kind, gauge or length of the wire used; some useful figures are given below:

Approximate Resistance per metre, in Ohms.

Gauge (S.W.G.)	Eureka Wire	Nichrome Wire
24	2·0	4·7
26	2·8	7·2
30	6·1	14·8
36	16·2	41·0

The maximum current that will flow in a circuit when our resistance is included is easily calculated from the relationship:

$$\text{amperes} = \text{volts}/\text{ohms}.$$

Thus, if we are using a 12-volt supply a resistance of 6 ohms will limit the current to a maximum of 2 amperes. Such a resistance is provided by about a metre of 30-gauge Eureka wire, or by about 40 cm of 30-gauge nichrome wire.

The "former" is a 10-cm length of 1-cm diameter dowel rod. The resistance wire is wound on this so that adjacent turns are not touching. The ends of the wire are secured to small brass screws, which are also used to fasten the dowel rod to a wooden baseboard. The ends of the dowel rod should be drilled beforehand to take these screws.

A brass strip, 8 cm × 1 cm × 2 mm, drilled at one end with a length of connecting wire soldered to the same end, pivots on a screw fixed in the baseboard so as to move radially over the resistance spiral. Washers are provided as shown in the diagram, and the strip should be filed and rubbed smooth where it slides over the resistance wire.

Current is led in through a wire connected to one end of the coil; mark this end "zero" and the other end "full resistance". When using the instrument always have the moving arm set at "full" when the circuit is first completed.

Note: Ammeters and voltmeters are not all constructed to give the same range of readings. If 10 amperes is sent through an instrument designed to read from 0 to 1 ampere, the coils inside will be burnt out. Before passing current through any instrument an estimate should be made of the maximum possible current or voltage, and an instrument of

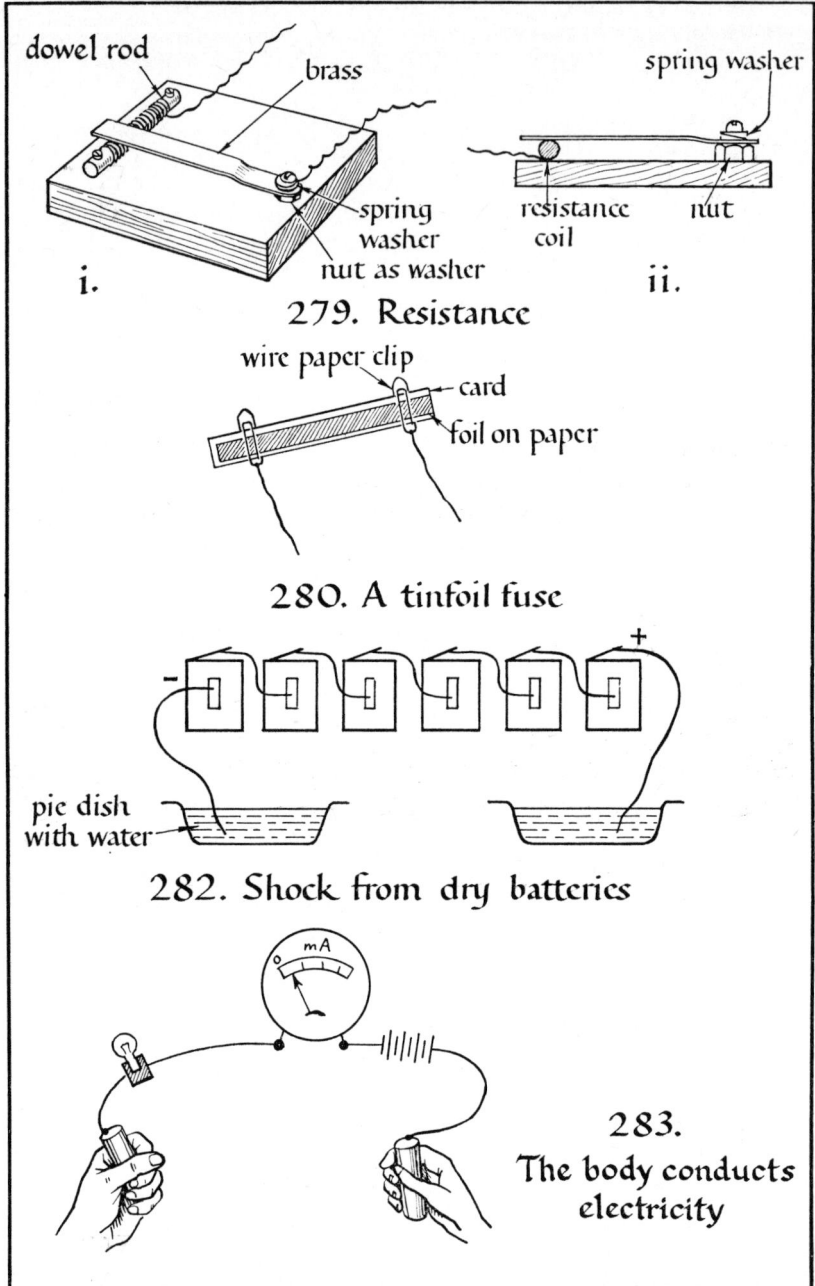

279. Resistance

280. A tinfoil fuse

282. Shock from dry batteries

283. The body conducts electricity

suitable range then chosen. For complete safety it is wise to include a large variable resistance in circuit until the recording instrument has been tested.

280 *Action of a Fuse*
Stick metal foil, e.g. from chocolate wrappers, on to gummed paper and cut it into strips about 8 cm long and of various widths (e.g. 3 mm, 6 mm, etc.). Grip each end of a strip in a wire paper clip and connect the clips to a battery (4 volts) and simple switch as in Expt. 277. Test different widths of foil in this way. Include a variable resistance (Expt. 279) in circuit and try again, noting what happens as the resistance is steadily cut out.

Topics: Examination of heating devices used in the home (the list can be a long one—immersion heater, oven and grill, fire, hair drier, thermostat, soldering iron, infra-red lamp, etc.). Repair of a fuse.

Low and High Voltage

281 *The Accumulator*
An old accumulator may be taken apart and examined; any liquid inside must be CAREFULLY poured away first and the cell washed out.

Prepare some "accumulator acid" by pouring one volume of concentrated sulphuric acid VERY SLOWLY and with constant stirring into four volumes of cold water in a large beaker standing in a trough of cold water; the temperature may rise almost to boiling point and GREAT CARE is necessary. The TEACHER should prepare this acid beforehand and have it cooled and bottled ready for the lesson.

Cut two strips of thin sheet lead, about 12 cm $\times$ 2 cm $\times$ 2 mm—old gas piping, hammered out, will serve. Stand them in a jam jar three parts filled with accumulator acid, bending the upper ends over the edge of the jar to keep the plates apart. Connect one plate to the positive terminal of a 4-volt supply and the other plate to the negative terminal of the supply. Allow current to pass for 10–15 minutes and observe any colour changes on the plates and the liberation of gas. Now disconnect from the charging supply and connect the plates to a torch bulb—which will light up for perhaps half a minute. The discharged accumulator may then be recharged, and after each successive charge the model will give longer service.

Using a voltmeter reading 0–3 volts, measure the voltage across the terminals of the model accumulator (a) immediately after charging, (b) after discharge.

282 *Difference between Battery and Mains Supply (voltage):*
An electric shock may be obtained from batteries if a sufficient number are placed in series. Six cycle batteries, giving about 18 volts, or nine accumulators, or a mixture of accumulators and cycle batteries, will serve. Connect

the batteries up, positive terminal to negative terminal, and connect the end terminals by copper wire to water in two pie dishes. One hand is placed under the water in each dish, so making a good connection to the whole surface of the hand. A slight shock is felt, especially if the water is somewhat warm. Young children, with thin skin, experience a more powerful shock than do adults.

Thus the mains supply at 230 volts (more than twelve times the voltage used in our experiment) is VERY DANGEROUS to handle and should not be tampered with. The danger is particularly great if hands are moist or if equipment is damp—e.g. in a bathroom.

283 *To Show that our Bodies Can Conduct Electricity*
Two tin handles have connecting wire soldered to them and are joined to a milliammeter or galvanometer and a 6-volt supply; a torch bulb is included in the circuit to protect the meter. When the handles are gripped, one in each hand, a small current is registered although no shock is felt. After washing the hands well in warm soapy water, so as to moisten the skin thoroughly, a considerably larger current is registered.

Dry skin is a poor conductor of electricity; the body fluids conduct much more efficiently.

Topics: Care and use of the accumulator, including testing (hydrometer) and charging. Treatment of person suffering from electric shock. Safety precautions in using or repairing household electrical appliances.

The House Lighting Circuit

284 *Fairy Lamps (connection in series)*
Use three home-made bulb-holders (Expt. 271), three flash-lamp bulbs and a torch battery or other source of current. Select the voltage to be right for one lamp by itself and observe the brightness of the lamp. Now introduce a second lamp, and then a third, in series with the first; notice how all the lamps are dimmed. An ammeter may be put into the circuit to confirm the reduced flow of current.

Keeping the three lamps in circuit, put a second battery in series with the first (DO NOT REMOVE ANY OF THE LAMPS) and notice the increase in brightness. Unscrew one lamp from its socket; all go out.

It is evident that a string of fairy lamps may require quite a high voltage source. Christmas tree lamps are, therefore, a possible danger if the insulation becomes faulty. Moreover, if one lamp fails all go out; and the faulty one can only be discovered by testing each lamp in turn.

285 *Lamps in Parallel*
Here (and in Expt. 284) the cards of Expt. 272 may be used (with lamp

ELECTRICITY IN THE HOME 231

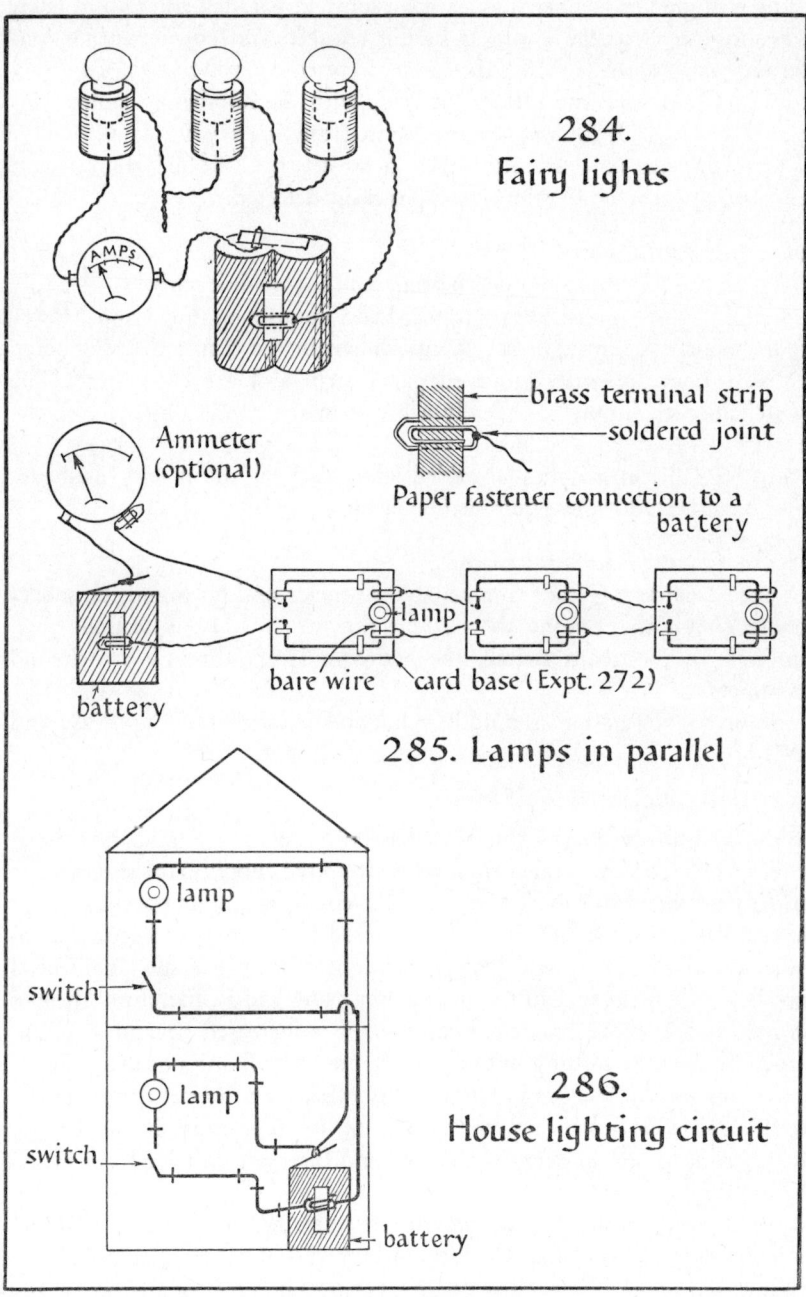

284. Fairy lights

brass terminal strip
soldered joint
Paper fastener connection to a battery

Ammeter (optional)

battery
bare wire   card base (Expt. 272)
lamp

285. Lamps in parallel

lamp
switch
lamp
switch
battery

286. House lighting circuit

holder and connecting wires permanently attached). Begin as in Expt. 284, using a single lamp. Then add a second lamp in parallel, and a third later. The brightness of the lamps is hardly reduced and equal current runs through each (provided that the lamps have equal resistances). The total current taken from the battery increases with the number of lamps; this may be shown by including an ammeter in the main circuit.

Unscrew one of the lamps; the others are not affected. In such an arrangement, therefore, a faulty lamp is easily detected.

286 (a) *House Lighting Circuit*
Keep the model simple in order to bring out the principles clearly.

Cut a "house" shape from cardboard and indicate an upper and a lower room in pencil. Arrange the circuits shown in the diagram, using torch bulbs, connecting wire, gummed paper strip and a cycle battery. The switch in each "room" is merely a break in the connecting wire (Expt. 272).

Additional features may be added later—and the meter and fuse-boxes may be indicated by neat gummed-on labels.

286 (b) *Current Round the Circuit*
Connect wandering leads to a suitable ammeter and go round the model house circuit to examine the current flowing in various sections—e.g. through the bedroom switch, the bedroom lamp, through switch and lamp, etc.

Similar investigations should be made in the circuits of Expts. 284 and 285.

287 *Overloading*
We have already seen (Expt. 285) that every additional lamp in parallel circuits increases the total current taken from the supply. House lamps are usually arranged in sub-circuits, each sub-circuit containing several lamps in parallel; thus one sub-circuit might serve the kitchen and scullery, another the dining-room and lounge, etc. The wiring in a sub-circuit need not be so heavy as that in the main supply line and is, therefore, cheaper to install. But if the current in any circuit is increased beyond a certain amount, either by putting in too many lamps or by fixing unsuitable appliances (e.g. an electric fire in a lighting circuit), then there is danger of the connecting wire heating up, with a risk of fire. To diminish this danger, fuses are included in every sub-circuit and there are heavier fuses in the main supply circuit.

Screw two terminals into a board (cf. Expt. 277) and stretch 5-A fuse wire between them. Make a holder for four 12-volt car headlamp bulbs by fixing four small Terry clips side by side in one edge of the board and screwing a metal plate (tin-plate) underneath the board so that it projects

ELECTRICITY IN THE HOME

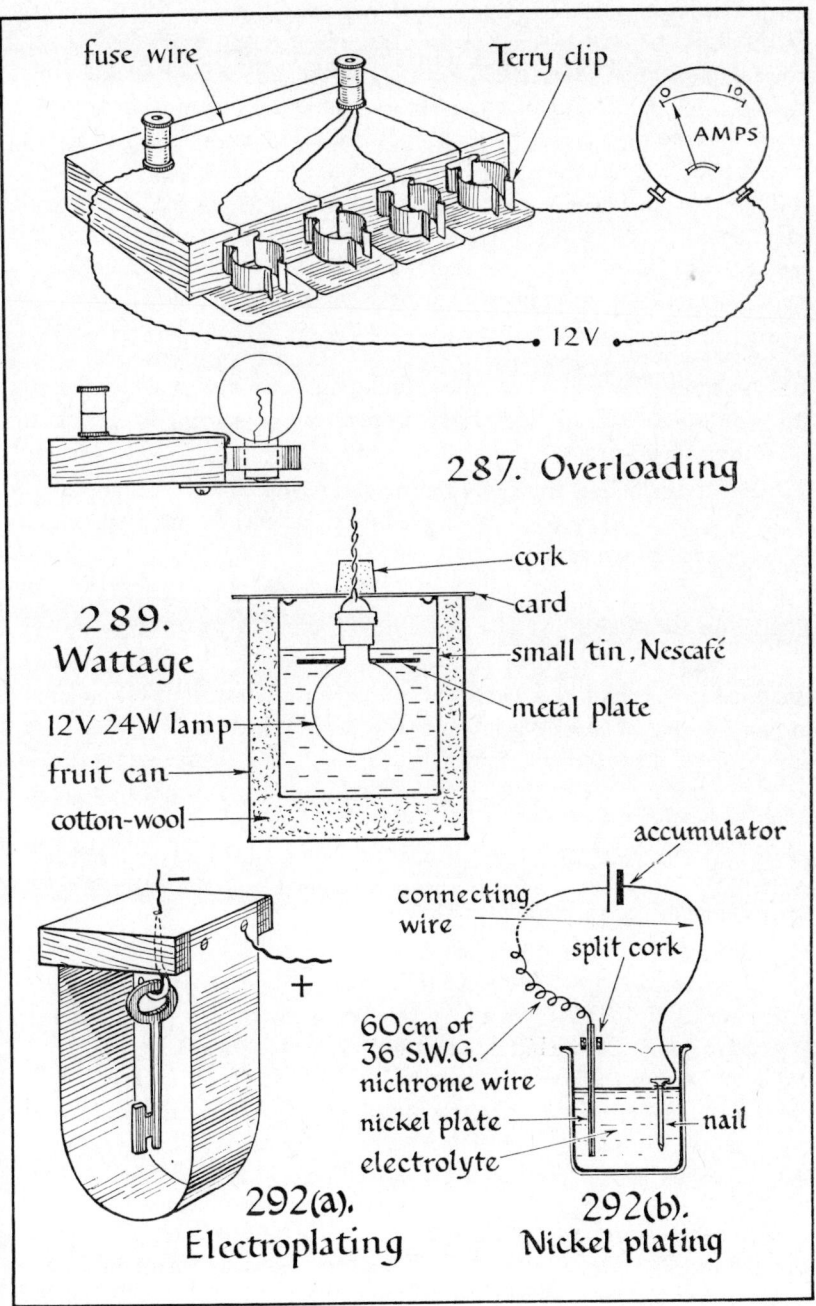

out under the clips. The plate is cut part-way through between the clips to form four lugs. When a bulb is pushed into a clip it presses down on to one of the lugs. A wire soldered to the plate leads via an ammeter (0–10 A) to a 12-volt supply, whilst the Terry clips are joined via the fuse-wire to the supply. Plug the lamps into the holder one at a time and note that the ammeter reading steps up at each addition. The fuse-wire begins to heat up at about 5 A and finally fuses when about 8 A is reached.

Take out all but one of the lamps and fit a fresh length of fuse-wire. Place a metal object (e.g. a two pence piece) across a Terry clip and the metal plate, thus causing a "short-circuit". The ammeter momentarily registers a heavy current but will survive since the fuse "blows" instantly.

288 *Electric cables*

Examine twin flex and other cables; each pupil may dissect a short length, using a pocket-knife and lens. Draw a cross-section, naming the layers and indicating their purpose.

Topics: Examination of actual lighting and power circuits at home and in school; practice in drawing circuit diagrams. Actual experience of repairing a fuse.

Paying for Electricity

289 *Wattage*

Examine lamps of various wattage. Compare brightnesses by putting lamps in parallel—e.g. by plugging into a two-way lamp holder.

Set up the arrangement shown in the diagram. A lamp, suspended by twin flex through a cardboard cover, dips into 200 g of water in a lagged home-made calorimeter, the glass bulb being just covered by water. The lamp may conveniently be 12-volt 24-watt, but smaller voltage lamps will serve. The initial temperature of the water is noted and the water is gently stirred during the experiment. The lamp is fed from a 12-volt supply; if accumulators are used a variable resistance is included and the voltage across the lamp is adjusted to 12 volts. The time taken (seconds) for a rise in temperature of $10°$ C. is observed. The experiment is repeated using a lamp of the same voltage but different wattage (say, 36-watt).

The two times are inversely proportional to the rates of heating. Within the limits of experimental error it will be found that they are also inversely proportional to the wattages of the lamps. Thus wattage is a measure of the rate at which electrical energy is used—i.e. of electrical "power".

290 *Heat Equivalent of Electricity*

Use the results of the previous experiment to find the number of calories produced by a 1 watt appliance operating for 1 second.

Suppose the 24-watt lamp took 360 seconds to raise 20 g of water through

10° C.; then 24×360 watt-seconds of electrical energy produce 200×10 calories; and 1 watt-second of electrical energy is equivalent to 0·23 calories.

In experiments made by Joule over a hundred years ago he found that 1 watt-second supplied 0·24 calories. In honour of Joule the unit of energy, equivalent to 1 watt-second, is called 1 joule and this is in fact the unit adopted in SI (see p. 142). The joule will thus replace the calorie in time as the unit of heat energy:

$$1 \text{ joule} = 0.24 \text{ calorie}; 1 \text{ calorie} = 4.2 \text{ joule}.$$

291 *Efficiency of Electric Kettle*

Read the wattage marked on the kettle; it may be 1500 watts. Measure 1000 cm^3 (1000 g) of water into the kettle and note its temperature. Find the time, in seconds, required to bring the water to the boil. Suppose starting temperature = 20° C and final temperature = 100° C. Then heat supplied to the water = 1000×(100−20 calories = 80 000 calories.

Wattage of kettle = 1500 watts. Time to boil water = 4½ minutes. Electrical energy used = 1500×4½×60 = 405 000 watt-seconds.

Thus 405 000 joules of electrical energy supply 80 000 calories of heat to the water in the kettle; whence, 1 joule supplies about 0·2 calories. The rest of the heat produced is used in heating the kettle or is wasted. The efficiency of the kettle is, therefore, 0·2/0·24×100 = 83 per cent.

Topics: The electricity bill; how to read the meter; how to calculate the cost of running an appliance. The UNIT is 1000 watts of power for 1 hour, often known as the kilowatt-hour. The cost per unit may vary from perhaps ½–3p, depending upon the locality and the particular tariff operating.

The rate at which various appliances use electrical energy (i.e. their "power") might be:

Radio set	100 watts.	Vacuum Cleaner	130 watts.
Two-bar fire	2000 ,,	Immersion Heater	2000 ,,
Electric Iron	400 ,,	Oven and Hot-plate	4000 ,,

In all cases, the amount of electric energy consumed (and for which we must pay) is given by:

$$\text{Units} = \frac{\text{Wattage} \times \text{Hours}}{1000}$$

The cost is given by: Cost = Units × Cost per Unit.

Note: The power equation (watts = amperes × volts) might be given to the more able pupils. It is very useful for calculating the maximum load which can safely be applied in a given circuit. Thus, in stage lighting, we might wish to calculate how many 230-volt lamps can safely be put in parallel on a 5-A lighting circuit. If each lamp is 100 watts, then:

One lamp takes $100/230$ A $= 0.42$ A. On a 5-A circuit, therefore, we might have $5/0.42$, or 12 lamps.

At home the danger is usually that of putting an electric fire on a lighting circuit; but manufacturers often mark the amperage on the fire and pupils should come to see that to put a 4·4-A fire (say) on a 5-A circuit which already carries a number of lamps is asking for trouble.

Electro-Plating

Electricity can be used to split up chemical compounds into their elements. In electro-plating a current is passed through a solution of a metal compound (e.g. copper sulphate) and the metal which is set free is deposited upon the negative electrode.

292 (a) *Copper-plating*

Use a small steel object such as a key. Any rust should be removed with emery paper and grease by washing in hot soda solution followed by good rinsing; it is most important that the surface should be thoroughly clean—even contact with fingers should be avoided.

The anode (connected to the positive terminal of the battery) is a 20-cm ×5-cm strip of thin copper sheet bent into a U-form and tacked to a small wooden block. Under the block is a small brass hook from which the object to be plated is suspended within the U. A small hole drilled through the block carries the connecting wire from the hook to the negative terminal of the battery. The block rests across the top of a beaker containing a solution of copper sulphate prepared by dissolving about 100 g of crystals in a litre of water and adding a little sulphuric acid.

The current should be small—0·1 to 0·2 A—and the circuit might consist of an accumulator, ammeter and variable resistance. Allow current to flow for 30 minutes and then remove the plated object, dry it, and polish.

(b) *Nickel Plating*

Nails to be plated may be cleaned as described above or more conveniently as follows: heat the nails until they tarnish in a Bunsen flame, then warm them in diluted hydrochloric acid, allowing strong effervescence to continue for half a minute. Pour away the acid, rinse the nails thoroughly in running water and handle the cleaned nails only in filter paper.

The arrangement of apparatus is shown in the diagram. The nichrome wire provides a suitable resistance and the anode is a thin nickel plate or a nickel rod. The electrolyte is made up to the following formula: 150 g hydrated nickel sulphate. 5 g boric acid (cryst). 7·5 g hydrated nickel chloride. 500 cm³ water. (Instead, nickel ammonium sulphate alone may be used.)

Topics: Commercial applications of electrolysis—electro-plating, electro-
    typing, production of aluminium and other metals.

Chapter Fifteen

The Generation and Distribution of Electricity

Science Models and Science Clubs

The majority of books relating to the teaching of Science with average pupils lay emphasis on the importance of practical work. The idea is often interpreted in terms of model-making and it would appear that due consideration has not always been given to three factors:
(a) the very short time available for Science in most schools;
(b) the limited ability of average pupils working in large groups to carry through a detailed programme of operations demanding fair skill;
(c) the fact that many teachers, even though keenly interested in science, have little personal experience of model-making and of the great demands which it makes upon skill and patience.

Our syllabuses must be most carefully prepared if we are to give our pupils some idea of the many ways in which science impinges upon modern life; it seems indefensible in such circumstances to allot several weeks to the production of an electric motor. Practical work is not, in Science, an end in itself. There are questions to be answered, conclusions to be drawn, principles to be established. Our class experiments must be simple, so that they can be understood in some measure even by the weakest pupils; they must generally be short, so that the teacher has time to drive his point home in a reasonable unit of time; and they must be varied, so that interest is constantly refreshed. What, then, is the place of the more elaborate model?

The answer would appear to lie with the Science Society or Club, held after school (or even during the dinner interval). The appeal of model-making to most boys and to many girls (if the models are well chosen) is very great, but in any case only those pupils will come to the club who have a special interest. It is well to keep numbers low—to be in some sense exclusive—so that members do in fact receive individual attention, so that they learn to co-operate in small groups, and so that a sense of purpose and of responsibility can be developed. The society should have rules to regulate its conduct—as, for example, in the proper use of tools and the storage of material—and it should work to a programme, so that everyone has a definite job to do. Individual members can be made responsible for special tasks—for checking stock, keeping tools in good repair, collecting scrap materials of many kinds, keeping records of the club's activities, supplying the notice-board with interesting pictures and cuttings, painting "backgrounds" and lettering descriptive cards. The year's programme will include short talks by members—especially descriptions of their own work—and the occasional demonstration by a visiting expert (Science teachers from other schools will often undertake such a job with pleasure and profit to themselves as well as to the club). An end-of-term exhibition of work will attract interest and support from the rest of the school. In this latter connection Head Teachers and Science teachers may find the Science "At Home" a valuable extension of the exhibition idea.

It is commonplace to observe that too many teachers must work in comparative isolation. They are often tied to the classroom and to their own school and see little of the methods of teachers, facing similar problems elsewhere. The Science "At Home" can go some way towards solving this difficulty. Through the local authority's bulletin to schools or otherwise, the Head Teacher invites Heads of neighbouring schools and their Science teachers to spend an evening together. In the laboratory boys and girls demonstrate experiments which are an actual part of the normal Science course, and the place of their work in the school Science scheme is made clear to the visitors by such means as wall charts and cyclostyled notes. Sometimes the experiments may represent a cross-section of a whole year's work with a particular class; alternatively they may focus attention upon some selected topic. Apparatus and materials are clearly labelled, and often the source of these things is shown, and even their prices. Visual materials of all kinds, including science textbooks and library books, wall-charts, film-strips and demonstration apparatus, are other centres of interest. Pupils' note-books are on show, both the poorest and the best, so that methods of recording may be discussed and methods of marking commented upon. Members of the school Science Society are privileged to be present and to act as guides and stewards, and they may have a corner for their own models; but the display is essentially one of normal school work, and the "staged" atmosphere of the usual Parents' Open Day is carefully avoided.

The evening may open with a few words from the Head outlining the background against which the school works—the type of pupil, the range of ability, the kind of jobs to which the school leavers will go. Next, the Science teacher will describe the problems which he faces with his own subject and the methods by which he tries to overcome them. He will sketch the nature of his schemes, the place of Science in the school curriculum, and his aims in teaching the subject. To follow this, an hour in the laboratory will prove all too short a time in which to observe and note all that can be seen there. After light refreshment (served from the House-craft room) the visitors break up into discussion groups charged with the task of formulating material for the questions forum. During this last session of the evening the Science teacher and his Head Teacher will try to answer some of the queries thrown up in the discussion groups. Questions will be many and varied: the following are examples which have been put at actual "At Home" evenings:

"How much written work is demanded in Science?"

"Are labelled diagrams the answer for the slower pupil?"

"How much free time does the Science teacher get for laboratory preparation?"

"What amount of demonstration work is done as compared with pupils' own practical work?"

"Do you have half-classes for Science?"

"How do you issue instructions for group work?"

"What system do you adopt for setting out and clearing away apparatus?"

"Has your scheme a bias towards any particular type of career?"

"Is it biased towards the teacher's own special subject?"

"To what extent is Science correlated with Geography, Handicraft, Mathematics ... ?"

"How do you prepare for works' visits?"

"Are there separate schemes for boys and girls?"

"How do you make use of your Science library?"

As a change, questions may be put into a hat and lots may be drawn so that members in the body of the meeting are called upon to attempt to answer on subjects of general interest. Alternatively again, instead of a questions' forum, the Science teacher may demonstrate one or two of his favourite "home-made" experiments or devices, and he may even so arrange matters that his visitors are given an opportunity to carry through some "ten-minute experiment" themselves. Such an evening is an inspiration to the staff who arrange it and to the men and women who come as visitors.

In what follows the main series of experiments is designed, as usual, for individual or group practical work, or for teacher demonstration; but a few models are added at the end of the chapter as an indication of the type of work which is more suitable for a Science club. The teacher will have no difficulty in finding descriptions of the construction of models of this kind in the many practical work-books now available.

Permanent Magnets

The earliest special-steel magnets employed tungsten or chromium; later, cobalt-steel was used and it is still the material from which common **permanent magnets are made**. Complex alloys of aluminium, cobalt, nickel and iron were introduced in the nineteen-twenties, under the name "Alnico", and these have been further developed until we can now buy very powerful magnets capable of withstanding the effects of heat, vibration and long usage to a remarkable degree. Teachers are well advised to specify some of these when ordering; the extra expense is well justified in view of the very superior performance obtained. Cobalt-steel magnets about 10 cm × 1 cm × ½ cm are suitable, along with a few small horse-shoe magnets of the same kind. They should be stored with the keepers supplied by the makers.

It is, nevertheless, very convenient if magnets of ordinary steel can be demagnetized or re-magnetized in the laboratory. In Expt. 293 a magnetizing coil working on only 12 volts is described, which can be handled with safety by the pupils themselves.

293 *Low Voltage Magnetizing Coil*
Use a brass tube about 20 cm long and 2·5 cm diameter. Wind on three layers of 22 S.W.G. insulated copper wire, each of about 170 turns and about 15 cm long. Secure the coils with insulating tape, mount the apparatus on the wall (Terry clips) in a convenient position and connect through a switch with a 12 volt supply capable of giving 6 amperes. (The resistance of the coil will be nearly 2 ohms). For demagnetizing, 12 volts A.C. is required.

(i) Demagnetizing: Steel knitting needles and steel rods generally usually have some magnetisation when kept in the laboratory. To thoroughly demagnetize, simply slip the rod into the brass tube, switch on A.C. and (with the current still on) withdraw the rod along the axis of the tube.

(ii) Magnetizing: Insert the steel rod, switch on the current (either D.C. or A.C.), switch off and then withdraw the rod.

(iii) To distinguish soft iron from steel (similar rods): Insert the steel rod so that one end projects from the brass tube; wedge it in position with paper. Switch on D.C. and see how many tacks can be hung from the end of the rod. Switch off: how many remain? Then repeat using the soft iron rod.

(iv) Retentive power of special alloy magnets: Insert the north pole of a steel magnet into the magnetizing coil, leaving the south pole protruding. Switch on D.C. The magnet is drawn into the coil. The same thing happens if we begin with the south pole in the coil. Repeat the experiment using an alloy magnet (Alnico, ticonal, etc.).

The coil is powerful enough to reverse the magnetism of an ordinary steel magnet, so that the steel is always drawn into the brass tube. But in the case of the alloy magnets this is not the case: the magnet is sucked in or ejected according to which pole is inserted into the coil.

294 (a) *Magnetic Attraction*
Supply each group of pupils with a small box containing bits of aluminium, lead, tin-plate, pure tin, copper, metal alloys, wood, glass, plas-

GENERATION AND DISTRIBUTION OF ELECTRICITY

tic, card, wool, cotton, etc. They will also require a supply of small iron boot-nails.

Sprinkle the boot-nails on a sheet of paper and roll a bar-magnet among them; notice the distribution of nails clinging to the magnet when it is lifted horizontally. Mark off the magnet in centimetres (chalk) and find out how many nails can be hung from each section; draw a diagram to show the results.

Make a list of materials which are attracted by the magnet; what have they in common? All kinds of objects on the person and in the laboratory may be tested in addition to those supplied in the box. "Brass" drawing pins, "tin" lids, etc. give rise to useful discussion.

(b) *Repulsion*
Use a stirrup of paper or wire and suspend a small bar-magnet by a thread at least 30 cm long. The magnet eventually comes to rest in a north–south line, which may be marked in chalk on the bench beneath.

Cautiously bring the north pole of a second magnet towards the north pole of the suspended magnet. Repeat using south poles, and finally using dissimilar poles.

As a demonstration, two magnetized knitting needles may be pushed through a match-box, which is then impaled on the blackboard by a hat pin; the arrangement should rotate freely and be roughly balanced. The repulsion between similar poles is demonstrated—by bringing up a bar-magnet.

295 (a) *Making Magnets*
Stroke a darning needle, knitting needle, straightened piece of clockspring, or other strip of hard steel from end to end with one pole of a bar-magnet. Twenty strokes may be given, always in the same direction. Test the polarity of the new magnet against the suspended magnet of Expt 294, and its strength by its power to lift boot-nails.

295 (b) *Loss of Megnetism*
Magnetize a fretsaw-blade either by stroking or by using a magnetizing coil (Expt. 293). Test its strength (boot-nails) and then hammer it well on a block of wood and test again.

Remagnetize the blade. Now grip it in pliers and heat it to redness. Finally, cool the blade and see whether it is still magnetized.

296 *Making a Compass*
(a) Magnetize two darning needles. Fold a 5-cm × 3-cm card into halves lengthwise and fix the needles into the V-holder (see diagram). The two north poles must point in the same direction. Pivot the card on the sharpened point of a short piece of pencil standing upright in a lump of Plasticine. Set the arrangement at the centre of a ring of card marked out with the points of the compass

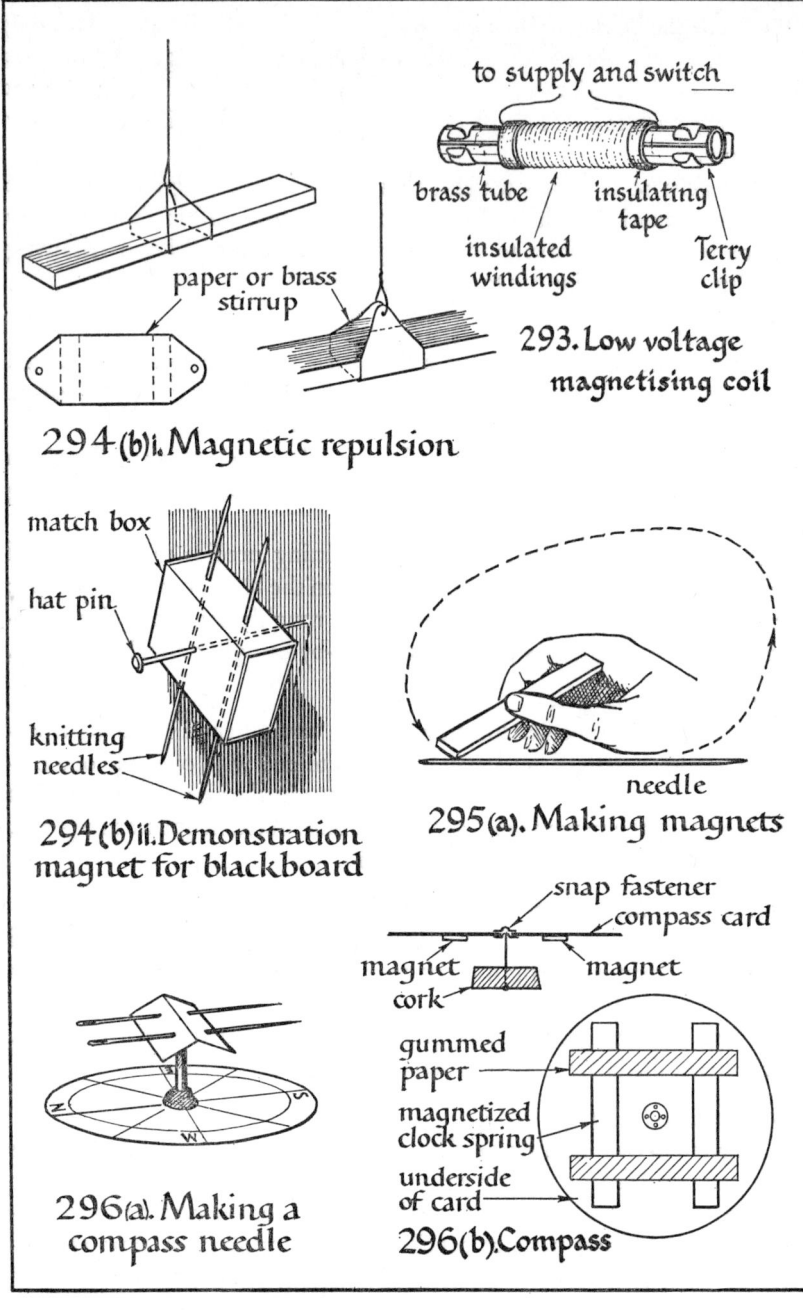

GENERATION AND DISTRIBUTION OF ELECTRICITY

(b) Prepare a compass card about 5 cm in diameter and attach two pieces of magnetized clock spring or crate binding strip to the back by gummed paper strip. Use a snap fastener as the pivot; punch a small hole in the centre of the card and snap the two halves of the fastener together with the card between them and with the hollow side of the fastener underneath the card. Use a pin pushed upwards through a cork as a support and pivot the fastener upon it. With some fasteners it is an advantage to punch a tiny dent in the inside of the hollow pivot using a small nail.

A Bakelite ink-bottle cap may be used as a case for a smaller compass card, and a Perspex cover may be cemented on.

297 (a) *Magnetic Fields*

Sprinkle iron filings on a sheet of Perspex or glass or card. Support the sheet over a strong bar-magnet and tap it gently.

The experiment may be repeated (i) using a single pole (magnet on end beneath the sheet); (ii) using the two poles of a horse-shoe magnet.

297 (b) *Making a Permanent Record*

Arrange packing pieces (e.g. layers of hardboard) on either side of the magnet, lay a sheet of waxed paper, from a cornflakes packet, over the top and sprinkle on iron filings, tapping to produce the "map". Then lay a double thickness of newspaper over the map and lower an electric iron, set at "warm", carefully on to the newspaper. Do *not* slide the iron sideways, but bring it down vertically and leave it undisturbed for half a minute; then lift it off and carefully remove the newspaper. Alternatively, wave a Bunsen flame over the waxed paper and "map".

298 *Floating Magnets*

(a) Magnetize half a dozen needles by stroking, making all the points (say) north poles. Cut flat discs from bottle corks, pass a needle through the centre of each disc, and so float the needles upright in a trough of water. About three-quarters of each needle should be below the cork.

(i) Bring the pole of a bar-magnet down towards the surface of the water; then try the opposite pole. Notice how the floating poles react in each case.

(ii) Remove all the floating magnets but one. Hold a bar-magnet horizontal and at water-level against the outside of the trough. Start with the north pole of the floating magnet against the north pole of the bar-magnet, release it and observe the path it takes.

(b) Tiny boat shapes may be cut from plywood or cork. A short piece of magnetized needle is laid along the "deck" and fixed in position with gummed paper. Such boats, floated on water, may be steered hither and thither by a remote magnet.

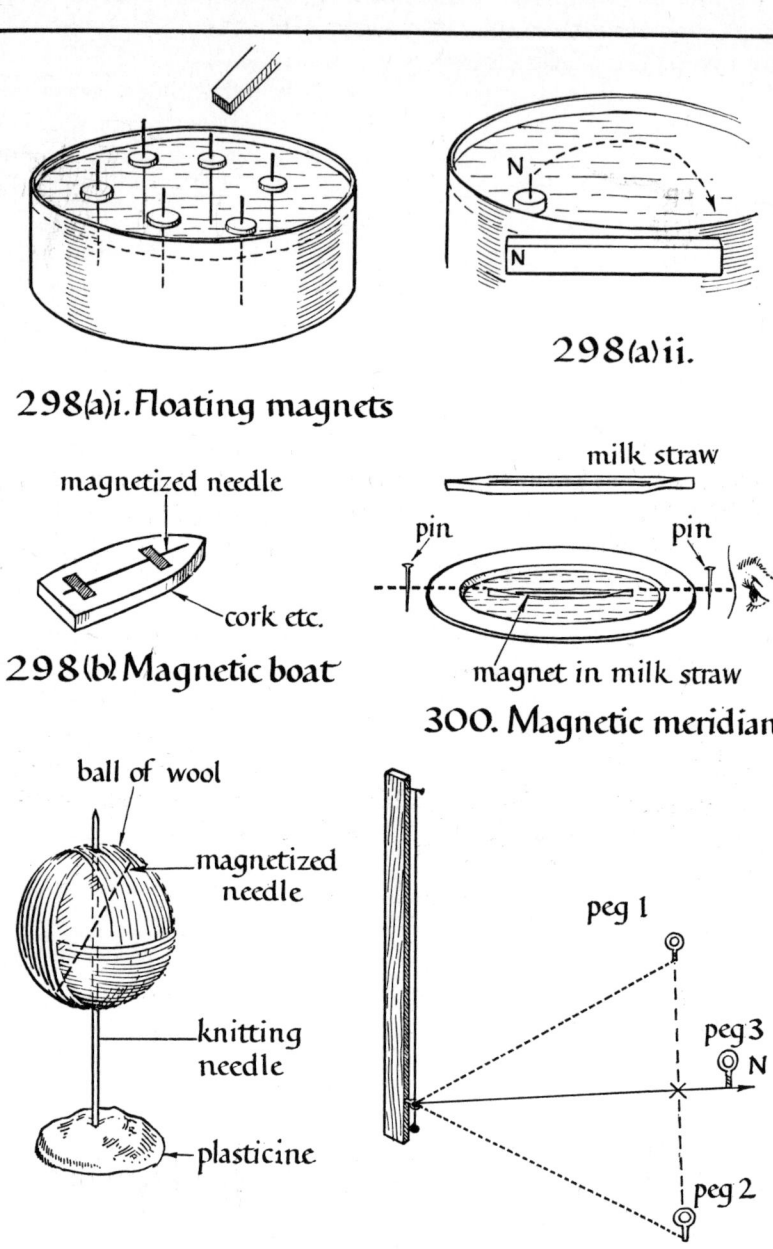

298(a)i. Floating magnets

298(a)ii.

298(b) Magnetic boat

300. Magnetic meridian

299. Earth's magnetism 301. Geographical meridian

The Earth's Magnetism

299 Earth Model
Stick a non-magnetic knitting needle through a large ball of wool and fix the needle upright in a lump of Plasticine. Cut a length of steel needle equal to the diameter of the ball, magnetize it, and stick it obliquely through the ball of wool to represent the magnetic axis of the earth. Use a "charm" compass to investigate the magnetic field round the ball. Make a diagram.

300 Magnetic Meridian
Magnetize a darning needle. Cut a milk straw in half, squeeze one end between the fingers to close it, slip the needle into the open end, and close this end also by squeezing. Float the straw on water in a soup plate; when it comes to rest, sight along its length, using two large pins. Remove the plate and join the feet of the pins with a pencil line. In the absence of disturbing factors, this will be the line of the magnetic meridian.

The result of the experiment may be quite misleading in a room where there are iron or steel fittings, but it may work well on the kitchen table at home.

301 Geographic Meridian
The experiment requires a sunny day, and is best performed in summer when the sun rises high in the sky at noon.

Erect a straight wooden rod, a metre or more high, on level ground out-of-doors. There should be a screw-eye just above ground-level and a nail near the top of the rod. A plumb line (thread and small weight) hangs from the nail and passes centrally through the screw eye when the rod is vertical.

As early as convenient in the morning, mark the end of the shadow of the rod with a small peg (meat skewer). Join the head of the peg by string, pulled taut, to the screw eye. Watch the shadow of the rod shorten as noon approaches and lengthen again after noon, and notice that it gradually moves round in a clockwise direction (northern hemisphere). When, in the afternoon, the shadow is again approaching the length marked off in the morning, swing the peg round (noting its first position with a second peg), keeping the string taut, and wait until it can again be used to mark the end of the shadow. Stick the peg into the ground at this point.

Measure the distance between the two pegs and so find the midpoint between them. Swing the peg and string round until the string passes through this point and fix it in this position. The string now marks geographic north–south.

Set a bowl of water over the string and repeat Expt. 300 (a whole straw may be used). The "variation" between magnetic and geographic north is evident.

Topics: Lodestone. Ship's Compass. Use of a compass with an Ordnance Survey map. Mention of uses of permanent magnets (e.g. in telephone receivers, loudspeakers, magnetos, cycle dynamos, gramophone pick-ups).

Electro-magnets

302 *Annealing and Hardening*

Iron or steel can be made relatively soft and pliable by heating it to redness and allowing it to cool slowly. The opposite process—hardening—is achieved by heating to redness and cooling very quickly, but the metal may then be very brittle and may require moderate heat treatment to remove this weakness. Ability to anneal or to harden a piece of metal (e.g. a tool) is useful to the handyman at home.

Try filing a steel needle, a piece of clock-spring, a nail file, or a hacksaw blade; success will be small, for the metal is very hard. Support the metal and make it red-hot in a flame; then plunge it into a can of hot sand and allow it to cool there; in this way it will cool only very slowly. Next lesson test it by bending it in the fingers.

A whole class may use the same (large) can of sand, which should be heated up beforehand. At home, pupils may anneal iron bolts or nails by putting them into the fire at night and letting them cool overnight in the ashes.

To reharden the metal, again make it red-hot, but this time cool it by plunging it into cold water. Now try bending it; its brittleness will be obvious.

To get hardness allied with toughness, the hardened steel must be tempered. Rub part of it with emery to polish it. Then warm it gently and evenly in a flame, watching the shiny part; the colour changes through straw to light-brown and purple; as soon as the blue tint appears plunge the metal into cold water.

A nail-file may be annealed, ground to give a blade, hardened and tempered, and finally sharpened on an oil-stone to a cutting edge.

303 *Magnetic Field Produced by Electric Current*

(a) Connect about a metre of gauge 26 D.C.C. copper wire with a switch and accumulator. The circuit card of Expt. 272 may be used. Hold a short length of the wire over a compass needle in the same direction as the needle. Switch on the current while watching the needle. Try the effect of moving the wire closer to the compass.

(b) Repeat, but use a single loop of wire round the compass; then try the effect of making a coil of about a dozen turns round the compass.

(c) Now wind the wire continuously in a single layer on a 10-cm length

GENERATION AND DISTRIBUTION OF ELECTRICITY 247

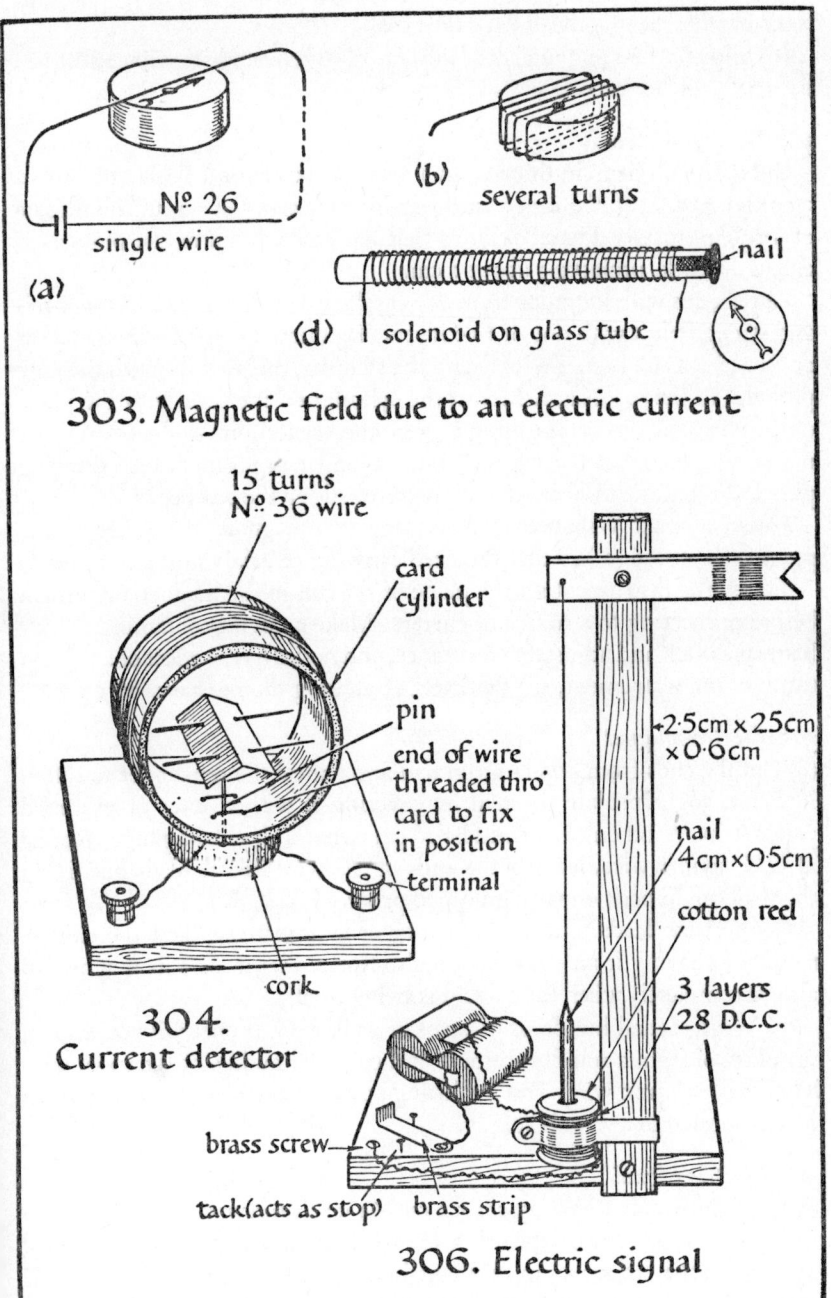

303. Magnetic field due to an electric current

304. Current detector

306. Electric signal

of glass tubing. Switch on the current and notice how the compass needle behaves when held at the ends of the tube.

(d) Slip an iron nail (annealed) into the glass tube and see what effect this has on the deflection of the compass needle.

304 Current Detector

Cut a disc about 1 cm thick from a 3-cm diameter cork. Push a pin about 3 cm long through the centre and cement the cork, flat, on to the middle of a square plywood baseboard, so that the pointed end of the pin stands above the cork, projecting about 2 cm.

Cut a 3-cm wide cylinder from the cardboard centre of an old toilet-roll and strengthen it with one or two layers of gummed paper. Wind 15 turns of No. 36 D.C.C. copper wire round the cylinder, carrying the ends through pinholes in the cardboard. Mount the cylinder on the cork with the plane of the wire coil vertical, pushing it on to the vertical pin whilst taking care not to foul the insulated wires. Fix the cylinder in position with drawing pins and run the leads from the coil to terminals on the baseboard.

Mount a small V-shaped card carrying two magnetized needles on the pin (cf. Expt. 296 (a)) so that the needles swing centrally in the cylinder.

To use the instrument set the plane of the coil in the magnetic meridian before connecting to a source of current. Make a circuit containing a cycle battery, switch and adjustable resistance, and notice (i) the effect of a current through the instrument, (ii) the effect of altering the resistance in circuit.

305 Electro-magnet

(a) Cut the ends from a 15-cm iron nail and anneal the remainder to soften it (Expt. 302). Insulate the nail by covering it with a layer of gummed paper-strip. Wind on to the middle 10 cm two neat layers of gauge 26 or 28 D.C.C. copper wire, leaving the ends of the wire free as leads but fixing the winding in position with gummed paper.

Connect the leads to an accumulator or cycle battery. Test the electro-magnet by laying it amongst boot-nails. Notice that it loses its magnetism almost completely when the current is switched off.

(b) Wrap several hundreds of turns of 30 S.W.G. copper wire on a spare metal spool from a roll-film camera and pack the middle of the spool with lengths of soft iron wire. Test the lifting power of this electro-magnet when it is connected to a 12-volt supply.

306 Electric Signal

An upright wooden post, 25 cm $\times$ 2 cm $\times$ 1 cm is screwed to one edge of a 12 cm $\times$ 8 cm $\times$ 1 cm baseboard. 5 cm from the top of the post the signal arm, 9 cm $\times$ 2 cm $\times$ 0.5 cm and suitably coloured, is pivoted on a small screw 2 cm from one end. Small washers on either side of the signal arm help towards free movement. Suspended from the short end of the signal

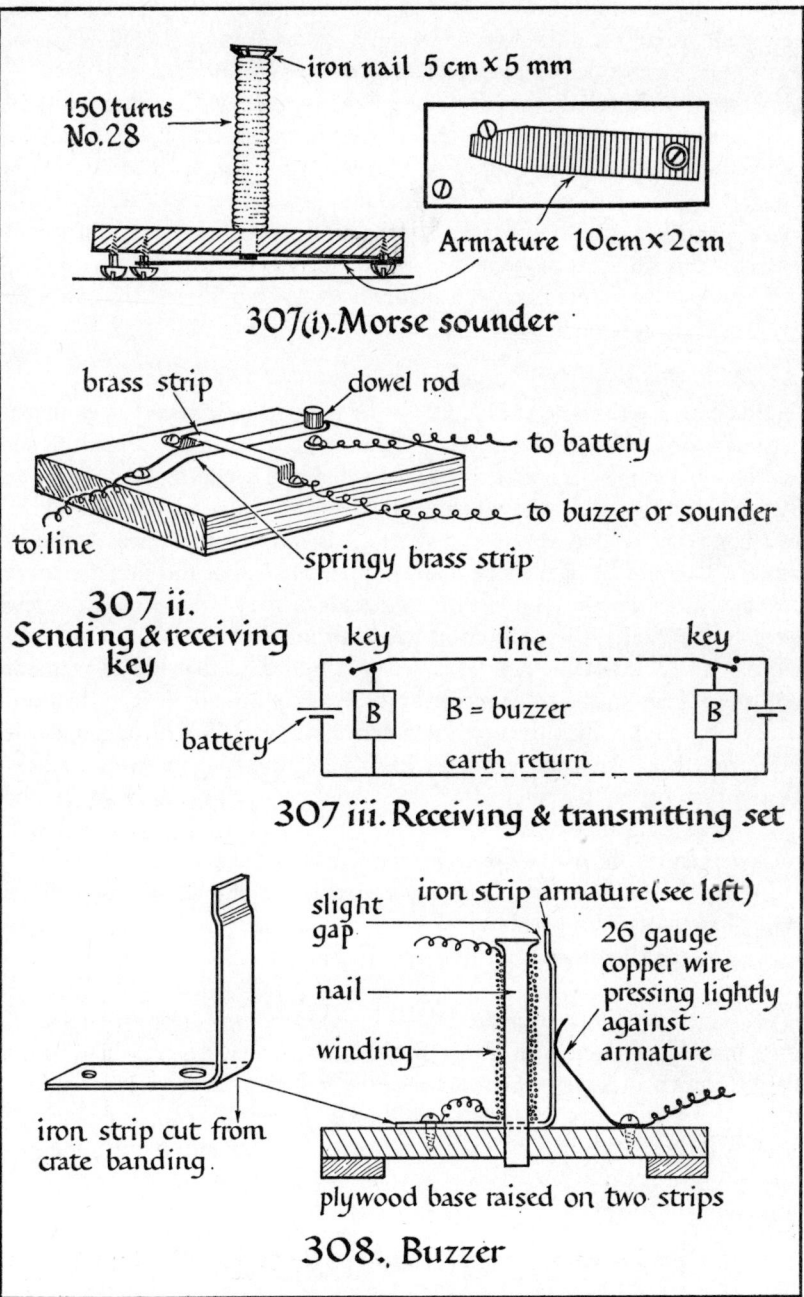

arm is a length of thin wire (about 15 cm) soldered at its lower end to one end of an armature. This armature, 4 cm long, is cut from a 15-cm iron nail and moves freely in and out of the central hole in a cotton reel fixed at the bottom of the upright post. The reel is wrapped with 100 turns of 28 D.C.C. wire connected to a switch (on the baseboard) and cycle battery.

The signal arm should move upwards when the current is switched on, and fall again as it is switched off; final adjustment can be made by hammering small nails into either end of the arm. The only other adjustment is that of ensuring that the armature moves freely in the hole in the reel.

If the armatures are prepared beforehand, such a signal can easily be made within a double lesson.

307 *Morse Sounder*
Wind about 150 turns of 28 D.C.C. copper wire on an iron core, 5 cm long, cut from the head end of a big nail (about 0·5 cm diameter). Press the cut end of the core into a hole drilled in a wooden baseboard (see Figure) so that the electromagnet projects upward. Beneath the base is a strip of iron, 10 cm × 2 cm, drilled at one end where it is screwed to the baseboard as shown. The middle of the strip passes under the end of the electromagnet and the free end presses against the underside of the head of a second screw fixed in the board (the position of the head in relation to the strip is obviously easily adjustable). A third screw is added so that the instrument will stand firm on the three screw heads, leaving a shallow space beneath the baseboard in which the armature strip can move. When the magnet is energized, the armature is pulled up against the magnet with a click. When the current is switched off, the armature springs away again, the free end striking the screw with another click. A paper disc gummed over the lower end of the magnet prevents the armature from sticking.

Use a simple tapping key (springy brass strip tapping down on to a brass screw-head, mounted on plywood base); the key may be in one room and the sounder in another, the instruments being connected through a dry battery.

Messages may be sent and received in each room by using two sets of instruments arranged as in Diagram (iii). In this case, tapping keys of the design shown in Diagram (ii) are necessary; when the brass strip springs upwards (breaking contact with the "home" battery) it comes against the brass "bridge" and so puts the "home" sounder into circuit with the distant key and battery.

308 *Buzzer*
The same kind of electro-magnet, fixed upright in a wooden baseboard, is used as in the sounder of Expt. 307. A piece of packing strip or tin strip is bent and fixed so that when the magnet is energized the upright part of the strip is drawn against the head of the nail and in doing so breaks contact

with the piece of copper wire which rests lightly against it. Current passes in through the magnet winding and thence to the metal strip, leaving via the copper wire. Thus we have a make-and-break arrangement which will give continuous "buzzing" when connected with a cycle battery.

309 *Microphone*

This instrument can be used either (i) in conjunction with a wireless set and loudspeaker, or (ii) in conjunction with the telephone described in Expt. 310. It is easily made in a very short time and the method of construction is practically foolproof.

The following two parts should be prepared in advance of the lesson, preferably by the boys in Woodwork lesson:

(i) A wood block, 8 cm × 5 cm × 2 cm; none of the dimensions in this model is critical. 3 cm from the top of one face drill a 2-cm diameter cavity about 1 cm deep. Clean out the hole with sandpaper. Drill two holes, about 1 cm between centres, from the top end of the block down into the cavity. These should be of the same diameter as the carbon rods from a cycle battery.

(ii) A wooden block, 5 cm × 5 cm × 1 cm, through the centre of which is drilled a 2-cm diameter hole.

For the practical lesson itself the pupils require, in addition:

Two carbon rods, with brass caps, from an old cycle battery. Carbon granules, which they may prepare for themselves in advance by hammering up old cycle battery carbons in a piece of cloth and sieving off the fine dust through butter muslin. Thin card and scissors, to make spacing rings. Small piece of thin tin-plate. Connecting wire.

With pencil or scriber and using a 10p piece, trace out two circles on the card and one on the tin-plate; cut these out. Cut the centres out of the cardboard circles so as to leave two rings of card.

Push the carbon rods down into the holes provided for them in the larger wood block, so that they project into the hole. Pack this hole with carbon granules, tapping them well down. Put one cardboard spacing ring round the hole, add a few more granules, cover with the tin-plate circle (diaphragm) and a second spacing ring, and screw the second wood block over so that the hole in it exposes the metal diaphragm. Two rubber bands can be used in place of screws to hold the parts of the microphone together. Solder connecting wires to the caps on the carbon rods. The microphone is now complete.

For use with a wireless set, proceed as follows. Wire the microphone through a cycle battery to the 8-volt terminals of a bell-transformer. Connect the 230-volt terminals to the gramophone terminals on the wireless set. Reproduction from a loudspeaker in another room is remarkably clear and strong.

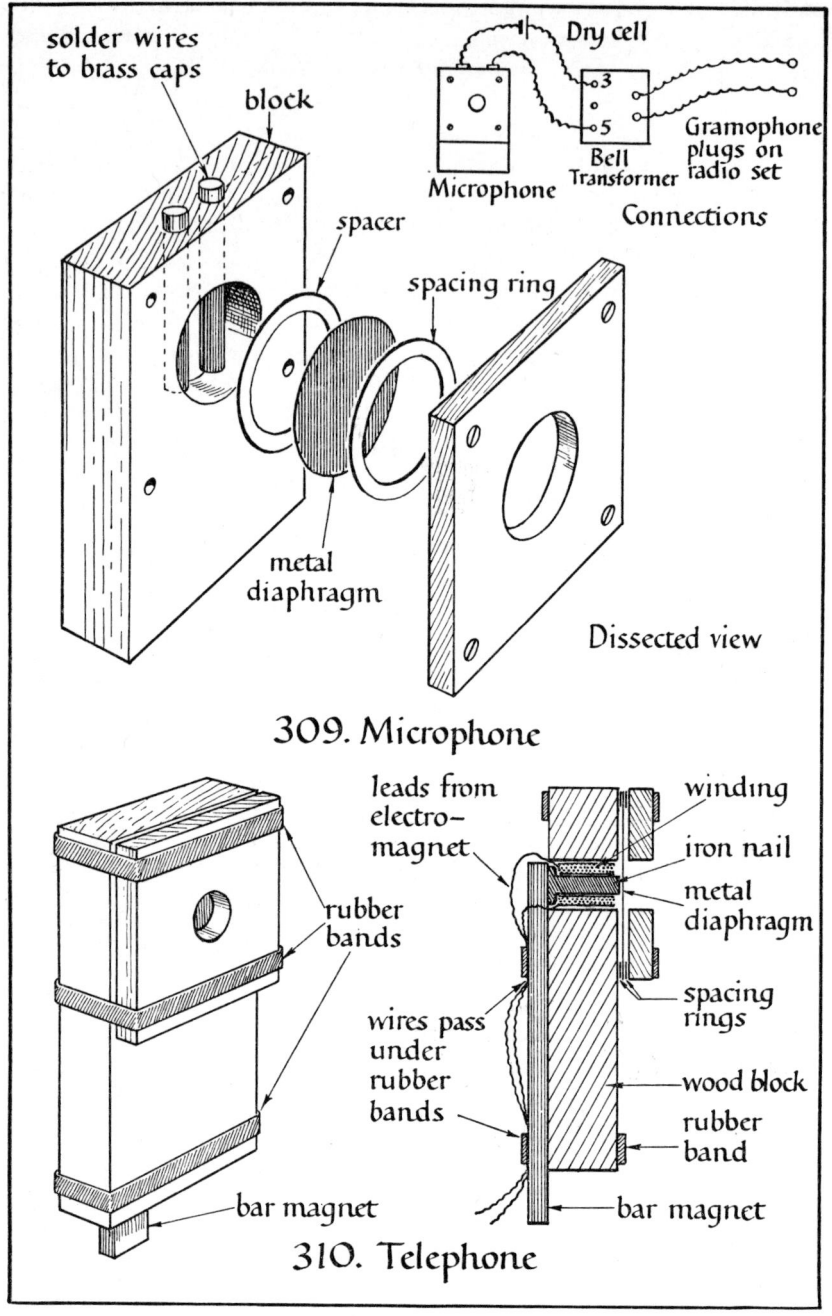

309. Microphone

310. Telephone

310 Telephone

This model is very suitable for a Science Club, but it is also a most effective example for teacher demonstration. The electro-magnet should be prepared beforehand.

For the magnet use a 10-cm round nail (about 5 mm diameter), previously annealed—see Expt. 302. Cover with a layer of gummed paper and fit on two card end-discs (5 cm diameter), one flush with the nail-head and the other about 2 cm farther along the nail. The second one may be kept in position by a little more gummed paper. Grip the pointed end of the nail in a hand drill, clamp the drill in a vice, and by turning the handle of the drill rotate the nail whilst winding on as much D.C.C. wire (28 or 36) as will fill the space between the end-discs. Cover the coil with gummed paper, carrying the ends of the wire out as leads at the head end of the nail. Cut off the other end of the nail beyond the second end-disc, leaving an electro-magnet 2 cm long.

Drill a 1·5-cm diameter hole through a wood block (10 cm × 5 cm × 2 cm), centre about 2 cm from one end of the block. Drill a similar hole through the centre of a 5 cm × 5 cm × 1 cm block. Prepare a pair of card rings and a thin tin-plate diaphragm, all 5 cm diameter, the hole in each ring being about 3 cm diameter. The diaphragm may be cut from the thin metal lid of a tin can.

Press the magnet into the hole in the larger block; it should be a tight fit, and more gummed paper packing can be used as required. Fit the diaphragm between the card rings and clamp centrally over the sawn-off end of the magnet, using the second block as a cover and using rubber bands to bind the blocks together. Finally, fit a cobalt-steel bar-magnet behind the instrument so that one pole covers the head of the magnet nail; the bar-magnet can be held by rubber bands (e.g. cut from an old cycle innertube).

Test the instrument by connecting it through a cycle battery with the microphone in another room. It may be necessary to reverse the bar-magnet so that the other pole covers the electro-magnet; this depends upon the direction of flow of current in the electro-magnet windings.

Topics: The electric bell and circuits employing it: many interesting devices can be set up in the Science Club—e.g. house bells, room indicators, door-mat alarms, fire-alarms, etc. Uses of electro-magnets in industry—in cranes, magnetic separators, magnetic chucks, automatic switches, etc., as well as in motors, dynamos, and transformers.

The Electric Motor

311 Moving-coil meter

The pointer is a light wooden spill. It is bound to the side of a 2·5 cm dia-

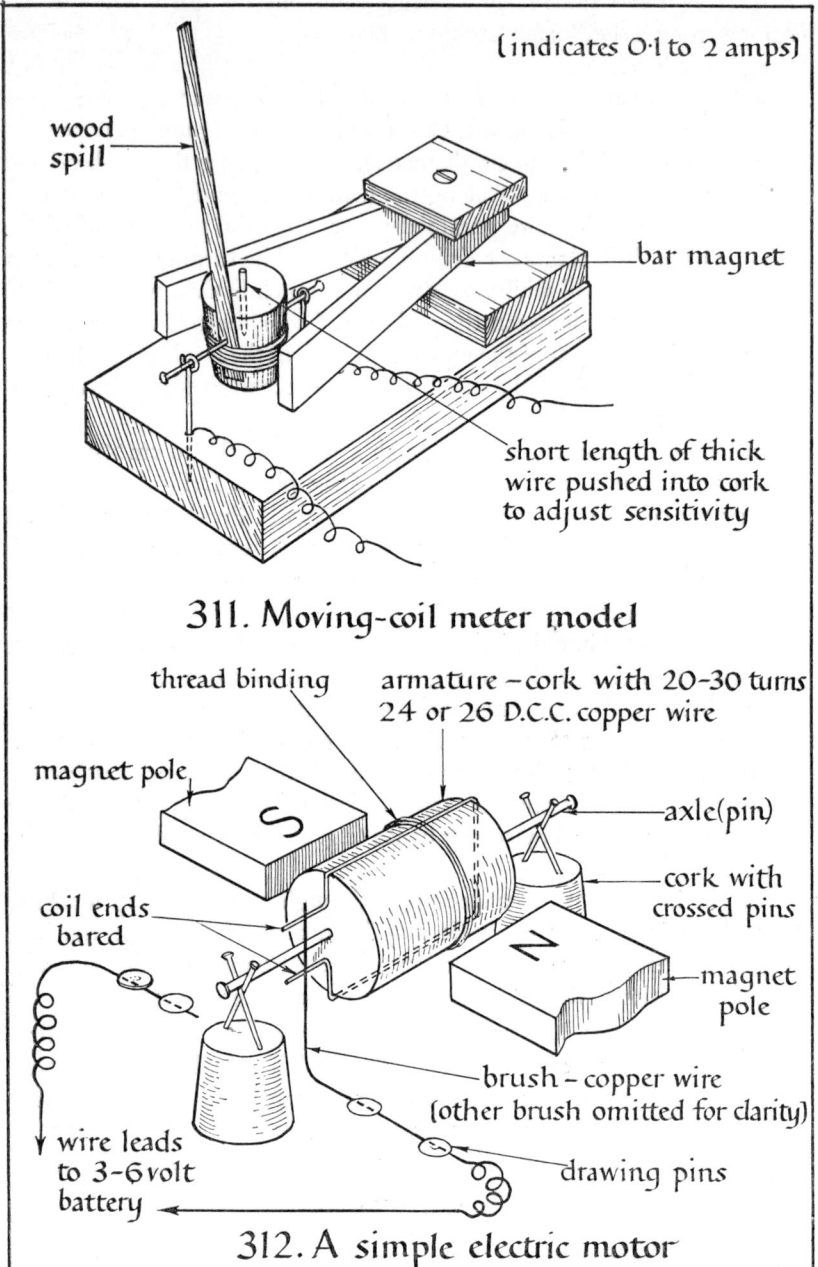

311. Moving-coil meter model

312. A simple electric motor

meter cork by 10 turns of No. 28 D.C.C. wire wound round the narrower end. Two pins pushed into opposite sides of the cork (along a diameter) between the coil wires serve as the axle and the ends of the coil are bound tightly round these pins, which also act as terminals. Each bearing for the axle is made by bending No. 16 copper wire into a narrow loop in which an axle pin will run. These bearing wires are fixed upright in holes drilled in the wooden baseboard. A bar-magnet fixed on each side of the cork completes the model.

The meter may be tested by connecting the bearing wires to a cycle battery and torch bulb (0·3 A) or to a 6-volt source and a 12-volt, 6-watt car bulb (0·5 A). Its sensitivity may be increased by cutting off cork below the axle, or by adjusting a No. 16 copper-wire weight pushed into the top of the cork.

312 *Model Motor*

This well-known design allows pupils to construct their own working model within a lesson period.

The armature consists of 30 turns of gauge 24 or 26 D.C.C. wire wrapped longitudinally round a 2·5-cm diameter cork, half the turns being put on at one side of the axle pins and half at the other. These pins, one at each end of the cork, are stuck in as centrally as possible so that the armature will spin smoothly. The coil is made secure by binding it with thread or with gummed paper. Its free ends are bent over at one end of the cork and then again at right angles so that they are in the same plane as the winding and parallel with the axle pin and about 5 mm from it on either side. These ends are bared and cleaned with emery paper.

Each bearing is made by pushing two pins into one end of a cork so that they form a cross, in the top V of which the axle may run. The armature is mounted on the bearings, and bar-magnets (opposite poles) are mounted on either side of it, the magnets being raised on small blocks of wood to the level of the armature. The magnets should just clear the armature as it spins.

Each contact-brush consists of a thin wire fixed to the base with drawing-pins and bent upwards at right angles so as to just touch the outside of the commutator wires as they spin; there is one brush on each side of the axle.

Connect the brush wires to a cycle battery or to the accumulators and spin the armature by hand; if the motor does not start try spinning it the other way. When the brushes are correctly adjusted, so that they just make contact, the motor will run at high speed; a drop of oil on each bearing helps.

Topics: Demonstration of actual working motors, including those built at the Science Club (see later). The factors that make for power.

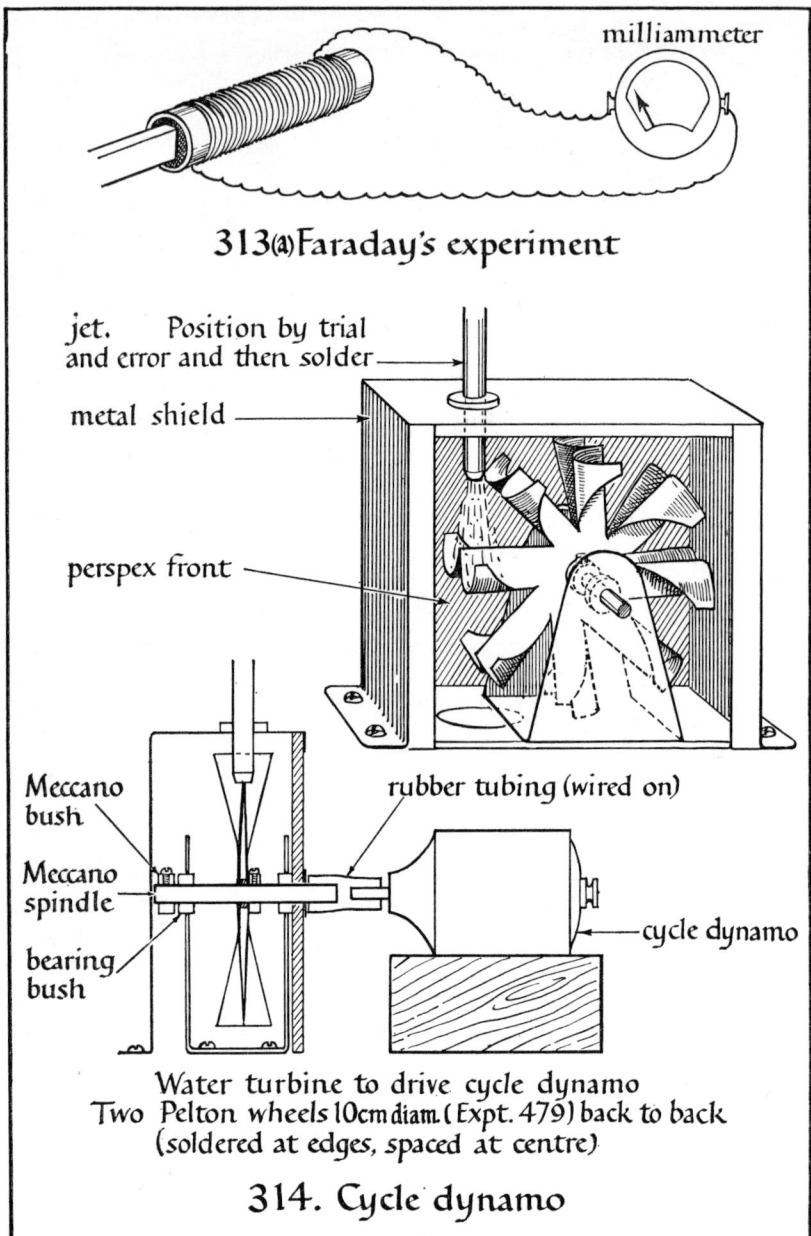

313(a) Faraday's experiment

314. Cycle dynamo

Water turbine to drive cycle dynamo
Two Pelton wheels 10cm diam. (Expt. 479) back to back
(soldered at edges, spaced at centre)

The uses of motors at home (e.g. electric washer, vacuum cleaner, radiogram, hair dryer) and in the world outside (e.g. trains, cranes, farming machinery, pumps, lathes, fans).

The Dynamo
A model motor (e.g. one of the Science Club models) will generate enough current when turned by hand to affect a centre-zero milliammeter connected in series with the motor leads.

313 *Principle of the Dynamo*
(a) Faraday's experiment: Prepare a solenoid by wrapping 100–200 turns of fine insulated copper wire on a cardboard tube large enough to admit of a bar-magnet being thrust inside it. Connect the ends of the coil to a centre-zero milliammeter.

Using a bar-magnet, thrust (i) a north pole, (ii) a south pole into the solenoid. Note what happens to the meter pointer when the magnet is thrust into the coil, when it is at rest within the coil, and when it is withdrawn. Try also the effect of a more powerful magnet, and of speeding up the movement.

Try a similar experiment using the current detector of Expt. 304 instead of the milliammeter and using a solenoid carrying a similar coil to that of the detector itself.

(b) Wind a coil of perhaps 700 turns of 22 S.W.G. copper wire in six layers on a cardboard tube about 10 cm long and 4 cm in diameter. Join the coil in series with a flash-lamp bulb. Bind together several Alnico magnets, push the bundle into the tube and then pull it smartly out: the lamp flashes.

314 *Cycle Dynamo*
Expose the interior. Observe the circular permanent magnet driven by a knurled nut which fits against the cycle tyre; the coil of many turns of fine wire built on a U-shaped core within which the circular permanent magnet rotates; and the single lead to the cycle lamp, the return path of the current being through the frame of the machine. Test the permanent magnet with a charm compass and notice that it is magnetized along a diameter.

Mount the dynamo on blocks on a wooden baseboard alongside a water turbine with a 10-cm diameter wheel (Expt. 478) so that the axles of the two machines are in line. Join the axles by a short length of pressure tubing. A shield will be needed round the turbine (see Fig. 314) and a hole must be cut in the baseboard beneath it to carry off water. More power is obtained by using the double wheel shown in Fig. 314 with a jet of 3 mm diameter.

Connect the dynamo with several bulb holders arranged in parallel, set the turbine going and note the resistance to movement as soon as a 6-volt bulb is inserted. The drop in speed and in voltage is most marked as more bulbs are inserted, i.e. as the dynamo is over-loaded.

315 Model Alternator

This is a demonstration model which should be made in the Science Club, but which is an essential part of the Science course in that it exhibits dynamo action so clearly.

Construct the model according to the details shown in the diagram. An 8-cm × 2-cm slot is cut in the 20-cm × 15-cm baseboard to allow rotation of the Alnico magnet. The magnet, 7 cm × 1·5 cm × 1 cm, is held in a groove across one end of a cotton reel by means of a light metal strap, and it rotates between the arms of a "stator" formed from two doubly bent mild steel strips, each 18 cm × 1 cm × 0·3 cm, strapped together on to the baseboard. The stator is wrapped with five layers of 22 D.C.C. copper wire, the ends of which are connected with a torch bulb (1½ volts) or, alternatively, with a centre-zero voltmeter. The reel and magnet are turned by working a 10-cm diameter plywood driving wheel which bears against a length of rubber tubing on the spindle which carries the reel. The reel should be bushed at each end with aluminium so that the spindle (a large nail) is a tight fit. The driving wheel must be cut true (e.g. with a washer cutter); it turns on a coachbolt (5 cm × 6 mm) held in a double bracket as shown.

Start with the magnet vertical. On rotating the wheel rapidly the lamp is seen to light up. If a centre-zero voltmeter is substituted for the lamp the alternating nature of the output is clearly demonstrated.

316 Hum from the 50-cycle mains

Connect a 3-volt A.C. supply to the nail electro-magnet of Expt. 305. The magnet may rest horizontally on a wood block. Bring the bottom of an empty tin can into contact with one pole of the magnet. The noise which can be heard is caused by the rapid changes in the magnetization of the nail occurring each half-cycle.

If low-voltage A.C. is not distributed to the pupils' benches, the experiment may be performed as a demonstration, using a bell-transformer plugged in to the mains. Such a transformer often has tappings of 3, 5, and 8 volts on the output side.

The Transformer

Only properly wired and covered-in transformers should be used by pupils where mains current is concerned. The ordinary bell transformer and the laboratory microprojector are useful. As a preliminary it is worth showing that a bell-transformer, fed from the mains, will light three torch bulbs (2·5-volt) in series, or a car side-lamp (6-volt); whilst a microprojector

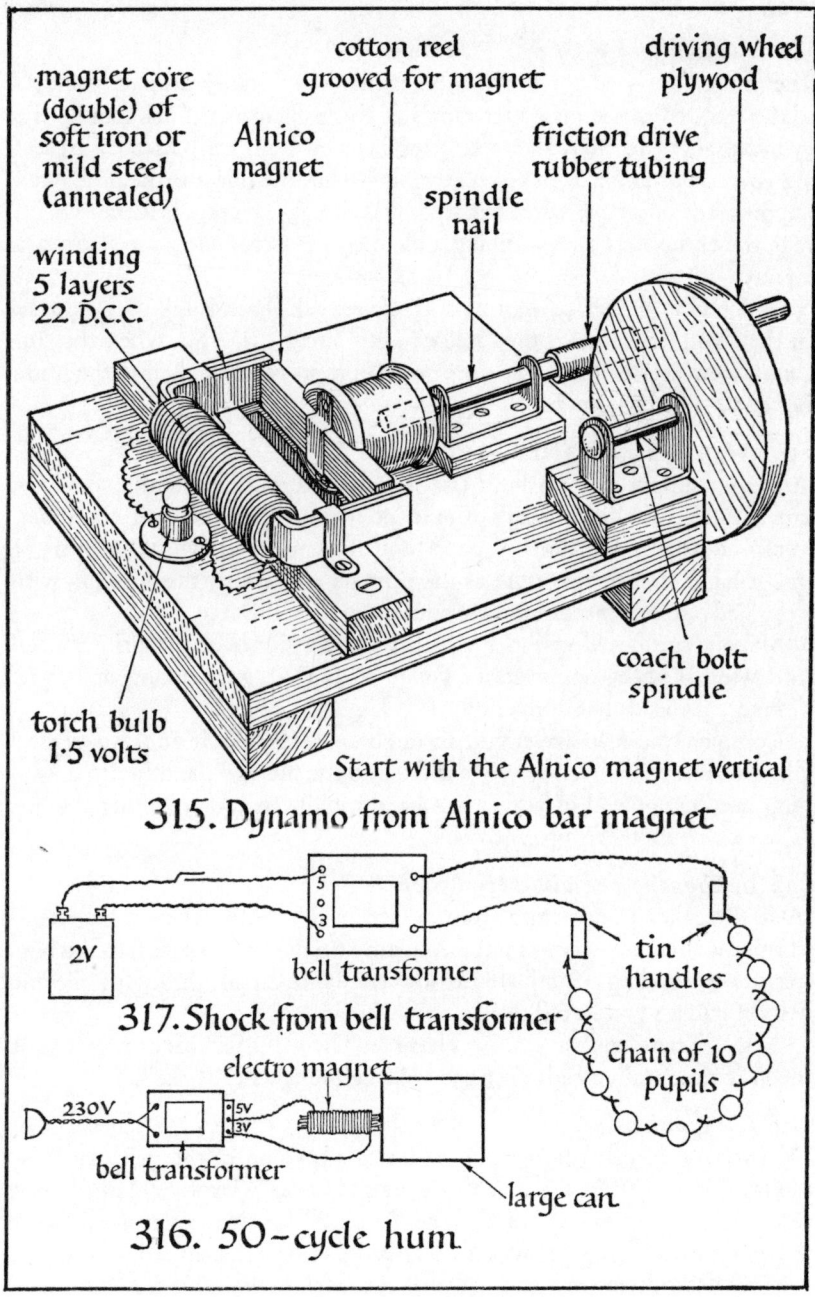

315. Dynamo from Alnico bar magnet

317. Shock from bell transformer

316. 50-cycle hum

transformer giving 12 volts will light two headlamp bulbs (12-volt, 24-watt) in parallel.

317 *Electric Shock from Bell Transformer*
The mains supply is not used in this experiment. Solder tin-plate handles to the leads from the mains terminals of the transformer. Each handle is a cylinder, about 10 cm × 2 cm diameter, bent up from scrap metal. Connect a 2-volt accumulator to the 8-volt terminals and include a make and break (tapping key or simple wire switch) in this circuit. Ten pupils form a chain, with the end pupils each gripping a handle so as to complete the secondary circuit.

Switch the primary current on and off; a weak shock is felt by the pupils in the chain, but only at the "make" and "break" (i.e. not when the current is flowing steadily). Try the effect of progressively reducing the number of pupils in the chain.

318 (a) *Interrupted Supply*
Anneal a supply of 7-cm nails (Expt. 302) and make a bundle about 1·5 cm diameter—half the heads should point one way and half the other. Wrap on a layer of gummed paper and then wind on two neat layers of gauge 24 D.C.C. copper wire as the primary coil, fixing the winding with gummed paper or insulating tape but leaving the ends free.

Make a cardboard cylinder which will just slip over the primary coil and wind it with two layers of gauge 26 D.C.C. wire, fixing as before. Connect the leads to a torch bulb.

Complete the primary circuit through an accumulator and a new steel file; one of the connecting wires is fixed to the file and the other to a knitting needle, one end of which is rubbed rapidly to and fro along the file. The torch bulb lights up.

318 (b) *Transformer with a High Step-up Ratio*
A loudspeaker transformer from a valve radio, T.V. set or a bell transformer is suitable. Connect any neon lamp (mains or indicator) to the high resistance winding. Complete the low resistance circuit through a file and a spike and a 1½-volt cell.

Note: Transistor transformers have too few turns for this experiment. A neon lamp usually needs over 150 volts before it will "strike".

319 *Car Ignition Coil*
A 6-volt or 12-volt car ignition coil is used. Connect the primary (low-voltage) terminals in series with the nail "buzzer" (Expt. 308) and 3 or 6 accumulators (or other source). The "buzzer" for this experiment should be wound with gauge 20 wire so that it does not seriously reduce the voltage to the ignition coil; and "silver" contacts are desirable for continuous working.

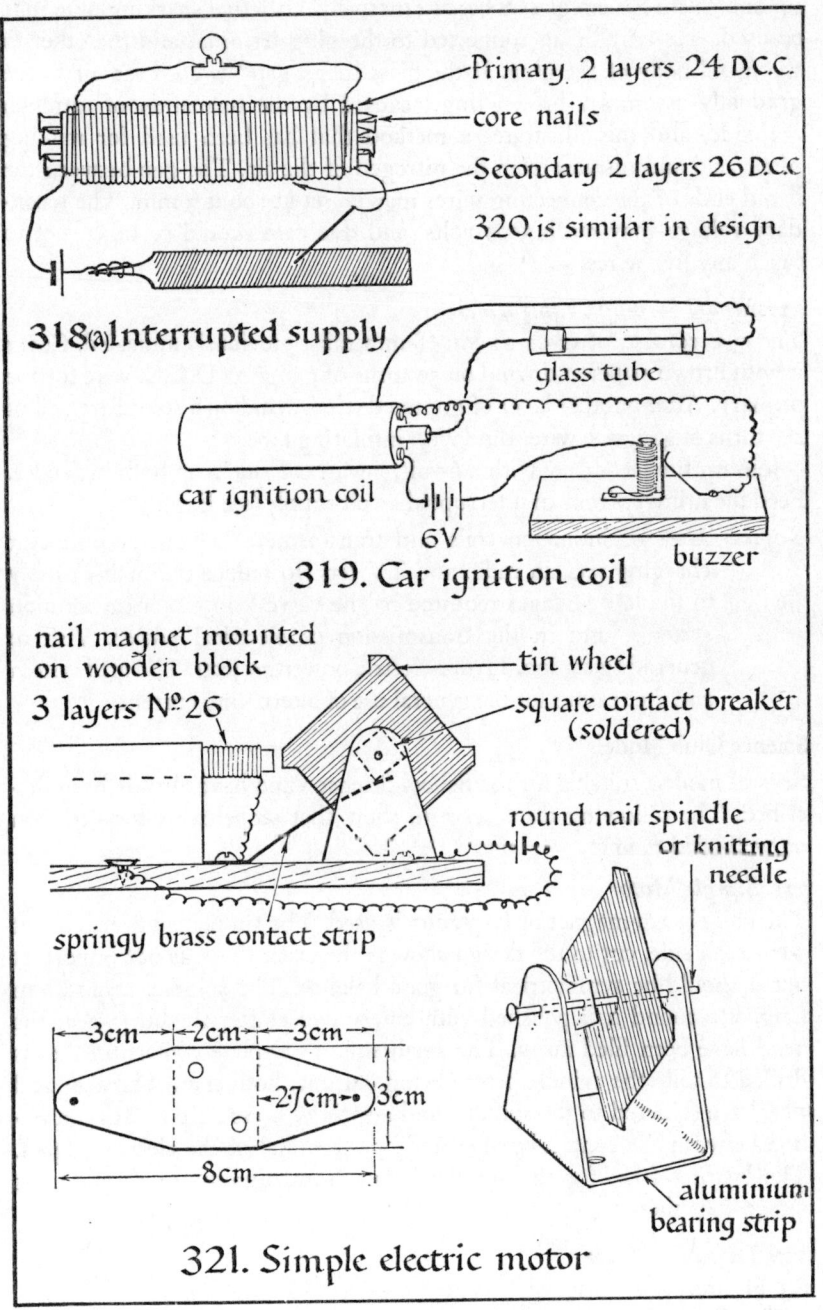

318(a) Interrupted supply

319. Car ignition coil

321. Simple electric motor

The secondary terminals of the coil are connected to a spark gap, made up in an 8 cm × 2 cm glass tube; alternatively, an actual sparking plug may be used, one wire being connected to the plug terminal and the other to the metal body of the plug. If the glass tube "gap" is used the air inside gradually assumes a brown tinge, caused by the formation of nitrogen peroxide, and this illustrates a method that has been used for making nitric acid and nitrates from the nitrogen of the air. The gap between the bared ends of the connecting wires may be set at about 3 mm. The secondary voltage may reach 5000 volts, and due care should be taken not to touch any live wires.

320 *Model Step-up Transformer*
The core consists of seven 20-cm × 8-mm rails, previously annealed. Cover it with brown paper and wind on 50 turns of gauge 22 D.C.C. wire for the primary. After another layer of gummed paper wind on a secondary coil of 200 turns of gauge 26 wire. Bind with insulating tape.

Join up the secondary with a 6-volt, 3-watt car sidelamp bulb in holder. Feed the primary from an interrupted 2-volt supply (see Expt. 318).

Topics Uses of induction coils and transformers—e.g. in accumulator charging sets, in radio and TV sets (to reduce the mains supply to the low voltages required by the valves), in motor-car ignition systems, and in the transmission of electrical power. Visit to generating station. Hydro-electric power projects. The grid system and the reasons for the general use of alternating current.

Science Club Models
Several models suitable for the School Science Club have already been described. The following three serve to show that scope exists for variation on well-tried themes.

321 *Simple Motor*
The nail electro-magnet of Expt. 305 is used. The tin-plate wheel is about 5 cm each side, cut to the design shown; the exact shape is not important but it should be symmetrical for good balance. The spindle, about 4 cm long, is a round nail polished with emery paper after the burrs near the head have been filed away. The small square tin-plate contact-breaker is drilled to take the spindle before being cut out; both contact-breaker and wheel are soldered to the spindle, and a springy brass strip makes connection between the contact-breaker and one terminal of the electro-magnet. The bearing strip for the spindle is cut from aluminium sheet to the dimensions shown.

322 *Two-pole Motor*
See Figure.

The dimensions are:

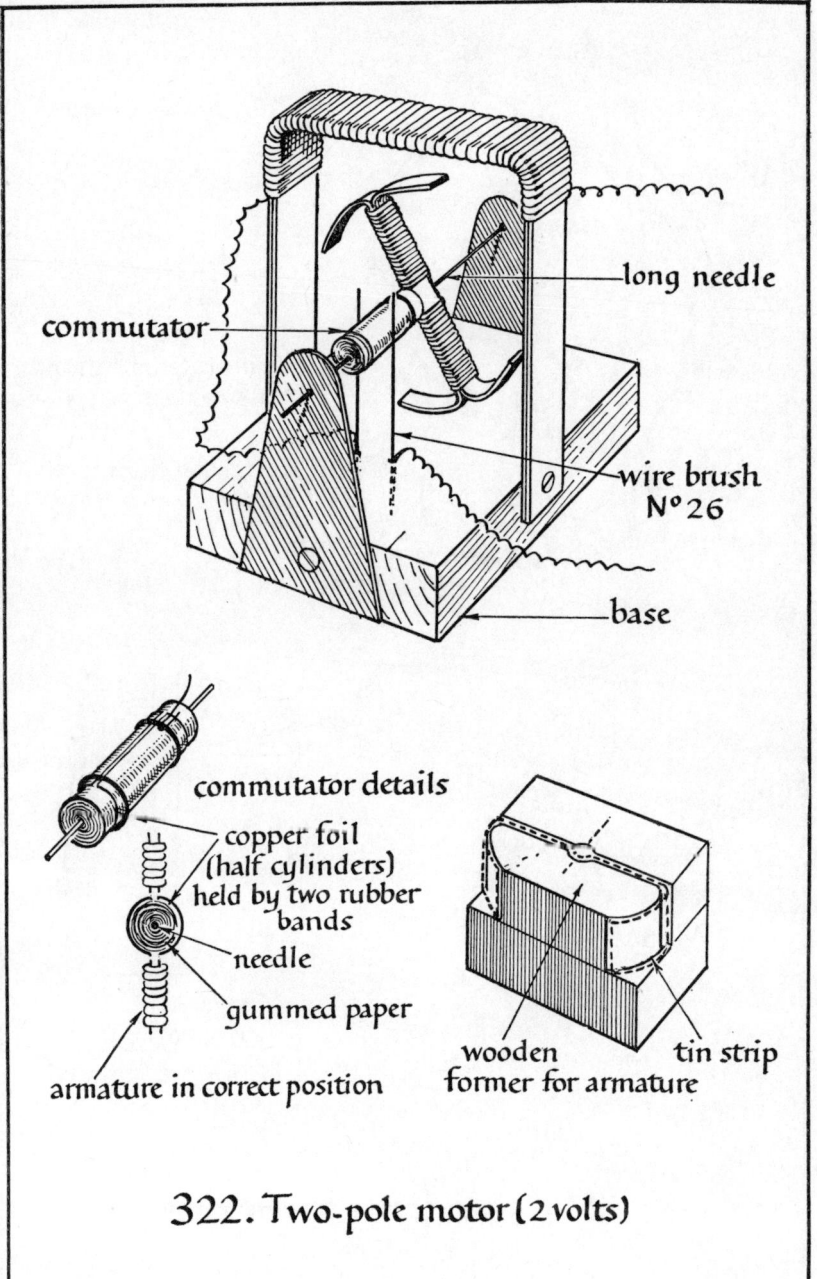

322. Two-pole motor (2 volts)

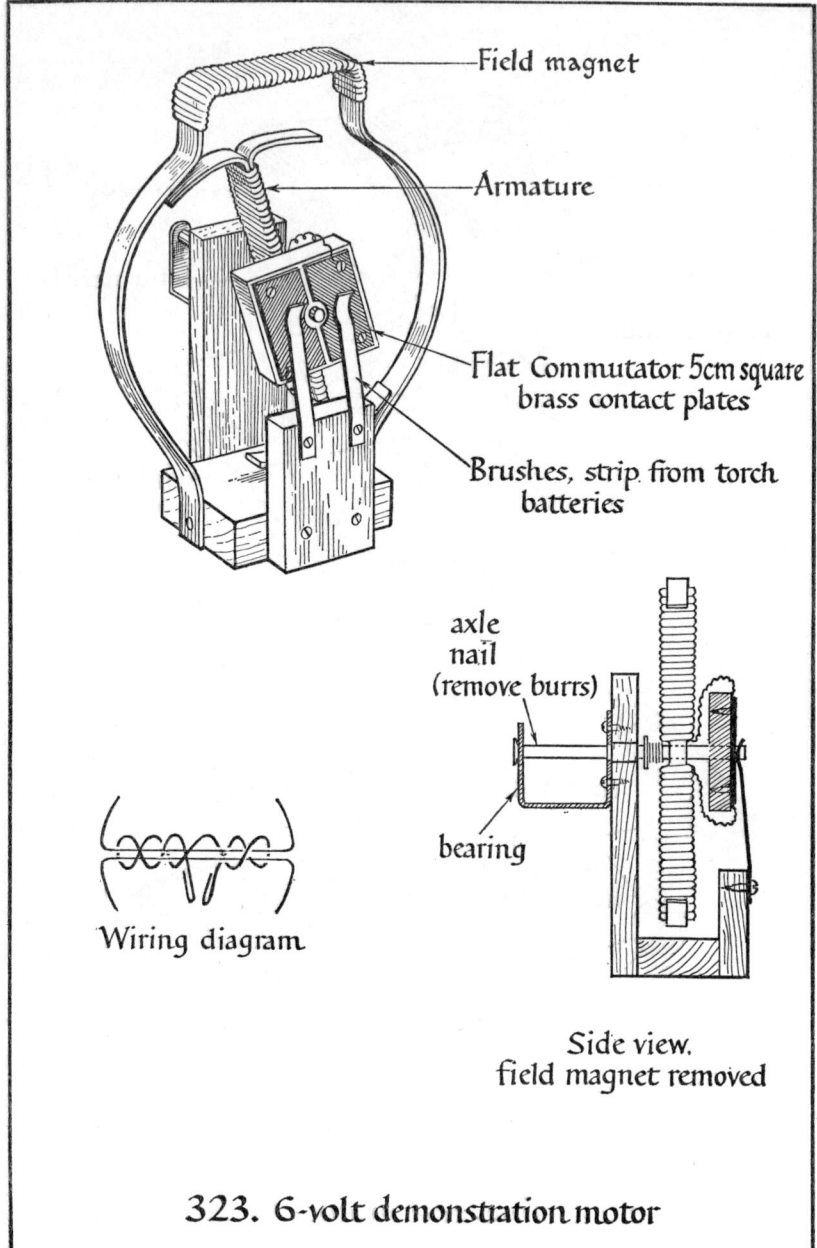

323. 6-volt demonstration motor

Armature: Diameter 3·5 cm, made from two tin strips each 6 cm × 1·5 cm, with two layers of 26 D.C.C. wire wound (start and finish at the middle) over brown paper. Field magnet: Core 7 cm high × 4 cm wide × 1·5 cm deep, made from 2 tin strips. Coil is two layers of 26 D.C.C. wire wound over brown paper.

Base: 4 cm × 5 cm × 1 cm.

323 *Large Motor for Demonstration*

See Figure

The dimensions are:

Armature: Diameter 15 cm; made from two tin strips each 25 cm × 1 cm × 3 mm, with two layers of 26 D.C.C. wire on brown paper (start and finish at the middle).

Field Magnet: Core made from strip 50 cm × 1 cm × 2 mm covered by three layers of 24 D.C.C. wire wrapped over brown paper.

Base: 8 cm × 4 cm × 2 cm.

Axle: 10 cm nail. Bearing strip: 15 cm × 1 cm × 2 mm.

Uprights: Plywood 1 cm thick.

Excellent books are available giving detailed instructions on how to make electrical (and other) models suitable for the Science Club. Examples are:

T. E. Haynes: *Model Engineering for Schools* (John Murray: 3 vols)
Sims (revised Armac, 1965): *The Boy Electrician* (Harrap)
Rumming: *Make and Use Models* (U.L.P.: 4 vols)
Boothroyd: *How and Why it Works* (Schofield and Sims: 3 vols)
Tweddle: *Science Teacher's Handbook* (Harrap)
Bulman: *Model-making for Young Physicists* (John Murray)

Chapter Sixteen

Music and Noise

The Teacher's Schemes and Records

Any teacher is well advised to keep careful and continuous records. By doing so he can avoid confusion and duplication of effort, profit by experience, and ensure that the time allotted to his subject is most economically used. He will also save himself time in the long run.

The records which the Science teacher needs, apart from some common to every subject (mark lists, progress reports, etc.), are described below. The list is formidable, but it should be remembered that only the day-book demands frequent and regular attention. Schemes and directions for experiments are usually worked out "at leisure"; the reference file and the shortages book are used only as occasion demands; the stock-book must be made up periodically; and the library catalogue can be assigned to an interested pupil.

(a) A Science Syllabus: We distinguish here between a syllabus, which lists the main subject headings of a course, and a scheme of work, which analyses the subjects of the syllabus in much more detail and indicates an order in which the various matters are intended to be tackled.

What science is included in the syllabus ought to be decided, in agreement with the Head of the school, on the basis of an assessment of actual needs of the pupils to whom the syllabus will refer. Too often in the past it has been determined by the syllabus of an external examining body on which the majority of teachers had little effective voice. With the growth of regional examinations for Modern schools in the fifties and now especially with their replacement by the Certificate of Secondary Education examinations, there is a prospect of radical change. Examinations Bulletin No. 1 (1963) of the Schools Examinations Council gets to the root of the problem:

". . . the proper context for the discussion of these matters is the schools' work itself, which in content and teaching method must constantly seek to marry the needs of society, and of particular interests within it, with those of the individual pupil. The C.S.E. examinations are intended to be . . . a reflection of this school work, involving the same reconciliation of general and individual needs, and not a convenient means of imposing a pattern upon the schools. It follows that whoever is entrusted with the last word in matters of school work must also control the examinations which measure its achievements. The teachers must, therefore, be in effective control of the C.S.E. examinations."

In 1964 the S.S.E.C. was replaced by the Schools Council for the Curriculum and Examinations—a change which suggests that curricula, teaching methods and examinations are closely inter-related parts of the educational system. Meanwhile teachers were made aware of yet another forward move, being given the option through Mode III of the examinations system of determining their own individual examination syllabuses, setting and even marking the examinations for their own pupils, subject only to moderation by the Examinations Board. For well understood reasons the majority of candidates have so far been entered for centrally-set papers, under Mode I, but it is very much to be hoped that more and more teachers will avail themselves of the opportunities which Mode III offers, not least for the average and somewhat below average pupils.

What topics to include and which to omit cannot be laid down here, since they depend so much upon the circumstances of individual schools. But there seems no reason to depart greatly from the list of subjects dealt with in the first edition of this book, from which each teacher may make his choice. In the present edition some topics have been enlarged upon or added (e.g. weather, radio and the transistor, and space science).

Those for whom this book is intended are unlikely to overlook the many boys and girls for whom a public examination would be quite inappropriate. Syllabus-making and the working out of a scheme is a matter requiring particular care in the case of less-able or much-retarded pupils. It can also be very rewarding; for Science, practically presented, has much to offer. That this is the case with school gardening, for example, is well known, but it is true in other areas too. Slow youngsters can come to life when the subject is their own bodies, or the machines of the space age, or the homely applications of science which they recognize as part of their own experience. Not infrequently the backward classes in school contain a high proportion of socially disadvantaged children, for whom practical work in science can make up some of the gaps. Not the weakest, but the best teachers are needed for this work; those with knowledge and experience if possible, but above all those with imagination, sympathy and patience.

(b) A Detailed Scheme of Work: A good scheme is the outcome of much experience (the teacher's or another's) and few teachers of any subject will claim that they have yet written one which completely satisfies them. Revision and re-writing are part of the game. But it may often occur that a newcomer to a Staff will be obliged to take over from a predecessor and in such a case he would do well to make a thorough investigation of the kind and extent of the work which has been done before proceeding to sweeping changes; the pupils may be questioned concerning the experiments which have been undertaken, work-books and textbooks should be examined, and an assessment of the stock of apparatus should be made. The time allowance for each class must be considered, and the facilities for practical work taken into account. Where a teacher resolves to undertake group practical work with his pupils for the first time, circumstances may compel him to begin in modest fashion. It is no bad thing initially to select a few experiments such as may be suitable for more than one class, so that the experiment which Class S.III has just performed may be repeated by S.II in the following lesson. There are obvious limitations upon this, but a thoughtful teacher can give himself time to become experienced in handling the practical problems by this means. Gradually, as the details of experiments are worked out, as pupils become accustomed to fending for themselves in the laboratory, and as the teacher develops confidence, more pupils' experiments may be added to the repertoire. In some cases, where little or no Science has previously been taught, it may even be wise to introduce only a First Year Scheme at the beginning, applying it to all classes. In the second year a Second Year Scheme would be started, and so on, so that the full five-year practical course would only come into operation over a period of five years. The system gives the young teacher (or any teacher) time to build up his stock, develop his techniques and crystallize his methods. It is not so reactionary as might at first sight appear since, where little Science has been done previously, the method of tackling the work is so much more important than the actual subject-matter.

Whatever the scheme, it must be prepared in the greatest detail. The sequence of practical work and demonstration, discussion and record must be clearly foreseen. There must be a clearly defined aim for every lesson and a well-marked path towards it. No teacher needs to be told that the actual lessons will frequently fall short of the ideal, that the best-laid plans may oft-times go awry. But a practical subject without a carefully thought out scheme is like a ship without a rudder and is as likely to run on the rocks.

(c) *Directions for Experiments*: A book should be kept giving the details of all experiments, or references to them. Beside each description or reference should be listed the apparatus and materials necessary for the experiment. This book is one which the laboratory assistant will consult regularly.

For pupils' practical work the system described on p. 221 may recommend itself. It is relatively easy to make alterations or additions to the duplicated filed notes of experiments there advocated. Some form of filing cabinet will be useful.

(d) *Teacher's Day-book*: This is the teacher's book of lesson notes:

the place where he translates an item in the scheme into an actual lesson plan. Lesson notes may be brief, but in making them the teacher should ensure that he clearly visualizes in his mind the course of the lesson, anticipating its needs and foreseeing its possibilities. Looking back on previous work, he will consider how to link up the new work. He may note any current developments of topical interest. He will consider what recording work, and what materials and apparatus will be needed for the lesson. In time much of this will become automatic, so that only new work will demand the same detailed preparation; but the need to think ahead through a lesson will always remain.

The day-book should also record what has actually been achieved. It should remind the teacher of work to be carried over to the next lesson, of points needing attention and of any departures from the normal scheme.

(e) *Breakages and Shortages*: Information on these points should be noted as it arises. It may be kept in the day-book, but some prefer a separate record. Without such a system it is easy to overlook some requirement when requisitioning. The book also provides the teacher with a check on "apparatus consumed" at stocktaking time.

(f) *Stock-book*: To be of maximum value to the teacher the Science stock-book should show everything which is normally described as either apparatus or materials, whether it was bought or not. It should also indicate (possibly by a system of coding) where the items may be found. The columns showing amounts consumed during the year should be of great value in estimating future requirements. Cross-references are essential, thus: "Stands, filter, retort, test-tube, etc.—see under Filter, Retort, Test-tube, etc."

Loose-leaf stock-books may not appeal to an auditor but they are very much to be preferred from the standpoint of the teacher who uses his stock-book as a direct help in his work.

(g) *Reference File*: This may be a loose-leaf or card-index file in which the teacher notes down ideas and information as he comes across them. Here he will record the addresses and telephone numbers of publishers, firms and individuals supplying materials of all kinds; book and magazine references; notes on films and filmstrips; descriptions of gadgets or experiments that seem likely to prove useful; laboratory recipes; and data referring to materials stocked in the school (e.g. the resistances of the particular wires in store).

(h) *Science Library Catalogue*: Even though the library may be small it is worth cataloguing, if only to give one or more pupils the opportunity to undertake a useful and responsible task. Most of the books ought to be available to pupils on loan, and a system of cataloguing is essential for this purpose. A pupil-librarian should be appointed. The teacher will be wise to include a card for "Recommended Books" in his reference file, so that he may note there suitable new books as they appear.

Movement and Sound

Innumerable examples of the connection between movement and sound will occur to the teacher. The class may be asked to write down as many words as possible which associate sound and movement—e.g. banging, scratching, hammering, ringing, rubbing, whispering, rustling, rattling, rolling, etc.

324 *Vibrating Bodies*

The small experiments listed below may be set out on different benches; class groups circulate to try each in turn. A cheap violin is most useful as a piece of permanent laboratory stock, but for many experiments the one-string fiddle (Expt. 337) will serve instead.

(a) Use a table-tennis ball suspended from a thread (to fix the thread use sealing-wax, or pass the thread through the ball by means of a sewing needle). Bring the ball against a sounding tuning-fork; the ball flies off and bounces to and fro repeatedly until the sound of the fork dies away.

Observe the effect of increasing the vibrating surface; touch the shaft of a sounding fork against the bench, a door panel, a box lid, etc.

(b) Use the table-tennis ball again to experiment with a hand-bell. Sound the bell and investigate its circumference with the ball to find whether some parts are vibrating more than others. An electric bell may be used instead of the handbell.

(c) Bow the G String of a violin and observe the wave loops. Put a tiny paper rider on any string, bow the string gently and observe that the rider is thrown off. Try the rider in various positions.

(d) Put a "mute" on the bridge of the violin and explain the effect. Sound a drum, or a tuning-fork, or a piece of tin-plate, and notice the immediate effect of "damping" the vibrations by touching with the fingers.

(e) Fix a strip of steel (e.g. hacksaw blade) so that part of it projects from a clamp or vice; or one end of the strip may be held under a weight, with the other end projecting over the edge of the bench. Pluck the free end. Shorten this end progressively by pushing the strip further into the clamp. Observe the increasing speed of vibration and the rise in pitch of the sound emitted.

325 *Resonance*

Just as a given pendulum, or a garden swing, has a natural period of vibration, so has a tuning fork, a violin or piano string, a steel strip or a column of air. The analogy of the garden swing may be used to show that small but properly timed impulses can set large masses into considerable mo-

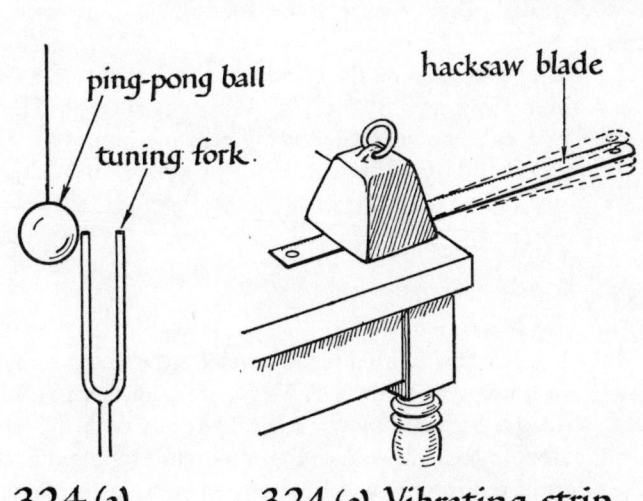

324 (a).   324 (e). Vibrating strip

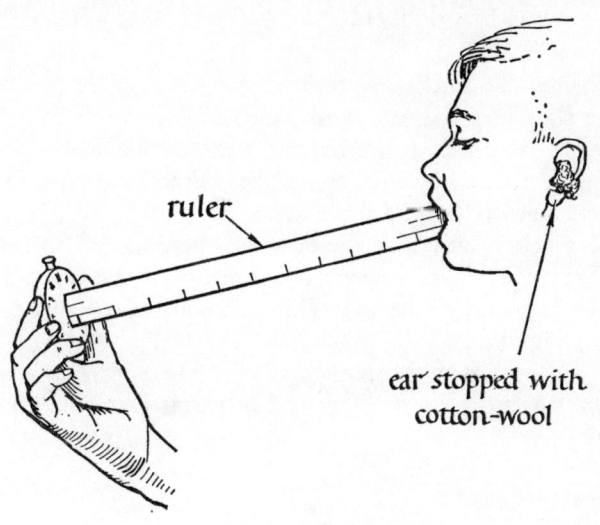

327 (c).
Bone conduction

tion; sound waves in air may cause a string or an air column to vibrate and so to "resound".

(a) Depress the "loud" pedal on a piano, best with the front board of the instrument removed. Utter a pure vowel sound in a loud voice, close to the strings.

(b) Put a small paper rider on the middle of the A string of a violin and sound an A tuning-fork against the belly of the instrument. The rider is thrown off, but a rider on any other string remains unmoved. Tune the A string down to G and try again with the A fork; then try with a G fork. Try riders on the normal G string, using a fork one octave higher.

How Sound Travels

326 *Sensitivity of Hearing*

Blindfold the subject. Start with a ticking watch near to the right ear and gradually move it away from the ear. Measure the distance at which the sound can no longer be heard by the subject. Repeat with the left ear. It is worthwhile stopping one ear with cotton-wool while testing the other.

Try the effect of putting the watch within a paper "megaphone", or of using a paper "ear-trumpet".

Differences between the two ears are often quite marked; a cold in the head may result in near-deafness.

327 *Conduction through Various Substances*

(a) Let the class note the ease with which sound travels through water when next they visit the baths. Hammer a metal tube (e.g. a pipe) under water and ask pupils at the other end of the bath to listen (i) with the head under water, (ii) with the head above water.

(b) Place a ticking watch on the floor well beyond the normal hearing distance (Expt. 326). Stand a wooden rod gently on the watch and apply an ear to the top end of the rod. This technique may be used to locate noises in car engines.

(c) Stop up the ears with cotton-wool. Put one end of a wooden rule against a watch and grip the other end between the teeth. This is bone conduction.

328 *String Telephone*

With a hammer and nail punch a hole in the base of each of two similar tin cans. Take a piece of string several metres long and pass it through the two holes, knotting an end inside each can. One can is used as a mouthpiece and the other as an earpiece, two operators standing at a distance from one another so that the string is taut.

Refer to Expt. 140 (model stethoscope).

329 *The Silence of Empty Space*
No sound reaches us from the sun or the stars.

Use a round 500 cm³ resistance-glass flask and choose a rubber stopper to fit. Push a small hook (bent pin) into the underside of the stopper and use this to suspend a little bell on a rubber cord (thin rubber band). Boil a little water in the flask until all the air has been expelled, remove the source of heat and simultaneously insert the stopper so that the bell hangs freely in the middle of the flask. Allow the flask to cool.

Set up a similar arrangement in a second flask but do not drive out the air in this case.

Shake both flasks gently, in turn, and listen.

330 *Wave Motion*
(a) Fit a sheet of glass into a large picture-frame and seal it in with putty. Mount the frame horizontally on wood blocks and place a headlamp bulb underneath the glass. Pour water into the shallow "tank".

Generate waves by dipping a finger or a pencil into the water and removing it smartly. A series of waves will spread out from the dipper and will be reflected from the sides of the tank. When the headlamp is lit it projects a shadow of the waves on the ceiling if the room is darkened.

Waves may also be generated by allowing water to drop from a burette above the tank. If two burettes are used, the effect of one set of waves upon another can be studied. Light fragments of cork floating on the water can be used to show that the water does not move outwards with the ripples.

Sound a tuning-fork and touch one prong on to the surface of the water in the tank.

(b) Water waves, and waves in a skipping rope, are "up-and-down" (transverse) waves, but they are similar in many respects to the "push-and-pull" (longitudinal) waves of sound. Longitudinal waves can be clearly demonstrated by means of a Weinhold's spring, which may be made from about 20 metres of stout iron wire wrapped into a long coil of about 10 cm diameter, with the turns about 2 cm apart and each suspended independently from two long wooden laths fixed horizontally 10 cm apart. The "walking spring" (Slinky) toy made by Randall Ltd. of Potters Bar is an excellent alternative. Waves may be sent along such a spring by pressing one end sharply: successive compressions and rarefactions are seen, and it is also clear that the coil as a whole does not move forward.

The moving film is peculiarly well-suited to help with this kind of work; "Sound Waves" (530/A2) covers the field well.

(c) Turn on a gas tap on the demonstration bench. Pupils hear the sound of escaping gas immediately, but the smell may only reach them after several seconds. The fact demonstrates that the *sound* is not carried by the bodily forward movement of the gas.

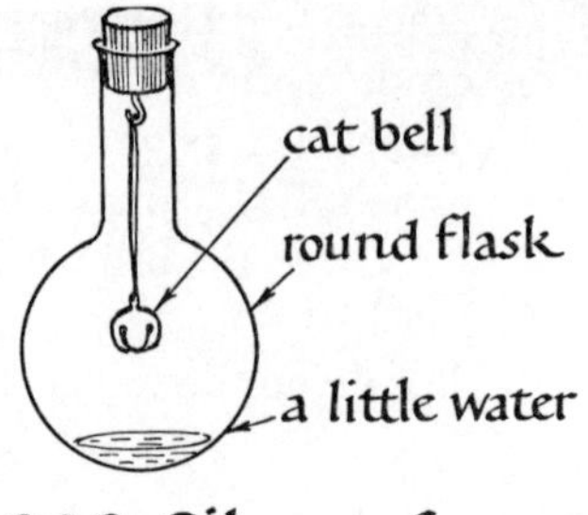

329. Silence of space — cat bell, round flask, a little water

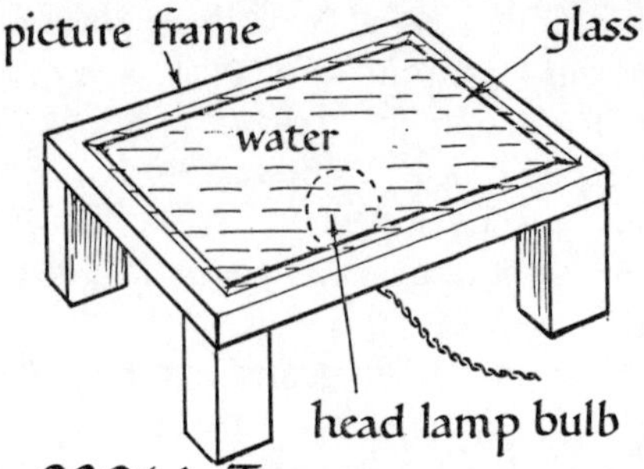

330(a). Transverse waves — picture frame, glass, water, head lamp bulb

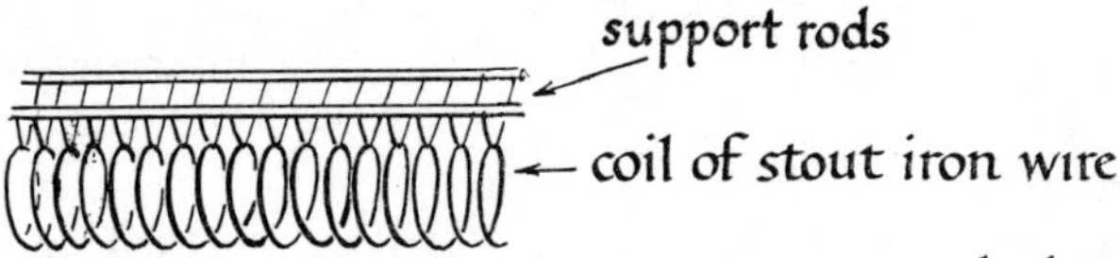

330(b). Longitudinal waves — support rods, coil of stout iron wire

335. Wave length — glass tube, milk bottle

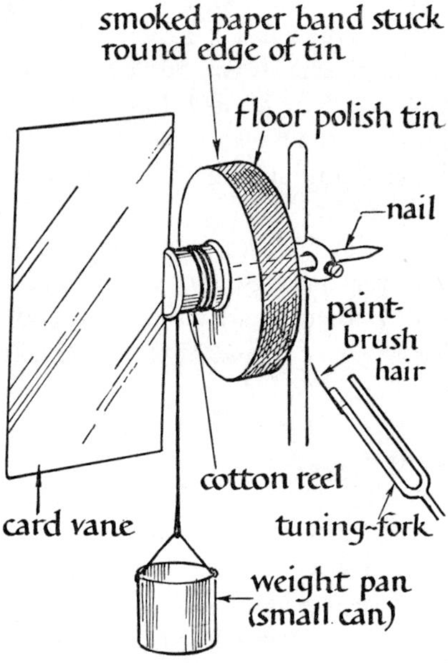

334. Frequency of tuning-fork — smoked paper band stuck round edge of tin, floor polish tin, nail, paint-brush hair, cotton reel, tuning-fork, card vane, weight pan (small can)

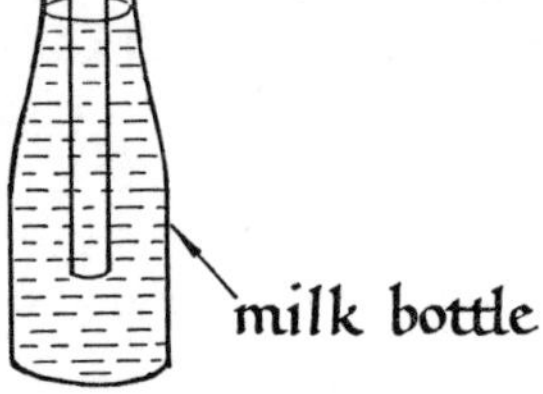

Speed of Sound

331 *Direct Method*

A direct determination of the speed of sound is easily the most convincing method for the ordinary pupil. It can also provide a fruitful discussion on sources of error and degrees of accuracy in scientific experiments.

A large open space is required, the bigger the better, and a school journey to the country might provide the opportunity. A stop-watch and a starting pistol are required. Useful work can be done with the observers a kilometre or more apart; an Ordnance Survey map must be used to determine the exact distance. A still day is desirable. The air temperature should be noted.

The pistol is fired and the distant observer starts his watch when he sees the smoke; he stops it when he hears the report. It is assumed that the interval is the time taken for sound to travel over the measured distance. The experiment should be repeated in the reverse direction to minimize error due to wind velocity.

332 *Distance of Thunder*

Whenever a thunderstorm occurs during school hours the opportunity should be seized to note the time interval between a lightning flash and the thunder which follows. For purposes of this calculation it is sufficient to assume that the speed of sound is one third of a kilometre per second.

333 *Echoes*

The fact that sound is reflected from large surfaces, such as the walls of buildings, cliffs, or even the edge of a wood, is well known. The rolling of thunder is caused by echoing among the clouds. Places where a good echo is obtained are often known to pupils; let us assume that we can reach such a spot. Stand 50 to 100 metres in front of the wall or cliff producing the echo and strike a sheet of metal with a mallet (at a pinch a hand-clap will serve). Listen for the echo. Then so arrange the striking that you hear "sound—echo—sound—echo" alternately and at equal intervals, like the ticking of a clock. When, after practice, a steady rate of striking has been achieved, time the interval between (say) 20 strikes. Then, with a tape or chain, measure the distance to the wall or cliff. Thence calculate the speed of sound.

334 *Frequency of Tuning-fork*

Use as a drum a floor-polish tin, perhaps 10 cm diameter and about 4 cm deep. Cover the circumference with a strip of gummed paper and smoke the paper by using a candle-flame with a chip of naphthalene near the wick. Use as an axle a large round nail (head removed and all burrs carefully filed away); the holes in the drum must be accurately centred. A cotton reel also runs on the axle and is fixed to one side of the drum with two small screws: in the other (outer) end of the reel is a fine saw-cut carrying a card wind-vane (see Expt. 3) about 20 cm × 12 cm. Wrap a length of fine string several times round the reel, anchoring one end with a tack and tying a weight pan (small can) to the free end. Load the pan until the drum averages 1 revolution per second when timed for 10 revolutions; if the speed is too high, remove some weight; if too low, a strip may be cut from the wind-vane.

Attach a paint-brush bristle to one prong of the tuning-fork, using sticky tape. Sound the fork and hold it so that the hair just touches the smoked paper while the drum is revolving. Many wavy traces can be so obtained on a single piece of paper, and the best should be selected. Remove the paper and mark off measured lengths of wavy line. Using a magnifying glass if necessary, count the number of complete waves per centimetre. Measure also the length of the circumference of the drum.

Suppose that the number of waves per centimetre is 30 (average), and the circumference of the drum is 16 cm. Then the number of vibrations of the fork per second is 16 × 30 = 480.

335 *Wave-length*

Since a sounding body will generate one complete wave for each complete vibration, the product of the frequency (per second) of the vibrations and the length of each wave (the wave-length) must be the distance travelled by the sound in one second, i.e. its speed per second:

$$\text{Speed} = \text{Frequency} \times \text{Wave-length}.$$

Suppose we begin with a glass tube, perhaps 2 cm diameter and 30 cm long, standing in a tall jar of water so that the tube is practically full of water. Gradually withdraw the tube from the water whilst holding the prongs of a sounding fork just above the mouth of the tube. A point will be reached when the sound grows distinctly louder but diminishes again if the tube is raised further. Measure the length of the air column in the tube (i.e. above the water) at this point.

The "resonance" (Expt. 325) occurs because the length of the air column exactly harmonizes with the air waves produced by the fork. In any wave there are points of no-motion and points of maximum motion. In our experiment we have reached the (first) point where the air at the bottom of the tube (against the water surface) is motionless and the air at the top of the tube (which is free to move) is in maximum motion. The length of the air column is, therefore, one-quarter of a wave-length. Four times this is the full wave-length, and this multiplied by the frequency of the fork gives us the speed of sound in air.

If hot water is used in the experiment a distinct increase in the speed of the sound appears (the measured column may be of the order of 2–3 cm longer).

The fact that the air column is in tune with the fork when resonance occurs may be confirmed by blowing across the top of the tube; the note emitted is the same as that given by the fork.

336 *Speed of Sound in Air and in Coal-gas*

Feed a whistle with coal-gas by attaching it via a fairly long rubber tube to a gas tap. When the gas is first turned on the whistle sounds its normal note, but as coal-gas comes along the pitch rises.

Set up a one-string fiddle (Expt. 337 (d)) and tune the wire (by varying the bridge position) first to the normal whistle note, than to the "coal-gas note", keeping the tension the same.

If C air and C gas are the speed of sound in air and gas respectively, and if l air, l gas are the corresponding lengths of wire, then:

$$\frac{C_{gas}}{C_{air}} = \frac{l_{air}}{l_{gas}}$$

Topics: Modern uses of echo-sounding (e.g. locating fish shoals). Relationship to radar. Discussion of the speed of sound as it relates to aircraft; the "sound barrier". Explosion waves. The change in pitch of a bell or hooter sounded by a vehicle as it approaches and passes (Doppler effect).

Musical Instruments

Pupils should see and handle for themselves as many instruments of the orchestra as possible. Those who play an instrument may be given an opportunity to explain its working to others. Some local authorities have sponsored visits by groups of professional musicians to schools; in this way pupils not only learn to appreciate good playing but are introduced to each instrument individually by an expert.

337 *Simple Musical Instruments*

(a) Make a "milk bottle organ", using eight bottles containing various amounts of water; the notes of the scale are obtained by trial, water being poured out or added as required. Strike the bottles with a wooden hammer.

(b) Clamp 5-cm lengths of old Acme hacksaw blades, in pairs between a wooden bar (16 cm × 2 cm × 2 cm) and smaller wood blocks (4 cm × 2 cm × 2 cm), each block being screwed to the bar with one strip on each side of the screw. The bar is itself screwed down on a wooden baseboard (at least 20 cm × 15 cm × 1 cm) raised on end-pieces. Without the baseboard very little sound is produced, and the volume of sound is also diminished by standing the apparatus on soft cloth.

Tune the instrument by adjusting the lengths of the exposed parts of the strips; a scale may be obtained in which the free lengths vary from about 2–3 cm. Pluck with a wooden plectrum.

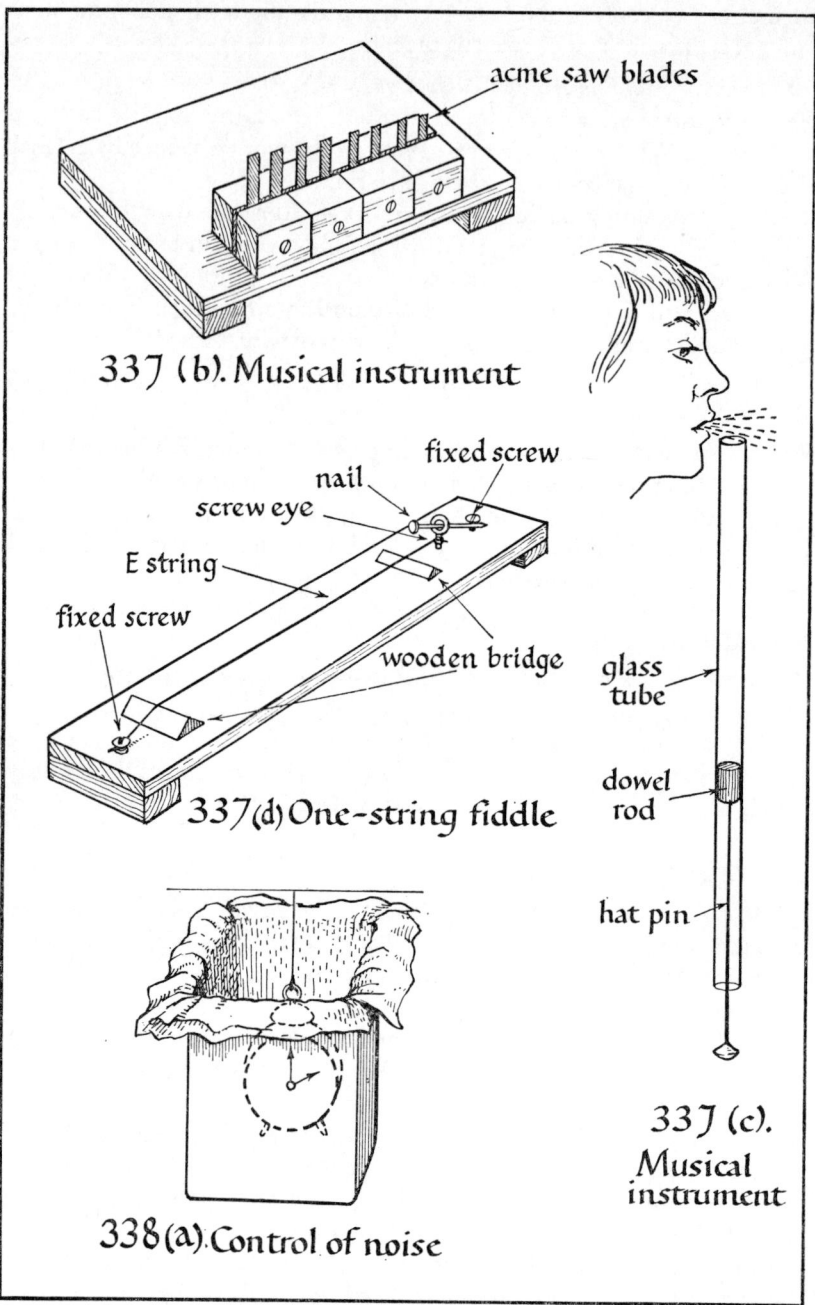

337 (b). Musical instrument

337 (d) One-string fiddle

337 (c). Musical instrument

338 (a). Control of noise

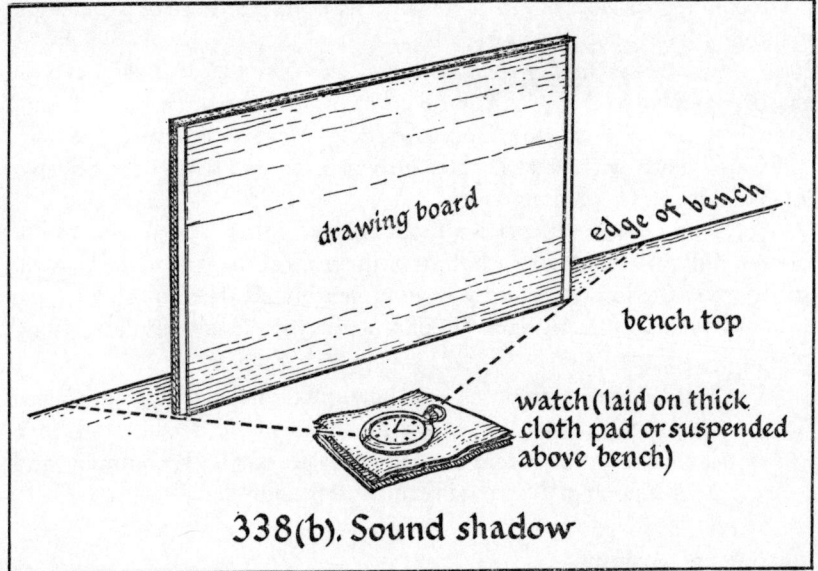

338(b). Sound shadow

(c) Choose a piece of glass tubing in which a length of 1-cm dowel rod will just fit easily. Cut off a 20-cm length of the tubing and a 2-cm length of rod. Stick the point of a hat pin into one end of the short piece of rod and use the pin to work the rod up and down in the glass tube like a piston. Blow across the open end of the tube (see diagram).

Many school groups have undertaken the making of pipes and recorders; the time required makes this a suitable after-school activity. A tin-whistle or recorder should be available in the Science room so that pupils may understand how the sound is produced and how the length of the vibrating column of air is altered by stopping holes in the tube. A visit "behind the scenes" to see a church organ may be arranged.

(d) Use a wooden baseboard, say 50 cm × 10 cm × 1 cm, raised on end-pieces as shown in the diagram: the screw-eye, used for tuning, is prevented from slipping by a nail which bears against a fixed screw. Under the wire place two low wooden wedges (1–2 cm high). Sound the string between the bridges by plucking or by bowing.

Observe the effect of (i) tightening the string, (ii) moving one of the bridges so as to shorten the effective length of string, (iii) shortening the effective length by pressing the string against the baseboard as in fingering a violin. Mark on the baseboard the correct finger positions for the notes of a simple scale, calling the "open" string Doh. Play simple tunes.

Observe that when the string is fingered at its mid-point the note given is Doh, an octave above the open string note. Measure the lengths of string corresponding to Me, Soh, and Doh, and work out the ratio of each length to the length of the open string (Doh).

Stretch a second, similar string between screws so that it is parallel with the first and 1 cm from it. Tune both strings to the same pitch. Sound combinations such as Doh/Doh Doh/Soh, Me/Soh; contrast the harmonious sounds with what is obtained when the two strings are fingered haphazardly and bowed together.

All the above experiments can be performed using an ordinary violin. On the violin we notice also the effect of the mass of the string; the heaviest string gives the lowest note. By bowing gently and then strongly on the G string observe that loudness is connected with the amplitude of vibration of the string.

Topics: How sound is produced and how pitch and loudness are altered in organ pipes and other wind instruments, in reed instruments, brass instruments and percussion instruments. Recognition and appreciation of different instruments (quality).

Hearing and Acoustics

A study of the structure of the inner ear may be inappropriate for some pupils, for whom it will be sufficient to describe the eardrum as a delicate membrane via which sounds collected by the ear are transmitted to the brain. The analogy of the microphone should not be pressed too far. Voice production is too complicated a process to merit more than passing mention. But the value of clear and good enunciation should be insisted upon by the Science teacher as much as by the teacher of English.

338 (a) *Control of Noise*

Suspend a loudly ticking clock by a length of string. Take a deep cardboard box (e.g. 30 cm square by 50 cm deep) and line it loosely with a double layer of cloth; an old blanket laid across the top of the box and pushed down into it is very effective. Lower the clock into the box without touching the cloth lining; the ticking almost disappears. Lower the clock a similar distance outside of the box; the ticking is clearly heard. The experiment is equally effective if the alarm of the clock is set ringing; the change in volume when the clock is lowered into the box is most noticeable.

338 (b) *A Sound Shadow*

Arrange a loud-ticking watch or clock behind a drawing board which is supported vertically a few cm from the edge of the bench, as indicated in Fig. 338 (b). Blindfold a pupil and let him bring his ear along the edge of the bench to discover the limits of the sound shadow, marking the points with chalk.

339 *Reflection of Sound*

The experiment should be carried out by a small group of pupils working in a quiet room (e.g. a storeroom). Use the same cloth-lined box as in Expt. 338 (a). Set the box on a stool and put the ticking clock at the bottom of the box. Now use a large sheet of cardboard as a sounding-board, trying it in various angles above the opening of the box until pupils standing three or four metres away announce maximum sound. Sheets of three-ply wood, hardboard, metal, glass and cloth-covered wood may be tested in place of the cardboard.

Topics: Reduction of noise by the use of absorbent materials—curtain, carpets, special ceiling slabs, rubber feet for chairs, etc., and by designing rooms and concert halls so that echos are minimized. Concentration of sound by sounding-boards, megaphones, and the modern use of loud-speaker systems. Reproduction of sound by the gramophone.

The Science lesson can provide the teacher of English with useful exercises in the meanings and derivations of words—words of which the pupil has come to know something through his practical work but which he can appreciate more fully if he is given opportunity to use them, both in oral and written work. The meaning of words such as acoustics, audibility, intonation, discord, harmony, gamut, syncopation and sonorous, might be searched out and discussed. A short list of words ending in "-phone" can be written down and their relationship studied. The subtle differences in meaning between words sometimes spoken of as synonyms may be illustrated by examples such as rap, snap, tap; silence, hush, peace; unison, harmony, concord. Finally the poet's use of sound, whether in the special sense of onomatopoeia or in the wider meaning of his general use of words, can best be introduced by actual examples.

Chapter Seventeen
Optical Instruments

The Use of Visual and Aural Aids in Science Teaching
Television
During recent years a great change has occurred in the attitude of teachers to the use of audio-visual aids in the classroom. In Science this has stemmed partly from a shortage of subject specialists, but more from the increasing availability of machines and programmes, the nationwide moves to improve science syllabuses and the growing demands on teachers to keep abreast of modern discovery. Today it cannot be doubted that television in particular has much to offer, and will have more. As new schools are built with laboratories and lecture rooms equipped to meet the needs of a new age, television will bring the world into the classroom, providing the teacher with lesson material otherwise quite beyond him in its range and current interest. Some teachers are afraid: Is television to displace the teacher? Will it deprive him of his pupils' confidence? Even if the logistics of teacher supply are not sufficient to convince them otherwise, teachers ought to be reassured by their own experience. The finest mechanical aid is unlikely ever to rival the potentiality of person to person contact and those individual methods of presentation which can vary so subtly from class to class and even from pupil to pupil. Teachers have long made use of charts, diagrams and pictures; of exhibits and displays; of visits to museums, workshops and country lanes. Now they are learning to make use of television—and to adapt it and improve it for their purpose. To view it simply "as a source of alien material, sometimes a welcome interruption but seldom as an integral part of the learning situation" is not good enough. Until now the classroom has been the private kingdom of the teacher, and broadcasting studios have been equally self-contained. That day too is passing.

None who have read this book so far will doubt the authors' conviction that "learning by doing" must remain central in teaching the great majority of boys and girls. But the method *is* time-consuming (other methods may be time-wasting) and the facility which television offers to widen the scope of the teaching syllabus, fill in the background and reinforce practical work is especially to be welcomed. In the future indeed it is likely to contribute much more directly, as it is doing already in colleges and universities: L. J. Lawler has written recently that "for several hundred pounds industrial standard television equipment can now be bought which will allow all pupils to see the demonstration in great detail on a large screen without leaving their seats. With a little ingenuity the equipment can act as blackboard, wall-chart, overhead projector, slide projector, epidiascope and microprojector. The camera can peer into a cage of rats or an aquarium with impunity and will allow the most foolhardy child to look inside dangerous apparatus without burns, electrocution or other injury."

Most schools are likely to have to wait many years to enjoy all the facilities that Lawler describes, but in Glasgow and a few other areas closed circuit television is already demonstrating some of the possibilities. In Glasgow in 1967 a television centre reconstructed from an old building at a cost of £50 000 had been linked by a 100-miles network of underground cable to more than 300 schools and colleges, each equipped with 27-inch receivers. From a fully equipped studio programmes were being transmitted which had been prepared and produced by teachers seconded for the work, with the assistance of permanent administrative and technical staff. To overcome the time-table barrier programmes were repeated four or five times in the week. The objectives of the Glasgow E.T.V. Service have been stated to be (i) to complement the day-to-day work of the schools through direct teaching programmes deliberately geared in content and pacing to school syllabuses; (ii) to provide in-service training for teachers in the rapidly changing content and methods of many curricular subjects.

Meanwhile the national and regional broadcasting agencies, guided by their Educational Advisory Councils, on which teachers, local education authorities and the Department of Education and Science are strongly represented, broadcast on each school day programmes chiefly designed to complement and re-inforce classroom work. Series such as *Science in Use* (ITV) and *Science Session* (BBC) are typical and information about these and other science television broadcasts can be obtained from the addresses given below:

> The Independent Television Schools Broadcasting Secretariat,
> 4 and 5 Grosvenor Street, London W.1

> The School Broadcasting Council,
> 3 Portland Place, London, W.1.

Sound Broadcasting

The BBC has put out sound-only science programmes for many years. They are supplemented by excellent notes for teachers and illustrated booklets for pupils. The series *General Science* and *Science and the Community* have much to offer the teacher of the Ordinary Pupil.

Video-tape

Permission to record sound broadcasts is given provided that the tapes are used only in school and are destroyed at the end of the year. The advantage of this for schools is obvious but the high cost of the equipment for recording television has hitherto ruled out any similar arrangement in the visual field. Video-tape machines are however now becoming available at prices which may bring them within the economy of large schools or of groups of schools. This could solve the major problem of fitting broadcast material into school time-tables, since tapes can be stored for use just when they are required and of course they may be played over and over again.

Video-tape also offers wider scope for the development of team teaching. Lessons prepared and produced by top-class teachers and recorded on video-tape may be televised to large audiences (e.g. a whole year group) while the time saved to other colleagues in the science team is used in preparation, follow up and practical sessions with pupils in small groups.

Film and Filmstrip

Film has been used as a teaching aid for almost half a century, but it is only in recent years that professional educationists have been brought in alongside professional film-makers to ensure that what is produced fits the needs of schools. There are many desiderata of the ideal film: clear aim; accuracy and relevance; well-ordered sequence; pace and content appropriate to the audience; suitable length; good photography; and (in the case of sound films) concise and clearly spoken commentary. Seldom are all achieved, but the work of the National Committee or Audio-Visual Aids in Education since its establishment in 1946 has done much to raise standards. The catalogue *Educational Films 1946–66* lists films made with the co-operation of the National Committee and which may be bought through the Educational Foundation for Visual Aids at 33 Queen Anne Street, London W.1, or hired from the Foundation's Film Library, Brooklands House, Weybridge, Surrey. Information about prices and hire charges is given in the national catalogue of films and filmstrips called *Visual Aids*, which is a most comprehensive list of available material, though obviously less selective than the National Committee publication. Science teachers should ask for Part 5 (mathematics and physical sciences) and Part 6 (life sciences) of *Visual Aids*: supplements to both have appeared in the Foundation's monthly magazine *Visual Education*.

Film shares with television (which, of course, also makes great use of film) the ability to record scenes beyond normal reach: not only far-distant places, but the inside of a machine or the organs of a living creature. The cartoon or animated diagram, presented on film, can give an integrated picture of the flow of blood round the body, the nitrogen cycle in nature, or the birth of a volcano. Films can show processes too quick, or too slow, for the unaided eye to appreciate: the advance of a lightning flash, the shape of a falling drop or the growth movement of a plant. They can reveal the minutely small, bringing before us the marvels of cell division and the microstructure of metals. But perhaps it is the power of being able to show many things at once in their relationship to each other, and yet to emphasize what is significant, which is especially important for the science teacher when he uses films. He must of course, be very careful in his choice: films are not cheap and he should always pre-view before ordering. Their advantage is that they are permanent and that the photography and presentation can be of very high quality. Many local authorities have set up their own film libraries, further enabling teachers to use film as a flexible tool available just when it is wanted.

Today the 16-mm projector, sound or silent, is standard; and the quality is better than that of 35-mm of only a few years ago. In the not-distant future we may look forward to 8-mm sound equipment, lightweight, easy to handle and relatively cheap.

Many teaching films are too long and attempt too much; they may fail to focus the lesson or to provide the repetitive stimulus which is sometimes needed. The modern 8-mm (silent) loop-films, contained in plastic cassettes, have been developed to deal with particular topics, experiments or techniques. Running for only a few minutes, they allow the teacher to integrate the material into his lesson very easily. The Technicolor E projector, or a similar instrument, may be bought for less than £100 and cassettes may cost £2 to £3 each: the apparatus operates by back projection, requires no black-out, repeats the showing of the film automatically and can be stopped or started at any point. Loading consists simply in slipping the cassette into a slot and can be carried out by pupils working individually or in groups. Cassette loops are included in the catalogue *Visual Aids*.

Filmstrip too is valuable as a lesson aid. The projector is cheap and operation is simple. Unfortunately many strips of very indifferent quality have been produced, but there is scope for the kind of strip which provides pictures or drawings not readily available otherwise, or which are frequently required. Long strips often become boring just because many of the frames are not really relevant or significant. It is a great advantage to cut out selected frames and mount them as slides, chosen for their value in illustrating particular lessons. A library of slides can enable pictures to be shown with a minimum of trouble.

Appraisals of films, film loops and filmstrips appear regularly in educational journals: *The School Science Review, Natural Science in*

Schools and *The Science Teacher* should be consulted, in addition to *Visual Education* and the catalogue *Visual Aids*.

The *Visual Education Year Book* includes a register of teachers' audio-visual aid groups and of other societies with similar interests. It surveys audio-visual equipment of all kinds—cameras, projectors, tape recorders and accessories—and supplies details too of materials such as pens, paints, stencils, ink, paper and adhesives useful in making non-projected aids. *Visual Education* throughout the year carries reliable technical reports on current apparatus, as well as reviews and articles on the teaching aspects.

The Blackboard and its Modern Counterpart

The blackboard (more accurately, today, the chalkboard) is still an effective teaching aid. "Chalk and talk" is rightly decried, but no experienced teacher will deny the power of well-timed and well-executed blackboard work—emphasizing exactly the right thing at exactly the right time. Use of the blackboard, or of its modern counterpart the overhead projector, is an art to cultivate and one which can have a marked influence upon the records of the pupils themselves.

The overhead projector, still a luxury, is a device which could do away with the dust and inconvenience of the chalkboard. E.F.V.A. make a descriptive booklet available, but essentially a lens system and a mirror project, backwards from the demonstration bench, an image of whatever the teacher writes or draws on a transparent plastic sheet. The teacher faces the class the whole time and can add to or subtract from his picture as he goes along.

Other pictorial aids are useful in science teaching. Pictures, diagrams and graphs cut from newspapers and magazines may be displayed week by week on the notice board and the right boy or girl will be glad to take charge: most of this material may safely be scrapped thereafter but items of lasting worth should be mounted on standard size card and filed, to be used later with the episcope as required. Collections of postcards, such as those issued by the British Museum (famous scientists), and the series of scientific advertisements produced from time to time by firms such as Shell and I.C.I., are also good episcope material. Permanent laboratory pictures and charts should be kept to a minimum: the best wall displays are records of current work and experiments in progress. The accumulation of dust on a chart or museum specimen is too often the measure of its ineffectiveness.

It is the business of all education to foster interests, but the ability of a teacher to be interesting seldom depends mainly upon the material aids at his disposal but rather upon his personality and enthusiasm, and upon the long- and short-term preparation that has gone into his lesson. Unless he has a complete grasp of what he is aiming at he will never distinguish the significant. By a wise choice of visual material he may rivet his pupils' attention, or forge a link with the outside world, or elucidate a particular difficulty. But it is in the daily give and take between teacher and pupil that the real business of teaching lies—in question and answer (whether the pupils' part be oral or written) and in the arrangements for practical work. We must do everything in our power to encourage the pupil to be an active partner in the teaching-learning relationship.

Natural and Artificial Lighting

For much of the work of this and the following chapter it is very desirable that the room should be darkened, in part at least.

The subject of lighting might be opened by a discussion of the light sources available to man; as many as possible should be listed. A demonstration of what is seen when an electric fire is switched on in a darkened room is a useful introduction to the idea that heat and light are intimately connected.

340 *Reflecting Power of Different Surfaces*

Cut a window, say 15 cm wide × 10 cm high, in the middle of one side of a breakfast cereal box and stick tracing paper over the hole. Divide the box into two "rooms" (each having half of the window) by a sheet of card fitted down the centre. Line the sides and back of each room with a half-cylinder of paper—dull-black in one case and light-coloured in the other. Turn the box so that the "window" side is away from the light.

Fix a lamp (12-volt will serve) in a tin-can lampshade, the can being painted dull-black inside. Hold the lamp centrally above the card partition so as to throw light equally into both "rooms"; tilt the lamp so that light does not fall directly on the windows. The window in one room appears much brighter than that in the other room. Repeat the experiment using other shades and textures of lining paper.

341 *Illumination at Different Distances*

Cut out a 16-cm square of cardboard and rule it in 2-cm squares. Cut a 2-cm square hole in the middle of a second sheet of card. Support each card vertically by pinning (drawing pins) to blocks of wood.

Set up a 12-volt car headlamp bulb in a lamp-holder on a small baseboard and mask it with a cylindrical tin can in which have been cut (curved tin-snips) two circular holes, each about 2 cm in diameter, at the level of the filament and diametrically opposite to one another. The lamp filament and the circular holes should be centred 8 cm above the bench. Such a lamp-house can be set up between two groups of pupils and so be shared between them. For an alternative design see Expt. 379.

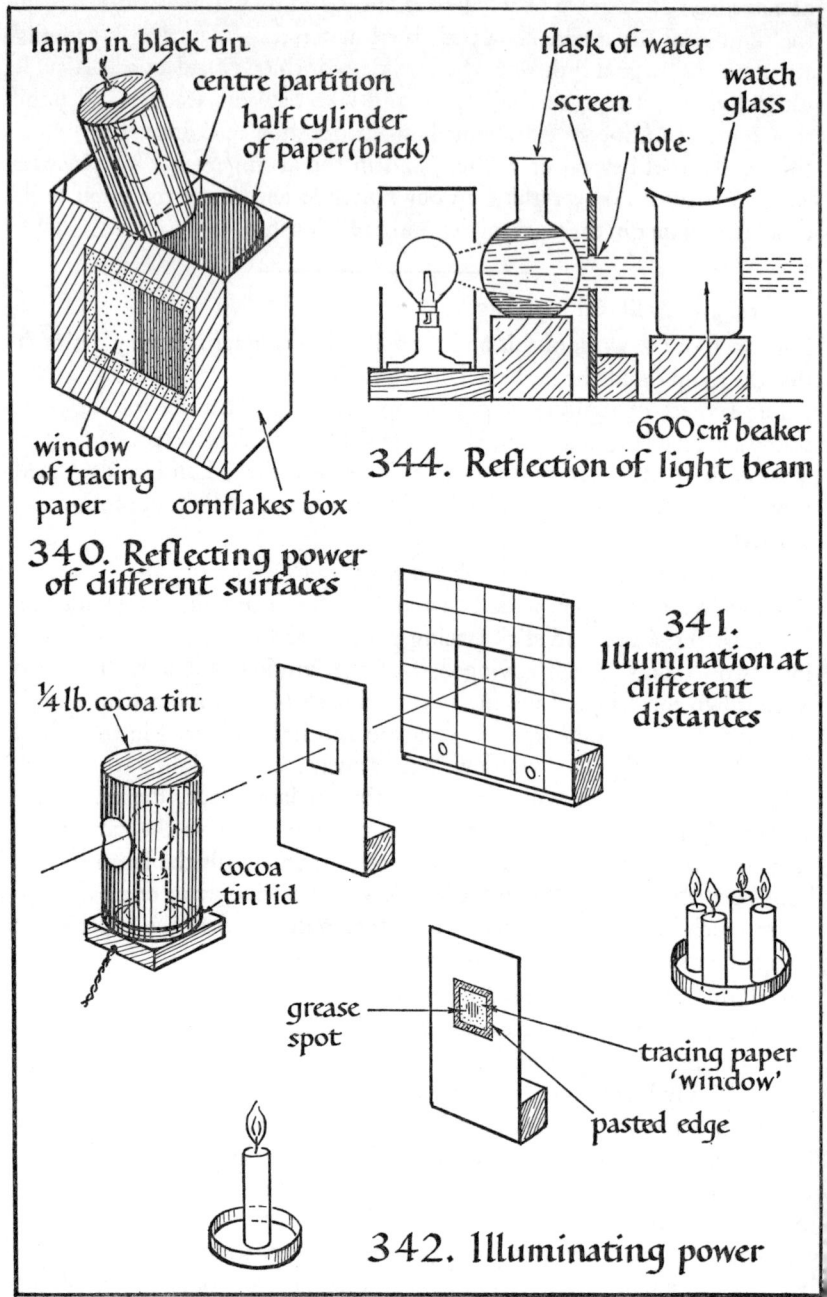

Set the card with the hole 15 cm from the lamp-house (measure from the lamp filament) so that light shines through the hole. Now move the ruled card backwards and forwards and up and down, on the side of the hole away from the lamp, until exactly four squares are illuminated by the light beam coming through the hole. Measure the distance from the ruled card to the lamp filament. In a similar way find the distances for the illumination of (i) 9 squares (ii) 16 squares. The results will show that at twice the distance the light is spread over four times the area—i.e. the intensity of illumination is only one quarter. Thus four times as powerful a light source is required to maintain the intensity of illumination if the distance from the source is doubled. Nine times the illuminating power is needed to give the same illumination at three times the distance.

342 *Illuminating Power*

Refer back to Expt. 95 (grease-spot test for an oil or fat). Use a mounted card with a 2-cm square hole cut in it, as in Expt. 341. Paste the edges of a 3-cm square piece of duplicating paper and stick the paper over the hole. Spot one drop of oil on to the centre of this paper. The arrangement is called a "grease-spot photometer". Work with it away from windows.

(a) Stand a lighted candle (flame at same height as grease spot) 15 cm from one face of the photometer and observe the appearance of the grease spot, first from one side and then from the other. Now put another, similar, candle on the other side of the photometer and move it away from or toward the grease spot until the spot is least easily distinguishable from the rest of the paper. Each side of the spot is now equally illuminated and, as would be expected, the candles are equidistant from the grease spot if the flames are of equal brilliance.

(b) Replace the second candle by four similar candles and again adjust the distance for equal illumination. The four candles, each perhaps 8 cm long, are best mounted together in a tin lid.

The illuminating power of the four candles is about four times that of one. Use the result of the experiment to show that the illuminating power of a source is proportional to the square of the distance from the photometer.

(c) Find the "candle power" of a flash lamp bulb by measuring its illuminating power against that of a single candle, using the formula:

$$\frac{\text{Illuminating power of lamp}}{\text{Illuminating power of candle}} = \frac{(\text{Distance of lamp from grease spot})^2}{(\text{Distance of candle from grease spot})^2}$$

If we call the illuminating power of the candle "one candle-power", and if we call the distance from candle to grease spot 1 unit, then: Candle-power of lamp = (Distance of lamp from grease spot)^2, the distance being measured in the agreed units.

343 *Glare*

Light the blackboard with a shaded lamp so that no direct light reaches the eyes. Walk away from the board until writing on it is only just legible. Now remove the shade (which may be a paper cone): the writing becomes undecipherable owing to the excessive brightnes of the direct light from the lamp to the eyes.

Topics: Value of light colours in interior decoration. Concealed lighting. Importance of adequate illumination to avoid eye-strain (varying requirements for different occupations.

Reflection from Plane mirrors

Provide pupils with a mirror each; handbag mirrors can be accumulated. Let pupils confirm for themselves that the image is (i) the same size as the object, (ii) laterally inverted. Draw attention to the fact that the light beams between the object and the mirror, and between the mirror and the eye, cannot be seen (Expt. 344); only when light actually strikes the eye do we get the sensation of "seeing". Refer to the beam of light in the cinema, which is only rendered visible because of the smoke and dust in the atmosphere.

344 *Reflection of Light Beam*

Use the lamp-house described in Expt. 341, with a 12-volt straight vertical filament headlamp bulb.

Fill a 100 cm^3 flat-bottomed flask with water and interpose it in the beam from the lamp-house by raising it on a wooden block. Just beyond the flask put the screen of Expt 341 (2-cm hole in the centre) and adjust the distance of the lamp from the flask until the beam emerging through the hole in the card is reasonably parallel (test by holding a postcard in the beam at varying distance from the flask).

Stand a clean 600 cm^3 tall glass beaker in the beam and check that the light passes right through, from side to side, by holding a card on the far side of the beaker. If the air is fairly free from dust the beam inside the beaker will be practically invisible; it can be made completely so by smearing a little Vaseline on the bottom of the beaker (inside, to act as a dust trap) and covering the top of the beaker with a watch glass or card. Blow a little smoke into the beaker—the beam is strongly outlined as light is reflected in all directions by the smoke particles.

When the smoke has settled, lower a strip of white card into the beaker; it can be seen equally well from any angle because it reflects light from the beam in all directions, but the light is scattered and does not dazzle the eye. Remove the card and introduce in its place a strip of mirror. Light is now reflected in one direction only, and the concentrated beam dazzles the eye.

345 *Law of Reflection*

(a) Use the lamp-house described in Expt. 341, and stand in front of it a

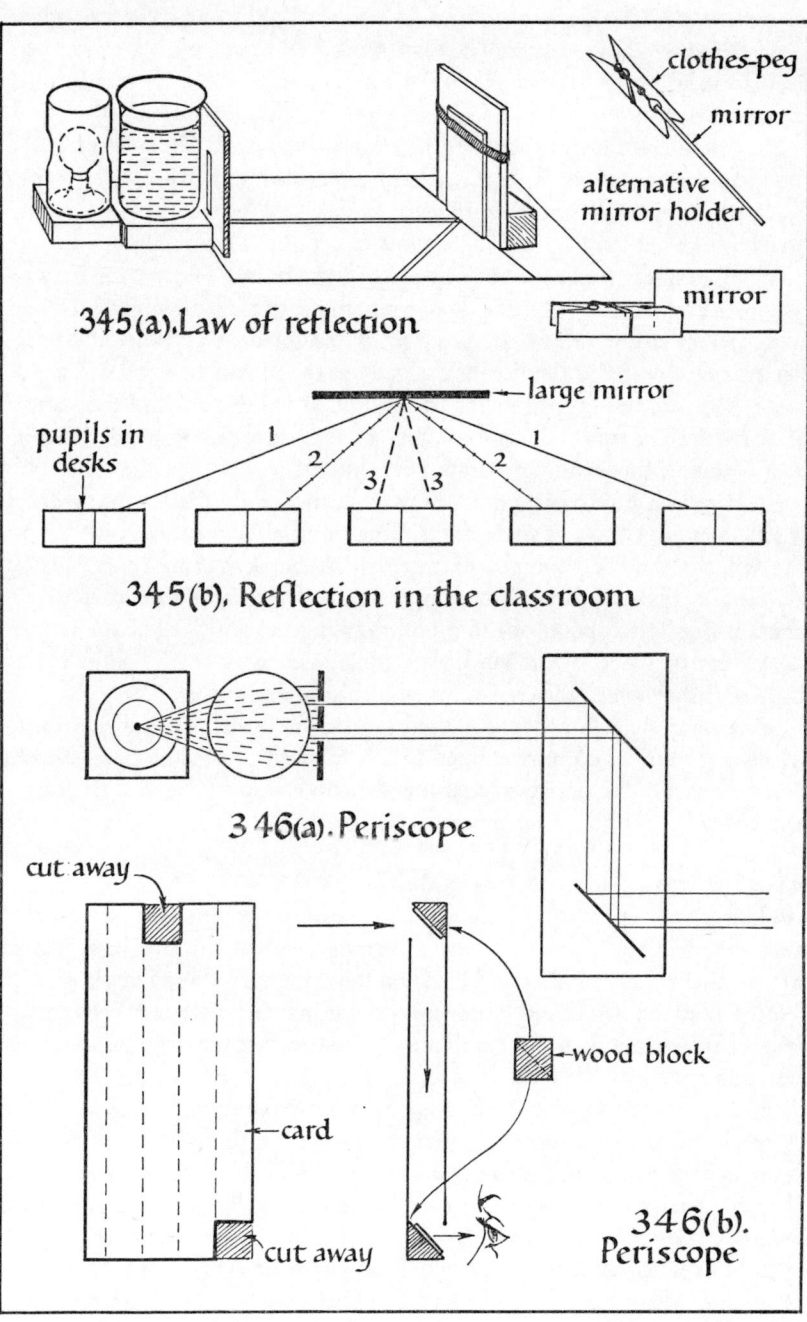

345(a). Law of reflection

345(b). Reflection in the classroom

346(a). Periscope

346(b). Periscope

600 cm³ tall-form beaker three parts filled with water. Adjust the position of the lamp and beaker to get a parallel beam of light along a sheet of white paper lying on the bench. Stand a sheet of aluminium, with a single vertical slit in it, against the beaker so that a narrow pencil of light is formed along the paper.

Slits may be cut in sheet aluminium as follows: Take a piece of the metal, say 15 cm × 10 cm, and grip it between four nails driven into a block of wood (Fig. 347, ii) so that the metal is slightly curved. Cuts may now be made quite easily with a hacksaw.

Stand a handbag mirror upright in the light beam. The mirror may be supported by a spring clothes-peg or by fixing it to a simple plywood stand with rubber bands. Mark the position of the incident ray and of the reflected ray; mark also the line of the back of the mirror (the reflecting surface). Measure with a protractor the "angle of incidence" and the "angle of reflection". Repeat for other angles of incidence (by moving the mirror). Tabulate the results and draw a conclusion.

(b) Fix a large mirror against the wall at the height of the pupils' faces when they are sitting at their desks. One pupil after another is invited to say who he can see through the mirror (the pupil may move slightly as required). The equality of the angles of incidence and reflection is evident. If duplicated plans of the room, showing the positions of the pupils' desks, are prepared beforehand, the pupils may mark in the paths of the light beams by which they see other pupils through the mirror.

(c) A lamp held in a clamp is used to throw a horizontal beam through a slit on to a pivoted mirror fixed to a cardboard protractor (see Figure). Mirror *and* protractor are rotated together on a screw pivot and the directions of incident and reflected beams observed.

346 *Periscope*

(a) Use the ray apparatus (Expt. 345 (a)) but have two slits, one narrow and one wider, in the aluminium sheet. Arrange so that the two light beams are parallel to one another and let them fall on a mirror at an angle of 45°. Notice how the two beams cross one another in being reflected. Set another mirror facing the first and parallel to it. Notice that the original direction and order of the two beams is restored.

(b) Cut a 3-cm wooden cube diagonally to make two 45° prisms. Glue a small square of mirror on the cut face of each (such squares may be bought in sheets at picture frame shops under the name of Mirroflex). Take a piece of card, 30 cm × 13 cm, mark it carefully into four 3-cm wide lengths, and bend it to form a 3-cm square tube, 30 cm long (there will be a little overlap, which may be glued down). Cut away a depth of 3 cm from one side of one end of the tube, and the same amount from the opposite side of the other end of the tube. Fix one of the 45° prisms in each end

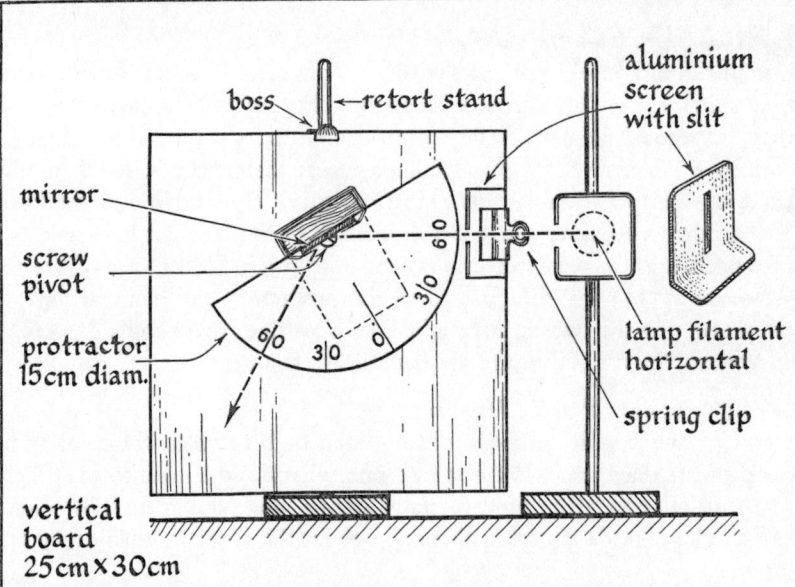

345(c). Demonstration of Law of Reflection

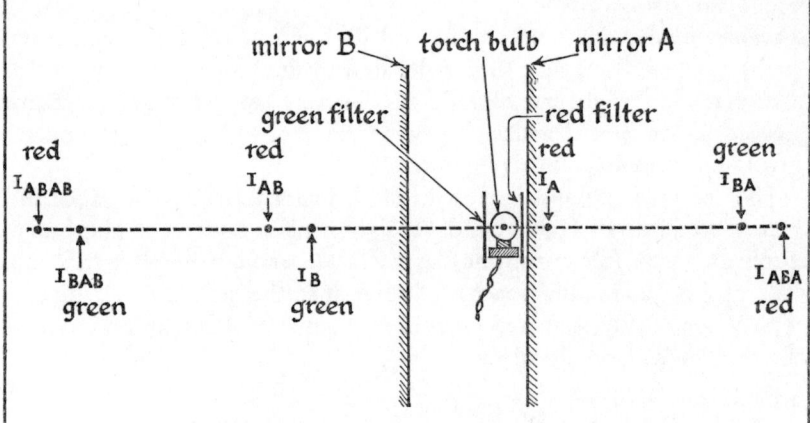

348. Reflections in parallel mirrors

of the tube so that the mirrors face the gaps and one another. Use the periscope so formed.

347 *Tracking Down the Rays*
Use the lamp-house (Expt. 345) without the beaker of water. Lean a multiple slit (sheet of aluminium with several slits) against the lamp-house so that the vertical filament throws a fan of light pencils on a sheet of paper laid on the bench. Set a plane mirror across these pencils. Mark in the track of each pencil and of its reflection. Mark also the line of the back of the mirror. Remove the paper and produce the incident and reflected rays back to their points of origin (apparent origin in the case of the reflected rays). Having thus identified the position of the filament and of its image, join the two by a straight line. This line is perpendicular to the mirror, and object and image are equidistant from the mirror.

348 *Reflections in Parallel Mirrors*
Arrange two parallel mirrors with a torch bulb between them, as indicated in the diagram. Look first into one mirror and then into the other, inserting red and green light filters as shown while doing so. The colour of the images leads to useful discussion about the order in which they are formed.

Topics: Uses of plane mirrors at road junctions, for advertising signs, in kaleidoscopes, etc. Polished metal, plane glass, and water surfaces as reflectors. The moon and planets seen by reflected light.

Curved Mirrors

349 *The Driving Mirror*
Provide pupils with soup spoons and let them polish them with metal polish. Let them examine their reflections in the convex side, noting that the image is upright but diminished in size. Now use a convex mirror instead of the spoon; notice the "wide angle of vision" that the mirror gives—hence its use as a driving mirror.

Use the ray-track apparatus with an ordinary comb as a multiple slit, and so produce a divergent bundle of light pencils; let these impinge upon a convex mirror (the mirror may be held at the end of a bench so that only half projects above the bench). Observe that the reflected rays diverge widely, apparently from a point behind the mirror. Look at the image of the lamp filament in the mirror.

350 *Concave Mirror*
Look into the bowl of a polished spoon: an inverted image of the face is seen. Bring the spoon very close to one eye; an upright and enlarged image of the eye is seen. Repeat using a concave mirror of large focal length (i.e. a fairly flat mirror). The image of a distant object can be caught on a screen in the case of the concave mirror; prove this by using it to direct light

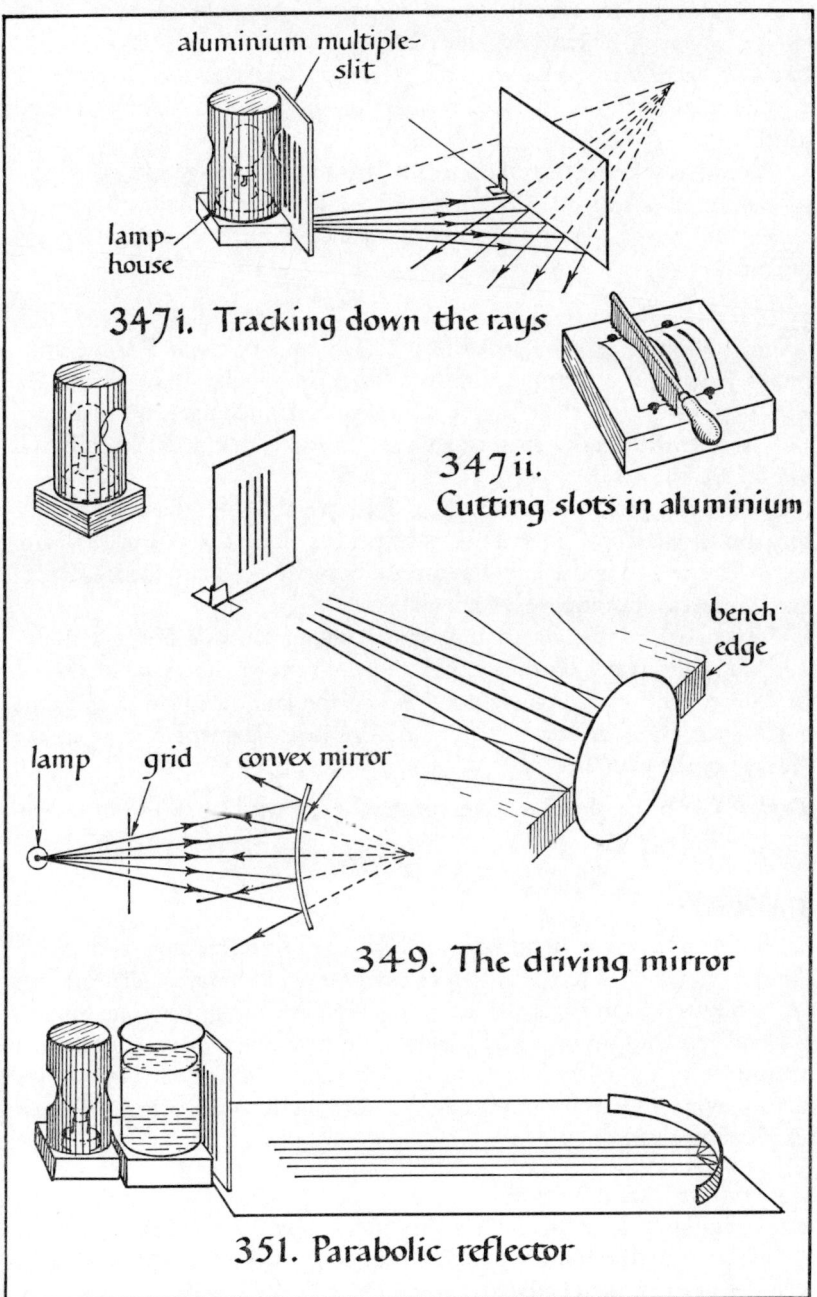

from a distant window on to a sheet of paper held in front of the mirror—a tiny inverted picture of the window is seen on the paper. Large concave mirrors are used in reflecting telescopes to collect the light from distant stars and bring them to a focus on a photographic plate. Use the ray-track apparatus to show that parallel rays are brought to a focus by a concave mirror.

When the object is very near to the mirror, the image can no longer be caught on a screen. In the mirror it appears bigger than the object; hence the use of concave mirrors for shaving mirrors and "make-up" mirrors.

351 *Parabolic Reflector*
Bought reflectors or car headlamp reflectors may be used. For the abler pupils it is an excellent exercise to let them draw the graph of $x = y^2$, $x = \frac{1}{2}y^2$, etc. From their curves they may make templates in thick card and use them to bend a strip of aluminium sheet, 30 cm $\times$ 1 cm, into a parabolic curve.

Use the ray-track apparatus with a multiple slit and adjust the beaker for parallel pencils of light. Direct the pencils along the axis of the parabolic reflector and notice how they are all brought to a sharp focus (sharper than in the case of the concave mirror).

Move a lighted flash-lamp bulb slowly along the axis of the reflector (laid on white paper on the bench) and notice how the shape of the reflected beam changes. At one point, when the lamp is fairly close to the mirror, the reflected beam is parallel; the lamp filament is than at the "focus" of the parabola.

Topics: Use of parabolic reflectors in motor car headlamps and in searchlights.

The Camera
A photographic club, rightly handled, can be of great benefit both to individual pupils and to the school as a whole. Here pupils will learn the art of taking pictures and the techniques of developing, printing, enlarging and reproducing on slides. Colour film and cine work are additional attractions today. Class lessons in the laboratory do not lend themselves to such work, but every pupil may be introduced to the principles upon which photography depends.

352 *Printing from a Negative*
The operation is so useful and exciting that it is worth attempting in class. Simple printing frames about 12 cm $\times$ 10 cm, with an 8-cm $\times$ 5-cm aperture, can be made in Woodwork lessons. Open the back of the frame and lay a negative (one of the pupil's own) glossy side down on the glass. Place the

sensitized side of a sheet of "gaslight" printing paper (the side which curls inwards slightly) against the dull side of the negative and replace the back of the frame. Hold the frame at about 30 cm from a 40-watt electric lamp for perhaps 15 seconds; the time will depend upon the distance, on the negative, on the quality of the printing paper, etc. Remove the frame from direct light, extract the print and immerse it at once face upwards in a bath of gaslight paper developing solution at the proper temperature (a soup plate will serve as a bath, and full directions for the making up and use of developer are given by the manufacturers). As soon as the image has attained the desired depth (perhaps after 30–40 seconds), the print is rinsed in a bath or cold water and is then plunged into a "fixing bath"; here the essential chemical is sodium thiosulphate or "hypo", which dissolves away the silver salts that have not been acted upon by light and the developer. The print should be kept moving for a few seconds and then left for a quarter of an hour with occasional movement. Finally the print is placed in a trough kept full and overflowing with running water (the trough standing in a sink). After an hour's washing the print is removed and pressed on to cheese-cloth or similar material to dry it.

The work can be carried out in a partially dimmed laboratory; complete darkness is not necessary. Printing paper should not be removed from its packet until required, but one sheet may be supplied to each group of pupils in a separate dark envelope. When each group has prepared its frame for exposure, lights can be switched on and the exposure made, the lights being switched off again afterwards. The teacher should make a preliminary test for a suitable time, and he should demonstrate the whole printing process to the class before pupils attempt it. Full instructions are to be found in handbooks produced by the photographic suppliers.

353 *Box Camera*

Get pupils to bring box cameras (unloaded) to school; they can work in groups according to the number of cameras available. Open the camera, as though to load it, and note the lens, shutter action (time and instantaneous), the various stops, the film rollers, how the film is fitted (a roll of paper may be used), and the view-finder. Fit a piece of tracing paper in place of the film (it need not be fitted to the rollers), point the opened camera at a distant scene (e.g. houses), and view the paper with the head and the back of the camera enveloped in dark cloth. Try (a) an "instantaneous" exposure (b) a "time" exposure (c) a time exposure with each of the different stops in succession, noting how the quantity of light reaching the paper is increased as the lens aperture is increased. Why is the interior of the camera painted dull black?

354 *Pin-hole Camera*

(a) Darken the room and then use the lamp-houses (Expt. 344) shared between groups of pupils. Provide each group with a sheet of paper, a sheet of cardboard and a pin.

Make a pin-hole in the centre of the card and hold the card between the lamp and the paper (used as a screen). An image of the lamp filament appears on the screen. Try the effects of altering the relative positions of lamp, hole and screen.

(b) Drill a 1-cm hole in the base of a cylindrical tin box which has an overlapping lid. Paste tinfoil over the hole, inside the tin, and paint the inside of the tin dead-black. Pierce a fine hole through the metal foil using a sewing needle. Select (or make) a card tube at least 20 cm long, which will just slide inside the tin; household cleanser boxes can be matched up to selected tins and serve admirably. Stretch and fix tracing paper over one end of the tube and push this end into the tin. Apply the eye to the open end of the tube, pointing the pin-hole towards a window or other well illuminated object. A clearly defined image is obtained on the tracing paper. Vary the distance between pin-hole and screen.

Then enlarge the hole by stages (needle, compasses point, etc.). Later again, pierce a second fine hole near to the larger hole. Try multiple holes. Finally, tear off the metal patch. Throughout these operations, observe the effects on the size and clarity of the image.

(c) Use the same tin, painted black inside, and stick in a new patch of foil. Pierce a fine hole in the foil. Cut out a circle of single-weight bromide paper to fit exactly inside the lid of the tin, working in a dark room. Fit the lid and paper circle on to the tin and cover the pin-hole with a finger while the camera is taken out of doors and fixed facing a brightly lit scene. An exposure of $1-1\frac{1}{2}$ minutes can be tried. The bromide paper will give a negative picture after developing and a positive may be obtained by contact printing with a second piece of paper in a simple frame.

355 *Stops*

(a) Use a thick convex lens (bull's-eye) to examine millimetre-squared paper; notice how the much magnified lines are distorted into curves. Now view through a small hole in a piece of black paper held immediately in front of the lens, so that only the middle of the lens is in action; the lines are no longer distorted.

(b) Use the pin-hole camera of Expt. 354 (b) again, but make a larger hole in the base—say 3-cm diameter. Put a convex lens of focal length about 10 cm inside the tin and resting over the hole. Fix the lens in position by means of a cardboard ring just big enough to fit tightly into the tin; the central hole has a diameter of 3 cm and the ring is pressed down on to the lens. Now cut three card rings, each of which will just fit within

OPTICAL INSTRUMENTS 299

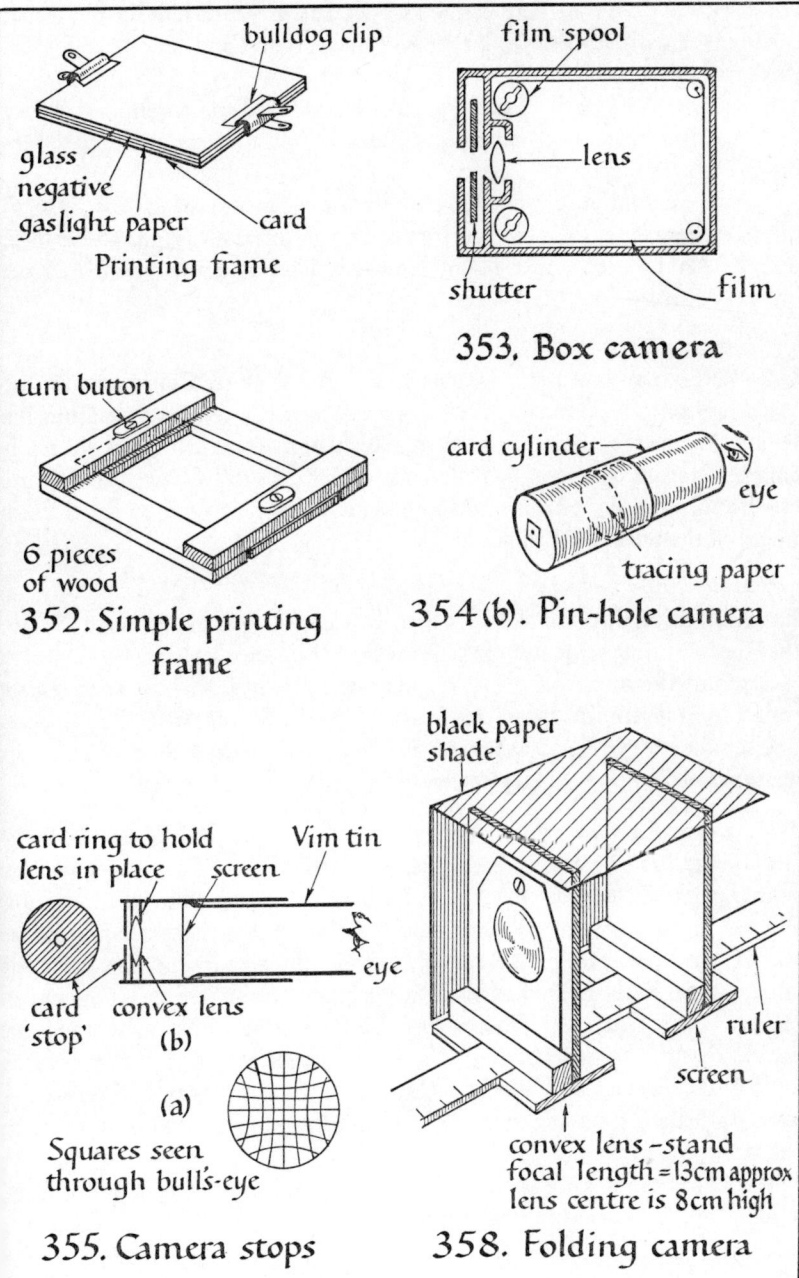

Printing frame — bulldog clip, glass negative, gaslight paper, card

352. Simple printing frame — turn button, 6 pieces of wood

353. Box camera — film spool, lens, shutter, film

354 (b). Pin-hole camera — card cylinder, eye, tracing paper

355. Camera stops — card ring to hold lens in place, screen, Vim tin, eye, card 'stop', convex lens (b); (a) Squares seen through bull's-eye

358. Folding camera — black paper shade, ruler, screen, convex lens–stand focal length = 13 cm approx, lens centre is 8 cm high

the outside rim at the bottom of the tin. Cut a 15-mm diameter hole at the centre of one, a 9-mm hole in the second, and a 3-mm hole in the third; cork borers will cut the two larger holes, and a bradawl will serve for the smallest.

Use the camera as in Expt. 354 (b) focusing a distant window. Apply each stop in turn and compare (a) brightness (b) sharpness of image ("definition").

The diameter of a stop is often expressed as a fraction of the focal length of the camera lens; thus the aperture of an f.8 stop is one-eight of the focal length. An f.8 stop on a 10-cm lens will have a diameter of 10/8 cm = $12\frac{1}{2}$ mm.

356 *Burning Glass*
On a sunny day use a convex lens as a burning glass. Concentrating the sun's rays on one spot on a piece of paper, measure the distance from the lens to the paper. This distance, at which light from a distant source is concentrated by the lens, is called the "focal length" of the lens. In the absence of sun, light from a distant window may be used to get a sharp image of the window at the focal distance.

357 *Magnifying Glass*
Examine print through the lens used in the previous experiment. Notice that the lens must be nearer to the print than the focal distance.

Examine the surface of ordinary paper with the lens; why does such paper reflect light in all directions? Look also at fabric, flower parts, the skin, etc.

Use other magnifiers: (a) water in a watch-glass (b) a drop of water in a 2-mm hole in a metal plate (the early magnifiers were like this).

358 *Folding Camera*
Set up the model shown. It consists of a front screen carrying a convex lens (f = 10 cm approximately) and a back screen of white card; a ruler is used to measure the distance between the screens. Black paper covers the top and one side of the model, leaving the remaining side open for observation. Face the lens towards the window and move the front screen until a sharp image is obtained on the card. The distance between the screens is now the focal length of the lens (approximately). Next, focus on a near object: a brightly lit picture about a metre away will serve. Repeat with the object still nearer. In each case measure the distance from lens to image.

Box cameras, lacking such a focusing device, are suitable only for "distant" objects—i.e. objects 3 metres or more away.

359 *Action of a Convex Lens*
Use the ray-track apparatus. Half-lenses can be bought and are convenient.

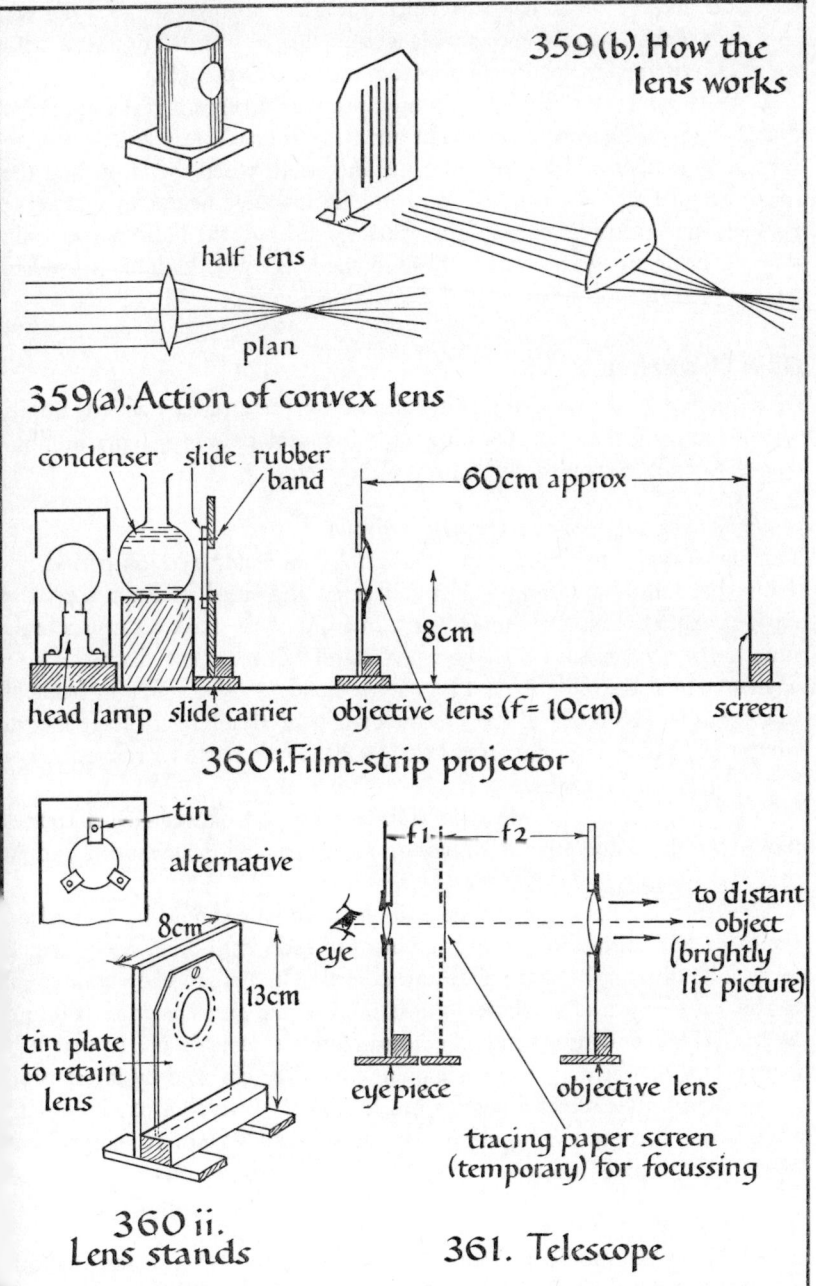

(a) With lamp, multiple slit, and beaker set the apparatus for parallel rays and observe what happens when these are thrown on to a convex lens (half-lens). Measure the focal length in this way and compare it with the value obtained by focusing light from the Sun (Expt. 356).

(b) With lamp and multiple slit only, produce divergent rays and notice that as the distance between lamp and lens is made less and less these rays focus farther and farther from the lens, until when the lamp is at the focal distance they are parallel. With the light source nearer than this the rays are made to diverge even after passage through the lens and the only way to see an image is to look through the lens towards the lamp, when a magnified view of the source will be obtained.

Other Optical Instruments

Once having understood the principles of mirror and lens action, pupils will be interested in the working of the school episcope, lantern, film-strip projector, microprojector, film projector, etc.

360 *Projection Lantern or Filmstrip Projector*
This apparatus (Fig. 360, i) can be assembled in a single lesson period.

Use the lamp-house and 100 cm³ flask as described in Expt. 344; the flask of water is the "condenser" lens. In front of the flask set up a simple slide carrier, consisting of a plywood stand with a 4-cm diameter hole against which the slide is held by rubber bands. A short way in front of this again is the objective lens—a convex lens of about 10-cm focal length (simple lensholders are shown in Fig. 360, ii). The screen is arranged 60 cm beyond the objective lens.

Slides may be single filmstrip frames mounted between card frames (bound with Sellotape), or drawings made on cellophane with Indian ink.

The lamp filament, flask, slide and objective lens should be centred on the same horizontal line, with the centre of each item 8 cm above bench level. The distance between slide and objective lens should be about equal to the focal length of the latter *plus* 2 cm, but the exact position is found by trial. The condenser bends the beam from the lamp-house so that it is focused on the objective lens; this point should be checked by interposing a white card. The screen image is much brighter than that obtained with an episcope because the highlights on the slide allow almost 100 per cent of the light to pass through.

361 *Astronomical Telescope*
The object-glass should measure about 5 cm across, with a focal length of not less than 30 cm. The eye-piece is 2–3 cm diameter with a focal length of about 2–3 cm (e.g. a botanical magnifier).

Measure the focal length of each lens by focusing the image of a distant object on paper (Expt. 356). Then set up the objective lens to face a *clear* electric bulb at the other side of the half-darkened laboratory (a mains carbon-filament lamp is best). Focus the image on a temporary screen (a sheet of tissue paper) at the focal distance of the lens.

Now set up the eye-piece at its focal length from this image and adjust its position until a clear image of the object is seen through it. The observer's eye should be moved backwards and forwards in relation to the eye-piece until a large field of view is obtained.

The object should appear much nearer than it actually is because the objective brings together far more light than would otherwise reach the eye and the eye-piece magnifies the image so formed.

Plane-convex lenses may be used with advantage. For both eye-piece and objective the plane side should face the eye.

It is essential for the success of this work that the object and lens centres should lie in one line and that the lenses should be parallel. Once the preliminary experiment has been done, pupils may be shown how to fix the lenses within cardboard tubes, sliding within each other. Details have been provided by R. I. Shewell (*School Science Review*, June 1951, pp. 383–4). Such home-made instruments are remarkably good.

Historical Note: Teachers today are spared the "Pin and Parallax" methods of a former generation of science teaching. One of the pioneers in the use of light beams was F. A. Meier of Rugby, and his original paper appears in *S.S.R.* No. 13 (September, 1922), p. 12. Later, J. P. Stephenson of the City of London School developed the famous "ray box" bearing his name: see *S.S.R.* No. 52 (June, 1932), p. 371.

Chapter Eighteen
Sight and Colour

Experiments Demonstrated by the Teacher

It is a main aim of this book to emphasize the importance of allowing boys and girls of average ability to carry out practical work themselves, either individually or in small groups. To this end an attempt has been made to show something of the wide range of simple experiments available for such work. Until a real attack is made in this direction many pupils in non-selective schools, and not a few in grammar schools, will continue to regard Science as just another burden, with results long familiar.

It would, however, be entirely wrong to conclude that there is no longer a place for experiments done before the class and under the direct control of the teacher. Some experiments are best demonstrated; for example, those requiring expensive or complicated apparatus, or manipulative skill beyond the capabilities of the average pupil; those which could scarcely be tackled otherwise because of the amount of preparation or follow-up needed; and (very commonly) those for which the laboratory does not possess sufficient apparatus for class practical work. There is another category, commented upon by Fowles:

" . . . small, perhaps unpremeditated experiments, to settle a question raised in discussion . . . Of such there is only one thing to note—namely, that they should be made visible to the whole class. An experiment which would ordinarily be done in a test-tube should be done in a gas jar . . ."

But even apart from all these, there is bound to be much teacher demonstration so long as large classes and a meagre time allotment continue to be the rule in many places. A happy blend of practical work by the pupils and of demonstration by the teacher is a flexible compromise which can suit itself to the special conditions of individual schools. The determining factors, besides the abilities and aptitudes of the teaching staff and the particular range of material in the syllabus, include considerations such as laboratory equipment and accommodation, storage space, the amount of teaching time and the availability of laboratory assistance.

Experiments carried out in front of a class provide many pitfalls for the unwary. Yet upon the success or failure of his demonstration may hang the reputation of a teacher with his pupils. According to the way in which they are conducted, discipline and interest will go hand in hand or the lesson will end in disorder and failure. The following hints may help those new to this kind of work.

(a) Careful preparation and rehearsal are essential. Always try out any new experiment beforehand, and do not use it until you are confident that you can carry it through to the satisfaction of the class. The teacher is in one sense a showman: he demonstrates not only physical phenomena but also manipulative techniques and experimental method.

If a failure does occur, avoid the too easy snare of assigning imaginary reasons: seek the cause quickly and keep in mind Faraday's remark—"We learn most from our failures." For a schoolmaster, however, it is well if demonstrations succeed.

(b) Have all necessary apparatus and materials ready before the lesson begins. Know where to put your hand on spares, should these be required. Water may be boiled, or ice crushed, or containers weighed, before the lesson is due to start—if by so doing a break in the pace of the demonstration can be avoided. Nothing causes interest to flag more than unexciting chores holding up the development of the main theme, unless it be the retirement of the teacher backstage to seek something that has been overlooked—especially if, as may often happen, it cannot immediately be found. Nothing either is more subversive of discipline.

(c) As with experiments by the pupils, stick to familiar apparatus and materials as far as possible. If pupils see the tools which are being used as familiar objects, they are more likely to accept the reality and significance of the results. At the same time they are better able to comprehend the course of the experiment.

(d) Ensure that every member of the class can see what is going on. A thoughtful mounting of the apparatus will usually ensure that there is no need for pupils to crowd forward in order to see.

(e) Even if pupils are brought round the lecture table, they should never be so crowded that they cannot move easily. For one reason, they will need to join in the demonstratiion from time to time. It is most important that pupils be encouraged to play an active part in what is going forward. The ordinary pupil will not sit quiet for long. If he knows that there may come, at any moment, an opportunity for him to take a hand he will be keener, he will be more readily convinced that the work has significance for him, and he will be anxious to demonstrate to his fellows that he is no fool.

(f) Keep the experiment going with the give and take of question and answer and comment. Capitalize any special development. In no form of teaching is there greater need for practical training, manual dexterity, wide background knowledge, and the ability to think on one's feet.

Structure and Action of the Eye

362 *Bullock's Eye*
The experiment is best demonstrated by the teacher to a small group of pupils. Wear rubber gloves. Cut away any flesh and fat around the eye with a very sharp knife. Find on the outside of the eye the place where the optic nerve leaves the eyeball. Holding the eye over a small dish, cut it across midway between the optic nerve and the cornea, and collect the colourless transparent fluid which escapes. On the inner wall of that half of the eye containing the optic nerve notice the dark film of the retina, broken at the spot where the optic nerve leaves. From the other half carefully cut out the lens of the eye; notice its convex shape and use it as a magnifying glass. Finally, observe the iris and the cornea of the eye.

363 *Action of the Iris*
Pupils may work in pairs for this experiment, one observing the eye of the other. The person under examination should look at a bright window. Notice the white of the eyeball, the coloured iris and the dark pupil, the latter two being visible through the transparent window called the cornea. Look at the eye from the side and see how the cornea bulges outwards. Now cover the eye for a few moments with a dark cloth and then observe the size of the pupil. Turn a bright light upon the eye (e.g. an electric torch or other lamp) and note how the iris expands to diminish the size of the pupil.

Observe how, every few seconds, the upper eyelid flicks over the surface of the eye, washing its surface with moisture; and how the eyelids can help protect the eyes from dust.

364 *The Blind Spot*
Supply each pupil with a small piece of paper or card. Mark on it a cross (X) and a black spot (●) 10 cm apart, with the cross on the left. Close the left eye and stare at the cross. Move the paper slowly backwards and forwards about 25–30 cm in front of the face and find a distance at which the black spot disappears. Holding the card at this distance, move it to the right and to the left.

Repeat with a cross and spot 5 cm apart (use the other side of the card). At what distance does the spot disappear now?

Draw a diagram to incorporate both results.

365 *Reversal of Imprint on Retina by the Brain*
Make a pin hole in a sheet of brown paper or card, hold it up to a strong light and look through it at a distance of 8–10 cm. Move the point of a pencil, or the end of a ruler, slowly up in front of the eye and as near to the eye as possible (touching the lashes); pupils wearing spectacles will have to remove them. As the obstacle moves up in front of the eye it

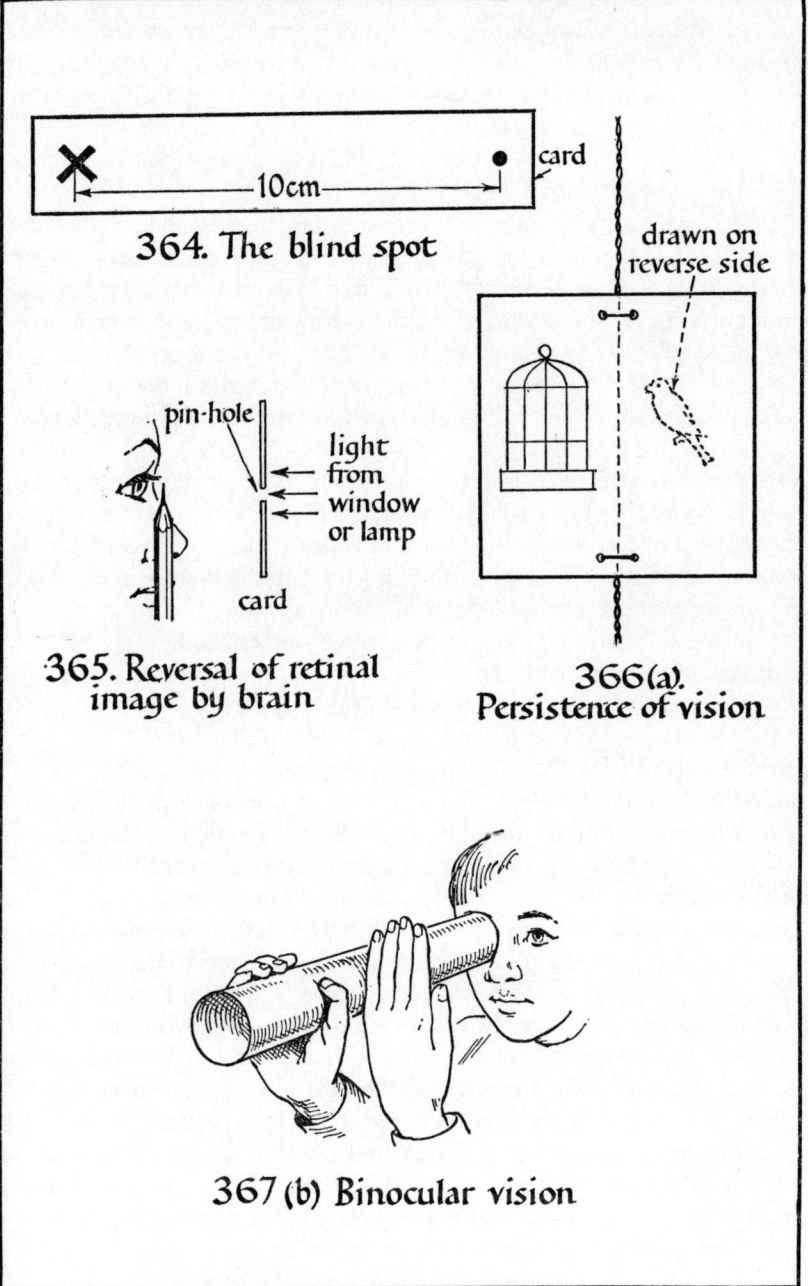

obstructs some light from the pin hole and an upright shadow (not an image) of the pencil or ruler is cast on the retina. As the obstacle moves upward, so does its shadow. But the brain reverses the impression, so that although the experimenter is well aware that the obstacle is being moved upwards he appears to see it moving downwards against the background of the pin hole.

366 Persistence of Vision
(a) Take a card about 7 cm square and draw on one side a bird and on the other a bird cage (this is the classic combination, but pupils may suggest alternatives). Suspend the card between two loops of thin string threaded through holes in opposite edges of the card. Put one loop over a hook and while holding the second loop in one hand use the other hand to turn the card round forty or fifty times, until the strings on either side are twisted as far as they will go. Release the card; the bird appears to be in the cage.

(b) Make a "flicker" book. Take an old pack of playing cards having plain backs and draw on one end of each card a picture, say of a man on horseback. The pictures should form a series, each picture differing slightly from the next. Thus we may begin with the horse galloping, then jumping, rising over a fence, landing, and galloping away. Hold the cards in one hand and flick through the pictures with the other hand.

Instead of using playing cards, pupils may staple together 50–100 pieces of paper, each about 4-cm square, to make a little book.

367 Binocular Vision
(a) With the right eye closed, hold a pencil at arm's length and align it with a line on a distant wall. Open the right eye and close the left; the pencil seems to move far to the left. Repeat the experiment with the pencil held closer to the eye; the movement this time appears even greater. The experiment shows that each eye gives a slightly different view of any object.

(b) To show that images formed by the two eyes are blended together, roll a sheet of paper into a tube, put the tube to the right eye and, with both eyes open, look at some distant object. Bring the palm of the left hand in front of the left eye and move it backwards and forwards alongside the paper tube. The pictures seen by the two eyes blend so that the distant scene is apparently viewed through a hole in the hand.

(c) Point with a finger at a distant tree and look fixedly at the tree. In a moment or two, two fingers are seen pointing. When we look directly at anything we see it singly, the two eyes adjusting themselves to bring it into the same focus; but things nearer (or farther away) appear double.

(d) Hold a pencil upright in the left hand almost at arm's length. Close one eye and quickly try to touch the pencil point with the index finger of the right hand. Notice how easy it is to misjudge distance if only one eye is used.

The slightly different views of objects at different distances help us to judge the distance between them. In stereoscopic pictures we see two slightly different (prepared) views, so that we get the impression that not all points of what is really a flat picture are at the same distance; the picture therefore appears "solid" or three-dimensional.

Topics: Reference to eyes of other animals (e.g. cat, bee) and to animals without eyes. Care of the eyes; tears; how to remove dust from the eye. Application of persistence of vision in the cinema. Optical illusions. It is a useful revision exercise for children to list the similarities and the differences between the eye and a camera.

Defects of the Eye and their Correction

368 Model Eye

First make a lens carrier as follows: use a square of tin-plate about 3 cm wider than the convex lens which is to be used. A lens of about 20 cm focal length is suitable. In the plate cut a circular hole (curved tin-snips) of 5 mm smaller radius than the lens, and cut four tags as shown, each about 6 mm wide by 1 cm deep. Bend the tags up at right angles to the plate, drop the lens into place, and turn the tags down over the lens. Solder two stiff wires, bent as shown, to the sides of the plate (Fig. 368, ii).

Now blow up a balloon to a diameter about 2 cm greater than the focal length of the lens. Paste strips of newspaper all over the balloon and when they are dry paste on more strips until the ball is sufficiently rigid. Cover finally with white tissue paper, pasted on in strips. When the ball is dry, deflate and remove the balloon and cut openings on opposite sides of the ball to represent the cornea and the retina respectively. The retina opening should be large enough to admit the lens.

Insert the lens in its carrier, pushing the front ends of the wires through holes pricked in the papier-maché on either side of the cornea and squeezing the other ends slightly together until they are within the ball and then pushing them back through holes pricked on either side of the retina opening. Now, by pushing the wires to and fro slightly, the lens may be moved nearer or farther from the cornea opening. Finally, paste a patch of tracing paper over the retina aperture.

Mount the model eye to face a brightly lit window and focus the image on the retina; note that the image is inverted. The model may be used for some of the work described in Expts. 369 and 370. See also the *School Science Review*, No. 151, p. 739.

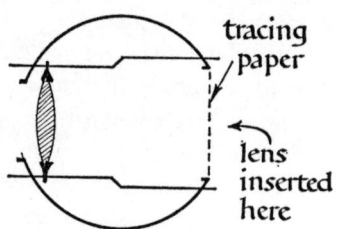

368 i. Plan of papier-mâché eye

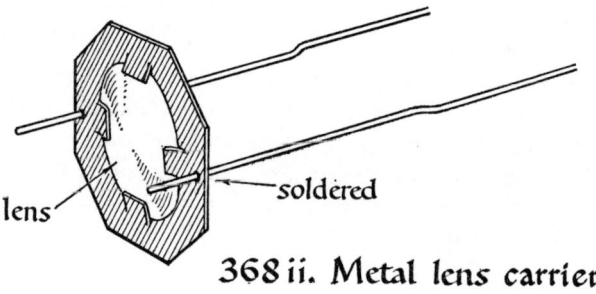

368 ii. Metal lens carrier

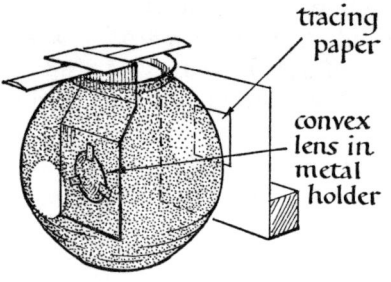

369. Short sight & long sight

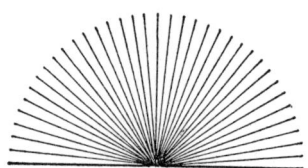

371. Astigmatism

369 Short Sight

Paint a small goldfish bowl dull black except for 2-cm diameter patches on opposite sides, one to represent the cornea and the other the retina of an eye. Bring up a ground glass or tracing-paper screen immediately behind the retinal patch. Lay a ruler across the top of the bowl and suspend from it a convex lens in a tinplate carrier, so that the lens hangs between the "cornea" and the "retina". The lens should be of such a focal length that it can be adjusted to throw a sharp image of a distant window on the retina.

Now move the lens slightly farther from the retina: the image of the window becomes blurred because the light now focuses in front of the retina (as can be shown by lowering a strip of ground glass into the bowl). This is the condition of short-sighted people. But they can focus nearer objects; bring a clear lamp towards the bowl and show that the image of the filament can be focused sharply on the retina.

Finally, mount a long focus (i.e. fairly flat) concave lens in front of the cornea. This probably throws the image of the window so far back that the screen has to be moved back from the bowl to catch it. Adjust the eye-lens (inside the bowl) until the image focuses on the retina; notice that it is farther from the retina than when the concave lens was not used. Thus a concave spectacle lens can be used to correct short sight.

370 Long Sight

Repeat the first part of Expt. 369, and then move the suspended lens slightly towards the retina. The ground glass screen has to be moved away from the bowl to catch the image of the distant window. The image of a lamp brought nearer to the cornea is farther away still. Long-sighted people cannot focus near objects properly, although they may be able to focus distant objects by using the ciliary muscles.

Mount a thin convex lens in front of the cornea. This will bring the image of the window nearer to the retina than its position when focusing the window without the convex lens. Thus long sight can be corrected by using convex spectacle lenses.

371 Astigmatism

Make an eye-testing chart by drawing radial lines in Indian ink at 5 degree intervals on a cardboard semicircle 30 cm in diameter. Set this up under a strong light and get pupils who wear glasses to look at it (with one eye closed) without their glasses and then when wearing them. Other pupils may also record their impressions.

Examine print through a spectacle lens designed to correct astigmatism. Turn the lens slowly through 360° and observe how the print is distorted. Notice the cylindrical grinding of the lens.

Refraction and the Spectrum

We have already seen how light can be refracted (changed in direction) when it passes through a lens.

372 *Everyday Examples*
(a) Put a coin at the bottom of a basin and stand away from the basin until the coin just disappears from view. Now let an assistant pour water gently into the basin, being very careful not to disturb the coin. The coin comes into view.

(b) Stand a ruler vertically in 8 cm of water. Notice that the part under water seems much shortened; estimate its apparent length by comparison with the scale marking above the water.

(c) Incline the ruler to an angle of 45° or more in the water and notice that it appears to bend at the water surface.

373 *Refraction of Light between Air and Water*
(a) Fill a medicine bottle with water and lay it on the bench on one of its narrower sides with a sheet of paper underneath it. Pencil round the bottle to mark its position on the paper. Set a ruler on edge obliquely to one side of the bottle and sight the top edge through the bottle, setting a second ruler in line with the sighting. One boy should hold the first ruler whilst a second boy sights. Mark the position of both rulers on the paper, remove the bottle, and study the position of the lines that have been drawn. Repeat the experiment with the first ruler (i) at a greater inclination to the bottle (ii) at right angles to the bottle.

(b) Screw a lamp-house (Expt. 344) and a lens-stand (with convex lens) on a wooden base so as to give a parallel beam of light. Pass a fairly tightly fitting bolt through the centre of the base so that when the bolt is gripped in a clamp the base can be pivoted and held in any desired position. Direct the beam downwards into a trough filled with water containing a little fluorescein or milk. The path of the beam above the water may be outlined by smoke from burning brown paper; the path in the water will be very clear in a partially darkened room. Vary the angle of incidence of the light beam on the water surface.

374 *Refraction Through Glass*
(a) Outline the position of a rectangular glass block standing on paper and then direct a pencil of light obliquely towards one face of the block. Mark the path of this pencil and also of the light emerging from the opposite face of the block. Repeat for various angles of incidence (including the case where the pencil is at right angles to the glass face). Remove the block and draw in the path of the light through the glass corresponding to each incident pencil.

(b) Repeat the experiment, using a 60° glass prism. The prism must be

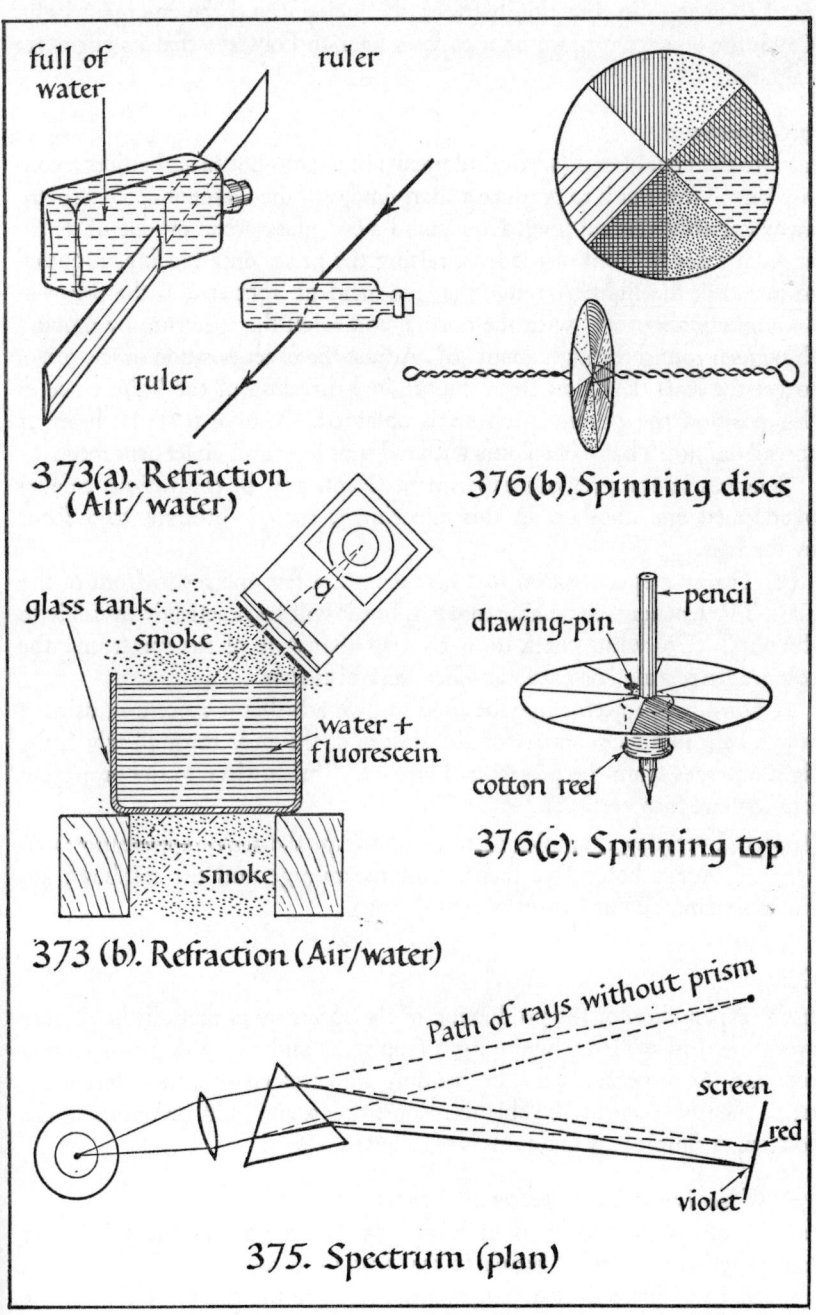

rotated in the light pencil until an emergent beam is obtained. Notice the marked change in direction between the incident and the emergent light. Catch the emergent beam on a paper screen and observe that its edges are coloured.

375 *Spectrum*
(a) Use the usual lamp (vertical filament) in a lamp-house and adjust a convex lens in front of it to produce a sharp image of the filament about a metre away (narrow vertical line). Now stand a 60° glass prism on one of its triangular faces in front of the lens, raising the prism on a block as required to intercept the light. Arrange that the incident light strikes the prism at an angle of about 45° with the normal and catch the spectrum by moving the screen round through about 40°. Adjust the exact position of the prism to get the least deviation from the original direction of the light, since in this position the purest spectrum is obtained. Observe that the beam is spread out into a band of colours with red bent least and violet bent most.

Whereas in the previous experiment (Expt. 374, b) the various colours overlapped one another, in this experiment each is brought to a focus by the lens.

(b) Throw a spectrum on to a blackboard, a few metres in front of the class. The teacher will be able to see it, but it will be practically invisible to the pupils. Use white chalk to mark strip after strip of the spectrum: the colours are revealed one after another, very distinctly.

A film-strip projector may be used to give a brilliant spectrum, using a vertical slit in a 5-cm square of aluminium as the slide through which the light emerges from the projector. Place a 60° prism close to the projection lens (square face vertical).

Topics: Everyday examples of refraction (e.g. the wavy appearance seen over a hot stove; mention of the mirage and the rainbow; apparent enlargement of setting Sun).

Colour
If the explanation of the production of the spectrum is that all the colours are present in ordinary white light (sunlight) and that the prism merely separates or disperses them, by bending different colours to different extents, then we ought to be able to reconstitute white light by remixing the colours. A simple way to do this is as follows:

376 *White Light from Spectrum Colours*
(a) Set up the spectrum as in Expt. 375. Then remove the prism and move the lens somewhat nearer to the lamp until the image on a screen is a broad band instead of a narrow line. Replace the prism. The beam is bent round as before but the band of light is white with one red edge and

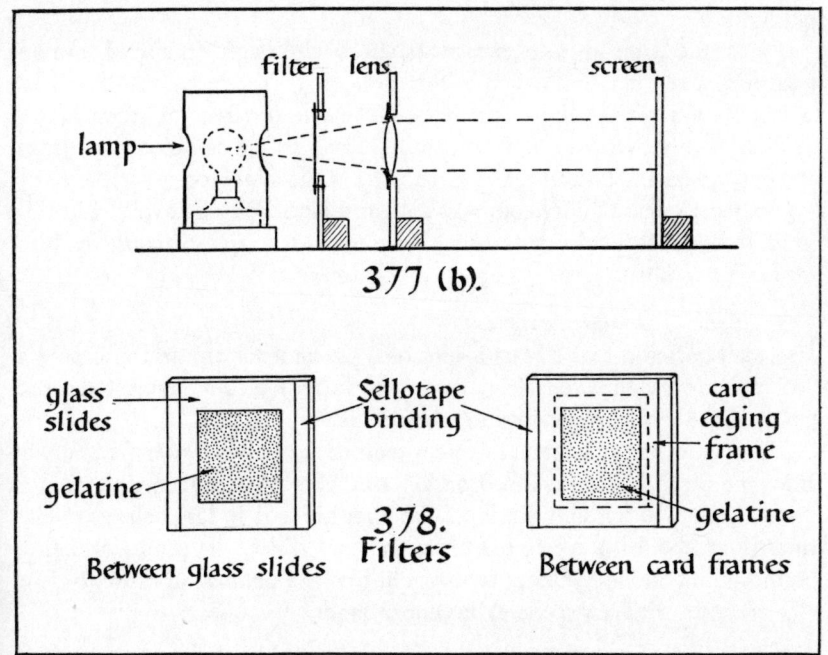

377 (b).

378. Filters — Between glass slides / Between card frames

one bluish edge. This is because the broad bands of colour overlap except at the very edges, where red (bent least) and violet (bent most) are still visible.

(b) Paint the main spectrum colours on sectors marked out on a circle of card. It is convenient to have 8 sectors, one of which is left blank for later colour adjustment (more blue may probably be required). Pass about a metre of fine string through two holes near the centre of the card (Fig. 376 (b)), knot the ends together and hold the two ends of the loop so that the disc can be spun by first twisting the string and then alternately increasing and relaxing the pull on it. The colours on the card merge (persistence of vision) and a near approach to white can be obtained.

(c) Push a pencil through a cotton reel into which it fits tightly, until the reel is near to the pencil point. Colour a 20-cm diameter card as for the previous experiment, pierce it through the centre and push the blunt end of the pencil through the hole, fixing the card to the top of the reel with a drawing pin. Spin the top so formed.

377 *Colour of Transparent Materials*
(a) Insert a red filter (see Expt. 378) between the lamp and lens of the spectrum apparatus (Expt. 375) (a)). All the spectrum except the red end is blotted out. Evidently the filter appears red because it allows only red light

to pass through it. Repeat the experiment with other filters (e.g. green, blue).

(b) Use the lamp and lens to cast a patch of white light on a screen. Interpose first a red filter and then a blue one. Next interpose both filters together; practically no light now reaches the screen, since the second filter absorbs all light that the first transmits. Try also the combinations green and red, green and blue, etc. and discuss the results obtained.

It is recommended that common coloured glass slides be avoided in this kind of work; they seldom transmit pure colours, so that their use leads to confusing results.

378 Colour of Opaque Materials

Use the lamp and lens to cast a spot of light on a screen, and interpose a red filter. View materials (e.g. wools) of various colours against the red patch on the screen. Repeat using other filters.

Either gelatine or Cinemoid filters may be used. The latter (obtainable from the Strand Electric Co., London and Manchester) are much stouter and can be used without binding. Cinemoid is sold in large sheets. Gelatine filters should be mounted between glass slides, the sandwich being bound with Sellotape. Either type of filter is held against an ordinary lens stand (screen with central hole) by rubber bands.

379 Mixing Primary Colours

Three lights—red, green and blue—cannot be produced by mixing other lights. They are called "primary colours". All other colours may be produced by mixing two or three of the primaries in suitable proportions.

A convenient type of lamp-house is shown in Fig. 379, i; it consists of the usual 12-volt headlamp bulb (straight vertical filament) mounted on a wood base. The cover is a powder-paint tin with rectangular holes cut in three sides at the height of the lamp filament (Fig. 379, ii), i.e. centres 8 cm high. Colour filters may be placed in front of the apertures, and mounted mirrors may be arranged so that the light from all three apertures is cast on a single screen (Fig. 379, iii). Always place the blue filter in the direct beam.

(Fig. 379, i shows how such apparatus (lamp-house, slide-carrier, lens carrier, screen, mirror, etc.) may be mounted on wooden feet to slide along a metre rule, thus forming a simple optical bench. Such a bench is useful in building the filmstrip projector (Expt. 360) or the telescope (Exp. 361).)

Use two apertures only of the lamp-house at first, and cast a red and a green patch on to the screen; arrange for the patches partly to overlap. Notice that the overlapping part appears yellow. Repeat using green and blue (peacock blue overlap), and then blue and red (magenta overlap). Yellow, peacock blue and magenta are called "secondary colours".

Now use all three apertures. Confirm that when the three primary

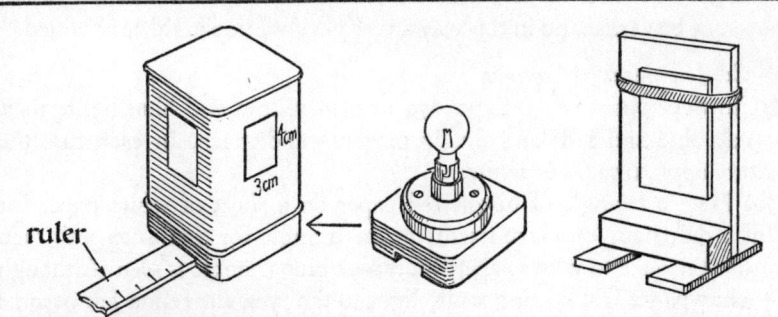

Alternative lamp box
(rectangular powder colour tin 10cm × 8cm × 8cm

3J9 i. Lamp-house & stand for other apparatus

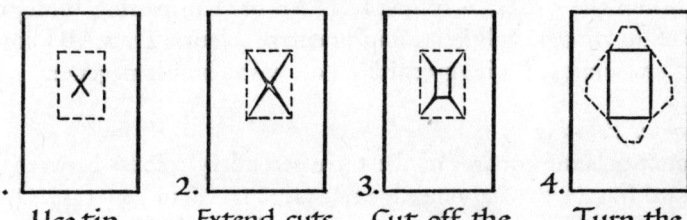

1. Use tin opener
2. Extend cuts with tin snips
3. Cut off the points
4. Turn the flaps inside

3J9 ii. Cutting a rectangular hole in a tin

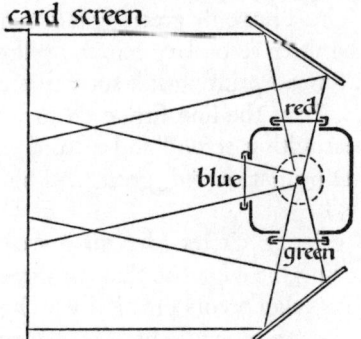

Plan of lamp box with two mirrors used for colour mixing

3J9 iii.

colours overlap, the screen appears white or near-white; by adjusting the distances of the mirrors from the lamp-house the relative intensity of the lights may be varied and in this way a very good white should be obtained.

380 *Complementary Colours*
(a) Use the apparatus of Expt. 379 to mix yellow and blue light; then peacock blue and red; and finally magenta and green. In each case the mixture approximates to white.

(b) Paste a triangle of bright red paper on a sheet of white paper (or paint a red triangle). Gaze fixedly at the triangle for 2 minutes and then transfer the gaze to white paper; a peacock blue triangle is seen. Although the white paper is reflecting white light to the eyes, the retina has become fatigued in respect of red and appreciates the remainder of the spectrum better. Repeat the experiment using first a blue triangle and then a green one.

(c) Construct a colour triangle (see diagram). The colours may be painted into the circles. Any line (e.g. AB or XY) passing through the centre of the triangle will join complementary colours. Thus AB joins blue and yellow, while XY joins greenish yellow with a bluish magenta.

381 *Colour Printing*
(a) Mount gelatine squares of the three secondary colours between glass or in card frames, leaving one edge free (see Figure) in each case. Overlap the free edges of two secondaries and examine by holding over a white paper or by projecting on a screen.

If the two colours were yellow and peacock blue, then the yellow will absorb all but red and green light, whilst the peacock blue will absorb all but blue and green light. Thus only green light is transmitted.

(b) Printers use the three secondary colours, yellow, turquoise (peacock blue) and magenta. Spread printing ink such as is used for lino cuts over 5-cm squares of lino. Press the lino firmly on to white paper; a coloured square results. Repeat with a second and a third colour, overlapping the squares slightly. The primaries, red, green and blue, are obtained at the overlaps.

(c) Mount three gelatine circles (the three secondaries) between two squares of glass (binding the edges) so that the three overlap in the centre. Where the complete overlap occurs practically no light can come through; this is "black"—ie. absence of any light. The printer finds in practice that he gets only a poor black by overlapping secondary inks and he therefore often adds a "black printer" to the three secondary inks.

382 *Effect of Light Source on Colour*
Construct a simple two-compartment wooden or cardboard box: fix a lamp-holder on the lid above each compartment and remove the lower half

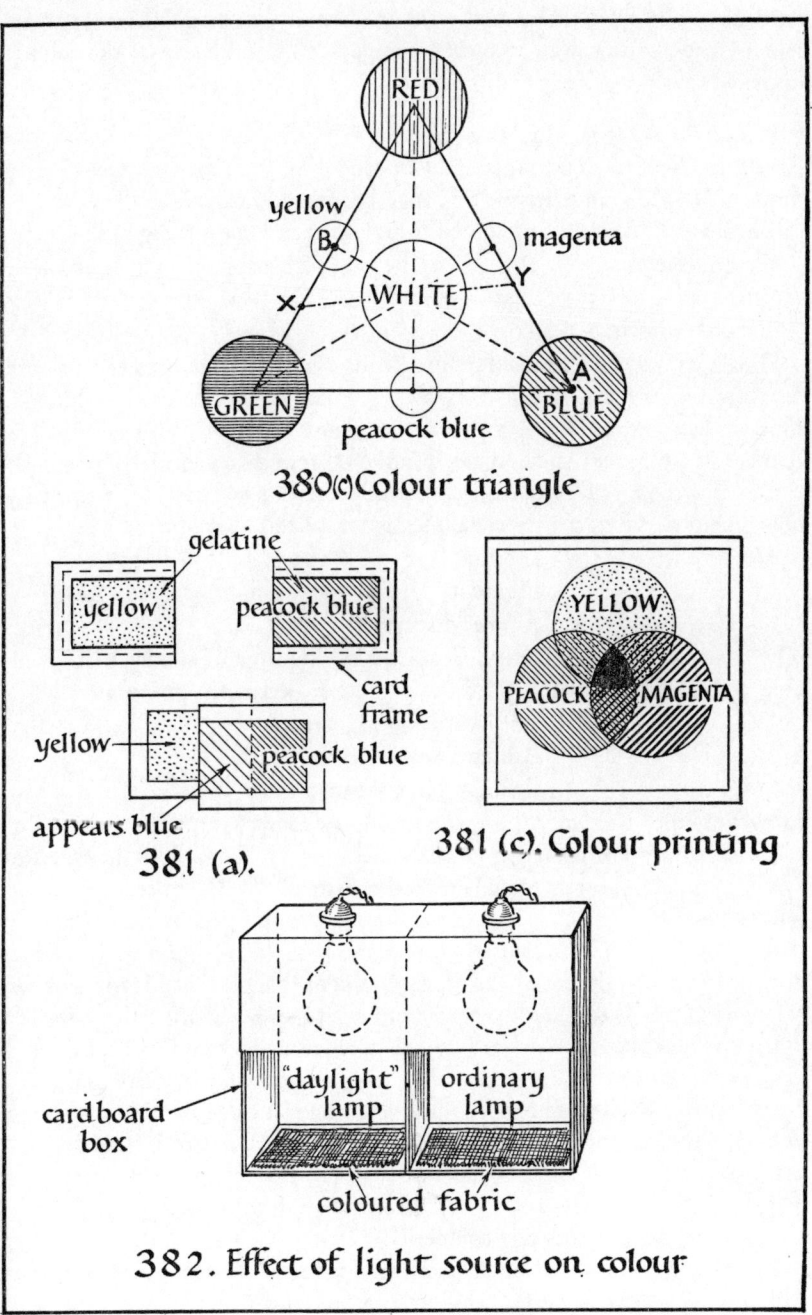

380(c) Colour triangle

381 (a).

381 (c). Colour printing

382. Effect of light source on colour

of the front side of the box. Fit a "daylight" bulb in one compartment and an ordinary bulb of equal power in the other. Put samples of the same fabric (wool, cotton, etc.) into each compartment and compare the colours under the different lamps.

383 *The Preparation of Lipsticks*

Reference back to Expt. 119 should be made for notes on the general technique of weighing out and melting together fats and oils.

The lipstick base is compounded from waxes and non-drying oils:

Ceresine wax	25 g	Lanolin	28 g
Olive oil	5 g	Vaseline	31 g
Liquid paraffin	11 g		

Hardness may be increased by increasing the ratio of wax to oils. Weigh out the mixture into a can on which a small spout has been fashioned. Heat it to about 80°C. in a pan of hot water. Stir well and when all is melted add pigment to the base. Manufacturers disperse the pigment by using roll mills, but simple stirring will serve our purpose. The quantity of pigment required may be calculated from the following formula:

Lipstick base	87 parts
Pigment	12 parts
Acid eosin 17369	1 part

The eosin confers indelibility. From the wide range of shades then available in the I.C.I. pigments, the following were used by the authors:

Brilliant Tangerine 13030
Brilliant Scarlet 13032
Brilliant Rose A21232

However, enquiries must be made through chemical suppliers to find out what pigments are currently available. A note in the *School Science Review*, No. 162 (March, 1966) gave the firm of D. F. Anstead Ltd., of Victoria Road, Romford, Essex, as a source of appropriate pigments.

The moulds, three or four at a time, are prepared in a manner similar to that used for styptic pencil (Expt. 147), except that (i) the thickness of the wooden former is selected to correspond with the size of the empty lipstick holders available; (ii) the end of the former is rounded. The coloured molten base is poured carefully direct from the can to fill each mould and the sticks are allowed to cool thoroughly. The last stage consists in cutting the stick to the required length, stripping off the metal foil, inserting the stick into its holder and wiping away any imperfections with a scrap of paper tissue. The whole operation, from weighing to mounting, is easily carried out within a single lesson period.

In passing it is interesting to comment upon the very large cooling contraction which occurs, often leading to a hole down the centre of the cast stick.

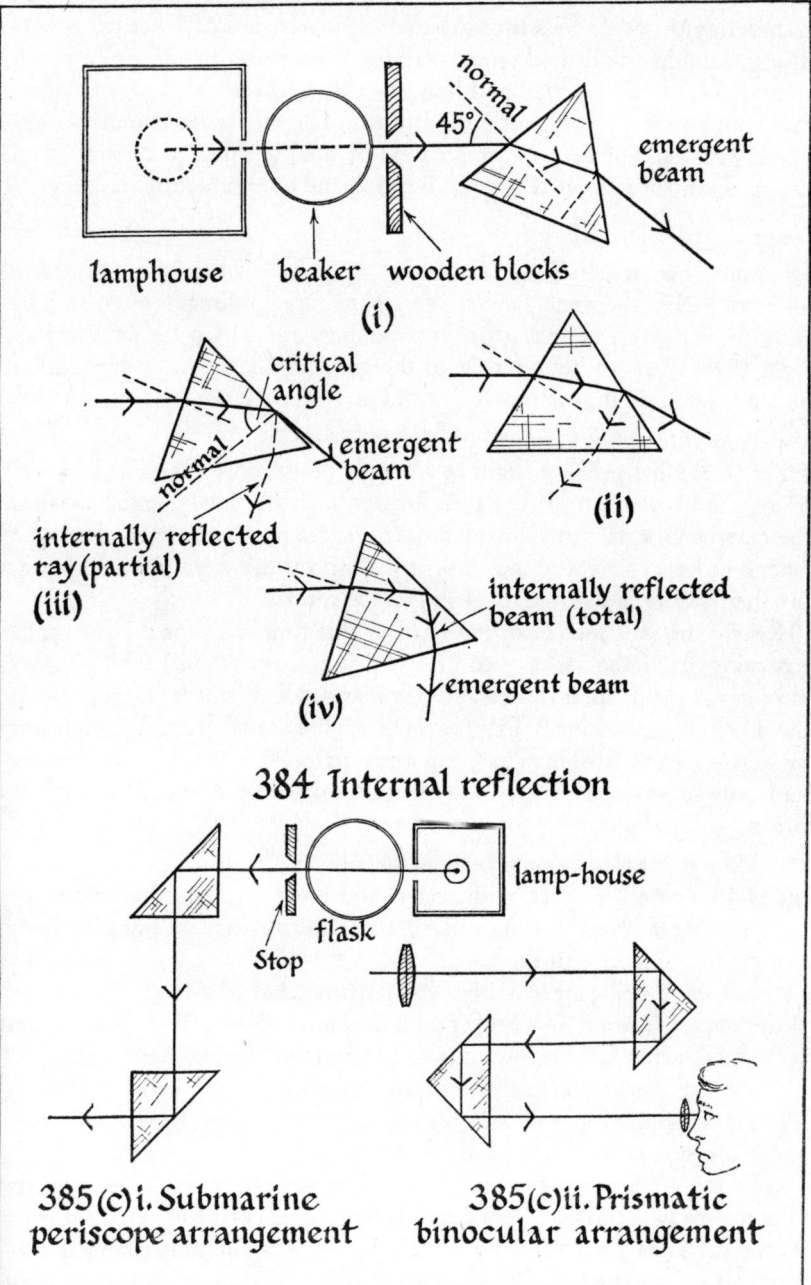

384 Internal reflection

385(c)i. Submarine periscope arrangement

385(c)ii. Prismatic binocular arrangement

The experiment can form an original and valuable introduction to the study of colour. A series of pairs of lips is drawn on white card and coloured with the various lipsticks that have been made. The card is now illuminated, in a darkened room, with light from a sodium flame (asbestos rope soaked in salt solution and hung in a large Bunsen flame), a daylight lamp, and a mercury vapour lamp in turn. The effects are extremely convincing and should lead to a discussion of the matching of colours when shopping and of stage effects, street lighting and interior decoration.

Internal Reflection of light

Diamonds owe much of their brilliance to the fact that light is reflected to and fro, within the stone, between the many facets. Mirages, often seen by motorists on the road ahead in hot weather, are caused by reflection of light from layers of hot air near to the ground. Glass prisms are used as very efficient reflectors in binoculars and periscopes.

384 *Total Internal Reflection*

Direct a parallel pencil of light at an angle of 45° on to one face of a 60° triangular glass prism (Fig. 384, i). Rotate the prism slowly, anticlockwise: the emergent beam turns downwards (Fig. 384, ii). Continue turning: the emergent beam moves round until it just grazes the prism face (Fig. 384, iii), then it disappears from that face (Fig. 384, iv).

Repeat the sequence of operations but this time look for a faint pencil emerging from the lower face of the prism (Fig. 384, ii) which grows stronger as the prism is turned and becomes suddenly much brighter just as the other emergent pencil disappears (Figs. 384, iii and 384, iv). This lower emergent pencil is light which has been reflected internally: it becomes suddenly brighter at the position where total reflection occurs within the prism.

385 *More Examples of Total Internal Reflection.*

(a) Hold a tumbler, filled with water, above eye level and look upwards at the water surface: it shines like a silver mirror because light is totally reflected from it to your eyes.

(b) Drive a nail part-way into the narrower end of a cork stopper and float the cork in water in a beaker with the nail projecting downwards from it. View the cork from below: the nail appears to be standing upright.

(c) Set up the arrangements indicated in Figs. 385 (c), i and 385 (c), ii. The former finds application in the submarine periscope; the latter in prismatic binoculars.

The red reflectors at the back of a motor vehicle are built up of many tiny prisms which reflect light from the headlamps of a following car back to the driver of that car. Tiny spherical glass beads possess a similar property: they are used in ciné screens and, suspended in paint, for marking road lines.

Chapter Nineteen
Stars and Space

Textbooks and Science Libraries
It is generally more difficult to find a class-book suitable for less able pupils than for boys and girls who have a public examination in mind. A textbook may serve the purpose of a written syllabus and prove a useful revision guide; but its didactic statements are often unattractive. Too often the subject-matter is presented only as a body of knowledge to be memorized, whereas science is better displayed as something inviting participation. Even teachers may too easily accept the contents of a book as a substitute for teaching.

One of the obstacles that must be faced by teachers is the wide range of ability and interest often found within a class, making text-book selection doubly difficult. With the weakest pupils vocabulary alone may be a serious stumbling block. Today a flood of new books is coming on to the market for C.S.E. and Nuffield courses, but the problem of the ordinary youngster, for whom Science is just another subject until it is lifted out of the rut by inspired teaching, is far from solved. The authors' own series of class-books (*Practical Science for Secondary Schools*: in 4 vols: Univ. of London Press) is specifically designed for average and below-average pupils; yet teachers will be well advised to use even these books with discretion—not blindly accepting the contents as their own work scheme, but making a careful selection to meet particular needs. It is only through his own effort that the teacher can match subject-matter and standards to the needs of the pupils he teaches, exploit the resources of his department (which may be only his own classroom), and exercise his personal bent and skill most profitably. The freedom of the teacher to pursue his own ideas, in his own unique situation, is a privilege that should on no account be surrendered.

A class library is valuable for immediate reference purposes, even though Science may be well represented in the main school collection. Well-chosen books, close at hand, can support day to day teaching in more than one way, of which not the least important is that they may be useful to fill in spare moments such as inevitably come at times. The purposes of a classroom library are exemplified by the following list of recommended categories of books:

(a) Books of reference data (formulae, recipes, physical constants, etc.).

It is extremely useful to have at hand, for example, the resistances of wires of various kinds and gauges; the calorific values of foodstuffs; and the boiling points of commonly used liquids. The best arrangement may be to have a few copies of a home-produced booklet containing data known to be needed, with space for additions. New tables can be pasted in from time to time. If such booklets are made up by interested pupils their value is greatly increased.

(b) Well illustrated books for the identification of plants, land animals, rocks, shells, fossils, clouds, star constellations and the like. Such books are seldom cheap today and it is well to see that they are fitted with strong plastic covers before they are released for class use. The following, among many, are recommended for consideration:

Step:	*Wayside and Woodland Blossoms*
	Wayside and Woodland Trees (Warne).
Philips:	*Garden Flowers* (Warne).
Whitehead:	*Flowering Trees and Shrubs* (Warne).
Sandars:	*Beast Book for the Pocket*
	Insect Book for the Pocket
	Bird Book for the Pocket
	Butterfly Book for the Pocket (OU.P.).
Skene:	*Flower Book for the Pocket* (O.U.P.).
Various authors:	Observer's Books: *Ferns, Grasses, Geology, Birds' Eggs, Mosses, Fishes*, etc. (Warne).
Forbes:	*British Fossils* (Black).
Daglish:	*Name This Bird*
	Name This Insect (Dent).
Peterson and others:	*Field Guide to the Birds of Britain and Europe* (Collins).
Biggs:	*Discovering Weather* (U.L.P.).
Grigson:	*The Shell Country Book* (Phoenix House).
Menzel:	*Field Guide to the Stars and Planets* (Collins).

Remembering the more backward pupils, it is well to include picture books of the Puffin Series type (e.g. *Animals of the Countryside*); books for the identification of cars, trains and aircraft; and easy readers such as Haworth's *The Sea Shore* (U.L.P.).

(c) Books which serve as a background to and an extension of the topics of the Science course. Three main categories may be noted: (i) books relating to the history of a topic; (ii) popular expositions of the science of a topic; (iii) books dealing with everyday applications. Books of this kind should be found also in the main school library (see later).

Many of the large industrial and commercial firms produce booklets and pamphlets excellent for classroom reference purposes—those of Shell, Unilever and the British Iron & Steel Federation are typical. Also outstanding are the BBC Nature Study pamphlets, while Her Majesty's Stationery Office is a rich source of reference material on many subjects.

(d) Practical work-books. These are useful for the Science Club and in suggesting ideas for development either in school or at home. The short list which follows is indicative only:

Tweddle: *Everyday Science Topics* (Harrap).
Boothroyd: *How and Why it Works* (Schofield and Sims).
Parish: *Simple Working Models* (Wheaton).
Rumming: *Make and Use Models* (U.L.P.).
Knight: *Field Work for Young Naturalists* (Bell).
Ford: *How to Begin your Fieldwork* (Murray).
de Vries: *The First (Second, Third) Book of Experiments* (Murray).
Belham: *Projects in Physics for the Secondary School* (Batsford).

The Main School Library

It is the duty of those who teach science to recommend books for inclusion in the main school library: the librarian will be glad to receive suggestions.

Two classes of books are particularly appropriate for the central collection: those which lay emphasis upon the history and the personalities of science; and those which deal with applications of science in the modern world.

A number of publishing houses produce series of biographies of great scientists, e.g.:

Aicken: *Galileo* and *Newton* (E.U.P.).
Wymer: *Lives of Great Men and Women* (O.U.P.).
Crowther: *Six Great Scientists*
         Six Great Inventors (Hamish Hamilton).
Various
authors: *British Men of Science* (Nelson).

Books on applied science are usually attractive if well illustrated and if the reading matter is within the pupils' range. Much depends upon the presentation: some years ago (1956) the Grosvenor Press issued *Practical Car Owner Illustrated*, and more recently (1966) John Baker has published *The Shell Book of How Cars Work*; both are models of the excellent use of visual material. The devices employed in such books include cut-away drawings in full colour, transparent colour film (overlaid), up-to-date photographs, and "exploded" pictures of complex working parts. Although the book is generally too advanced for our ordinary pupils, *The Human Body* by Barnett *et al.* (E.U.P.) exemplifies the minimum use of words and their replacement by ingenious and often original techniques of diagrammatic description.

Much the most comprehensive list of book reviews relating to school science teaching is to be found in the pages of the *School Science Review*, published by the Association for Science Education. The same Association has produced the booklet *Science Books for a School Library* (Fifth Edition 1968, with later supplements): this classifies recommended books by subjects. *Science For All* (National Book League), an annotated reading list for the non-specialist, is also valuable.

As with other subjects, the price of school library books on scientific topics has risen alarmingly and care in selection is more than ever necessary. It is most unwise to rely solely on the evidence of the publisher's catalogue. The teacher should actually see and handle books he proposes to buy. Much the best thing is for him to keep his eyes open in bookshops, at publishers' exhibitions (often mounted in connection with teachers' conferences), in public libraries and when visiting other schools. He would do well to keep in touch with publishers (a list of addresses appears in *Science Books for a School Library*) and to send for inspection copies of likely items on their periodic lists.

It is, of course, most important that the teacher should provide opportunities and incentives for his pupils to use the library: the worst fate that can befall a library is that it should become a museum. Guidance is needed on how to set about looking up a particular subject, and boys and girls require specific practice. Pupils may use the library in pursuing their own interests, in answering questions on a set topic, in preparing for classroom debates and lecturettes, and in the working out of projects. Our average pupil often needs to be persuaded about the value of books.

The Teachers' Library

There should be available in every school, a teachers' library which in the case of Science at least, might include books on teaching method and laboratory technique, on the philosophy of science and on the history of the subject. Here also one would hope to find volumes of the *School Science Review* and of *Natural Science in Schools* (formerly *School Nature Study*). A collection of modern text-books will prove useful.

Although published in 1929, Westaway's *Science Teaching* is still worth reading. Among books specifically concerned with teaching for the less academically inclined pupils the following may be noted:

A.S.E.: *Teaching Science at the Secondary Stage* (Murray).
UNESCO: *Source Book for Science Teaching*.
Nunn: *Handbook for Science Teachers in Secondary Modern Schools* (Murray).

Tweddle: *Science Teacher's Handbook* (Harrap).
Lewis and
Potter: *The Teaching of Science in the Elementary School* (Prentice-Hall).

The series of booklets *Science Teaching Techniques* (Murray) assembles articles by practising teachers on a wide range of topics, presented in a most practical fashion.

For refreshment and inspiration nothing is more effective than the occasional re-reading of the scientific classics, some of which (e.g. Faraday's *Chemical History of a Candle*) are available in modern editions, and others of which may be found in second-hand bookshops. Harvey's *The Motion of the Heart and the Blood* (Everyman) and Darwin's *Vegetable Mould and Earthworms* may be quoted with effect in modern classrooms: so can passages from Gilbert White's *Natural History of Selbourne*. Selected extracts from scientific writers appear in *Readings from the Scientists*, by J. E. Mason (Macmillan); *Science and Literature*, by Eastwood (Macmillan); and *The Major Achievements of Science*, by McKenzie (O.U.P.).

Books on the meaning, philosophy and modern development of science are legion. Every teacher of science must do what he can to keep his own thinking and background knowledge alive and some suggestions as to how he might attempt the task are made in Chapter 23. At this point it may be helpful to draw attention to three books which are typical of many which could usefully find a place on the shelves of a teachers' library:

Rapport and
Wright: *Science: Method and Meaning* (New York University Press).
Beveridge: *The Art of Scientific Investigation* (Mercury Books).
Brierley: *Science in its Context* (Heinemann).
Weatherall: *Scientific Method* (E.U.P.).

Astronomy is one of the subjects which the man-in-the-street reads with interest. Popularized by such men as Jeans, Hoyle and Patrick Moore, it has captured the imagination of many who can understand little if anything of its mathematical background. The teacher will certainly discover that his "ordinary pupil" often shares this interest and he will find an eager audience for accounts of the stars and the solar system and, of course, for modern exploration of space. Yet it is sad to think how many boys and girls may have "learned" about eclipses without ever having seen one, or answered examination questions on the seasons without any real understanding of the causes of the changing year. This is why we would direct particular attention to the experiments and experiences described below. Some may be undertaken by pupils as an enjoyable form of homework; others are perhaps suitable for the Science Club, or for demonstration; but a number are entirely appropriate for individual or group work in the laboratory.

The science of space is the subject of Chapter XIV in Book Four of our *Practical Science for Secondary Schools* (U.L.P.), to which we direct attention. Teachers interested in the mathematics of space flight will find the following two books valuable:

A Handbook of Astronautics (U.L.P., 1966).

From Here, Where? (U.S. National Aeronautics and Space Administration, 1965).

The Spinning Earth

The apparent motion of the sun in the sky is beautifully and very quickly shown by the following experiment. Pupils also form an excellent first idea of how celestial objects can be sighted and their position determined.

386 *Daily Motion of the Sun*

Roll a sheet of stiff paper into a tube 50 cm long and about 3 cm diameter; fix with gummed paper. Cover one end with gummed paper and pierce a pin-hole at the centre of this end. Cut two circles from an old negative to rest over the other end of the tube and hold them in position by a collar of gummed paper stuck round the tube and overlapping the end somewhat. Stick a pin through one side of the tube very near this end, so that the point projects to the centre of the tube.

Choose a window which opens by pushing it outwards and upwards (the type of upper window common in modern houses). Open it slightly and grip the tube between one side of the window and the fixed frame; it will be found that the tube is readily held at any desired angle. In the laboratory, a retort stand may be used instead. Point the "pin" end of the tube at the sun and sight through the pin-hole at the other end, adjusting the tube until the pin-point is at the centre of the sun's disc. Within seconds the apparent movement of the sun is noticeable, and in a few minutes the sun passes out of sight altogether. It is easy to see whether the sun is rising or falling in the sky and to confirm that it appears to travel from east to west.

387 *The Earth Turns Round*

The most satisfactory demonstration is certainly by means of a Foucault pendulum and an account of how one was constructed from simple materials and used in a school where there was a deep staircase well has

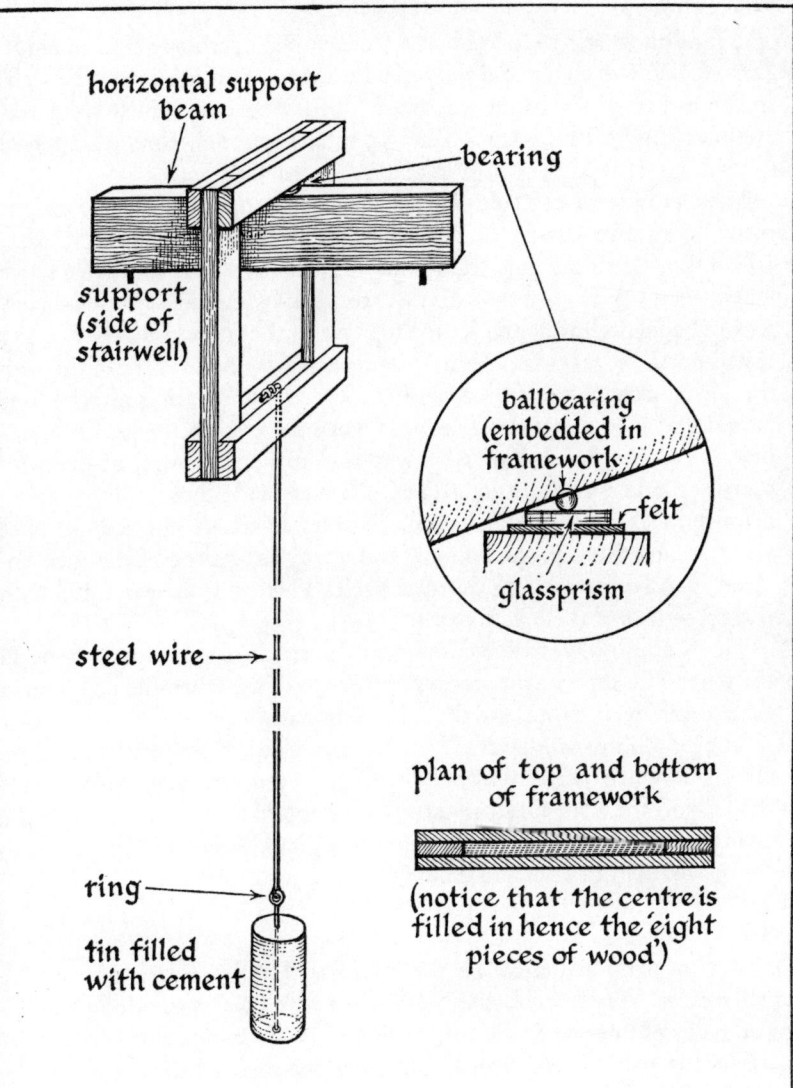

387. Foucault's pendulum

been given by R. H. Smith (*School Science Review*, No. 33, pp. 43-5), from which the following account is taken:

> The pendulum was supported on a wooden beam, cross-section 18 cm × 4 cm, which was clamped tightly in a horizontal position across the well. In the centre of the beam was fixed a bed of felt on which lay a rectangular glass prism, 8 cm × 4 cm × 5 mm. Projection rims were raised to hold the felt and the prism in place.
>
> The pendulum was made of a rectangular wooden framework of eight pieces of 13 mm wood (see Figure 387), nailed securely together, from which the wire hung; the frame was large enough to leave ample space when swinging around the beam. A steel ball-bearing, 22 mm diameter, was embedded centrally under the top part of the frame, and the bearing rested on the glass prism. A narrow hole was drilled centrally through the lower part of the frame, and through it the pendulum wire was passed and wound symmetrically. It was held in place by small staples driven into the wood. The wire was steel pianoforte wire, of diameter 0.91 mm, and was 20 m long. The bob was made thus: a large cylindrical tin was taken, height 15 cm, diameter 14 cm. A stout copper wire was fastened through the bottom, and a ring in the top of the wire enabled it to be fastened to the steel wire. Then the tin was filled with cement, which was allowed to set.
>
> The pendulum was allowed to hang for 24 hours to remove torsion in the wire. The experiment was performed at a time when the doors upon the staircase were closed and draughts eliminated.
>
> The pendulum was started by drawing it out of the vertical and releasing it when perfectly steady—perhaps by drawing it aside with a thread and then burning the thread. The initial and final phases of the swing were determined by placing a straight-edge on the floor beneath the bob and sighting it from the staircase above.

388 *Circumpolar Stars*

Draw a 30-cm radius circle on the blackboard and divide it into twelve equal sectors. Very near to the centre show the Pole Star. Along the circumference of one sector set out the five stars of Cassiopeia to form a W with its top to the Pole. Spread out over one and a half sectors on the opposite side of the Pole, show the Great Bear. The Little Bear may be added, and perhaps Cepheus. Let the pupils make such a chart for themselves on a 15-cm diameter card, drawing a 10-cm diameter circle on it as a guide and using their protractors to mark out the sectors. Then let them set out a 24-hour clock-face on a 20-cm diameter card, with the hours marked round the circumference so that they are still visible when the star-chart is fixed centrally over the clock-face with a paper-fastener.

Pupils now identify the constellations in the sky at night for themselves,

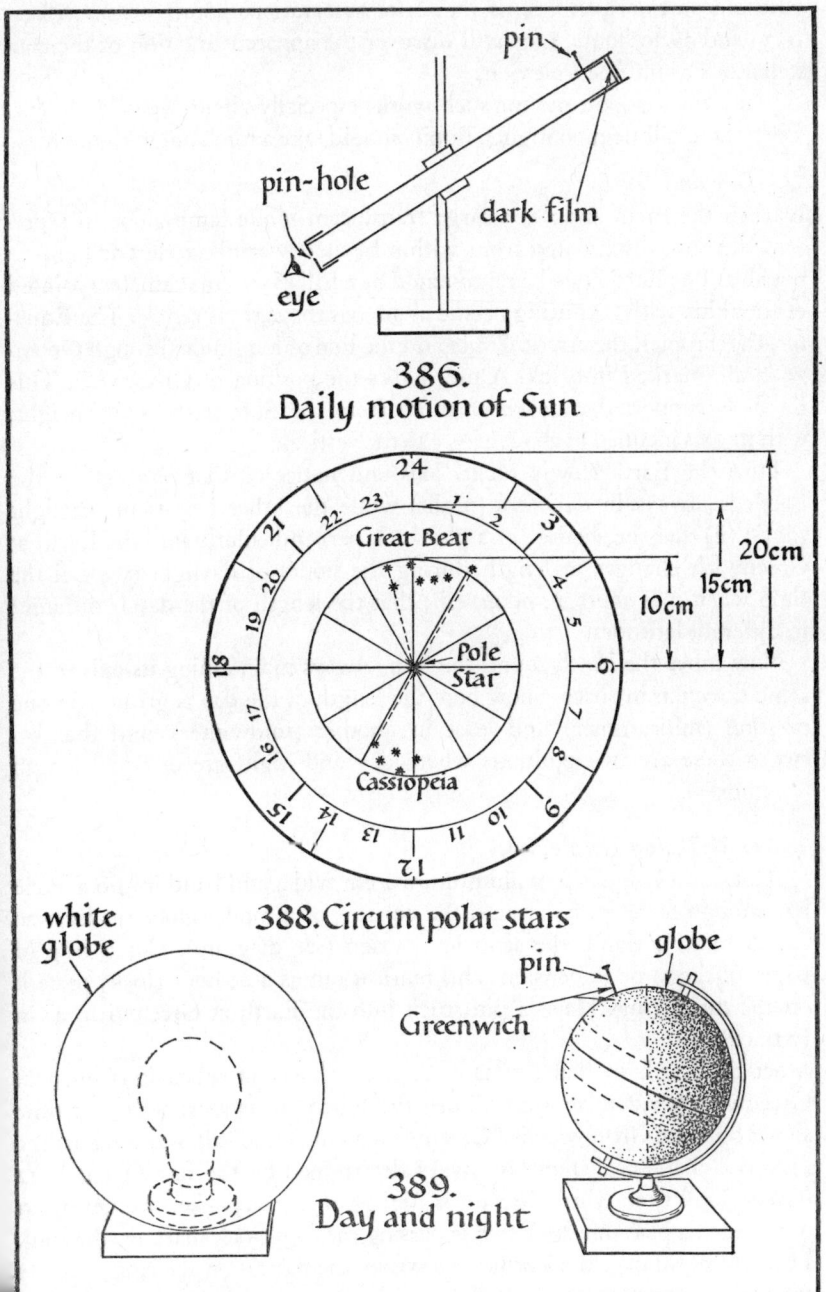

noting the hour of observation and turning the star-chart to the appropriate positions on the clock-face. If they take observations hourly at, say, 18.30, 19.30 and 20.30 hours, they will discover the apparent rotation of the constellations round the Pole Star.

Winter is a good time for such work, especially about New Moon (i.e. when there is little moonlight). Pupils should take a torch out with them.

389 *Day and Night*

Darken the room and use a large translucent white lamp-globe to represent the Sun, illuminated from within by as powerful an electric lamp as possible. The Earth may be represented by a ball (8–10 cm diameter) painted dead white, with a knitting needle as an axis through its centre. The Equator, the Tropics, the Arctic Circle and the line of longitude through Greenwich are marked in black. A pin marks the position of Greenwich. This Earth is supported a metre or more from the Sun at the same height, with its axis inclined at about $23\frac{1}{2}°$ to the vertical.

Turn the Earth slowly on its axis and notice (i) that one half of the Earth is always in darkness (night) while the other half is in the light (day); (ii) that the shadow of a pin stuck perpendicularly into the Earth at Greenwich changes in length during the hours of daylight (we call the time when it is shortest, noon; (iii) that the length of the day is different in different latitudes.

Now move the Earth round the Sun, always maintaining its axis in the same direction in space. Show how the length of the day is greatest in one position (midsummer) and least in another (midwinter), and that between these are two positions where day and night are of equal length (equinoxes).

390 *G.M.T. and Local Time*

(a) Cut out a long strip of aluminium 2 cm wide, and band it into a circle big enough to fit loosely round the equator of a model globe (at least 20 cm diameter); clamp the strip in position (see diagram). Cut a ring of paper of the same dimensions and mark it out as a 24-hour clock; paste it on the metal ring. Have a pin stuck into the Earth at Greenwich, as in Expt. 389.

Set the Earth so that the 24-hour clock shows 12 when it is noon at Greenwich (shadow shortest). Turn the Earth on its axis; whatever time shows opposite Greenwich is "Greenwich Mean Time" all over the Earth.

Notice that Local Time is always determined by the fact that it is 12 o'clock local time when the Sun is highest in the sky—i.e. whenever, on our model, a place on the Earth is passing the 12 o'clock mark on the ring. Local Time all over the Earth is shown by the figures on the ring opposite the places concerned.

(b) Longitude: Since the 24 hours of day and night cover the 360° into which we divide the Earth for purposes of stating longitude, the Earth turns through 1° every four minutes. Show that if a mariner can observe local noon (by the time of "southing" of the sun) and if he knows Greenwich Time (from his accurate chronometer or from radio signals), then he can determine his longitude. For example, if the Local Time is behind Greenwich Time, his longitude is West and equal to D/4 degrees, where D is the number of minutes Local Time is behind.

Using the Earth and Sun models, show from the 24-hour clock that the times of sunrise and sunset at Greenwich vary as the Earth moves round in its orbit (cf. last part of Expt. 389).

391 Latitude

At the North Pole the Pole Star is directly overhead, and we say that its "altitude" is 90°. As we move from Pole to Equator the altitude of the Pole Star steadily decreases until it is zero at the Equator, the star being then on the horizon. The altitude of the Pole Star at any particular place measures the latitude of that place.

Cut out a quarter-circle of card, radius 30 cm, and mark out the circumference into 90°, e.g. using the blackboard protractor. Fix a plumb-line to the corner of the card (thin string with metal weight, suspended from brass paper-fastener) and sight the Pole Star along one edge of the card, holding the 90° mark about 15 cm from the eye. Whilst doing this, allow the plumb-line to swing freely just clear of the card and when it settles press it on to the card with the free hand. Observe the angle marked where the plumb-line crosses the scale. This is the latitude of the place of observation.

392 Sundial

The theory of the construction of a sundial (e.g. the factors which determine the spacing of the hour marks) are beyond the ordinary pupil, but he will appreciate the general idea of the instrument and he will enjoy making and using one.

Mark out on thin sheet metal or stout card a triangle ABC such that AB = 10 cm, angle A = 90°, and angle B = Latitude of the place at which the dial is to be used (look this up in the atlas). Mark a rectangle ABXY below AB with BX = 1 cm. Cut out ACBXY and bend it at right angles along AB. This cut-out is the "style" of the sun-dial, ABXY being merely a flap for fixing the style to the base.

Use as base a 20-cm square of wood or card. Screw or glue the style to it, setting B at the midpoint of one side and BA at right angles to this side. Set the dial with BA pointing exactly north (Expt. 301) and the base horizontal. BC (the top of the style) then points to the Pole Star. Observe the shadow of the style on a sunny day, marking in the shadow of C every hour. Join these markings to B and label each hour-line, the central one (BA produced) being XII. Use Greenwich Time.

393 *Ellipse*

Fix two drawing-pins 25 cm apart in a sheet of paper covering a drawing board. Tie the ends of a metre of fine string together to make a loop and lay the loop on the board so as to enclose the two pins. Now pull the loop taut by means of a pencil held in one hand and move the point of the pencil so as to trace a path on the paper round the pins, always keeping the loop taut. Repeat with the pins at other distances apart.

The figures obtained are ellipses, the pins being at the foci. The earth's path round the sun is almost circular but is actually an ellipse, with the sun at one of the foci (Kepler's First Law). The other planets also move in elliptical paths (of varying "eccentricity").

394 *The Seasons*

Fold a postcard across the middle and bend the two halves backwards and forwards several times so that the "hinge" works smoothly. Hold the card about a metre below a strong light and gradually swing one half upwards so that it lies more and more in line with the rays of light, Observe both halves through half-closed eyes and notice that the part which remains at right angles to the rays is more brightly illuminated.

Two major effects account for the seasons. First, in summer the days are longer and the nights are shorter, so that more heat is received and less radiated away. Second, in summer the Sun is more nearly overhead, so that its heating effect is more intense.

395 *Models of the Solar System*

(a) Relative sizes of Sun and planets: Approximate relative diameters (Earth = 1) are given in the table below:

Sun	109	Earth	1	Saturn	9·4
Mercury	0·4	Mars	0·5	Uranus	3·7
Venus	1	Jupiter	11	Neptune	3·5

Let the pupils model the planets in any suitable material, making the diameter of the model Earth 1 cm. Alternatively, they may draw circles on paper. In either case, comparison should be made with a circle 109 cm in diameter (representing the Sun) drawn on the blackboard or on the floor. (b) Distances of planets from the Sun: Actual distances, in millions of kilometres, are shown below:

Mercury	58	Mars	228	Uranus	2869
Venus	108	Jupiter	778	Neptune	4496
Earth	150	Saturn	1426	Pluto	5905

Let pupils scale the distances, using 1 cm to represent 1 million km. Then go outdoors and use pupils to represent the planets, arranging them

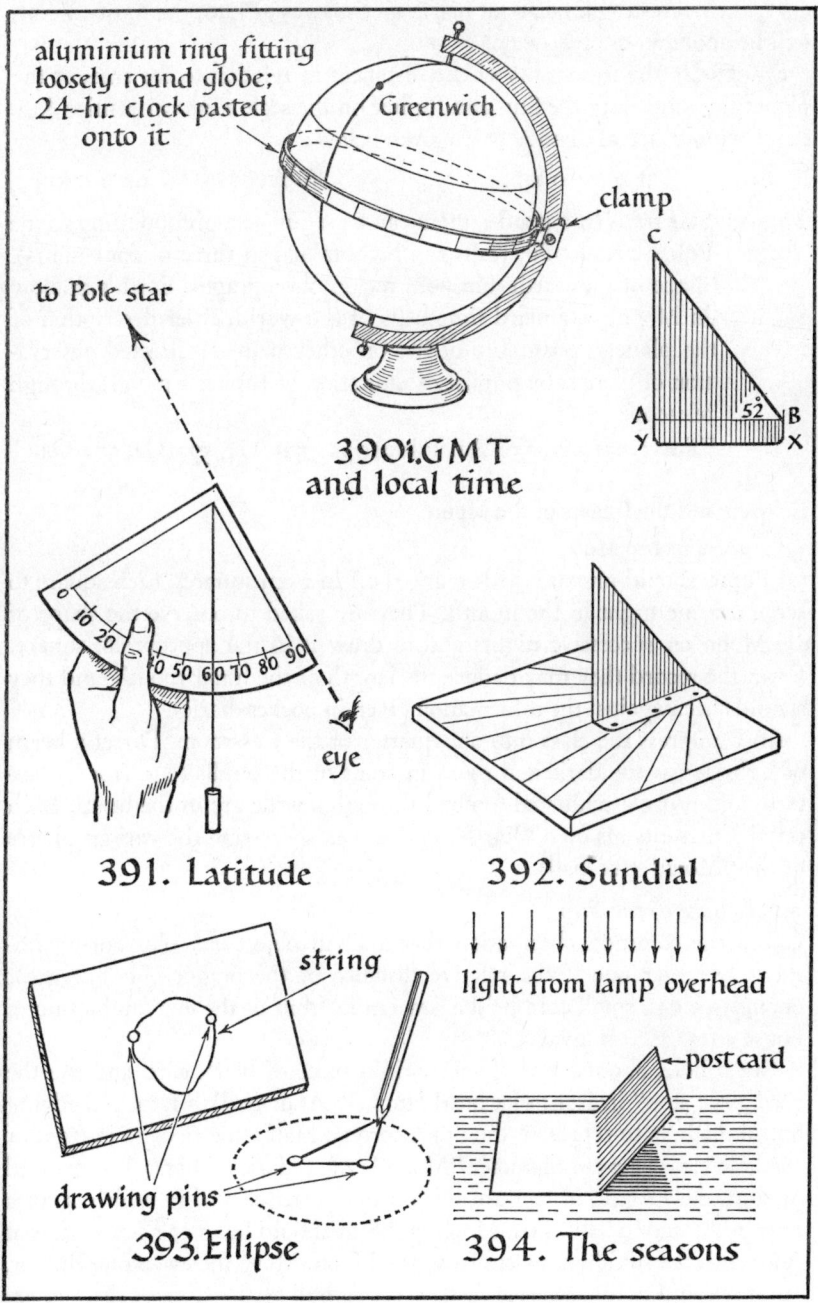

390i. GMT and local time

391. Latitude

392. Sundial

393. Ellipse

394. The seasons

at the correct relative distances from a pupil representing the Sun. Mercury, the nearest, will be about half a metre away; Pluto, the most distant, will be about 60 metres away.

Emphasize the immensity of the distances in relation to the sizes of the planets by modelling the Sun and Jupiter on the scale 1 cm = 1 million km. Approximate actual diameters are given below:

Sun   1 400 000 km.   Jupiter   140 000 km

Topics: Star trails (if a good camera can be set up at night, pointing to the Pole Star, circular trails can be obtained in three or four hours). Shape of the Earth (horizon, rocket photographs, Earth's shadow on Moon). Standard time belts of the world. Brief description of the planets; possibility of life on other planets; directed observation of planets by pupils; examination of Jupiter's moons through telescope.

Films: 571/A1, 572/A1. Filmstrips: 571/G4, 572/G2, 572/G4.

Eclipses and the Phases of the Moon

396 *Phases of the Moon*

(a) Pupils should prepare cards marked off in 2-cm squares, each square to serve for one night in the month. They are asked to observe the shape of the Moon on successive nights and to draw it in the appropriate square. From the record they may deduce the length of the lunar month, and they should check against the information given in pocket diaries.

(b) Compress the class into one-quarter of the classroom. Direct a beam of light across the darkened room in front of the pupils (e.g. from a lantern) and move a whitened football through a wide arc in the beam. Each pupil represents his own "Earth" and sees in succession the various phases of the "Moon" (football).

397 *Eclipse of the Sun*

Check the common observation that a small object can blot out an immensely larger one if the relative distance of the bigger object is great enough—e.g. a small coin held a few cm in front of the eye can blot out a house a few metres away.

Cut a hole, about 3 cm diameter, in a piece of black card and use the card as a "stop" in front of a pearl lamp. Paint or chalk a faint red edging round the hole to represent the Sun's corona. Half a metre or so in front of the hole set up a 2-cm diameter "Moon" (e.g. a dark rubber ball supported on a needle). Again in front of this set up a vertical card in which is cut a narrow horizontal slit. Slit, Moon and Sun should be in the same straight line, with the slit about 25 cm from the Moon. Move the eye along the slit, from one end to the other; successive stages of a total eclipse of the Sun are seen and each should be carefully drawn. Notice that when the "Sun" is

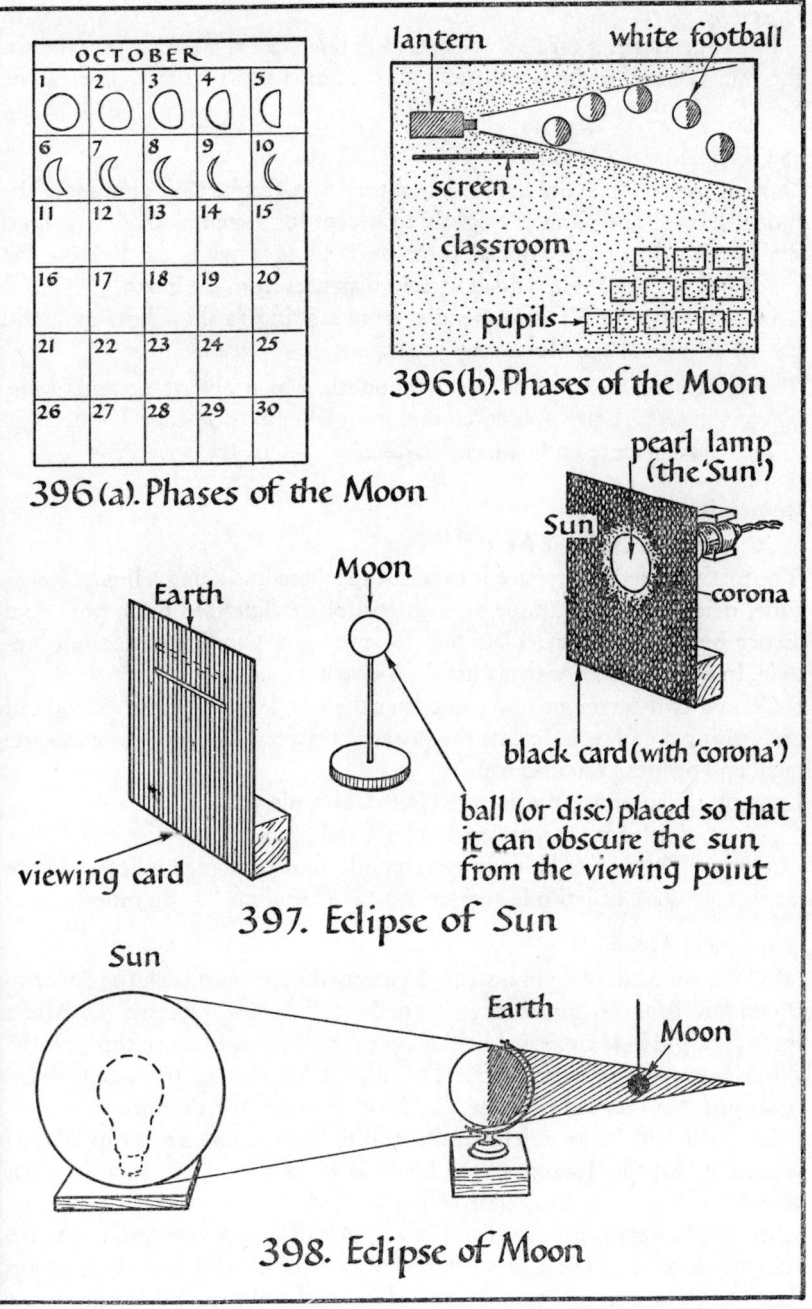

396(a). Phases of the Moon
396(b). Phases of the Moon
397. Eclipse of Sun
398. Eclipse of Moon

totally eclipsed the corona becomes visible, being at all other times obscured by glare.

Raise the viewing card somewhat, so that as the eye moves along the slit the Sun is never entirely eclipsed; this represents a partial eclipse of the Sun.

398 *Eclipse of the Moon*

Darken the room. Now let the laboratory Sun (Expt. 389) illuminate the model Earth. The room is brightly lit except for a conical shadow behind the Earth. Identify its conical form by holding a white card across the shadow at various angles and at various distances from the Earth.

Now use a 2-cm Moon suspended from a string to show how total and partial eclipses of the Moon may occur.

Topics: Lunar month and calendar month. Moon always presents same face to Earth (observation through public telescope if possible). Occurrence and paths of eclipse.

Immensity of Space

399 *Circumference of the Earth*

The method used in practice is to measure a base-line along a line of longitude, determine the latitude at each end of the line (see Expt. 391), and thence by proportion calculate the distance corresponding to $360°$ of latitude. In the classroom we may use the following method:

Choose two towns on the same meridian and read off the latitude of each, using an atlas. Calculate the distance between the towns by measurement and by using the map scale.

Example: Taunton, latitude $51°$; Gretna, latitude $55°$.

    Distance apart (from map) 288 miles.

    Thus $4°$ of latitude corresponds to 463 km (288 miles), whence $360°$ of latitude corresponds to 41 670 km (25 920 miles).

400 *Size of Moon*

(a) Cut a slit 2 cm wide in a strip of gummed paper and stick the paper to a window between the observer and the full Moon. Observe the Moon through a pin-hole in a card held close to one eye and thence through the slit. Move nearer or closer to the slit until the Moon, seen through the pinhole, just fills the width of the slit. Now measure the distance from pinhole to slit and hence calculate the approximate diameter of the Moon, assuming that the distance of the Moon is 385 000 km (240 000 miles). An assistant with a measuring tape will be needed. (b) An alternative arrangement is indicated in Fig. 400 (b). Fix a square of card to one end of a metre rule as shown and use a pencil fitted with a pocket-clip as a slider along the rule. Point the rule towards the Moon and sight the Moon through a pin-hole in the card. Then slide the pencil until the thickness of the

STARS AND SPACE 339

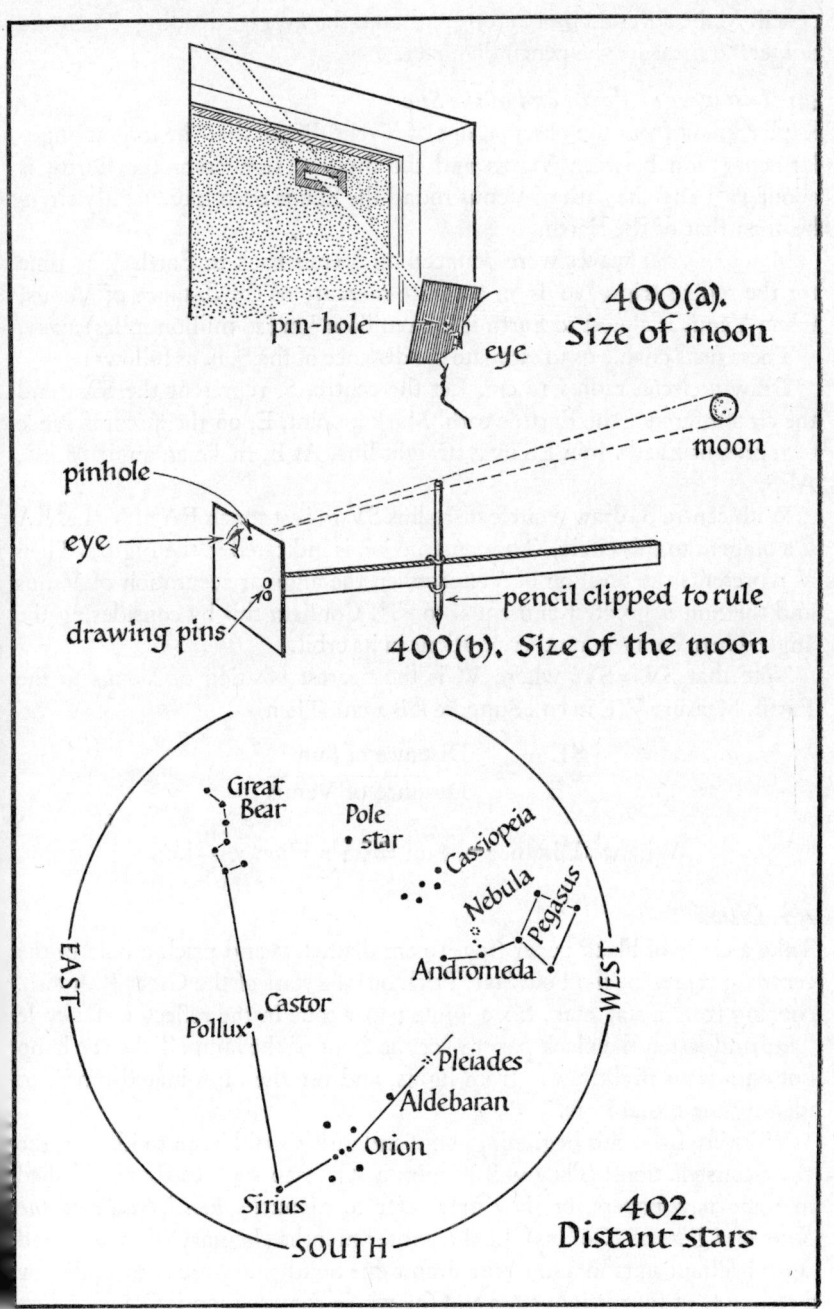

400(a). Size of moon

400(b). Size of the moon

402. Distant stars

pencil *just* covers the Moon. Read the distance from the pin-hole to the pencil. Make several observations and take the average reading. Then use calipers to measure the pencil diameter.

401 *Distances of Venus and of the Sun*
Kepler knew from the observations of Tycho Brahe that the largest angular separation between Venus and the Sun, as seen from the Earth, is about 48°; and the path of Venus round the Sun is even more nearly circular than that of the Earth.

In 1961, radar waves were bounced off Venus back to Earth. The time for the return trip gave us an accurate measure of the distance of Venus; when Venus is closest to Earth it is 42 million km (26 million miles) away.

These facts enable us to estimate the distance of the Sun, as follows:

Draw a circle, radius 10 cm. Let the centre, S, represent the Sun, and the circumference the Earth's path. Mark a point, E, on the circumference to represent Earth. Join ES by a straight line. At E, make an angle of 48°, AES.

With centre S, draw a circle of radius SV to just touch EA at V (i.e. EA is a tangent to this circle). The construction is indicated in the Figure. Then V represents the position of Venus when the angular separation of Venus and the Sun is greatest and equal to 48°. Confirm this by considering the angle when Venus is at other positions in its orbit.

Note that $SV = SV'$ where V' is the nearest position of Venus to the Earth. Measure V'E in cm. Suppose it is x cm. Then

$$\frac{SE}{V'E} = \frac{\text{Distance of Sun}}{\text{Distance of Venus}}$$

Whence Distance of Sun $= 42$ million $\times \frac{10}{x}$ km.

402 *Distant Stars*
Take a circle of black paper (say, 10 cm diameter) and prick a hole in the centre to represent the Pole Star. Prick out the stars of the Great Bear also, copying from a star map. Fix a white paper cone in the reflector of a cycle lamp and fasten the black paper over the front of the lamp. Take the lamp out on a clear night, away from lights, and use the illuminated model to identify the actual stars.

Working from this beginning, boys and girls should learn to identify the chief constellations. They will require a star map such as that published in some newspapers, or they may refer to Menzel's *Field Guide to the Stars and Planets* (Collins). In the winter months (January) they will find three brilliant stars in a line and almost due South; they are surrounded by a rectangle of four bright stars and the whole constellation is Orion. A line upwards through the belt of Orion passes almost through Aldebaran, the

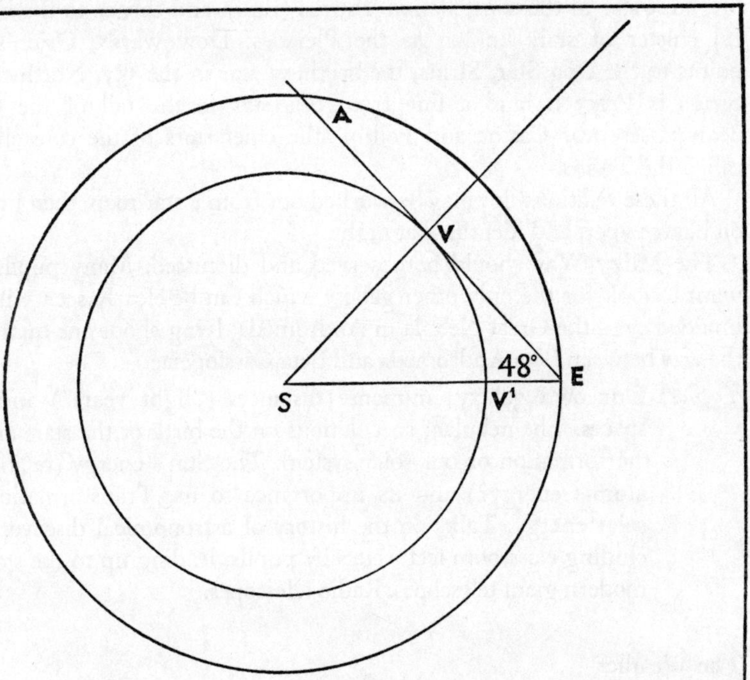

401. Distances of Venus and the Sun

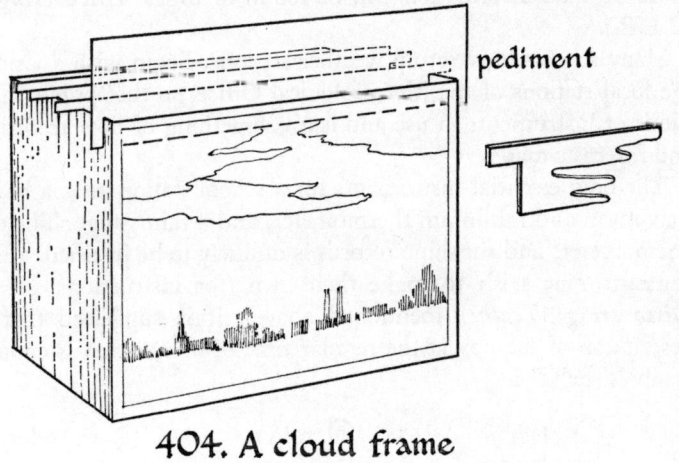

404. A cloud frame

brightest star in the constellation Taurus (Bull), and thence to the beautiful cluster of stars known as the Pleiades. Downwards, Orion's belt points to the Dog Star, Sirius, the brightest star in the sky. North-east of Sirius is Procyon, and a line from this star to the tail of the Great Bear passes near Castor and Pollux—the chief stars of the constellation called the Twins.

All these relationships may be worked out from a star map, then pricked on black paper, and identified at night.

The Milky Way should be observed and discussed. Many pupils will want to look for the only other galaxy which can be clearly seen with the unaided eye—the Great Nebula in Andromeda, lying about one-quarter of the way between Beta Andromeda and Beta-Cassiopeiae.

Topics: Our own galaxy; immense distances ("light years") and vast spaces. The nebulae; speculations on the birth of the stars and on the formation of our solar system. The Sun's energy (relation to atomic energy?) and its importance to us. Transformations of solar energy. Talks on the history of astronomical discovery, including classroom lecturettes by pupils, leading up to the story of modern giant telescopes. Radio telescopes.

The Weather

An extended practical treatment of the subject of weather constitutes Chap. XV of Book Four of our *Practical Science for Secondary Schools*. More detailed information will be found in Biggs' *Discovering Weather* (U.L.P.).

Many schools have set up weather stations. Begin with a visit to one of the local stations of the Meteorological Office, so that pupils may see the kinds of instruments in use and learn something of how records are kept and forecasts made.

The only essential instruments for a school station are: a barometer, a maximum and minimum thermometer, and a rain gauge. The expense of anemometers and sunshine records is unlikely to be justified, although enthusiasts may wish to make their own (for instructions, see the book *Discovering Weather* mentioned above). It is suggested that a simple description of the day at the regular time of observation is enough, using symbols such as:

      Ⓞ clear   Ⓡ rain   Ⓣ thunder
      ◍ cloudy   Ⓢ snow   etc.
      ⊜ foggy   Ⓕ frost

Wind can be described from observations of the movement it causes, using the Beaufort Wind Scale, a copy of which will be found in the *Ox-*

ford Junior Encyclopaedia, Vol. III, p. 490. Thus speed 4 is "Moderate", raising dust, loose paper, etc. and moving small branches. On charts, the wind is indicated by arrows showing its direction. A full-length feather on an arrow represents two steps on the Beaufort Scale, half a feather being used for one step.

403 Keeping a Weather Record

At a fixed time each day (say, 11.00 hours), take the following observations at the weather station:

(a) The barometer reading, in mm of mercury. (Current practice in England of using inches may be continued for some time).

(b) The temperature at the time, together with the readings shown by the maximum and minimum indicators. Reset these indicators.

(c) The rain-gauge reading. Remove the funnel, pour any water into the measuring jar, stand the jar on a level surface and take the reading in mm (or inches).

(d) Observe the direction of the wind as shown by a local vane, and its strength by reference to the Beaufort Scale.

(e) Observe the appearance of the day—sunny, cloudy, rain etc. Record the type of cloud, if any.

Put down all this information in a book kept for the purpose, ruled into columns for the various data. Each week, graph the temperature, pressure and rainfall figures, recording the wind and general appearance of each day alongside.

404 A Cloud Frame

This consists of a box open in front and at the top, in which are mounted cloud shapes to build up a sky scene.

The back wall is made of hardboard covered with p.v.c. sheet, to which cut-out shapes of cumulus type clouds may be made to adhere. Stratus-type clouds may be suspended by tabs from the top of the frame. A silhouette of buildings or the countryside is prepared and placed across the bottom of the frame, while a pediment across the top conceals the tabs from which cloud silhouettes hang.

Pupils should sketch and colour cloud pictures (on a scale to fit the frame), working from their observations of real clouds, afterwards mounting them for use in the frame. In this way a library of cloud types may be built up, each example being labelled on the back.

During a period of work on weather, pupils attempt to match the cloud type they see out of doors by building up a picture in the frame, using the extensive library. Those who have used this technique will appreciate what a powerful incentive to careful observation and identification it can provide.

Topics: Study of Meteorological Office weather charts—often to be found in newspapers. Study particularly a series of such charts, marking the positions of the "low" and "high" areas on a map showing the British Isles and a good deal of the Atlantic and Western Europe. If small flags are used as markers, the advance of the "low" or "high" areas is clearly seen. Compare this with pupils' own records of the weather during the period.

The relation between barometric pressure variations and weather. Cyclones and anti-cyclones, "fronts", etc.

Chapter Twenty
Force and Movement

The More Able Among the Ordinary Pupils
Great changes have often taken place in the organization of secondary education since the publication of the first edition of this book in 1957. Many schools are now comprehensive, admitting pupils over a wide ability range. Curricula are being re-examined, through the medium of curriculum development projects, Nuffield programmes and in other ways. A new examination has been introduced, the Certificate of Secondary Education, which may encourage more enlightened teaching and which is designed to meet the needs of pupils of quite average academic achievement. Finally, more and more young people are electing to stay longer at school. Regardless of the decisions of governments, the leaving age is rising.

Reorganization, new curricula, new-type examinations and a longer school life will not of themselves solve the problems which the education of ordinary pupils present, though they may make significant contributions. The tone and attitudes within schools, and the relationships between teachers and taught, remain all-important. Teachers in comprehensive schools often remark that the real challenges are neither with the ablest nor the least able, but with pupils in the intermediate ranges— especially those whose potential is not realized through conventional approaches. Nevertheless, increasing numbers of these very boys and girls are being influenced to continue their education longer. Sometimes ambition is the spur, to match the progress of contemporaries who formerly would have been in a different school. Parents want more for their children. Adolescents set their eyes on better jobs. Those who leave school turn more often to evening classes, or enjoy the opportunities of day release under industrial training schemes. It would be utterly wrong to hold ambition in check: such youngsters should be encouraged to stretch themselves to the full extent of their capabilities.

The present chapter has the needs of the more able of the ordinary pupils in mind, in the sense that underlying scientific principles are given a greater emphasis and extensions of the work are indicated. Concepts such as those of inertia, centrifugal force or elasticity, for example, are capable of more precise and detailed treatment than is generally permissible with average pupils. Experiments offering a suggestion of quantitative development are available in connection with friction, elasticity and the study of the pendulum. An introduction to the notion of compounding and resolving forces through scale drawings may have significant vocational links. Many pupils today may find their interest in space flight a help to the study of gravitation, projectiles, velocity, acceleration and friction. The use of formulae and of graphical methods may be integrated with work done in mathematics lessons.

Having said this, it must be emphasized that the basic material is entirely suitable for inclusion in any science course. Although perhaps of greater interest for boys, the ideas are of universal application and much depends upon the particular approach employed by the teacher. Two rather more detailed examples of what is envisaged may be helpful:

Elasticity

The phenomenon is of more general significance than is realized by children. In addition to its obvious application to metal springs of various kinds, it plays an essential part in the bending of beams, in the resistance of trees to the force of the wind, in the reinforcement of concrete and safety glass, and in the action of muscles and cartilage. The vibrations which are responsible for sound (e.g. those of string, reeds or skins on musical instruments) are elastic in nature; and Boyle's Law is an expression of elastic behaviour in gases.

The teacher may introduce the idea by contrasting the rebound of an old and "soft" tennis ball with that of a new ball; and that of a lump of Plasticene (nil) with that of a ball bearing. He may lead his pupils to the conclusion that rebound is not to be expected in a body unless it offers considerable resistance to change of shape. At this point he may devise an experiment to compare the heights of rebound of balls of various metals (copper, brass, iron, steel, aluminium, lead, etc.) when dropped on to a block of glass from (say) a height of about a metre. The balls should all be of the same size and they may be released down a short glass tube fixed vertically above the block; an adjustable pointer may be used to measure the rebound. The mean of several trials is taken. The balls may subsequently be examined under a lens. After this kind of investigation pupils should begin to understand why billiard balls are regarded as highly elastic, in spite of the fact that they feel very hard and unyielding.

The simple experiments with a spiral spring (pp. 352-3) have limitations; with abler pupils, and where time permits, the teacher may wish to examine the behaviour of a straight wire under load. Badcock (*School Science Review*, No. 74, pp. 296-7) has described simple apparatus which enables the small extensions within the elastic region to be appreciated, while yet coping with the very much greater elongations beyond the yield point.

We are indebted to Robert Hooke (1635-1703) for the Law which bears his name. He demonstrated it with a straight wire, a spiral spring and a cantilever, just as we may. He worked first as an assistant to Robert Boyle and there is reason to think that his experiments on the elasticity of air may have been the basis of the discovery which we call Boyle's Law. Hooke was a remarkable man: his great work *Micrographia* (1665) is concerned not only with microscopic objects (he was the first to use the word "cell" in connection with plant structures) but also with topics as diverse as the nature of heat and light, thermal expansion, capillarity, crystal structure and astronomy. His life and achievements would be an appropriate theme for a lecture by a pupil to the school Science Society.

The Pendulum and the Metric System
For more than a century attempts have been made to secure support for the general adoption of metric weights and measures in the United Kingdom. In a lecture to the Leeds Astronomical Society in 1863 Sir John Herschel began with the words: "The attention of the public has of late been strongly drawn to the subject of a proposed alteration of our national system of weights and measures, by the attempt made during the last session of Parliament to carry through a bill, having for its object the abolition of our existing system . . . and the introduction . . . of what is known as the French Metrical System." Herschel called his paper "The yard, the pendulum and the metre", a title which even today may suggest to teachers a useful starting point for discussion of a theme of current interest. Unlike the decimalization of our coinage, "going metric" is still a matter for governmental decision, but there now seems little doubt that British industry will adopt metric units on a very considerable scale during the next decade. The use of the International System of Units (SI) now adopted for scientific work is reflected in the current change-over to this system for specialized Science courses in schools, and here metrication is of course fully accepted.

Teachers may find help on the historical side in an article by McKie, printed in *Endeavour*, No. 85 (January, 1963), which takes us back to the days of the French Revolution and the work of French scientists in measuring the Earth's meridian as a basis for the standard of length. The National Assembly had earlier (1790) decreed that the unit should be related to the length of a seconds pendulum. In the event the metre was an arbitrary standard—the length of a certain metal bar—but the story of its origin is a fascinating one. The search for an invariable universal natural standard to replace quite irrational measures (many of which persist even today) has only ended recently, with the adoption of the wave-length of a line in the spectrum of krypton-86 as the basis of the international unit of length.

It is a worthwhile practical exercise for pupils to examine some of the many different systems of measurement which have been used in this and other countries, to speculate upon their origins and to discover by trial something of the relationships between units. What was, and whence came, the cubit, barleycorn, rood, bushel, grain . . .? What is the connection between quire and quarto? How did our "English units", such as mile, foot and inch, originate? Pupils may complete the following table for themselves:

$$\ldots \text{digits} = 1 \text{ palm}$$
$$\ldots \text{palms} = 1 \text{ span}$$
$$\ldots \text{spans} = 1 \text{ cubit}$$

Variety lay not only in different systems of units, but in differences between the value of the units themselves. The English pound, in the year 1704, was apt to vary throughout the country; and to be very different from the pound in other countries. The unscrupulous found ample scope for profit. As early as 1671 the astronomer Jean Picard had proposed reform based on the pendulum, and fifty years later another astronomer, Cassine, suggested as an alternative a specified fraction of the Earth's meridian. There proved to be objections to each, quite apart from difficulties of measurement as such: the length of the seconds pendulum depends upon the place of observations, and the meridian varies at different longitudes—both because the Earth is not a perfect sphere.

Simple as is the theory, the practical difficulties in the way of arranging that a small bob attached to a thin thread shall have a period of exactly 1 second are very considerable. Teachers who are interested in constructing a seconds pendulum as a laboratory standard, against which stop-watches, etc. may be tested, should refer to No. 28 of the *School Science Review* (June, 1926).

Inertia (Newton's First Law)

The subject is best introduced by reference to personal experiences on buses and trains—how one is thrown backwards when a vehicle starts suddenly, and forwards when it suddenly stops.

405 *Bodies at Rest*
(a) Stand six coins, or six draughtsmen, one on top of another on a sheet of paper and draw round the bottom of the column with a pencil. Strike away the bottom coin or draughtsman by a sharp blow from the side with the back of a knife-blade. The rest of the column remains intact and drops into the pencilled circle. Repeat the experiment until only one coin or draughtsman remains.

(b) Draw a 5-cm diameter circle on paper and cover it with a flat tin box (e.g. tobacco-tin). Put a penny on top of the box. Move the box smartly to one side; the penny drops into the circle.

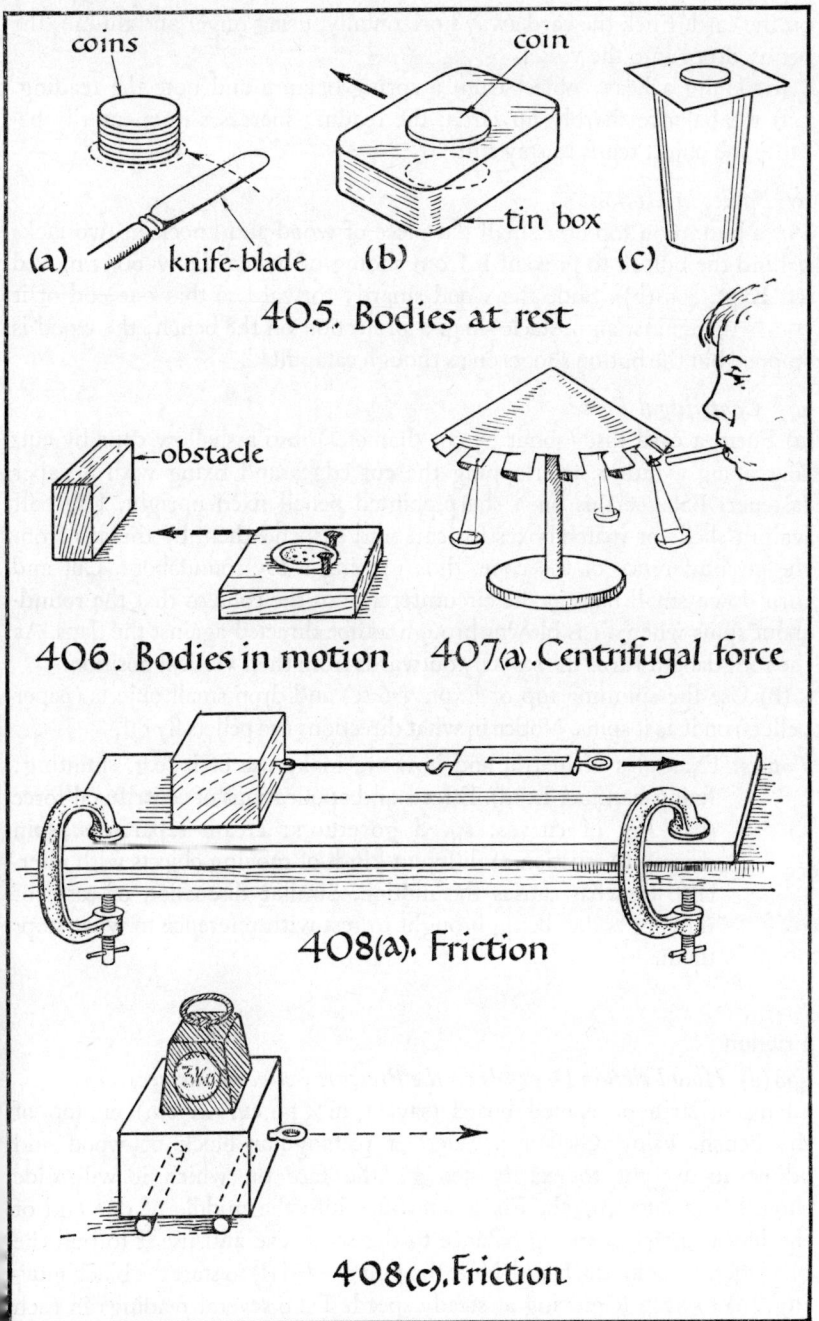

405. Bodies at rest
406. Bodies in motion
407(a). Centrifugal force
408(a). Friction
408(c). Friction

(c) Lay a card over the open top of a tin-can or tumbler and put a penny on the card. Flick the card away horizontally, using finger and thumb; the penny drops into the vessel.

(d) Hang a heavy object from a spring balance and note the reading. Lift the balance sharply upwards; the reading increases momentarily because the object tends to stay still.

406 *Bodies in Motion*

Put a button on top of a small flat piece of wood and knock in two tacks behind the button to prevent it from sliding off when the wood is moved (cf. Expt. 405 (b)). Slide the wood smartly forward so that one end of it comes up against an obstacle—e.g. a projection on the bench; the wood is stopped but the button shoots on as though catapulted.

407 *Centrifugal Force*

(a) Form a card disc (about 25 cm diameter) into a shallow cone by cutting along a radius, overlapping the cut edges and fixing with a paper fastener. Balance this on a sharp-pointed pencil fixed upright. Use half walnut shells or match-boxes for cars and suspend them by threads from the circumference of the cone, thus making a toy roundabout. Cut and turn down small flaps at the circumference of the cone so that the roundabout spins when air is blown through a tube directed against the flaps. As the roundabout turns the seats fly outwards from their vertical position.

(b) Use the spinning top of Expt. 376 (c) and drop small objects (paper pellets) on it as it spins. Notice in what directions the pellets fly off.

Topics: Examples of inertia and how we make use of it (e.g. shunting; fixing hammer head). Effects and applications of centrifugal force (banking of curves; speed governors; cream separators, spin driers). Discussion of different kinds of moving objects with reference to what causes the motion. Similar discussion of cases of moving bodies being brought to rest with reference to what stops them.

Friction

408 (a) *How Friction Depends on the Pressure between Surfaces*

Clamp a strip of planed board (say, $1 \text{ m} \times 15 \text{ cm} \times 2 \text{ cm}$) on top of the bench, using G-clamps. Select a rectangular block of wood and adjust its weight to exactly 500 g: the face on which it will slide should be made smooth. Fix a screw-eye into the middle of one end of the block, attach a spring balance to the screw-eye and use it to pull the block gently along the board. Note the pull needed (i) to start the block moving, (ii) to keep it moving at steady speed. Take several readings in each case, averaging them. Hence get values for "starting" friction and "sliding" friction. In reporting, the nature of the materials in contact and the weight of the block should be stated.

Stand a 1-kg weight on the block and repeat the experiment. Then use still heavier loads.

408 (b) *How friction Depends on the Kind of Surfaces in Contact*
Repeat Expt. 408 (a), but substitute sheets of glass, metal, linoleum, carpet, rough board... for the planed base-board.

408 (c) *How Friction may be Reduced*
Stand a 3-kg weight on the wood block and repeat Expt. 408 (a). Now place two short lengths of dowel rod between block and board to act as rollers. Determine "starting friction" and "rolling friction". Compare "rolling friction" with "sliding friction".

408 (d) *Another Way of Reducing Friction*
Repeat Expt. 408 (a) after waxing and polishing the contact surfaces.

409 *Water as a Lubricant*
Use a reagent bottle with a ground-in stopper. First show that the stopper does not turn very easily—there is much friction between the ground-glass surfaces. Then stand the bottle on a level surface, fill it brimful with water and allow the stopper to fall gently into the neck. With a suitable bottle (not difficult to find) the stopper can be made to spin freely in the neck. The water film promotes rolling friction; but if the film is broken by pressing the stopper in firmly, friction greatly increases.

410 *Hovercraft Principle*
(a) Heat a small plastic tub (e.g. one of those in which the milkman delivers cream) by sinking it in hot water. Then empty the tub and at once invert it on a smooth, slightly sloping tile. The air in the tub expands as it is heated by the plastic envelope and lifts the tub, which glides downwards over the tile. (A similar phenomenon is observed when a glass tumbler is inverted on a smooth draining board after being washed in hot water).

(b) Make up the apparatus shown in the diagram. Any squat tin can will serve: the lid is removed and the rim must be smooth. Drill a 1-cm hole in the centre of the base and select a 5-cm length of rubber tubing that tightly fits the hole. Plug one end of this tube with a short (1 cm) length of dowel rod which has been pierced with a 2-mm hole. Push the other end of the tube through the hole in the can, from the inside. Stand the can, open end down, on a smooth formica surface and try pushing it about with a finger.

Inflate a toy rubber balloon, slip the neck over the free end of the tubing and again test the movement of the can over a smooth surface.

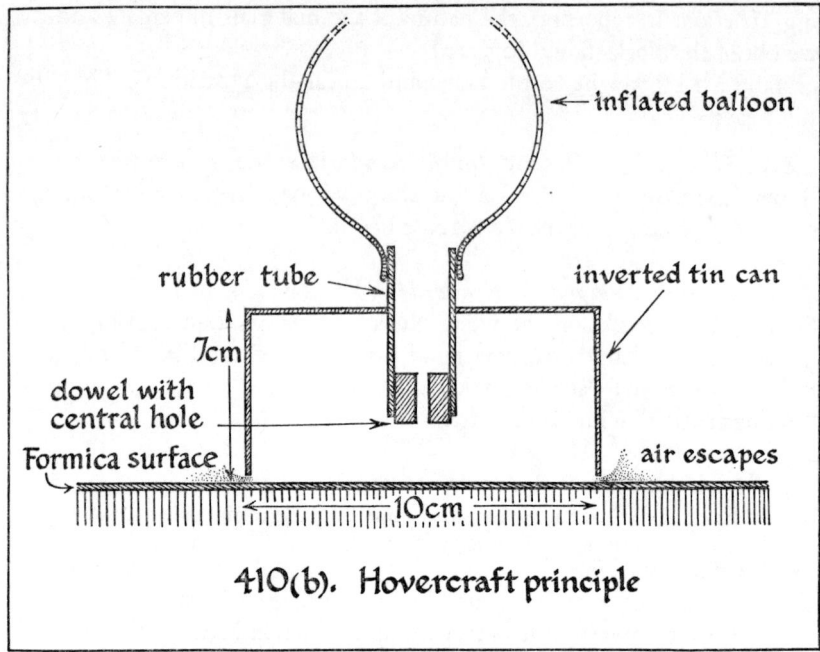

410(b). Hovercraft principle

The function of the dowel rod is to slow down the rate of escape of air from the balloon into the can and pupils may experiment with holes of various sizes in relation to the particular tin can that is being used.

Topics: Examples where friction acts as a drag on movement (rusty lock, bolt, or hinge; shuffling old playing-cards; speed of motor-boat through water compared with speed of motor-car on land). The application of friction to check motion (belt and rope drives; clutches). Abrasives (grinding and polishing in industry and in the home). Danger where friction is too small (mat on linoleum; icy roads; worn tyres). Use of lubricants and of ball and roller bearings. See also Chapter 23.

Elasticity

411 (a) *Spring Balance*

Grip the pointed end of a large nail (15-cm) and one end of a length of steel wire in the chuck of a hand-drill. Hold the drill in a vice and wind the tightly-held wire in a neat layer on the nail by turning the handle of the drill.

Detach the spiral and bend a short length of the wire at each end into a small loop. Hang up the spring so formed by one loop and suspend nails from the other by a double loop of light string. If a small piece of cord is

FORCE AND MOVEMENT 353

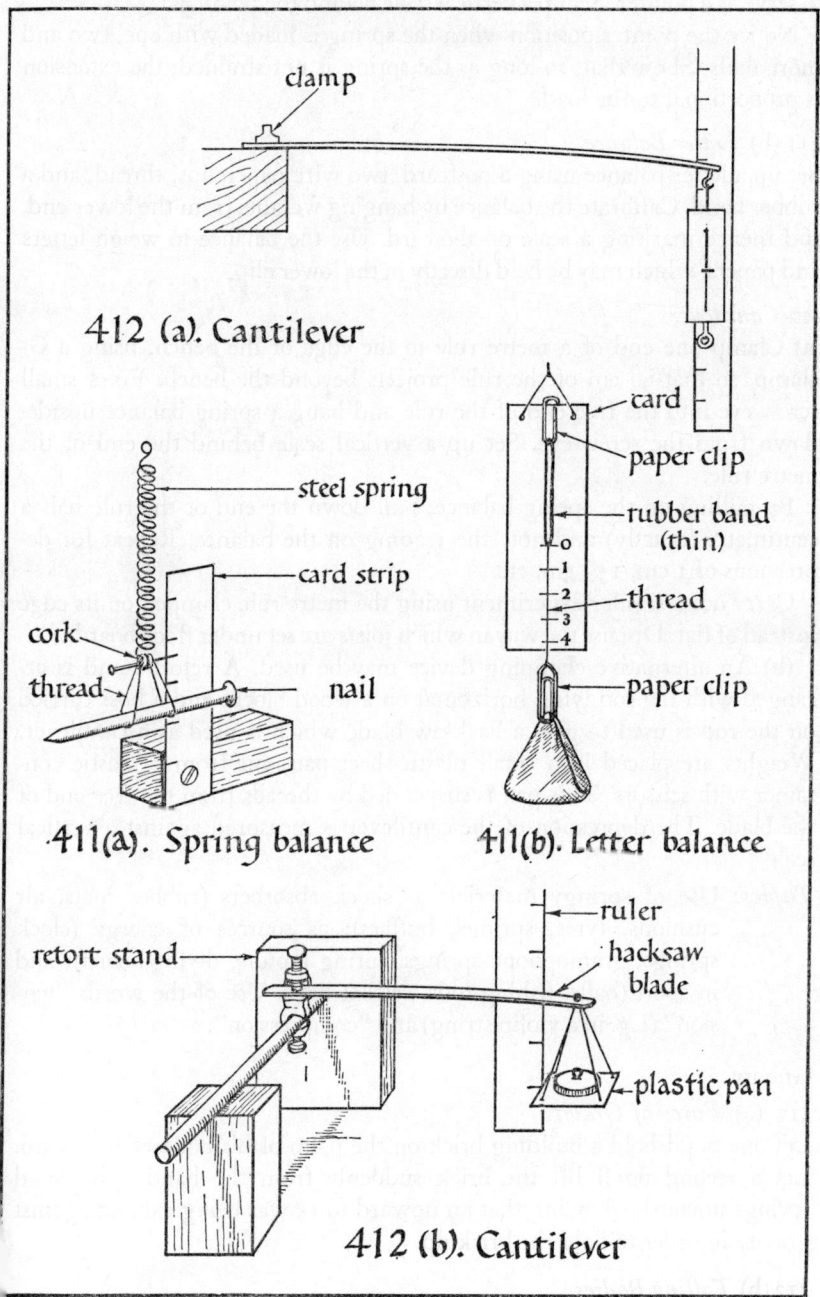

412 (a). Cantilever

411(a). Spring balance

411(b). Letter balance

412 (b). Cantilever

squeezed into the lower loop a pin can be pushed horizontally through it to serve as a pointer. Set up a vertical scale behind the pointer.

Notice the pointer position when the spring is loaded with one, two and more nails. Show that, so long as the spring is not strained, the extension is proportional to the load.

411 (b) *Letter Balance*
Set up a letter balance using a postcard, two wire paperclips, thread, and a rubber band. Calibrate the balance by hanging weights from the lower end, and thence marking a scale on the card. Use the balance to weigh letters and papers, which may be held directly in the lower clip.

412 *Cantilever*
(a) Clamp one end of a metre rule to the edge of the bench, using a G-clamp, so that 90 cm of the rule projects beyond the bench. Fix a small screw-eye into the free end of the rule and hang a spring balance upside-down from the screw-eye. Set up a vertical scale behind the end of the metre rule.

By pulling on the spring balance, pull down the end of the rule half a centimetre (exactly) and note the reading on the balance. Repeat for depressions of 1 cm, 1½ cm, etc.

Carry out a similar experiment using the metre-rule clamped on its edge instead of flat. Discuss the way in which joists are set under floor-boards.

(b) An alternative clamping device may be used. A retort stand is arranged with the rod lying horizontal on a wood block, and a boss carried on the rod is used to grip a hacksaw blade which is used as a cantilever. Weights are placed in a small plastic-sheet pan, cut from a plastic container with scissors. This pan is suspended by threads from the free end of the blade. The depression of the cantilever is measured against a vertical scale.

Topics: Use of springy materials as shock absorbers (rubber mats, air cushions, tyres, springs, buffers); as sources of energy (clock springs, gramophone springs, spring motors, diving-board); and in sport (balls, fishing-rods, cricket bats). Use of the words "tension" (e.g. in a violin string) and "compression".

Gravity

413 (a) *Force of Gravity*
Let one pupil hold a building brick on the palm of his outstretched hand. Let a second pupil lift the brick suddenly from the hand. The hand springs upwards, showing that an upward force was being exerted against gravity in order to hold the brick up.

413 (b) *Falling Bodies*
Arrange a horse-shoe electro-magnet high above the floor of the labora-

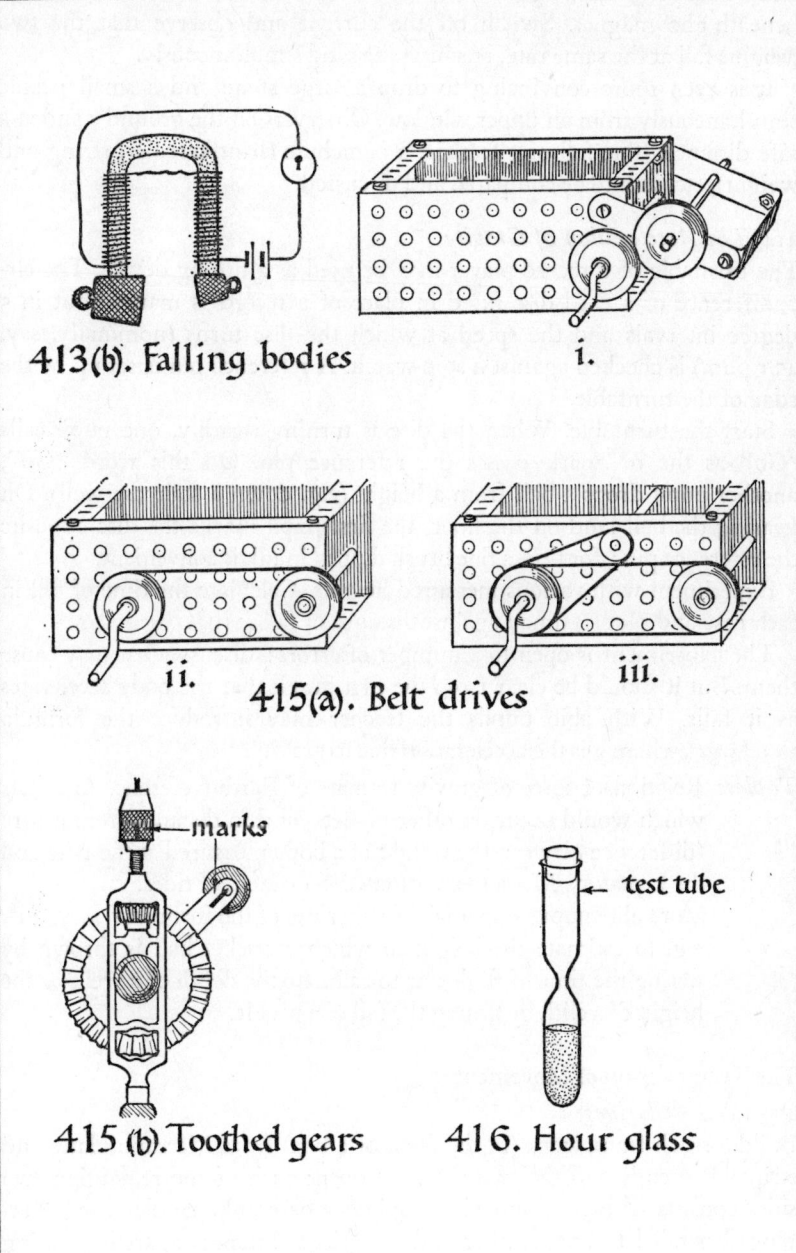

413(b). Falling bodies

i.

415(a). Belt drives

ii.   iii.

415 (b). Toothed gears   416. Hour glass

tory. Energize the magnet and attach a small iron weight to one leg and a much heavier weight to the other. Place a bucket of sand on the floor beneath the magnet. Switch off the current and observe that the two weights fall at the same rate, reaching the sand simultaneously.

It is even more convincing to drop a large stone and a small pebble simultaneously from an upper window. Observers on the ground stand at a safe distance. The fall of a feather, a parachute (handkerchief, string and weight), etc. should be compared and discussed.

414 *The Acceleration of Gravity*

The turntable of a record-player may be used as a timing device. The circumference of a card disc fitted in place of a record is marked out in 5 degree intervals and the speed at which the disc turns (nominally, say, 45 r.p.m.) is checked against a stop-watch. A reference pin is set up by the edge of the turntable.

Start the turntable. When the disc is turning steadily, one pupil calls "Go" as the 0° mark passes the reference pin. On this word "Go", another pupil drops a ball from a height (e.g. down a staircase well). On hearing the ball land on the floor, the first pupil marks the disc opposite the reference pin: for this, a fine brush dipped in ink is convenient.

Experiment with various measured heights. Calculate the time of fall in each case and plot (i) time t against distance of fall s; (ii) t^2 against s.

The experiment is open to a number of errors: discuss what may cause them. But it should be clear from the first graph that the body accelerates as it falls. With able pupils the teacher may introduce the formula $s = \frac{1}{2} gt^2$, where g is the acceleration due to gravity.

Topics: Relation of force of gravity to mass of Earth (reference to effects which would occur on other planets) and to distance from centre (difference between the weight of a body measured at the Pole and the Equator). Elementary discussion of cause of tides.

More able pupils may make further use of the formula $s = \frac{1}{2} gt^2$, e.g. to estimate the height to which a cricket ball is thrown by noting the time of flight; or to estimate the depth of a well, or the height of a cliff, by timing the fall of a pebble.

The Transmission of Movement

415 (a) *Belt Drives*

Build a small framework (in the form of a box) from Meccano plates and strips. The ends and the two sides are open; each of the remaining two sides consists of a Meccano plate. Spindles or crank handles can be arranged parallel to one another and at various distances apart by passing them through holes in the plates. Fix two strips at one end of the box (with a supporting cross-piece) so that they project at an angle (Fig. 415 (a), i).

Use the arrangement shown in Fig. 415 (a), i. Each pulley has a wide rubber band stretched round it (to prevent slip) and there is a rubber band tightened over the two spindles to hold the pulleys in contact. Mark with chalk the point of contact of the pulleys. Turn the handle so that one pulley makes one complete turn; observe that the other pulley does so also, but in the opposite direction.

Now replace one pulley by one of larger size and repeat the experiment. What happens when one pulley has (say) twice the diameter of the other?

Next set up the arrangement of Fig. 415 (a), ii, where the pulleys are some distance apart and are connected by a rubber band. Make observations on the number of turns of one pulley as compared with the other, using (i) pulleys of equal size, (ii) pulleys of different size. Notice that the pulleys now turn in the same direction. Try "crossing" the driving belt.

Finally, set up the arrangement of Fig. 415 (a), iii, where one pulley is used to drive two shafts at different speeds. In each case mark the pulleys with chalk so that the revolutions are easily observed.

415 (b) *Toothed Gears*

Count the number of teeth on the driving-wheel of a hand-drill and on the smaller gear-wheel which it drives. Turn the handle of the drill into the position where it passes over the chuck and make chalk marks on the handle and chuck opposite one another. Now turn the handle and count how many turns must be made to bring the chalk marks opposite one another again. Get a second pupil to count the number of turns made by the chuck.

Multiply:

(i) Number of turns of handle × Number of teeth on driving wheel

(ii) Number of turns of chuck × Number of teeth on smaller gear-wheel.

Discuss how the relative numbers of teeth on the gear-wheels affect the speed of the drill.

Topics: Examination of gears on machines of various kinds: clocks and watches, cranes, gas and electricity meters, egg whisks, the shuttle-winder of a sewing machine, etc. Demonstrate the *rack & pinion*, e.g. on a pedestal spring balance, the *worm drive*, and the use of bevelled gears (use Meccano). Interested teachers may develop the subject of gears through a study of the motor car.

The Pendulum and Time

416 *Hour Glass*

Soften a small test-tube (soda-glass) half-way along its length by holding it and turning it in a Bunsen flame; when the glass has obviously softened, draw it out to form a narrow neck in the middle of the tube.

Pour fine, dry sand into the tube, and then cork the tube. Find how many seconds it takes for the sand to drop from one end of the tube into the other. Adjust the amount of sand to get a 4-minute egg-timer.

417 *Pendulum*
(a) Suspend three different-sized iron nuts (or other weights) by threads from a horizontal rod gripped in a boss-head. Adjust the centres of the nuts to the same level by using slip-knots on the threads. Start the pendulums swinging by tilting the base of the retort stand slightly to one side for a moment. The three pendulums keep time with one another.

(b) It is possible, by twisting the rod and boss through a small angle, to get the three pendulums swinging together but with different amplitudes. Notice that they still keep in step provided that the swings are small.

(c) Lengthen the middle pendulum and start all three swinging again as in (a). The longer pendulum lags behind the others.

418 (a) *Timing a Pendulum*
Refer to Expt. 136 (seconds ticker). Hang a pendulum (Expt. 417) from a drawing pin stuck into the edge of the bench, making the thread about half a metre long. Measure the length from the pin to the centre of the bob. Using a watch with seconds pointer, find the time of swing by timing 100 complete to-and-fro movements.

Fill the hole in the nut with solder (it is easily hammered in) and again time the pendulum.

Confirm that the "period" does not vary with the extent of swing ("amplitude") provided that the latter is not too large.

Lengthen the pendulum (and later shorten it), and thus find out what effect this has on the period of swing.

418 (b) *The Law of the Pendulum*
Use Galileo's method of timing a pendulum—against the human pulse.

Steadman (*School Science Review*, No. 150, p. 477) describes the construction of an easily adjusted simple pendulum which is readily set up for experiment and which can be stored as a whole.

Using in turn various pendulum lengths, take the time of 50 short swings, in pulse beats. Plot length (l) first against time (t), then against t^2. Hence show that the period of swing is proportional to the square root of the length of the pendulum.

419 *Effect of External Force on a Pendulum*
It is not possible, in our laboratory, to alter the gravitational force, but the effect of a change may be simulated by using a magnet beneath a pendulum with an iron bob. Set the poles of an electro-magnet just under the bob (it is even better to have a row of three or four magnets) and measure the time for 50 swings with and without magnetic force in action.

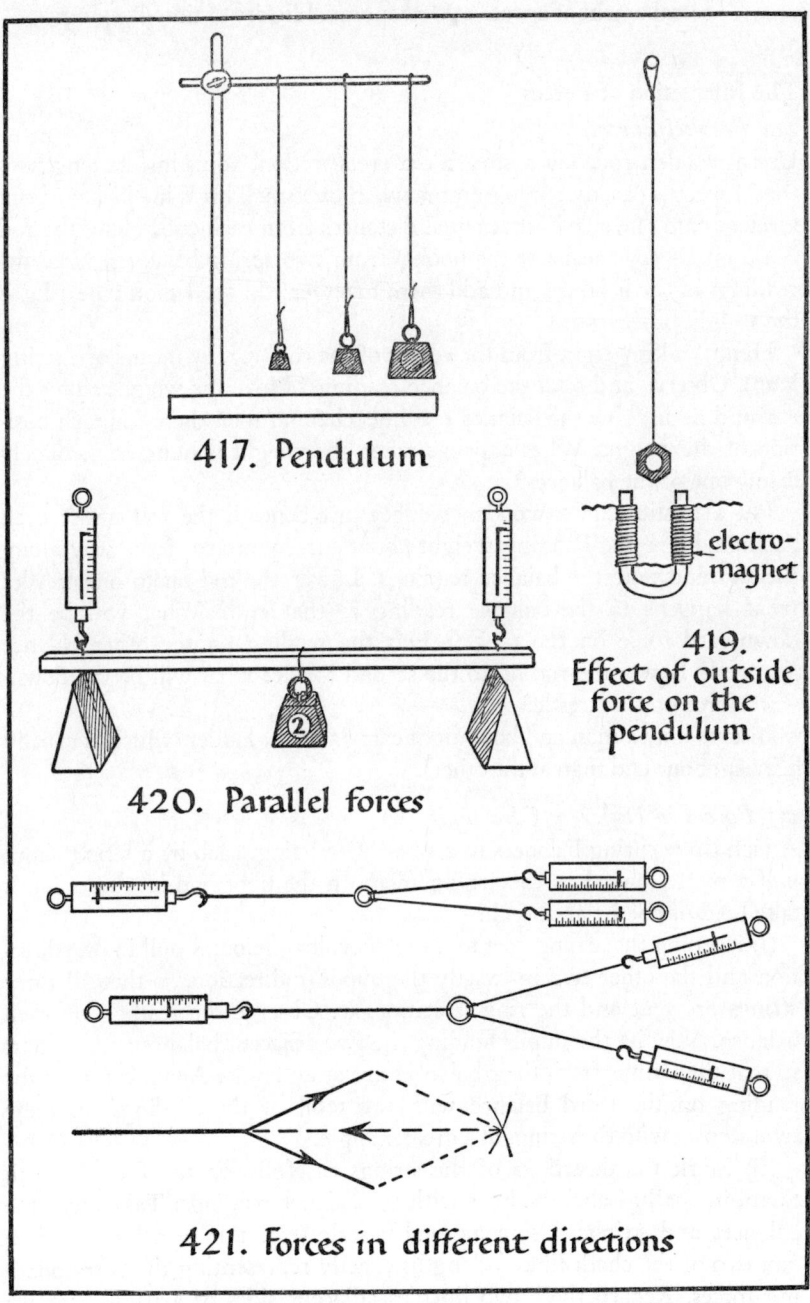

417. Pendulum

419. Effect of outside force on the pendulum

420. Parallel forces

421. Forces in different directions

Topics: Pendulum clock, including the escapement. Balance wheel and escapement of a watch. Metronome. History of time-keeping.

The Interaction of Forces

420 *Parallel Forces*

Use a wooden rod, say 2 cm × 2 cm cross-section, adjusting its length so that it weighs exactly 1 kilogramme when two small brass hooks have been screwed into one side of it at equal distances from each end. Hang the rod horizontally (by means of the hooks) from two spring balances. Note the readings of the balances and add them together; the total should be 1 kg—the weight of the rod.

Hang a 2-kg weight from the centre of the rod (e.g. by means of a string loop). Observe and total the balance readings. Move the weight along the rod and notice how the balance readings change; total them for each position of the weight. What happens when the weight is hung immediately below one of the balances?

Put a trestle (e.g. a wooden wedge) just beneath the rod under each balance. Have the hanging weight about threequarters of the way along the rod and note the balance readings. Lower the rod on to one trestle; what happens to the balance reading at that end? What will be the downward force on the trestle? Has the reading on the other balance changed? Lower the rod on to the second trestle; what will be the downward force on this trestle?

Discuss how a man and boy might carry a heavy ladder (which is usually heavier at one end than at the other).

421 *Forces in Different Directions*

Attach three spring balances to a small metal ring, each by a string about half a metre long. Lay the arrangement on the floor and let three pupils take hold of one balance each.

(i) Keeping the arrangement on the floor, let one pupil pull in one direction and the other two in exactly the opposite direction, so that all three strings are taut and the ring is stationary. Observe the reading on each balance. Now let the pupils holding the two adjacent balances move apart so that the strings from their balances are at an angle. Again compare the reading on the third balance with the total of the readings on these two. Repeat with the strings at a greater angle.

(ii) Mark the directions of the strings carefully on the floor beneath them, in chalk. Label the lines with the balance readings. Take away the balances and strings. Using a suitable scale (e.g. 1 m = 2 kg), produce any two of the chalk lines to lengths exactly representing the corresponding forces. Regard these two lines as adjacent sides of a parallelogram; complete the parallelogram (e.g. by striking arcs with the blackboard compasses) and draw the diagonal which divides the angle between the first two sides. Notice that this diagonal lies in the direction of the chalk line which represented the third force. Measure it, and note that its length corresponds with the value of the third force.

Topics: General discussion of bodies under the action of various forces, e.g. a suitcase standing on the floor (weight and upward thrust of floor); a train running steadily on the level (weight balanced by upthrust; friction balanced by forward thrust of engine); a steamship directed south against a westerly current; aeroplanes and wind velocity; the planets round the Sun. The discussion may be entirely qualitative for the less able pupils; or quantitative, with the aid of scale drawings, for the more able.

Chapter Twenty-One
Balance and Stability

The Storage of Equipment

There can seldom be too much storage space in or associated with laboratories; usually far too little has been provided, and even about new buildings one hears frequent complaints that store-rooms have been sacrificed to meet the exigencies of cost limits. The problems of storage have in any case been increased as secondary schools have grown larger, for multi-streaming may mean the frequent movement of apparatus between rooms. Modern methods of laboratory organization, demanding perimeter services (so that bench-tables may be switched from one position to another to suit particular purposes), restrict the use of space under benches. Finally, if pupils are to enjoy real scope for experiment, and for the display of their efforts, maximum working surfaces are essential.

All this means that much material must be housed in store- and preparation-rooms rather than round the laboratory; and the ideal may be open storage bays. Teachers who are called upon to take any part in the design of science facilities for new schools are referred to two valuable booklets: (i) *Designing for Science* (Building Bulletin No. 39. H.M.S.O.); (ii) *Storage of Apparatus* (Nuffield Foundation Science Teaching Project: Association of Science Education). However, for the majority of teachers questions of how best to use quite limited space will remain and the comments which follow are relevant whether storage is within or without the laboratory.

Unless equipment is so stored that resources of apparatus and materials are readily accessible, time is wasted and practical work is correspondingly restricted. It is also of the utmost importance that any item missing or damaged can be spotted easily; a quick glance should be sufficient to check that material has been returned completely and in good condition. Storage should enable pupils to collect and return apparatus directly—a valuable aspect of training, as well as a great saving of teachers' or assistants' time. No attempt will be made here to survey methods of storing equipment in detail, since the problems are highly individual, but a number of fairly general considerations are discussed.

So far as possible, all small pieces of apparatus should be kept in boxes or trays, labelled to show the nature and number of the items inside. Today, cardboard boxes may with advantage be replaced by cheap plastic trays and boxes, of sizes chosen to fit conveniently on to shelves or into drawers. These will be useful not only for stocks of single items (thermometers, lenses, magnets, scissors, etc.), but also for sets of apparatus ("kits") relating to particular experiments. Examples of the latter may be labelled, for example: "Air resistance, B2; 2 sets". Needless to say, sets must not be robbed; the temptation to borrow spring clips, glass T-pieces and other items in frequent demand should be resisted firmly. Corks, nails and similar things are best stored in drawers divided into nests (e.g. fitted with plastic boxes) for the various sizes.

Increasingly in future, certain items such as lenses, thermometers and other glassware may be marketed in pre-formed expanded polystyrene "gloves", making for safety and for simplicity of checking.

The larger, simpler (and unbreakable) items of equipment, such as cans, tripods, pie-dishes, wood blocks, Bunsen burners and stands of various kinds, may be kept in cupboards near to floor level. On the other hand, simple racks are easily devised which may better solve the problem: thus retort stands, tripods and Bunsen burners may hang, base upwards, in holes drilled in 7-cm × 3-cm wood battens fixed to the wall or between the legs of benches. It is unwise to store anything on the laboratory floor, since cleaners have their work to do and apparatus left about in this way not only gets dirty but makes sweeping doubly difficult. Open shelves are satisfactory only if equipment is stored in covered trays and if it is unlikely to be stolen. The aim should be to get everything into stores or cupboards which can be locked at night and at other times when the laboratory is not in use.

With proper storage facilities it should be possible to clear bench tops completely at the end of the lesson (except for 'experiments in progress'). It is excellent training if pupils are taught to regard their work as unfinished until the bench is clear and clean. Dusters and polishing rags should be freely available (boys and girls will bring them from home if they are encouraged to do so) and furniture polish and scouring powder (for sinks), part of the Science requisition, should be used by pupils in periodical sprucing-up sessions.

Biology material requires special attention. Something has been said already about Nature Tables and the exhibition of wild flowers. Anatomical models, specimens in transparent cases, and mounted collections, may profitably be kept in a glass fronted cupboard within the laboratory so that they are on permanent display. "Dry" materials, such as seeds and fruits, may be kept in plastic boxes; "wet" material (e.g. stems for sectioning) should be preserved in 4% formalin in stoppered wide-mouthed bottles.

Sensitive and costly instruments (e.g. electrical meters, microscopes), as well as dangerous chemicals, are properly kept in the store-room, inaccessible to any except nominated pupils. Winchester bottles and other large containers should be kept near floor level. Solid chemicals are best transferred from paper bags to bottles or stone jars.

Metal rod, strip and tubing is conveniently stored horizontally on a long narrow shelf with a batten along the front edge. A similar arrangement serves for long lengths of glass tubing. Plywood, hardboard, perspex and formica sheets may be supported parallel to a wall (perhaps behind a door) by means of battens.

Tools for class use are best kept in sets in stands or racks, which may either be issued as required or screwed down to the benches. A useful set of 10 tools consists of a bradawl, small screwdriver, light hammer, light hacksaw, tinsnips, small scissors, file, large (15-cm) pointed nail, pliers (with wire cutters), and half-metre rule. Larger or less-frequently used tools may be kept in a shallow wall-cupboard lined with peg-board and fitted with clip supports.

In the teacher's bench (or near to it) there should be a range of equipment for demonstration work; files, cork-borers (and sharpener), flat-flame burner, tapers and matches, scissors, tongs, string and thread, set of tools and roll of dissecting instruments, soldering equipment, fuse-wire, etc.—in addition to a basic selection of stands and glassware, a Bunsen burner and the like. One or two stout trays are very useful for carrying apparatus from store to laboratory.

Lenses, scalpels, torch bulbs, miniature compasses and other small items attractive to boys and girls should be counted each time after use. It is a good plan to assign the distribution and collection of such things to accredited monitors who appreciate their responsibilities. But it is important that every pupil should be given opportunities to share in the running of the laboratory, assembling and putting away routine equipment at least. Only so will it prove possible to maintain regular practical work where ancillary help is inadequate, especially, of course, if classes are large.

Charts and diagrams may be rolled in light tubes, suspended vertically from battens projecting from the wall. Alternatively (and preferably if room permits) they should be stored flat in a large drawer or set of drawers. Ordinary paper may be treated in the same way.

Laboratory designers frequently overlook one important item—a cupboard for the reception of class note-books, with space sufficient for every class using the laboratory.

Muscles and Levers

422 *Arm and Leg Movements*

(a) Bare an arm. As the forearm is raised and lowered feel the strong tendons inside the elbow joint, and the contraction and relaxation of the biceps muscle on the upper arm. (b) Stretch the arm outwards and move the fingers; notice the movements of the muscles under the skin below the elbow and of the tendons at the inside of the wrist. Spread out the fingers as widely as possible and trace down the back of the hand the tendons that are straightening the fingers. (c) Grip the back of the thigh and notice the thickening of the muscle as the leg is bent at the knee to bring the heel up towards the thigh. (d) Cut out of thick cardboard models of the upper and lower arm, and pivot them together at the elbow, using a small nut and bolt. Screw the top of the upper arm to a baseboard. Attach stout rubber bands to represent the biceps and triceps muscles; they may be looped through small holes drilled in the forearm near the elbow and over nails fixed in the baseboard (which represents the shoulder) at the top of the upper arm. A similar model may be contrived to show the action of the foot.

423 *Crowbar*

(a) Fill a strong wooden box with bricks or stones and screw the lid on firmly; or use some other large heavy object which cannot easily be lifted. Push a crowbar (metal or wooden rod, a metre long) some 15 cm under the box and notice how easy it is to lever the box upwards using only one hand at the other end of the bar. Slide the hand nearer to the box and again try to lift the box. (b) Put a brick under the crowbar near to the box and lever the box upwards by pressing downwards on the free end of the bar. Again try the effect of sliding the hand nearer to the box. (c) Lay the crowbar on the floor with one end under the box; get someone to stand on the other end. Grasp the middle of the bar and try to lift the box. Slide the hand nearer to the box and try again.

Make diagrams of all the experiments. Show the "fulcrum" (the spot where the bar hinges, whether on the floor or on the brick), the "load" (the weight of the box, represented by a downward arrow), and the "effort" (the force of the hand, represented by an arrow).

(d) An alternative arrangement for this series of experiments is to lay a broom-handle across a horizontal bar (e.g. one of the cross-bars between the legs of an inverted stool) and to hang a pail, loaded with stones, from one end of the pole while holding the other end. Various positions of the fulcrum are tried, and it is established that the pail is most easily raised when the fulcrum is near to it and when the "effort" is applied as far away from the fulcrum as possible. The experiment is repeated with one end of the pole resting on the top of a stool and (i) the free end held in the hand, with the pail suspended between hand and stool; (ii) the pail suspended from the free end of the pole, the hand gripping the pole between pail and stool. In each case the effect of moving the hand and pail nearer together or farther apart is examined.

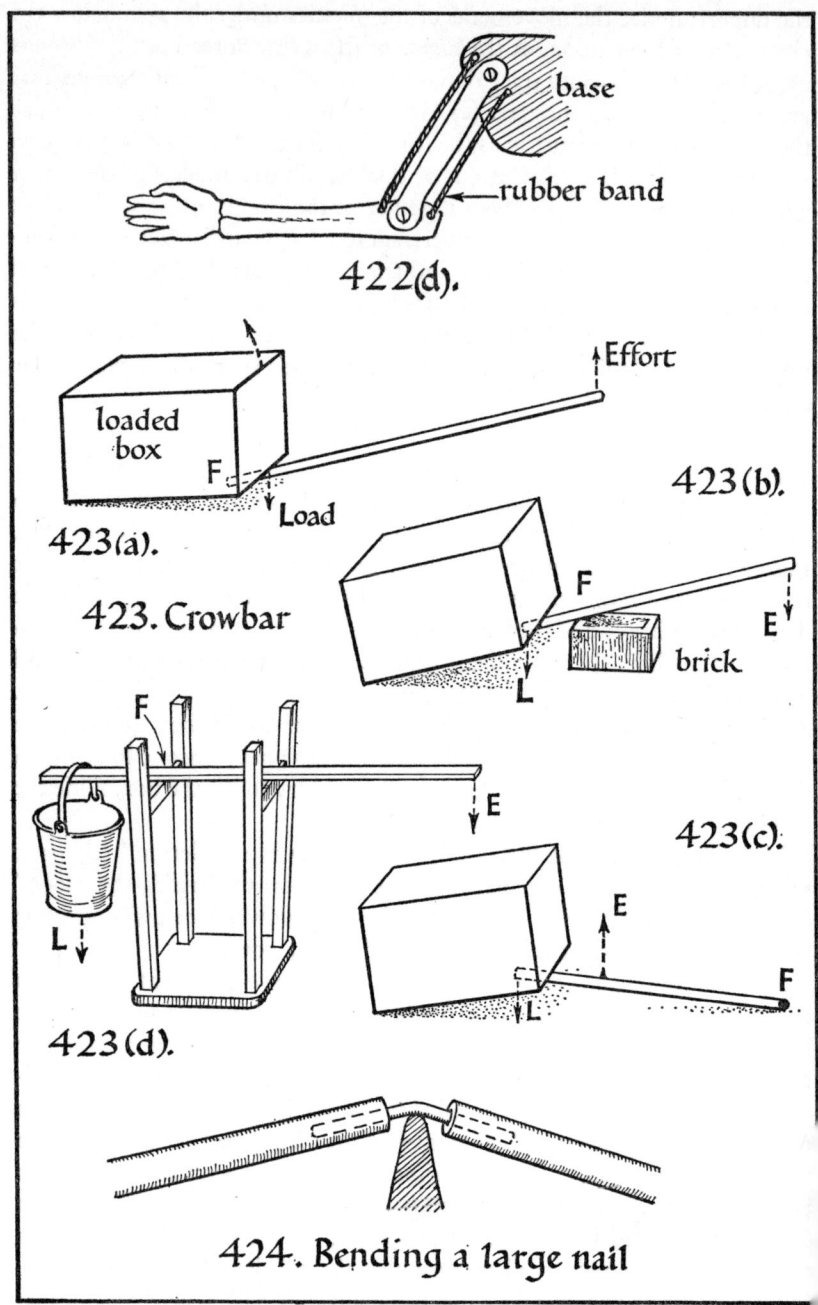

422(d).

423(a). 423. Crowbar 423(b).

423(c).

423(d).

424. Bending a large nail

BALANCE AND STABILITY 367

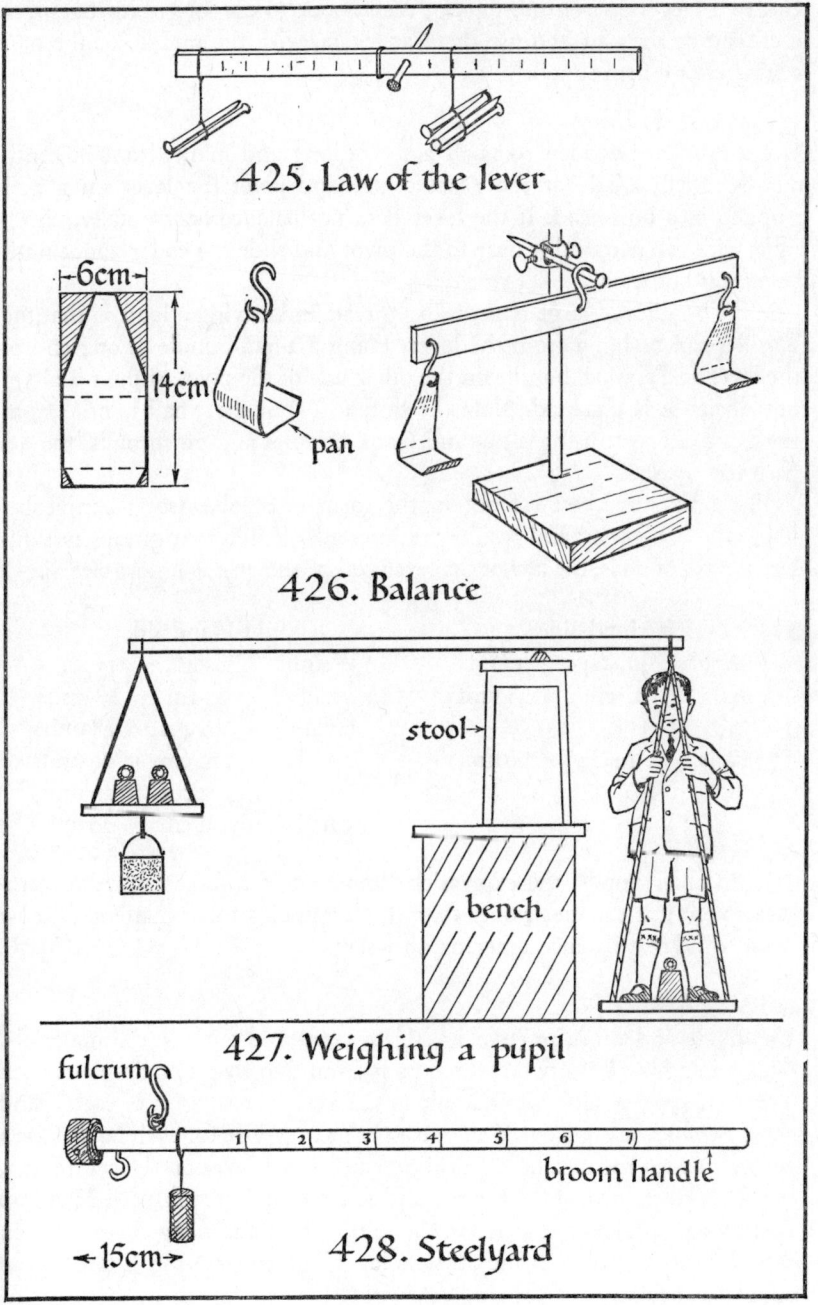

425. Law of the lever

426. Balance

427. Weighing a pupil

428. Steelyard

424 *To Bend a Large Nail at Right Angles*

Cut two pieces of iron gas-piping, each about 30 cm long. Slip one over each end of the nail and use them as levers, with the middle of the nail resting over a firm support.

425 *Law of the Lever*

Use a uniform wooden rod half a metre long and marked out in centimetres. Drill a hole at the exact centre and pivot the lever on a nail gripped in a boss-head. If the lever does not balance horizontally, clip a light wire collar round it near to the pivot and slide the collar about until balance is obtained.

Make bundles of large nails, using thread and leaving a loop so that the bundles can be hung from the lever. Hang a 2-nail bundle at one end of the lever and a 3-nail bundle on the other side of the pivot, sliding it along until balance is obtained. Note the distance (l) of the 3-nail bundle from the pivot. Repeat, using 2-, 4- and 6-nail bundles and go through the experiment again.

The results are best set out in the form of a table (see example below, where a few typical results are inserted). If different groups use different sizes of nails, the law of the lever will be shown even more clearly.

Left-Hand Side			Right-Hand Side		
Weight	Distance	$w \times l$	Weight	Distance	$w \times l$
2 nails	24 cm	48 units	4 nails	12 cm	48 units
			6 nails	8 cm	48 units
2 nails	10 cm	20 units	2 nails	10 cm	20 units
			4 nails	5 cm	20 units
			5 nails	4 cm	20 units

With abler pupils, the expression "moment of a force" may be introduced; but it is the idea rather than the terminology that matters. Discuss how a child may balance a man on a see-saw.

426 *The Balance*

Use pliers and tin-snips (two levers) to bend and cut out the materials. Cut out and bend up two balance pans from two sheets of tin-plate, each 6 cm × 14 cm, piercing a small hole in the top of the support of each. Bend three S-hooks, using 8 cm of stout copper or iron wire for each hook. Use a 30-cm wooden rod as a beam, drilling three small holes on the centre line, one 2 cm from each end of the rod and one exactly in the middle. Hang up the rod on an S-hook attached to the middle hole and hang the pans from S-hooks suspended from the other holes. Use a collar, as in Expt. 425, to adjust the balance.

Use the balance: e.g. find the weight of each of the new coins.

427 *Weighing a Pupil*

The beam is a stout wood or metal rod, 2 metres long and 5 cm × 5 cm in cross section, and the fulcrum is a short length of broom handle on which a flat lower face has been planed. The fulcrum rests on a tall stool standing on the bench near one edge. The scale pans are thick wood boards, securely hung from the ends of the beam, each by four ropes. The one on the long end of the beam has a can suspended beneath it; the other is only two or three centimetres above the floor when the beam is balanced.

The beam is first balanced, with the fulcrum about 25 cm from one end, by putting a metal weight in the lower pan and stones in the can hanging from the other pan. Then the pupil to be weighed stands on the lower pan, grasping the ropes above his chest (not the beam). Weights are now added to the other pan until balance is obtained. The ratio of the balance arms is carefully measured (it may conveniently be arranged to be $5:1$), and hence the weight of the pupil is found at once.

428. *Steelyard*

Hammer old lead piping into strip and wrap about a kilogramme of it round one end of a broom handle, forming a cylinder perhaps 5 cm long. The lead may be tacked in position.

Suspend a lead weight (about ½ kg) from the rod by a loop of fine string, at about 15 cm from the weighted end. By picking up the rod between thumb and forefinger, find the approximate point about which the rod will balance. Insert a stout screw-eye here and suspend the rod by an S-hook (meat hook) passing through the eye. A slight movement of the ½ kg weight should now balance the rod exactly.

Insert a screw-hook underneath the rod 5 cm nearer to the main weight than the screw-eye. Objects to be weighed will be hung from this hook.

First balance the steelyard by adjusting the position of the ½ kg balancing weight; mark this position "0". Then hang various known weights (½, 1, 2 . . . kg) from the S-hook, balancing the steelyard each time and marking the successive positions of the balancing weight "1", "2" . . . etc., the scale being in kg. Subdivisions can be added.

Use the steelyard to find the weight of a building brick, a litre of water, etc.

429 *Oblique Forces*

Fix screw-eyes 15 cm apart along a horizontal line across a door. Using a spring balance, find the least pull required to just move the door on its hinges when the balance is attached at each screw-eye in turn. What is the direction of pull relative to the door in each case? Try pulling on the outer screw-eye at a very oblique angle; then gradually reduce the angle until the pull is perpendicular to the door.

Topics: The many applications of levers, both in the home (e.g. knives, scissors, nut-crackers, sugar-tongs, claw-hammer) and outside (wheelbarrow, pump handle, girder crane, car brake system, garden shears, gate, etc.). Use of levers to increase movement (forearm, fishing rod). Value of exercise to develop muscles. Source of energy for muscular work. Muscular fatigue and need for rest; sleep.

Balance and Stability

430 *Spinning-top*

Use an irregularly shaped sheet of stiff card and a light plumb-line (thread and small weight). Prick three or four holes in the card, spacing them out round the edges. Hang the card at each hole in turn from a nail in the wall, suspending the plumb-line from the nail in front of the card. For each position of the card mark the track of the plumb-line; both card and line must hang freely. All the lines thus marked will cross at one point, which is the centre of gravity of the card. Punch a hole in the card at this point, using a sharp pencil, and convert the card into a spinning top as described in Expt. 376 (c). No matter how irregular the shape of the card, the top will spin well.

431 *Bus Stability*

Take a large rectangular wooden block and suspend a light plumb-line from a drawing pin stuck in the exact centre of one of the largest faces. Stand the block on end, with this face vertical and overhanging the edge of the bench so that the plumb-line swings freely. Gradually tilt the block on one edge (Fig. 431, ii) and notice that if released it always falls back into its original position provided that the tilt does not carry the plumb-line (i.e. the vertical through the centre of gravity) beyond the edge on which the block is resting; but that if the plumb-line does pass this edge the block falls over when released.

Buses are tested for stability by a method similar to this. But buses are more stable than the block because the engine and other heavy parts are placed low down.

432 *Centre of Gravity Toys*

Examples of these are illustrated. (a) Balance a pencil on its point on a finger, using a partly opened penknife to lower the centre of gravity. (b) Make a perching parrot, fixing a piece of metal to the tail. (c) Make a prancing horse, using a long cork, card, pins, wire and a metal nut. (d) Balance a key and heavy metal tube as shown.

> *Topics:* Discuss the design of ornaments and furniture in relation to stability. Stability of towers, chimneys, etc., and of ships and road vehicles. Need for good foundations in building. Balance of the body.

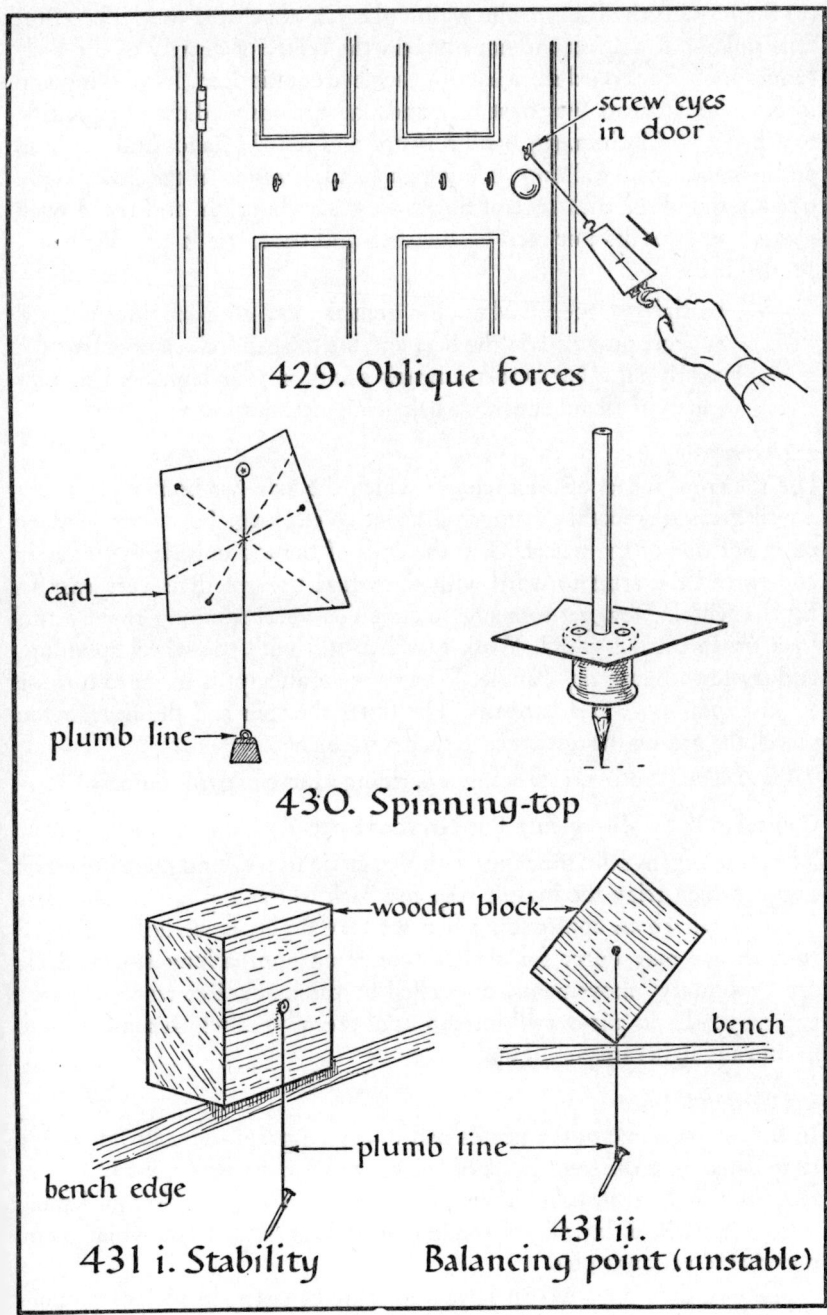

429. Oblique forces

430. Spinning-top

431 i. Stability

431 ii. Balancing point (unstable)

433 *Body Balance*

(a) Stand with the back to the wall and try to touch the toes. The effort fails so long as the feet are not moved: the centre of gravity of the body cannot move backward sufficiently to achieve equilibrium. In walking and in other movements we constantly and unconsciously adjust our position to achieve equilibrium. (b) Bend forward and rest the hands and forehead on the handle of a walking stick which stands upright on the floor. Walk quickly round the stick several times. Now stand upright and try to walk along a straight line; or pick up the stick and try to use it to strike a suspended ball.

Topics: Upright stance of Man; the arched foot, with its three-pointed support provided by the heel and the toe-pads (cf. camera tripod); nearly all other land mammals stand on four legs. Semicircular canals of the inner ear as a balancing mechanism.

434 *Gyroscope*

Use the front wheel of a bicycle, in which the axle has been replaced by a well greased smoothly fitting rod about 30 cm long. Fit a large washer on either side of the wheel. Grip the ends of the rod outside the washers and extend the arms forward with the wheel upright. It is very easy to tilt the wheel. Now get someone to start the wheel spinning rapidly and then try to tilt the wheel. Walk forward, still with the wheel spinning, and try to turn at a right angle. Whenever an attempt is made to turn or tilt the spinning wheel it resists. The faster the spin and the heavier the wheel, the greater the resistance to such movements.

Topics: Toy gyroscope; spinning-top, riding a bicycle; gyro-compass.

Control of Body Movement: The Nervous System

The sense organs send messages to the brain via nerves, and there are other nerves which relay the brain's response back to the appropriate muscles. Thus, if we see an approaching lion we take flight; if we hear a clap of thunder we may hurry for shelter against an approaching storm. Such are "voluntary" movements, controlled by the brain. Reference to Expt. 327, and to Expts 362–7, will remind us of the ways in which some stimuli (sound and light) are picked up.

435 *Sense of Taste*

In the tongue some of the nerves end in special groups of cells known as taste buds. Test different parts of the tongue for the sensations of bitter, salt, sour, and sweet, using a few grains of salt or sugar, a drop of lemon juice, etc. Make a drawing of the tongue and mark the parts which seem sensitive to various tastes.

Many of the things we eat have a mixture of tastes, in various proportions. Flavour often depends upon smell as well as upon taste. Blindfold

BALANCE AND STABILITY 373

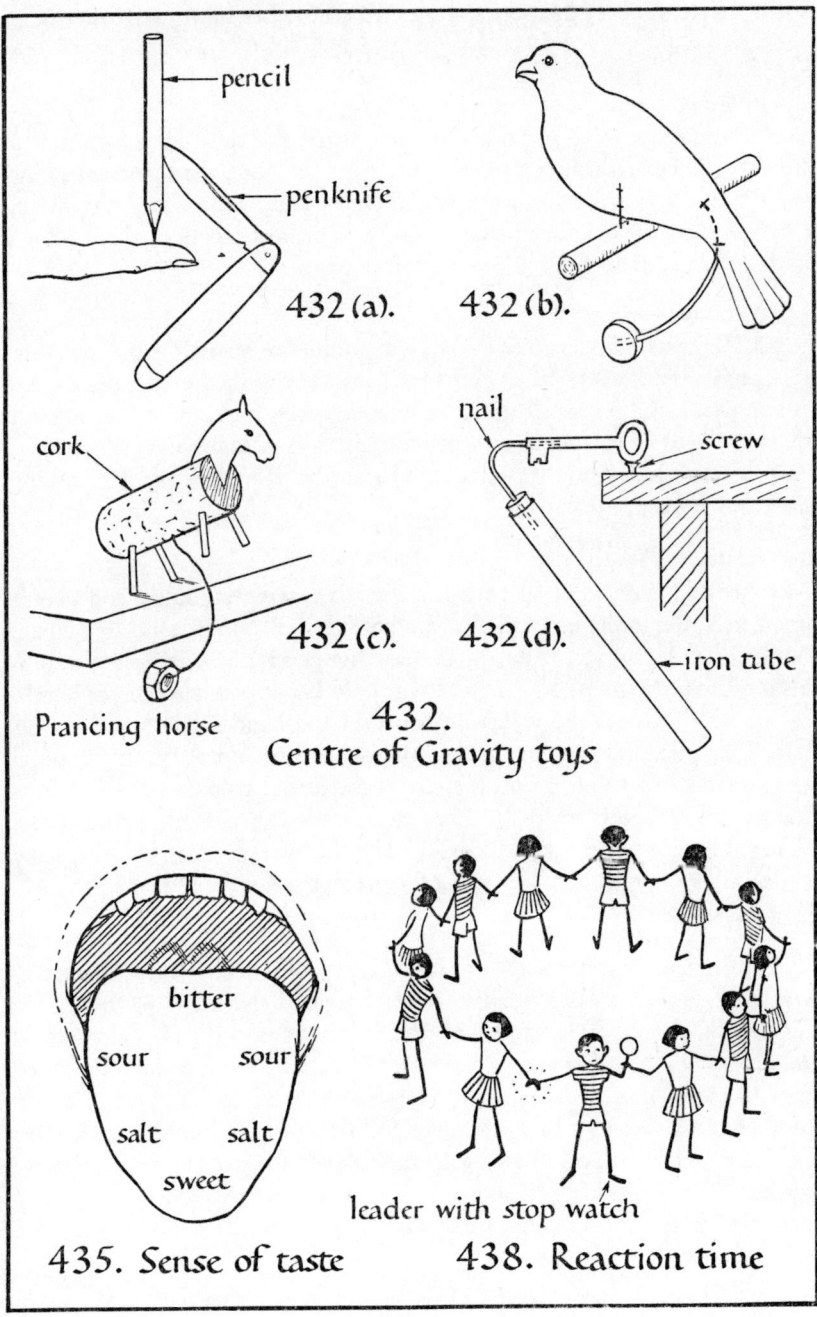

432 (a). 432 (b).

Prancing horse — cork

432 (c). 432 (d).
nail — screw — iron tube

432. Centre of Gravity toys

435. Sense of taste
bitter, sour, sour, salt, salt, sweet

438. Reaction time
leader with stop watch

a pupil and put a small piece of apple into his mouth while letting him smell a slice of pear; then reverse the two fruits. Let him guess what he is eating.

436 *Sense of Smell*
Soak strong ammonia on to a cloth and shake the cloth in one corner of the laboratory. Ask pupils to raise their hands when they first smell the gas. In this way trace the passage of the gas molecules through the room. Comment on the molecular theory; on the warning function of our noses; and on the use of respirators against poison gases.

437 *Sense of Touch*
Bend the arms of a hairpin so that the points are about 5 cm apart. Let one pupil blindfold another and touch his skin with the two points, repeating with the points closer and closer together. Determine the smallest distance apart of the points at which a sensation of *two* points can be felt. Try the experiment on the back of the hand, the palm, the forearm and the back of the neck.

438 *Reaction Time*
Measure the time interval between receiving some stimulus and acting upon it, in the following way. Let a whole class of pupils stand in a circle, holding hands and facing outwards. Call one pupil the leader and give him a stopwatch (the pupil on his right will hold his arm instead of his hand). As the leader starts the watch he squeezes the hand of the pupil on his left. This pupil, as soon as he feels the squeeze, passes it on to the pupil on his left; and so on round the circle, the leader stopping the watch as soon as the squeeze returns to him. Repeat the experiment several times, doing it both ways round the circle. Take the average time and divide by the number of pupils in order to get the average individual "reaction time".

439 *Reflex Actions*
These are automatic responses—involuntary but not necessarily unconscious. Expt. 363 dealt with the reflex action of the pupil of the eye in response to bright light, and with another involuntary and often unconscious action—the sweeping of the upper eyelid over the surface of the eye. In connection with Expt. 115 reference was made to the reflex action of salivation. Two further examples follow: (a) Let one pupil clap his hands, or strike an anvil with a hammer, near to another pupil; observe the automatic "blinking response. (b) One pupil sits with one knee crossed over the other and another taps his leg just below the knee-cap; observe the "knee jerk".

Topics: Diagram (very simple) of reflex arc, showing sense organ, sensory nerves, brain (or other nerve centre), motor nerves and energized muscles. Discussion of functions of brain and its supreme importance. Spinal cord and other nerve centres (e.g. solar plexus). Involuntary actions (coughing, breathing, sweating, glandular secretion, etc.). How nervous disorders can result in lack of complete control. Use of anaesthetics. Chemical messengers in the body—hormones.

Movements Made by Plants

Reference to Expt. 82 will recall how roots are attracted earthwards and how shoots seek the light. Comment on the way in which many flowers "follow the Sun" during the day (e.g. Sunflower) and how others (e.g. daisy, dandelion) close up at night. The opening of stomata is another response to particular conditions.

440 Climbing Plants

(a) Plant Scarlet Runner Beans in each of two or three pots. When shoots appear fix light canes as supports. Notice the direction of twining. (b) Grow Sweet-peas similarly and observe the way in which the tendrils grip the support. (c) Stroke tendrils of White Bryony, say 20 times; then note the movement of the tendrils during the next five minutes.

Topics: Other examples of climbing plants (Convolvulus, Hop, Honeysuckle; Vine, Virginia Creeper; Rose, Blackberry) to illustrate various adaptations. Discussion of how plants spread by "runners" and of how roots penetrate the soil. Contrast between plants and animals in relation to their mobility and nutrition.

Chapter Twenty-Two

Common Materials

Discipline in the Laboratory

Effective practical work is impossible unless the teacher is in complete control of his class. Unruly behaviour spells not only waste and inefficiency but also danger; there can be no room in a laboratory for anything which distracts attention from the job in hand. Nor is repressive discipline the answer; unless there is freedom of action, within well understood limits, the joy of doing things and of finding out things will disappear; organization will lack spontaneity and initiative will not develop. To boys and girls a Science teacher should be something of an idol—an "expert" at an exciting job; someone to whom they can turn with their questions; the author of lessons which they like. How can this be achieved? The following suggestions are offered to the less-experienced teacher in the full knowledge that one thing alone will finally determine the teacher-pupil relationship, namely, the personality of the one who teaches. They may help the beginner to develop his own methods successfully more quickly than he would otherwise do.

(a) Arrive in time to meet the class; or dismiss one class promptly so that the next is not howling in the corridor or peeping in at the door. See that every pupil knows his place at the benches and that the positions are maintained.

(b) See that pupils have a place to put their gear so that it neither clutters up the bench tops nor interferes with free passage on the floor. Insist upon tidiness in everything, and especially at the close of the lesson; institute the invariable rule that no pupil leaves until the work of his group is properly cleared away, with bench rubbed down, sink cleaned and waste in the waste-box. Allow sufficient time at the end of each lesson to carry this out.

(c) Have everything ready so that the lesson can start at once. The main thing here is to have the plan of the lesson fully worked out. There is no greater aid to good discipline than the knowledge that one knows exactly what one is going to do. To "muddle through" a lesson is to invite loss of interest and boredom. Apart from the occasional misfortune, experiments ought not to fail. Failure means interruption at the least, but it is damaging also to the pupils' confidence in the subject and to the teacher's prestige. Every time the teacher departs into the store to fetch something that has been forgotton, he runs a risk in leaving his class unattended.

(d) Organize a laboratory routine, familiar to all. The more pupils who have some clearly seen responsibility in the laboratory the better. There will be those who maintain aquaria, nature tables, vivaria, etc., or keep records, arrange displays, and keep the notice board up-to-date. These people have a vested interest in the laboratory—it is *their* work-room. And within the ordinary lessons encourage pupils to do things for themselves —to fetch and clear away the apparatus they need, to carry out straightforward adjustments or repairs to the apparatus they are using, and to apply directly to books for necessary information. Movement must be quiet and unhurried; conversation, of which there will be plenty, should be reasonably subdued. Where pupils have freedom to work hard at interesting tasks they can easily be persuaded of the importance of good class behaviour.

(e) Speak quietly but forcefully; and refuse to be ruffled. When a teacher shouts, or sends a boy out, or commits a flagrant injustice on the class as a whole for the sins of one, pupils are not slow to exploit his weakness or to resent his unfairness. The teacher's own attitude and behaviour are all-important. He must insist by example as well as by precept upon the best of which each pupil is capable. If he and his laboratory are untidy he may expect the same of his pupils' notebooks; if his demonstrations are slap-dash, so will be the practical work of his class; if he is prepared to accept second-rate work he will certainly get it. Good teachers build up, over the years, standards of work and behaviour which pupils automatically accept for the teachers concerned.

(f) There is bound to be noise in a busy laboratory, and the teacher must always be in a position to call the class immediately to attention. A small electric bell with a press button on the demonstration bench is invaluable. At its sound, pupils simply stop talking and stand still, without necessarily interrupting their work.

(g) Keep the laboratory alive—a place of interesting activity. Biological material, periodic displays, up-to-date notice boards, new books in the library—all help to focus and maintain interest. Exhibit both the practical work and the notebooks of pupils, so that others may see what good work is like.

(h) Show concern for the efforts of individual pupils and respect their point of view. Be prepared to listen as well as to inform.

The above standards may not be reached easily. Where practical science runs smoothly and efficiently the teacher may justly be proud of his achievement.

Rocks and Building Stones

Teachers will find a useful introductory article, "Geology in the Science Course", in the booklet *Science Teaching Techniques, VII* (John Murray).

441 *Rock Collections*

Named collections of common rocks are reasonably cheap, and one of these, together with a good reference book or two in the classroom library, can help the beginner over many difficulties. Working contact with a local museum is even better of course. It is not to be expected that most boys and girls will get far beyond a very simple classification of the stones they find, but they have a strong collecting instinct and they like to label their specimens.

It may help if the teacher prepares a small collection and suggests that pupils try to make their own similar collections; in this way the chosen rocks can be those likely to be found by the pupils in a particular district. Spaces may be left in the pupils' collecting cabinets for "extra" rocks outside the standard collection. Boys and girls working together on such a project will "swap" rocks just as they do foreign stamps.

The collecting cabinet is merely a shallow cardboard or plastic box, perhaps 25 cm x 15 cm x 5 cm, into which matchbox trays are fitted. Neat labels are printed and stuck into the trays. Twelve common rocks which might be included in every collection are:

Igneous (formed by fire)	Sedimentary (deposited in layers)
Granite	Sandstone
Quartz	Clay
Pumice	Chalk
Basalt	Limestone
	Coal
	Pebble-rock (conglomerate)

Metamorphic (changed by heat and pressure)
Marble
Slate

Fragments the size of the palm of the hand are good for classroom observation but too heavy for the cabinet. Senior boys and girls may learn to use a hammer to produce tidy specimens of suitable size. Rock outcrops, stream beds, road cuttings and cultivated fields are among the places where finds may be expected, but even the least enterprising pupil should find six of the twelve rocks mentioned above without difficulty. Each rock should be examined with a lens, tested with dilute hydrochloric acid (chalk, limestone and marble all effervesce, being carbonates), and scratched with a knife blade to make an estimate of hardness.

442 Granite

Break a piece of granite and examine the freshly broken surface under a lens. Observe its three chief constituents: a glass-like substance (quartz), a whitish or pink material (felspar), and a very lustrous component in thin layers (mica). Have specimens of the three minerals on exhibition. By breaking granite up it is possible, with the help of a lens, to separate the material into three unequal heaps, each representing one more or less pure mineral.

Discuss the use of the terms *rock* and *mineral*—the latter having reference to a single chemical substance.

443 Minerals

Collect and arrange on labelled trays such common minerals as quartz, Iceland spar, rock-salt, iron pyrites ("fool's gold" in coal), galena, magnetite, haematite, mica. All of these and many others can be bought cheaply, and it is worthwhile to allow pupils to form their collections of half-inch specimens from laboratory supplies, since in so doing they will certainly come to know much more about the materials they are handling. In labelling they may add useful information, e.g. Haematite—Iron oxide —Source of iron.

Determine the density of Iceland spar (2·7), magnetite or haematite (about 5), and galena (7·5) by weighing a fairly large piece (compression or lever balance) and finding its volume by displacement (Expt. 204).

Topics: Origin of chief classes of rocks as related to ideas about the history of the earth; the formation of continents and oceans; the sedimentation of shells, sand, and clay; the laying down of coal measures; the drying-up of inland seas; volcanic action; weathering. The connection between the geography of the homeland and the rocks of which it is built—occurrence of limestone, chalk, sandstone, clay, coal, slate and granite. Use of rocks for building purposes; observation of local buildings.

Artificial Building Materials

In addition to the natural building stones (marble, limestone, sandstone, slate, etc.), many building materials are manufactured; among them we might mention brick, mortar, cement, concrete, glass and plastics. Most of these are made from such substances as clay, sand, chalk, limestone and soda; but the primary sources of plastics are petroleum and coal.

444 Limestone Burning

Bore a 2-mm hole (a twist drill held in the fingers) through the middle of a piece of natural chalk the size of a chestnut. Suspend the chalk on a wire passed through the hole and heat directly in a Bunsen flame. Quicklime is produced in 15 minutes and glows brilliantly while hot. After cooling, test it by putting a lump on a metal lid and allowing water to drip on it. The water is greedily absorbed, much steam is formed, and the lid gets very hot; the lump disintegrates, forming "slaked lime". Shake a little of the slaked lime in a bottle with much water, allow the liquid to stand, and blow breath through a sample of the clear "lime-water" (Expt. 51).

445 (a) *Bricks and Pottery*
Knead clay with a little water and form it into small bricks; in some incorporate finely chopped straw. Allow some of the bricks to dry out slowly and thoroughly in hot sunshine; fire others standing on a bed of broken pot in a muffle, which may be contrived from bricks and a Bunsen burner. Refer to Exodus v. 7–19. Roll "worms" of pottery clay and coil them to make a small clay vessel. Fire the vessel. Then sprinkle salt over it and refire; see whether any part has taken a glaze.

445 (b) *Mortar*
Mix 1 part by weight of freshly slaked lime with 3 parts of dry sand. Add water a little at a time, with stirring, to produce a thick paste. Spread over a brick and press another brick on top of it. Allow to dry.

445 (c) *Concrete*
Use a tin can as a measure. Mix together 1 part of cement and 3 parts of sand. Tip the mixture on to a stone or concrete floor, scoop out a hollow in the heap, pour in water and gradually mix all in until a thick paste is obtained. Run the mixture into a large baby food can, setting up a broom handle in the centre. When the concrete has set hard the weighted rod may be found useful as a laboratory stand.

Experiment with other proportions of cement and sand (e.g. 1 to 6). Try also the effect of replacing part of the sand by small limestone or marble chips.

To introduce the idea of reinforced concrete, use narrow cardboard tubes, corked at one end, as moulds. After filling with wet mix, insert thin steel wires into some of the tubes. After setting, devise means of comparing the strengths of ordinary and reinforced concrete.

446 (a) *Phenol-formaldehyde Plastic*
Mix together in a test-tube 2 cm^3 of formalin, 1 g of phenol and 2–3 drops of strong caustic soda solution. Warm, with stirring, over a small flame. To complete the polymerization of the sticky red mass, heat it for several hours at about 50°C. in an oven. After cooking, the glass tube may be broken away from the hard plastic.

446 (b) *Moulding with Plastic*
The teacher may already have used Vinamold (Expt. 116 (b)), a thermosoftening plastic. Polythene pellets may be bought and are useful for

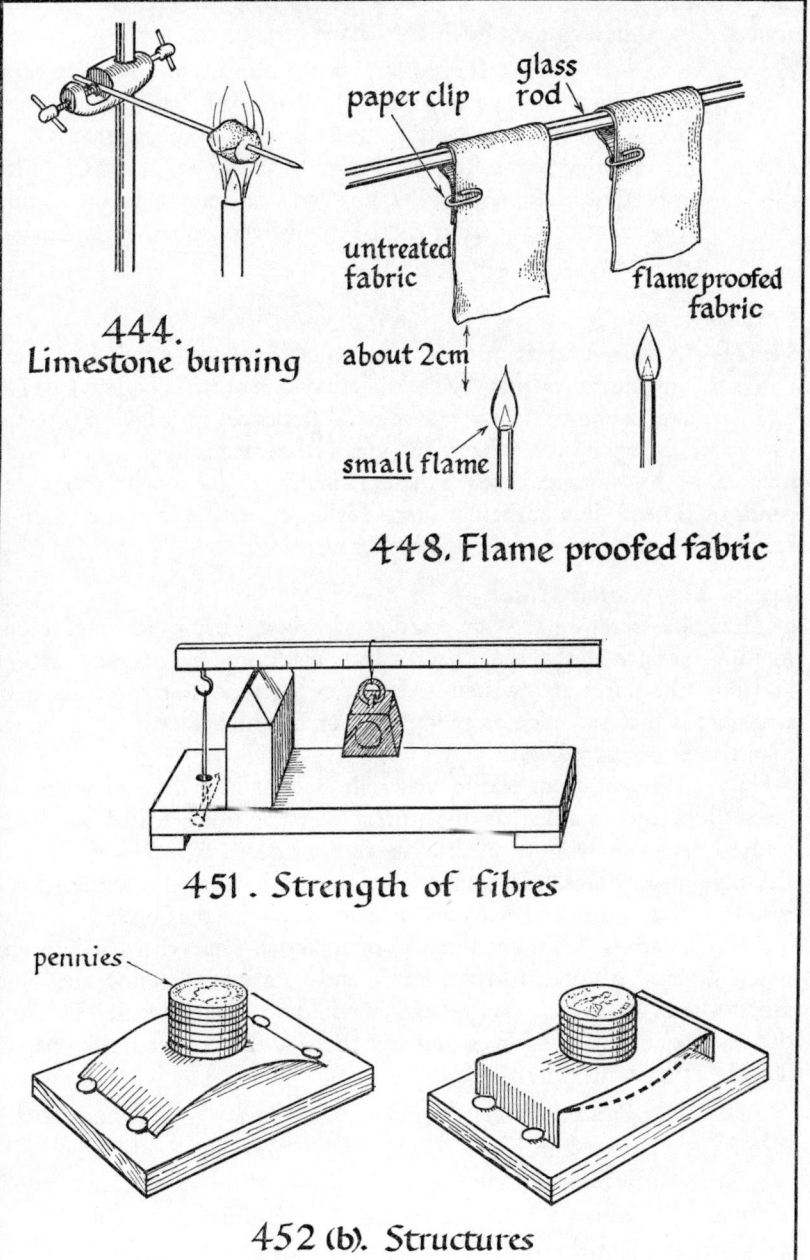

moulding. Polythene melts easily, but care should be taken to avoid charring when it is being heated (e.g. in a boiling tube). It may be run into plaster of Paris moulds and pressed into shape as required.

Topics: Uses of slaked lime (for mortar, plaster, cement, bleaching powder manufacture and as a fertilizer). Plaster of Paris (Expts. 80, 116). Plastics: thermosetting and thermosoftening; uses. Glass (manufacture; uses for vessels, lenses, building units, etc.); its property of softening under heat will be known to the pupils who have made stirring rods, bent delivery tubes, or fashioned egg-timers (Expt. 416).

Textiles

Textile—"A woven fabric, or a material suitable for weaving."

Natural textile fibres may be animal (wool, mohair, silk, etc.), vegetable (cotton, linen, ramie, etc.) or mineral (asbestos) in origin. Synthetic fibres include rayon, nylon, Terylene, etc. The existence of glass-fibre cloth reminds us that whether or not a material is suitable for weaving often depends on it being in a particular form. Nylon, for example, can be manufactured in rigid form quite unsuitable for weaving.

447 *Fibres of Various Kinds*
(a) Examine scraps of paper, cardboard, rope, string, sacking, coco-matting, various cloths, etc. under a lens, observing their fibrous nature and how the fibres are twisted and woven together. For comparison, a non-fibrous material such as cellophane, or the rubber of a toy balloon, may also be examined.

Unravel threads from textile materials, mount in a drop of water on glass slides and examine on the microprojector: fibres teased out from undyed yarn are recommended. Observe the smooth cylinders of silk and the man-made fibres, the bamboo-like fibres of linen, the flattened appearance of cotton and the scaly nature of wool. Sketch the fibres.

(b) Use narrow strips (or threads) of material. Observe what happens when a flame is applied to the lower end of a strip hanging above an asbestos mat. Does the material burn, smoulder or merely melt? Describe the residue. Smell any fumes and test them with the wet litmus paper. Tabulate the results e.g.:

Material	*Effect of flame*	*Residue*	*Smell*	*Litmus test*
Wool	Slow-burning or smouldering	Black, soft.	"Burning hair"	Alkaline
Cotton	Burns quickly	Grey ash	"Burning paper"	Acid
Natural Silk	Melts as it slowly burns	Black bead.	—	Alkaline

Nylon	Melts, but does not burn.	Pale brown bead.	"Celery"	Neutral

List as many materials as possible. "Unknown" materials may then be tested, using the list as a guide to identification. Scraps of fur, camel-hair, angora, alpaca, carpet, etc. should be accumulated for the purpose.

(c) The protein test (Expt. 98) may be tried. The teacher may demonstrate an alternative: treat a scrap of material in a dish or test-tube with just one or two drops of concentrated nitric acid. A yellow colour is produced with protein, turning pink or orange when the material is warmed with two drops of strong ammonia solution. Vegetable and man-made fibres do not contain protein.

448 *Flame Proofing*

Cut two strips, 10 cm × 2 cm, from the same piece of cotton material. Dissolve ½ g borax in 100 cm^3 water and bring to the boil. Soak one of the cotton strips in the boiling liquid for 1 minute; then remove with tongs, squeeze out as well as possible, and allow to dry naturally (or in an oven at 60°C.).

Hang the two strips over a horizontal glass rod, each about 2 cm above small, similar flames. Compare the times taken to catch fire.

449 *Water Proofing*

(a) Stretch fine nylon across the mouth of a jam jar, holding the fabric in position with a rubber band. Arrange i. Terylene, ii. water-proofed cotton, similarly. Drop water (pipette) from a height of about 15 cm on to each fabric and observe what happens.

Wash out the fabrics in detergent solution, squeeze (do not rinse) and dry; then repeat the test with falling drops of water.

(b) Stand a wax candle in turpentine or white spirit until you can see that some of the wax has dissolved. Immerse fabric in the solution and stir for two or three minutes, making sure that all of it is wetted. Allow to dry away from flames and then test as in Expt. 449 (a).

Nylon and Terylene are naturally water-repellant, and hence stain-resisting. Provided that they are washed carefully, they will retain these properties. Other fabrics can have a water-repellant finish applied, but this may be destroyed by washing so that sooner or later re-proofing may be necessary.

450 *Dyeing*

Immerse squares of cotton, linen, wool and real silk cloth in a hot solution of picric acid (about 20 g acid per half litre). Simmer for half an hour and then rinse the squares thoroughly in water. Observe that whilst the wool and silk are dyed, the cellulose materials fail to hold the colour.

Now soak squares of cotton and linen in 10 per cent alum solution, wring out and immerse in weak ammonia. Wash, and then repeat the mordanting process. Finally, immerse the washed, mordanted cloth in hot picric acid solution and show that it is now capable of holding the dye.

Remember that whilst picric acid solution is perfectly safe, the dry solid is explosive (Expt. 153, c).

451 *Strength of Fibres*

Set up the simple testing machine shown in the diagram: it consists of a wooden rod half a metre long, marked off in centimetres, pivoting on a wedge screwed down to a baseboard. There is a shallow cut across the rod 10 cm from one end, where it rests on the pivot, and a hook is screwed into the rod, underneath, 3 cm from the same end. Under this hook a 1-cm diameter hole is drilled in the baseboard. The baseboard is raised above the bench on two cross-pieces of wood.

Pass a loop of thread over the hook, push it through the hole in the baseboard and push a nail through the loop under the board; now fasten the loop whilst holding the lever horizontal. Take off the loop and cut a length of thick cardboard or wood so that the loop will just slip over it. Use this gauge to prepare loops of cotton, linen, silk, artificial silk, nylon, hair, thin string, etc.

Suspend a 1 kg weight by a loop of string from the long arm of the lever, near to the pivot, and fix one of the loops to be tested on the hook and through the hole as described above. Move the weight along the lever until the loop breaks. Using the "law of the lever" (Expt. 425), calculate the breaking strength of the test-loop. Repeat for the other test materials.

Remember that this experiment compares only the strength of the threads used; the strength depends upon the thickness of the threads as well as upon the nature of the materials. Examine threads of wool, silk, cotton, etc. under a lens; observe how the fibres are twisted together (spun).

Topics: Sources of textile materials (e.g. ramie, hemp, jute, sisal, mohair, cashmere, nylon, Orlon, Terylene). Spinning, weaving and dyeing. Reference to and extension of earlier work: bleaching (Expt. 231); stain removal (Expt. 96); insulating power (Expt. 155); heat absorption (Expt. 267); inflammability (Expt. 447 (b))—samples of wool, cotton and flannelette can be tested and the danger emphasized.

Structural Design

452 *Structures*

(a) Use 15-cm × 4-cm strips of newspaper. Fold two of them twice to make two strips, 15 cm × 1 cm, each four layers thick. Roll two more into 15-cm tubes by wrapping round a pencil, and make another pair into tubes of triangular section. In all cases the paper may be held in position by using tiny strips of gummed paper.

Place two similar books on the bench 10 cm apart, and lay the two folded strips across them about 2 cm apart. Rest a piece of tin or stout cardboard 5 cm square, centrally across the strips to form a platform. Load weights on the platform and so find the maximum load that the strips will carry.

Repeat the experiment, substituting first the cylindrical tubes and then the triangular tubes for the folded strips. (b) Bend two postcards into the shapes shown and hold the bottom edges in position on a board by putting drawing-pins in as stops. Pile coins on to the top of each "bridge" and so find out which is the stronger structure. (c) Use Meccano strips to make the shape shown; notice that the triangular shapes are firm under a shearing load, whereas the rectangular shape collapses.

Topics: Design of bridges (observation of types of arch). Structural framework in buildings in course of construction. Refer also to Chapter 21 ("Balance and Stability"). Spider's web.

Metals

Let pupils list common objects which are made of metal, stating alongside each what the metal is. Point out that some of the metals are mixtures (alloys) and refer to Expt. 235 (solder).

453 *Action of acids on metals*

Use equal parts concentrated nitric acid and water in a small glass or porcelain dish standing in a sink. Put an old copper coin into the acid. In seconds the dirty surface is removed, the liquid turns green (copper nitrate) and a brown gas (nitrogen peroxide) escapes. At once pour off the acid into a second dish (in the sink) and flood the coin in the first dish with water. Dry the coin and polish it with a dry cloth.

Refer to another example of similar action (Expt. 45).

The corrosion of metals in air and ways of preventing it have already been discussed (Expts. 33–36). Refer to ways of removing rust by mechanical means—emery, steel wool, abrasive powders, etc. Consider the tarnishing of metals and their staining by fruit juices and the modern use of stainless platings and rustless alloys.

454 *Polishing Metals*

Metals can be very highly polished, and the polished surface has the unmistakable appearance which we call "metallic lustre".

Provide each pupil with a useful task in the laboratory, polishing brass (taps), aluminium (pans), iron and steel (retort stands), etc. Discuss the best means of polishing each metal and compare results. Polish strips of

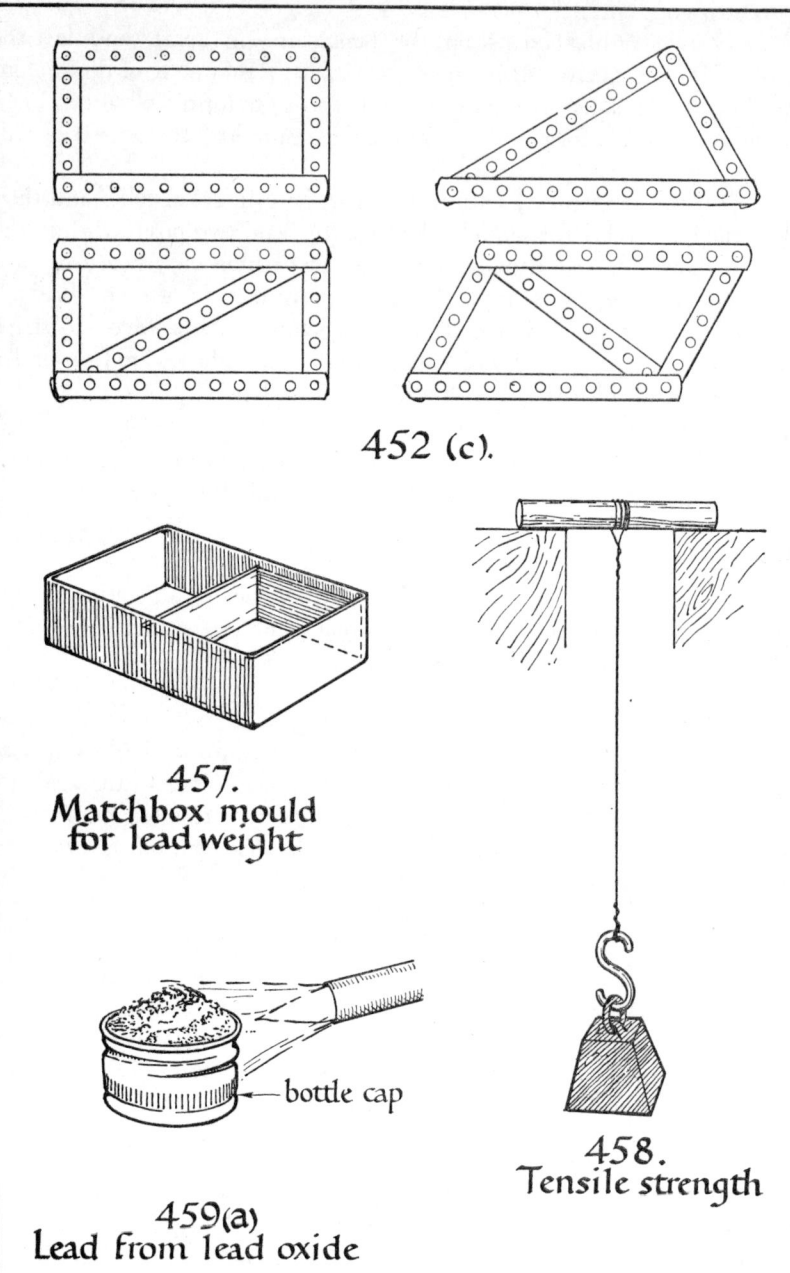

452 (c).

457.
Matchbox mould for lead weight

458.
Tensile strength

459(a)
Lead from lead oxide

bottle cap

various metals with metal polish and compare. Metal polish has both an acid and an abrasive action.

455 *Ductility*
Weigh a small coin on the simple lever balance (Expt. 160). Weigh out the same weight of gauge 36 (uncovered) copper wire. Uncoil the wire and measure its length.

Calculate the length per kilogram of wire.

Topics: Standard Wire Gauge (S.W.G.); uses of wires. Metal sheet (rolling mills); tinning and galvanizing; gold leaf.

456 *Gilding*
Pupils often make their own folders for notes and exercises. They may do the cover title in gold as follows. Outline the letters in pencil and then block in the letters with gum-arabic, being very careful to follow the lines exactly. Leave the gum until it is almost dry—just sticky enough to feel tacky to the fingers but not to stick to them. Lift a sheet of gold leaf carefully with a dry paint brush and lower it on to the gummed letters; avoid breathing on the work. Press the leaf down gently with a wad of cotton-wool. The gold will stick to the gummed parts and the overlapping leaf can easily be brushed away.

457 *Casting a Metal Weight (fusibility of metals)*
Use a match-box as a mould; a strip cut from the lid may be put across the tray at any point to get different sizes of mould. Melt up old lead or solder in a tin lid and allow it to cool until it is beginning to solidify; then pour it at once into the mould (which may stand in a tray of sand), lifting the lid with tongs or pincers. If time is short, cool the cast block in water. It may be used in the laboratory as a weight: a hole for suspension can be made with a matchstick before the metal solidifies in the mould.

458 *Tensile Strength*
Use in turn steel wire and other wires of the same gauge (e.g. 36). Wrap one end of the wire several times round a strong bar (iron gas pipe) and fasten by twisting. Wrap the other end of the wire similarly round an iron meat-hook. There may be half a metre or more of wire between the bar and the hook (the more the better), but the bar should be laid horizontally across two supports so that the wire and hook hang down to within a short distance of the floor. Hang weights from the hook and determine the weight which just breaks the wire.

The diameter of the wire may be obtained by using a micrometer screw gauge or from tables, and the breaking load should be calculated in g per square cm. The rapid elongation of copper wire after the elastic limit has been passed will be apparent in this experiment. See also p. 346.

Topics: Refer to the elasticity of metals (Expts. 214, 411, 412); their expansion and contraction (Expts. 28, 29); their power of conducting heat (Expts. 260–262) and electricity (Expt. 272). Discuss uses of metals which illustrate the various characteristics. Alloys for special purposes.

How Metals are Obtained from Ores

459 (a) *Lead from Litharge*
Heat litharge (PbO) or red lead Pb_3O_4) mixed with powdered charcoal in a small crucible or metal bottle cap, stirring with a wood splint. Holding the crucible in tongs, pour the product into water; silvery metallic lead can be seen.

459 (b) *Iron from Haematite*
Use the crushed ore or use ferric oxide powder. Mix it with twice its bulk of powdered coke or charcoal and fill a fireclay crucible with the mixture. Embed the crucible in the middle of a forge fire (Metalwork shop) and keep the fire well blown for half an hour. The iron will be found at the bottom of the crucible as a grey mass; test it with dilute hydrochloric acid and show that it liberates hydrogen from the acid.

Topics: Production of copper (Expt. 292) and of aluminium by electrolysis. Blast-furnace. Manufacture of steel from iron.

Preparation and Identification of Metal Salts

Refer to Expt. 123 (preparation of common salt by neutralization); and to Expt. 161 (a) (identification of iron).

460 *The "Vitriols"*
Discuss "oil of Vitriol" and its importance in industry. Refer to the notes following Expt. 122.

(a) Epsom Salt from Magnesium Metal: Use not more than 10 cm³ of dilute sulphuric acid ("normal" strength is suitable; about 25 cm³ concentrated acid added very cautiously to a litre of water). Put the acid in a small dish and add short lengths of magnesium ribbon until no more will dissolve. Filter, and allow the clear solution to cool. Set the liquid aside; long, colourless crystals of magnesium sulphate form. Wash one with water and then taste it.

The experiment is expensive of material, but only one or two groups of pupils need do it; all may taste the product.

(b) White Vitriol: Use about 25 cm³ of dilute sulphuric acid, add granulated zinc in small quantities, and warm when the action begins to slow down. When no more metal dissolves, filter and crystallize as with Epsom salts. Zinc sulphate is poisonous.

(c) Green Vitriol: Repeat Expt. 459 (b) using clean iron strip, iron wire or nails, etc. DO NOT do more than gently warm the liquid; otherwise, oxidation will occur (liquid turns brown).

461 Copper Sulphate from Copper Oxide

Add black copper oxide little by little to dilute sulphuric acid in a dish; warm gently. When no more solid dissolves, filter and cool. Evaporate the solution slightly if crystals fail to appear; then cool again.

The gas given off in the previous experiment was hydrogen. Why is hydrogen *not* evolved when copper oxide is used?

Pupils may "grow" crystals of copper sulphate (or of alum, etc.) by selecting a well formed crystal, immersing it in cold saturated solution and setting it aside in a cool cupboard. Temperature fluctuations should be avoided, and the crystal should be turned over daily; only cold saturated solution should be added in topping up. When the crystal is big enough it may be hung in the solution from a thread.

462 Lead Iodide from Lead Nitrate

Use dilute solutions of lead nitrate and potassium iodide. Take a few cubic centimetres of each in separate test-tubes; then mix the solutions together. Observe the dense yellow precipitate of the insoluble lead iodide. The salt is soluble in hot water; pour a little of the yellow suspension into a test-tube, add water and heat to boiling—the solid dissolves to give a colourless solution. On cooling (under tap), beautiful yellow spangles form.

463 (a) *Analysis for Lead*

Test solder, lead piping, lead shot, the sheathing of an electric cable, dry white paint, etc. Warm scrapings with dilute nitric acid, cool and add potassium iodide solution. A yellow precipitate indicates the presence of lead in the original material.

463 (b) *Analysis for Copper*

Use brass, German silver, a drawing pin, etc. Dissolve a little by treatment with warm dilute nitric acid, pour off some of the liquid into a clean tube and add excess of ammonia solution; a blue colour indicates copper.

A test for iron has been given in Expt. 161 (a). Use it to identify iron in a pen-nib, tinplate, black ink, etc. Nitric acid may be used. A test for potassium is given in Expt. 102 (b).

Topics: Chemical compounds in everyday life, e.g. as fertilizers, pigments and dyes, explosives, drugs. The importance of the analytical chemist (e.g. Public Analyst). Living matter built from very complex compounds. A simple idea of the distinction between elements, compounds and mixtures (no formal list of properties); reference to Expt. 150. Many non-metallic elements have been handled in the experiments described earlier—e.g. carbon, iodine, sulphur and the gases oxygen, nitrogen, hydrogen and chlorine.

Chapter Twenty-Three
Machines and Engines

Keeping up-to-date

The problem of keeping up-to-date has a special urgency for the science teacher because of the extraordinary growth of knowledge in scientific fields. Not only must he try to keep the content of his lessons abreast of modern ideas and essay a convincing answer to the questions of pupils growing up in a scientific age; he must also be ever ready to cash in on current interest, and to exploit the value of the apt reference and the up-to-the-minute example. This is not to say that the teacher should never confess ignorance: the need to walk humbly is nowhere more evident than in the domain of modern science. But he should be able to direct attention to possible sources of information and to make use of apparatus and techniques designed and developed in recent years to increase the effectiveness of science teaching.

Two things seem essential. First, the teacher's continuing and developing interest in his particular branch of science, so that his scholarship and craftsmanship are maintained. Second, a lively awareness of the main lines of progress in other fields.

Membership of the Association of Science Education is undoubtedly the best single means of keeping in touch with developments in science teaching at school level. The Association (A.S.E.), which traces its origins to the foundation of the Association of Public Schools Science Masters in 1901, was formed in 1963 by a union between the Science Masters' Association and the Association of Women Science Teachers. Membership is open to science teachers in schools of all kinds. Students in University Departments of Education and in Colleges of Education are eligible for Associateship. Enquiries should be adddessed to the General Secretary at College Lane, Hatfield, Hertfordshire.

The Association's journal, *The School Science Review*, contains major articles of interest to science teachers, but no less valuable are the copious notes, correspondence and descriptions of practical work. From time to time selected experiments and techniques from the Review are published in the well-known series of Science Masters' Books; and some of the articles of most general interest have been reprinted as the *Modern Science Memoirs*. A.S.E. also publishes, through John Murray, *Science Teaching Techniques*, a series of booklets containing practical information particularly useful to teachers of our ordinary pupils. The Bulletin of the A.S.E., *Education in Science*, aims to keep members abreast of activities in the main Association and in the regional Branches. At the famous Annual Meetings and at Branch meetings teachers find a forum for their ideas and opportunities to share experiences with fellow practitioners.

The School Natural Science Society, formerly the School Nature Study Union (General Secretary): Miss M. J. Sellers, 2 Bramley Mansions, Berrylands Road, Surbiton, Surrey), and the National Rural Studies Association (General Secretary: R. F. Morgan, Chorley College of Education, Union Street, Chorley, Lancs.) are of particular help to teachers of nature study in its many aspects. The journal of the S.N.S.S. is *Natural Science in Schools*, occasional articles from which are reissued as the *Natural Science Leaflets*. *Countryside*, the magazine of the British Naturalists' Association, is addressed to both adults and young people. *Wildlife and the Countryside* is a monthly magazine written specially for use in schools and contains many suggestions for the active participation of teachers and pupils.

Education in Chemistry, Physics Education and *The Journal of Biological Education* are recently established magazines with a somewhat more specialized content, in which, nevertheless, the teacher of the ordinary pupil may often discover material of interest to him.

Science Progress, Endeavor (published by I.C.I. Ltd.), *New Scientist* and *The Scientific American* are magazines which review the progress of science in ways which the teacher may often find helpful. In 1966 *Science Journal* incorporated *Discovery*; back numbers of both are still a mine of information. A visit to the reading room of a public library is likely to reveal a range of general magazines and newspapers from which up-to-date lesson material may be culled. The contributions by the science correspondents of papers such as *The Times, The Guardian* and *The Daily Telegraph* are noteworthy. *The Listener* prints some of the best broadcast talks: here may be found articles on the history of science (often on the occasion of some anniversary), on developments in pure and applied science (e.g. astronomy, atomic energy, communications, world food supply) and on the philosophy of science. It is not, of course, implied that any one teacher should attempt to read all these journals, but even occasional reference to some of them will keep a teacher's thinking alive. When he comes to answer a question or to argue a problem he will do so in the light of ideas which he could not perhaps expound in detail but which condition his approach. The Esso Petroleum Company now produce, and circulate free, a series of *Science abstracts* which should be of further help to the teacher.

Reference has been made in earlier chapters to the work and publications of the Schools Council. A useful summary is provided in the booklet *The First Three Years* (H.M.S.O., 1968). The Schools Council *Integrated Science Project* (S.C.I.S.P.) is intended for 13–16 year old pupils and aims at strong links with the social sciences, geography, history and technology. Many teachers will now be acquainted with the invaluable texts, teachers' guides and source books of the Nuffield Foundation. *Combined Science, The Junior Science Teacher's Guides* and the source books *Animals and Plants* and *Apparatus* (all published by Collins) have particular relevance to the ability ranges with which the present book is concerned.

Much valuable material is available from the Stationery Office bookshops. It includes publications from the following sources:
(a) Ministry of Agriculture and Fisheries.
    e.g. *Manual of Nutrition*; *Wild Birds and the Land*; *Identification of Common Water Weeds*.
(b) Department of Education and Science
    (formerly Ministry of Education).
    e.g. *Science in Secondary Schools* (1960); Reports on Education, No. 46, *Changing School Science and Technology*.
(c) British Museum (Natural History).
    e.g. *History of the Primates: Succession of Life through Geological Time*; several booklets on fossil animals, such as *Dinosaurs*; *Natural History of Snakes*.
(d) The Science Museum.
    e.g. *Time Measurement*; series of Illustrated Booklets, including *Ship Models*, *Aeronautics*, *Making Fire*, *Cameras*, etc.
(e) U.N.E.S.C.O.
    e.g. Booklets on the race question in relation to modern science, such as *Race and Biology*, *Racial Myths*, etc.

No attempt is made here to discuss the enormous range of books, constantly being enlarged, on the various branches of science. Teachers will, however, find great help in selecting their reading if they turn to the book review columns of many of the journals already cited. Meanwhile, we draw attention to a small number of outstanding volumes dealing with the methods and techniques of science teaching. Among these, Westaway's *Science Teaching* (1929) is a classic. The A.S.E. Handbook *Teaching Science at the Secondary Stage* replaces the earlier *Secondary Modern Science Teaching*. Tweddles's *Science Teacher's Handbook* (Harrap) and the U.N.E.S.C.O. *Source Book for Science Teaching* are still very useful. Among American books, *The Teaching of Science in the Elementary School*, by Lewis and Potter (Prentice-Hall), 1961 is of considerable interest for its up-to-date content.

The Guinness Awards for Science Teachers in Training and for Science Teachers in Service are offered annually for description of work of a practical nature. Results are published in the magazine *The Science Teacher* and prizes range up to £250 each. Imperial Chemical Industries Limited offer Endeavour Prizes, each year totalling more than £200, for essays on scientific subjects. The competition is run in collaboration with the British Association; pupils may enter, and ages are taken into account. University College, London, in association with Shell, has instituted the Shell Chemistry Teachers Fellowship to enable experienced teachers in secondary schools to renew their acquaintance with developments in research and teaching and to see something of modern applications of chemistry. The Fellowship carries a stipend of £2000 and is tenable at University College for one year. Further information may be obtained from the Secretary, Shell Grants Committee, Shell Centre, London, S.E.1.

Science Fairs, organized by the British Association in collaboration with *The Sunday Times*, are staged in various centres up and down the country for the encouragement of science projects in schools. A visit to one of these exhibitions of practical work, like a visit to the Members' Exhibition at the A.S.E. Annual Conference, can scarcely fail to suggest new possibilities to the teacher. The British Association also organizes, through its area committees, a Science Lecture Service to schools which can provide lecturers on almost every conceivable topic (The British Association for the Advancement of Science, Lecture Service, 3 Sanctuary Buildings, 20 Great Smith Street, London, S.W.1.).

The Department of Education and Science publishes each year its *Programme of Short Courses* for teachers, which invariably includes many courses for teachers of science. Applications should be made through the teacher's local education authority, from whom the programme may be obtained. Vacation courses for teachers are organized also by universities, colleges and institutes of education and by teachers' associations. The Educational Development Association (General Secretary: A. Zimmerman, 8 Windmill Gardens, Enfield, Middlesex) encourages practical methods of teaching, through its long-established summer schools and through its local branches. Curriculum development centres, recently established in many towns, present valuable opportunities for men and women interested in the development of science subjects. Radio and television series which present aspects of science to the layman are usually excellent in presentation and authority and can offer much to teachers.

For inexperienced teachers a course in the simple laboratory arts is well worth undertaking; such courses are available at the larger technical colleges. But the teacher who adopts practical work by the pupils as the basis of his method is not likely to lag far behind in his laboratory techniques. He will constantly find opportunities to make and mend and to devise and adapt. New twists to old ideas will suggest themselves, with the need to experiment and to improve. There can be nothing better than the day-to-day practice of a craft for the development of skill and dexterity.

SI Units of Force, Energy and Work
SI, the International System of Units in science, has been recommended for all British scientific publications. A booklet, *SI Units, Signs, Symbols and Abbreviations* was published by the Association for Science Education in 1969 and reprinted with amendments in 1970.

SI employs the newton (N) as the universal unit of force. 1 newton is the force required to give a mass of 1 kilogramme an acceleration of 1 metre per second per second. The gravitational pull of the Earth is sufficient to give 1 kilogramme mass an acceleration of about 9.8 m s^{-2} and is thus equal to about 9.8 newtons. That pull we call the weight of the mass on Earth:

1 kg weight (on Earth) = 9.8 newtons

Even on the Earth the gravitational pull is different (very slightly) at different places on the surface; and on the Moon, for example, the gravitational pull on 1 kg (mass) is only about 1.6 newtons:

1 kg weight (on the Moon) = 1.6 newtons

Evidently the "weight" of a body—defined as the gravitational pull upon it—is far from being a universal constant; whereas the newton is, by definition, "the same size of force everywhere".

Many teachers, anxious to fall into line with SI, will seek ways of beginning the teaching of force in terms of the newton, and they will find support in the Combined Science scheme of the Nuffield Teaching Project. On the other hand, the Nuffield Physics (O-level) course reserves the general use of the newton to the fourth year, preferring gravitational units in the earlier stages. For the Ordinary Pupil we believe that gravitational units offer distinct advantages, yet pose no bar to the later introduction of the newton.

Much the same is true of the units of energy and work—both of which are the joule in SI. The joule is the work done (energy dissipated) when a force of 1 newton acts through 1 metre:

1 joule = 1 newton-metre

Thus 1 kg (weight)-metre (on Earth) = 9.8 joules.

Uses of Pulleys
Metal pulleys such as are sold in the cheap stores for use with clothes-lines and airing-racks are excellent for laboratory work.

464 *Home-made Pulleys*
(a) Cotton-reel Pulley: The axle is one half of a large nail and the suspension is formed from gauge 16 copper wire (see diagram). (b) More Efficient

Pulley: Plug the hole in a cotton reel with a length of pencil, after removing the lead either by soaking in water or by drilling. Cut off a suitable length of knitting-needle for the axle, and bend up a 15-cm length of crate banding strip for the support. Assemble with a washer at each end of the reel. (c) Large Pulley: Cut out two 15-cm squares of plywood, mark the diagonals and describe a circle on each piece of wood using the crossing point of the diagonals as centre: the diameter should be that of an available floor-polish tin (about 10 cm). Drill a hole at the centre of each sheet of wood large enough to take a large (c. 15 cm) nail. Set the tin between the sheets, centred exactly on the marked circles, to form a sandwich. Grip the sandwich in a vice, drill through the tin at the centre and pass the nail through to ensure that the sandwich does not slip. Now drill three more holes through the sandwich, symmetrically spaced round the centre and about 5 cm from it. Pass bolts through these holes and fit nuts to hold the tin and wood sheets together. The corners of the wood squares may be marked off and cut away; reasonable care is required so that the balance of the pulley is not upset, for the pulley must run smoothly on its axle. Suspend the pulley by a stiff wire loop as shown; with strong wire it will operate under heavy loads.

465 Hoisting Pulley

Hang the large pulley (Expt. 464, c) from a hook some distance above the floor (e.g. in the edge of a shelf). Pass a cord over it and hang a can or small bucket from each end of the cord; one can should hang just below the pulley when the other is at floor level. Use the arrangement to move a heap of stones from shelf to floor.

Replace one bucket by a spring balance. Put successively increasing weights (1, 2, 3 ... kg) in the remaining bucket and observe the pull on the balance required to lift each weight. In recording results add the weight of the bucket in with the "load" in each case; notice that the "effort" still exceeds the load somewhat.

Discuss cases in which a fixed pulley can be used with advantage: sash-windows, clothes-airers (Housecrafts room or kitchen), housebuilding, etc.

466 Raising Heavy Weights with Small Effort
(a) Suspend a single pulley by a cord from two balances as shown. Compare the reading of each balance with the total load (include the weight of the pulley in the load). (b) Set up the two-pulley tackle shown. Use the same load as in (a) and observe the two balance readings: (i) when the system is at rest, (ii) when the load is being raised slowly. Set up a ruler behind the load and another behind the effort; measure the distance the effort moves whilst the load rises 5 cm. (c) Using the same apparatus, vary the load and tabulate the effort required to maintain steady movement of

MACHINES AND ENGINES 397

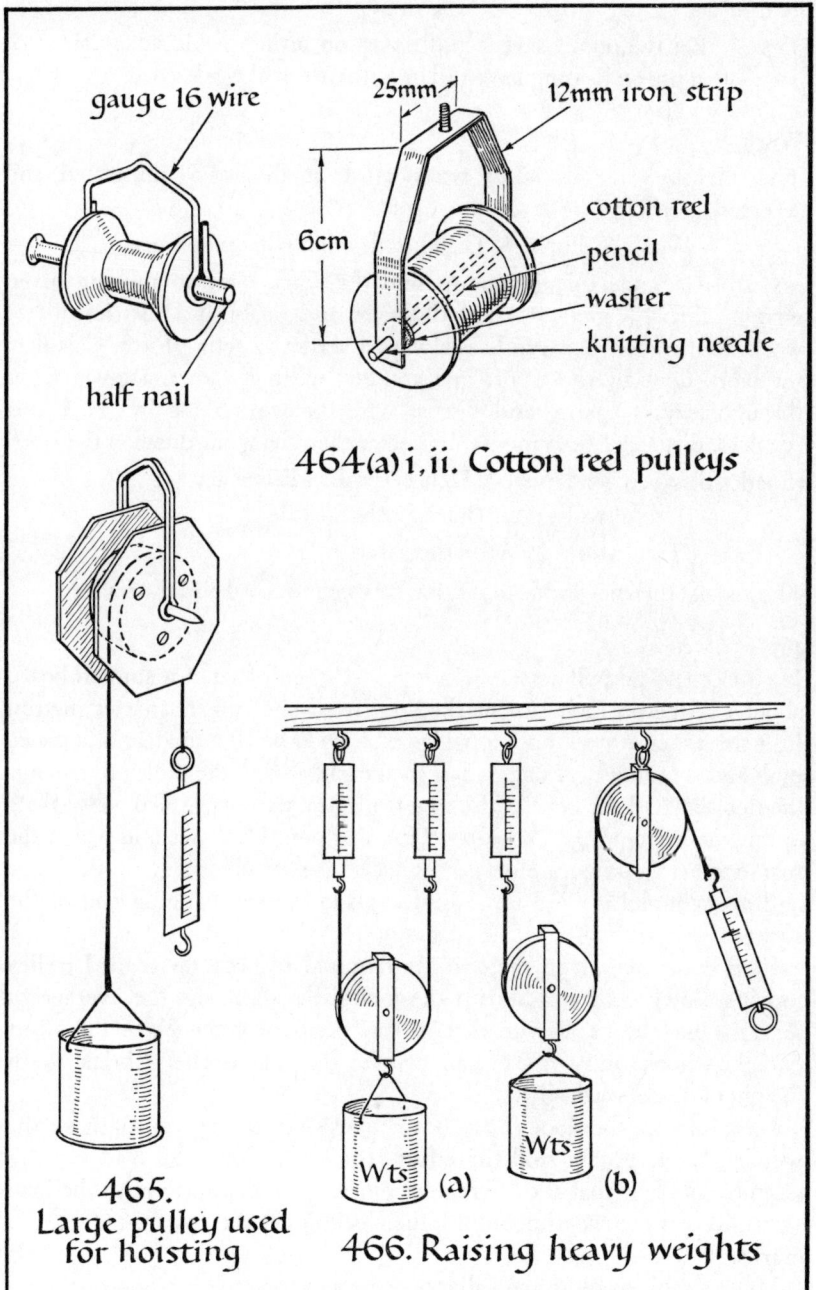

464(a) i, ii. Cotton reel pulleys

465. Large pulley used for hoisting

466. Raising heavy weights

each load. Calculate the mechanical advantage from each value of load/effort.

Topics: Let the pupils sketch and report on lifting tackle which they see in use on loading bays and in constructional work, etc.

Work

The scientist's definition of work must be discussed, illustrated and accepted:

Work = Force × Distance through which force acts.

Perform simple calculations to find the work done in moving given weights through given vertical distances and establish a metric unit of work. Remember that weight is always a vertically acting force. Calculate the work done by the Effort in Expt. 465 when it moves a given Load through (say) 1 metre, and discuss why the work done by the Effort (Effort × distance Effort moves) is greater than the work done on the Load (Load × distance Load moves). Hence, speak of Efficiency as:

$$\frac{\text{Useful work done (moving the Load)}}{\text{Total work done (by the Effort)}} \times 100\%.$$

The loss of efficiency is due to friction between the cord and the pulley.

467 Inclined Plane

Fix a clothes-line pulley (screw-in type) to an end face of a smooth board about 2½ metres long and marked out from one end in quarter metres. Rest the 2 metre mark on a top edge of a wood block a quarter of a metre high and standing near one end of the bench, so that the pulley overhangs the floor beyond the bench. Use as a trolley either a well-oiled roller-skate or one made from Meccano parts. Tie a brick on the trolley and weigh the two together (in kilogrammes). Pass a string from the trolley up the plane and over the pulley, and tie a light hook to the free-hanging end of the string.

Find what weight on the hook is required to keep the loaded trolley moving slowly and steadily up the inclined plane; take the average of several observations. Notice that in this position of the plane the effort (weight + hook) must move 2 m to raise the load (trolley + brick) ¼ m (height of block) vertically.

Now increase the slope of the board by resting the 1¾ m mark on the wooden block. Again find the effort required to keep the load moving steadily. Observe that the effort now moves only 1¾ m to raise the load ¼ m. Repeat the experiment with the block under the 1½ m, 1¼ m, . . . marks.

Make a table to show the value of the effort for each position of the inclined plane, and the work done in each case by the effort in raising the

MACHINES AND ENGINES 399

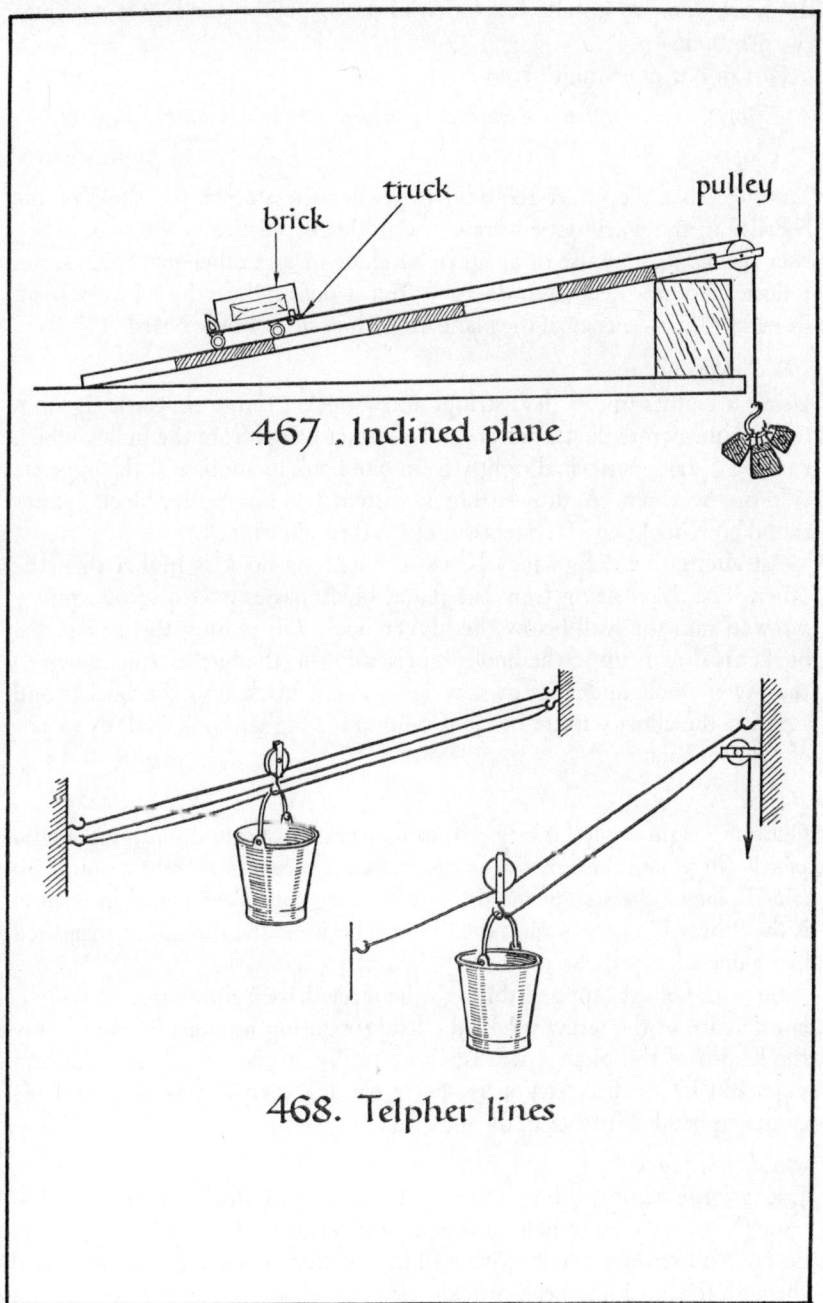

467. Inclined plane

468. Telpher lines

load through $\tfrac{1}{4}$ m (measured vertically). If the total load is 4 kg, then the work done on it in each position of the inclined plane is $4 \times \tfrac{1}{4}$ kg-m ($= 9\cdot 8$ joules).

Part of our table might read:

Effort	*Distance moved by effort*	*Work done by effort*
1 kg	$1\tfrac{1}{4}$ m	$1 \times 1\tfrac{1}{4}$ kg-m

Notice that the effort required is greater the steeper the slope of the board; but the work done to raise the trolley is practically the same whatever the slope. The use of an inclined plane or any other machine cannot reduce the work needed to do a job; but it does reduce the effort needed. Calculate the efficiency of the plane for each position of the board.

468 *Telpher Line*

Using a clothes-line pulley, string, and a bucket (large tin-can), rig up a telpher line across the laboratory. The bucket hangs from the pulley which runs on a string stretched tightly from one hook to another at the opposite side of the room. A draw-string is fastened to the pulley-block, passes round both hooks and is fastened again to the pulley-block.

An alternative design may be used when one hook is higher than the other. The draw-string from the pulley-block passes over a second pulley screwed into the wall below the higher hook. On pulling this string, the bucket is drawn up to the hook; on releasing it, the bucket runs down to the lower hook under its own weight. Put a brick into the bucket and measure the effort required to pull it up to the higher hook (pull by means of a spring balance).

469 *Screw*

Cut out a right-angled triangle from a piece of paper and wrap it round a pencil (Fig. 469); the model suggests that a screw is merely a spiral inclined plane. The side of the triangle running round the pencil in a spiral is the "thread" of the screw; the distance between the threads as measured along one edge of the screw is the "pitch".

Since the effort (applied through the screwdriver) moves round the circumference of the screw whilst the load (opposing motion) is moved only the length of the pitch, there is, theoretically, a great mechanical advantage. But in practice friction is very great and increases as the screw becomes embedded further in the material.

470 *Lifting-jack*

Use a large carriage bolt (c. 20 cm long) and drill a hole, just big enough to take the bolt, through the centre of a block of wood 20 cm × 20 cm × 5 cm, counter-sinking so that when the bolt is passed through the block the head is flush with the wood surface. Screw a nut on the bolt tight down to the wood. Now screw on a second nut, followed by a

MACHINES AND ENGINES 401

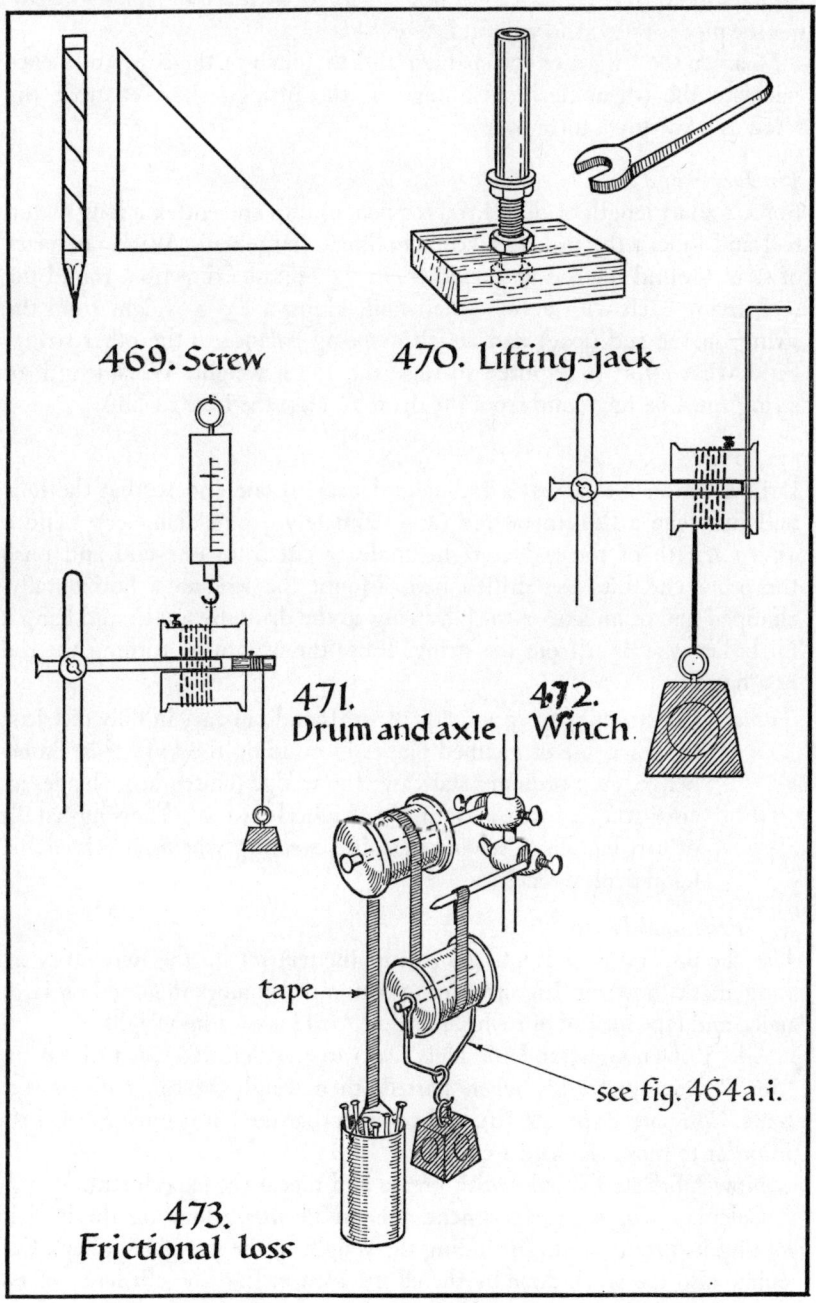

469. Screw 470. Lifting-jack

471. Drum and axle 472. Winch

tape

see fig. 464a.i.

473. Frictional loss

stout washer and a 12-cm length of iron piping just wide enough to slip over the bolt. When the second nut is turned with a long-handled spanner the pipe is raised and will lift heavy loads.

Measure the length of the spanner and the pitch of the bolt, and hence calculate the (theoretical) advantage of the lifting-jack. Note that the screw is evidently a form of lever.

471 *Drum and Axle*

Force a short length of dowel rod (or pencil) into one end of a long cotton reel and mount the reel on a horizontal axle (large nail). Wind one piece of string round the rod and another, in the opposite direction, round the reel, fixing each with a very small nail. Hang a 100 g weight from the string on the rod (axle) and attach a spring balance to the other string. Find what effort is required to raise the 100 g weight. What length of string must be unwound from the drum to raise the load 10 cm?

472 *Winch*

Drill a cotton reel across a radius and near to one end so that the hole will just take a thin metal rod (approximately 3 mm diameter). Bend a 15-cm length of the rod at right angles 3 cm from one end and push the other end into the drilled hole. Mount the reel on a horizontally-clamped nail as an axle. Attach a string to the drum by a tack and hang a fairly heavy weight from the string. Raise the weight by turning the rod as a handle.

Topics: Construction of easy-gradient roads and railways in hilly districts; supposed use of inclined planes in building the Pyramids, Stonehenge, etc.; ordinary staircase; the wedge (chisel, knife-blade, incisor teeth); further examples of wheel and axle (starting-handle of car, handle of sewing-machine, steering wheel, bicycle crank, hand-drill, wrench).

473 *Frictional Loss*

Use the apparatus of Expt. 466 (b); or (better) set up the two-pulley arrangement shown in Fig. 473, using cotton-reel pulleys mounted on large nails, and tape instead of string. For the "load" use a 1 kg weight.

Add just enough sand (or nails, etc.) to the "effort" can to keep the "load" moving steadily when started; then weigh the can with its contents. Compare Expt. 466 (b), and confirm that the effort must move 2 cm in order to move the load 1 cm.

Now lubricate the axles with grease and repeat the experiment.

Calculate, for each experiment, the useful work done on the load in raising it through 1 cm (including the weight of the movable pulley). Calculate also the work done by the effort. Hence, find the efficiency of the mechanism before and after lubrication.

Specimen results are set out below:
Before greasing:
- Load = 470 g   Distance moved = 1 cm
- Work done on load = 470 × 1 g-cm units
- Effort = 342 g   Distance moved = 2 cm
- Work done by effort = 342 × 2 g-cm units

$$\text{Efficiency} = 100 \times \frac{\text{Useful work done}}{\text{Total work supplied}} = 100 \times \frac{470}{684} = 69\%$$

After greasing: $\text{Efficiency} = 100 \times \dfrac{470}{620} = 76\%$

Thus, greasing has considerably reduced frictional losses.

Horse-power

In spite of metrication and the introduction of SI units the term "horse-power" is likely to continue in use. In any case it is part of the history of engineering. On both counts it should be explained to pupils. When Matthew Boulton and James Watt were marketing their new steam engines they might often be asked "How many horses will one of your engines replace?" It is said that an English brewer drove a horse to exhaustion in attempting to find out; but Watt's own experiments with a farm-horse raising a load in a mine shaft led him to propose "1 horse-power" as the work needed to lift 550 lbs. vertically at the rate of 1 foot per second. Thus, a 1 h.p. engine could (theoretically) lift about 1 cwt through 5 ft in 1 second.

474 *Climbing Power*
Measure the vertical height of a staircase and the time taken by a pupil to run upstairs at top speed; if possible, allow a flying start and use a stop-watch. Weigh the pupil on the school weighing machine.

Results from an actual experiment are given below:

Weight of pupil	= 112 lb
Time taken	= 5 secs
Height of stairs	= 12 ft
Work done in 5 secs	= 12 × 112 ft-lb
	= 1,340 ft-lb
Work per second	= 268 ft-lb
Horse-power developed	= 268/550 = 0·5 h.p.

0·5 h.p. is well above the average horse-power developed by a man working continuously, and is likely to be achieved even in the experiment described only when the staircase is a short one.

475 *Pulling Power*
Attach a light tow-rope to the steering pillar of a bicycle through a spring

balance. Let one pupil pull another (who rides the cycle without pedalling) along a smooth, level road at a normal speed of about 10 miles per hour. When the machine is moving steadily let other pupils time the cycle over a measured distance (say 50 yards). An example of the kind of result to be expected is given:

Pull on balance (approx.)	= 4 lb
Time taken	= 11 secs
Distance covered	= 150 ft
Work done in 11 secs	= 150 × 4 ft-lb
	= 600 ft-lb
Work per second	= 55 ft-lb
Horse-power developed	= 55/550 = 1/10th h.p.

To drive the machine at the same speed the cyclist would have to work a little harder than this, because some of his effort is lost as friction on the chain and pedals.

Topics: Energy defined as capacity for doing work. Examples of energy sources and storers; conversion of one form of energy to another; energy chains; Sun as ultimate source.

476 *Toy Windmill*

Cut out a 10-cm square of paper, mark the diagonals, draw a 2-cm radius circle at the centre of the paper and cut inwards along the diagonals to this circle. Bend alternate corners of paper over and inwards so that they overlap slightly at the centre of the circle. Gum these corners down where they overlap and pass a pin through the centre of the windmill to act as an axle. Hold the pin in the fingers or mount it on a stick. Run with the windmill facing forward; it revolves at high speed. (See Expt. 494 for conversion of windmill to helicopter.)

477 *Waterwheel*

Use a surgical-tape spool for the wheel. Punch six evenly spaced slits in the central ring of metal (plug the centre hole with dowel rod, and use a screwdriver blade as a punch). Cut six vanes to the shape shown (i) and of a size to fit the wheel. The small lugs are to pass through the slits in the central ring, so holding the vanes firmly (ii). Bend the top edge of each vane over at right angles where it sticks out beyond the wheel, and then bend the corners over the edges of the wheel and solder them down. Drill a hole centrally through the wooden plug and fix a round nail or a Meccano rod through it as an axle (iii). Mount the wheel over a sink. A mill "race" may be contrived if desired.

478 *Pelton Wheel (water turbine)*

The construction should be clear from the drawings. Small wooden chocks tacked on to the baseboard keep an inverted jam jar in position;

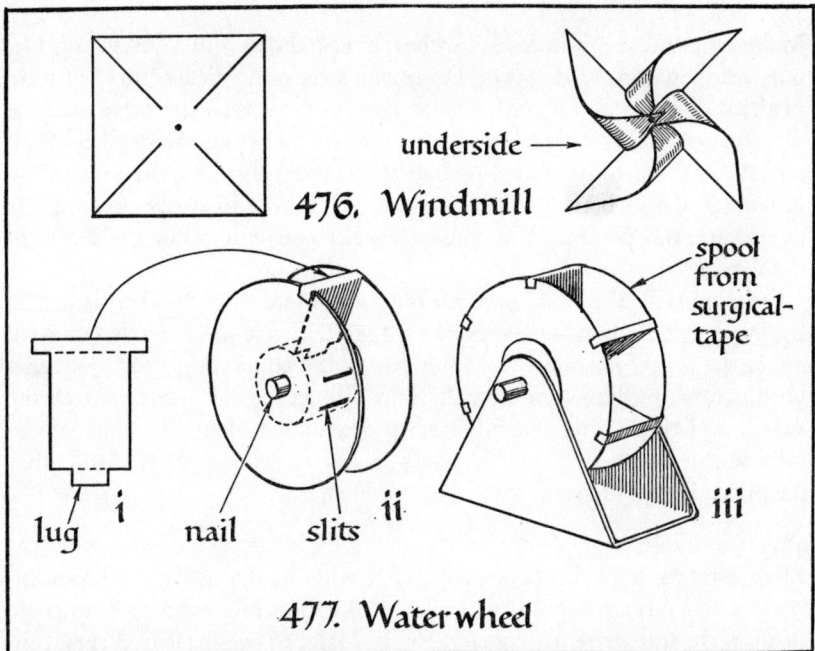

476. Windmill

477. Waterwheel

this cover prevents water from splashing outwards. A glass tube jet passes up through a hole in the board and through this water is directed at the vanes. Spent water leaves via a hole in the bearing-plate and baseboard. In bending the vanes a suitable wooden "former" (e.g. dowel rod) should be used.

Topics: Modern windmills (e.g. for pumping water). Use of the water turbine in hydro-electric power stations.

The Steam Engine

The social and economic history of England during the eighteenth and nineteenth centuries was profoundly affected by the discoveries of Newcomen, Watt, Stephenson and their associates. Unlike the story of the conquest of disease germs or of the development of flying, the principal discoveries were almost all British. But there is the same lesson to be learned: the discoveries made by one man are based on the discoveries of his predecessors.

Study the reciprocating engine by means of a model engine in action. Notice the boiler, safety valve and steam whistle (if one is fitted). Observe the piston working in the end of the cylinder, the connecting rod and crank which convert the longitudinal movement of the piston into a rotary movement, and the crank shaft which carries the flywheel and driving wheel.

479 Slide-valve Action

Make a flat model from thick cardboard tacked down to a baseboard. Details are shown in the diagram. Dimensions are not critical until the fitting of the slide-valve and its operating rod is reached; then the valve must be placed at one of its extreme positions, the rod laid from the flywheel to it, and the position for the pivoting bolt marked. At the same time the piston must be half-way between the top and the bottom of its stroke, making the connecting-rod pivoting bolt come vertically above or below the centre of the flywheel.

Small nuts and bolts are used for the connections. The flywheel is turned by hand to demonstrate the cycle of operations; it has no axle (so as to avoid the need for cranks from the axle to the connecting rods) but turns within four guiding tacks. Small tacks also guide the movement of the valve; and thin strips of cardboard, tacked down along the sides of the cylinder so as to overlap the edges of the piston slightly ensure that the piston is kept in position.

480 Steam Turbine

Here rotary motion is obtained directly, without the use of reciprocating parts. Use a large syrup tin as a boiler. Make the wheel from an 8-cm circle of tin-plate and scribe a 5-cm circle on it. Make 16 evenly spaced cuts from circumference to inner circle and twist each vane so formed through 45°. Punch a hole with a thin nail through the centre of the wheel, and solder half a knitting needle through it as an axle, leaving half an inch projecting one one side. Punch two similar holes along a diameter of the boiler lid from the underside, each 1 cm from the rim. As bottom bearing, use a nail-made dent in the middle of the lid; the top bearing is a small hole in a tin strip, soldered or wired to the boiler.

Put a little water in the boiler and heat it until steam issues freely from the two jets. The jets strike the turbine blades and the wheel revolves at high speed.

Topics: Steam locomotives. Use of steam turbines in ships and in power stations.

Internal-combustion Engines

Refer to Expt. 254 (b) on the explosion of a gas/air mixture; use it to introduce the idea of the explosion of petrol vapour with air in a car cylinder.

Refer to Expt. 319 for the action of a sparking plug; outline the ignition system of a motor-car.

Refer to Expt. 495 on the lifting power of a stream of air. Use a scent spray, or the spray supplied with certain liquid insecticides, to learn how petrol is vaporized and mixed with air in the carburettor. Use a diagram or a film to study the action of the car accelerator pedal and of the choke.

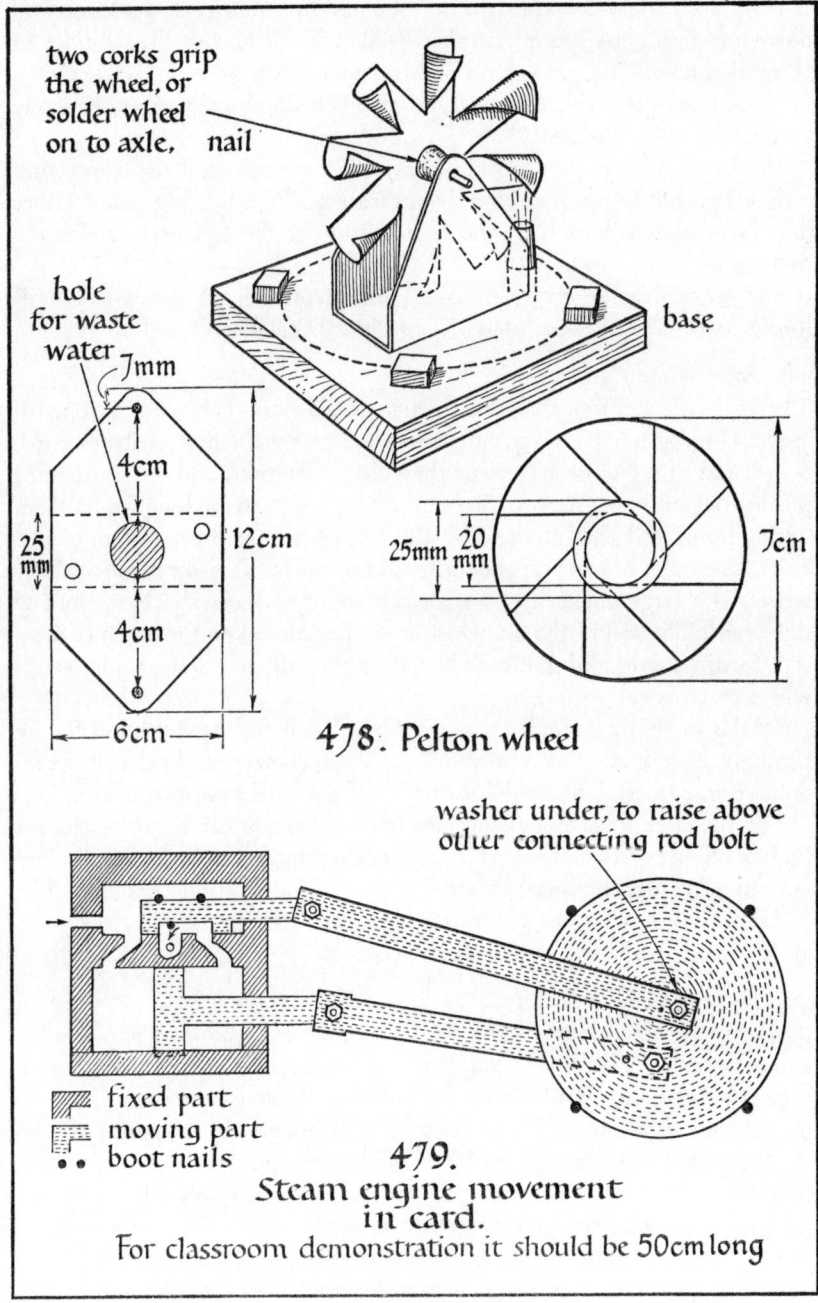

478. Pelton wheel

479. Steam engine movement in card.
For classroom demonstration it should be 50cm long

481 *Petrol-engine Model*

A cork, with a wire loop pushed into the middle of one end, works up and down inside a glass specimen tube. Rubber bands anchor the cylinder to a wooden base. The connecting rod is a safety pin, and the flywheel is a circle of thick plywood. The flywheel axle is a wood screw; another screw serves as the crank pin.

Turn the flywheel gently and observe the movements of the connecting rod and piston. In a real engine the pressure of the exploding gases pushes the piston down, and then the momentum of the flywheel carries the motion on.

For smooth working (i) remove all burrs from the axle screw (file); (ii) lubricate the plywood bearing with a blacklead pencil.

482 *Four-stroke Cycle*

The cycle of operations can be explained with the help of a cardboard model (Fig. 482, i). The cylinder sides are grooved (three strips of cardboard, the middle one narrower than the other two) and the cardboard piston runs in these grooves. The connecting rod is 16 cm long for an 8-cm wide piston, and the little-end and big-end bearings are small nuts and bolts. The main bearing (at the centre of the 16-cm diameter cardboard flywheel) is a large wood screw, with cardboard washers above and below the wheel. The rest of the model is drawn or painted on the baseboard except for the valves and guides. The valves slide up and down under strips which serve as valve guides.

Set the valves by hand in the correct position for each stroke and follow through the induction, compression, explosion (power) and exhaust operations (Fig. 482, ii). The model is durable if made of stout cardboard.

The diesel engine, though heavier than the motor-car engine, achieves higher efficiency by raising the compression ratio (volume of cylinder/volume of compressed gas) to a point where heavy oil will explode. The oil is sprayed in when the piston is at the top of its compression stroke; the air is very hot and complete combustion occurs.

483 *Heating by Compression*

(a) Pump up a bicycle tyre or football as rapidly as possible. The pump becomes very hot at the lower end. (b) Fit a cycle pump, a thermometer and a glass jet respectively to the three limbs of a T-piece by means of wired-on rubber connections. Work the pump; although air escapes at the jet the thermometer shows a considerable rise of temperature. (c) Replace the thermometer by a copper/eureka thermocouple joined up to a sensitive milliammeter. The rise in temperature shows as a deflection on the meter.

The couple is made by soldering copper wires to each end of a length of eureka resistance wire and carrying the copper leads to the meter. The wires adjacent to each junction may be twisted together for a few

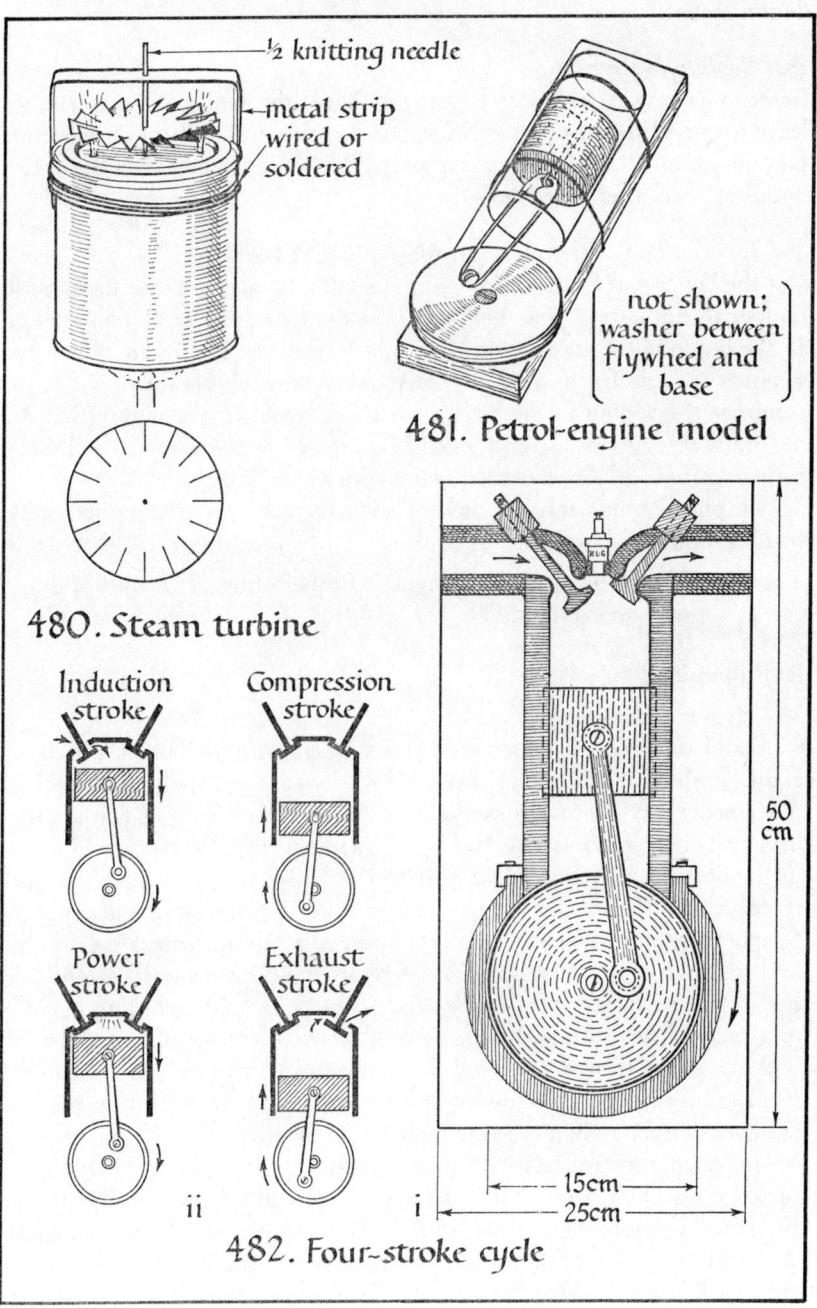

480. Steam turbine

481. Petrol-engine model

482. Four-stroke cycle

centimetres. One junction is kept cold (e.g. in ice); the other is used as a thermometer.

484 *Cooling by Expansion*
Refer to Expt. 200. Pump up a cycle tyre hard; this will make it warm, so leave it to cool for 10 minutes. Moisten the valve and pull it out only just far enough to allow air to escape rapidly. A ring of ice forms on the valve but disappears after a few seconds.

485 *Ignition by Compression* (DEMONSTRATION ONLY)
Cut the lower end from a cycle pump (Expt. 11) and fit it into the mouth of a small but strong glass bottle (ink bottle) by means of a rubber ring. In the bottle put a little cotton-wool which has been soaked in carbon bisulphide containing a trace of dissolved yellow phosphorus. Suddenly compress the vapour in the bottle by a sharp stroke of the pump (the piston must be a good one and should be greased). The carbon bisulphide vapour ignites and the wool catches fire with a blue flash.

The phosphorous solution ignites spontaneously on evaporation; any surplus should be burnt.

Topics: The motor-car. Diesel engines. Liquefaction of air and of other gases; uses of liquid air.

Jet Propulsion

486 *Action and Reaction*
(a) Stand on roller-skates or on a truck fitted with well-oiled wheels (a child's push-chair will serve). Try to move forward by any kind of jerking movement; it will prove impossible. Then throw away from you a fairly heavy object (e.g. an old football loaded with stones); the truck will move in the opposite direction. (b) Stand on the school weighing machine and throw a football upwards as hard as you can. The machine will register, temporarily, an increased weight. (c) Suspend a tin-can, with a press-in lid and containing a little water, from a retort stand by two wire slings (see Figure). Use 28-gauge copper wire and Sellotape to hold each sling in place on the can. The can might hang about 1 metre below the support. A 2-cm wide strap, cut from sheet metal, is bent to form a clip to hold the can lid in place. With the clip removed and the lid well pressed in, heat the can (Bunsen burner) to boil the water and cause the lid to fly off. The lid may be projected 3 metres or more, while the heavier can moves slowly in the opposite direction. Repeat the experiment after attaching the clip. When the steam pressure loosens the lid (which cannot fly away), the can shudders and then remains stationary. The momentum (mass × velocity) of the lid exactly balances that of the can. (This experiment is due to W. E. Pearce.)

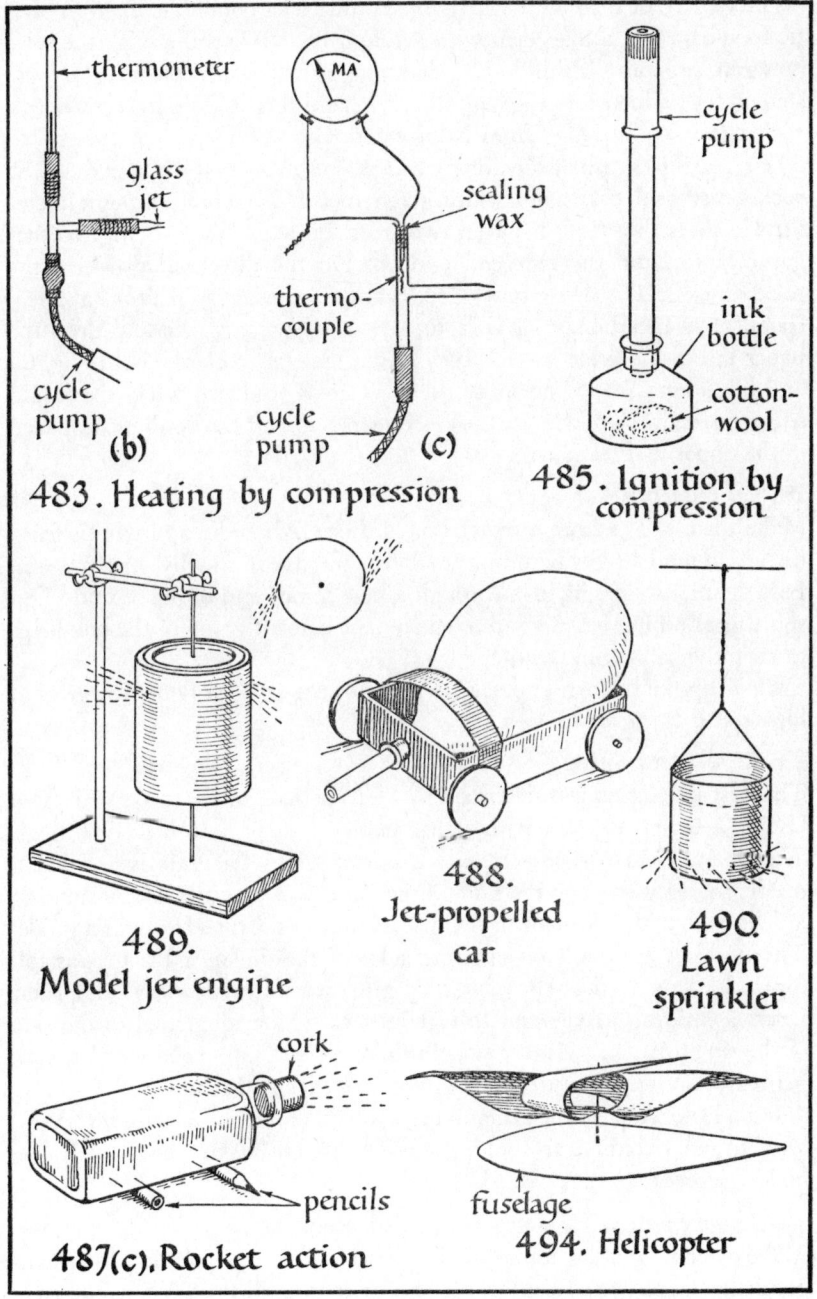

483. Heating by compression

485. Ignition by compression

489. Model jet engine

488. Jet-propelled car

490. Lawn sprinkler

487(c). Rocket action

494. Helicopter

487 Rocket Action

(a) Hook two or three wire paper-clips in line down one side of a thin plastic food-bag, run a long thin wire through the clips, and stretch the wire between supports with the bag hanging downwards. Push a sausage-shaped toy balloon into the bag, inflate it, and then release it. (b) Model a rocket (say 15 cm long) from balsa wood. Bore a hole in the tail end to take a Sparklets carbon dioxide cartridge. Fix two small screw-eyes in the rocket-case and pass a long string (20 metres or more) through them. Stretch the string tight between two trees. Puncture the cartridge so that gas escapes from the rear end and observe the direction in which the rocket moves. The string may be fixed at quite a steep angle. (c) Put a teaspoonful of bicarbonate of soda in a twist of tissue paper and drop the paper into a medicine bottle. Add a little vinegar, cork the bottle lightly and lay it across two pencils as rollers. Gas is produced when the liquid soaks through the paper, the cork is blown out, and the bottle is propelled in the opposite direction.

488 Jet-propelled Car

Make the carriage from a match-box and use light axles and wheels from discarded model-railway rolling-stock (the pupils can usually supply these). Pass the mouth of a balloon through a hole in one end of the box and fit a short glass-tubing jet. A strap of sticky tape across the top of the box helps to keep the balloon in position.

Blow up the balloon and release the car on a smooth floor. It moves at high speed as the air escapes.

489 Model Jet Engine

The first jet engine was described by Hero of Alexandria, 2000 years ago. Use as a boiler any can with tight seams. A small hole drilled through the lid and then corked serves as a safety valve. The axle is a knitting needle soldered through the lid and the bottom of the can. It may stand in a dent in the lid of a small tin, whilst its upper end runs freely in a guide. The two jets are made on opposite sides of the tin, near the top, as follows: Make a vertical cut (about 1·5 mm) with a bradawl or tin-opener. Insert a knitting needle and turn it into a position tangential to the side of the tin; this will twist the opening into a jet pointing more or less tangentially. Both jets should point clockwise or both anti-clockwise.

Put a little water in the can and press the lid on firmly. Heat with a Bunsen burner, avoiding the soldered joint. When steam issues freely the boiler revolves rapidly.

490 Lawn Sprinkler

Make a series of holes round the lower edge of a can, pointing them tangentially (Expt. 489). Suspend the can by string, fill it with water (over a sink), and observe the rotation produced as the jets of water escape.

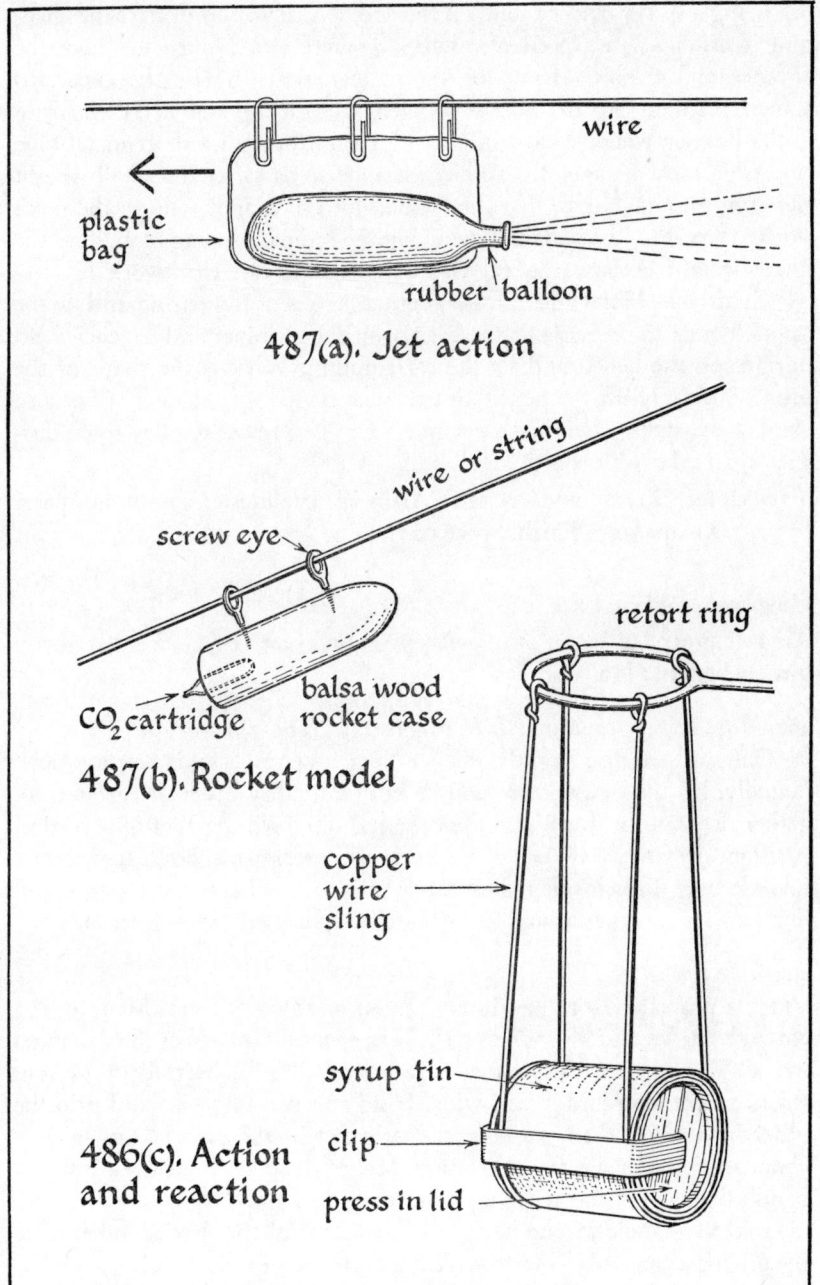

487(a). Jet action

487(b). Rocket model

486(c). Action and reaction

491 *Forces Acting on a Body in Orbit*
(a) Swing a heavy object round on the end of a rubber cord. Feel the changing tension as the speed of circling is increased. Notice too how the distance of the object from the centre increases. (b) Use the apparatus shown in Figure 491 (b). The small weight at the top is joined by a string to the heavier weight below, the string passes through a short metal tube (top edge must be smooth). Whirl the tube so as to set the small weight swinging round. Notice that the farther out the weight swings, the more slowly it rotates. Try suddenly reducing the radius of swing by pulling the lower weight downwards. (c) Use a toy model car, clockwork or electrically driven. Make a loop from about 2 metres of thin string and tie the knotted ends to one *side* of the car. Loop the string round a pencil held upright on the bench and set the car running. What is the shape of the orbit? Suddenly lift the pencil away: what happens to the car? (Try also looping the string round *two* uprights—e.g. two retort stands—some distance apart; the orbit is now an ellipse).

Topics: Jet aircraft and rockets. Artificial satellites. Gravity in space. Escape from Earth. Space travel.

How an Aeroplane Flies

Aircraft propelled by an airscrew depend upon air resistance; they therefore fly better at low altitudes.

492 *More Experiments on Air Resistance* (*cf. Expt. 3*)
(a) Cut a paper disc slightly smaller than a penny. Hold a penny horizontally, lay the disc on top, and let both fall; they reach the ground together. Repeat, but start with the coin and disc held together in a vertical position. (b) Cut away part of the cork of a specimen tube so that the remainder just slides inside the tube. Start the cork at the top of the tube and find how long it takes to sink to the bottom: it may take several seconds.

493 *The Propeller*
Cut the propeller from an aluminium strip, 11 cm × 3 cm. Make it 1¼ cm wide in the middle and cut a slit here about 6 mm across, filed smooth inside. The starting axle is made from steel ("tin") sheet about ½ mm thick, 20 cm long and 5 mm wide. Hold one end in a vice and grip the other in pincers; then, keeping the strip flat in the pincer jaws, give it about 10 twists in the same direction. Make a loop at one end, or attach a handle firmly. The metal driving tube is 2–3 cm long.

Hold the handle in one hand and, by means of the driving tube, force the propeller upwards. If well-made it will rise to the housetops.

Notes: (i) the "leading" edge of each blade should be rounded with a file; (ii) each blade should be made slightly convex.

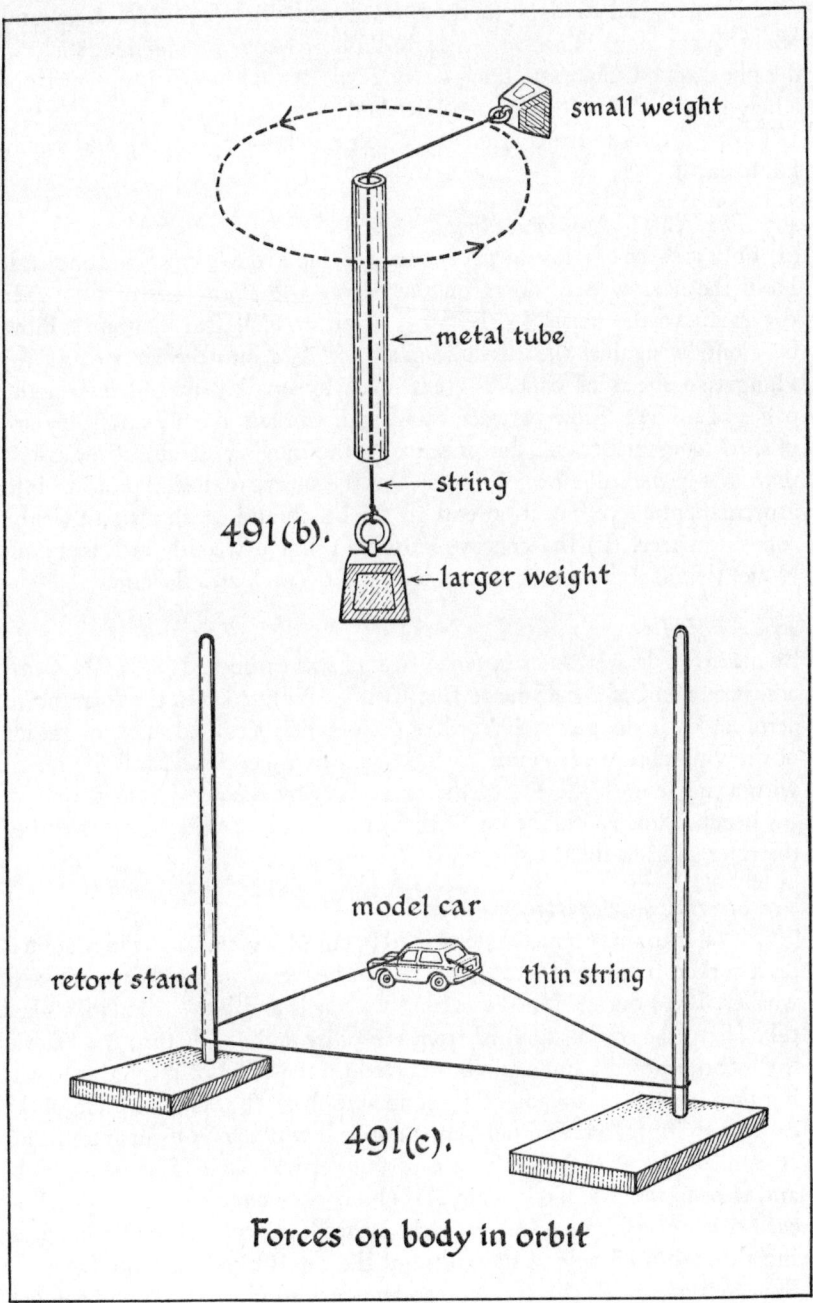

Forces on body in orbit

494 Helicopter Landing

Cut out a model fuselage in thick cardboard, the shape of a cigar and about 10 cm long. Fix the model windmill of Expt. 476 above it, sticking the pin through the centre point of the card. Release the "helicopter" from a height and observe its controlled descent.

Throw sycamore fruits into the air and watch their spinning and steady fall to earth.

495 The "Lift" of Moving Air

(a) Fold a sheet of exercise paper along a line about 2 cm from one end. Hold the narrow strip down on the bench so that the rest of the paper curves above the bench in the form of an aerofoil (see diagram). Blow horizontally against the curved surface; it rises into the air stream. (b) Hang two sheets of paper 2–3 cm apart by holding them between the pages of a book. Blow between them as if to blow them apart; they are pushed together because the pressure in the moving stream of air is less than that in the still air on the outside of the sheets. (c) Roll a postcard into a permanent curve. Set it on end on the bench and brush air past (i) the convex surface, (ii) the concave surface, using a second card as a fan. Notice that in each case the curved card falls over *towards* the fan.

496 Aerofoil

By means of drawing-pins fasten a sheet of stiff cardboard (15 cm × 5 cm) across one end of a half-metre rule. Bend a postcard into the form of an aerofoil, lay it along the stiff card, and maintain its curved shape by means of drawing-pins at each end. Lay the ruler on a pencil and roll the pencil with a finger until the end of the ruler carrying the aerofoil just sinks to the bench. Blow across the top of the aerofoil; it lifts, and the other end of the ruler sinks to the bench.

497 Steering an Aeroplane

(a) Elevators: Pivot a rectangle of card (5 cm × 2½ cm) on a pin mounted on a corked bottle (Fig. 497(a)); a button between card and cork acts as a washer. Bend one end of the card downwards and blow through a glass tube along the top of the card from the other end. Then turn the "elevator" strip upwards, and again blow. Deduce the effect of raising or lowering the elevators on the tail-plane of an aeroplane. (b) Bend a section of the card up to form a vertical tail-plane; notice that it always turns into the air stream. Then bend the back strip of the vertical plane, first to the right and then to the left; blow again and observe the effect of the "rudder" in each case. (c) Ailerons: Cut out a cardboard T. Suspend it by thread passing through a pinhole at the centre of the top. Raise it steadily from the floor by the thread; the T shows no tendency to spin. Now bend the bottom edges of the two arms of the T, one forward and the other backward.

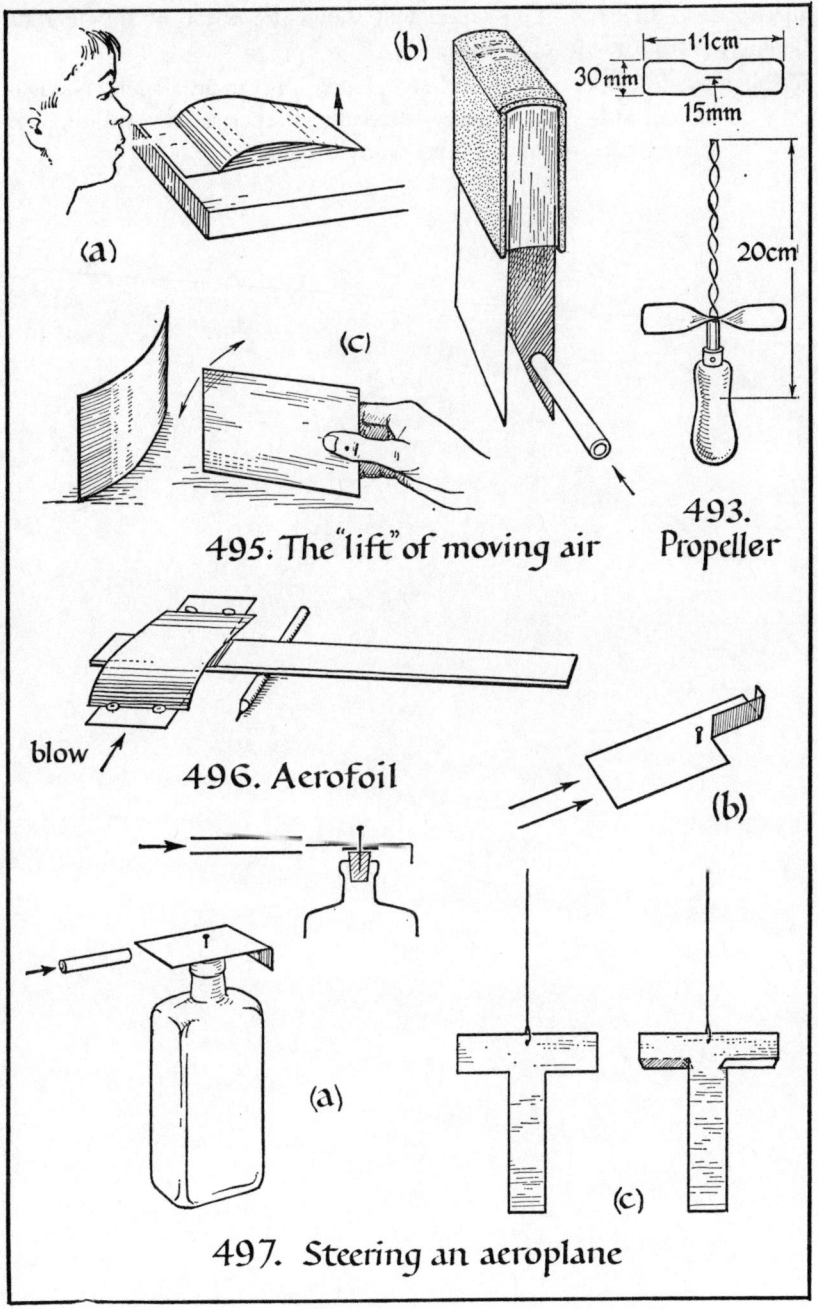

495. The "lift" of moving air

493. Propeller

496. Aerofoil

497. Steering an aeroplane

Raise the T again and note how it spins. Reverse the bends; the T spins in the opposite direction. The experiment shows the action of the ailerons behind the front wings of a plane.

Topics: Model gliders and model aeroplanes. Visit to an airport. Navigational aids. Importance of weather reports. Streamlining of planes, cars, submarines, etc. Speed records.

Chapter Twenty-Four
Soil

Think On These Things...

"Our contemporary problem is not to bring science to the intellectuals: that is already being done well and effectively; it is to bring science to the great majority of the British people who have not been selected for grammar school education, in such a way that they feel themselves to be an integral part of the scientific age, and not merely gaping onlookers."
  Sir Eric Ashby (British Association Granada Lecture, 1959).

"I wanted, for educational reasons, to grow everything from seed. ..."
  Margaret Hutchinson.

"... there should grow on him a sense of a number of different directions to be explored, realms to be penetrated and worlds which, if he wishes, he can increasingly make his own; but one and all, whether to do with engines or aeroplanes or animals or plants or burning and melting or rivers and mountains or the ways of different human beings: one and all parts of the same one world, constantly expanding for him. ..."
  Nathan Isaacs (*Early Scientific Trends in Young Children*, 1958).

"... all knowledge of reality starts from experience and ends in it."
  Albert Einstein.

"Guessing has gone out of fashion in science; it was at best a poor substitute for knowledge, and modern science ... confines itself, except on very rare occasions, to ascertained facts, and the inferences which, so far as can be seen, follow unequivocally from them."
  Sir James Jeans.

"We all say we want to teach for understanding, but what does that mean for the general pupil?"
  Prof. E. M. Rogers (CELC report, *School Science Teaching*: HMSO, 1964).

"The content of a science course should vary according to the circumstances."
  Report of a Joint Committee of the I.A.A.M. and the S.M.A. (*The Teaching of Science in Secondary Schools*, 1947).

"Teaching is such a personal art that it would be wrong to suggest any single, rigid approach."

> Nuffield Biology (*Teachers' Guide*, 1966).

"The evidence summarized in the (Crowther) report showed that there were many pupils who did not live up to their promise because the courses they followed failed to hold their interest, rather than because they had exhausted their capacity to learn."

> Schools Council (*Curriculum Bulletin* No. 2, 1967).

"For many pupils between 11 and 15 an education involving, or at any rate stressing, abstract thought, seems inappropriate. As their curiosity becomes more satisfied their interest will tend to revolve more and more around the useful. Such pupils are to be found in all types of school..."

> *Science in Secondary Schools* (Ministry of Education Pamphlet No. 38, 1960).

"The hope now at last to be realized of giving a longer school life to many children ... increases the importance of securing teachers and conditions that will enable good and full use to be made of the time thus redeemed."

> *Natural Science in Education* (Report of Committee on the position of Natural Science in the educational system of Great Britain, 1918).

"Students who are to become teachers need definite information (a) as to the quite simple material equipment needed, (b) as to the methods of using it in the field."

> *Science in Senior Schools* (Board of Education, Pamphlet No. 89, 1932

"European Conservation Year 1970 is your business. It is about the coast and countryside you use, enjoy and ill-treat. Everywhere you can find dismal and often tragic evidence of how, with our increased numbers and powerful technology, we are demanding too much of our environment. We are failing to work with nature and are rapidly degrading our surroundings."

> R. E. Boote (Chairman of the European Committee for the Conservation of Nature and Natural Resources).

"The plough is one of the most ancient and most valuable of man's inventions; but long before he existed the land was in fact regularly ploughed, and still continues to be thus ploughed, by earthworms. It may be doubted whether there are many other animals which have played so important a part in the history of the world as have these lowly organized creatures."

   Charles Darwin (*The Formation of Vegetable Mould through the Action of Worms*, 1881).

Nature of Soil

498 *Soil Profiles*

A visit to a quarry face, to road and railway cuttings, etc., may be arranged. In this way much may be learned of the ways in which rocks are laid down and of the relationship between soil, subsoil and the underlying rock. A sample profile may be obtained by clearing a vertical soil face (e.g. in a deep hole dug in the ground) and hammering into it a piece of half-round metal guttering, which is then dug out and the surface cut smooth. The resulting "soil monolith" may be preserved by pouring on perspex dissolved in a plastic solvent and allowing to dry.

499 *Nature of Soil*

(a) Soil types: Collect samples of various soils in normal conditions (i.e. neither excessively wet nor excessively dry). Classify them according to the following scheme:

1	Soil feels gritty	....	(2)
	Soil not gritty	....	(4)
2	Soil can be pressed in hand to form a cohesive ball	....	Light Loam.
	Soil will not form a cohesive ball	....	(3)
3	Soil stains fingers	....	Loamy Sand.
	Soil does not stain fingers	....	Light Sand.
4	Soil feels sticky or silky	....	(5)
	Soil neither sticky nor silky	....	Loam.
5	Soil can be polished between the fingers	....	(6)
	Soil cannot be so polished	....	(7)
6	Soil very difficult to deform between finger and thumb	....	Clay
	Soil less difficult to deform	....	(8)
7	Soil markedly silky	....	Light Silt.
	Soil only slightly silky	....	Silty Loam.
8	Soil fairly easily deformed	....	Heavy Loam.
	Soil deformed with some difficulty	....	Medium Loam.

 (b) Solid Constituents: Refer to Expt. 2 (air in soil). For the present experiment use a glass tube about 20 cm long and 2–3 cm wide, corked at one end, or a measuring cylinder. One-third fill the tube with garden soil and then fill it almost to the top with water. Shake well and allow to stand. Observe that fine gravel sinks to the bottom immediately, followed by sand and (more slowly) by silt. Particles of humus may float on the surface of the water. The muddy liquid clears only very slowly; the tube should be left for several days in order that the clay may settle.

By measuring the depth of each layer an estimate of the percentage of clay and of gravel, sand and silt (combined) in the soil may be obtained. Relate the descriptions "light", "medium", or "heavy" to the relative proportions of sand and clay in a soil and to the working properties of the soil.

Draw off a portion of the pale yellow liquid which is left after the clay has settled (use a glass tube as a pipette), and demonstrate the mineral salts content by the method of Expt. 220.

(c) Moisture in Soil: Heat a little garden soil in a tin lid, gently at first and then as strongly as possible. Observe the steam which escapes and the changes in colour and texture that occur as the organic matter burns away. Weigh about 10 g of crushed air-dried soil into a tin lid and heat over a steam-bath (e.g. syrup tin) or in a steam-oven for half an hour. Reweigh and then reheat; after a further 15 minutes the weight should not change. The clock-spring balance of Expt. 214 may be used in this experiment. Calculate the percentage of moisture in the original air-dried soil.

(d) Humus in Soil: Heat the residue of moisture-free soil over an open flame until it is a uniform light colour. Cool and weigh. Calculate the percentage of humus in the original soil.

Good garden soil may contain up to 10 per cent of organic matter; farm soil may have 5 per cent. Repeat the experiments on a sample of subsoil and show that the humus content is very low.

500 *Water-retaining Power of Soil*

Allow samples of clay and of various soils to dry out thoroughly in sunshine or over a warm radiator; then powder them and store in separate labelled bottles.

Put a loose plug of cotton-wool in the stem of each of three funnels and stand each funnel in the top of a medicine bottle or small milk bottle. Transfer a level eggcupful (about 40 cm^3) of dry sand to one funnel, of dry soil to a second, and of dry powdered clay to the third. Then gently pour an eggcupful of water into each funnel. Note that drainage through the sand stops after about 5 minutes, but water will continue to drip from the clay even after an hour; the corresponding time for soil is between these two. Measure the final volumes of water in the bottles and hence calculate the amounts of water retained by the different materials.

Topics: Types of soil, including discussion of terms in common use

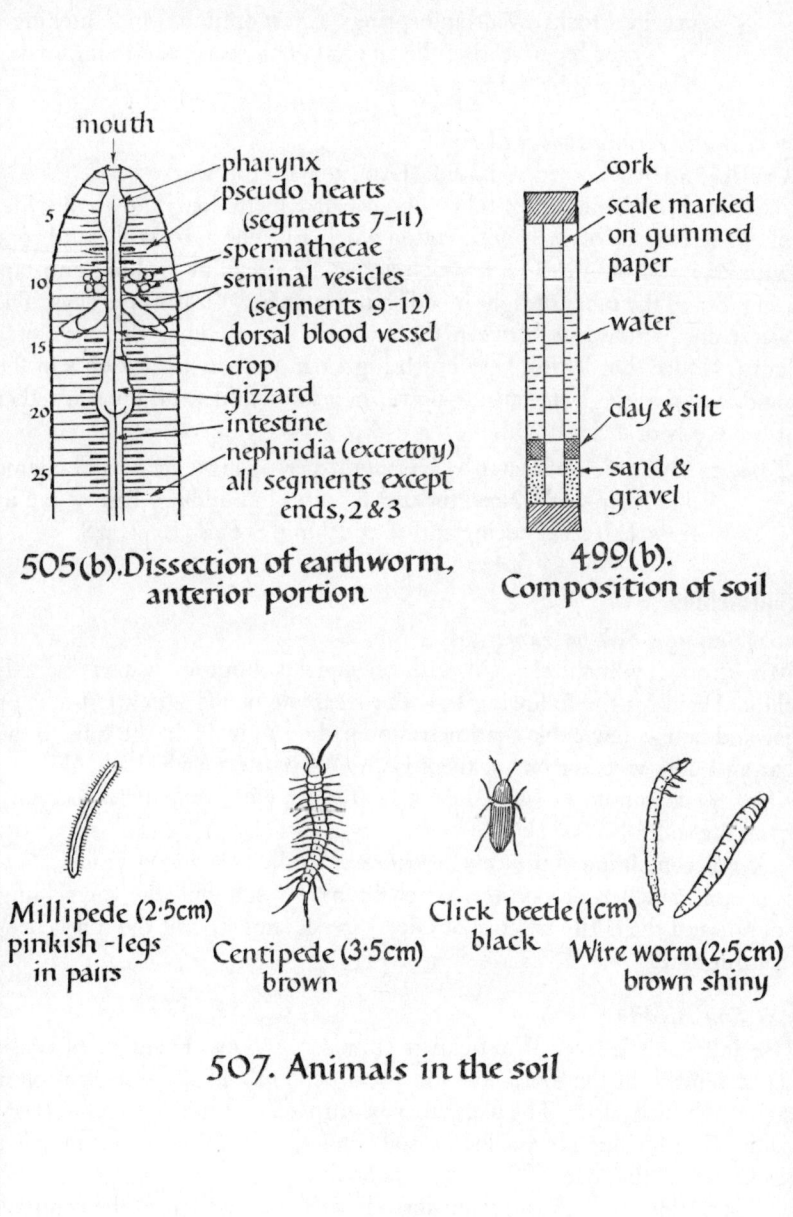

505(b). Dissection of earthworm, anterior portion

499(b). Composition of soil

507. Animals in the soil

("cold" soil, loam, etc.). Open-cast mining—importance of returning rock, subsoil and top-soil in proper order. Permeable and impervious rocks; wells and springs. Effect of humus in lightening a heavy soil by increasing the amount of air space, and in improving a sandy soil by holding water.

501 *Water-raising Power of Soil*

Use dry and finely powdered solids (Expt. 500) for this work.

Select three similar glass tubes, about half a metre long and 1 cm wide; plug the bottom of each with cotton-wool. Fill one tube with sand, one with clay and the third with soil; remove air spaces by shaking and tapping. Stand the tubes upright in a dish of water for at least three days. The water creeps upwards between the particles as oil climbs the wick of a lamp. Notice that it rises very much higher in the clay than it does in the sand, and that the water-raising power of a soil will depend upon whether it is a sandy or a clayey soil.

Topics: Absorption of water by blotting-paper, sponge, etc. Candle flame and lamp-wick. Need for damp-course in building. Rise of sap in trees. Effects of hoeing and of mulching. See also Expt. 248.

Soil Acidity

502 *Testing a Soil for Lime*

Mix strong hydrochloric acid with an equal volume of water; use this diluted acid for the following test. Put a sample of soil into a test-tube or jar and pour a few cubic centimetres of acid on to it. Hold the tube to the ear and note whether or not there is an effervescence (which should continue for a minute or two; do not confuse it with air bubbles escaping from the soil).

A soil containing 1 per cent or more of chalk will give a visible effervescence. Smaller proportions of chalk may result only in a crackling sound; and the entire absence of effervescence suggest that the soil is deficient in lime.

503 *Soil Acidity*

Use Johnson's Universal test-papers (Johnson & Sons, Hendon, N.W.4). Take a pinch of the moist soil and use a pen-knife blade to press it on a strip of the test paper. The paper may be turned any tint between red (very acid soil) and blue (very alkaline soil), but the desirable colour is green (indicated on the cover of the test-paper book).

Test various soils in this way; include peat, material from the compost heap, recently limed soil, etc.

When plant materials rot down, acids are formed which check plant growth. The farmer and gardener add lime to soil partly to neutralize these acids (see also Expt. 504); about 100 g per square metre once a year is usually sufficient.

504 Flocculating Effect of Lime
(a) Take two jam jars. Put powdered clay into one, and powdered clay to which a little slaked lime has been added in the other. Fill up the jars with water and stir vigorously. Observe the time required for the solid material in each jar to settle. (b) Shake some soil well with water, allow to settle for a few minutes and then decant some of the still-muddy liquid into two jars or tubes. Add a little lime-water to one and observe that this greatly assists the speed with which the liquid clears.

Animals in the Soil
Refer to Expt. 60 (the wormery) and to the various suggestions. Class experiments with worms taken from a jar and distributed to pupils on pieces of paper are seldom successful; children are not unnaturally repelled by the slimy (and often smelly) material presented to them. The worm in its natural environment—soil—is quite a different proposition. Let pupils collect their own worms and make their own wormeries, using two or three small worms only to a jam jar. When they have become interested in such work they will be ready to make a closer examination of the creatures they have cared for themselves.

505 Earthworm
(a) External features:
Observe the animal's movements on a piece of rough drawing-paper. Put an ear to the paper; rub a finger along the underside of the worm from back to front, noting the bristles; and describe the way in which the worm contracts and expands its body when it moves. Use a lens to see the mouth (turn the worm over), the segments (with their bristles and pores), and the anus. The dark line running the length of the body on the upper (dorsal) side is a blood vessel. Notice the saddle (about 30 segments from the head) and look for openings on the underside of the worm about midway between the head and the saddle; these are the ducts concerned with reproduction.

(b) *Dissection of Earthworm*
Only a very simple dissection should be attempted with the average pupil. Use small enamel pie-dishes with a layer of wax in the bottom; the wax is easily remelted by running a flame over its surface. Ordinary pins serve to anchor the specimen. The teacher should kill the worm previously, using, for example, hot 20 per cent salt solution.

Pin the worm down, dorsal side uppermost, stretched lengthways; just cover it with water. Nip up the body-wall with forceps and make a careful cut with fine, sharp-pointed scissors along the mid-dorsal line of the front third of the worm's length. The cut should be as shallow as possible. Turn back the flaps of skin and pin them down, exposing the alimentary canal. Make out the chief parts of the canal (pharynx, gullet, gizzard, intestine) and prod the gizzard to feel the hard particles of gravel with which food is crushed. Look for blood vessels covering the intestine; discuss their function. Find the swollen blood vessels round the gullet ("hearts"). Other details (e.g. reproductive organs and excretory organs) may be seen with a lens if desired.

506 *Soil Brought to Surface by Worms*
Estimate the depth of top-soil in a field or garden. Weigh a cubic decimetre of soil and so make a rough estimate of the weight of soil over a square kilometre. Now collect together worm casts from a square metre of lawn each morning and weigh them. Thence estimate the amount of soil brought to the surface by worms over a square kilometre in the course of a year. Compare the results with those obtained by Charles Darwin.

507 *Other Animals in the Soil*
Examine a trowelful of soil, spreading it out on a newspaper. Remove any living creatures to a dish covered with a glass plate. The likely finds include:

(i) The Leather-jacket (larva of the Cranefly or Daddy Long-legs); about $2\frac{1}{2}$ cm long and $\frac{1}{2}$ cm broad, and of a dirty greenish- or greyish-brown colour. The segmented body has a tough skin. There are no legs. The small black head has very powerful jaws (lens).

(ii) The Wireworm (larva of the Click Beetle); about 2 cm long; shiny yellow segmented body, and with three pairs of legs near to the head end. Use a lens to observe the jaws. The animal is often found sticking half out of a root on which it is feeding.

(iii) The Centipede is flatter than the Wireworm, may be yellow, pink, brown, or black, and has a pair of legs on each segment.

(iv) The Millipede is round in section and has two pairs of legs on each segment; in colour it resembles the Centipede.

All of these animals, except the Earthworm and the Centipede, are garden pests, destroying roots. The Centipede is carnivorous and feeds upon slugs and insects, so that it is the gardener's friend. (See Ministry of Agriculture leaflets.)

508 *Soil Bacteria*
Refer to Chapter 10. Put a little fresh milk in each of two test-tubes and sterilize by boiling gently for a few minutes. Plug the tubes with cotton-wool which has been passed quickly through a flame and leave them to cool. Then add a few grains of garden soil to one lot of milk (opening the

tube for as short a time as possible), leaving the second tube as a "control".
After a day or two smell the contents of the two tubes.
See Expt. 185.

509 *Soil Population*
Expose the Leather-jackets in a square metre of lawn by watering it with a solution of ortho-dichlor-benzene (sold for the purpose). The Leather-jackets come to the surface and can be swept into a heap and counted (see Ministry of Agriculture leaflet 179).
Topics: Garden friends and foes. Man's war against soil and insect pests. The Locust problem.

Natural and Artificial Manures
The need for certain elements in the soil has been shown by means of culture solutions (Expt. 172). The preparation of a compost heap was described in Expt. 175.

510 *Fertilizers*
(a) Make a collection of small samples of the chief natural and artificial manures, storing each in a screw-topped bottle. Label each bottle; e.g.:

> Sulphate of ammonia. By-product from gas-works. Manufactured from atmospheric nitrogen by Haber process. Converted to nitrate by lime and bacteria in soil. Contains 21 per cent nitrogen. Apply 10 g per sq. m when planting. Stimulates leafy growth.

Pupils should be encouraged to seek such information for themselves and to prepare the appropriate labels. A small collection might include:

Farmyard manure (dry)	Soot	Nitrate of soda
Garden compost	Dried blood	Sulphate of ammonia
National Growmore	Bone meal	Superphosphate
Seaweed	Basic slag	Kainite

(b) Take 25 cm^3 of dilute sulphuric acid in an evaporating dish or beaker and drop in a litmus paper. Add dilute ammonia solution slowly and with stirring until the test-paper just turns blue; any excess of ammonia will boil off during the later evaporation. Gently evaporate the liquid until it will crystallize on cooling. To test this, remove one drop on the end of a glass rod; if the drop crystallizes as it cools, so will the whole solution. Now leave the liquid to stand overnight (cover to protect from dust) and then filter off the fine white crystals. Allow them to dry, and store in a labelled box.

511 *Mixing Manures*
Leafy growth is stimulated by nitrogen; roots by phosphates; flowers by potash. In compounding manures care must be taken that the speed of

action of each constituent is similar (thus basic slag, which is very slow-acting, should not be mixed with nitrate of soda); and that the constituents do not have an undesirable reaction upon one another.

(a) Mix a little sulphate of ammonia with dry slaked lime in a small dish; notice the smell of ammonia, which is increased by the addition of a little water.

(b) Mix superphosphate and nitrate of soda. Smell. Try the effect of gentle heat.

(c) Put a little soot into a test-tube and add an equal quantity of slaked lime. Shake to mix, and then warm and test for ammonia by smell and by moist red litmus paper. Soot often contains as much as 7 per cent of ammonia.

512 Bacterial Decomposition Assisted by Nitrates
Put finely-chopped straw in three jam jars. Leave one lot dry; this does not rot. Moisten the second sample thoroughly; this rots very slowly. Moisten the third sample with 1 per cent sodium nitrate solution; decomposition into dark-brown humus is rapid. All the jars should be loosely covered during the course of the experiment.

Topics: Rotation of crops. Scientific manuring (use of artificials on school plots). The nitrogen cycle (in simple terms). For most pupils the chemistry of these processes must be kept to a minimum, but with the more able it will be possible to extend the work to include such subjects as nitric acid, ammonia, sulphuric acid and their important salts. Refer to Expt. 319 in connection with the synthesis of nitric acid from air and water.

The Formation and Conservation of Soils
The work might be introduced by speculation upon the way in which the Earth was formed. The breakdown of rocks into soil may be illustrated by reference to Expt. 232 (expansion of water on freezing), and to the practice of "rough-digging" a garden in the autumn. Note the effects of wind and rain upon old buildings; get pupils to examine headstones in an old graveyard, relating the degree of weathering both to the kind of stone and to the date on the stone. Discuss why tar-filled spaces are left between the sections on concrete roads. Observe cases where flagstones have been lifted, or walls moved, by the pressure of tree roots.

513 Acid Conditions Produced by Growing Roots
Use the germination sandwich (Expt. 82). Soak the (white) blotting paper in blue litmus solution and set radish seeds in the sandwich. Observe the effect of the growing roots on the colour of the litmus over the course of several days.

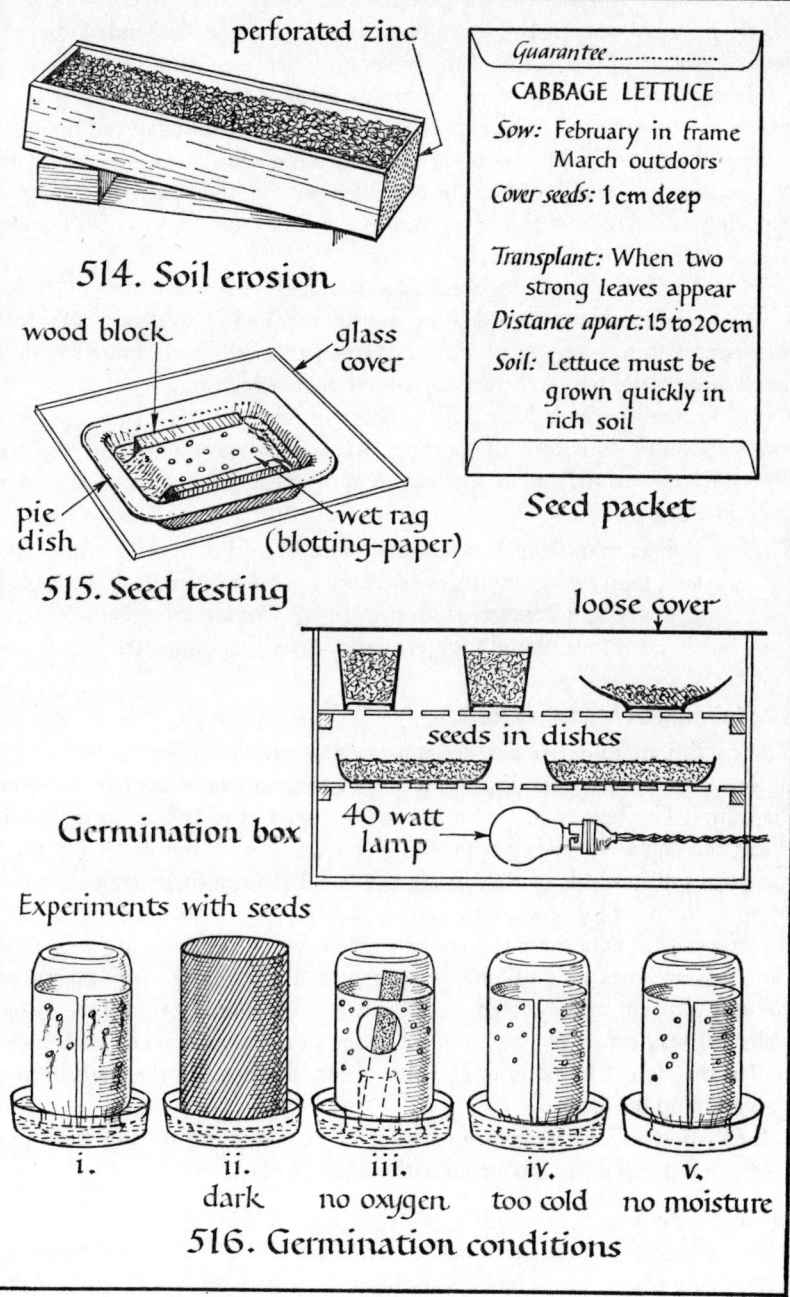

514. Soil erosion

515. Seed testing

Seed packet

Guarantee..................
CABBAGE LETTUCE
Sow: February in frame
  March outdoors
Cover seeds: 1 cm deep

Transplant: When two strong leaves appear
Distance apart: 15 to 20 cm
Soil: Lettuce must be grown quickly in rich soil

Germination box

Experiments with seeds

i. ii. dark iii. no oxygen iv. too cold v. no moisture

516. Germination conditions

514 *Soil Erosion*

Make a pair of wooden troughs, each about 75 cm long × 15 cm wide × 10 cm deep; leave one end of each box open and cover this end with perforated zinc. Seal the inside of the boxes with putty or paint or tar. In use, the boxes are set so that they slope downwards towards the open end, which overhangs a pail. The experiments are best performed out-of-doors.

(a) Fill one box with loose soil and the other with firmly packed soil. Allow them to stand out in heavy rain; or simulate rain by using a watering-can. Contrast the effect on the soil in the two boxes, and the appearance of the run-off water.

(b) Fill one box with soil and sow it thickly with mustard or cress; keep it warm and moist until there is a thick carpet of seedlings. Observe the effect of heavy rain (watering-can) upon this box as compared with a box of open soil. Discuss the protective action of vegetation.

(c) Fill one box with loose soil and square off the surface; then press a few milk-bottle tops into the surface. Expose to heavy rain and observe how the unprotected soil is washed away, leaving columns of soil under the bottle tops.

Topics: Soil as man's greatest material asset. World danger of erosion by sun, frost, water, wind, over-cropping and over-grazing. Effects of destruction of forests (industry, fires). Conservation by afforestation, contour ploughing, terracing, cover-cropping, etc.

The Conditions Necessary for Life

The conditions under which seeds germinate are an indication of the requirements of life generally. Study the instructions on a seed packet (see diagram). The best months for sowing are related to temperature conditions; the depth of sowing is probably concerned with moisture; the need for good soil reminds us that living things all require food; transplanting suggests the need for space, with light and air.

Germination experiments may be carried out at any time of the year if the seeds are kept at a suitable temperature. Fit a wooden box (about 50 cm long × 25 cm wide × 30 cm deep) with a ledge running round the inside walls halfway down the box. On the ledge fit a plywood shelf, with holes drilled through it to allow circulation of air. Underneath the shelf keep a 40-watt lamp burning.

Small flower-pots, ice-cream cartons, or saucers stand on the shelf and the open top of the box is covered with a sheet of glass.

515 *Seed Testing*

Place 20–30 seeds in a germination sandwich (Expt. 82), or on blotting-paper lying over a wood block standing in a dish of water (the ends of the paper dip down in the water); if the latter arrangement is used (see diagram), the dish should be covered with a sheet of glass. Keep the seeds warm and count how many germinate after several days. Try this experiment with new and with old seeds.

516 *Germination Conditions*
(i) Control experiment: Moisten the inside of a jam jar, lay the jar on its side and sprinkle radish seeds round the walls. Then line the jar with moist blotting-paper (so that the seeds are between the paper and the glass) and invert the jar in a dish of water. Keep the jar in a warm room (or in the germination box described above). The seeds germinate in 3 days and grow vigorously for several weeks. (ii) Repeat, but keep the jar completely covered with a removable black paper case. The seeds germinate but become yellow and unhealthy and soon die. (iii) Repeat part (i), but include under the jar a strip of card covered with moist iron filings (the card may stand in a meat paste jar); the seeds do not germinate and the water level rises one-fifth of the way up the jam-jar, because the oxygen of the air has been absorbed by the rusting iron. (iv) Set up Expt. 516 (i) in a north window before Easter; germination is unlikely because of the low temperature. (v) Try to germinate seeds without moisture; the attempt fails.

Notice that a minimum temperature is necessary (certainly it must be above freezing-point); light is not essential for germination but is required for continued healthy growth; food is supplied for the first stages of growth from the food stores within the seeds.

Topics: Growing seasons; value of greenhouse and garden frame; how the gardener achieves the best conditions for his crops (thinning, transplanting, staking, earthing-up, conserving moisture, etc.). World food problem; irrigation schemes for desert areas. Possibility of life on other planets.

Chapter Twenty-Five
How Life is Handed On

Aims of Biology Teaching with Ordinary Pupils

It will be generally agreed that one aim of Biology teaching in schools is to arouse a love of Nature, "a respect and feeling for all living things"; to inculcate an attitude indicative of the good citizen. For many of our ordinary pupils the study may become a hobby if properly tackled, and one that may bring much pleasure into lives where daily work is often only dull routine.

Again, through Biology as through Physical Science, we may hope to give our pupils some conception of the scientific method of enquiry, at however humble a level, so that they may realize the importance of first-hand experience, of a critical approach to evidence, and of directed enquiry as a basis for sound conclusions. We want them to appreciate that there are many unanswered questions (many, indeed, at present unanswerable); that the accumulation of knowledge must be accompanied by the formulation and testing of hypotheses, many of which will prove faulty; and that the pursuit of truth today is an international affair, the outcome of which is dependent upon researches by many minds working in many different fields.

Thirdly, we do well to emphasize the importance of an informed public opinion on matters which affect health and well-being: this is the point we made in our introduction to Chapter 10. Essentially we are concerned here with the interdependence of living things.

Finally, there is today more than ever before, and largely because of popular education and the communications explosion, widespread interest in subjects such as man's place in the universe, evolution, heredity and the nature of living matter. Here the mind of man reaches out for an answer to its most fundamental problem: "Why am I here?" To such a question Science can give no answer, and we should not hesitate to say so: to confess the limitations of our subject as well as extol its triumphs. We do well to teach our pupils that to knowledge must be added insight and faith. But it is equally our duty to give them confidence in Science; to indicate some of the remarkable advances that have been made in recent years and to assure them that the possibilities are boundless for further progress in extending man's understanding of the world in which he lives, and of bettering his condition in that world.

Sex Education in School

In the first edition of this book we wrote that "sex teaching . . . is a question on which opinion remains much divided", and that is still true today. Few teachers of Science would doubt the *need* for sex education; the problem is always that of how and by whom it is to be tackled. Those interested should read Chapter 11 of the Department of Education and Science *Handbook of Health Education* (1968), which provides a most perceptive analysis of the difficulties and very practical advice on how to overcome them. Help is available too from other sources. The Nuffield Foundation Science Teaching Project, in its Combined Science programme, has a useful section on reproduction in small mammals and in Man; and films may be found appropriate to particular circumstances, including television series.

Flowers, Pollination and Fertilization

Refer to the notes at the beginning of Chapter 5, where it is suggested that every pupil should at some time grow a plant for himself and record its complete life-history with pen and brush.

517(a) *A Wild-flower Collection*

Select only one or two flowers of each kind, along with a leaf or two, and carry them home carefully in a tin lined with damp moss. Press immediately between several thicknesses of good white blotting-paper in a sandwich with two planed wooden boards, perhaps 25 cm × 15 cm × 2 cm, as the outer covers. Fasten the sandwish carefully together with tape and lay it aside under a fairly heavy weight (e.g. a pile of books).

When the flowers are quite dry (this may necessitate one or two changes of position on the blotting-paper) mount them on white card, using tiny drops of good gum (e.g. "Spot-Stick") or very narrow strips of transparent adhesive paper. Label each flower with its name, its place of origin and the date.

(b) A Flower Calendar: Make cards for each month of the year. On them mount pressed specimens of flowers in bloom in the appropriate months, or make careful sketches of flowers and colour them. Record also on the calendar the name and origin of each flower.

518 *A Simple Flower*

Using a dissecting needle and a hand-lens, examine a Buttercup flower. Observe and count the sepals and petals, and notice the many stamens. Pull away some of the petals and stamens to see the many carpels, each consisting of a rounded ovary or seed-box and a pointed tip, the stigma.

Cut across a carpel with a sharp blade and look with a lens for the ovule within the ovary. Look at the inner side of the base of the petals to see the shining nectaries. Sketch a vertical cross-section of the flower.

Discuss the function of each part of the flower. It is a most useful exercise also to mount the various parts of a simple flower on a postcard, labelling them neatly. If the anther of a stamen is rubbed lightly across black paper traces of yellow pollen may often be seen.

519 *How Pollen is Carried About*

Keep a flower indoors, in water, overnight. Next day, remove an anther and press it on to a microscope slide, using a pen-knife blade. Pollen grains are forced out on to the slide. Put the slide (uncovered) on the microscope stage, illuminate it, and adjust the mirror so that the grains appear as shining particles under the low power. Now change to high power and observe the grains carefully.

Pollen grains of insect-pollinated plants often have hairs (e.g. the daisy family). How might these hairs assist transport of the pollen? In the case of wind pollination (e.g. hazel, birch) the grains may have tiny air-filled wings.

520 *Cross-pollination*

More highly evolved flowers have developed means of ensuring cross-pollination.

Examine a Wallflower by the method of Expt. 519, noticing that the petals are extended into a tube, closed at the top against the entry of small crawling insects by the stamen heads (anthers). Pull away part of the tube and find the nectaries; obviously only long-tongued insects can reach them.

Examine Deadnettle; note that the five petals are joined to form a tube but that one petal grows out to form a landing stage for insects and two others form a hood which shelters the four stamens and the forked stigma just beneath it. Discuss the special mechanism which ensures cross-pollination in this flower (when the bee pushes its head into the flower the stigma is forced down on to its back first, so that pollen brought from other flowers is transferred to the stigma; then the anthers descend, sweeping their pollen on to the bee's back).

Flowers of Snapdragon or Sweet Pea may be examined similarly.

521 *Pollination by Wind*

Bring Hazel catkins into school in early spring, when the long yellow flowers are in bloom. Shake a catkin over black paper and note the cloud of pollen. Look closely at the green buds on the same twig; some of them have red threads (stigmas) protruding from their tips. Open a bud and look for the seed-box at the base of a pair of stigmas. Look at the class

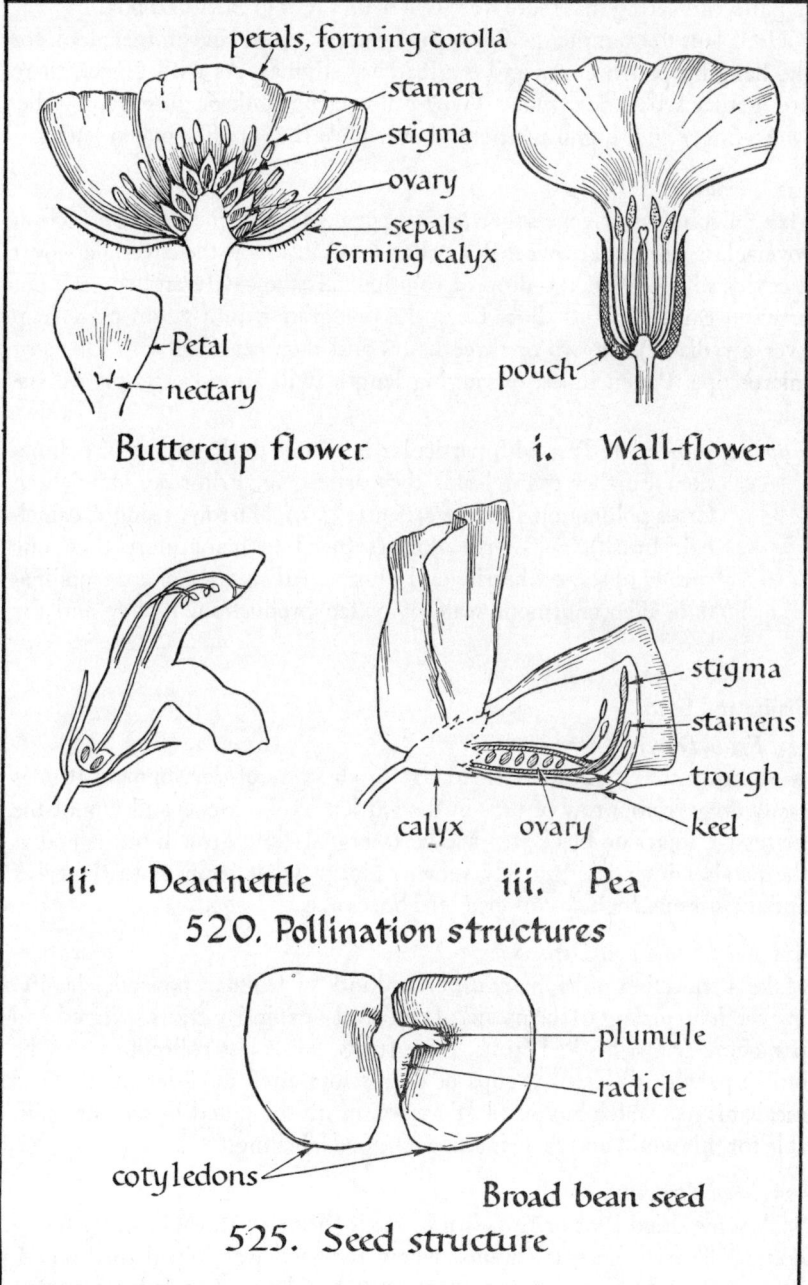

520. Pollination structures

525. Seed structure

collection of fruits from a previous year and notice how the Hazel nuts grow in pairs, indicating that there were two ovules within each seed-box.

Use a lens to examine the flowering heads of grasses in summer; look for the hanging pollen boxes and the feathery stigmas. As with Hazel, there are neither sepals nor petals. Twirl a flowering stalk of grass rapidly between finger and thumb and notice how slowly the very fine pollen settles.

522 *Fertilization*
Make a solution of cane-sugar (10–15 per cent), put one drop on a clean cover-glass, and shake Sweet Pea pollen on to it. Invert the cover-glass over a cavity slide so that the drop of solution fills the cavity and spreads out between cover-slip and slide. Keep the preparation in a warm place (e.g. over a radiator) for two or three hours and then examine with a lens or microscope. Pollen tubes, of varying length, will almost certainly be visible.

Topics: Flower studies, with particular reference to the means of pollination. Further examples as they arise—e.g. Primrose, Dandelion. Cross-pollination in the garden (e.g. of Marrow, using a camel-hair brush). Self-sterile flowers (need to plant more than one variety of some Cherries and Plums). Advantages of cross-pollination. The enormous scale of pollen production. Honey and the bee.

Fruits and Seeds

523 *Fruit Development*
In summer collect garden Pea flowers in all states of development (this is easily done from a row of peas in the garden or allotment) and mount the successive stages on black paper. The emergence and growth of the pod as the petals wither is effectively shown. Notice what happens to the calyx and the stigma. Include cut-open seed-boxes at each stage.

524 *Seed and Fruit Dispersal*
Make a collection of as many different kinds of fruits as possible, classifying them according to the means of dispersal—explosive fruits, winged and parachute fruits, hooked fruits, juicy fruits, etc. Class collections may be built up, with different groups of pupils interested in different dispersal mechanisms. Match-box or plastic trays, neatly mounted in sets, are suitable for this work, and there is scope for good labelling.

525 *Seed Structure*
Soak some dried Peas or Broad Bean seeds (from a packet) in water for 24 hours. Observe the scar (hilum) where the seed was joined to the pod. Peel off the seed-coat and separate the two seed-leaves (cotyledons), noting how they were joined together at one point and how the seed-coat has a

pocket there which encloses the young root or radical. Notice also the young shoot (plumule) lying between the seed-leaves.

Test the seed-leaves for starch (Expts. 92, 93).

If desired, similar examination of other seeds may be made. The Castor Oil seed is worth investigation, both for its food store (oil) and for the fact that the food is stored outside the seed-leaves. It is necessary to cut the soaked seed crosswise and lengthways to see the beautifully veined thin seed-leaves and the embryo within.

526 *Growth of Seedlings*

Sow Broad Beans or Peas out-of-doors, or indoors in boxes or pots but with a good depth of soil. When the first seedlings appear, dig them and some others up and examine the parts. Observe the hooked plumule and the way in which it straightens out when it reaches the light. Notice also that the seed-leaves remain below ground, supplying food to the seedling until it is able to feed itself. Continue to watch growth; the development of the tap-root and of lateral roots, and the production of leaves, buds, flowers and fruits can all be observed during the summer term.

Plant also seeds of Sunflower, Wheat, Oats, Grass, Cress, Sycamore, Horse-chestnut, Maize, etc. Small seeds may be grown in a germination sandwich (Expt. 82); larger ones between a layer of moist blotting-paper and the glass of a jam jar, keeping a little water standing in the bottom of the jar. For the Horse-chestnut the blotting-paper may be supported by half-filling the jar with sawdust.

Find out which seeds come above the surface of the ground during early growth (e.g. Sunflower, Marrow, Sycamore), thus protecting the plumule.

Topics: Fertilization and fruit formation. Annual plants. Man's use of seeds for food and other purposes.

Other Methods of Plant Increase

527 *Growth from Cuttings*

Propagate the classroom Geranium plants by cutting off stems (about 10 cm long and carrying leaves) just below a node. Leave only two or three top leaves on each stem. Plant each in a small hole in a sand/soil/leaf-mould compost, pressing the compost firmly round the stem. Several stems may be planted round the edge of a single plant-pot. Keep the soil moist: one way is to enclose the whole pot in a polythene bag, tying the neck. Warmth is needed but it must be gentle.

Dig the cuttings up after a month or so and examine the parts that were (i) below ground, (ii) above ground. If roots have developed, plant each cutting in a separate pot and keep it moist.

Plants which strike readily are Balsam ("Busy Lizzie"), Tradescantia and twigs of Willow.

528 *Runners*

Examine Creeping Buttercup out-of-doors (it is common on rough lawns). Notice how roots and new shoots are produced, so that a creeping stem may have several plants along its length. Creeping Jenny and Strawberry show the same method of propagation.

Dig up a long underground runner of Couch Grass and observe how it forms new roots and shoots underground, just as Strawberry does above ground.

529 *Biennials*

Cut off a slice (about 1 cm thick) from the top of a Carrot or Radish and stand it in a saucer of water. Notice how within a few days the buds at the top of the section of swollen root grow into stems and leaves.

Pound up a few scrapings from Carrot or Radish, pour on a little boiling water, filter the liquid, and test the solution (Chapter 6) for the food which biennials store for seed production in the second year.

530 *Perennials*

Examine a Potato which has been allowed to sprout, a Crocus corm, and an Iris rhizome. Look for buds and discuss the function of the food stored in the swollen stems. Cut an Onion vertically and observe that in this case it is the leaves which are swollen with food; notice the stem from which they grow and separate the fleshy Onion leaves to find the bud which grows between the stem and a leaf. The thin brown outer leaves are called "scale" leaves.

Refer to the experience of growing bulbs in the classroom. If possible, dig up the old bulb after flowering. Some children will have lifted potatoes and will recall the appearance of the old tuber (see Expt. 108).

Topics: Trees and shrubs as woody perennials; man's use of timber. Other methods of plant propagation—e.g. grafting. Reference to the results of growing Geraniums from cuttings (Expt. 527), noting that the new plants are always similar in type (e.g. in flower colour) to the parent plants. Reference to Chapter 4: the healing of wounds, the regeneration of lost parts (e.g. Earthworm) and the "budding" of Hydra as examples of vegetative growth in animals.

The Evolution of Plants

Refer to experiments with very simple plants (Expt. 70—Spirogyra; Expt. 72—Pleurococcus), and with moulds and fungi (Expts. 173, 177, 178, 180).

531 *Bladderwrack*

(a) Look for brown "bladderwrack" sea-weed between tide levels and collect specimens that have swollen, warty ends. Note the flexible blade

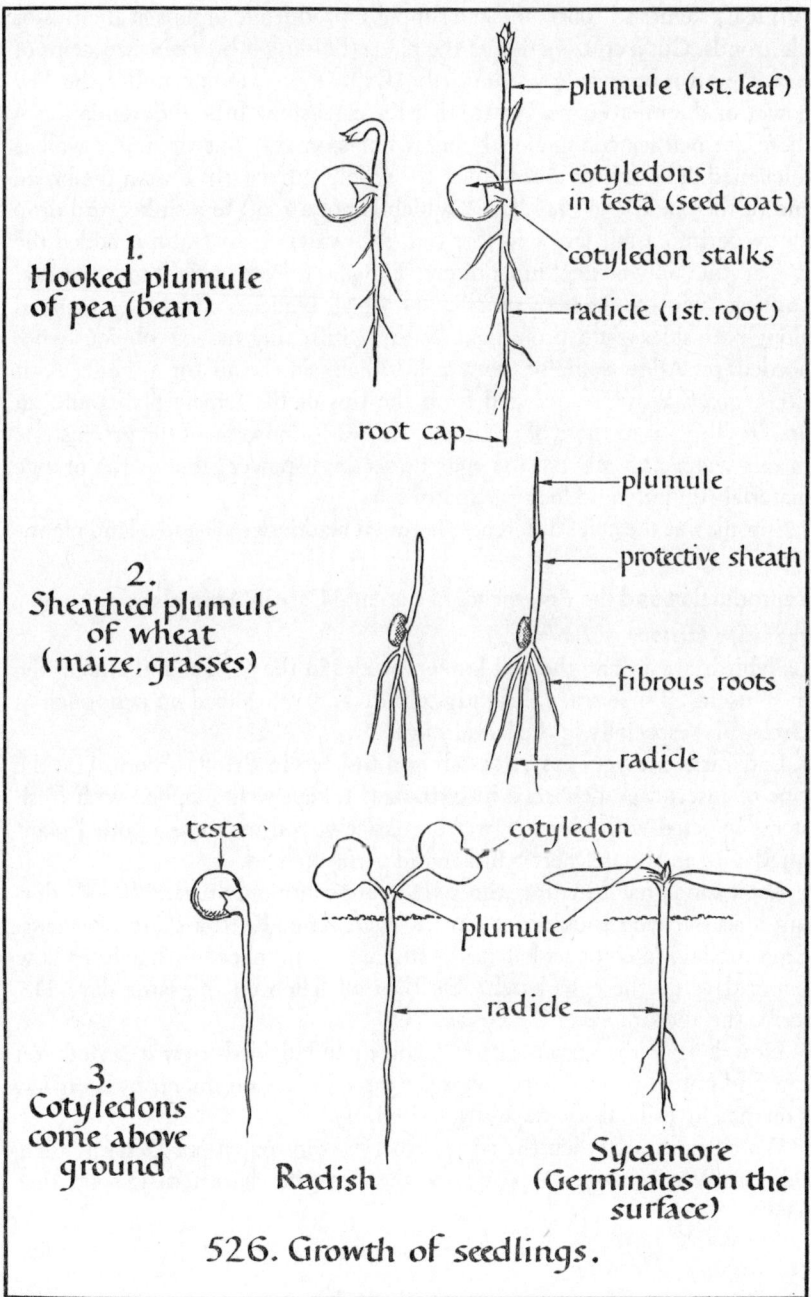

526. Growth of seedlings.

(absence of stiffening tissue), the undifferentiated structure (no division into leaf, stem and root), and the simple reproductive organs at the tips of the fronds. Cut a cross-section of the blade (holding it between two strips of carrot) and mount in glycerine jelly (Expt. 67); examine under the low power of the microscope. Notice that the cells show little differentiation—there are neither conducting bundles nor stomata—but the outer wall is thickened. The fronds absorb over the whole surface. (b) Fasten the broad end of the blade (the "holdfast", which is not a root) to a sinker and drop the weed into a tall jar of 0·8 per cent salt water; if formalin is added the preparation may be kept indefinitely. The plant floats upright to its natural position owing to the buoyant effect of the air-bladders which are arranged along both sides of the prominent mid-rib. Stiffening tissue is obviously not needed. (c) Allow some of the wrack to hang in the air for a while. As it dries, green slime is squeezed from the tips of the female plants and an orange slime from those of the male plants. Mount some of the green slime in salt water and observe the eggs under high power; mount the orange material similarly and look for sperms.

Summarize the chief differences between bladderwrack and a land plant.

Reproduction and the Emergence of Parental Care in Animals

532 *Life History of Ladybirds*

Ladybirds are among the best known beetles in the garden and among the most useful. These small, brightly-coloured creatures feed on pests such as Green Fly, especially in the larval stage.

Ladybirds are very easy to catch and to keep in the classroom. Use the type of insect-cage described in Exp. 62 (b), kept well supplied with fresh stems infected with Green Fly. Alternatively, you may use a potted plant fitted with an acetate-sheet cylinder and perforated lid.

Look for signs of mating. Since there are commonly several broods during a season, you should not have to wait long. Keep a diary of events. Eggs are laid in compact batches: estimate the number in a batch. In how many days do the eggs hatch? Do they all hatch on the same day? Describe the appearance of the larvae.

How long is the larval stage? If you mate ladybirds over a period you can find out whether this period is the same in late summer as it is earlier. You may investigate the pupal stage similarly.

Watch carefully when the adults emerge from pupation. Describe their colours. What changes appear and when are the characteristic spots first seen?

533 *Study of Herring*

(a) *Dissection*: Use herring from the fishmonger's shop. Discuss the stream-lined shape; the scales serving as a tough but smooth and flexible

HOW LIFE IS HANDED ON 441

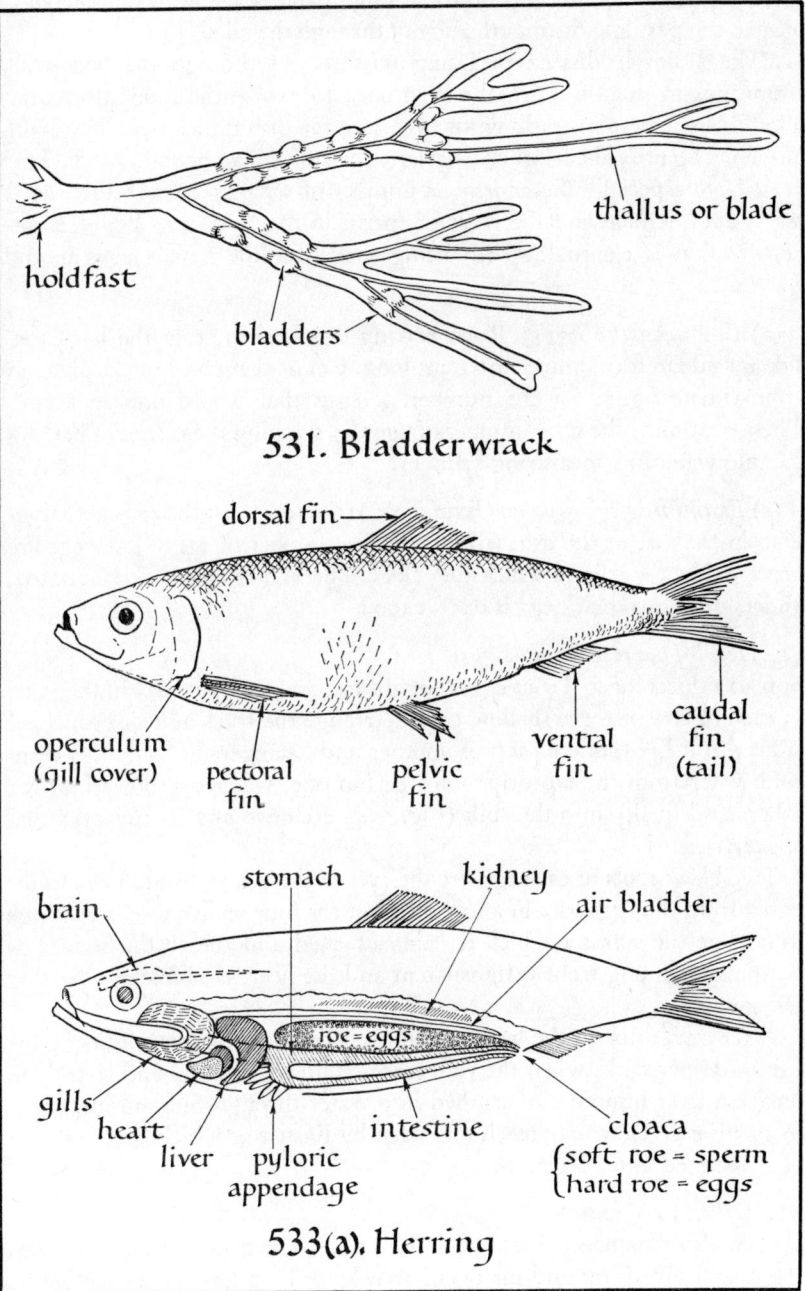

covering; and the fins and tail with which the fish propels and directs itself. Open the mouth and note the huge gape; see how water carrying oxygen can pass into the mouth and out through the gills.

Make a simple dissection. Using scissors, cut through the body-wall from anus to mouth. Turn the flesh back to expose the internal organs. The fish may be pinned down on wax in a pie-dish under a shallow layer of water. Identify the heart and various parts of the alimentary canal (Fig. 533). Note especially the enormous number of separate eggs in the "hard roe" of the female and the mass of sperm in the "soft roe" of the male. Fertilization is external, sperm being shed over the female eggs in the water.

(b) *Counting the Eggs*: Place herring eggs, taken from the hard roe, side by side to form a line just 1 cm long. Count them and so calculate an approximate figure for the number of eggs that would occupy 1 cm^3. Thence estimate the total number of eggs by scraping them from a herring roe into water in a measuring cylinder.

(c) *Examining Frogspawn* (Expt. 61(c)): Note (i) that the eggs are larger than in the case of the fish; (ii) the smaller number of eggs. The eggs are protected by the jelly in which they float. The lighter coloured yolk on the underside of each black egg is reserve food.

534 *Development of Trout Eggs*

Spread a dozen or so Trout eggs (bought from a hatchery early in the year) in each of two or three shallow trays. Arrange the trays in a sink shielded from direct light, one on top of another and "staggered" so that as clean cold water from the tap drips into the top one, water overflows into the others and finally into the sink (Fig. 534). Remove any cloudy eggs that appear.

Two black spots in each egg are the eyes of the young trout. The alevins hatch from the egg cases in a few days but for four or five weeks continue to feed on the yolk sac which remains attached underneath the body. For a time each young trout is transparent and the heart is visible as a beating red spot.

After a week or so the back of the trout begins to darken. Remove the fish to deeper tanks when the yolk sacs are almost used up and feed them on fresh liver minced and crushed into water through fine muslin, or on Water Fleas. They may reach this stage by Easter, at which time they are best liberated into a stream.

535 *Other Vertebrates*

(a) See also Chapter 3. Lizards, and even a Grass Snake, may be kept in the school vivarium; and many children keep Tortoises at home. Reptiles lay shelled eggs and, since fertilization must take place before the shell is

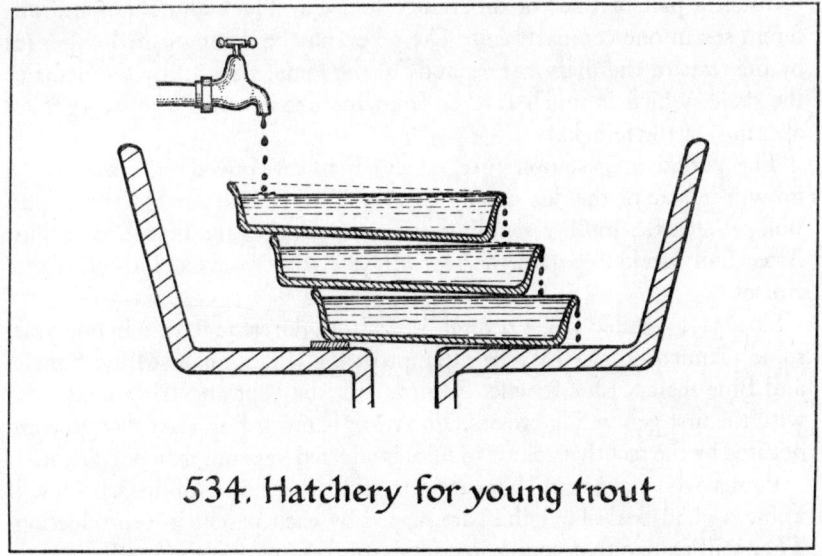

534. Hatchery for young trout

formed, it is evidently internal. The shelled egg means that the embryo is protected, fed and can develop on land without needing external water (contrast the Frog). The female Ringed Snake guards her eggs. In some snakes hatching occurs while the egg is still within the mother's body. Recall the obvious features of a hen's egg; the large quantity of reserve food ("white" and yolk) for the tiny speck which is the embryo; the skin-like envelopes that can be seen when a boiled egg is cracked open; and the porous, brittle shell. The mother's care of her eggs and chicks is proverbial.

(b) Mice: (cf. Hamsters, Chapter 3). Mice are easy to handle but their cages must be kept clean if objectionable smell is to be avoided. Scrub out each cage with water and disinfectant once a week and spread a good layer of clean sawdust or peat moss when the cage is thoroughly dry. Provide plenty of wood wool or finely torn newspapers for the nests. Dust everything inside the cage with louse powder.

Water can be provided from an inverted bottle with a bent glass tube leading into the cage, so that the mice may take what water they require from the end of the tube. Food is best enclosed in a fine-mesh wire basket suspended from the lid of the cage. Rat cake is a complete diet for mice, but whole wheat, dry bread soaked in water and Dandelion leaves may be given, with a little milk and codliver oil occasionally to supply vitamins.

A double, hardwood cage is suitable, about 30 cm square and 15 cm high, divided down the middle with a zinc partition, and with a glass front. In this two families may be kept. Perforated zinc sheet is used for the top of each section, held down by metal clips.

Install a pair of mice of different colour (say Black and Blue) and different sex in one compartment. The sexes may be distinguished either (a) by the teats of the mammary glands in the female; or (b) by the penis of the male, which is much further from the anus than the vulva (genital opening) of the female.

The period of gestation (pregnancy) is twenty-one days. Observe the growth in size of the doe during this time but handle her as little as possible. Watch the mother suckling her young during the first three weeks. After four weeks separate the sexes if you wish to avoid indiscriminate crosses.

Since it is possible to get several litters from the same female in one year, some planned crosses may be attempted; e.g. Black male × Blue female, and Blue male × Blue female. Records must be kept and trials made also with the first-generation crosses. The work is rewarding even though complicated by the fact that colour in mice is affected by more than one factor.

Pupils who have kept hamsters or rabbits at home or in school will know a good deal about the part played by each parent in reproduction. They will realize that young mammals are kept within the mother's body for a considerable time, and that parental care goes on even after birth. Post-natal care is obvious with dogs and cats and horses; but it reaches an infinitely higher level in the case of Man.

Topics: The main vertebrate groups, leading to a study of the characteristics of mammals. Evolution of plants and animals. Adaptations for survival. The interdependence of living things; outdoor excursions to observe some typical plant and animal communities.

Adaptation in the Human Body

536 Upright Stance

(a) The human foot is a highly specialized organ for walking. Walk over a heap of coke in plimsolls, or over any very uneven surface; or walk along the "balancing bars" in the gymnasium. Notice how the foot adjusts itself to maintain the body upright. (b) Moisten the sole of the bare foot and make footprints on paper. Discuss what is seen. (c) Press a hand against the muscle by the trouser pocket opening and take the body weight first on one leg and then on the other; the muscle (the iliacus) can be felt reacting to the strain as the weight shifts. (d) Keeping the hand at the same level, move it round to the back of the leg and repeat the experiment of shifting the weight on to one leg; this time the buttocks muscle is felt in action. (e) Grasp the calf muscle with one hand and stand on that leg; then stand on tip-toe. The muscular movements are very marked.

537 The Human Hand

(a) Count all the bones that can be felt in the hand (compare with the drawing); 14 bones can be felt in the fingers and thumb, 5 more in the

HOW LIFE IS HANDED ON 445

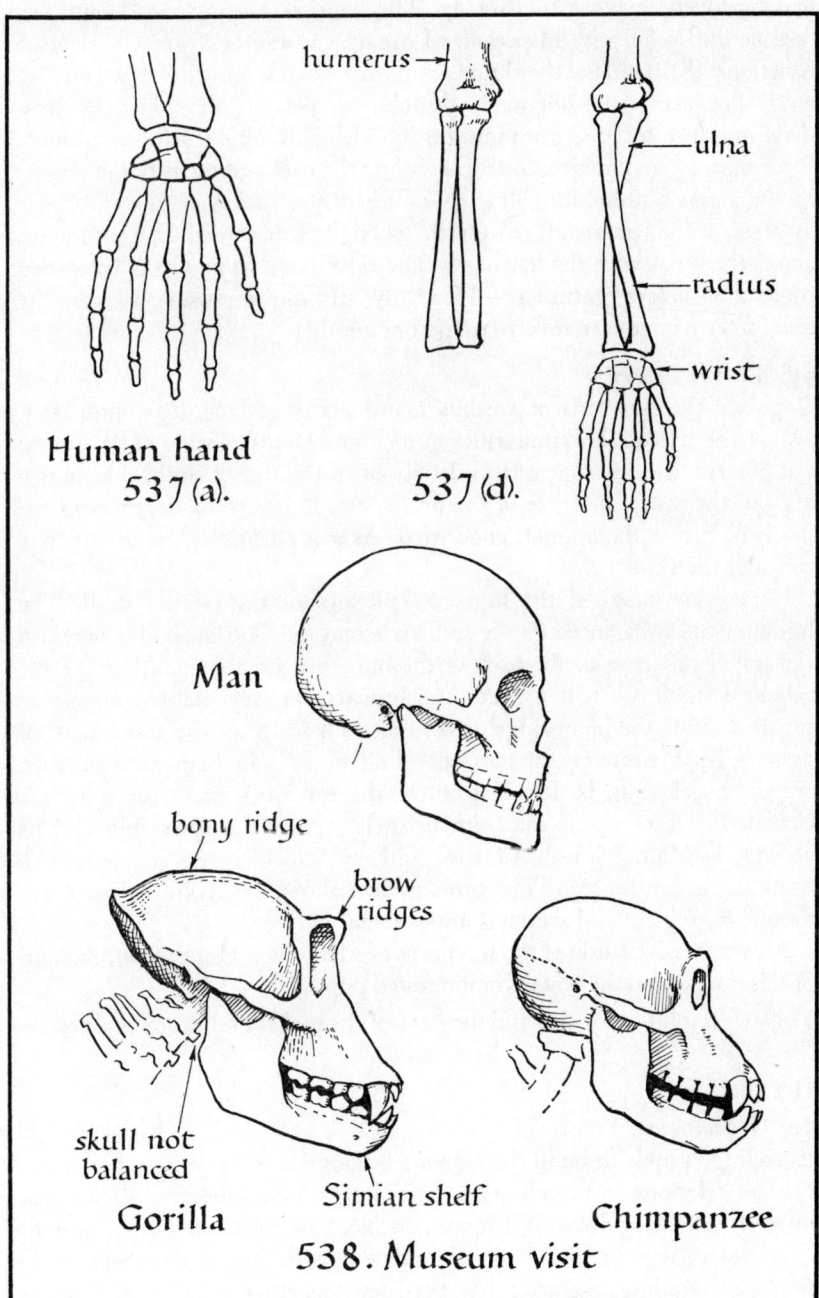

538. Museum visit

back of the hand, and these, with 8 in the wrist which cannot all be identified by touch, make a total of 27. The hand is a complicated but very flexible and relatively unspecialized organ, capable of a great variety of functions. (b) Bandage the thumbs, or wear gloves, and then try to tie up your shoe-laces. The opposable thumb was possibly developed by tree-dwelling ancestors for grasping. (c) The hand is very sensitive to touch. Place various small objects on a tray; close the eyes and identify the objects by touch. As a more difficult exercise, identify a variety of unseen objects as glass, wood, or metal. (d) Grasp the right forearm a few centimetres above the wrist with the left hand. The right hand cannot now be turned more than a few centimetres. Normally, turning is possible because the two forearm bones can revolve round one another.

538 *Visit to Museum*
Compare the skeletons of various mammals—e.g. Dog, Ape and Man. Notice the remarkable similarities in the number and placing of the bones; but observe also the contrasts in detail—as in the size of skull, the appearance of the jaws, the form of the pelvis, etc. Relate the differences to the mode of life of the animals concerned. As a particular example, we may consider the skull.

Draw side views of the human skull and of the Gorilla skull. The human skull is balanced on the spine whereas the Gorilla skull is not, and the spinal processes at the back of the human neck are small because the balanced skull does not need attachments for very large supporting muscles. Note the bony ridge across the ape's scalp for the attachment of powerful jaw muscles (the corresponding muscles in Man need no such ridge; muscles can be felt in front of the ear lobes when the teeth are clenched). Observe also the "simian shelf" under the ape's chin and its absence in Man. Look in a mirror and say "clock": very active tongue movements can be seen. The Simian chin allows no room for such free tongue movement and speech is impossible.

A comparative study of the forelimbs of Man, Ape, Horse, Dog, Bat and Seal is not beyond the powers of interested pupils.

Topics: Evolution; fossils and the story of the rocks. Prehistoric reptiles.

Heredity

539 *Genealogical Tree*
Encourage pupils to build their own genealogical trees, showing as many of their relations and forebears as possible; parents sometimes show great interest in such projects. Wherever possible, hair colour and type (straight or wavy), eye-colour, and height should be shown. Discuss also cases where some outstanding character has persisted—whether a talent for art or craft, or a following of trade or profession. Consider the influence of the

circumstances of life upon, for example, health, length of life and trade or profession.

Topics: The significance of the sexual method of reproduction in relation to variation (the dangers can be mentioned by reference to mental deficiency, haemophylia, etc.). Improvement of plants (e.g. wheat) and of animals (hens, for laying; sheep, for wool; cattle, for beef or for milk-yield; race-horses for speed). Contrast the asexual method (Expt. 527).

Chapter Twenty-Six

Transistors and Radio

A New Discovery in Electronics

On July 15, 1948, there appeared in the *Physical Review* a letter which began:

"A three-element electronic device which utilizes a newly discovered principle ... is described. It may be employed as an amplifier, oscillator, and for other purposes for which vacuum tubes are ordinarily used. The device consists of three electrodes placed on a block of germanium..."

Eight years later, in 1956, the three men responsible for this letter shared the Nobel Prize for Physics. William Shockley, John Bardeen and Walter Brattain of the Bell Telephone Laboratories, New Jersey, had made a major break-through in the field of electronics. They had invented the transistor.

In 1823 Berzelius identified silicon, a crystalline element related chemically to carbon; and in 1906 Pickard invented the "cat's whisker" which was used to "tickle" a silicon crystal in the earliest radio sets, providing a rectifying device or valve. Winkler meanwhile (1886) had discovered germanium, and in 1915 Benedicks used germanium instead of silicon in a rectifier. This is the basic history behind the invention of the transistor in 1948. It reminds us once again that scientific advance is dependent upon the efforts of many people.

A transistor is a device that can be used to increase the strength of weak radio signals. It may consist of a wafer of the metal germanium with small blobs of another material, such as the metal indium, on either side. The three leads to the transistor are respectively the collector (output; marked with a spot), the base (input; the middle lead), and the emitter (common to both input and output circuits, and normally earthed).

The transistor is comparable in action to a radio valve, but it is very small and light and it will work at much lower voltages than the ordinary valve. It also uses very little power, needing no heater current. Wherever space and weight must be kept down, and power conserved, transistors offer great advantages and already they are the basis of an enormous industry. Not only in such things as transistor radios and transistorized hearing aids, but on a much vaster scale in computers, telephone switch gear, aircraft, guided missiles and Earth satellites men are learning the far-ranging possibilities of this new discovery.

It is the purpose of the present Chapter to enable any interested teacher to construct a number of simple transistorized devices for him- (her-)self, to investigate some of their characteristics, and to employ them in the laboratory in ways which will certainly interest many of our ordinary pupils. We treat the subject entirely practically, but we hope that teachers will read for themselves, in the many books that are available, enough of the underlying theory to enable them to build on the foundation presented here.

For school purposes, individual transistors can be mounted on small wooden bases with connecting tags, so arranged that a series of units automatically connect together when inserted into a suitable block. This unit method allows transistors to be added into a circuit one by one, and the effects observed. The units can be kept in stock and, with little modification, used over and over again and in a variety of circuits.

The best starting point for the work is a radio crystal set using a crystal diode detector, which incorporates a germanium crystal and acts like a valve because it allows current to pass in one direction only.

540 How to Make A Crystal Set

We first describe essential components:

The "earth": Make a strong soldered connection to a length of iron piping which is then hammered into the ground; or bury a sheet of galvanized iron (about 30 cm square) leaving a corner with the soldered wire connection exposed. A gallon oil can is satisfactory but not very durable. Gas or water pipes are sometimes useful.

Earphones: A high resistance pair (2000 ohm) is needed; this is the only expensive item. (Earpieces supplied for "personal listening" sets are often unsuitable since they may not conduct direct current.)

Crystal diode detector: Any germanium diode is suitable. Radio signals generate high frequency alternating currents, the effect of which on a telephone diaphragm would be zero (since the positive and negative impulses would cancel each other out). The current through the diode is unidirectional and the high frequency pulses add up to produce a response in the earphone. A capacitor is often added to provide a smoothing effect (although the connecting cords of the earphones may serve this purpose).

Tuning capacitor: A compression tuner value ·0005 μF is suitable. It is compact and cheap, consisting of several thin metal plates connected in two groups insulated from one another by plastic interleaving. Any ·0005 μF air-spaced variable capacitor will serve however.

Tuned coil: Signal strength is much improved by connecting a coil from aerial to earth and tuning it by means of a variable capacitor. Wind 60 to 70 turns of No. 28 D.C.C. copper wire on a cardboard cylinder of about 5 cm diameter, so as to occupy a length of 3–4 cm. With a normal aerial such a coil should cover the B.B.C. medium wave band. A more compact coil may be made by winding 60 turns of the same wire on a paper-covered ferrite rod 5 cm long × 1 cm diameter.

Aerial: Carry copper wire (15 or more metres long) to the top of the building, preferably on the side facing the B.B.C. transmitter (since the building would probably have some shielding effect). Suspend it from an insulated support (e.g. perspex or waxed wood fixed to the chimney or an upper window) and carry the lower end into the laboratory or workroom, wrapping the wire with polythene where it comes into contact with any part of the building.

Assembly: See Figs. 540 (i)–(iii). The wooden base (9 cm × 6 cm × 1 cm) has tinplate contact pieces (about 8 mm wide) screwed down to it on three edges. The set components are arranged on the base as shown. Aerial, earth and phone leads terminate in small tin connectors bent round the leads (Fig. 540 (iii), with the free ends inserted between the base and a contact piece. The wire leads from the other components are inserted directly between base and contact piece.

At distances of up to 30 kilometres loud clear signals should be received on the earphones. Some results should be expected even up to 70 or 80 kilometres.

541 Action of a Diode

Connect a diode in series with a 0–15 milliammeter and a 1½-volt cell, joining the red (positive) end of the diode to the positive of the cell. Read the meter. Then reverse the cell connections: does any current now flow?

542 How to Solder a Transistor into a Circuit

Transistors and diodes are easily damaged by heat, so that special care must be taken when soldering them into a circuit. If a small pair of pliers is used to grip the lead between the soldering point and the transistor (or diode), the mass of metal in the pliers will act as a heat shunt, conducting heat away. If the pliers are kept closed by means of a stout rubber band, both hands remain free for manipulation in the soldering process. The pliers are left in position until the soldered joint has cooled. Use cored solder (flux at centre) and a small, 15-watt, soldering iron with a pencil bit. The secret of soldering success is to use an iron sufficiently hot to make the join at the first touch.

It is convenient to solder a short length (2–3 cm) of tinned copper wire to

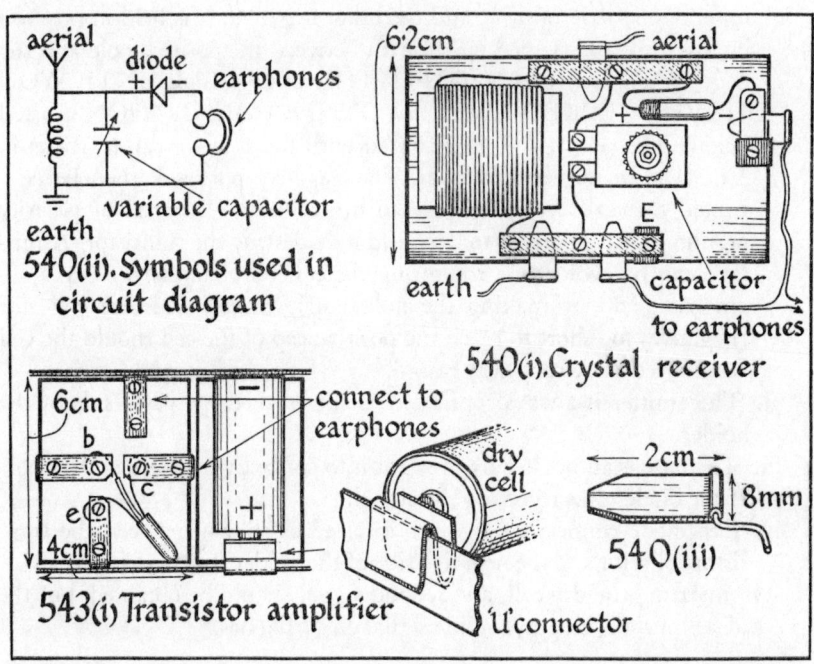

each point in the circuit to which the transistor is to be connected. The free end of the wire is then bent round the tip of the appropriate lead of the transistor and soldered to it using the heat shunt.

543 *A Transistor-Amplifier for a Crystal Set*
An OC71 or OC72 (Mullard) transistor is suitable. Mount it on a wooden base, 6 cm × 4 cm × 1 cm, fitted with four tin-plate connecting strips (thin metal, about 1 cm wide × 2.5 cm long) screwed down and then bent down over the edges as indicated (Figs. 543 (i)–(iii)). It is easier to drill screw-holes in a large plate from which short lengths are cut as required. Each screw is driven in just 5 mm from the edge of the base after starting a hole in the base with an awl.

A special tray is now required, made by tacking 2-cm wide tin strip to the two long sides of a wooden board so that the strip projects 1 cm above the top surface of the board. The board is 20 cm long × 6.2 cm wide (important) × 1 cm thick. The crystal-set and the transistor-amplifier fit into the tray between the metal strips, with which they make electrical contact through the right-angled connecting strips when the circuit is complete (Fig. 543 (iv)). A short right-angled strip must be added to the crystal set, labelled E in Fig. 540. Note the following points:
i. A 1½-volt dry-cell is to be fitted between the metal strips of the tray,

making one strip positive and the other negative. It is held in position by inserting a U-shaped piece of tin between the positive pole and the edge of the tray. DO NOT FIT THE DRY CELL UNTIL YOU HAVE CHECKED ALL THE OTHER CONNECTIONS, listed below. The cell MUST be inserted with the positive cap (carbon) in contact with the earthed strip. The negative pole will then be connected through the ear-phones to the collector. Reversal of polarity permits a heavy current to flow and may destroy the transistor. A mistake can be avoided by mounting the cell on a standard 6-cm × 4-cm base, and by making the holder-strip linked with the collector (negative) too short to reach the positive cap of the cell should the cell be inserted the wrong way round.

ii. The emitter is always connected to the earthed, positive, side of the holder.
iii. The base is automatically brought into contact with the negative pole of the diode, thus receiving the signal.
iv. Ear-phone connecting tags are inserted as shown between the transistor collector and the negative side of the holder (Fig. 543 (i)).

On inserting the dry cell, a very loud signal should be obtained, but the crystal set must provide an audible signal on earphones.

544 *Loud-speaker Receiver*

A single transistor may give a current magnification of about ×50, of which half is usable. Two transistors may thus provide useful amplification of perhaps $\times(30)^2$, sufficient to operate a loud-speaker. Suitable speakers can often be salvaged from surplus TV or radio sets. The resistance of these speakers is usually 3 ohm, while the output impedence (resistance to alternating currents) of a transistor may be of the order of 10,000 ohm. A matching output transformer must, therefore, be connected with the speaker and it is likely that this will have to be bought new, since transformers salvaged from radio sets are unsuitable. Ask for a transistor output transformer. Connect the two thicker leads to the loud-speaker.

Make up a second transistor unit exactly like the first. Plug it into the chain between the first transistor and the cell. Fix the loud-speaker in an upright position on a plywood base and mount the transformer on the same base, connecting it up to the speaker. Insert the speaker/transformer unit between the collector of the final transistor and the negative strip of the holder. Between the collector of the first transistor and the negative strip interpose a 2200 ohm resistor. The resistor is held is position temporarily and its effect observed; other values are then tried (e.g. 1500 ohm, 3900 ohm . . .) until the most suitable one is found. 2200 ohm is generally satisfactory to supply the small current required to feed the collector, but as the same source must also supply current to the base of the second

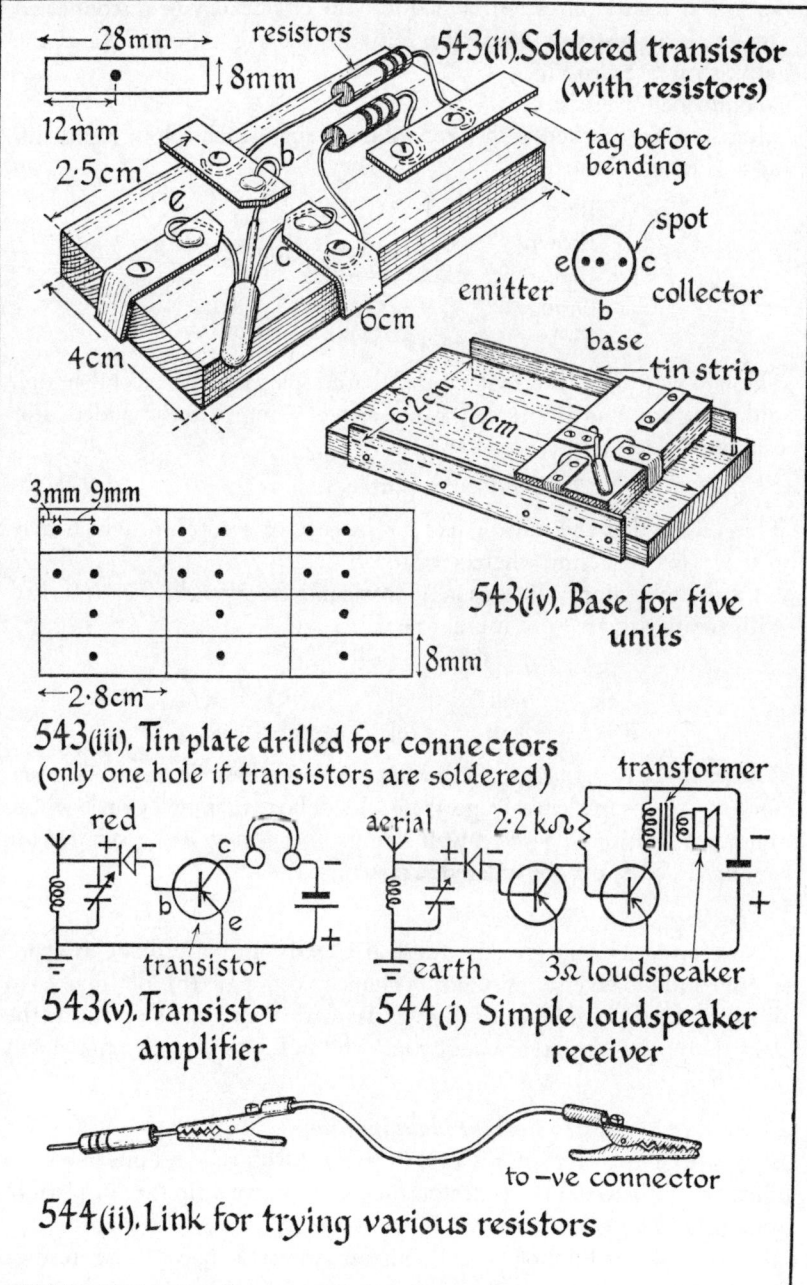

transistor, ideally at a lower voltage, compromise is necessary. See also Expt. 548. A resistor already fastened into the circuit may be disconnected by inserting a plastic or card strip between the tag concerned and the negative strip. See also Fig. 544 (ii).

Colour code for Resistors:

Resistors are marked with three coloured rings, each colour representing a different number:

Black	0	Green	5
Brown	1	Blue	6
Red	2	Purple	7
Orange	3	Grey	8
Yellow	4	White	9

The end ring gives the first figure, the middle ring the second figure, and the third ring indicates the number of noughts to be added. For example:

Yellow (end ring), purple, red . . . 4700

This means that the resistor has a resistance of 4700 ohm, which may also be written 4·7k ohm, where k = 1000.

Of the following values usually obtainable from stock, those marked with an asterisk are most useful to us:

1k*	1·2k	1·5k*	1·8k	2·2k*
3·3k	3·9k*	4·3k	4·7k*	5·6k
6·8k*	8·2k	10k	100k*	

The accuracy is ±10%, sufficient for most purposes. These carbon resistors are so cheap that salvage from old radio sets is not worth while. They are sold in ½, 1 and 2-watt ratings, the ½-watt being suitable for our needs. They may be ordered in dozens.

545 Testing Diode Resistance

(a) An ohm-meter will give the "forward" resistance of a diode as about 200 ohm and the reverse resistance as about 10,000 ohm. (b) Join up a 0–10 milliammeter and a 1½-volt cell in series with the diode. Current in the forward direction should be about 7 mA and in the reverse direction about a fiftieth of this.

546 Testing Transistor Current Magnification

Use your mounted transistor. Connect to a 1½-volt cell and put in a 0–10 milliammeter between the collector and the negative strip (i.e. in place of earphones). The current shown is known as the leakage current and is only a small fraction of a milliampere. Insert a 15 000 ohm resistor mounted on a 6 cm × 4 cm base between the transistor base and the negative strip (Fig. 546): the meter may now read 5 mA.

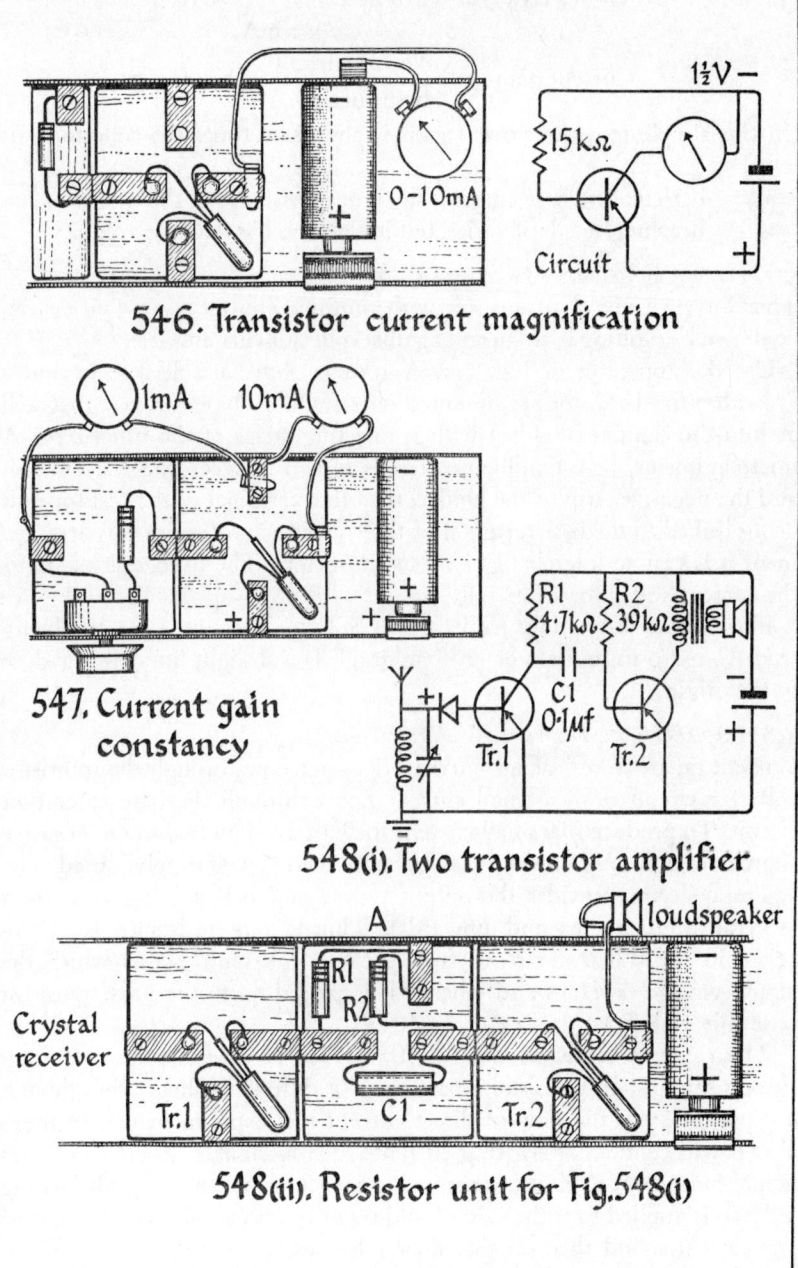

546. Transistor current magnification

547. Current gain constancy

548(i). Two transistor amplifier

548(ii). Resistor unit for Fig. 548(i)

Collector current = 5 mA.
By Ohm's Law, base current = $1\frac{1}{2}/15\,000$ A.
= 0·1 mA.

$$\text{Current gain} = \frac{\text{collector current}}{\text{base current}} = 5/0\cdot1 = 50.$$

(In this simple test, the current gain is always 10 times the collector current.)

Note: In calculating base current, the input resistance of the transistor has been neglected: it varies, but it is always less than 1000 ohm.

547 Testing Constancy of Current Gain

The Current Gain of a transistor with common emitter is constant, as can be shown by plotting base current against collector current.

Use the apparatus of Fig. 547. A 100 000 ohm variable resistor and a 4700 ohm fixed resistor are mounted on a standard base (i.e. one that will fit into the standard holder) with connecting strips of the usual type. A micro-ammeter, or 0-1 milliammeter, is linked between the resistor unit and the negative strip of the holder, the other terminal of the resistor unit being linked to the base terminal of the transistor unit; with this arrangement it is easy to interchange various transistors. The fixed resistor limits the current and is for safety only.

Plot a series of readings for base and collector currents, the latter being read from a 0-10 milliammeter. The graph is a straight line passing close to the origin.

548 Amplifier with Improved Voltage Control

Current (apart from leakage current) does not flow through the transistor collector circuit until a small current flows through the base to emitter circuit. To produce this small current the base is connected to the negative source through a *high* resistor; say 39k ohm if a $1\frac{1}{2}$-volt supply is used.

The collector provides the output power and passes a higher current (several milliamperes and upwards). Thus a *low* resistance is appropriate in the collector circuit, from 2·2k to 10k ohm, across which the signal voltage develops and whence it is passed on to the next transistor base (Fig. 548 (i)).

The capacitor between the two transistors is necessary because transistor 1 output and transistor 2 base work at different voltages; but though a capacitor stops the flow of direct current this experiment demonstrates that it will conduct alternating currents such as signals. There can be no actual movement of electrons across the capacitor, but when an alternating voltage is applied to it there is a build-up of electrons first on one plate of the capacitor and then on the other (alternately, at high frequency), so that the effect of an alternating current is transmitted.

While the two resistors and the capacitor can be added directly to the transistor units, it is preferable to mount them on a separate base (Fig. 548 (ii)). When two leads are connected to the same point, washers or short tin strips should be inserted under the screw heads.

549 *A Capacitor can Store Electricity*

In one of its simplest forms a capacitor consists of two metal plates separated by an insulator (dielectric) which may be mica, waxed paper, polythene ... or even air. Usually there are many layers of metal foil linked alternately to give the effect of two very large plates; variable capacitors often have two sets of aluminium vanes which may be turned on an axle to vary the amount of overlap (the air between is the dielectric). When a capacitor is joined to a source of electromotive force, electrons are accumulated on the plate attached to the negative pole and drawn away from the other plate. Although electrons cannot flow across the dielectric, a state of strain is set up there which is only relieved when the capacitor is discharged. The ability of a capacitor to store charge depends upon the area of the plates, their distance apart and the nature of the dielectric. The unit of capacity is the farad (F); for practical purposes the micro-farad (μF), a millionth of a farad, is often convenient.

Connect a 4μF capacitor with a pair of phones as shown in Fig. 549. Put the phones on your head and touch the leads X and Y to the terminals of a 12-volt D.C. supply. Listen for the single "click" as the capacitor is charged. Then disconnect from the supply and touch X and Y together; another click indicates the discharge. Replace the phones by a centre-zero milliammeter and repeat the operations of charge and discharge.

Examine the power of the capacitor to hold its charge by allowing time to pass between charging and attempting the discharge.

550 *A Capacitor and Alternating Voltage*

The ability of the capacitor to transmit the effect of alternating voltage (Expt. 548) may be demonstrated as follows:

Make a capacitor from two flat cooking tins and a slightly larger sheet of polythene or thin paper. Use crocodile clips to join leads to the two metal plates. Set up a crystal set with earphones (Expt. 540) and check that a signal is being received. Then disconnect one phone lead from the set and insert the capacitor in series with set and phones. The signal is still audible, though weaker than before.

551 *A Three-Transistor Receiver*

The circuit shown in Fig. 551 (i) makes a sensitive receiver, easily set up using units already described with the addition of two resistors and a 25μF capacitor in the crystal receiver circuit. The aerial may be a 2-metre length of wire at ceiling height and the earth a metal plate laid on the floor.

The value of the resistor (called a feed-back resistor) between the final collector and the first base is somewhat critical: 330k ohm is usually satisfactory with the circuit shown. Sensitivity is increased if the first transistor is of a high-frequency type (OC44) and then the feed-back resistor may need to be larger. If a 1-megohm variable resistor is used as a temporary feed-back, the best value can be determined and a fixed resistor then substituted. Selectivity, and sometimes volume, is increased by connecting the diode to an aerial tapping (point X, Fig. 551 (i)) so as to include only about one-fifth of the coil in the diode circuit.

Note on D.C. (direct current) "feed-back" and "phase reversal":
The feed-back resistor from the final collector to the first base stabilizes the D.C. voltages on all three transistors. This is necessary because when a transistor warms up the current increases, so causing the temperature to rise further. The cumulative result may be sufficient to overheat and so destroy the transistor.

D.C. Feed-back with One Transistor: In Fig 551 (ii) a high resistor (200k ohm) is connected across the base and collector of the same transistor. If the collector current increases, the voltage drop across the collector resistor will increase and the collector will become less negative. The base voltage will then become less negative also and this effect, called feed-back, will reduce the current through the transistor and check any tendency to overheat. Thus direct feed-back in a transistor from collector to base has a stabilizing effect.

Phase Reversal in Transistors: Positive pulses at the base (input) are converted to negative pulses at the collector. This change of polarity is known as phase reversal and is inherent in the action of a transistor.

Feed-back across Two Transistors: If feed-back is used from the final collector to the first base, the two phase reversals cancel and so, feed-back is in phase (positive feed-back). The current builds up until the circuit oscillates continuously. The arrangement is used to generate audio-frequency oscillations (see Expt. 552).

Feed-back with Three Transistors: With three phase reversals, feed-back from the final transistor to the first base is negative and so can be used for stabilization.

552 Audio-frequency Oscillator

Use the apparatus shown in Figs. 548 and 552. Remove the crystal receiver unit and replace it by the 100k ohm variable resistor used in Expt. 547. Connect the resistor through a 0·1 μF capacitor to the collector of the second transistor (the capacitor may be made a part of the resistor unit). Use a 3-volt cell. An audible note is generated, which can be varied over a wide range by varying the resistor. To extend the range to the upper limit of audibility a 500k ohm variable resistor is needed.

The circuit is shown in Fig. 552. Greater volume can be obtained by

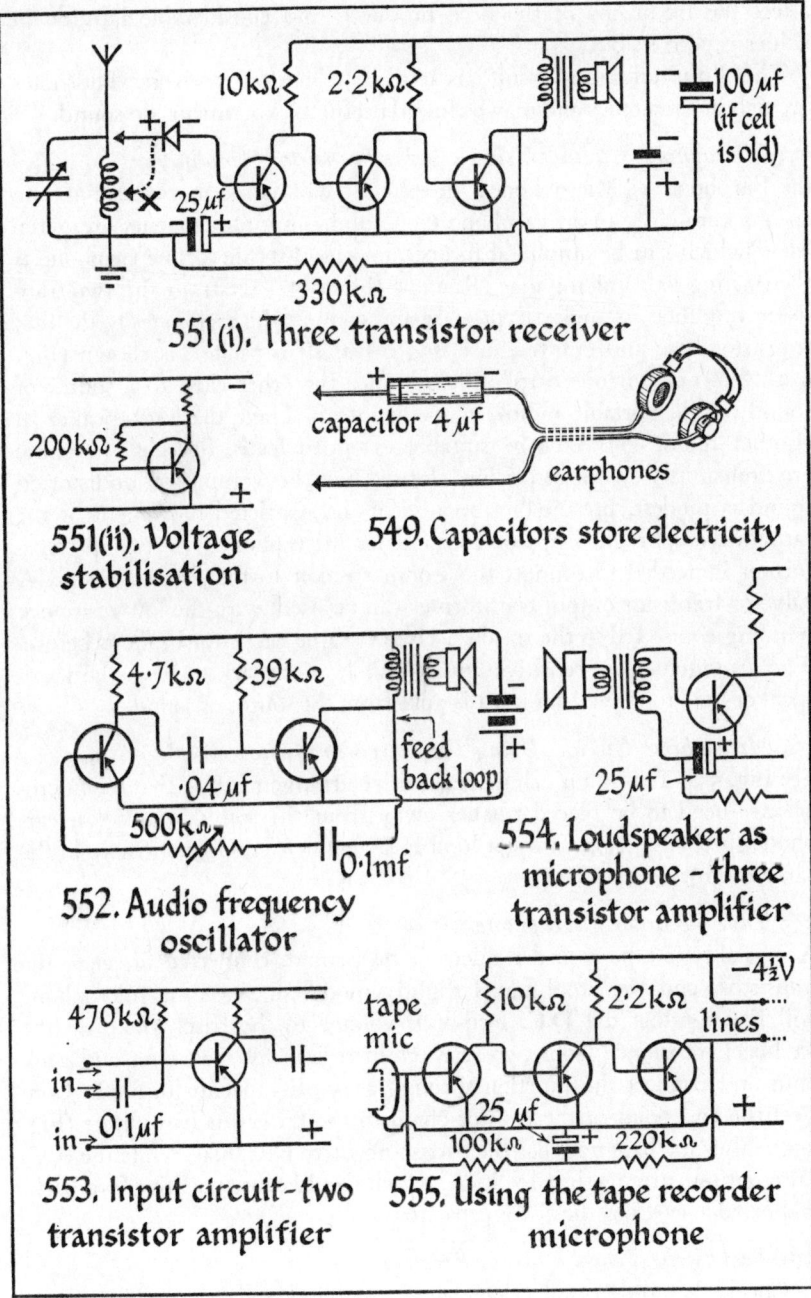

increasing the cell voltage up to about 7.5 volts. Most of the components affect the frequency of the note produced and considerable latitude in values is permissible.

This "multivibrator circuit" is used in television receivers. The notes are rich in harmonics and may be found useful in experiments on sound.

533 *Microphone Circuits Using a Two-Transistor Amplifier.*
(a) Earphone as Microphone: Earphones will work in reverse; if one speaks very close to an earphone (2000 ohm), minute currents are generated which can be amplified to operate a loud-speaker. The earphone is then acting as a microphone. Remove the crystal set from the two-transistor amplifier assembly (Expt. 548) and connect the earphones to the first transistor base and emitter, inserting a 0·1 μF capacitor as shown (Fig. 553). Short-circuit one earphone and place the other close to a source of sound (clock, portable radio), or speak into it. Have the loud-speaker in another room, connected by suitably extended leads. Speech and music are transmitted with surprising clarity, but the volume of undistorted sound is modest, presumably because of the restricted movement of the earphone diaphragm. (b) Loud-speaker as Microphone: A step-up transformer is needed to connect the 3-ohm speaker to the first transistor. A valve or transistor output transformer can be used, with the low resistance winding connected to the speaker. Use the same capacitor input as before. The arrangement is sensitive and it will be necessary to have the loud-speaker "microphone" at some distance from the source of sound.

554 *Microphone Circuits Using the Three-Transistor Amplifier.*
See Fig. 554. This is a much more sensitive arrangement, so that the microphones need to be placed further away from the sound source (an earphone, perhaps 10 cm away; a loud-speaker microphone, anywhere in the same room).

555 *Tape Recorder Microphone*
A crystal-type tape recorder microphone is used, connected direct to the transistor, and the amplifier is slightly modified, since the microphone will not conduct the D.C. feed-back voltage to the base. Make up the feed-back resistance from two resistors in series, say 100k ohm and 220k ohm and connect the junction through a 25 uF capacitor to earth. Connect the end point of the resistor chain to the transistor base direct (Fig. 555). Thus the base now has the correct negative D.C. bias, while the A.C. (alternating current) signal voltage, which would cause negative feed-back, is shorted to earth by the 25 uF capacitor.

556 *Testing the Two-Transistor Receiver Circuit*
1. Check that the crystal circuit alone is giving a clearly audible phone signal.

TRANSISTORS AND RADIO 461

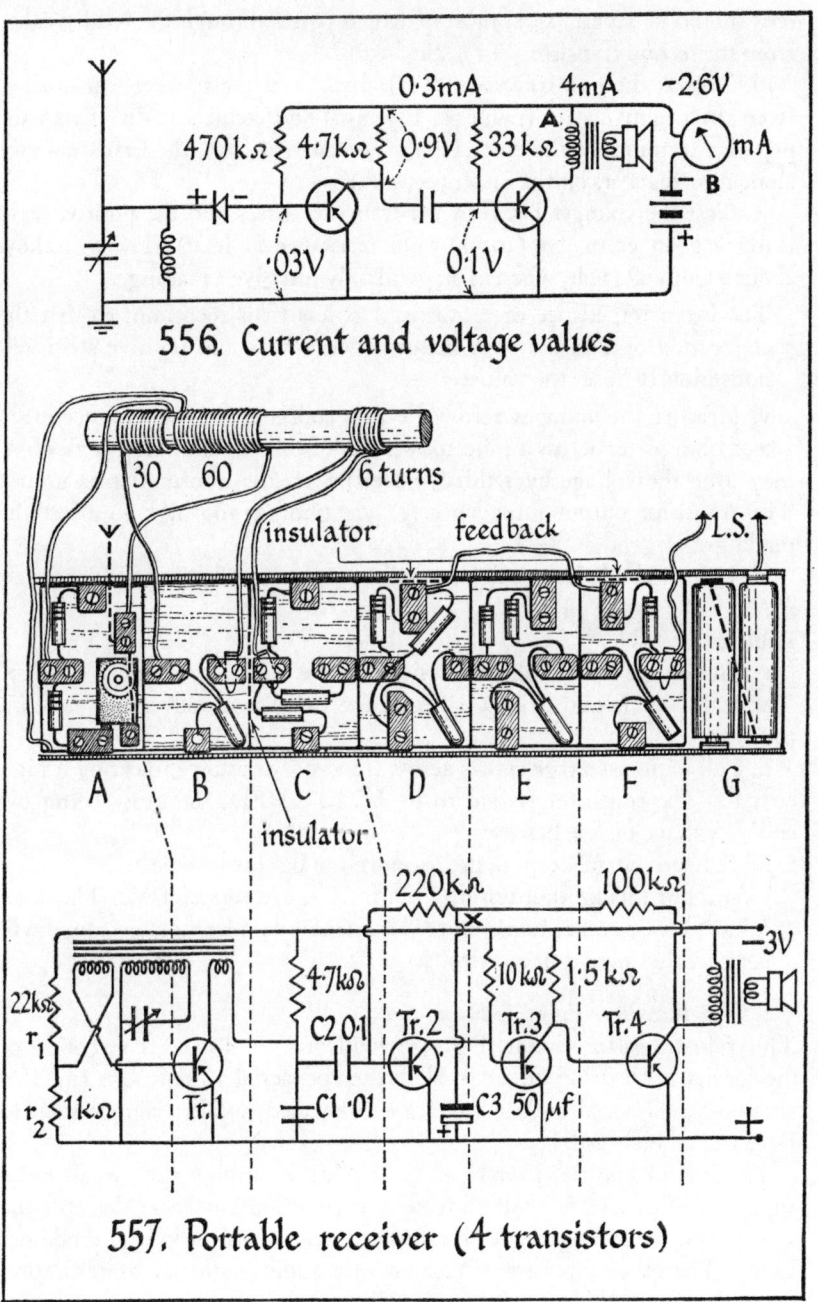

556. Current and voltage values

557. Portable receiver (4 transistors)

ii. Connect a 0–10 milliammeter in the negative battery lead. The current should be several mA, most of which passes through the loud-speaker from the second transistor (Tr_2) (Fig. 556).

iii. To test the first transistor (Tr_1), disconnect the speaker transformer from the negative strip (point A, Fig. 556) and connect it directly to the negative terminal of the battery (B). The current from the first transistor alone now registers on the meter (0·3 mA).

iv. Test the voltages between the transistor bases and the positive strip using a 0–10 voltmeter (10,000 ohm resistance at least). Tr_2 will show about a tenth of a volt, whereas Tr_1 will only just give a reading.

> The input impedance of a transistor is less than 1000 ohm so that the connection of a 10,000 ohm meter between base and positive strip will not seriously upset the values.

v. Measure the voltages across the first collector resistor. Connecting a 10,000 ohm meter across a collector resistor of comparable value (4·7k ohm) may drop the voltage by a third; nevertheless, the information is useful. The transistor output impedance (c. 30k ohm) is too high to affect the readings.

vi. Using Ohm's Law, calculate collector currents flowing in Tr_1 (¼–1 mA).

Faults:

i. No voltage across collector resistor means that no current is flowing. The transistor is said to be OFF and the cause is usually no voltage on the base.

ii. Full battery voltage shows across transistor resistor, indicating a high current. The transistor is said to be BOTTOMED, the cause being excessive voltage on the base.

iii. Battery voltage drops in use: a worn-out battery is indicated.

> Note: For this kind of testing, multimeters are very suitable. The Avo-minor, for example, fulfils all requirements; its microampere range will indicate the current in a crystal set.

557 Four-transistor Portable Radio Set

This four-transistor circuit (Fig. 557) will give loud-speaker reception of the local station using an internal ferrite rod aerial 10 cm × 1 cm. If a short external aerial and an earth are connected, weaker signals such as Radio 3 can be heard.

The first OC44 transistor has a dual role: it amplifies the weak radio signal, making use of positive feed-back (reaction); it also "detects" the signal, and the arrangement gives better results than the crystal diode detector. The other three transistors provide audio-frequency amplification using the almost unchanged circuit of Fig. 555.

The very small current of Tr_1 is controlled by a potential divider ($r_1 =$

22k ohm; r_2 = 1k ohm), which puts a small voltage on the Tr_1 base through the 30-turn coil, wound from 32 D.C.C. wire on a ferrite rod. The tuned 60-turn coil is wound close to the base coil and is also earthed. Feed-back, or reaction, is provided by a 6-turn coil on the same ferrite rod, connected between the transistor collector and the 4·7k ohm resistor; the two tags concerned are separated by a card insulator. A coupling unit, C, is provided between the first transistor and the amplifier; high frequency ripple remaining after detection is shorted to earth via the capacitor C_1.

The junction (X) of the three components of the feed-back link is anchored to the top tag of block D. This tag is not otherwise used and is separated from the negative strip by a card insulator.

The battery supply is 3 volts. The reaction coil will slide along the ferrite rod and moving it towards the 60-turn coil should increase signal strength; if this is not the case, remove the reaction coil and having turned it round replace it with the connections reversed. The coupling should not, however, be too close, else the signal will be distorted and interference may occur in other receivers. The reaction coil is finally fixed in position with wax. Reaction can be increased, if necessary, by using more turns in the coil, or by increasing the capacity of C_1.

The ferrite rod aerial is too long for convenient mounting on the units, but it may be held in two cardboard loops pinned to the loud-speaker board.

There will be a delay of up to 10 seconds before the signal is heard. This is the time taken for the feed-back capacitor C_3 to charge up through the high resistance of 100k ohm.

In testing the circuit, always use new batteries. Old ones have increased resistance which is common to all the transistor circuits and which may cause positive feed-back and distortion. Temperature extremes can also be a source of trouble. Current and voltage values to be expected with a 3-volt battery are indicated below:

	Collector resistor (R)	Voltage (E) on collector resistor	Current = E/R
Tr_1	4·7 ohm	1·2 volt	0·25 mA
Tr_2	10k ohm	2·2 volt.	0·22 mA
Tr_3	1·5k ohm	2·2 volt	1·5 mA
Tr_4	—	—	8–10 mA

The value of the Tr_4 collector current varies markedly with change in the value of the feed-back resistor.

Transistor types: At the time of going to press, the transistors used in these circuits were freely available from advertisers in the practical wireless journals. OC71 and OC72 are audio frequency amplifiers, and any similar transistors may be used in their place. The 300 000 ohm feedback resistor may need to be changed. Modern equivalents recommended by Mullard are ACY20 and ACY21.

The first transistor (OC44) is a radio frequency type and substitution of any other R.F. transistor (Mullard ASY26 or 27) may affect reaction. This can be increased by using more than 6 turns on the reaction coil, or by increasing C_1 the by-pass capacitor or by connecting a small capacitor across r_2 (1k ohm).

If silicon transistors are used, the battery polarity as a rule must be reversed.

Sources of supply of radio components: Local radio service shops and shops dealing in surplus equipment; advertisers in the practical radio periodicals. Loud-speakers (3-ohm) may be salvaged from discarded radio or TV sets.

Advertisers in the *School Science Review* sometimes offer to supply catalogues free to educational establishments (e.g. Radiospares, 13 Epworth Street, E.C.2; and Hardmans, Baillie Street, Rochdale). The *Mullard Reference Manual of Transistor Circuits* will be found very useful.

Index

Index

Abler pupils 345
Absorption of food 114
Acceleration of gravity 356
Accumulator 229
Acid burn, treatment 32
Acidity of soil 424, 428
Acids, common 111
　properties 112
Acoustics 280
Action and reaction 410
Adhesive tape, uses 31
Aerial 450
Aerofoil 416
Aeroplane, controls 416
　flight 414
　lift 416
　propeller 414
　steering 416
Agar jelly 159
Aims of Science teaching 170, 188, 432
Air, altered during burning 34
　and nature of matter 9
　and rusting 34
　convection in 22
　expansion of 24
　from lungs 11
　in soil 11
　in water 124
　lift of moving 416
　moisture in 172
　pressure 11, 12, 22
　oxygen in 34
　resistance 11, 414
　weight of 12
Alcohol distillation 167
Alderfly larva 54
Alimentary canal 106
Alkalis, emulsifying action 108
　properties of 111
Alternator model 258
Alum 128
Ammonia 427
Ammonium sulphate 427
Ammeter 228
Amoeba 63
Amphibians 57

Amplifier, transistor 451
Aneroid barometer 14
Animals, in soil 425
　reproduction in 440
Annealing 246
Annual rings 81
Antiseptics 164
Ants 58
Apparatus and equipment for Science teaching 27
Aquarium 48, 57
　aerator 122
Aquatic animals 47, 51
　plants 47, 48
Arm movements 364
Arteries, and first aid 127
　and pulse 126
Artificial manures 427
Association of Science Education 391
Astigmatism 311
Astronomical telescope 302
Atmosphere, knowledge of 9
Atmospheric pressure 14
Atomic theory 10
Audio-frequency oscillator 458
Aural aids to teaching 282

Bacteria, growth of 160
　infection by 160, 161
　in soil 426
　of decomposition 428
　on legumes 160
　useful 166
Baking powder 112
Balance, and stability 370
　letter 354
　lever 140, 368
　of body 372
　spiral spring 352
　spring strip 180
　to weigh pupil 369
Balanced meals 150
Barometer 21
　and atmospheric pressure 22
　aneroid 14
　mercury 22

468 INDEX

Bath salts 181
Beaks of birds 102
Beaufort wind scale 342
Belt drive 356
Bending nails 368
  glass tubing 29
Biennials 438
Bimetal-strip alarm 31
Binocular vision 308
Biological material, storage of 363
Birds, feet and beaks 102
  footprints 104
Blackboard 286
Bladderwrack 438
Bleaching powder, chlorine from 192
  use of 192
Blind spot 306
Blood, and oxygen 128
  capillaries and corpuscles 127
  circulation 130
  nature of 128
  smear 128
  temperature 134
Blowing hole in glass tube 132
Bodies, at rest 348
  falling 356
  in motion 350
Body, balance 372
  conducts electricity 229
  movement, control of 372
  outer defences of 166
Boiling point, and pressure 198
  of water 197
Bone, nature of 72
Books for Science teaching 120, 323, 393
Boring corks 29
Botanical key 78
Bourdon gauge 18
Box camera 297
Bread-making 93
Breakages and shortages book 269
Breathing, carbon dioxide exhaled 42
  movements of fish and frog 122
  movements of man 18
Bricks and pottery 380
British Thermal Unit 144
Building materials 379
Bullock's eye 306
Bunsen burner 205
Buoyancy of water 178
Burgundy mixture 166
Burn treatment 32
Burner, Bunsen 205
  spirit 204
Burning and rusting 34
  glass 300
Bursts due to freezing 194

Buttercup flower parts 433
Buzzer 250

Caddis-fly larva 54
Calorie 144
Calorific value 144
Camera, box 297
  folding 300
  pinhole 298
  stops 298
Canadian Pondweed (Elodea) 51
Candle, burning 36
  making 194
  -power 289
Cantilever 354
Capacitor, and alternating voltage 457
  stores electricity 457
Capillaries, blood 127
Capillarity 204
Capillary tube, making 12
Car ignition coil 260
Carbon dioxide, and exercise 42
  from burning 40
  from living things 42
  preparation 38
  properties 38
Casting a metal (lead) 387
Casts, plaster 78
Cells, electric, 134, 224, 229
  in series 229
  living, from mouth 64
  plant 64
  size 66
Cellulose 89
Centipede 426
Centre of gravity 370
Centrifugal force 350
Certificate of Secondary Education 98
Cheese-making 92
Chemical decomposition 132
Chemical reaction, 132, 134
  speed 136
Chicken fountain 12
Chlorine 192
Chlorophyll, from leaves 94
  in starch formation 94
  light absorption 97
Cinemoid filters 316
Circumpolar stars 330
Classroom library 323
  plants 74
Cleaning metals 386
Clinical thermometer 136
Clothing, drying of 84
  absorption of heat by 215
Clouds, atlas 343
  formation 174

INDEX

frame 343
Coal gas, bubbles 40
   flame 205
   manufacture 206
Collapsing vessels 14
Collone 108
Colour mixing 314, 316
   of opaque materials 315
   of transparent materials 315
   printing 318
   triangle 318
Colours, complementary 318
   in various lights 318
   primary 316
Compass, magnetic 241
Composition of foods 140
Compost heap 158
Concave mirror 294
Concrete 380
Conditions necessary for life 430
Conductors, of electricity 222, 226, 230
   of heat 211
   of sound 272
Contact printing 296
Convection, in air 214
   in liquids 210
Convex lens 300
   mirror 294
Cooling, by evaporation 198
   by expansion 410
Copper, oxidation of 132
   plating 236
   sulphate 389
   test for 389
   -zinc cell 134
Copper oxide, reduction of 132
   synthesis 132
Cork boring 29
Corpuscles, blood 127
Cosmetics 108, 116, 320
Cracking of vessels by heat 212
Creeping Jenny 51
Cross-pollination 434
Crowbar 366
Crustaceans 51
Crystal radio set 449
Crystals 388
Culture solution 153
Current detector 153
   measurer 254
Custard making 89
Cutting glass bottles 18, 30
   glass tubes 30
   metal tubes 31
Cuttings, growth from 437
Cycle lamp 224
Cyclops 51

Damping-off fungus 158
Daphnia 63
Davy lamp 212
Day and night 332
Day-book, teacher's 268
Dead-nettle flower parts 434
Demonstration, bench equipment 364
   hints for teacher 304
Density of floating bodies 176
   gas 176
   rocks 379
   solids 175
   water 176
Dental formula 100
Detergents 182
Dew formation 172
Diaphragm, action of 18, 20
Diesel engine 408
Diet 148
Digestion in mouth 100, 104
   of cream 113
   of fats 107
   of proteins 113
   of starch 104
   significance of 107
Digestive system 106
Diode, action of 450
   resistance 454
Discipline in laboratory 376
Disease and decay, prevention of 162
Disinfectants 164, 192
Dissection of earthworm 425
   rat 68
Distillation of alcohol 167
   water 184
Diving bell 137
Dragonfly larva 54
Dramatisation as teaching aid 119
Draughts 214
Drying conditions 172
   oils 116
Duckweed 48
Ductility 387
Dyeing 383
Dynamo, cycle 257
   model 258
   principle of 257
Dytiscus larva 54

Earth, circumference of 338
   magnetism 245
   rotation 328
Earthworm, dissection of 425
   external features 425
   soil raised by 426
   wormeries for 56, 425
Echoes 275, 281

Eclipse of Moon 338
  Sun 336
Educational television 283
Efficiency, electrical 235
  heating 145
  mechanical 398, 403
  reduced by friction 403
Elasticity 346, 352
Electric battery 229
  buzzer 250
  cables 234
  circuit 222, 232
  current detector 248
  fire model 226
  kettle, efficiency of 235
  low voltage units 220
  meter, moving coil 254
  motor model 256, 262
  motor, demonstration model 265
  shock 229
  signal 248
  torch 224
Electrical energy 134
  heat 234
  resistance 224
  resistance, variable 228
  resistance wire 224
Electricity, conductors of 222, 226
  cost of 234
  fuses 229
  heat equivalent of 234
  in Science syllabus 219
  insulators 222
  mains danger 229
  overloading 232
  power equation 236
  unit of 235
  voltage 229
  wattage 234
Electrolysis of brine 192
  copper sulphate 236
  nickel salts 236
Electro-magnets 246
  -plating 236
Elements essential for plants 152
Ellipse 334
Elodea 51
Emulsions 108
Energy, electrical, from chemical action 134
  units, electrical 235
  heat 142
  mechanical 395
  value of foods 146
Engines, diesel 408
  internal combustion 406
  steam 405
Epsom salts 388

Equipment, for teacher's bench 364
  storage of 362
  tools for class use 364
Erosion of soil 430
Evaporation and boiling 197
  cooling effect of 198
  of solids 196
Evolution of plants 438
Examinations 98
Exercise and carbon dioxide 42
Expansion, cooling effect of 410
  of air 24
  of glass 212
  of liquids 24
  of metals 24
Experiments, directions-book 268
Explosion of coal-gas 206
  hydrogen 39
  picric acid 134
Eye, blind spot 306
  bullock's 306
  defects 310
  iris action 306
  long sight 311
  lotion 164
  model 310
  short sight 311

Fairy lamps 230
Falling bodies 354
Faraday's expriment (dynamo) 257
Fats, display of 107
  emulsification of 108
  extraction of 90
  in diet 150
  tests for 90
Feet of birds 102
Fermentation, sugar 166
Fertilisation, in plants 436
  animals 442
Fertilisers 427
Fibres, dyeing 383
  flame-proofing 383
  flammability 382
  strength 384
  structure 382
  textile 382
Field work 45
Fifty-cycle hum 258
Film in Science teaching 284
  -loops 285
  -strip 284
Filmstrip projector 302
Filter, sand 191
  light 316
Filtration 107, 181, 191

INDEX 471

Finger prints 166
Fire alarm 31
  -making 202, 205
  precautions 205, 232
  -proofing 383
Fire extinguisher,
  carbon dioxide 38
  foam 39
  for petrol fire 186
First-aid 32
Fish, aquarium 56
Flicker book (vision) 308
Floating bodies 178
Flocculation of soil 425
Flour, gluten from 92
  paste 159
Flower parts 433, 434
Flushing tank 191
Focal strength 300
Fog 174
Food, calorific values 144
  composition of 140
  digestion of 107
  energy values 146
  growth of moulds on 156
  preservation of 162
  soluble and insoluble 107
  test for iron in 140
  used up in growth 97
  values per pennyworth 146
  water content 140
Footprints, bird 104
Force, centrifugal 350
Forces, interaction of 360
  oblique 369
  on body in orbit 414
  on moving bodies 350, 361, 414
  parallel 360
  units 395
Formicarium 58
Foucault's pendulum 328
Fountain 174
  -pen filler 12
Four-stroke cycle 408
Freezing and melting 194
  bursts caused by 194
  mixtures 196
  with ether 198
Frequency and wave-length 276
  of tuning fork 275
Friction and nature of surfaces 351
  and pressure 350
  losses 402
  reduction of 351
Frogspawn 57, 442
Fruits, development 436
  dispersal of 436

Fuels, products of burning 40
  and foods 142
Fungi, growth of 159
  in useful roles 166
  spores 160
Fuses, action of 229

Galvanometer (current detector) 248
Garden, school 75
Gas (see also Coal-gas)
  -bill 208
  explosion 206
  -fire model 208
  -holder 208
  making and by-products 208
  -meter reading 208
  pressure 21
  -works visit 208
Gear wheels 357
Gelatine nutrient 159
Genealogical tree 446
General Science question 168
Geographic meridian 245
Geotropism 80, 152
Germination box 430
  conditions for 430, 431
  experiments 430
  requires oxygen 42
  sandwich 80
Germs, spread of 160
Geyser, hot-water 212
Gilding, 387
Gills 124
Glare 289
Glass jet 12
Glucose test 88
Gluten, extraction of 92
Gnat larva 54
  development from eggs 162
Grain in wood 81
Granite 379
Grass snake, 442
Grasses, flowers of 436
  sugar in 88
Gravity, acceleration by 356
  and falling bodies 354
  force of 354
Greenhouse effect 74, 215
Group work in Science 221
Growth, essential elements 153
  factors affecting 152
  from cuttings 437
  in animals and plants 152
  of seedlings 437
  of stick insects 152
Gummed paper, uses of 31
Gyroscope 372

H.M.S.O. publications 393
Hair cream 108
Hamsters 58
Hardening steel 247
Hardness of water 180
  curd formed 181
  measurement 182
  softening 182
Harlequin-fly larva 54
Hazel catkins 434
Health education 154
  salts 112
Hearing and acoustics 280
  sensitivity 272
Heart, beat 126
  model 130
  position of 68, 72
  sheep's 124
Heat, absorption by clothing 215
  by glass 218, 269
  by surfaces 215
  by water 216
  and SI units 142
  conductors 211
  equivalent of electricity 234
  filter 216
  insulation 136, 212
  measurement 144
  of chemical reaction 132, 134
  radiant 214
  -sensitive paper 212
  units 144
Heating by compression 408
  effect of electric current 224, 226
Helicopter landing 416
Heredity 446
Hero's engine 412
Herring, dissection 440
  eggs 442
History as aid to Science teaching 118
Hoisting pulley 396
Holes in cans 30, 31
Horse leech 56
Horse-power, definition of 403
  of cyclist 403
  of pupil 403
Hot air rises 22, 214
Hot-water geyser 212
  supply 210
Hour glass 357
House lighting circuit 230, 232
  ventilation 214
  water supply 190
Housefly, 58, 161
Hovercraft principle 352
Hum, 50-cycle 258

Human adaptation 444
  body conducts electricity 230
  chin 446
  circulation 130
  energy requirements 146
  foot 372
  hand 444
  heredity 446
  horse-power 403
  organs 68
  skeleton 72
  skull 446
  stance 444
  reaction time 374
  teeth 100
Humidity 172
Humus 422, 428
Hydra 63
Hydraulic lift 178
Hydrogen bubbles 40
  explosion 39
  forms water 40
  preparation 39
Hygrometer 172

Ice 196
Iced drinks 197
Ignition, by compression 410
  coil 260
  temperature 202
Illuminating power 289
Illumination 288
Immensity of space 338
Improvised apparatus 27, 188
Inclined plane 398
Indicators (chemical) 112
Inertia 348
Infection of nutrient jellies 161
Inflammability 202, 382
Insect cages 57
Insulating power 212
Insulation, heat 211
Insulators, electrical 222
Internal combustion engine 407
  cycle 408
  model 408
Inverse square law 218, 289
Involuntary action 374
Iodine, in starch test 89
  tincture of 164
Iris action 306
Iron from haematite 388
  lung 20
  ship floats 178
  sulphate (green vitriol) 389
  test for 140

Jet engine model 412
 -propelled car 412
 propulsion 410
Joule's equivalent 235
Junket 113

Keeping up-to-date 391
Kinetic theory of matter 10, 374

Laboratory assistance 199
 discipline 376
 techniques 29
Ladybirds 440
Lamphouse 288
Lamps, cycle and torch 273
 fairy 230
 in parallel 230
 in series 230
 overloading 232
Latent heat 197
Latitude 333
Lawn sprinkler 412
Law, Hooke's 346
 Newton's First 348
 Newton's Third 410
 of inverse squares 218, 289
 of reflection 290
 of the lever 368
 of the pendulum 358
Laying a fire 202
Lead, from litharge 388
 iodide 389
 test for 389
Leatherjackets 426
Leaves and carbon dioxide 96
 contain starch 94
 give out water 82
 shapes of 76
 stomata in surface of 97
Leg movements 364
Legumes, root nodules on 160
Lens, concave 311
 convex 300, 311
 magnification 66
Lenticels 80
Less-able pupils 99, 187
Letter balance 354
Lever balance 140
 law of the 368
Levers, applications of 364, 400
Libraries, school Science 324
Lift, hydraulic 178
 of moving air 416
 pump 16
Lifting jack 400
Light, coloured 314
 complementary colours 318

 effect on colour 318
 filters 316
 glare 289
 internal reflection 322
 reflection of 290, 294
 refraction of 312
 spectrum 314
Lighting, natural and artificial 288
Lime, flocculating effect 425
 in soil, test for 424
Limestone burning 379
Lime-water and carbon dioxide 38
 from slaked lime 380
Linoleum 117
Lipstick 320
Living things in classroom 46
Lizards 442
Long sight 311
Longitude 332
Loop films 285
Loudspeaker receiver 452
Low-voltage supply 220
Lubrication 351, 402
Lung capacity 20
 iron- 20
 model 19
 pressure 21

Machines 395, 398
Magnesium sulphate 388
Magnetic attraction 240
 compass 241
 field of current 246
 Earth 245
 magnets 243
 meridian 245
 repulsion 241
Magnetising coil 240
Magnetism, loss of 241
 terrestrial 245
Magnets electro- 248
 floating 243
 making 240, 241
 permanent 239
 uses of 246
Magnifiers 61
Magnifying glass 300
 power 66
Mammals, organs of 68
Man, organs (model) 68
 skeleton (model) 72
Manures 427
Matches 204
May-fly larva 54
Mechanical advantage of simple machines,
 inclined plane 398
 lifting jack 400

Mechanical advantage of simple machines
—*continued*
  pulley systems 396
  screw 400
  wheel and axle 402
Melting point 194
  under pressure 196
Mercury barometer 22
Meridian, geographic 245
  magnetic 245
Metals, action of acids 39, 386
  casting 387
  cleaning 386
  ductility of 387
  extraction of 388
  fusibility of 387
  gilding 387
  polishing 386
  rusting of 34
  strength of 387
Meter, moving-coil 254
Methods of teaching Science 170, 187, 288
Methylated spirit burner 204
Metric system 347
Mice 443
Microphone 252
  circuits 460
  tape recorder 460
Micro-projector 61
Microscope 61
  sections 62
  slide 62
Milfoil 51
Milk, pasteurisation 162
Milk-bottle organ 278
Milky Way 342
Milling wheat 93
Millipede 426
Mineral salts in plant material 94
Minerals, common 379
Mirrors, curved 294
  parabolic 296
  plane 290
Mist 174
Modelling material 106
Moisture in air 172
Molecular theory 374
Moment of a force 368
Moon, eclipse of 338
  phases of 336
  size of 338
Morse sounder 250
Mortar 380
Mosquito 162
Moulds 156, 159
Movement in animals 364
  plants 375

Mucor 156
Muscles and levers 364
Mushroom spores 160
Musical instruments 278

Nature rambles 45
  records 75
  table 75
Nature-study 44
Negatives, printing from 296
Nervous system 372
Neutralisation 112, 427
Newsom Report 86
Newton's laws of motion 348, 410
Newts 57
Nickel plating 236
Nitric acid and nitrates from air 262
Noise, control of 280
Non-metals 390
Nuffield project 86
Nutrient gelatine 159
  jellies 158

Observation of living things 46
Ohm's law 228
Oils and fats 90, 107
  drying and non-drying 116
One-string fiddle 279
Optic nerve 306
Oral work 138
Ordinary pupils and Science 186, 267
Organs of mammals 68
  man, model 68
Oscillator 458
Overflow can 175
Overhead projector 286
Overloading (electrical) 232
Oxidation of copper 132
  iron 34, 38
Oxygen, and blood 128
  burning elements in 38
  essential for life 42
  from waterweed 96
  preparation 36
  properties of 38
  proportion in air 34

Paint 116
Parabolic reflector 296
Parallel connection 230
Parallelogram of forces 361
Paramoecium 63
Parental care 440
Pasteurisation 162
Pelton wheel 404
Pendulum and metric system 347
  and time 357

effect of external force 358
factors affecting period 358
Foucault 328
law of 358
Penicillium 158
Perennials 438
Periodicals, scientific 391
Periscope 292
  submarine 322
Persistence of vision 308
Petrol engine 406
  fire 205
Phases of Moon 336
Photographic club 296
Phototransistors 216
Phototropism 152
Picric acid 134
Pitch, of screw 400
  of sound 280
Planets, distances 334, 340
  sizes 334
Plant cells 64
  culture solution 153
  growth factors 152
  movements, automatic 375
  runners 438
Plants, and photosynthesis 94
  biennial 438
  climbing 375
  evolution of 438
  food storage in 87
  in the classroom 75
  perennial 438
  reproduction in, sexual 433
    vegetative 437
  roots and stems of 80
  water and 82
Plaster casts 78, 106
Plastics 380
Pleurococcus 64
Pollen dispersal 434
  tubes 436
Pollination, cross- 434
  by wind 434
Pond life 47
  skater 54
  snails 56
  weed 51
Popgun 14
Potassium test 94
Potato jelly 159
  starch 88
Potometer 82
Pottery 380
Preservation of food 164
Pressure and depth 137
  atmospheric 16

cooker 198
  meaning of 178
Primary colours 316
Printing, colour 318
  from negatives 296
Projection lantern 302
Projects in Science 86, 93
Propeller (airscrew) 414
Proteins, classes of 148
  digestion of 113
  in fibres 383
  in flour 92
  in milk 92
  structure of 148
  tests for 92, 383
Puffball spores 160
Pulleys, home-made 395
  systems of 396
  uses of 395
Pulse, arterial 126
Pump, lift 16
  vacuum 14
Putty 116

Question and answer board 224
Quicklime 379
Quotations for Science teachers 419

Radiant heat, absorption of 215, 216
  characteristics 214
Radiating power 215
Rat, dissection 68
  organs 68
Ray-tracks 290, 300, 303
Reaction time 374
Receiver, crystal radio 449
  loud speaker 452
  transistor 451, 452, 457, 462
Records, pupils' 138
  teachers' 266
Reference file 269
  books 323
Reflecting power 288
Reflection in curved mirrors 294
  in parallel mirrors 294
  in plane mirrors 290, 294
  internal 322
  laws of 290, 294
Reflection of sound 275, 281
Reflex actions 374
Refraction of light 312
Refrigeration with ether 198
Reproduction in animals 440
  in plants 433, 437
Reptiles 57, 442
Resistance, adjustable 228
  of metals 224

Resistor colour code 454
Resonance 270
Respiration 40, 130
Retinal image reversal 306
Rhubarb wine 167
Ripple tank 274
Rocket action 412
Rocks, collection of 378
  density of 379
  types 378
Roots, absorption by 82
  functions 82
  growth 80
    produces acid 428
  nodules 160
  structure 80, 81
Rose-hip syrup 142
Roundabout model 350
Rubber sucker 12
Ruminants' teeth 102
Runners (plant) 438
Rust, relation to air 34
  prevention 36

Safety First in the laboratory 31
Salad dressing 164
Saliva and digestion 104
Salts, preparation of 388
  identification of 388
Sand filter 191
Scalds 32, 197
Schemes of work 267
School garden 75
  Science publications 392
  Science Review 391
  Science societies 237, 262
Science 'At Home' 238
  library 323
  library catalogue 269
  models 237
  schemes and records 266
  supply of teachers for 185
  teaching aims 170, 188, 432
Screw 400
Sealing a glass tube 34
Seasons 334
Seaweed 438
Secondary colours 318
Seconds ticker 122
Seedlings, growth of 437
Seeds, dispersal of 436
  germination conditions 431
  need oxygen 42
  storage of 164
  structure of 436
  testing 430

Sense of hearing 272
  sight 306
  smell 374
  taste 372
  touch 374
Series connection 229, 230
Sex education 433
Shelled egg 443
Shock from batteries 229
Short courses for teachers 394
  sight 311
Sight, astigmatism 311
  binocular vision 308
  inversion of images 306
  long 311
  persistence of vision 308
  short 311
Silence of space 274
Silk, artificial 89
Silkworm 57
Simian shelf 446
Sink waste-pipe 191
SI units 142, 395
Skeletons 72, 446
Skin 166
  touch spots 374
Skull 102, 446
Slide-valve action 406
Soap, preparation of 110
  solution 182
Social biology 44, 154
  value of Science 40, 154, 187
Soda-water syphon 38
Soil acidity 424, 428
  air in 11
  animals 425, 426
  bacteria 426
  conservation 428
  constituents 421
  erosion 430
  formation 428
  humus in 422
  identification scheme 421
  mineral salts in 422
  moisture 422
  population 427
  profile 421
  testing for lime in 424
  water-raising power of 424
  water retention 422
Solar system, models 334
Solder 194
Soldering 31, 450
Solution 107
Sound, absorption of 280
  broadcasts 283
  conduction of 272

INDEX 477

echoes 275, 281
frequency 275
reflection of 275, 281
shadow 280
sources 270
speed of 275, 278
transmission 274
-waves 274
Space science 328
immensity of 338
Spectrum 314
Speed of sound 275, 278
Spiders 58
Spinning Earth 328
top 370
Spirogyra 64
Spring balance 180
Stability of bus 370
Starch, digestion by saliva 104
in foodstuffs 89
in plants 94
in potato 88
paste 88
test 89
used by plants 96
Starch-formation, carbon dioxide necessary 96
chlorophyll necessary 94
light needed 94
Stars, circumpolar 330
identification of 330, 340
trails (photographic) 336
Starting a Science course 267
Startwort 51
Steam engine 405
from kettle 197
sterilisation by 158
turbine 406
Steelyard 369
Steering an aeroplane 416
Stem growth 80
structure 81
Stereoscopic pictures 310
Sterilisation of vessels 158
Stethoscope, model 126
Stick insects 152
Sticklebacks 56
Stock-book 269
Stomata 97
Stone-fly larva 54
Storage of equipment 362
Straw, rotting of 428
String telephone 272
Structural design 384
Styptic pencil 129
Sugar, detection in foods 87
fermentation 166

kinds of 87
test 8
Sulphate of ammonia 427
Sulphur, burning 38
union with iron 132
Sulphuric acid 111, 229
Sun, distance of 340
eclipse of 336
motion of 328
Sundial 333
Supply of Science Teachers 185
Surface tension 162
Sweat, cooling effect of 166
Sweet Pea flower 435
Syphon 190

Tadpoles 57
Talcum powder 180
Tap-washer renewal 190
Teacher's bench equipment 364
library 326
schemes and records 267
Teachers of Science, supply of 185
Techniques, laboratory 29
Teeth, animal 102
decay of 102
human 100
Telephone 254
string- 272
Telescope, astronomical 302
Television 283
closed circuit 283
Telpher line 400
Temperature and chemical action 136
ignition 202
of boiling water 197
Tensile strength of fibres 384
of metals 387
Textbooks 323
Textiles 382
Therm 144
Thermocouple 408
Thermometer, clinical 136
readings 24
Thunder, distance of 275
Tidal capacity of lungs 20
Time allowance for Science 170, 201
chart (historical) 118
Greenwich Mean and local 332
Tin cans as beakers 31
Tinplate from cans 31
Tinder-box 205
Tools for pupils' benches 364
Toothed gears 357
Topics in Science course 86, 100
Torch-bulb holder 222
Total internal reflection 322

Transformer 258
  bell-, shock from 260
  principle 260
  step-up- 260, 262
  uses 262
Transmission devices 356
Transistor 448
  -amplifier 451
  current gain 454, 456
  feed-back 458
  phase reversal 458
  soldering 450
  circuits, testing 460
  types 463
  voltage control 456
Transmission of movement 356
Transparent materials 315
Transpiration 82
Trees, census 76
  leaves of 76
  recognition 78
  Winter twigs 78
Tropical Moonmoth 57
Trout eggs, development 442
Tuned coil 450
Tuning fork frequency 275
Turbine, water 404
  steam 406
Twigs, age of 81
  in Winter 78

Union of iron and sulphur 132
Upright stance in Man 444

Vacuum, no sound in 274
  -pump 14
Valves in veins 126
  mechanical 14, 130
Vanishing cream 116
Variable resistance 228
Vascular bundles 81
Vegetative propagation 437
Veins **126**
  valves in 126
Ventilation 214
Venus, distance of 340
Vibrating bodies 270
Video-tape 284
Vinamold 106
Violin, use in laboratory 270
Vision—*see* Sight
Visits 87, 155
  to fire station 205
  to museum 446
  to quarry-face 421
Visual aids 282

Vitamins 142
Vitriols 388
Vivaria 48, 56, 58, 442
Voltage 229
  control 456
Voltmeter 228

Wallflower parts 434
Warm and cold blood 134
Water, animals 51
  as lubricant 351
  atmospheric 172, 343
  Boatman 54
  buoyancy of 178
  capillary rise of 204
  conducts sound 272
  convection in 210
  Crowfoot 51
  density of 176
  detergents and 183
  dissolved air in 124
  dissolved solids in 183
  distillation 184
  essential for life 430
  evaporation and boiling 197, 198
  -filter 191
  fleas 51
  formed from hydrogen 40
  freezing and melting 194, 196, 198
  Great Beetle (Dytiscus) 51
  hardness in 182
  house supply 190, 210
  in foods 140
  in plants 82
  in soil 422
  internal reflection in 322
  leaves give out 82
  levels 174
  plants 48
  pressure 137, 174
  purification of 191
  refraction in 312
  roots take up 82
  Scorpion 54
  Shrimp 51
  Slater (Louse) 51
  softening of 182
  spiders 54
  sources 174
  supply 188
  supporting action of 176
  surface tension of 162
  -tap 190
  transpiration of 82
  -turbine 404
  waste of 190
  -wheel 404

Wattage 234
Wave motion 274
  sound- 274
Wave-length 276
Weather charts and records 343
  station 342
Weighing a pupil 369
Wet and dry bulb hygrometer 172
Wetting action 183
Wheat project 93
Wheel and axle 402
Whirligig beetle 54
White from coloured light 314
White Vitriol 388
Wild-flower calendar 433
  collection 433
Winch 402

Wind pollination 434
Windmill, toy 404
Winter twigs 78
Wireworm 426
Wood, grain and knots 81
Woody bundles 82
Work and simple machines 398
  definition of 398
  units of 395
Wormery 56, 425
Wounds, treatment of 32
Written work 139

Yeast cells 167

Zinc-copper cell 134
Zinc sulphate 388

Q
181
L48
1972